THE EDUCATION
OF HENRY ADAMS

Edited with an Introduction and Notes by

Ernest Samuels

Jayne N. Samuels, *Assistant Editor*

HOUGHTON MIFFLIN COMPANY • BOSTON

Atlanta • Dallas • Geneva, Illinois • Hopewell, New Jersey • Palo Alto • London

Printed in the U.S.A.

Library of Congress Catalog Card Number 73–6411

ISBN: 0–395–16620–9   PAPERBOUND
ISBN: 0–395–16810–4   HARDBOUND

Contents[2]

Introduction.   *By Ernest Samuels*   vii
Acknowledgements   xix
Textual Note   xxi

Editor's Preface.   *By Henry Cabot Lodge*   xxvii
Preface   xxix

I	*Quincy (1838–1848)*	3
II	*Boston (1848–1854)*	23
III	*Washington (1850–1854)*	40
IV	*Harvard College (1854–1858)*	54
V	*Berlin (1858–1859)*	70
VI	*Rome (1859–1860)*	82
VII	*Treason (1860–1861)*	98
VIII	*Diplomacy (1861)*	110
IX	*Foes or Friends (1862)*	128
X	*Political Morality (1862)*	145
XI	*The Battle of the Rams (1863)*	167
XII	*Eccentricity (1863)*	180
XIII	*The Perfection of Human Society (1864)*	194
XIV	*Dilettantism (1865–1866)*	208
XV	*Darwinism (1867–1868)*	224
XVI	*The Press (1868)*	237
XVII	*President Grant (1869)*	255
XVIII	*Free Fight (1869–1870)*	268
XIX	*Chaos (1870)*	284
XX	*Failure (1871)*	299
XXI	*Twenty Years After (1892)*	314

Contents

XXII   *Chicago (1893)*   331

XXIII   *Silence (1894–1898)*   346

XXIV   *Indian Summer (1898–1899)*   362

XXV   *The Dynamo and the Virgin (1900)*   379

XXVI   *Twilight (1901)*   391

XXVII   *Teufelsdröckh (1901)*   403

XXVIII   *The Height of Knowledge (1902)*   416

XXIX   *The Abyss of Ignorance (1902)*   426

XXX   *Vis Inertiae (1903)*   436

XXXI   *The Grammar of Science (1903)*   449

XXXII   *Vis Nova (1903–1904)*   462

XXXIII   *A Dynamic Theory of History (1904)*   474

XXXIV   *A Law of Acceleration (1904)*   489

XXXV   *Nunc Age (1905)*   499

Appendix A   507

Appendix B   519

Selected Bibliography   537

Notes   539

Index   689

Introduction

In a time of alienation and deepening crisis, the denunciatory voice of Henry Adams has a singularly contemporary resonance. His self-description at the opening of the twentieth century as a "conservative Christian anarchist" indicates that the distempers of our modern world have deep roots in the American experience. Even in his own day he saw the eighteenth century American dream of unlimited opportunity and indefinite progress turning into a waking nightmare of the moral dilemmas of a capitalist society. He saw too that though science was indeed making tremendous advances in the conquest of Nature, winning every battle in that age-old contest, the odds were growing that a dehumanized mankind might lose the war.

It is true that Henry Adams's quarrel with things as they are, with conventional values and with the establishment of his time, took a different direction from that of critics of a later day; however, like many of them he believed that the solution of the staggering problems of a science-dominated society must begin with the radical reform of university education.

Whatever else *The Education of Henry Adams* may be—and it is indeed many things else—it is, by expressed intention, as the author declared in his initial preface, a kind of handbook to prepare "young men, in universities and elsewhere, to be men of the world, equipped for any emergency." The small carefully selected group of readers of the original private printing quickly discovered that this description fitted the ultimate aim but not the method of the book. In consequence, in the "Editor's Preface" which Adams prepared for Henry Cabot Lodge's signature in 1915, eight years later, Adams acknowledged that he had cast a far wider net for his inquiry, that he had in fact proposed for himself nothing less than a "study of twentieth century multiplicity," for it was obvious to him that the reform of higher education must begin with the reordering of one's conception of the world process.

When he wrote his first preface Adams was approaching seventy. A half-century had gone by since his graduation from Harvard College, and his mind dwelt on that time of hope and idealism fifty years before when he had been stirred by Thomas Carlyle's *Sartor Resartus,* the tailor re-tailored. Carlyle had then challenged him to "know thy work and do it," and to give over the futile counsel of Socrates to "know thyself." As the ambitious scion of a great Boston family Adams had tried to find his work; more than half of the *Education* is the dramatic account of that frustrating quest. In age, looking back through the lens of his youthful expectations he had reason to consider that he had failed, regardless of what less idealistic observers might make of his remarkable literary career. Whether one finds his ambition inordinate or not may well depend on the daring of one's own aspirations.

In the homely metaphor which he borrowed from Carlyle he tells us that he has used his own personal history as a tailor's manikin, that his life's experiences are merely the garment "meant to show [the student] the faults of the patchwork fitted on their fathers." It is this angle of vision which gives such brilliant play to the retrospective irony of his story and the Voltairean wit of his satire. But if he is unduly harsh in his judgments of others, he is hardly less harsh upon himself.

Adams was by no means the first writer to believe that the record of his experiences might be instructive. He himself cites Benjamin Franklin and Jean Jacques Rousseau, but neither of them in his view could serve as guides for they had not foreseen the coming transformations of the Industrial Revolution. Their worlds were relatively stable and as men of the Enlightenment they could expect society to be improved by rational means, whether with Franklin through the improvement of street lighting and the founding of lending libraries or with Rousseau through child-centered education and the recognition of the equality of men.

The end of the nineteenth century showed a radically altered environment, one in which recurring economic and international crises had become the norm. Europe and America were already well advanced into the age of the machine and mass production, and the rivalry for world markets and raw materials foreshadowed world wars to come. In scarcely more than two generations an agricultural America had become a predominantly urban industrial society, complete with a city proletariat and corrupt political machines. This new world, as Adams saw it, was propelled at ever-increasing speed by the new energies released through scientific discovery. The feeling of passionate urgency which lies behind the *Education* breaks out in one of the many picturesque tirades with which he delighted his friends during the writing of the book:

> If I could live to the end of my century—1938—I am sure I should see the silly bubble explode. A world so different from that of my childhood or middle-life can't belong to the same scheme. It shifts from one motive to another, without sequence. . . . Out of a medieval, primitive, crawling infant of 1838, to find oneself a howling, steaming, Marconiing, radiumating, automobiling maniac of 1904 exceeds belief. (To Mrs. Edward Fell, June 27, 1904, Adams Papers.)

In its paradoxes and contradictions the book accurately reflects the man. He was a supreme conversationalist and often a dangerous one, in spite of his soft anglicized tone. He was given to sardonic chaff, wearing his pessimism with a rakish tilt and playing devil's advocate with tongue in cheek and flaming exaggeration. He speaks of himself as addressing young men in universities and elsewhere, yet he distributed the *Education* only to a circle of friends and relatives, many of whom like President

Theodore Roosevelt, Henry Cabot Lodge, and Justice Oliver Wendell Holmes held high office. He insisted that the book was only a draft sent out for correction, but only two or three took him at his word and returned their precious copies. A few years later, more confident of its worth, he made abortive plans to issue it broadcast to university professors of history as a contribution to the reform of university education.

This odd mixture of reticence and ambition, of his dread of public notoriety and his sense of mission as a "teacher of teachers" explains some of the ambivalences of the *Education.* He knew that in the world of men the capacity and the will to act must coexist, and yet what lifelong observation taught him was that, as Hannah Arendt has written, "the capacity to act is the most dangerous of all human abilities." The tension between thought and action became the central problem of his search. As he grew older the role of bystander appealed more and more to him, and he liked to think of himself as looking on above the battle. Like the hero of his friend Henry James's novel *The American* he had the paralyzing habit of second thoughts, recurring sessions of anxious introspection. What he wrote of the heroine of his own novel *Democracy* could well be said of him: he had a passion for "discussing things and hunting first principles" and an impulse to remove his "mental clothing" and examine it "as though it belonged to someone else." In the irreverent words of Ed Howe, the famous Kansas editor, Henry Adams was "the only man in the world who could sit on a fence and watch himself go by."

It is that quality of mind that gives an arresting piquancy to Adams's narrative; it is the source of the ironic detachment that cloaks a sensitive and emotional nature in the third person voice of the novelist. Beneath the brilliant artifice of his style lie depths of feeling the more intense for their repression and understatement. It is a voice with which, as has been said, the dramatizing eloquence of age transforms the past nearer to the mind's desire.

More than ironic second thought modulates the story. Never far distant is the philosophical theme. The note is sounded early in the first chapter: "From the cradle to the grave this problem of running order through chaos, direction through space, discipline through freedom, unity through multiplicity, has always been and must always be, the task of education, as it is the moral of religion, philosophy, science, art, politics, and economy." That note rises to its highest pitch in the complex coda of the "Dynamic Theory of History" and "A Law of Acceleration" of the final chapters.

If a philosophy of history or of world process forms, as it were, one pole of Adams's design, the other pole is a pragmatic concern with the conditions of worldly success. One might say of him as James Russell Lowell said of the philosophic Ralph Waldo Emerson:

> A Greek head on right Yankee shoulders, whose range
> Has Olympus for one pole, for t'other the Exchange.

Money might be the lowest common denominator of success, but it was not to be scorned in the total calculus. Reviewing his own educated generation Adams wrote (p. 347): "Education must fit the complex conditions of a new society, always accelerating its movement, and its fitness could be known only from success." Of the three typical cases he could think of all owed their free hand to having married wealthy wives. He was even more explicit in a letter to his brother Charles in 1903 (Ford, II, 417):

> I am rather surprised to see, on looking back fifty years, how few of our college mates, with all their immense advantages, seem to have got or kept their proportional share in the astounding creation of power since 1850. I should say that ten out of a thousand would cover them. We ought all to have rolled in millions, but nearly every one of my friends in college is now dead, and none was powerful or rich, except Lewis Cabot who married it.

To a very large extent the *Education* furnishes its own persuasive credentials, though it assumes much and suppresses more. To be an Adams in the Boston of his boyhood was to know fame

—as well as envy—long before they were earned. In a single generation in the eighteenth century his family had become one of the most prominent in the young republic. After a century and a quarter of respectable obscurity as New England yeoman farmers, the family sprang into the political foreground with great-grand-father John Adams, the farmer-lawyer who feared God but no one else and who from a sense of moral duty faced down public wrath to defend the British soldiers accused of the Boston Massacre. His precise signature appears along with that of his militant second cousin Samuel Adams on the Declaration of Independence for which he was a chief advocate. He served eight years under Washington as Vice President and followed him in the Presidency. However, after a single term he was displaced by Thomas Jefferson, leaving office so embittered by factional politics that he avoided greeting his successor. Reconciled in their old age, the two statesmen exchanged letters which became classics of political analysis of the American system: Adams arguing for a conservative democracy, Jefferson for a liberal one.

Henry Adams's grandfather John Quincy Adams inherited his father's moral fervor and intellectual ability and improved the inheritance. When as a Federalist senator he supported Jefferson's foreign policy he was read out of his party, exercising the Adams privilege, as grandson Henry called it, of forming a party of one. Under President Monroe, John Quincy Adams, as secretary of state, drafted the document setting forth what became known as the Monroe Doctrine. It set the United States on a course of determined opposition to the colonial imperialism of the European concert of powers in the American hemisphere. John Quincy Adams became President but like his father served only a single term, being swept under by the shirtsleeves democracy of Andrew Jackson's supporters. Undaunted by this rejection of his patrician leadership, John Quincy went back to the House of Representatives and for twenty years as "Old Man Eloquent" fought the infamous "Gag Rule" with which the representatives of the slave states stifled debate. His intellectuality and philosophic bent re-appeared in a more literary and speculative form in Henry Adams, as Henry's younger brother Brooks was to argue long afterwards in his essay "The Heritage of Henry Adams" with which he prefaced a posthumous collection of Henry's philosophical writings.

In the *Education* Henry Adams takes up the family story as an eyewitness observer with his father's entrance into politics as a congressman from the Fifth District of Massachusetts. Charles Francis Adams served in the crucial post of Minister to Great Britain during the Civil War with a success for which his son has only the highest praise. His diplomatic career was capped with his triumphant management of the Alabama Claims Arbitration. Yet by the end of his life the vying for political prizes disenchanted him. Under President Grant he saw the rise of a new breed of predatory politicians and businessmen. In his four sons, however, the impulse toward moral politics, though chastened by family disappointments, flared up with an intenser flame only to be quenched at last by the "Triumphant Democracy" of steel magnate Andrew Carnegie.

At twenty-five Henry wrote with buoyant hopefulness to his brother Charles in the Union Army: "We want a national set of young men like ourselves or better, to start new influences not only in politics, but in literature, in law, in society, and throughout the whole social organism of our country—a national school of our own generation. . . ." Only when we juxtapose the contemporary record of these letters filled with high principle can we measure the full curve of Henry Adams's own disenchantment. In the back of his mind he always had to face the hard fact, as he was wont to reflect, that with two older brothers ahead of him he stood third in line of "promotion."

Important to the understanding of the singular nature of this "autobiography" are the large reticences and omissions in the recital. In truth, as he wrote to his friend Henry James, he con-

sidered the *Education* "a mere shield of protection in the grave."
Self-depreciation, as he freely admitted, was one of his vices; indeed it served itself as a kind of emphasis. The largest gap in the
narrative, the twenty years which Adams passes over so summarily in Chapter XXI, "Twenty Years After," were years of
remarkable productivity. They established him as a leading
American historian and led to his being elected president of the
American Historical Association, albeit its shyest president, to
the point of delivering his presidential address by proxy. By the
middle of the period he had published a meticulously documented
biography of Albert Gallatin, Jefferson's secretary of the treasury,
and a brilliant if partisan biography of John Randolph of Roanoke,
the famed adversary of President John Quincy Adams. His nine-
volume masterpiece *The History of the United States during the
Administrations of Jefferson and Madison* (1889–1891) climaxed
his work as an American historian. In the intervals stolen from
these works he published anonymously two novels, *Democracy*
and *Esther,* minor classics in their way. *Democracy,* published
in 1880, unmercifully satirized the political corruption of Grant's
Washington and became a sensational success in England and
America. The secret of its authorship, like that of *Esther* (1884),
did not become known until after Adams's death.

The first half and more of that twenty-year period were the
years of his marriage to Marian Hooper, the intellectual and witty
daughter of a famous Boston oculist, widowed when Marian was a
child. Henry James, who had been a member of her Boston circle
in his law school days, admired her for her "intellectual grace."
The marriage took place in 1872. After Henry Adams resigned
from the Harvard history department in 1877, she presided over
their famous salon in Lafayette Square opposite the White House.
Here to their intimate dinners of six and eight came statesmen,
diplomats, and distinguished foreign visitors like Matthew Arnold,
Edward Augustus Freeman, and Henry James. Invitations to
dinner were envied marks of distinction. Here the noted "Five of

Hearts" held their gay inquest over Washington society and politics—John Hay and his easily scandalized wife, Clarence King, geologist and man of the world, and Adams and his wife. And here in Lafayette Square tragedy struck on December 6, 1885, when Marian Adams during a period of deep mental depression following the death of her father took her own life.

The tragedy, which became front page news, broke Adams's life in halves as he afterwards said, and thereafter he lived a "posthumous" existence, a double life, one "behind the veil" whose only outward sign would be the unmarked St. Gaudens Memorial in Rock Creek cemetery and the other in the great world as a semi-recluse eagerly cultivated at his twelve o'clock breakfasts by the great and the near-great.

The *Education* germinated for a long time during the crisis-ridden nineties while he and his younger brother Brooks tried to understand the underlying causes of the economic collapse of 1893. Brooks challenged their conservative Boston world with his *Law of Civilization and Decay* (1895), a sweeping attack upon the commercial spirit of the modern world. Henry Adams went on to bury his distaste for the ugliness and violence of the contemporary scene in the passionate study of the Middle Ages in France, professing to find in the art and religion of that period the social and spiritual unity which he made the theme of his *Mont-Saint-Michel and Chartres*. That exquisite and learned masterpiece, privately printed in 1904 for his nieces and "nieces-in-wish," was, after much urging from friends that he publish it, finally donated by him to the American Institute of Architects which published it in 1913, five years before Adams's death at the age of eighty.

The *Education* came into being as an experimental afterpiece to the *Chartres,* the last few chapters of the book—relating to his "Dynamic Theory of History"—being, according to Adams the Q.E.D. and complement of the last three philosophical chapters of the *Chartres*. Knowledge of the existence of the *Education* and of its provocative mixture of recent history and autobiography, of politics, philosophy and science, spread in ever-widening circles. However, many even among those initial readers who could supply for themselves the personal omissions found themselves both fascinated and baffled by Adams's style and thesis. William James declared to him: "The boyhood part is really superlative. It and the London part should become classic historic documents," but he went on, "There is a hodge-podge of world-fact, private fact, philosophy, irony, (with the word 'education' stirred in too much for my appreciation!). . . . A great deal of the later diplomatic history is dealt with so much by hint and implication, that to an ignoramus like W[illiam] J[ames] it reads obscurely." A younger friend, the famed art historian Bernard Berenson, confessed to his wife Mary, "It is not easy reading, for the style is over-Jamesian for my intelligence and assumes too much knowledge of nineteenth century history and personalities. Yet it fascinates me beyond telling. . . ."

Adams, driven to explaining and defending the book to his friends, deepened the obscurities, if anything, with further illustrative analogies. The difficulty, as always with a work of profound intuition, was that no explanation could convey the Protean nature of the art which had attempted a unique fusion of a narrative and didactic theme or could translate the subtle implications of his exuberant metaphors. He forewarned in the *Education* that "no one means all he says, and yet very few say all they mean, for words are slippery and thought is viscous." Nevertheless there are rewarding clues in Adams's commentaries, some of which have been collected in an appendix to this volume, for they emphasize the prophetic and yet provisional nature of his ideas. Particularly significant is the letter which he drafted that was to have accompanied the distribution of the *Education* to leading professors in the country inviting their comment and collaboration in the revitalization of higher education. He gave up the idea and sent out instead a small book in 1910 called *A Letter to American*

Teachers of History in which he proposed that the analysis of energy embodied in the Second Law of Thermodynamics (the principle of entropy) be applied to all social phenomena as he believed that all the energies of the world, physical and societal, were being steadily degraded to lower energy levels and would ultimately be unusable.

On its posthumous publication by the Massachusetts Historical Society and Houghton Mifflin Company in 1918, the *Education* elicited the highest praise and became a best seller. In the following year it was awarded the Pulitzer Prize. The focus of the book was somewhat blurred by the subtitle "An Autobiography" which was added by the publisher. As an addict of paradox and contradiction Adams would have wryly relished his posthumous reputation. In his youth and middle age he had sought fame and power, but these had eluded him. His single sensational success, *Democracy*, had flourished as the anonymous orphan of his oversensitive scruple. He had been dedicated to the dream of making life rationally predictable; his experience taught him that unpredictability was the rule of life rather than the exception, that the unchanging law of life is its irony.

The multitude of allusions and private references which confounded so many of his friends have become, after nearly three-quarters of a century, even more enigmatic. Yet in the shifting pattern of metaphor and symbol they play a role too easily overlooked, adding a level of meaning that is like a fourth dimension in the geometry of his style. Moreover, the intellectual and social ambiance in which the book was conceived at the opening of the twentieth century differs radically from that in which we live in the closing decades of the century. The annotations which have been supplied in the "Notes" section at the back of this edition have been provided to help the reader recover that half-forgotten past. They also identify the instances in which Adams's memory altered the facts and thus provide a kind of psychological parallax on the shaping power of his imagination. No one is likely to make the mistake of looking up every note on his first reading, but it is suggested that he might profitably scan the notes of each chapter en masse as a kind of running commentary to sound Adams's erudition in a dozen fields and to feel the ceaseless thrust of his intellectual awareness.

The 1918 edition which Adams authorized to be published after his death did not, despite the best intentions of the editors, carry out Adams's intentions as stated in the "Editor's Preface" with entire accuracy. Collation of the authorized edition with the original private printing of 1907 as revised by Adams has made it possible to present a definitive text of the *Education*. The results of that collation are reported in the Textual Note. The substantive variations are listed in Appendix B.

ERNEST SAMUELS
NORTHWESTERN UNIVERSITY

Acknowledgements

It is a pleasure to acknowledge the assistance of the many persons who responded to my inquiries and to those whose serendipity rescued me from many a blind alley. Some of the early reconnaissance was carried out by the members of Seminar E35 who tracked their quarry with admirable zeal: Dominic Bazzanella, Paul Grawe, Alex Hammond, Daniel Lindsey, Carol Long, James Meade, Arthur Miller, Kermit Moyer, Paul Psilos, Susan Sibbett, James Stupple, Elizabeth Taylor, and Raquel Totaro. I am especially indebted to the reference staff of the Northwestern University Library and to Miss Marjorie Carpenter in charge of Interlibrary Loans. Materials have also been generously supplied by the Massachusetts Historical Society, the Regenstein Library of the University of Chicago, the Houghton and Widener Libraries of Harvard University, the Boston Public Library, the Boston Athenaeum, and the Abernethy Library of Middlebury College.

The edition has benefited from the perceptive reading of the manuscript by James Cox of Dartmouth College, Earl Harbert of Tulane University, J. C. Levenson of the University of Virginia, and James Nagel of Northeastern University. Howard Munford of Middlebury College kindly made available to me his article on the long-missing second copy of the 1907 *Education* containing corrections by Henry Adams. Charles Vandersee of the University of Virginia deserves special thanks for his analysis of the recently discovered third revised copy of the 1907 *Education*. To Malcolm Freiberg, editor of publications of the Massachusetts Historical Society, and Ruth A. Frager, his assistant, I wish to express my thanks for their expeditious help in completing the collation of the corrected copies of the 1907 edition.

xix

Acknowledgements

As always I have found colleagues at my university and elsewhere extremely generous in sharing the special and often recondite knowledge of their fields whenever I have called upon them.

I wish to thank the Council of the Massachusetts Historical Society for its approval of this edition and particularly the director, Stephen T. Riley, for his friendly interest and many courtesies. I have profited also from the counsel of Lyman Butterfield, editor in chief of *The Adams Papers* and of his associate Marc Friedlander. Winifred Collins, assistant librarian of the Society, has also helped in providing access to elusive documents. Here too I should like to thank Ron Schroeder for his help in the exacting work of collation.

My debt to my wife, Jayne Newcomer Samuels, at every stage in the preparation of this edition is indicated on the title page.

E. S.

Textual Note

The copy text adopted for this edition is that of the trade edition published in September, 1918, by Houghton Mifflin Company (the copyright being entered in the name of the Massachusetts Historical Society) and frequently reprinted thereafter as the standard text. Adams died late in March of 1918 at the age of eighty. He had explicitly authorized a posthumous edition early in 1916 in a letter addressed to Senator Henry Cabot Lodge, the president of the Society, requesting that the book be published on behalf of the Society, with which his family had been closely identified for generations. The letter accompanied a sealed packet containing a corrected copy of the 1907 private printing and an "Editor's Preface," which Adams himself composed but to which he affixed in a shaking hand the initials "H. C. L.," with the puzzled but indulgent acquiescence of Lodge. In this Preface Adams has the nominal editor assert that the *Education* is being published "as it was printed in 1907, with only such marginal corrections as the author made." That statement was scrupulously respected in all substantive matters by the actual editors of the trade edition: Worthington Chauncey Ford, editor of the Massachusetts Historical Society and a longtime friend of Adams; Henry Cabot Lodge, once a doctoral candidate in history at Harvard under Adams; and Ferris Greenslet, editor of Houghton Mifflin Company. They were obliged to obey his wishes, however, in a manner that Adams had not foreseen. Immediately after his death they discovered that some years earlier, before his stroke in 1912, Adams had made a much more comprehensive revision in another copy of the 1907 printing. This contained more than 100 changes, ranging from a single word to a few sentences, added or deleted. The copy which Adams worked on in a rather cursory fashion early in 1916 and sent to Lodge contained only about 25 corrections. Adams at that late period was under the mistaken impression that the earlier corrected copy had unaccountably disappeared. In fact he had given it to William Roscoe Thayer to use in connection with the writing of his biography of John Hay which was published in 1915. About a month after Adams's death Thayer agreed to an exchange of copies, so that the more heavily annotated copy came into the possession of the Massachusetts Historical Society; both copies thus became available to the editors. The great majority of the revisions were naturally adopted from the copy which Adams had corrected before his crippling illness in 1912.

The copy deposited with Lodge eventually found its way from the Thayer estate to the Abernethy Library of Middlebury College, where it was discovered by Professor Howard M. Munford. For a valuable analysis of it see his article, "Thayer, Ford, Goodspeed's, and Middlebury: A Missing Copy of The Education of Henry Adams Found," in the *Proceedings* of the Massachusetts Historical Society, LXXXIII, 148–153.

In a few instances the editors in 1918 adopted changes marked only in the later copy. The editors also corrected some but not all typographical errors and one or two errors in dates. All of the changes authorized by Adams's markings and marginal annotations and those made additionally by the editors are identified in Appendix B. They have been adopted in this edition in all cases where they demonstrably follow Adams's final intention. In two instances the editors did not adopt Adams's corrections. One, of particular interest, concerned his confusion of Wolcott Gibbs with Willard Gibbs. Both of these have been included in this edition as indicated and explained in Appendix B, Table 2. Our collation of the 1918 edition with the 1907 printing revealed a substantial number of misprints and misreadings, some of which significantly altered the meaning of a passage or rendered it unintelligible. These have been corrected and the 1907 readings, as revised by Adams, have been restored as shown in Appendix B, Table 4.

It now appears that Adams began to think of a corrected edition of the *Education* sometime before he revised the copy which he lent to Thayer. A third copy of the 1907 printing with corrections and annotations in the firm handwriting which antedates his illness was recently found by Peter Haack of the Boston Athenaeum among uncatalogued books from the Adams Mansion in Quincy, books which were deposited at the Athenaeum sometime before 1946. These corrections were probably made in 1908 or very shortly thereafter. Adams was in Paris in the summer of 1908 and was making an intensive study of the scientific works which he cites in the marginal annotations. He was then revising his "Rule of Phase Applied to History," an essay which he planned to send out to professors of history as a kind of circular to accompany the *Education*. (See Appendix A and Samuels, III, 416 ff.) One of the sources—Brunhes, *La Degradation de l'Energie*—had just been published. Most of the sources were in French and thus readily available. The annotations show him chiefly concerned with demonstrating how recent scientific writing confirmed his own analysis. He soon abandoned his plan to distribute the *Education* in this fashion and turned instead to the writing of *A Letter to American Teachers of History* which he circulated in 1910.

As the pressure upon him to publish the *Education* continued to grow he decided to make a more thorough revision with a view to eventual publication and thus began again with an unmarked copy of the 1907 printing, the copy which he afterwards lent to Thayer. In this second revision Adams spread his net far wider among the chapters of the *Education*, and he was now more concerned with subtleties of style and expression. He adopted some of the corrections of the preceding revision and some of the deletions but rejected the nearly 20 changes—including deletions and insertions of sentences—which he had contemplated making. The reader may study the greatly broadened scope of Adams's second revision by comparing Tables 1 and 2 in Appendix B with Table 5 which tabulates the corrections in the earliest revision. As the changes in that copy, the Athenaeum copy, represent only an intermediate stage of the process of revision none of its changes have been incorporated in the present text. Adams's annotations citing supporting authorities are listed in Appendix B, Table 6.

Adams was not always consistent in his spelling, punctuation, capitalization, or use of italics. He tended to punctuate very heavily in the older style, especially favoring the semicolon, the semicolon dash, and the comma dash to articulate longer sentences. He often omitted completing the pointing of parenthetical phrases. In his spelling he usually employed one of the more conservative English forms as, for example, "eat" for "ate" and "ise" for "ize" in such words as "realize," "civilize," etc., thus giving point to the remark of a fellow journalist, Henry Watterson, that "in manners, tone and cast of thought" Adams was "delightfully English" and to that of his publisher-friend Henry Holt that Adams spoke with an "Anglicized accent," the result of his long residence in England in his twenties (Samuels, I, 331, n. 2). He also capitalized with great but not always consistent freedom. These features were largely normalized in 1918, although a few spellings still current in American usage were allowed to stand, like "defence" and "offence." These typographical modifications have been retained.

In the spelling of such collective pronouns as "anyone," "anybody," "everyone," and "everybody" Adams's usage has been restored in place of "any one," "any body," "every one," and "every body" as more accurately conveying the meaning of the great number of references to his contemporaries or to society as a collectivity which is so marked a feature of the *Education.*

The subtitle "An Autobiography" which was printed on the title page of the 1918 edition without authorization in either of the corrected copies or in Adams's letter to Lodge has been deleted as a misnomer. For Adams's own provisional subtitle "A Study of Twentieth-Century Multiplicity" see his "Editor's Preface."

Textual Note

The circumstances surrounding the initial printing of the *Education* and the steps leading up to the publication of the posthumous edition in 1918 are given in full detail in Samuels, III, 332–345, 559–571. In a few particulars this account is corrected by the later information supplied above and in the notes to the "Preliminaries."

E. S.

Editor's Preface

This volume, written in 1905 as a sequel to the same author's "Mont-Saint-Michel and Chartres," was privately printed, to the number of one hundred copies, in 1906,[3] and sent to the persons interested, for their assent, correction, or suggestion. The idea of the two books was thus explained at the end of Chapter XXIX:—

"Any schoolboy could see that man as a force must be measured by motion from a fixed point. Psychology helped here by suggesting a unit—the point of history when man held the highest idea of himself as a unit in a unified universe. Eight or ten years of study had led Adams to think he might use the century 1150–1250, expressed in Amiens Cathedral and the Works of Thomas Aquinas, as the unit from which he might measure motion down to his own time, without assuming anything as true or untrue, except relation. The movement might be studied at once in philosophy and mechanics. Setting himself to the task, he began a volume which he mentally knew as 'Mont-Saint-Michel and Chartres: a Study of Thirteenth-Century Unity.'[4] From that point he proposed to fix a position for himself, which he could label: 'The Education of Henry Adams: a Study of Twentieth-Century Multiplicity.' With the help of these two points of relation, he hoped to project his lines forward and backward indefinitely, subject to correction from anyone who should know better."

The "Chartres" was finished and privately printed in 1904.[5] The "Education" proved to be more difficult. The point on which the author failed to please himself, and could get no light from readers or friends, was the usual one of literary form. Probably he saw it in advance, for he used to say, half in jest, that his great ambition was to complete St. Augustine's "Confessions,"[6] but that St. Augustine, like a great artist, had worked from multiplicity to unity, while he, like a small one, had to reverse the method and

work back from unity to multiplicity. The scheme became unmanageable as he approached his end.

Probably he was, in fact, trying only to work into it his favorite
theory of history, which now fills the last three or four chapters of
the "Education," and he could not satisfy himself with his work-
manship.[7] At all events, he was still pondering over the problem in
1910, when he tried to deal with it in another way which might
be more intelligible to students. He printed a small volume called
"A Letter to American Teachers," which he sent to his associates
in the American Historical Association, hoping to provoke some
response. Before he could satisfy himself even on this minor point,
a severe illness in the spring of 1912 put an end to his literary
activity forever.[8]

The matter soon passed beyond his control. In 1913 the Institute of Architects published the "Mont-Saint-Michel and Chartres."[9] Already the "Education" had become almost as well known,
as the "Chartres," and was freely quoted by every book whose
author requested it. The author could no longer withdraw either
volume; he could no longer rewrite either, and he could not publish that which he thought unprepared and unfinished, although in
his opinion the other was historically purposeless without its sequel. In the end, he preferred to leave the "Education" unpublished, avowedly incomplete, trusting that it might quietly fade
from memory.[10] According to his theory of history as explained in
Chapters XXXIII and XXXIV, the teacher was at best helpless,
and, in the immediate future, silence next to good temper was the
mark of sense. After midsummer, 1914, the rule was made absolute.[11]

The Massachusetts Historical Society has decided to publish the
"Education" as it was printed in 1907, with only such marginal
corrections as the author made,[12] and it does this, not in opposition
to the author's judgment, but only to put both volumes equally
within reach of students who have occasion to consult them.

HENRY CABOT LODGE[13]

September, 1918

Preface

Jean Jacques Rousseau began his famous "Confessions" by a vehement appeal to the Deity: "I have shown myself as I was; contemptible and vile when I was so; good, generous, sublime when I was so; I have unveiled my interior such as Thou thyself hast seen it, Eternal Father! Collect about me the innumerable swarm of my fellows; let them hear my confessions; let them groan at my unworthiness; let them blush at my meannesses! Let each of them discover his heart in his turn at the foot of thy throne with the same sincerity; and then let any one of them tell thee if he dares: 'I was a better man!' "[14]

Jean Jacques was a very great educator in the manner of the eighteenth century, and has been commonly thought to have had more influence than any other teacher of his time; but his peculiar method of improving human nature has not been universally admired. Most educators of the nineteenth century have declined to show themselves before their scholars as objects more vile or contemptible than necessary, and even the humblest teacher hides, if possible, the faults with which nature has generously embellished us all, as it did Jean Jacques, thinking, as most religious minds are apt to do, that the Eternal Father himself may not feel unmixed pleasure at our thrusting under his eyes chiefly the least agreeable details of his creation.

As an unfortunate result the twentieth century finds few recent guides to avoid, or to follow. American literature offers scarcely one working model for high education. The student must go back, beyond Jean Jacques, to Benjamin Franklin,[15] to find a model even of self-teaching. Except in the abandoned sphere of the dead languages,[16] no one has discussed what part of education has, in his personal experience, turned out to be useful, and what not.[17] This volume attempts to discuss it.

xxix

As educator, Jean Jacques was, in one respect, easily first; he erected a monument of warning against the Ego. Since his time, and largely thanks to him, the Ego has steadily tended to efface itself,[18] and, for purposes of model, to become a manikin on which the toilet of education is to be draped in order to show the fit or misfit of the clothes. The object of study is the garment, not the figure. The tailor adapts the manikin as well as the clothes to his patron's wants. The tailor's object, in this volume, is to fit young men, in universities or elsewhere, to be men of the world, equipped for any emergency; and the garment offered to them is meant to show the faults of the patchwork fitted on their fathers.[19]

At the utmost, the active-minded young man should ask of his teacher only mastery of his tools. The young man himself, the subject of education, is a certain form of energy; the object to be gained is economy of his force; the training is partly the clearing away of obstacles, partly the direct application of effort. Once acquired, the tools and models may be thrown away.

The manikin, therefore, has the same value as any other geometrical figure of three or more dimensions, which is used for the study of relation. For that purpose it cannot be spared; it is the only measure of motion, of proportion, of human condition; it must have the air of reality; must be taken for real; must be treated as though it had life. Who knows? Possibly it had!

February 16, 1907[20]

THE EDUCATION OF HENRY ADAMS

THE EDUCATION
OF HENRY ADAMS

CHAPTER I

Quincy (1838–1848)

UNDER the shadow of Boston State House, turning its back on the house of John Hancock,[1] the little passage called Hancock Avenue runs, or ran, from Beacon Street, skirting the State House grounds, to Mount Vernon Street, on the summit of Beacon Hill; and there, in the third house below Mount Vernon Place, February 16, 1838, a child was born, and christened later by his uncle, the minister of the First Church after the tenets of Boston Unitarianism, as Henry Brooks Adams.[2]

Had he been born in Jerusalem under the shadow of the Temple[3] and circumcised in the Synagogue by his uncle the high priest, under the name of Israel Cohen, he would scarcely have been more distinctly branded, and not much more heavily handicapped in the races of the coming century, in running for such stakes as the century was to offer; but, on the other hand, the ordinary traveller, who does not enter the field of racing, finds advantage in being, so to speak, ticketed through life, with the safeguards of an old, established traffic. Safeguards are often irksome, but sometimes convenient, and if one needs them at all, one is apt to need them badly. A hundred years earlier, such safeguards as his would have secured any young man's success; and although in 1838 their value was not very great compared with what they would have had in 1738, yet the mere accident of starting a twentieth-century career from a nest of associations so colonial — so troglodytic — as the First Church, the Boston State House, Beacon Hill, John Hancock and John Adams, Mount Vernon Street and Quincy, all

3

crowding on ten pounds of unconscious babyhood, was so queer as to offer a subject of curious speculation to the baby long after he had witnessed the solution. What could become of such a child of the seventeenth and eighteenth centuries, when he should wake up to find himself required to play the game of the twentieth? Had he been consulted, would he have cared to play the game at all, holding such cards as he held, and suspecting that the game was to be one of which neither he nor anyone else back to the beginning of time knew the rules or the risks or the stakes? He was not consulted and was not responsible, but had he been taken into the confidence of his parents, he would certainly have told them to change nothing as far as concerned him. He would have been astounded by his own luck. Probably no child, born in the year, held better cards than he. Whether life was an honest game of chance, or whether the cards were marked and forced, he could not refuse to play his excellent hand. He could never make the usual plea of irresponsibility. He accepted the situation as though he had been a party to it, and under the same circumstances would do it again, the more readily for knowing the exact values. To his life as a whole he was a consenting, contracting party and partner from the moment he was born to the moment he died. Only with that understanding — as a consciously assenting member in full partnership with the society of his age — had his education an interest to himself or to others.

As it happened, he never got to the point of playing the game at all; he lost himself in the study of it, watching the errors of the players; but this is the only interest in the story, which otherwise has no moral and little incident. A story of education — seventy years of it — the practical value remains to the end in doubt, like other values about which men have disputed since the birth of Cain and Abel; but the practical value of the universe has never been stated in dollars. Although everyone cannot be a Gargantua-Napoleon-Bismarck and walk off with the great bells of Notre Dame,[4] everyone must bear his own universe, and most persons are moderately interested in learning how their neighbors have managed to carry theirs.

This problem of education, started in 1838, went on for three years, while the baby grew, like other babies, unconsciously, as a vegetable, the outside world working as it never had worked before, to get his new universe ready for him. Often in old age he puzzled over the question whether, on the doctrine of chances,[5] he was at liberty to accept himself or his world as an accident. No such accident had ever happened before in human experience. For him, alone, the old universe was thrown into the ash-heap and a new one created. He and his eighteenth-century, troglodytic Boston were suddenly cut apart — separated forever — in act if not in sentiment, by the opening of the Boston and Albany Railroad;[6] the appearance of the first Cunard steamers in the bay;[7] and the telegraphic messages which carried from Baltimore to Washington the news that Henry Clay and James K. Polk were nominated for the Presidency. This was in May, 1844; he was six years old; his new world was ready for use, and only fragments of the old met his eyes.

Of all this that was being done to complicate his education, he knew only the color of yellow. He first found himself sitting on a yellow kitchen floor in strong sunlight. He was three years old when he took this earliest step in education; a lesson of color. The second followed soon; a lesson of taste. On December 3, 1841, he developed scarlet fever.[8] For several days he was as good as dead, reviving only under the careful nursing of his family. When he began to recover strength, about January 1, 1842, his hunger must have been stronger than any other pleasure or pain, for while in after life he retained not the faintest recollection of his illness, he remembered quite clearly his aunt entering the sick-room bearing in her hand a saucer with a baked apple.

The order of impressions retained by memory might naturally be that of color and taste, although one would rather suppose that the sense of pain would be first to educate. In fact, the third recollection of the child was that of discomfort. The moment he could be removed, he was bundled up in blankets and carried from the little house in Hancock Avenue to a larger one which his parents were to occupy for the rest of their lives in the neighboring Mount Vernon Street. The season was midwinter, January 10, 1842,[9] and he never forgot his acute distress for want of air under his blankets, or the noises of moving furniture.

As a means of variation from a normal type, sickness in childhood ought to have a certain value not to be classed under any fitness or unfitness of natural selection;[10] and especially scarlet fever affected boys seriously, both physically and in character, though they might through life puzzle themselves to decide whether it had fitted or unfitted them for success; but this fever of Henry Adams took greater and greater importance in his eyes, from the point of view of education, the longer he lived. At first, the effect was physical. He fell behind his brothers[11] two or three inches in height, and proportionally in bone and weight. His character and processes of mind seemed to share in this fining-down process of scale. He was not good in a fight, and his nerves were more delicate than boys' nerves ought to be. He exaggerated these weaknesses as he grew older. The habit of doubt; of distrusting his own judgment and of totally rejecting the judgment of the world; the tendency to regard every question as open; the hesitation to act except as a choice of evils; the shirking of responsibility; the love of line, form, quality; the horror of ennui; the passion for companionship and the antipathy to society — all these are well-known qualities of New England character in no way peculiar to individuals but in this instance they seemed to be stimulated by the fever, and Henry Adams could never make up his mind whether, on the whole, the change of character was morbid or healthy, good or bad for his purpose. His brothers were the type; he was the variation.

As far as the boy knew, the sickness did not affect him at all, and he grew up in excellent health, bodily and mental, taking

life as it was given; accepting its local standards without a difficulty, and enjoying much of it as keenly as any other boy of his
age. He seemed to himself quite normal, and his companions
seemed always to think him so. Whatever was peculiar about
him was education, not character, and came to him, directly and
indirectly, as the result of that eighteenth-century inheritance
which he took with his name.

The atmosphere of education in which he lived was colonial,
revolutionary, almost Cromwellian, as though he were steeped,
from his greatest grandmother's[12] birth, in the odor of political
crime. Resistance to something was the law of New England nature; the boy looked out on the world with the instinct of resistance; for numberless generations his predecessors had viewed the
world chiefly as a thing to be reformed, filled with evil forces to
be abolished, and they saw no reason to suppose that they had
wholly succeeded in the abolition; the duty was unchanged. That
duty implied not only resistance to evil, but hatred of it. Boys
naturally look on all force as an enemy, and generally find it so, but
the New Englander, whether boy or man, in his long struggle with
a stingy or hostile universe, had learned also to love the pleasure
of hating; his joys were few.

Politics, as a practice, whatever its professions, had always
been the systematic organization of hatreds, and Massachusetts
politics had been as harsh as the climate. The chief charm of
New England was harshness of contrasts and extremes of sensibility — a cold that froze the blood, and a heat that boiled it
— so that the pleasure of hating — oneself if no better victim
offered — was not its rarest amusement; but the charm was a
true and natural child of the soil, not a cultivated weed of the
ancients. The violence of the contrast was real and made the
strongest motive of education. The double exterior nature gave
life its relative values. Winter and summer, cold and heat, town
and country, force and freedom, marked two modes of life and
thought, balanced like lobes of the brain. Town was winter

confinement, school, rule, discipline; straight, gloomy streets, piled with six feet of snow in the middle; frosts that made the snow sing under wheels or runners; thaws when the streets became dangerous to cross; society of uncles, aunts, and cousins who expected children to behave themselves, and who were not always gratified; above all else, winter represented the desire to escape and go free. Town was restraint, law, unity. Country, only seven miles away, was liberty, diversity, outlawry, the endless delight of mere sense impressions given by nature for nothing, and breathed by boys without knowing it.[13]

Boys are wild animals, rich in the treasures of sense, but the New England boy had a wider range of emotions than boys of more equable climates. He felt his nature crudely, as it was meant. To the boy Henry Adams, summer was drunken. Among senses, smell was the strongest — smell of hot pine-woods and sweet-fern in the scorching summer noon; of new-mown hay; of ploughed earth; of box hedges; of peaches, lilacs, syringas; of stables, barns, cow-yards; of salt water and low tide on the marshes; nothing came amiss. Next to smell came taste, and the children knew the taste of everything they saw or touched, from pennyroyal and flagroot to the shell of a pignut and the letters of a spelling-book — the taste of A-B, AB, suddenly revived on the boy's tongue sixty years afterwards. Light, line, and color as sensual pleasures, came later and were as crude as the rest. The New England light is glare, and the atmosphere harshens color. The boy was a full man before he ever knew what was meant by atmosphere; his idea of pleasure in light was the blaze of a New England sun. His idea of color was a peony, with the dew of early morning on its petals. The intense blue of the sea, as he saw it a mile or two away, from the Quincy hills; the cumuli in a June afternoon sky; the strong reds and greens and purples of colored prints and children's picture-books, as the American colors then ran; these were ideals. The opposites or antipathies, were the cold grays of November evenings, and the thick, muddy

8

thaws of Boston winter. With such standards, the Bostonian could not but develop a double nature. Life was a double thing. After a January blizzard, the boy who could look with pleasure into the violent snow-glare of the cold white sunshine, with its intense light and shade, scarcely knew what was meant by tone. He could reach it only by education.

Winter and summer, then, were two hostile lives, and bred two separate natures. Winter was always the effort to live; summer was tropical license. Whether the children rolled in the grass, or waded in the brook, or swam in the salt ocean, or sailed in the bay, or fished for smelts in the creeks, or netted minnows in the salt-marshes, or took to the pine-woods and the granite quarries, or chased muskrats and hunted snapping-turtles in the swamps, or mushrooms or nuts on the autumn hills, summer and country were always sensual living, while winter was always compulsory learning. Summer was the multiplicity of nature; winter was school.

The bearing of the two seasons on the education of Henry Adams was no fancy; it was the most decisive force he ever knew; it ran though life, and made the division between its perplexing, warring, irreconcilable problems, irreducible opposites, with growing emphasis to the last year of study. From earliest childhood the boy was accustomed to feel that, for him, life was double. Winter and summer, town and country, law and liberty, were hostile, and the man who pretended they were not, was in his eyes a schoolmaster — that is, a man employed to tell lies to little boys. Though Quincy was but two hours' walk from Beacon Hill,[14] it belonged in a different world. For two hundred years, every Adams, from father to son, had lived within sight of State Street,[15] and sometimes had lived in it, yet none had ever taken kindly to the town, or been taken kindly by it. The boy inherited his double nature. He knew as yet nothing about his great-grandfather, who had died a dozen years before his own birth: he took for granted that any great-grandfather of his must have always

9

been good, and his enemies wicked; but he divined his great-grand-father's character from his own. Never for a moment did he connect the two ideas of Boston and John Adams; they were separate and antagonistic; the idea of John Adams went with Quincy. He knew his grandfather John Quincy Adams only as an old man of seventy-five or eighty who was friendly and gentle with him, but except that he heard his grandfather always called "the President," and his grandmother "the Madam," he had no reason to suppose that his Adams grandfather differed in character from his Brooks grandfather who was equally kind and benevolent. He liked the Adams side best, but for no other reason than that it reminded him of the country, the summer, and the absence of restraint. Yet he felt also that Quincy was in a way inferior to Boston, and that socially Boston looked down on Quincy. The reason was clear enough even to a five-year-old child. Quincy had no Boston style. Little enough style had either; a simpler manner of life and thought could hardly exist, short of cave-dwelling. The flint-and-steel with which his grandfather Adams used to light his own fires in the early morning was still on the mantelpiece of his study. The idea of a livery or even a dress for servants, or of an evening toilette, was next to blasphemy. Bathrooms, water-supplies, lighting, heating, and the whole array of domestic comforts, were unknown at Quincy. Boston had already a bathroom, a water-supply, a furnace, and gas. The superiority of Boston was evident, but a child liked it no better for that.

The magnificence of his grandfather Brooks's house in Pearl Street or South Street has long ago disappeared, but perhaps his country house at Medford may still remain to show what impressed the mind of a boy in 1845 with the idea of city splendor. The President's place at Quincy was the larger and older and far the more interesting of the two; but a boy felt at once its inferiority in fashion. It showed plainly enough its want of wealth. It smacked of colonial age, but not of Boston style or plush curtains. To the end of his life he never quite overcame the prejudice thus drawn

in with his childish breath. He never could compel himself to
care for nineteenth-century style. He was never able to adopt
it, any more than his father or grandfather or great-grandfather
had done. Not that he felt it as particularly hostile, for he reconciled himself to much that was worse; but because, for some remote
reason, he was born an eighteenth-century child. The old house
at Quincy was eighteenth century. What style it had was in its
Queen Anne mahogany panels and its Louis Seize chairs and sofas.
The panels belonged to an old colonial Vassall who built the house;
the furniture had been brought back from Paris in 1789 or 1801
or 1817,[16] along with porcelain and books and much else of old diplomatic remnants; and neither of the two eighteenth-century styles
— neither English Queen Anne nor French Louis Seize — was comfortable for a boy, or for anyone else. The dark mahogany had
been painted white to suit daily life in winter gloom. Nothing
seemed to favor, for a child's objects, the older forms. On the
contrary, most boys, as well as grown-up people, preferred the
new, with good reason, and the child felt himself distinctly at a
disadvantage for the taste.

Nor had personal preference any share in his bias. The Brooks
grandfather was as amiable and as sympathetic as the Adams
grandfather. Both were born in 1767, and both died in 1848.[17]
Both were kind to children, and both belonged rather to the
eighteenth than to the nineteenth centuries. The child knew no
difference between them except that one was associated with
winter and the other with summer; one with Boston, the other
with Quincy. Even with Medford, the association was hardly
easier. Once as a very young boy he was taken to pass a few days
with his grandfather Brooks under charge of his aunt, but became
so violently homesick that within twenty-four hours he was brought
back in disgrace. Yet he could not remember ever being seriously
homesick again.

The attachment to Quincy was not altogether sentimental or
wholly sympathetic. Quincy was not a bed of thornless roses.

Even there the curse of Cain[18] set its mark. There as elsewhere a cruel universe combined to crush a child. As though three or four vigorous brothers and sisters, with the best will, were not enough to crush any child, everyone else conspired towards an education which he hated. From cradle to grave this problem of running order through chaos, direction through space, discipline through freedom, unity through multiplicity, has always been, and must always be, the task of education, as it is the moral of religion, philosophy, science, art, politics, and economy; but a boy's will is his life, and he dies when it is broken, as the colt dies in harness, taking a new nature in becoming tame. Rarely has the boy felt kindly towards his tamers. Between him and his master has always been war. Henry Adams never knew a boy of his generation to like a master, and the task of remaining on friendly terms with one's own family, in such a relation, was never easy.

All the more singular it seemed afterwards to him that his first serious contact with the President should have been a struggle of will, in which the old man almost necessarily defeated the boy, but instead of leaving, as usual in such defeats, a lifelong sting, left rather an impression of as fair treatment as could be expected from a natural enemy. The boy met seldom with such restraint. He could not have been much more than six years old at the time — seven at the utmost — and his mother had taken him to Quincy for a long stay with the President during the summer. What became of the rest of the family he quite forgot; but he distinctly remembered standing at the house door one summer morning in a passionate outburst of rebellion against going to school. Naturally his mother was the immediate victim of his rage; that is what mothers are for, and boys also; but in this case the boy had his mother at unfair disadvantage, for she was a guest, and had no means of enforcing obedience. Henry showed a certain tactical ability by refusing to start, and he met all efforts at compulsion by successful, though too vehement protest. He was in fair way to win, and was holding his own, with sufficient energy, at the bottom of the long staircase which led up to the door of the President's library, when the door opened, and the old man slowly came down. Putting on his hat, he took the boy's hand without a word, and walked with him, paralyzed by awe, up the road to the town. After the first moments of consternation at this interference in a domestic dispute, the boy reflected that an old gentleman close on eighty would never trouble himself to walk near a mile on a hot summer morning over a shadeless road to take a boy to school, and that it would be strange if a lad imbued with the passion of freedom could not find a corner to dodge around, somewhere before reaching the school door. Then and always, the boy insisted that this reasoning justified his apparent submission; but the old man did not stop, and the boy saw all his strategical points turned, one after another, until he found himself seated inside the school, and obviously the centre of curious if not malevolent criticism. Not till then did the President release his hand and depart.[19]

The point was that this act, contrary to the inalienable rights of boys, and nullifying the social compact, ought to have made him dislike his grandfather for life. He could not recall that it had this effect even for a moment. With a certain maturity of mind, the child must have recognized that the President, though a tool of tyranny, had done his disreputable work with a certain intelligence. He had shown no temper, no irritation, no personal feeling, and had made no display of force. Above all, he had held his tongue. During their long walk he had said nothing; he had uttered no syllable of revolting cant about the duty of obedience and the wickedness of resistance to law; he had shown no concern in the matter; hardly even a consciousness of the boy's existence. Probably his mind at that moment was actually troubling itself little about his grandson's iniquities, and much about the iniquities of President Polk,[20] but the boy could scarcely at that age feel the whole satisfaction of thinking that President Polk was to be the vicarious victim of his own sins, and he gave his grandfather credit for intelligent silence. For this forbearance he felt instinctive respect. He admitted force as a form of right; he admitted even temper, under protest; but the seeds of a moral education would at that moment have fallen on the stoniest soil in Quincy, which is, as everyone knows, the stoniest glacial and tidal drift known in any Puritan land.[21]

Neither party to this momentary disagreement can have felt rancor, for during these three or four summers the old President's relations with the boy were friendly and almost intimate. Whether his older brothers and sisters were still more favored he failed to remember, but he was himself admitted to a sort of familiarity which, when in his turn he had reached old age, rather shocked him, for it must have sometimes tried the President's patience. He hung about the library; handled the books; deranged the papers; ransacked the drawers; searched the old purses and pocket-books for foreign coins; drew the sword-cane; snapped the travelling-pistols; upset everything in the corners, and penetrated the President's dressing-closet where a row of tumblers, inverted on the shelf, covered caterpillars which were supposed to become moths or butterflies, but never did. The Madam bore with fortitude the loss of the tumblers which her husband purloined for these hatcheries; but she made protest when he carried off her best cut-glass bowls to plant with acorns or peachstones that he might see the roots grow, but which, she said, he commonly forgot like the caterpillars.

At that time the President rode the hobby of tree-culture, and some fine old trees should still remain to witness it, unless they have been improved off the ground; but his was a restless mind, and although he took his hobbies seriously and would have been annoyed had his grandchild asked whether he was bored like an English duke, he probably cared more for the processes than for the results, so that his grandson was saddened by the sight and smell of peaches and pears, the best of their kind, which he brought up from the garden to rot on his shelves for seed. With the inherited virtues of his Puritan ancestors, the little boy Henry conscientiously brought up to him in his study the finest peaches he found in the garden, and ate only the less perfect. Naturally he ate more by way of compensation, but the act showed that he bore no grudge. As for his grandfather, it is even possible that he may have felt a certain self-reproach for his temporary rôle of schoolmaster — seeing that his own career did not offer proof of the worldly advantages of docile obedience[22]— for there still exists somewhere a little volume of critically edited Nursery Rhymes with the boy's name in full written in the President's trembling hand on the fly-leaf. Of course there was also the Bible, given to each child at birth, with the proper inscription in the President's hand on the fly-leaf; while their grandfather Brooks supplied the silver mugs.

So many Bibles and silver mugs had to be supplied, that a new house, or cottage, was built to hold them. It was "on the hill," five minutes' walk above "the old house," with a far view eastward over Quincy Bay, and northward over Boston. Till his twelfth year, the child passed his summers there, and his pleasures of childhood mostly centred in it. Of education he had as yet little to complain. Country schools were not very serious. Nothing stuck to the mind except home impressions, and the sharpest were those of kindred children; but as influences that warped a mind, none compared with the mere effect of the back of the President's bald head, as he sat in his pew on Sundays, in line with that of President Quincy,[23] who, though some ten years younger, seemed to children about the same age. Before railways entered the New England town, every parish church showed half-a-dozen of these leading citizens, with gray hair, who sat on the main aisle in the best pews, and had sat there, or in some equivalent dignity, since the time of St. Augustine, if not since the glacial epoch. It was unusual for boys to sit behind a President grandfather, and to read over his head the tablet in memory of a President great-grandfather, who had "pledged his life, his fortune, and his sacred honor" to secure the independence of his country and so forth; but boys naturally supposed, without much reasoning, that other boys had the equivalent of President grandfathers, and that churches would always go on, with the bald-headed leading citizens on the main aisle, and Presidents or their equivalents on the walls. The Irish gardener once said to the child: "You'll be thinkin' you'll be President too!" The casuality[24] of the remark made so strong an impression on his mind that he never forgot it. He could not remember ever to have thought on the subject; to him, that there should be a doubt of his being President was a new idea. What had been would continue to be. He doubted neither about Presidents nor about Churches, and no one suggested at that time a doubt whether a system of society which had lasted since Adam would outlast one Adams more.

The Madam was a little more remote than the President, but more decorative. She stayed much in her own room with the Dutch tiles, looking out on her garden with the box walks, and seemed a fragile creature to a boy who sometimes brought her a note or a message, and took distinct pleasure in looking at her delicate face under what seemed to him very becoming caps. He liked her refined figure; her gentle voice and manner; her vague effect of not belonging there, but to Washington or to Europe, like her furniture, and writing-desk with little glass doors above and little eighteenth-century volumes in old binding, labelled "Peregrine Pickle" or "Tom Jones" or "Hannah More."[25] Try as she might, the Madam could never be Bostonian, and it was her cross in life, but to the boy it was her charm. Even at that age, he felt drawn to it. The Madam's life had been in truth far from Boston. She was born in London in 1775, daughter of Joshua Johnson, an American merchant, brother of Governor Thomas Johnson of Maryland; and Catherine Nuth, of an English family in London. Driven from England by the Revolutionary War, Joshua Johnson took his family to Nantes, where they remained till the peace. The girl Louisa Catherine was nearly ten years old when brought back to London, and her sense of nationality must have been confused; but the influence of the Johnsons and the services of Joshua obtained for him from President Washington the appointment of Consul in London on the organization of the Government in 1790. In 1794 President Washington appointed John Quincy Adams Minister to The Hague. He was twenty-seven years old when he returned to London, and found the Consul's house a very agreeable haunt. Louisa was then twenty.

At that time, and long afterwards, the Consul's house, far more than the Minister's, was the centre of contact for travelling Americans, either official or other. The Legation was a shifting point, between 1785 and 1815; but the Consulate, far down in the City,[26] near the Tower, was convenient and inviting; so inviting that it proved fatal to young Adams. Louisa was charming, like a Romney[27] portrait, but among her many charms that of being a New England woman was not one. The defect was serious. Her future mother-in-law, Abigail,[28] a famous New England woman whose authority over her turbulent husband, the second President, was hardly so great as that which she exercised over her son, the sixth to be, was troubled by the fear that Louisa might not be made of stuff stern enough, or brought up in conditions severe enough, to suit a New England climate, or to make an efficient wife for her paragon son, and Abigail was right on that point, as on most others where sound judgment was involved; but sound judgment is sometimes a source of weakness rather than of force, and John Quincy already had reason to think that his mother held sound judgments on the subject of daughters-in-law which human nature, since the fall of Eve, made Adams helpless to realize. Being three thousand miles away from his mother, and equally far in love, he married Louisa in London, July 26, 1797, and took her to Berlin to be the head of the United States Legation. During three or four exciting years, the young bride lived in Berlin; whether she was happy or not, whether she was content or not, whether she was socially successful or not, her descendants did not surely know; but in any case she could by no chance have become educated there for a life in Quincy or Boston. In 1801 the overthrow of the Federalist Party[29]drove her and her husband to America, and she became at last a member of the Quincy household, but by that time her children needed all her attention, and she remained there with occasional winters in Boston and Washington, till 1809. Her husband was made Senator in 1803, and in 1809 was appointed Minister to Russia. She went with him to St. Petersburg, taking her baby, Charles Francis, born in 1807; but broken-hearted at having to leave her two older boys behind. The life at St. Petersburg was hardly gay for her; they were far too poor to shine in that extravagant society; but she survived it, though her little girl baby did not, and in the winter of 1814–15, alone with the boy of seven years old, crossed Europe from St. Petersburg to Paris, in her travelling-carriage, passing through the armies, and reaching Paris in the *Cent Jours*[30]after Napoleon's return from Elba. Her husband next went to England as Minister, and she was for two years at the Court of the Regent.[31] In 1817 her husband came home to be Secretary of State, and she lived for eight years in F Street, doing her work of entertainer for President Monroe's administration. Next she lived four miserable years in the White House. When that chapter was closed in 1829, she had earned the right to be tired and delicate, but she still had fifteen years to serve as wife of a Member of the House, after her husband went back to Congress in 1833.[32] Then it was that the little Henry, her grandson, first remembered her, from 1843 to 1848, sitting in her panelled room, at breakfast, with her heavy silver teapot and sugar-bowl and cream-jug, which still exist somewhere as an heirloom of the modern safety-vault. By that time she was seventy years old or more, and thoroughly weary of being beaten about a stormy world. To the boy she seemed singularly peaceful, a vision of silver gray, presiding over her old President and her Queen Anne mahogany; an exotic, like her Sèvres china; an object of deference to everyone, and of great affection to her son Charles; but hardly more Bostonian than she had been fifty years before, on her wedding-day, in the shadow of the Tower of London.[33]

Such a figure was even less fitted than that of her old husband, the President, to impress on a boy's mind the standards of the coming century. She was Louis Seize, like the furniture. The boy knew nothing of her interior life, which had been, as the venerable Abigail, long since at peace, foresaw, one of severe stress and little pure satisfaction. He never dreamed that from her might come some of those doubts and self-questionings, those hesitations, those rebellions against law and discipline, which marked more than one of her descendants; but he might even then have felt some vague instinctive suspicion that he was to inherit from her the seeds of the primal sin, the fall from grace, the curse of Abel,[34] that he was not of pure New England stock, but half exotic. As a child of Quincy he was not a true Bostonian, but even as a child of Quincy he inherited a quarter taint of Maryland blood. Charles Francis, half Marylander by birth,[35] had hardly seen Boston till he was ten years old, when his parents left him there at school in 1817, and he never forgot the experience. He was to be nearly as old as his mother had been in 1845, before he quite accepted Boston, or Boston quite accepted him.

A boy who began his education in these surroundings, with physical strength inferior to that of his brothers, and with a certain delicacy of mind and bone, ought rightly to have felt at home in the eighteenth century and should, in proper self-respect, have rebelled against the standards of the nineteenth. The atmosphere of his first ten years must have been very like that of his grandfather at the same age, from 1767 till 1776, barring the battle of Bunker Hill, and even as late as 1846, the battle of Bunker Hill remained actual. The tone of Boston society was colonial. The true Bostonian always knelt in self-abasement before the majesty of English standards; far from concealing it as a weakness, he was proud of it as his strength. The eighteenth century ruled society long after 1850. Perhaps the boy began to shake it off rather earlier than most of his mates.

Indeed this prehistoric stage of education ended rather abruptly with his tenth year. One winter morning he was conscious of a certain confusion in the house in Mount Vernon Street, and gathered, from such words as he could catch, that the President, who happened to be then staying there, on his way to Washington, had fallen and hurt himself.[36] Then he heard the word paralysis. After that day he came to associate the word with the figure of his grandfather, in a tall-backed, invalid armchair, on one side of the spare bedroom fireplace, and one of his old friends, Dr. Parkman[37] or P. P. F. Degrand,[38] on the other side, both dozing.

The end of this first, or ancestral and Revolutionary, chapter came on February 21, 1848 — and the month of February brought life and death as a family habit — when the eighteenth century, as an actual and living companion, vanished. If the scene on the floor of the House, when the old President fell, struck the still simple-minded American public with a sensation unusually dramatic, its effect on a ten-year-old boy, whose boy-life was fading away with the life of his grandfather, could not be slight. One had to pay for Revolutionary patriots; grandfathers and grandmothers; Presidents; diplomats; Queen Anne mahogany and Louis Seize chairs, as well as for Stuart[39] portraits. Such things warp young life. Americans commonly believed that they ruined it, and perhaps the practical common-sense of the American mind judged right. Many a boy might be ruined by much less than the emotions of the funeral service in the Quincy church, with its surroundings of national respect and family pride. By another dramatic chance it happened that the clergyman of the parish, Dr. Lunt,[40] was an unusual pulpit orator, the ideal of a somewhat austere intellectual type, such as the school of Buckminster[41] and Channing[42] inherited from the old Congregational clergy. His extraordinarily refined appearance, his dignity of manner, his deeply cadenced voice, his remarkable English and his fine appreciation, gave to the funeral service a character that left an overwhelming impression on the boy's mind. He was to see many great functions — funerals and festivals — in after-life, till his only thought was to see no more, but he never again witnessed anything nearly so impressive to him as the last services at Quincy over the body of one President and the ashes of another.[43]

The effect of the Quincy service was deepened by the official ceremony which afterwards took place in Faneuil Hall, when the boy was taken to hear his uncle, Edward Everett,[44] deliver a Eulogy. Like all Mr. Everett's orations, it was an admirable piece of oratory, such as only an admirable orator and scholar could create; too good for a ten-year-old boy to appreciate at its value; but already the boy knew that the dead President could not be in it, and had even learned why he would have been out of place there; for knowledge was beginning to come fast. The shadow of the War of 1812 still hung over State Street; the shadow of the Civil War to come had already begun to darken Faneuil Hall. No rhetoric could have reconciled Mr. Everett's audience to his subject. How could he say there, to an assemblage of Bostonians in the heart of mercantile Boston, that the only distinctive mark of all the Adamses, since old Sam Adams's father[45] a hundred and fifty years before, had been their inherited quarrel with State Street,[46] which had again and again broken out into riot, bloodshed, personal feuds, foreign and civil war, wholesale banishments and confiscations, until the history of Florence was hardly more turbulent than that of Boston?[47] How could he whisper the word Hartford Convention before the men who had made it? What would have been said had he suggested the chance of Secession and Civil War?

Thus already, at ten years old, the boy found himself standing face to face with a dilemma that might have puzzled an early Christian. What was he? — where was he going? Even then he felt that something was wrong, but he concluded that it must be Boston. Quincy had always been right, for Quincy represented a moral principle — the principle of resistance to Boston. His

Adams ancestors must have been right, since they were always hostile to State Street. If State Street was wrong, Quincy must be right! Turn the dilemma as he pleased, he still came back on the eighteenth century and the law of Resistance; of Truth; of Duty, and of Freedom. He was a ten-year-old priest and politician. He could under no circumstances have guessed what the next fifty years had in store, and no one could teach him; but sometimes, in his old age, he wondered — and could never decide — whether the most clear and certain knowledge would have helped him. Supposing he had seen a New York stock-list of 1900, and had studied the statistics of railways, telegraphs, coal, and steel — would he have quitted his eighteenth-century, his ancestral prejudices, his abstract ideals, his semi-clerical training, and the rest, in order to perform an expiatory pilgrimage to State Street, and ask for the fatted calf [48] of his grandfather Brooks and a clerkship in the Suffolk Bank?

Sixty years afterwards he was still unable to make up his mind. Each course had its advantages, but the material advantages, looking back, seemed to lie wholly in State Street.

CHAPTER II

Boston (1848–1854)

PETER CHARDON BROOKS, the other grandfather, died January 1, 1849, bequeathing what was supposed to be the largest estate in Boston, about two million dollars, to his seven surviving children: four sons — Edward, Peter Chardon, Gorham, and Sydney; three daughters — Charlotte, married to Edward Everett; Ann, married to Nathaniel Frothingham, minister of the First Church; and Abigail Brown, born April 25, 1808, married September 3, 1829, to Charles Francis Adams, hardly a year older than herself. Their first child, born in 1830, was a daughter, named Louisa Catherine, after her Johnson grandmother; the second was a son, named John Quincy, after his President grandfather; the third took his father's name, Charles Francis; while the fourth, being of less account, was in a way given to his mother, who named him Henry Brooks, after a favorite brother just lost. More followed, but these, being younger, had nothing to do with the arduous process of educating.[1]

The Adams connection was singularly small in Boston, but the family of Brooks was singularly large and even brilliant, and almost wholly of clerical New England stock. One might have sought long in much larger and older societies for three brothers-in-law more distinguished or more scholarly than Edward Everett, Dr. Frothingham, and Mr. Adams. One might have sought equally long for seven brothers-in-law more unlike. No doubt they all bore more or less the stamp of Boston, or at least of Massachusetts Bay, but the shades of difference amounted to contrasts. Mr. Everett belonged to Boston hardly more than Mr. Adams. One of the most ambitious of Bostonians, he had broken bounds early in life by leaving the Unitarian pulpit to take a seat in Congress where he had given valuable support to J. Q. Adams's administration; support which, as a social consequence, led to the marriage of the President's son, Charles Francis, with Mr. Everett's youngest sister-in-law, Abigail Brooks. The wreck of parties which marked the reign[2] of Andrew Jackson had interfered with many promising careers, that of Edward Everett among the rest, but he had risen with the Whig Party to power, had gone as Minister to England, and had returned to America with the halo of a European reputation, and undisputed rank second only to Daniel Webster as the orator and representative figure of Boston. The other brother-in-law, Dr. Frothingham, belonged to the same clerical school, though in manner rather the less clerical of the two. Neither of them had much in common with Mr. Adams, who was a younger man, greatly biassed by his father, and by the inherited feud between Quincy and State Street,[3] but personal relations were friendly as far as a boy could see, and the innumerable cousins went regularly to the First Church every Sunday in winter, and slept through their uncle's sermons, without once thinking to ask what the sermons were supposed to mean for them. For two hundred years the First Church had seen the same little boys, sleeping more or less soundly under the same or similar conditions, and dimly conscious of the same feuds; but the feuds had never ceased, and the boys had always grown up to inherit them. Those of the generation of 1812 had mostly disappeared in 1850; death had cleared that score; the quarrels of John Adams, and those of John Quincy Adams were no longer acutely personal; the game was considered as drawn; and Charles Francis Adams might then have taken his inherited rights of political leadership in succession to Mr. Webster and Mr. Everett, his seniors. Between him and State Street the relation was more natural[4] than between Edward Everett and State Street; but instead of doing so, Charles Francis Adams drew himself aloof and renewed the old war which had already lasted since 1700. He could not help it. With the record of J. Q. Adams fresh in the popular memory, his son and his only representative could not make terms with the slave-power, and the slave-power overshadowed all the great Boston interests. No doubt Mr. Adams had principles of his own, as well as inherited, but even his children, who as yet had no principles, could equally little follow the lead of Mr. Webster or even of Mr. Seward.[5] They would have lost in consideration more than they would have gained in patronage. They were anti-slavery by birth, as their name was Adams and their home was Quincy. No matter how much they had wished to enter State Street, they felt that State Street never would trust them, or they it. Had State Street been Paradise, they must hunger for it in vain, and it hardly needed Daniel Webster to act as archangel with the flaming sword, to order them away from the door.

Time and experience, which alter all perspectives, altered this among the rest, and taught the boy gentler judgment, but even when only ten years old, his face was already fixed, and his heart was stone, against State Street; his education was warped beyond recovery in the direction of Puritan politics.[6] Between him and his patriot grandfather at the same age, the conditions had changed little. The year 1848 was like enough to the year 1776 to make a fair parallel. The parallel, as concerned bias of education, was complete when, a few months after the death of John Quincy Adams, a convention of anti-slavery delegates met at Buffalo to organize a new party and named candidates for the general election in November: for President, Martin Van Buren; for Vice-President, Charles Francis Adams.

For any American boy the fact that his father was running for office would have dwarfed for the time every other excitement, but even apart from personal bias, the year 1848, for a boy's road through life, was decisive for twenty years to come. There was never a side-path of escape. The stamp of 1848 was almost as indelible as the stamp of 1776, but in the eighteenth or any earlier century, the stamp mattered less because it was standard, and everyone bore it; while men whose lives were to fall in the generation between 1865 and 1900 had, first of all, to get rid of it, and take the stamp that belonged to their time. This was their education. To outsiders, immigrants, adventurers, it was easy, but the old Puritan nature rebelled against change. The reason it gave was forcible. The Puritan thought his thought higher and his moral standards better than those of his successors. So they were. He could not be convinced that moral standards had nothing to do with it, and that utilitarian morality was good enough for him, as it was for the graceless. Nature had given to the boy Henry a character that, in any previous century, would have led him into the Church; he inherited dogma and *a priori* thought[7] from the beginning of time; and he scarcely needed a violent reaction like anti-slavery politics to sweep him back into Puritanism with a violence as great as that of a religious war.

Thus far he had nothing to do with it; his education was chiefly inheritance, and during the next five or six years, his father alone counted for much. If he were to worry successfully through life's quicksands, he must depend chiefly on his father's pilotage; but, for his father, the channel lay clear, while for himself an unknown ocean lay beyond. His father's business in life was to get past the dangers of the slave-power, or to fix its bounds at least. The task done, he might be content to let his sons pay for the pilotage; and it mattered little to his success whether they paid it with their lives wasted on battle-fields or in misdirected energies and lost opportunity. The generation that lived from 1840 to 1870 could do very well with the old forms of education; that which had its work to do between 1870 and 1900 needed something quite new.

His father's character was therefore the larger part of his education, as far as any single person affected it, and for that reason, if for no other, the son was always a much interested critic of his father's mind and temper. Long after his death as an old man of eighty, his sons continued to discuss this subject with a good deal of difference in their points of view.[8] To his son Henry, the quality that distinguished his father from all the other figures in the family group, was that, in his opinion, Charles Francis

Adams possessed the only perfectly balanced mind that ever existed in the name. For a hundred years, every newspaper scribbler had, with more or less obvious excuse, derided or abused the older Adamses for want of judgment. They abused Charles Francis for his judgment. Naturally they never attempted to assign values to either; that was the children's affair; but the traits were real. Charles Francis Adams was singular for mental poise — absence of self-assertion or self-consciousness — the faculty of standing apart without seeming aware that he was alone — a balance of mind and temper that neither challenged nor avoided notice, nor admitted question of superiority or inferiority, of jealousy, of personal motives, from any source, even under great pressure. This unusual poise of judgment and temper, ripened by age, became the more striking to his son Henry as he learned to measure the mental faculties themselves, which were in no way exceptional either for depth or range. Charles Francis Adams's memory was hardly above the average; his mind was not bold like his grandfather's or restless like his father's, or imaginative or oratorical — still less mathematical; but it worked with singular perfection, admirable self-restraint, and instinctive mastery of form. Within its range it was a model.

The standards of Boston were high, much affected by the old clerical self-respect which gave the Unitarian clergy unusual social charm. Dr. Channing, Mr. Everett, Dr. Frothingham, Dr. Palfrey, President Walker, R. W. Emerson,[9] and other Boston ministers of the same school, would have commanded distinction in any society; but the Adamses had little or no affinity with the pulpit, and still less with its eccentric offshoots, like Theodore Parker, or Brook Farm, or the philosophy of Concord.[10] Besides its clergy, Boston showed a literary group, led by Ticknor, Prescott, Longfellow, Motley, O. W. Holmes;[11] but Mr. Adams was not one of them; as a rule they were much too Websterian. Even in science Boston could claim a certain eminence, especially in medicine, but Mr. Adams cared very little for science.

He stood alone. He had no master — hardly even his father. He had no scholars — hardly even his sons.[12]

Almost alone among his Boston contemporaries, he was not English in feeling or in sympathies. Perhaps a hundred years of acute hostility to England had something to do with this family trait; but in his case it went further and became indifference to social distinction. Never once in forty years of intimacy did his son notice in him a trace of snobbishness. He was one of the exceedingly small number of Americans to whom an English duke or duchess seemed to be indifferent, and royalty itself nothing more than a slightly inconvenient presence. This was, it is true, rather the tone of English society in his time, but Americans were largely responsible for changing it, and Mr. Adams had every possible reason for affecting the manner of a courtier even if he did not feel the sentiment. Never did his son see him flatter or vilify, or show a sign of envy or jealousy; never a shade of vanity or self-conceit. Never a tone of arrogance! Never a gesture of pride!

The same thing might perhaps have been said of John Quincy Adams, but in him his associates averred that it was accompanied by mental restlessness and often by lamentable want of judgment. No one ever charged Charles Francis Adams with this fault. The critics charged him with just the opposite defect. They called him cold. No doubt, such perfect poise — such intuitive self-adjustment — was not maintained by nature without a sacrifice of the qualities which would have upset it. No doubt, too, that even his restless-minded, introspective, self-conscious children who knew him best were much too ignorant of the world and of human nature to suspect how rare and complete was the model before their eyes. A coarser instrument would have impressed them more. Average human nature is very coarse, and its ideals must necessarily be average. The world never loved perfect poise. What the world does love is commonly absence of poise, for it has to be amused. Napoleons and Andrew Jacksons amuse it, but it is not amused by perfect balance. Had Mr. Adams's nature been cold, he would have followed Mr. Webster, Mr. Everett, Mr. Seward, and Mr. Winthrop[13] in the lines of party discipline and self-interest. Had it been less balanced than it was, he would have gone with Mr. Garrison, Mr. Wendell Phillips, Mr. Edmund Quincy, and Theodore Parker, into secession.[14] Between the two paths he found an intermediate one, distinctive and characteristic — he set up a party of his own.[15]

This political party became a chief influence in the education of the boy Henry in the six years 1848 to 1854, and violently affected his character at the moment when character is plastic. The group of men with whom Mr. Adams associated himself, and whose social centre was the house in Mount Vernon Street, numbered only three: Dr. John G. Palfrey, Richard H. Dana, and Charles Sumner.[16] Dr. Palfrey was the oldest, and in spite of his clerical education, was to a boy often the most agreeable, for his talk was lighter and his range wider than that of the others; he had wit, or humor, and the give-and-take of dinner-table exchange. Born to be a man of the world, he forced himself to be clergyman, professor, or statesman, while, like every other true Bostonian, he yearned for the ease of the Athenæum Club in Pall Mall or the Combination Room at Trinity.[17] Dana at first suggested the opposite; he affected to be still before the mast, a direct, rather bluff, vigorous seaman, and only as one got to know him better one found the man of rather excessive refinement trying with success to work like a day-laborer, deliberately hardening his skin to the burden, as though he were still carrying hides at Monterey. Undoubtedly he succeeded, for his mind and will were robust, but he might have said what his lifelong friend William M. Evarts[18] used to say: "I pride myself on my success in doing not the things I like to do, but the things I don't like to do." Dana's ideal of life was to be a great Englishman, with a seat on the front benches of the House of Commons until he should be promoted to the woolsack;[19] beyond all, with a social status that should place him above the scuffle of provincial and unprofessional annoyances; but he forced himself to take life as it came, and he suffocated his longings with grim self-discipline, by mere force of will. Of the four men, Dana was the most marked. Without dogmatism or self-assertion, he seemed always to be fully in sight, a figure that completely filled a well-defined space. He, too, talked well, and his mind worked close to its subject, as a lawyer's should; but disguise and silence it as he liked, it was aristocratic to the tenth generation.

In that respect, and in that only, Charles Sumner was like him, but Sumner, in almost every other quality, was quite different from his three associates — altogether out of line. He, too, adored English standards, but his ambition led him to rival the career of Edmund Burke.[20] No young Bostonian of his time had made so brilliant a start, but rather in the steps of Edward Everett than of Daniel Webster.[21] As an orator he had achieved a triumph by his oration against war;[22] but Boston admired him chiefly for his social success in England and on the Continent; success that gave to every Bostonian who enjoyed it a halo never acquired by domestic sanctity. Mr. Sumner, both by interest and instinct, felt the value of his English connection, and cultivated it the more as he became socially an outcast from Boston society by the passions of politics. He was rarely without a pocket-full of letters from duchesses or noblemen in England. Having sacrificed to principle his social position in America, he clung the more closely to his foreign attachments. The Free Soil Party fared ill in Beacon Street.[23] The social arbiters of Boston — George Ticknor[24] and the rest — had to admit, however unwillingly, that the Free Soil leaders could not mingle with the friends and followers of Mr. Webster. Sumner was socially ostracized, and so, for that matter, were Palfrey, Dana, Russell,[25] Adams, and all the other avowed anti-slavery leaders, but for them it mattered less, because they had houses and families of their own; while Sumner had neither wife nor household, and, though the most socially ambitious of all, and the most hungry for what used to be called polite society, he could enter hardly half-a-dozen houses in Boston. Longfellow stood by him in Cambridge, and even in Beacon Street he could always take refuge in the house of Mr. Lodge,[26] but few days passed when he did not pass some time in Mount Vernon Street. Even with that, his solitude was glacial, and reacted on his character. He had nothing but himself to think about. His superiority was, indeed, real and incontestable; he was the classical ornament of the anti-slavery party; their pride in him was unbounded, and their admiration outspoken.

The boy Henry worshipped him, and if he ever regarded any older man as a personal friend, it was Mr. Sumner. The relation of Mr. Sumner in the household was far closer than any relation of blood. None of the uncles approached such intimacy. Sumner was the boy's ideal of greatness; the highest product of nature and art. The only fault of such a model was its superiority which defied imitation. To the twelve-year-old boy, his father, Dr. Palfrey, Mr. Dana, were men, more or less like what he himself might become; but Mr. Sumner was a different order — heroic.

As the boy grew up to be ten or twelve years old, his father gave him a writing-table in one of the alcoves of his Boston library, and there, winter after winter, Henry worked over his Latin Grammar and listened to these four gentlemen discussing the course of anti-slavery politics. The discussions were always serious; the Free Soil Party took itself quite seriously; and they were habitual because Mr. Adams had undertaken to edit a newspaper[27] as the organ of these gentlemen, who came to discuss its policy and expression. At the same time Mr. Adams was editing the "Works"[28] of his grandfather John Adams, and made the boy read texts for proof-correction. In after years his father sometimes complained that, as a reader of *Novanglus* and *Massachusettensis*,[29] Henry had shown very little consciousness of punctuation; but the boy regarded this part of school life only as a warning, if he ever grew up to write dull discussions in the newspapers, to try to be dull in some different way from that of his great-grandfather. Yet the discussions in the *Boston Whig* were carried on in much the same style as those of John Adams and his opponent, and appealed to much the same society and the same habit of mind. The boy got as little education, fitting him for his own time, from the one as from the other, and he got no more from his contact with the gentlemen themselves who were all types of the past.

Down to 1850, and even later, New England society was still directed by the professions. Lawyers, physicians, professors, merchants were classes, and acted not as individuals, but as though they were clergymen and each profession were a church. In politics the system required competent expression; it was the old Ciceronian[30] idea of government by *the best* that produced the long line of New England statesmen. They chose men to represent them because they wanted to be well represented, and they chose the best they had. Thus Boston chose Daniel Webster, and Webster took, not as pay, but as *honorarium*, the cheques raised for him by Peter Harvey[31] from the Appletons, Perkinses, Amorys, Searses, Brookses, Lawrences, and so on, who begged him to represent them. Edward Everett held the rank in regular succession to Webster. Robert C. Winthrop claimed succession to Everett. Charles Sumner aspired to break the succession,[32] but not the system. The Adamses had never been, for any length of time, a part of this State succession; they had preferred the national service, and had won all their distinction outside the State, but they too had required State support and had commonly received it. The little group of men in Mount Vernon Street were an offshoot of this system; they were statesmen, not politicians; they guided public opinion, but were little guided by it.

The boy naturally learned only one lesson from his saturation in such air. He took for granted that this sort of world, more or

less the same that had always existed in Boston and Massachusetts Bay, was the world which he was to fit. Had he known
Europe he would have learned no better. The Paris of Louis Philippe, Guizot, and de Tocqueville,[33] as well as the London of Robert Peel, Macaulay, and John Stuart Mill,[34] were but varieties of
the same upper-class *bourgeoisie* that felt instinctive cousinship
with the Boston of Ticknor, Prescott, and Motley. Even the
typical grumbler Carlyle,[35] who cast doubts on the real capacity
of the middle class, and who at times thought himself eccentric,
found friendship and alliances in Boston — still more in Concord. The system had proved so successful that even Germany
wanted to try it, and Italy yearned for it. England's middle-class
government was the ideal of human progress.[36]

Even the violent reaction after 1848, and the return of all
Europe to military practices, never for a moment shook the true
faith.[37] No one, except Karl Marx,[38] foresaw radical change. What
announced it? The world was producing sixty or seventy million tons of coal, and might be using nearly a million steam-horse-
power, just beginning to make itself felt. All experience since the
creation of man, all divine revelation or human science, conspired to deceive and betray a twelve-year-old boy who took for
granted that his ideas, which were alone respectable, would be
alone respected.

Viewed from Mount Vernon Street, the problem of life was as
simple as it was classic. Politics offered no difficulties, for there
the moral law was a sure guide. Social perfection was also sure,
because human nature worked for Good,[39] and three instruments
were all she asked — Suffrage, Common Schools, and Press. On
these points doubt was forbidden. Education was divine, and
man needed only a correct knowledge of facts to reach perfection:[40]

"Were half the power that fills the world with terror,
    Were half the wealth bestowed on camps and courts,
Given to redeem the human mind from error,
    There were no need of arsenals nor forts."[41]

Nothing quieted doubt so completely as the mental calm of the Unitarian clergy. In uniform excellence of life and character, moral and intellectual, the score of Unitarian clergymen about Boston, who controlled society and Harvard College, were never excelled. They proclaimed as their merit that they insisted on no doctrine, but taught, or tried to teach, the means of leading a virtuous, useful, unselfish life, which they held to be sufficient for salvation. For them, difficulties might be ignored; doubts were waste of thought; nothing exacted solution. Boston had solved the universe; or had offered and realized the best solution yet tried. The problem was worked out.

Of all the conditions of his youth which afterwards puzzled the grown-up man, this disappearance of religion puzzled him most. The boy went to church twice every Sunday; he was taught to read his Bible, and he learned religious poetry by heart; he believed in a mild deism; he prayed; he went through all the forms; but neither to him nor to his brothers or sisters was religion real.[12] Even the mild discipline of the Unitarian Church was so irksome that they all threw it off at the first possible moment, and never afterwards entered a church. The religious instinct had vanished, and could not be revived, although one made in later life many efforts to recover it. That the most powerful emotion of man, next to the sexual, should disappear, might be a personal defect of his own; but that the most intelligent society, led by the most intelligent clergy, in the most moral conditions he ever knew, should have solved all the problems of the universe so thoroughly as to have quite ceased making itself anxious about past or future, and should have persuaded itself that all the problems which had convulsed human thought from earliest recorded time, were not worth discussing, seemed to him the most curious social phenomenon he had to account for in a long life. The faculty of turning away one's eyes as one approaches a chasm is not unusual, and Boston showed, under the lead of Mr. Webster, how successfully it could be done in politics; but in politics a certain number of men did at least protest.[43] In religion and philosophy no one protested. Such protest as was made took forms more simple than the silence, like the deism of Theodore Parker, and of the boy's own cousin Octavius Frothingham,[44] who distressed his father and scandalized Beacon Street by avowing sceptism that seemed to solve no old problems, and to raise many new ones. The less aggressive protest of Ralph Waldo Emerson, was, from an old-world point of view, less serious.[45] It was *naïf*.

The children reached manhood without knowing religion, and with the certainty that dogma, metaphysics, and abstract philosophy were not worth knowing. So one-sided an education could have been possible in no other country or time, but it became, almost of necessity, the more literary and political. As the children grew up, they exaggerated the literary and the political interests. They joined in the dinner-table discussions and from childhood the boys were accustomed to hear, almost every day, table talk as good as they were ever likely to hear again. The eldest child, Louisa, was one of the most sparkling creatures her brother met in a long and varied experience of bright women. The oldest son, John, was afterwards regarded as one of the best talkers in Boston society, and perhaps the most popular man in the State, though apt to be on the unpopular side. Palfrey and Dana could be entertaining when they pleased, and though Charles Sumner could hardly be called light in hand, he was willing to be amused, and smiled grandly from time to time; while Mr. Adams, who talked relatively little, was always a good listener, and laughed over a witticism till he choked.

By way of educating and amusing the children, Mr. Adams read much aloud, and was sure to read political literature, especially when it was satirical, like the speeches of Horace Mann and the "Epistles" of "Hosea Biglow,"[46] with great delight to the youth. So he read Longfellow and Tennyson as their poems appeared, but the children took possession of Dickens and Thackeray for themselves. Both were too modern for tastes founded on Pope and Dr. Johnson. The boy Henry soon became a desultory reader of every book he found readable, but these were commonly eighteenth-century historians because his father's library was full of them. In the want of positive instincts, he drifted into the mental indolence of history. So, too, he read shelves of eighteenth-century poetry, but when his father offered his own set of Wordsworth as a gift on condition of reading it through, he declined. Pope and Gray called for no mental effort; they were easy reading; but the boy was thirty years old before his education reached Wordsworth.

This is the story of an education, and the person or persons who figure in it are supposed to have values only as educators or educated. The surroundings concern it only so far as they affect education. Sumner, Dana, Palfrey, had values of their own, like Hume, Pope, and Wordsworth, which anyone may study in their works; here all appear only as influences on the mind of a boy very nearly the average of most boys in physical and mental stature. The influence was wholly political and literary. His father made no effort to force his mind, but left him free play, and this was perhaps best. Only in one way his father rendered him a great service by trying to teach him French and giving him some idea of a French accent. Otherwise the family was rather an atmosphere than an influence. The boy had a large and overpowering set of brothers and sisters, who were modes or replicas of the same type, getting the same education, struggling with the same problems, and solving the question, or leaving it unsolved much in the same way. They knew no more than he what they wanted or what to do for it, but all were conscious that they would like to control power in some form; and the same thing could be said of an ant or an elephant. Their form was tied to politics or literature. They amounted to one individual with half-a-dozen sides or facets; their temperaments reacted on each other and made each child more like the other. This was also education, but in the type, and the Boston or New England type was well enough known. What no one knew was whether the individual who thought himself a representative of this type, was fit to deal with life.

As far as outward bearing went, such a family of turbulent children, given free rein by their parents, or indifferent to check, should have come to more or less grief. Certainly no one was strong enough to control them, least of all their mother, the queen-bee of the hive, on whom nine-tenths of the burden fell, on whose strength they all depended, but whose children were much too self-willed and self-confident to take guidance from her, or from anyone else, unless in the direction they fancied. Father and mother were about equally helpless. Almost every large family in those days produced at least one black sheep, and if this generation of Adamses escaped, it was as much a matter of surprise to them as to their neighbors. By some happy chance they grew up to be decent citizens, but Henry Adams, as a brand escaped from the burning,[47] always looked back with astonishment at their luck. The fact seemed to prove that they were born, like birds, with a certain innate balance. Home influences alone never saved the New England boy from ruin, though sometimes they may have helped to ruin him; and the influences outside of home were negative. If school helped, it was only by reaction. The dislike of school was so strong as to be a positive gain. The passionate hatred of school methods was almost a method in itself. Yet the day-school of that time was respectable, and the boy had nothing to complain of.[48] In fact, he never complained. He hated it because he was herded with a crowd of other boys and compelled to learn by memory a quantity of things that did not amuse him. His memory was slow, and the effort painful. For him to conceive that his memory could compete for school prizes with machines of two or three times its power, was to prove himself wanting not only in memory, but flagrantly in mind. He thought his mind a good enough machine, if it were given time to act, but it acted wrong if hurried. Schoolmasters never gave time.

In any and all its forms, the boy detested school, and the prejudice became deeper with years. He always reckoned his schooldays, from ten to sixteen years old, as time thrown away. Perhaps his needs turned out to be exceptional, but his existence was exceptional. Between 1850 and 1900 nearly everyone's existence was exceptional. For success in the life imposed on him he needed, as afterwards appeared, the facile use of only four tools: Mathematics, French, German, and Spanish. With these, he could master in very short time any special branch of inquiry, and feel at home in any society. Latin and Greek, he could, with the help of the modern languages, learn more completely by the intelligent work of six weeks than in the six years he spent on them at school. These four tools were necessary to his success in life, but he never controlled any one of them.

Thus, at the outset, he was condemned to failure more or less complete in the life awaiting him, but not more so than his companions. Indeed, had his father kept the boy at home, and given him half an hour's direction every day, he would have done more for him than school ever could do for them. Of course, school-taught men and boys looked down on home-bred boys, and rather prided themselves on their own ignorance, but the man of sixty can generally see what he needed in life, and in Henry Adams's opinion it was not school.

Most school experience was bad. Boy associations at fifteen were worse than none. Boston at that time offered few healthy resources for boys or men. The bar-room and billiard-room were more familiar than parents knew. As a rule boys could skate and swim and were sent to dancing-school; they played a rudimentary game of baseball, football, and hockey; a few could sail a boat; still fewer had been out with a gun to shoot yellow-legs or a stray wild duck; one or two may have learned something of natural history if they came from the neighborhood of Concord;[49] none could ride across country, or knew what shooting with dogs meant. Sport as a pursuit was unknown. Boat-racing came after 1850.

For horse-racing, only the trotting-course existed. Of all pleasures, winter sleighing was still the gayest and most popular. From none of these amusements could the boy learn anything likely to be of use to him in the world. Books remained as in the eighteenth century, the source of life, and as they came out — Thackeray, Dickens, Bulwer, Tennyson, Macaulay, Carlyle, and the rest — they were devoured; but as far as happiness went, the happiest hours of the boy's education were passed in summer lying on a musty heap of Congressional Documents in the old farmhouse at Quincy, reading "Quentin Durward," "Ivanhoe," and "The Talisman,"[50] and raiding the garden at intervals for peaches and pears. On the whole he learned most then.

CHAPTER III

Washington (1850–1854)

EXCEPT for politics, Mount Vernon Street had the merit of leaving the boy-mind supple, free to turn with the world, and if one learned next to nothing, the little one did learn needed not to be unlearned. The surface was ready to take any form that education should cut into it, though Boston, with singular foresight, rejected the old designs. What sort of education was stamped elsewhere, a Bostonian had no idea, but he escaped the evils of other standards by having no standard at all; and what was true of school was true of society. Boston offered none that could help outside. Everyone now smiles at the bad taste of Queen Victoria and Louis Philippe [1]—the society of the forties — but the taste was only a reflection of the social slack-water between a tide passed, and a tide to come. Boston belonged to neither, and hardly even to America. Neither aristocratic nor industrial nor social, Boston girls and boys were not nearly as unformed as English boys and girls, but had less means of acquiring form as they grew older. Women counted for little as models. Every boy, from the age of seven, fell in love at frequent intervals with some girl — always more or less the same little girl — who had nothing to teach him, or he to teach her, except rather familiar and provincial manners, until they married and bore children to repeat the habit. The idea of attaching one's self to a married woman, or of polishing one's manners to suit the standards of women of thirty, could hardly have entered the mind of a young Bostonian, and would have scandalized his parents. From women the boy got the domestic virtues and nothing else. He might not even catch the idea that women had more to give. The garden of Eden was hardly more primitive.

To balance this virtue, the Puritan city had always hidden a darker side. Blackguard Boston was only too educational, and to most boys much the more interesting. A successful blackguard must enjoy great physical advantages besides a true vocation, and Henry Adams had neither; but no boy escaped some contact with vice of a very low form. Blackguardism came constantly under boys' eyes, and had the charm of force and freedom and superiority to culture or decency. One might fear it, but no one honestly despised it. Now and then it asserted itself as education more roughly than school ever did. One of the commonest boy-games of winter, inherited directly from the eighteenth-century, was a game of war on Boston Common. In old days the two hostile forces were called North-Enders and South-Enders. In 1850 the North-Enders still survived as a legend, but in practice it was a battle of the Latin School against all comers, and the Latin School, for snowball, included all the boys of the West End. Whenever, on a half-holiday, the weather was soft enough to soften the snow, the Common was apt to be the scene of a fight, which began in daylight with the Latin School in force, rushing their opponents down to Tremont Street, and which generally ended at dark by the Latin School dwindling in numbers and disappearing. As the Latin School grew weak, the roughs and young blackguards grew strong. As long as snowballs were the only weapon, no one was much hurt, but a stone may be put in a snowball, and in the dark a stick or a slungshot in the hands of a boy is as effective as a knife. One afternoon the fight had been long and exhausting. The boy Henry, following, as his habit was, his bigger brother Charles,[2] had taken part in the battle, and had felt his courage much depressed by seeing one of his trustiest leaders, Henry Higginson[3] — "Bully Hig," his school name — struck by a stone over the eye, and led off the field bleeding in rather a ghastly manner. As night came on, the Latin School was steadily forced back to the Beacon Street Mall where they could retreat no further without disbanding, and by that time only a small band was left, headed by two heroes, Savage and Marvin.[4] A dark mass of figures could be seen below, making ready for the last rush, and rumor said that a swarm of blackguards from the slums, led by a grisly terror called Conky Daniels, with a club and a hideous reputation, were going to put an end to the Beacon Street cowards forever. Henry wanted to run away with the others, but his brother was too big to run away, so they stood still and waited immolation. The dark mass set up a shout, and rushed forward. The Beacon Street boys turned and fled up the steps, except Savage and Marvin and the few champions who would not run. The terrible Conky Daniels swaggered up, stopped a moment with his body-guard to swear a few oaths at Marvin, and then swept on and chased the flyers, leaving the few boys untouched who stood their ground. The obvious moral taught that blackguards were not so black as they were painted; but the boy Henry had passed through as much terror as though he were Turenne or Henri IV,[5] and ten or twelve years afterwards when these same boys were fighting and falling on all the battle-fields of Virginia and Maryland, he wondered whether their education on Boston Common had taught Savage and Marvin how to die.[6]

If violence were a part of complete education, Boston was not incomplete. The idea of violence was familiar to the anti-slavery leaders as well as to their followers. Most of them suffered from it. Mobs were always possible. Henry never happened to be actually concerned in a mob, but he, like every other boy, was sure to be on hand wherever a mob was expected, and whenever he heard Garrison or Wendell Phillips speak, he looked for trouble. Wendell Phillips on a platform was a model dangerous for youth. Theodore Parker in his pulpit was not much safer. Worst of all, the execution of the Fugitive Slave Law in Boston — the sight of Court Square packed with bayonets, and his own friends obliged to line the streets under arms as State militia, in order to return a negro to slavery — wrought frenzy in the brain of a fifteen-year-old, eighteenth-century boy from Quincy, who wanted to miss no reasonable chance of mischief.[7]

One lived in the atmosphere of the Stamp Act, the Tea Tax, and the Boston Massacre.[8] Within Boston, a boy was first an eighteenth-century politician, and afterwards only a possibility; beyond Boston the first step led only further into politics. After February, 1848, but one slight tie remained of all those that, since 1776, had connected Quincy with the outer world. The Madam stayed in Washington, after her husband's death, and in her turn was struck by paralysis and bedridden. From time to time her son Charles, whose affection and sympathy for his mother in her many tribulations were always pronounced, went on to see her, and in May, 1850, he took with him his twelve-year-old son. The journey was meant as education, and as education it served the purpose of fixing in memory the stage of a boy's thought in 1850. He could not remember taking special interest in the railroad journey or in New York; with railways and cities he was familiar enough. His first impression was the novelty of crossing New York Bay and finding an English railway carriage on the Camden and Amboy Railroad. This was a new world; a suggestion of corruption in the simple habits of American life; a step to exclusiveness never approached in Boston; but it was amusing. The boy rather liked it. At Trenton the train set him on board a steamer which took him to Philadelphia where he smelt other varieties of town life; then again by boat to Chester, and by train to Havre de Grace; by boat to Baltimore and thence by rail to Washington. This was the journey he remembered. The actual journey may have been quite different, but the actual journey has no interest for education. The memory was all that mattered; and what struck him most, to remain fresh in his mind all his lifetime, was the sudden change that came over the world on entering a slave State. He took education politically. The mere raggedness of outline could not have seemed wholly new, for even Boston had its ragged edges, and the town of Quincy was far from being a vision of neatness or good-repair; in truth, he had never seen a finished landscape; but Maryland was raggedness of a new kind.

The railway, about the size and character of a modern tram, rambled through unfenced fields and woods, or through village streets, among a haphazard variety of pigs, cows, and negro babies, who might all have used the cabins for pens and styes, had the Southern pig required styes, but who never showed a sign of care. This was the boy's impression of what slavery caused, and, for him, was all it taught. Coming down in the early morning from his bedroom in his grandmother's house — still called the Adams Building — in F Street and venturing outside into the air reeking with the thick odor of the catalpa trees, he found himself on an earth-road, or village street, with wheel-tracks meandering from the colonnade of the Treasury hard by, to the white marble columns and fronts of the Post Office and Patent Office which faced each other in the distance, like white Greek temples in the abandoned gravel-pits of a deserted Syrian city. Here and there low wooden houses were scattered along the streets, as in other Southern villages, but he was chiefly attracted by an unfinished square marble shaft,[9] half-a-mile below, and he walked down to inspect it before breakfast. His aunt drily remarked that, at this rate, he would soon get through all the sights; but she could not guess — having lived always in Washington — how little the sights of Washington had to do with its interest.

The boy could not have told her; he was nowhere near an understanding of himself. The more he was educated, the less he understood. Slavery struck him in the face; it was a nightmare; a horror; a crime; the sum of all wickedness! Contact made it only more repulsive. He wanted to escape, like the negroes, to free soil. Slave States were dirty, unkempt, poverty-stricken, ignorant, vicious! He had not a thought but repulsion for it; and yet the picture had another side. The May sunshine and shadow had something to do with it; the thickness of foliage and the heavy smells had more; the sense of atmosphere, almost new, had perhaps as much again; and the brooding indolence of a warm climate and a negro population hung in the atmosphere heavier than the catalpas. The

impression was not simple, but the boy liked it: distinctly it remained on his mind as an attraction, almost obscuring Quincy
itself. The want of barriers, of pavements, of forms; the loose-
ness, the laziness; the indolent Southern drawl; the pigs in the
streets; the negro babies and their mothers with bandanas; the
freedom, openness, swagger, of nature and man, soothed his
Johnson blood. Most boys would have felt it in the same way,
but with him the feeling caught on to an inheritance. The softness of his gentle old grandmother as she lay in bed and chatted
with him, did not come from Boston. His aunt was anything
rather than Bostonian. He did not wholly come from Boston
himself. Though Washington belonged to a different world, and
the two worlds could not live together, he was not sure that he
enjoyed the Boston world most. Even at twelve years old he could
see his own nature no more clearly than he would at twelve hundred, if by accident he should happen to live so long.

His father took him to the Capitol and on the floor of the Senate, which then, and long afterwards, until the era of tourists,
was freely open to visitors. The old Senate Chamber[10] resembled
a pleasant political club. Standing behind the Vice-President's
chair, which is now the Chief Justice's, the boy was presented to
some of the men whose names were great in their day, and as
familiar to him as his own. Clay and Webster and Calhoun[11] were
there still, but with them a Free Soil candidate for the Vice-Presi-
dency had little to do; what struck boys most was their type.
Senators were a species; they all wore an air, as they wore a blue
dress coat or brass buttons; they were Roman. The type of
Senator in 1850 was rather charming at its best, and the Senate,
when in good temper, was an agreeable body, numbering only
some sixty members, and affecting the airs of courtesy. Its vice
was not so much a vice of manners or temper as of attitude. The
statesman of all periods was apt to be pompous, but even pomposity was less offensive than familiarity — on the platform as
in the pulpit — and Southern pomposity, when not arrogant, was

genial and sympathetic, almost quaint and childlike in its simple-mindedness; quite a different thing from the Websterian or Conklinian[12] pomposity of the North. The boy felt at ease there, more at home than he had ever felt in Boston State House, though his acquaintance with the codfish[13] in the House of Representatives went back beyond distinct recollection. Senators spoke kindly to him, and seemed to feel so, for they had known his family socially; and, in spite of slavery, even J. Q. Adams in his later years, after he ceased to stand in the way of rivals, had few personal enemies. Decidedly the Senate, pro-slavery though it were, seemed a friendly world.

This first step in national politics was a little like the walk before breakfast; an easy, careless, genial, enlarging stride into a fresh and amusing world, where nothing was finished, but where even the weeds grew rank. The second step was like the first, except that it led to the White House. He was taken to see President Taylor.[14] Outside, in a paddock in front, "Old Whitey," the President's charger, was grazing, as they entered; and inside, the President was receiving callers as simply as if he were in the paddock too. The President was friendly, and the boy felt no sense of strangeness that he could ever recall. In fact, what strangeness should he feel? The families were intimate; so intimate that their friendliness outlived generations, civil war, and all sorts of rupture. President Taylor owed his election to Martin Van Buren and the Free Soil Party.[15] To him, the Adamses might still be of use. As for the White House, all the boy's family had lived there, and, barring the eight years of Andrew Jackson's reign, had been more or less at home there ever since it was built. The boy half thought he owned it, and took for granted that he should some day live in it. He felt no sensation whatever before Presidents. A President was a matter of course in every respectable family; he had two in his own; three, if he counted old Nathaniel Gorham,[16] who was the oldest and first in distinction. Revolutionary patriots, or perhaps a Colonial Governor, might be worth talking about, but any one could be President, and some very shady characters were likely to be. Presidents, Senators, Congressmen, and such things were swarming in every street.

Everyone thought alike whether they had ancestors or not. No sort of glory hedged Presidents as such, and, in the whole country, one could hardly have met with an admission of respect for any office or name, unless it were George Washington. That was — to all appearance sincerely — respected. People made pilgrimages to Mount Vernon and made even an effort to build Washington a monument. The effort had failed, but one still went to Mount Vernon, although it was no easy trip. Mr. Adams took the boy there in a carriage and pair, over a road that gave him a complete Virginia education for use ten years afterwards.[17] To the New England mind, roads, schools, clothes, and a clean face were connected as part of the law of order or divine system. Bad roads meant bad morals. The moral of this Virginia road was clear, and the boy fully learned it. Slavery was wicked, and slavery was the cause of this road's badness which amounted to social crime — and yet, at the end of the road and product of the crime stood Mount Vernon and George Washington.

Luckily boys accept contradictions as readily as their elders do, or this boy might have become prematurely wise. He had only to repeat what he was told — that George Washington stood alone. Otherwise this third step in his Washington education would have been his last. On that line, the problem of progress was not soluble, whatever the optimists and orators might say — or, for that matter, whatever they might think. George Washington could not be reached on Boston lines. George Washington was a primary, or, if Virginians liked it better, an ultimate relation, like the Pole Star, and amid the endless restless motion of every other visible point in space, he alone remained steady, in the mind of Henry Adams, to the end. All the other points shifted their bearings; John Adams, Jefferson, Madison, Franklin, even John Marshall,[18] took varied lights, and assumed new relations, but

47

Mount Vernon always remained where it was, with no practicable road to reach it; and yet, when he got there, Mount Vernon was only Quincy in a Southern setting. No doubt it was much more charming, but it was the same eighteenth-century, the same old furniture, the same old patriot, and the same old President.

The boy took to it instinctively. The broad Potomac and the coons in the trees, the bandanas and the box-hedges, the bedrooms upstairs and the porch outside, even Martha Washington herself in memory, were as natural as the tides and the May sunshine; he had only enlarged his horizon a little; but he never thought to ask himself or his father how to deal with the moral problem that deduced George Washington from the sum of all wickedness. In practice, such trifles as contradictions in principle are easily set aside; the faculty of ignoring them makes the practical man; but any attempt to deal with them seriously as education is fatal. Luckily Charles Francis Adams never preached and was singularly free from cant. He may have had views of his own, but he let his son Henry satisfy himself with the simple elementary fact that George Washington stood alone.

Life was not yet complicated. Every problem had a solution, even the negro. The boy went back to Boston more political than ever, and his politics were no longer so modern as the eighteenth century, but took a strong tone of the seventeenth. Slavery drove the whole Puritan community back on its Puritanism. The boy thought as dogmatically as though he were one of his own ancestors. The Slave Power took the place of Stuart kings and Roman popes. Education could go no further in that course, and ran off into emotion; but, as the boy gradually found his surroundings change, and felt himself no longer an isolated atom in a hostile universe, but a sort of herring-fry[19] in a shoal of moving fish, he began to learn the first and easier lessons of practical politics. Thus far he had seen nothing but eighteenth-century statesmanship. America and he began, at the same time, to become aware of a new force under the innocent surface of party machinery.

Even at that early moment, a rather slow boy felt dimly conscious that he might meet some personal difficulties in trying to reconcile sixteenth-century principles and eighteenth-century statesmanship with late nineteenth-century party organization. The first vague sense of feeling an unknown living obstacle in the dark came in 1851.

The Free Soil conclave in Mount Vernon Street belonged, as already said, to the statesman class, and, like Daniel Webster, had nothing to do with machinery. Websters or Sewards depended on others for machine work and money — on Peter Harveys[20] and Thurlow Weeds,[21] who spent their lives in it, took most of the abuse, and asked no reward. Almost without knowing it, the subordinates ousted their employers and created a machine which no one but themselves could run. In 1850 things had not quite reached that point. The men who ran the small Free Soil machine were still modest, though they became famous enough in their own right. Henry Wilson, John B. Alley, Anson Burlingame,[22] and the other managers, negotiated a bargain with the Massachusetts Democrats giving the State to the Democrats and a seat in the Senate to the Free Soilers. With this bargain Mr. Adams and his statesman friends would have nothing to do, for such a coalition was in their eyes much like jockeys selling a race. They did not care to take office as pay for votes sold to pro-slavery Democrats. Theirs was a correct, not to say noble, position; but, as a matter of fact, they took the benefit of the sale, for the coalition chose Charles Sumner as its candidate for the Senate, while George S. Boutwell[23] was made Governor for the Democrats. This was the boy's first lesson in practical politics, and a sharp one; not that he troubled himself with moral doubts, but that he learned the nature of a flagrantly corrupt political bargain in which he was too good to take part, but not too good to take profit. Charles Sumner happened to be the partner to receive these stolen goods, but between his friend and his father the boy felt no distinction, and, for him, there was none. He entered into no casuistry on the matter. His friend was right because his friend, and the boy shared the glory. The question of education did not rise while the conflict lasted. Yet every one saw as clearly then as afterwards that a lesson of some sort must be learned and understood, once for all. The boy might ignore, as a mere historical puzzle, the question how to deduce George Washington from the sum of all wickedness, but he had himself helped to deduce Charles Sumner from the sum of political corruption. On that line, too, education could go no further. Tammany Hall stood at the end of the vista.

Mr. Alley, one of the strictest of moralists, held that his object in making the bargain was to convert the Democratic Party to anti-slavery principles, and that he did it. Henry Adams could rise to no such moral elevation. He was only a boy, and his object in supporting the coalition was that of making his friend a Senator. It was as personal as though he had helped to make his friend a millionaire. He could never find a way of escaping immoral conclusions, except by admitting that he and his father and Sumner were wrong, and this he was never willing to do, for the consequences of this admission were worse than those of the other. Thus, before he was fifteen years old, he had managed to get himself into a state of moral confusion from which he never escaped. As a politician, he was already corrupt, and he never could see how any practical politician could be less corrupt than himself.

Apology, as he understood himself, was cant or cowardice. At the time he never even dreamed that he needed to apologize, though the press shouted it at him from every corner, and though the Mount Vernon Street conclave agreed with the press; yet he could not plead ignorance, and even in the heat of the conflict, he never cared to defend the coalition. Boy as he was, he knew enough to know that something was wrong, but his only interest was the election. Day after day, the General Court balloted; and the boy haunted the gallery, following the roll-call, and wondered what Caleb Cushing[24] meant by calling Mr. Sumner a "one-eyed abolitionist." Truly the difference in meaning with the phrase "one-ideaed abolitionist," which was Mr. Cushing's actual expression, is not very great, but neither the one nor the other seemed to describe Mr. Sumner to the boy, who never could have made the error of classing Garrison and Sumner together, or mistaking Caleb Cushing's relation to either. Temper ran high at that moment, while Sumner every day missed his election by only one or two votes. At last, April 24, 1851, standing among the silent crowd in the gallery, Henry heard the vote announced which gave Sumner the needed number. Slipping under the arms of the bystanders, he ran home as hard as he could, and burst into the dining-room where Mr. Sumner was seated at table with the family. He enjoyed the glory of telling Sumner that he was elected; it was probably the proudest moment in the life of either.

The next day, when the boy went to school, he noticed numbers of boys and men in the streets wearing black crape on their arm. He knew few Free Soil boys in Boston; his acquaintances were what he called pro-slavery; so he thought proper to tie a bit of white silk ribbon round his own arm by way of showing that his friend Mr. Sumner was not wholly alone. This little piece of bravado passed unnoticed; no one even cuffed his ears; but in later life he was a little puzzled to decide which symbol was the more correct. No one then dreamed of four years' war, but every one dreamed of secession. The symbol for either might well be matter of doubt.

This triumph of the Mount Vernon Street conclave capped the political climax. The boy, like a million other American boys, was a politician, and what was worse, fit as yet to be nothing else. He should have been, like his grandfather, a protégé of George Washington, a statesman designated by destiny, with nothing to do but look directly ahead, follow orders, and march. On the contrary, he was not even a Bostonian; he felt himself shut out of Boston as though he were an exile; he never thought of himself as a Bostonian; he never looked about him in Boston, as boys commonly do wherever they are, to select the street they like best,

the house they want to live in, the profession they mean to practise. Always he felt himself somewhere else; perhaps in Washington with its social ease; perhaps in Europe; and he watched with
vague unrest from the Quincy hills the smoke of the Cunard
steamers stretching in a long line to the horizon, and disappearing
every other Saturday or whatever the day might be, as though the
steamers were offering to take him away, which was precisely what
they were doing.

Had these ideas been unreasonable, influences enough were at
hand to correct them; but the point of the whole story, when
Henry Adams came to look back on it, seemed to be that the ideas
were more than reasonable; they were the logical, necessary, mathematical result of conditions old as history and fixed as fate —
invariable sequence in man's experience. The only idea which
would have been quite unreasonable scarcely entered his mind.
This was the thought of going westward and growing up with the
country. That he was not in the least fitted for going West made
no objection whatever, since he was much better fitted than most
of the persons that went. The convincing reason for staying in
the East was that he had there every advantage over the West.
He could not go wrong. The West must inevitably pay an enormous tribute to Boston and New York. One's position in the East
was the best in the world for every purpose that could offer an
object for going westward. If ever in history men had been able
to calculate on a certainty for a lifetime in advance, the citizens
of the great Eastern seaports could do it in 1850 when their railway
systems were already laid out. Neither to a politician nor to a
business-man nor to any of the learned professions did the West
promise any certain advantage, while it offered uncertainties in
plenty.

At any other moment in human history, this education, including its political and literary bias, would have been not only good,
but quite the best. Society had always welcomed and flattered men
so endowed. Henry Adams had every reason to be well pleased

with it, and not ill-pleased with himself. He had all he wanted. He saw no reason for thinking that any one else had more. He finished with school, not very brilliantly, but without finding fault with the sum of his knowledge. Probably he knew more than his father, or his grandfather, or his great-grandfather had known at sixteen years old. Only on looking back, fifty years later, at his own figure in 1854, and pondering on the needs of the twentieth century, he wondered whether, on the whole, the boy of 1854 stood nearer to the thought of 1904, or to that of the year 1. He found himself unable to give a sure answer. The calculation was clouded by the undetermined values of twentieth-century thought, but the story will show his reasons for thinking that, in essentials like religion, ethics, philosophy; in history, literature, art; in the concepts of all science, except perhaps mathematics, the American boy of 1854 stood nearer the year 1 than to the year 1900. The education he had received bore little relation to the education he needed. Speaking as an American of 1900, he had as yet no education at all. He knew not even where or how to begin.

CHAPTER IV

Harvard College (1854–1858)

ONE day in June, 1854, young Adams walked for the last time down the steps of Mr. Dixwell's school in Boylston Place, and felt no sensation but one of unqualified joy that this experience was ended. Never before or afterwards in his life did he close a period so long as four years without some sensation of loss — some sentiment of habit — but school was what in after life he commonly heard his friends denounce as an intolerable bore. He was born too old for it. The same thing could be said of most New England boys. Mentally they never were boys. Their education as men should have begun at ten years old. They were fully five years more mature than the English or European boy for whom schools were made. For the purposes of future advancement, as afterwards appeared, these first six years of a possible education were wasted in doing imperfectly what might have been done perfectly in one, and in any case would have had small value. The next regular step was Harvard College. He was more than glad to go. For generation after generation, Adamses and Brookses and Boylstons and Gorhams had gone to Harvard College, and although none of them, as far as known, had ever done any good there, or thought himself the better for it, custom, social ties, convenience, and, above all, economy, kept each generation in the track. Any other education would have required a serious effort, but no one took Harvard College seriously.[1] All went there because their friends went there, and the College was their ideal of social self-respect.

Harvard College, as far as it educated at all, was a mild and liberal school, which sent young men into the world with all they needed to make respectable citizens, and something of what they wanted to make useful ones. Leaders of men it never tried to make. Its ideals were altogether different. The Unitarian clergy had given to the College a character of moderation, balance, judgment, restraint, what the French called *mesure;* excellent traits, which the College attained with singular success, so that its graduates could commonly be recognized by the stamp, but such a type of character rarely lent itself to autobiography. In effect, the school created a type but not a will. Four years of Harvard College, if successful, resulted in an autobiographical blank, a mind on which only a water-mark had been stamped.

The stamp, as such things went, was a good one. The chief wonder of education is that it does not ruin everybody concerned in it, teachers and taught. Sometimes in after life, Adams debated whether in fact it had not ruined him and most of his companions, but, disappointment apart, Harvard College was probably less hurtful than any other university then in existence. It taught little, and that little ill, but it left the mind open, free from bias, ignorant of facts, but docile. The graduate had few strong prejudices. He knew little, but his mind remained supple, ready to receive knowledge.

What caused the boy most disappointment was the little he got from his mates. Speaking exactly, he got less than nothing, a result common enough in education. Yet the College Catalogue for the years 1854 to 1861 shows a list of names rather distinguished in their time. Alexander Agassiz and Phillips Brooks led it; H. H. Richardson and O. W. Holmes helped to close it.[2] As a rule the most promising of all die early, and never get their names into a Dictionary of Contemporaries, which seems to be the only popular standard of success. Many died in the war. Adams knew them all, more or less; he felt as much regard, and quite as much respect for them then, as he did after they won great names and were objects of a vastly wider respect; but, as help towards education, he got nothing whatever from them or they from him until long after they had left college. Possibly the fault was his, but one would like to know how many others shared it. Accident counts for much in companionship as in marriage. Life offers perhaps only a score of possible companions, and it is mere chance whether they meet as early as school or college, but it is more than a chance that boys brought up together under like conditions have nothing to give each other. The Class of 1858, to which Henry Adams belonged, was a typical collection of young New Englanders, quietly penetrating and aggressively commonplace; free from meannesses, jealousies, intrigues, enthusiasms, and passions; not exceptionally quick; not consciously sceptical; singularly indifferent to display, artifice, florid expression, but not hostile to it when it amused them; distrustful of themselves, but little disposed to trust any one else; with not much humor of their own, but full of readiness to enjoy the humor of others; negative to a degree that in the long run became positive and triumphant. Not harsh in manners or judgment, rather liberal and open-minded, they were still as a body the most formidable critics one would care to meet, in a long life exposed to criticism. They never flattered, seldom praised; free from vanity, they were not intolerant of it; but they were objectiveness itself; their attitude was a law of nature; their judgment beyond appeal, not an act either of intellect or emotion or of will, but a sort of gravitation.

This was Harvard College incarnate, but even for Harvard College, the Class of 1858 was somewhat extreme. Of unity this band of nearly one hundred young men had no keen sense, but they had equally little energy of repulsion. They were pleasant to live with, and above the average of students — German, French, English, or what not — but chiefly because each individual appeared satisfied to stand alone. It seemed a sign of force; yet to stand alone is quite natural when one has no passions; still easier when one has no pains.

Into this unusually dissolvent medium, chance insisted on enlarging Henry Adams's education by tossing a trio of Virginians as little fitted for it as Sioux Indians to a treadmill. By some further affinity, these three outsiders fell into relation with the Bostonians among whom Adams as a schoolboy belonged, and in the end with Adams himself, although they and he knew well how thin an edge of friendship separated them in 1856 from mortal enmity. One of these Virginians[3] was the son of Colonel Robert E. Lee, of the Second United States Cavalry; the two others[4] who seemed instinctively to form a staff for Lee, were town-Virginians from Petersburg. A fourth outsider came from Cincinnati and was half Kentuckian, N. L. Anderson,[5] Longworth on the mother's side. For the first time Adams's education brought him in contact with new types and taught him their values. He saw the New England type measure itself with another, and he was part of the process.

Lee, known through life as "Roony," was a Virginian of the eighteenth century, much as Henry Adams was a Bostonian of the same age. Roony Lee had changed little from the type of his grandfather, Light Horse Harry.[6] Tall, largely built, handsome, genial, with liberal Virginian openness towards all he liked, he had also the Virginian habit of command and took leadership as his natural habit. No one cared to contest it. None of the New Englanders wanted command. For a year, at least, Lee was the most popular and prominent young man in his class, but then seemed slowly to drop into the background. The habit of command was not enough, and the Virginian had little else. He was simple beyond analysis; so simple that even the simple New England student could not realize him. No one knew enough to know how ignorant he was; how childlike; how helpless before the relative complexity of a school. As an animal, the Southerner seemed to have every advantage, but even as an animal he steadily lost ground.

The lesson in education was vital to these young men, who, within ten years, killed each other by scores in the act of testing their college conclusions. Strictly, the Southerner had no mind; he had temperament. He was not a scholar; he had no intellectual

57

training; he could not analyze an idea, and he could not even conceive of admitting two; but in life one could get along very well without ideas, if one had only the social instinct. Dozens of eminent statesmen were men of Lee's type, and maintained themselves well enough in the legislature, but college was a sharper test. The Virginian was weak in vice itself, though the Bostonian was hardly a master of crime. The habits of neither were good; both were apt to drink hard and to live low lives; but the Bostonian suffered less than the Virginian. Commonly the Bostonian could take some care of himself even in his worst stages, while the Virginian became quarrelsome and dangerous. When a Virginian had brooded a few days over an imaginary grief and substantial whiskey, none of his Northern friends could be sure that he might not be waiting, round the corner, with a knife or pistol, to revenge insult by the dry light of *delirium tremens;* and when things reached this condition, Lee had to exhaust his authority over his own staff. Lee was a gentleman of the old school, and, as every one knows, gentlemen of the old school drank almost as much as gentlemen of the new school; but this was not his trouble. He was sober even in the excessive violence of political feeling in those years; he kept his temper and his friends under control.

Adams liked the Virginians. No one was more obnoxious to them, by name and prejudice; yet their friendship was unbroken and even warm. At a moment when the immediate future posed no problem in education so vital as the relative energy and endurance of North and South, this momentary contact with Southern character was a sort of education for its own sake; but this was not all. No doubt the self-esteem of the Yankee, which tended naturally to self-distrust, was flattered by gaining the slow conviction that the Southerner, with his slave-owning limitations, was as little fit to succeed in the struggle of modern life as though he were still a maker of stone axes, living in caves, and hunting the *bos primigenius,*[7] and that every quality in which he

58

was strong, made him weaker; but Adams had begun to fear that even in this respect one eighteenth-century type might not differ deeply from another. Roony Lee had changed little from the Virginian of a century before; but Adams was himself a good deal nearer the type of his great-grandfather than to that of a railway superintendent. He was little more fit than the Virginians to deal with a future America which showed no fancy for the past. Already Northern society betrayed a preference for economists over diplomats or soldiers — one might even call it a jealousy — against which two eighteenth-century types had little chance to live, and which they had in common to fear.

Nothing short of this curious sympathy could have brought into close relations two young men so hostile as Roony Lee and Henry Adams, but the chief difference between them as collegians consisted only in their difference of scholarship: Lee was a total failure; Adams a partial one. Both failed, but Lee felt his failure more sensibly, so that he gladly seized the chance of escape by accepting a commission offered him by General Winfield Scott[8] in the force then being organized against the Mormons. He asked Adams to write his letter of acceptance, which flattered Adams's vanity more than any Northern compliment could do, because, in days of violent political bitterness, it showed a certain amount of good temper. The diplomat felt his profession.

If the student got little from his mates, he got little more from his masters. The four years passed at college were, for his purposes, wasted. Harvard College was a good school, but at bottom what the boy disliked most was any school at all. He did not want to be one in a hundred — one per cent of an education. He regarded himself as the only person for whom his education had value, and he wanted the whole of it. He got barely half of an average. Long afterwards, when the devious path of life led him back to teach in his turn what no student naturally cared or needed to know,[9] he diverted some dreary hours of faculty-meetings by looking up his record in the class-lists, and found himself graded precisely in the middle. In the one branch he most needed — mathematics — barring the few first scholars, failure was so nearly universal that no attempt at grading could have had value, and whether he stood fortieth or ninetieth must have been an accident or the personal favor of the professor. Here his education failed lamentably. At best he could never have been a mathematician; at worst he would never have cared to be one; but he needed to read mathematics, like any other universal language, and he never reached the alphabet.

Beyond two or three Greek plays, the student got nothing from the ancient languages. Beyond some incoherent theories of free-trade and protection, he got little from Political Economy. He could not afterwards remember to have heard the name of Karl Marx mentioned, or the title of "Capital."[10] He was equally ignorant of Auguste Comte.[11] These were the two writers of his time who most influenced its thought. The bit of practical teaching he afterwards reviewed with most curiosity was the course in Chemistry, which taught him a number of theories that befogged his mind for a lifetime. The only teaching that appealed to his imagination was a course of lectures by Louis Agassiz[12] on the Glacial Period and Palæontology, which had more influence on his curiosity than the rest of the college instruction altogether. The entire work of the four years could have been easily put into the work of any four months in after life.

Harvard College was a negative force, and negative forces have value.[13] Slowly it weakened the violent political bias of childhood, not by putting interests in its place, but by mental habits which had no bias at all. It would also have weakened the literary bias, if Adams had been capable of finding other amusement, but the climate kept him steady to desultory and useless reading, till he had run through libraries of volumes which he forgot even to their title-pages. Rather by instinct than by guidance, he turned to writing, and his professors or tutors occasionally gave his English composition a hesitating approval; but in that branch, as in all the rest, even when he made a long struggle for recognition, he never convinced his teachers that his abilities, at their best, warranted placing him on the rank-list, among the first third of his class. Instructors generally reach a fairly accurate gauge of their scholars' powers. Henry Adams himself held the opinion that his instructors were very nearly right, and when he became a professor in his turn, and made mortifying mistakes in ranking his scholars, he still obstinately insisted that on the whole, he was not far wrong. Student or professor, he accepted the negative standard because it was the standard of the school.

He never knew what other students thought of it, or what they thought they gained from it; nor would their opinion have much affected his. From the first, he wanted to be done with it, and stood watching vaguely for a path and a direction. The world outside seemed large, but the paths that led into it were not many and lay mostly through Boston, where he did not want to go. As it happened, by pure chance, the first door of escape that seemed to offer a hope led into Germany, and James Russell Lowell[14] opened it.

Lowell, on succeeding Longfellow as Professor of Belles-Lettres, had duly gone to Germany, and had brought back whatever he found to bring. The literary world then agreed that truth survived in Germany alone, and Carlyle, Matthew Arnold, Renan, Emerson,[15] with scores of popular followers, taught the German faith. The literary world had revolted against the yoke of coming capitalism — its money-lenders, its bank directors, and its railway magnates. Thackeray and Dickens followed Balzac[16] in scratching and biting the unfortunate middle class with savage ill-temper, much as the middle class had scratched and bitten the Church and Court for a hundred years before. The middle class had the power, and held its coal and iron well in hand, but the satirists and idealists seized the press, and as they were agreed that the Second Empire[17] was a disgrace to France and a danger to England, they turned to Germany because at that moment

Germany was neither economical nor military, and a hundred years behind western Europe in the simplicity of its standards. German thought, method, honesty, and even taste, became the standards of scholarship. Goethe[18] was raised to the rank of Shakespeare — Kant[19] ranked as a law-giver above Plato. All serious scholars were obliged to become German, for German thought was revolutionizing criticism. Lowell had followed the rest, not very enthusiastically, but with sufficient conviction, and invited his scholars to join him. Adams was glad to accept the invitation, rather for the sake of cultivating Lowell than Germany, but still in perfect good faith. It was the first serious attempt he had made to direct his own education, and he was sure of getting some education out of it; not perhaps anything that he expected, but at least a path.

Singularly circuitous and excessively wasteful of energy the path proved to be, but the student could never see what other was open to him. He could have done no better had he foreseen every stage of his coming life, and he would probably have done worse. The preliminary step was pure gain. James Russell Lowell had brought back from Germany the only new and valuable part of its universities, the habit of allowing students to read with him privately in his study. Adams asked the privilege, and used it to read a little, and to talk a great deal, for the personal contact pleased and flattered him, as that of older men ought to flatter and please the young even when they altogether exaggerate its value. Lowell was a new element in the boy's life. As practical a New Englander as any, he leaned towards the Concord faith[20] rather than towards Boston where he properly belonged; for Concord, in the dark days of 1856,[21] glowed with pure light. Adams approached it in much the same spirit as he would have entered a Gothic Cathedral, for he well knew that the priests regarded him as only a worm. To the Concord Church all Adamses were minds of dust and emptiness, devoid of feeling, poetry or imagination; little higher than the common scourings of State

Street; politicians of doubtful honesty; natures of narrow scope; and already, at eighteen years old, Henry had begun to feel uncertainty about so many matters more important than Adamses that his mind rebelled against no discipline merely personal, and he was ready to admit his unworthiness if only he might penetrate the shrine. The influence of Harvard College was beginning to have its effect. He was slipping away from fixed principles; from Mount Vernon Street; from Quincy; from the eighteenth century; and his first steps led toward Concord.

He never reached Concord, and to Concord Church he, like the rest of mankind who accepted a material universe, remained always an insect, or something much lower — a man. It was surely no fault of his that the universe seemed to him real; perhaps — as Mr. Emerson justly said [22] — it was so; in spite of the long-continued effort of a lifetime, he perpetually fell back into the heresy that if anything universal was unreal, it was himself and not the appearances; it was the poet and not the banker; it was his own thought, not the thing that moved it. He did not lack the wish to be transcendental. Concord seemed to him, at one time, more real than Quincy; yet in truth Russell Lowell was as little transcendental as Beacon Street. From him the boy got no revolutionary thought whatever — objective or subjective as they used to call it [23] — but he got good-humored encouragement to do what amused him, which consisted in passing two years in Europe after finishing the four years of Cambridge.

The result seemed small in proportion to the effort, but it was the only positive result he could ever trace to the influence of Harvard College, and he had grave doubts whether Harvard College influenced even that. Negative results in plenty he could trace, but he tended towards negation on his own account, as one side of the New England mind had always done, and even there he could never feel sure that Harvard College had more than reflected a weakness. In his opinion the education was not serious, but in truth hardly any Boston student took it seriously, and none of them seemed sure that President Walker himself, or President Felton[24] after him, took it more seriously than the students. For them all, the college offered chiefly advantages vulgarly called social, rather than mental.

Unluckily for this particular boy, social advantages were his only capital in life. Of money he had not much, of mind not more, but he could be quite certain that, barring his own faults, his social position would never be questioned. What he needed was a career in which social position had value. Never in his life would he have to explain who he was; never would he have need of acquaintance to strengthen his social standing; but he needed greatly some one to show him how to use the acquaintance he cared to make. He made no acquaintance in college which proved to have the smallest use in after life. All his Boston friends he knew before, or would have known in any case, and contact of Bostonian with Bostonian was the last education these young men needed. Cordial and intimate as their college relations were, they all flew off in different directions the moment they took their degrees. Harvard College remained a tie, indeed, but a tie little stronger than Beacon Street and not so strong as State Street. Strangers might perhaps gain something from the college if they were hard pressed for social connections. A student like H. H. Richardson, who came from far away New Orleans, and had his career before him to chase rather than to guide, might make valuable friendships at college. Certainly Adams made no acquaintance there that he valued in after life so much as Richardson, but still more certainly the college relation had little to do with the later friendship. Life is a narrow valley, and the roads run close together. Adams would have attached himself to Richardson in any case, as he attached himself to John LaFarge or Augustus St. Gaudens or Clarence King or John Hay, none of whom were at Harvard College.[25] The valley of life grew more and more narrow with years, and certain men with common tastes were bound to come together. Adams knew only that he would have felt himself on a more equal footing with them had he been less ignorant, and had he not thrown away ten years of early life in acquiring what he might have acquired in one.

Socially or intellectually, the college was for him negative and in some ways mischievous. The most tolerant man of the world could not see good in the lower habits of the students, but the vices were less harmful than the virtues. The habit of drinking — though the mere recollection of it made him doubt his own veracity, so fantastic it seemed in later life — may have done no great or permanent harm; but the habit of looking at life as a social relation — an affair of society — did no good. It cultivated a weakness which needed no cultivation. If it had helped to make men of the world, or give the manners and instincts of any profession — such as temper, patience, courtesy, or a faculty of profiting by the social defects of opponents — it would have been education better worth having than mathematics or languages; but so far as it helped to make anything, it helped only to make the college standard permanent through life. The Bostonian educated at Harvard College remained a collegian, if he stuck only to what the college gave him. If parents went on, generation after generation, sending their children to Harvard College for the sake of its social advantages, they perpetuated an inferior social type, quite as ill-fitted as the Oxford[26] type for success in the next generation.

Luckily the old social standard of the college, as President Walker or James Russell Lowell still showed it, was admirable, and if it had little practical value or personal influence on the mass of students, at least it preserved the tradition for those who liked it. The Harvard graduate was neither American nor European, nor even wholly Yankee; his admirers were few, and his critics many; perhaps his worst weakness was his self-criticism and self-consciousness; but his ambitions, social or intellectual, were not necessarily cheap even though they might be negative. Afraid of serious risks, and still more afraid of personal ridicule, he seldom made a great failure of life, and nearly always led a life more or less worth living. So Henry Adams, well aware that he could not succeed as a scholar, and finding his social position beyond improvement or need of effort, betook himself to the single ambition which otherwise would scarcely have seemed a true outcome of the college, though it was the last remnant of the old Unitarian supremacy. He took to the pen. He wrote.

The College Magazine printed his work, and the College Societies listened to his addresses. Lavish of praise the readers were not; the audiences, too, listened in silence; but this was all the encouragement any Harvard collegian had a reasonable hope to receive; grave silence was a form of patience that meant possible future acceptance; and Henry Adams went on writing. No one cared enough to criticise, except himself who soon began to suffer from reaching his own limits. He found that he could not be this — or that — or the other; always precisely the things he wanted to be. He had not wit or scope or force. Judges always ranked him beneath a rival, if he had any; and he believed the judges were right. His work seemed to him thin, commonplace, feeble. At times he felt his own weakness so fatally that he could not go on; when he had nothing to say, he could not say it, and he found that he had very little to say at best. Much that he then wrote must be still in existence in print or manuscript, though he never cared to see it again, for he felt no doubt that it was in reality just what he thought it. At best it showed only a feeling for form; an instinct of exclusion. Nothing shocked — not even its weakness.

Inevitably an effort leads to an ambition — creates it — and at that time the ambition of the literary student, which almost took place of the regular prizes of scholarship, was that of being chosen as the representative of his class — the Class Orator — at the close of their course. This was political as well as literary success, and precisely the sort of eighteenth-century combination that fascinated an eighteenth-century boy. The idea lurked in his mind, at first as a dream, in no way serious or even possible, for he stood outside the number of what were known as popular men. Year by year, his position seemed to improve, or perhaps his rivals disappeared, until at last, to his own great astonishment, he found himself a candidate. The habits of the college permitted no active candidacy; he and his rivals had not a word to say for or against themselves, and he was never even consulted on the subject; he was not present at any of the proceedings, and how it happened he never could quite divine, but it did happen, that one evening on returning from Boston he received notice of his election, after a very close contest, as Class Orator over the head of the first scholar, who was undoubtedly a better orator and a more popular man. In politics the success of the poorer candidate is common enough, and Henry Adams was a fairly trained politician, but he never understood how he managed to defeat not only a more capable but a more popular rival.

To him the election seemed a miracle. This was no mock-modesty; his head was as clear as ever it was in an indifferent canvass, and he knew his rivals and their following as well as he knew himself. What he did not know, even after four years of education, was Harvard College. What he could never measure was the bewildering impersonality of the men, who, at twenty years old, seemed to set no value either on official or personal standards. Here were nearly a hundred young men who had lived together intimately during four of the most impressionable years of life, and who, not only once but again and again, in different ways, deliberately, seriously, dispassionately, chose as their representatives precisely those of their companions who seemed least to represent them. As far as these Orators and Marshals had any position at all in a collegiate sense, it was that of indifference to the college. Henry Adams never professed the smallest faith in universities of any kind, either as boy or man, nor had he the faintest admiration for the university graduate, either in Europe or in America; as a collegian he was only known apart from his fellows by his habit of standing outside the college; and yet the singular fact remained that this commonplace body of young men chose him repeatedly to express his and their commonplaces. Secretly, of course, the successful candidate flattered himself — and them — with the hope that they might perhaps not be so commonplace as they thought themselves; but this was only another proof that all were identical. They saw in him a representative — the kind of representative they wanted — and he saw in them the most formidable array of judges he could ever meet, like so many mirrors of himself, an infinite reflection of his own shortcomings.

All the same, the choice was flattering; so flattering that it actually shocked his vanity; and would have shocked it more, if possible, had he known that it was to be the only flattery of the sort he was ever to receive. The function of Class Day was, in the eyes of nine-tenths of the students, altogether the most important of the college, and the figure of the Orator was the most conspicuous in the function. Unlike the Orators at regular Commencements, the Class Day Orator stood alone, or had only the Poet for rival. Crowded into the large church, the students, their families, friends, aunts, uncles and chaperones, attended all the girls of sixteen or twenty who wanted to show their summer dresses or fresh complexions, and there, for an hour or two, in a heat that might have melted bronze, they listened to an Orator and a Poet in clergyman's gowns, reciting such platitudes as their own experience and their mild censors permitted them to utter. What Henry Adams said in his Class Oration of 1858 he soon forgot to the last word, nor had it the least value for education; but he naturally remembered what was said of it.[27] He remembered especially one of his eminent uncles or relations remarking that, as the work of so young a man, the oration was singularly wanting in enthusiasm. The young man — always in search of education — asked himself whether, setting rhetoric aside, this absence of enthusiasm was a defect or a merit, since, in either case, it was all that Harvard College taught, and all that the hundred young men, whom he was trying to represent, expressed. Another comment threw more light on the effect of the college education. One of the elderly gentlemen noticed the orator's "perfect self-possession." Self-possession indeed! If Harvard College gave nothing else, it gave calm. For four years each student had been obliged to figure daily before dozens of young men who knew each other to the last fibre. One had done little but read papers to Societies, or act comedy in the Hasty Pudding, not to speak of all sorts of regular exercises, and no audience in future life would ever be so intimately and terribly intelligent as these. Three-fourths of the graduates would rather have addressed the Council of Trent[28] or the British Parliament than have acted Sir Anthony Absolute or Dr. Ollapod before a gala audience of the Hasty Pudding.[29] Self-possession was the strongest part of Harvard College, which certainly taught men to stand alone, so that nothing seemed stranger to its graduates than the paroxysms of terror before the public which often overcame the graduates of European universities. Whether this was, or was not, education, Henry Adams never knew. He was ready to stand up before any audience in America or Europe, with nerves rather steadier for the excitement, but whether he should ever have anything to say, remained to be proved. As yet he knew nothing. Education had not begun.[30]

CHAPTER V

Berlin (1858–1859)

A
FOURTH child has the strength of his weakness. Being of no great value, he may throw himself away if he likes, and never be missed. Charles Francis Adams, the father, felt no love for Europe, which, as he and all the world agreed, unfitted Americans for America. A captious critic might have replied that all the success he or his father or his grandfather ever achieved was chiefly due to the field that Europe gave them, and it was more than likely that without the help of Europe they would have all remained local politicians or lawyers, like their neighbors, to the end. Strictly followed, the rule would have obliged them never to quit Quincy; and, in fact, so much more timid are parents for their children than for themselves, that Mr. and Mrs. Adams would have been content to see their children remain forever in Mount Vernon Street, unexposed to the temptations of Europe, could they have relied on the moral influences of Boston itself. Although the parents little knew what took place under their eyes, even the mothers saw enough to make them uneasy. Perhaps their dread of vice, haunting past and present, worried them less than their dread of daughters-in-law or sons-in-law who might not fit into the somewhat narrow quarters of home. On all sides were risks. Every year some young person alarmed the parental heart even in Boston, and although the temptations of Europe were irresistible, removal from the temptations of Boston might be imperative. The boy Henry wanted to go to Europe; he seemed well behaved, when anyone was looking at him; he observed conventions, when he could not escape them; he was never quarrelsome, towards a superior; his morals were apparently good, and his moral principles, if he had any, were not known to be bad. Above all, he was timid and showed a certain sense of self-respect,

when in public view. What he was at heart, no one could say; least of all himself; but he was probably human, and no worse than some others. Therefore, when he presented to an exceedingly indulgent father and mother his request to begin at a German university the study of the Civil Law [1] — although neither he nor they knew what the Civil Law was, or any reason for his studying it — the parents dutifully consented, and walked with him down to the railway-station at Quincy to bid him good-bye, with a smile which he almost thought a tear.

Whether the boy deserved such indulgence, or was worth it, he knew no more than they, or than a professor at Harvard College; but whether worthy or not, he began his third or fourth attempt at education in November,[2] 1858, by sailing on the steamer Persia, the pride of Captain Judkins and the Cunard Line; the newest, largest and fastest steamship afloat. He was not alone. Several of his college companions sailed with him, and the world looked cheerful enough until, on the third day, the world — as far as concerned the young man — ran into a heavy storm. He learned then a lesson that stood by him better than any university teaching ever did — the meaning of a November gale on the mid-Atlantic — which, for mere physical misery, passed endurance. The subject offered him material for none but serious treatment; he could never see the humor of sea-sickness; but it united itself with a great variety of other impressions which made the first month of travel altogether the rapidest school of education he had yet found. The stride in knowledge seemed gigantic. One began at last to see that a great many impressions were needed to make a very little education, but how many could be crowded into one day without making any education at all, became the *pons asinorum*[3] of tourist mathematics. How many would turn out to be wrong, or whether any would turn out right, was ultimate wisdom.

The ocean, the Persia, Captain Judkins, and Mr. G. P. R. James,[4] the most distinguished passenger, vanished one Sunday morning in a furious gale in the Mersey, to make place for the drearier picture of a Liverpool street as seen from the Adelphi coffee-room in November murk, followed instantly by the passionate delights of Chester and the romance of red-sandstone architecture. Millions of Americans have felt this succession of emotions. Possibly very young and ingenuous tourists feel them still, but in days before tourists, when the romance was a reality, not a picture, they were overwhelming. When the boys went out to Eaton Hall,[5] they were awed, as Thackeray or Dickens would have felt in the presence of a Duke. The very name of Grosvenor struck a note of grandeur. The long suite of lofty, gilded rooms with their gilded furniture; the portraits; the terraces; the gardens; the landscape; the sense of superiority in the England of the fifties, actually set the rich nobleman apart, above Americans and shopkeepers. Aristocracy was real. So was the England of Dickens. Oliver Twist and Little Nell[6] lurked in every churchyard shadow, not as shadow but alive. Even Charles the First[7] was not very shadowy, standing on the tower to see his army defeated. Nothing thereabouts had very much changed since he lost his battle and his head. An eighteenth-century American boy fresh from Boston naturally took it all for education, and was amused at this sort of lesson. At least he thought he felt it.

Then came the journey up to London through Birmingham and the Black District,[8] another lesson, which needed much more to be rightly felt. The plunge into darkness lurid with flames; the sense of unknown horror in this weird gloom which then existed nowhere else, and never had existed before, except in volcanic craters; the violent contrast between this dense, smoky, impenetrable darkness, and the soft green charm that one glided into, as one emerged — the revelation of an unknown society of the pit — made a boy uncomfortable, though he had no idea that Karl Marx was standing there waiting for him, and that sooner or later the process of education would have to deal with Karl Marx much more than with Professor Bowen[9] of Harvard College or his Satanic free-trade majesty John Stuart Mill.[10] The Black District was a practical education, but it was infinitely far in the distance. The boy ran away from it, as he ran away from everything he disliked.

Had he known enough to know where to begin he would have seen something to study, more vital than the Civil Law, in the long, muddy, dirty, sordid, gas-lit dreariness of Oxford Street as his dingy four-wheeler dragged its weary way to Charing Cross. He did notice one peculiarity about it worth remembering. London was still London. A certain style dignified its grime; heavy, clumsy, arrogant, purse-proud, but not cheap; insular but large; barely tolerant of an outside world, and absolutely self-confident. The boys in the streets made such free comments on the American clothes and figures, that the travellers hurried to put on tall hats and long overcoats to escape criticism. No stranger had rights even in the Strand.[11] The eighteenth century held its own. History muttered down Fleet Street, like Dr. Johnson,[12] in Adams's ear; Vanity Fair[13] was alive on Piccadilly[14] in yellow chariots with coachmen in wigs, on hammer-cloths; footmen with canes, on the footboard, and a shrivelled old woman inside; half the great houses, black with London smoke, bore large funereal hatchments; everyone seemed insolent, and the most insolent structures in the world were the Royal Exchange and the Bank of England. In November,[15] 1858, London was still vast, but it was the London of the eighteenth century that an American felt and hated.

Education went backward. Adams, still a boy, could not guess how intensely intimate this London grime was to become to him as a man, but he could still less conceive himself returning to it fifty years afterwards, noting at each return how the great city grew smaller as it doubled in size; cheaper as it quadrupled its wealth; less imperial as its empire widened; less dignified as it tried to be civil. He liked it best when he hated it. Education began at the end, or perhaps would end at the beginning. Thus far it had remained in the eighteenth century, and the next step took it back to the sixteenth. He crossed to Antwerp. As the Baron Osy steamed up the Scheldt in the morning mists, a travelling band on deck began to play, and groups of peasants, working along the fields, dropped their tools to join in dancing. Ostade and Teniers[16] were as much alive as they ever were, and even the Duke of Alva[17] was still at home. The thirteenth-century cathedral towered above a sixteenth-century mass of tiled roofs, ending abruptly in walls and a landscape that had not changed. The taste of the town was thick, rich, ripe, like a sweet wine; it was mediæval, so that Rubens[18] seemed modern; it was one of the strongest and fullest flavors that ever touched the young man's palate; but he might as well have drunk out his excitement in old Malmsey,[19] for all the education he got from it. Even in art, one can hardly begin with Antwerp Cathedral and the Descent from the Cross. He merely got drunk on his emotions, and had then to get sober as he best could. He was terribly sober when he saw Antwerp half a century afterwards. One lesson he did learn without suspecting that he must immediately lose it. He felt his middle ages and the sixteenth century alive. He was young enough, and the towns were dirty enough — unimproved, unrestored, untouristed — to retain the sense of reality. As a taste or a smell, it was education, especially because it lasted barely ten years longer; but it was education only sensual. He never dreamed of trying to educate himself to the Descent from the Cross. He was only too happy to feel himself kneeling at the foot of the Cross; he learned only to loathe the sordid necessity of getting up again, and going about his stupid business.

This was one of the foreseen dangers of Europe, but it vanished rapidly enough to reassure the most anxious of parents. Dropped into Berlin one morning without guide or direction, the young man in search of education floundered in a mere mess of misunderstandings. He could never recall what he expected to find, but whatever he expected, it had no relation with what it turned out to be. A student at twenty takes easily to anything, even to Berlin, and he would have accepted the thirteenth century pure and simple since his guides assured him that this was his right path; but a week's experience left him dazed and dull. Faith held out, but the paths grew dim. Berlin astonished him, but he had no lack of friends to show him all the amusement it had to offer. Within a day or two he was running about with the rest to beer-cellars and music-halls and dance-rooms, smoking bad tobacco, drinking poor beer, and eating sauerkraut and sausages as though he knew no better. This was easy. One can always descend the social ladder. The trouble came when he asked for the education he was promised. His friends took him to be registered as a student of the university; they selected his professors and courses; they showed him where to buy the Institutes of Gaius and several German works on the Civil Law in numerous volumes; and they led him to his first lecture.

His first lecture was his last. The young man was not very quick, and he had almost religious respect for his guides and advisers; but he needed no more than one hour to satisfy him that he had made another failure in education, and this time a fatal one. That the language would require at least three months' hard work before he could touch the Law was an annoying discovery; but the shock that upset him was the discovery of the university itself. He had thought Harvard College a torpid school, but it was instinct with life compared with all that he could see of the University of Berlin. The German students were strange animals, but their professors were beyond pay. The mental attitude of the university was not of an American world. What sort of instruction prevailed in other branches, or in science, Adams had no occasion to ask, but in the Civil Law he found only the lecture system in its deadliest form as it flourished in the thirteenth century. The professor mumbled his comments; the students made, or seemed to make, notes; they could have learned from books or discussion in a day more than they could learn from him in a month, but they must pay his fees, follow his course, and be his scholars, if they wanted a degree. To an American the result was worthless. He could make no use of the Civil Law without some previous notion of the Common Law; but the student who knew enough of the Common Law to understand what he wanted, had only to read the Pandects or the commentators at his ease in America, and be his own professor. Neither the method nor the matter nor the manner could profit an American education.

This discovery seemed to shock none of the students. They went to the lectures, made notes, and read textbooks, but never pretended to take their professor seriously. They were much more serious in reading Heine.[20] They knew no more than Heine what good they were getting, beyond the Berlin accent — which was bad; and the beer — which was not to compare with Munich; and the dancing — which was better at Vienna. They enjoyed the beer and music, but they refused to be responsible for the education. Anyway, as they defended themselves, they were learning the language.

So the young man fell back on the language, and being slow at languages, he found himself falling behind all his friends, which depressed his spirits, the more because the gloom of a Berlin winter and of Berlin architecture seemed to him a particular sort of gloom never attained elsewhere. One day on the Linden[21] he caught sight of Charles Sumner in a cab, and ran after him. Sumner was then recovering from the blows of the South Carolinian[22] cane or club, and he was pleased to find a young worshipper in the remote Prussian wilderness. They dined together and went to hear "William Tell"[23] at the Opera. Sumner tried to encourage his friend about his difficulties of language: "I came to Berlin," or Rome, or whatever place it was, as he said with his grand air of mastery, "I came to Berlin, unable to say a word in the language; and three months later when I went away, I talked it to my cabman." Adams felt himself quite unable to attain in so short a time such social advantages, and one day complained of his trials to Mr. Robert Apthorp,[24] of Boston, who was passing the winter in Berlin for the sake of its music. Mr. Apthorp told of his own similar struggle, and how he had entered a public school and sat for

months with ten-year-old boys, reciting their lessons and catching
their phrases. The idea suited Adams's desperate frame of mind.
At least it ridded him of the university and the Civil Law and
American associations in beer-cellars. Mr. Apthorp took the
trouble to negotiate with the head-master of the Friedrichs-
Wilhelm-Werdersches Gymnasium[25] for permission to Henry
Adams to attend the school as a member of the Ober-tertia,[26] a class
of boys twelve or thirteen years old, and there Adams went for
three months as though he had not always avoided high schools
with singular antipathy. He never did anything else so foolish,
but he was given a bit of education which served him some purpose in life.

It was not merely the language, though three months passed
in such fashion would teach a poodle enough to talk with a cabman, and this was all that foreign students could expect to do,
for they never by any chance would come in contact with German society, if German society existed, about which they knew
nothing. Adams never learned to talk German well, but the
same might be said of his English, if he could believe Englishmen.
He learned not to annoy himself on this account. His difficulties
with the language gradually ceased. He thought himself quite
Germanized in 1859. He even deluded himself with the idea that
he read it as though it were English, which proved that he knew
little about it; but whatever success he had in his own experiment interested him less than his contact with German education.

He had revolted at the American school and university; he had
instantly rejected the German university; and as his last experience of education he tried the German high school. The experiment was hazardous. In 1858 Berlin was a poor, keen-witted,
provincial town, simple, dirty, uncivilized, and in most respects
disgusting.[27] Life was primitive beyond what an American boy
could have imagined. Overridden by military methods and bu-
reaucratic pettiness, Prussia was only beginning to free her hands
from internal bonds. Apart from discipline, activity scarcely

existed. The future Kaiser Wilhelm I, regent for his insane brother King Friedrich Wilhelm IV,[28] seemed to pass his time looking out at the passers-by from the window of his modest palace on the Linden. German manners, even at Court, were sometimes brutal, and German thoroughness at school was apt to be routine. Bismarck himself was then struggling to begin a career against the inertia of the German system. The condition of Germany was a scandal and nuisance to every earnest German, all whose energies were turned to reforming it from top to bottom; and Adams walked into a great public school to get educated, at precisely the time when the Germans wanted most to get rid of the education they were forced to follow. As an episode in the search for education, this adventure smacked of Heine.[29]

The school system has doubtless changed, and at all events the schoolmasters are probably long ago dead; the story has no longer a practical value, and had very little even at the time; one could at least say in defence of the German school that it was neither very brutal nor very immoral. The head-master was excellent in his Prussian way, and the other instructors were not worse than in other schools; it was their system that struck the systemless American with horror. The arbitrary training given to the memory was stupefying; the strain that the memory endured was a form of torture; and the feats that the boys performed, without complaint, were pitiable. No other faculty than the memory seemed to be recognized. Least of all was any use made of reason, either analytic, synthetic, or dogmatic. The German government did not encourage reasoning.

All State education is a sort of dynamo machine for polarizing the popular mind; for turning and holding its lines of force in the direction supposed to be most effective for State purposes. The German machine was terribly efficient. Its effect on the children was pathetic. The Friedrichs-Wilhelm-Werdersches Gymnasium was an old building in the heart of Berlin which served the educational needs of the small tradesmen or *bourgeoisie* of the neighborhood; the children were Berliner-kinder[30] if ever there were such, and of a class suspected of sympathy and concern in the troubles of 1848. None was noble or connected with good society. Personally they were rather sympathetic than not, but as the objects of education they were proofs of nearly all the evils that a bad system could give. Apparently Adams, in his rigidly illogical pursuit, had at last reached his ideal of a viciously logical education. The boys' physique showed it first, but their physique could not be wholly charged to the school. German food was bad at best, and a diet of sauerkraut, sausage, and beer could never be good; but it was not the food alone that made their faces white and their flesh flabby. They never breathed fresh air; they had never heard of a playground; in all Berlin not a cubic inch of oxygen was admitted in winter into an inhabited building; in the school every room was tightly closed and had no ventilation; the air was foul beyond all decency; but when the American opened a window in the five minutes between hours, he violated the rules and was invariably rebuked. As long as cold weather lasted, the windows were shut. If the boys had a holiday, they were apt to be taken on long tramps in the Thiergarten or elsewhere, always ending in over-fatigue, tobacco-smoke, sausages, and beer. With this, they were required to prepare daily lessons that would have quickly broken down strong men of a healthy habit, and which they could learn only because their minds were morbid. The German university had seemed a failure, but the German high school was something very near an indictable nuisance.

Before the month of April arrived, the experiment of German education had reached this point. Nothing was left of it except the ghost of the Civil Law shut up in the darkest of closets, never to gibber again before any one who could repeat the story. The derisive Jew laughter of Heine[31] ran through the university and everything else in Berlin. Of course, when one is twenty years old, life is bound to be full, if only of Berlin beer, although German student life was on the whole the thinnest of beer, as an

American looked on it, but though nothing except small fragments remained of the education that had been so promising — or promised — this is only what most often happens in life, when by-products turn out to be more valuable than staples. The German university and German law were failures; German society, in an American sense, did not exist, or if it existed, never showed itself to an American; the German theatre, on the other hand, was excellent, and German opera, with the ballet, was almost worth a journey to Berlin; but the curious and perplexing result of the total failure of German education was that the student's only clear gain — his single step to a higher life — came from time wasted; studies neglected; vices indulged; education reversed; — it came from the despised beer-garden and music-hall; and it was accidental, unintended, unforeseen.

When his companions insisted on passing two or three afternoons in the week at music-halls, drinking beer, smoking German tobacco, and looking at fat German women knitting, while an orchestra played dull music, Adams went with them for the sake of the company, but with no pretence of enjoyment; and when Mr. Apthorp gently protested that he exaggerated his indifference, for of course he enjoyed Beethoven, Adams replied simply that he loathed Beethoven; and felt a slight surprise when Mr. Apthorp and the others laughed as though they thought it humor. He saw no humor in it. He supposed that, except musicians, everyone thought Beethoven a bore, as everyone except mathematicians thought mathematics a bore. Sitting thus at his beer-table, mentally impassive, he was one day surprised to notice that his mind followed the movement of a Sinfonie.[32] He could not have been more astonished had he suddenly read a new language. Among the marvels of education, this was the most marvellous. A prison-wall that barred his senses on one great side of life, suddenly fell, of its own accord, without so much as his knowing when it happened. Amid the fumes of coarse tobacco and poor beer, surrounded by the commonest of German Haus-frauen,[33] a new sense burst out like a flower in his life, so superior to the old senses, so bewildering, so astonished at its own existence, that he could not credit it, and watched it as something apart, accidental, and not to be trusted. He slowly came to admit that Beethoven had partly become intelligible to him, but he was the more inclined to think that Beethoven must be much overrated as a musician, to be so easily followed. This could not be called education, for he had never so much as listened to the music. He had been thinking of other things. Mere mechanical repetition of certain sounds had stuck to his unconscious mind. Beethoven might have this power, but not Wagner, or at all events not the Wagner later than "Tannhäuser." Near forty years passed before he reached the "Götterdämmerung." [34]

One might talk of the revival of an atrophied sense — the mechanical reaction of a sleeping consciousness — but no other sense awoke. His sense of line and color remained as dull as ever, and as far as ever below the level of an artist. His metaphysical sense did not spring into life, so that his mind could leap the bars of German expression into sympathy with the idealities of Kant and Hegel.[35] Although he insisted that his faith in German thought and literature was exalted, he failed to approach German thought, and he shed never a tear of emotion over the pages of Goethe and Schiller.[36] When his father rashly ventured from time to time to write him a word of common sense, the young man would listen to no sense at all, but insisted that Berlin was the best of educations in the best of Germanies;[37] yet, when, at last, April came, and some genius suggested a tramp in Thüringen,[38] his heart sang like a bird; he realized what a nightmare he had suffered, and he made up his mind that, wherever else he might, in the infinities of space and time, seek for education, it should not be again in Berlin.

CHAPTER VI

Rome (1859–1860)

THE tramp in Thüringen lasted four-and-twenty hours. By the end of the first walk, his three companions — John Bancroft, James J. Higginson, and B. W. Crowninshield, all Boston and Harvard College like himself [2] — were satisfied with what they had seen, and when they sat down to rest on the spot where Goethe had written —

> " Warte nur! balde
> Ruhest du auch! " — [3]

the profoundness of the thought and the wisdom of the advice affected them so strongly that they hired a wagon and drove to Weimar the same night. They were all quite happy and lighthearted in the first fresh breath of leafless spring, and the beer was better than at Berlin, but they were all equally in doubt why they had come to Germany, and not one of them could say why they stayed. Adams stayed because he did not want to go home, and he had fears that his father's patience might be exhausted if he asked to waste time elsewhere.

They could not think that their education required a return to Berlin. A few days at Dresden in the spring weather satisfied them that Dresden was a better spot for general education than Berlin, and equally good for reading Civil Law. They were possibly right. There was nothing to study in Dresden, and no education to be gained, but the Sistine Madonna and the Correggios [4] were famous; the theatre and opera were sometimes excellent, and the Elbe was prettier than the Spree. They could always fall back on the language. So he took a room in the household of the usual small government clerk with the usual plain daughters, and continued the study of the language. Possibly one might learn something more by accident, as one had learned something of Beethoven. For the next eighteen months the young man pursued accidental education, since he could pursue no other; and by great good fortune, Europe and America were too busy with their own affairs to give much attention to his. Accidental education had every chance in its favor, especially because nothing came amiss.

Perhaps the chief obstacle to the youth's education, now that he had come of age, was his honesty; his simple-minded faith in his intentions. Even after Berlin had become a nightmare, he still persuaded himself that his German education was a success. He loved, or thought he loved the people, but the Germany he loved was the eighteenth-century which the Germans were ashamed of, and were destroying as fast as they could. Of the Germany to come, he knew nothing. Military Germany was his abhorrence. What he liked was the simple character; the good-natured sentiment; the musical and metaphysical abstraction; the blundering incapacity of the German for practical affairs. At that time everyone looked on Germany as incapable of competing with France, England or America in any sort of organized energy. Germany had no confidence in herself, and no reason to feel it. She had no unity, and no reason to want it. She never had unity. Her religious and social history, her economical interests, her military geography, her political convenience, had always tended to eccentric rather than concentric motion. Until coal-power and railways were created, she was mediæval by nature and geography, and this was what Adams, under the teachings of Carlyle and Lowell, liked.

He was in a fair way to do himself lasting harm, floundering between worlds passed and worlds coming,[5] which had a habit of crushing men who stayed too long at the points of contact. Suddenly the Emperor Napoleon declared war on Austria[6] and raised a confused point of morals in the mind of Europe. France was the nightmare of Germany, and even at Dresden one looked on the return of Napoleon to Leipsic as the most likely thing in the world. One morning the government clerk, in whose family Adams was staying, rushed into his room to consult a map in order that he might measure the distance from Milan to Dresden. The third Napoleon had reached Lombardy, and only fifty or sixty years had passed since the first Napoleon had begun his military successes from an Italian base.

An enlightened young American, with eighteenth-century tastes capped by fragments of a German education and the most excellent intentions, had to make up his mind about the moral value of these conflicting forces. France was the wicked spirit of moral politics, and whatever helped France must be so far evil. At that time Austria was another evil spirit. Italy was the prize they disputed, and for at least fifteen hundred years had been the chief object of their greed.[7] The question of sympathy had disturbed a number of persons during that period. The question of morals had been put in a number of cross-lights. Should one be Guelph or Ghibelline?[8] No doubt, one was wiser than one's neighbors who had found no way of settling this question since the days of the cave-dwellers, but ignorance did better to discard the attempt to be wise, for wisdom had been singularly baffled by the problem. Better take sides first, and reason about it for the rest of life.

Not that Adams felt any real doubt about his sympathies or wishes. He had not been German long enough for befogging his mind to that point, but the moment was decisive for much to come, especially for political morals. His morals were the highest, and he clung to them to preserve his self-respect; but steam and electricity had brought about new political and social concentrations, or were making them necessary in the line of his moral principles — freedom, education, economic development and so forth — which required association with allies as doubtful as Napoleon III, and robberies with violence on a very extensive scale. As long as he could argue that his opponents were wicked, he could join in robbing and killing them without a qualm; but it might happen that the good were robbed. Education insisted on finding a moral foundation for robbery. He could hope to begin life in the character of no animal more moral than a monkey unless he could satisfy himself when and why robbery and murder were a virtue and duty. Education founded on mere self-interest was merely Guelph and Ghibelline over again — Machiavelli[9] translated into American.

Luckily for him he had a sister[10] much brighter than he ever was — though he thought himself a rather superior person — who after marrying Charles Kuhn, of Philadelphia, had come to Italy, and, like all good Americans and English, was hotly Italian. In July, 1859, she was at Thun in Switzerland, and there Henry Adams joined them. Women have, commonly, a very positive moral sense; that which they will, is right; that which they reject, is wrong; and their will, in most cases, ends by settling the moral. Mrs. Kuhn had a double superiority. She not only adored Italy, but she cordially disliked Germany in all its varieties. She saw no gain in helping her brother to be Germanized, and she wanted him much to be civilized. She was the first young woman he was ever intimate with — quick, sensitive, wilful, or full of will, energetic, sympathetic and intelligent enough to supply a score of men with ideas — and he was delighted to give her the reins — to let her drive him where she would. It was his first experiment in giving the reins to a woman, and he was so much pleased with the results that he never wanted to take them back. In after life he made a general law of experience — no woman had ever driven him wrong; no man had ever driven him right.

Nothing would satisfy Mrs. Kuhn but to go to the seat of war as soon as the armistice was declared. Wild as the idea seemed, nothing was easier. The party crossed the St. Gothard and reached Milan, picturesque with every sort of uniform and every sign of war. To young Adams this first plunge into Italy passed Beethoven as a piece of accidental education. Like music, it differed from other education in being, not a means of pursuing life, but one of the ends attained. Further, on these lines, one could not go. It had but one defect — that of attainment. Life had no richer impression to give; it offers barely half-a-dozen such, and the intervals seem long. Exactly what they teach would puzzle a Berlin jurist; yet they seem to have an economic value, since most people would decline to part with even their faded memories except at a valuation ridiculously extravagant. They were also what men pay most for; but one's ideas become hopelessly mixed in trying to reduce such forms of education to a standard of exchangeable value, and, as in political economy, one had best disregard altogether what cannot be stated in equivalents. The proper equivalent of pleasure is pain, which is also a form of education.

Not satisfied with Milan, Mrs. Kuhn insisted on invading the enemy's country, and the carriage was chartered for Innsbruck by way of the Stelvio Pass.[11] The Valtellina, as the carriage drove up it, showed war. Garibaldi's Cacciatori[12] were the only visible inhabitants. No one could say whether the pass was open, but in any case no carriage had yet crossed. At the inns the handsome young officers in command of the detachments were delighted to accept invitations to dinner and to talk all the evening of their battles to the charming patriot[13] who sparkled with interest and flattery, but not one of them knew whether their enemies, the abhorred Austrian Jägers,[14] would let the travellers through their lines. As a rule, gaiety was not the character failing in any party that Mrs. Kuhn belonged to, but when at last, after climbing what was said to be the finest carriage-pass in Europe, the carriage turned the last shoulder, where the glacier of the Ortler Spitze[15] tumbled its huge mass down upon the road, even Mrs. Kuhn gasped when she was driven directly up to the barricade and stopped by the double line of sentries stretching on either side up the mountains, till the flash of the gun barrels was lost in the flash of the snow. For accidental education the picture had its value. The earliest of these pictures count for most, as first impressions must, and Adams never afterwards cared much for landscape education, except perhaps in the tropics for the sake of the contrast. As education, that chapter, too, was read, and set aside.

The handsome blond officers of the Jägers were not to be beaten in courtesy by the handsome young olive-toned officers of the Cacciatori. The eternal woman[16] as usual, when she is young, pretty, and engaging, had her way, and the barricade offered no resistance. In fifteen minutes the carriage was rolling down to Mals, swarming with German soldiers and German fleas, worse than the Italian; and German language, thought, and atmosphere, of which young Adams, thanks to his glimpse of Italy, never again felt quite the old confident charm.

Yet he could talk to his cabman and conscientiously did his cathedrals, his Rhine, and whatever his companions suggested. Faithful to his self-contracted scheme of passing two winters in study of the Civil Law, he went back to Dresden with a letter to the Frau Hofräthin von Reichenbach,[17] in whose house Lowell and other Americans had pursued studies more or less serious. In those days, "The Initials"[18] was a new book. The charm which its clever author had laboriously woven over Munich gave also a certain reflected light to Dresden. Young Adams had nothing to do but take fencing-lessons, visit the galleries and go to the theatre; but his social failure in the line of "The Initials," was humiliating and he succumbed to it. The Frau Hofräthin herself was sometimes roused to huge laughter at the total discomfiture and helplessness of the young American in the face of her society. Possibly an education may be the wider and the richer for a large experience of the world; Raphael Pumpelly[19] and Clarence King, at about the same time, were enriching their education by a picturesque intimacy with the manners of the Apaches and Digger Indians. All experience is an arch, to build upon.[20] Yet Adams admitted himself unable to guess what use his second winter in Germany was to him, or what he expected it to be. Even the doctrine of accidental education broke down. There were no accidents in Dresden. As soon as the winter was over, he closed and locked the German door with a long breath of relief, and took the road to Italy. He had then pursued his education, as it pleased him, for eighteen months, and in spite of the infinite variety of new impressions which had packed themselves into his mind, he knew no more, for his practical purposes, than the day he graduated. He had made no step towards a profession. He was as ignorant as a schoolboy of society. He was unfit for any career in Europe, and unfitted for any career in America, and he had not natural intelligence enough to see what a mess he had thus far made of his education.

By twisting life to follow accidental and devious paths, one might perhaps find some use for accidental and devious knowledge, but this had been no part of Henry Adams's plan when he chose the path most admired by the best judges, and followed it till he found it led nowhere. Nothing had been further from his mind when he started in November, 1858, than to become a tourist, but a mere tourist, and nothing else, he had become in April, 1860, when he joined his sister in Florence. His father had been in the right. The young man felt a little sore about it. Supposing his father asked him, on his return, what equivalent he had brought back for the time and money put into his experiment! The only possible answer would be: "Sir, I am a tourist!"

The answer was not what he had meant it to be, and he was not likely to better it by asking his father, in turn, what equivalent his brothers or cousins or friends at home had got out of the same time and money spent in Boston. All they had put into the law was certainly thrown away, but were they happier in science? In theory one might say, with some show of proof, that a pure, scientific education was alone correct; yet many of his friends who took it, found reason to complain that it was anything but a pure, scientific world in which they lived.

Meanwhile his father had quite enough perplexities of his own, without seeking more in his son's errors. His Quincy district had

sent him to Congress,[21] and in the spring of 1860 he was in the full
confusion of nominating candidates for the Presidential election
in November. He supported Mr. Seward. The Republican Party
was an unknown force, and the Democratic Party was torn to
pieces. No one could see far into the future. Fathers could
blunder as well as sons, and, in 1860, every one was conscious
of being dragged along paths much less secure than those of the
European tourist. For the time, the young man was safe from
interference, and went on his way with a light heart to take whatever chance fragments of education God or the devil was pleased
to give him, for he knew no longer the good from the bad.

He had of both sorts more than he knew how to use. Perhaps
the most useful purpose he set himself to serve was that of his
pen, for he wrote long letters, during the next three months, to
his brother Charles, which his brother caused to be printed in the
Boston Courier;[22] and the exercise was good for him. He had little
to say, and said it not very well, but that mattered less. The habit
of expression leads to the search for something to express. Something remains as a residuum of the commonplace itself, if one
strikes out every commonplace in the expression. Young men
as a rule saw little in Italy, or anywhere else, and in after life,
when Adams began to learn what some men could see, he shrank
into corners of shame at the thought that he should have betrayed his own inferiority as though it were his pride, which he
invited his neighbors to measure and admire; but it was still the
nearest approach he had yet made to an intelligent act.

For the rest, Italy was mostly an emotion and the emotion naturally centred in Rome. The American parent, curiously enough,
while bitterly hostile to Paris, seemed rather disposed to accept
Rome as legitimate education, though abused; but to young men
seeking education in a serious spirit, taking for granted that
everything had a cause, and that nature tended to an end, Rome
was altogether the most violent vice in the world, and Rome before 1870 was seductive beyond resistance. The month of May,

1860, was divine. No doubt other young men, and occasionally young women, have passed the month of May in Rome since then, and conceive that the charm continues to exist. Possibly it does — in them — but in 1860 the lights and shadows were still mediæval, and mediæval Rome was alive; the shadows breathed and glowed, full of soft forms felt by lost senses. No sand-blast of science had yet skinned off the epidermis of history, thought, and feeling. The pictures were uncleaned, the churches unrestored, the ruins unexcavated. Mediæval Rome was sorcery. Rome was the worst spot on earth to teach nineteenth-century youth what to do with a twentieth-century world. One's emotions in Rome were one's private affair, like one's glass of absinthe before dinner in the Palais Royal;[23] they must be hurtful, else they could not have been so intense; and they were surely immoral, for no one, priest or politician, could honestly read in the ruins of Rome any other certain lesson than that they were evidence of the just judgments of an outraged God against all the doings of man. This moral unfitted young men for every sort of useful activity; it made Rome a gospel of anarchy and vice; the last place under the sun for educating the young; yet it was, by common consent, the only spot that the young — of either sex and every race — passionately, perversely, wickedly loved.

Boys never see a conclusion; only on the edge of the grave can man conclude anything; but the first impulse given to the boy is apt to lead or drive him for the rest of his life into conclusion after conclusion that he never dreamed of reaching. One looked idly enough at the Forum or at St. Peter's, but one never forgot the look, and it never ceased reacting. To a young Bostonian, fresh from Germany, Rome seemed a pure emotion, quite free from economic or actual values, and he could not in reason or common sense foresee that it was mechanically piling up conundrum after conundrum in his educational path, which seemed unconnected but that he had got to connect; that seemed insoluble but had got to be somehow solved. Rome was not a beetle to be dissected and dropped; not a bad French novel to be read in a railway train and thrown out of the window after other bad French novels, the morals of which could never approach the immorality of Roman history. Rome was actual; it was England; it was going to be America. Rome could not be fitted into an orderly, middle-class, Bostonian, systematic scheme of evolution. No law of progress applied to it. Not even time-sequences — the last refuge of helpless historians — had value for it. The Forum no more led to the Vatican than the Vatican to the Forum.[24] Rienzi, Garibaldi, Tiberius Gracchus, Aurelian might be mixed up in any relation of time, along with a thousand more, and never lead to a sequence.[25] The great word Evolution had not yet, in 1860, made a new religion of history, but the old religion had preached the same doctrine for a thousand years without finding in the entire history of Rome anything but flat contradiction.[26]

Of course both priests and evolutionists bitterly denied this heresy, but what they affirmed or denied in 1860 had very little importance indeed for 1960. Anarchy lost no ground meanwhile. The problem became only the more fascinating. Probably it was more vital in May, 1860, than it had been in October, 1764, when the idea of writing the Decline and Fall of the city first started to the mind of Gibbon,[27] "in the close of the evening, as I sat musing in the Church of the Zoccolanti or Franciscan Friars, while they were singing Vespers in the Temple of Jupiter, on the ruins of the Capitol." Murray's Handbook had the grace to quote this passage from Gibbon's "Autobiography," which led Adams more than once to sit at sunset on the steps of the Church of Santa Maria di Ara Cœli,[28] curiously wondering that not an inch had been gained by Gibbon — or all the historians since — towards explaining the Fall. The mystery remained unsolved; the charm remained intact. Two great experiments[29] of Western civilization had left there the chief monuments of their failure, and nothing proved that the city might not still survive to express the failure of a third.

The young man had no idea what he was doing. The thought of posing for a Gibbon never entered his mind. He was a tourist, even to the depths of his sub-consciousness, and it was well for him that he should be nothing else, for even the greatest of men cannot sit with dignity, "in the close of evening, among the ruins of the Capitol," unless they have something quite original to say about it. Tacitus[30] could do it; so could Michael Angelo; and so, at a pinch, could Gibbon, though in figure hardly heroic; but, in sum, none of them could say very much more than the tourist, who went on repeating to himself the eternal question: — Why! Why!! Why!!! — as his neighbor, the blind beggar, might do, sitting next him, on the church steps. No one ever had answered the question to the satisfaction of anyone else; yet everyone who had either head or heart, felt that sooner or later he must make up his mind what answer to accept. Substitute the word America for the word Rome, and the question became personal.

Perhaps Henry learned something in Rome, though he never knew it, and never sought it. Rome dwarfs teachers. The greatest men of the age scarcely bore the test of posing with Rome for a background. Perhaps Garibaldi — possibly even Cavour [31] — could have sat "in the close of the evening, among the ruins of the Capitol," but one hardly saw Napoleon III there, or Palmerston[32] or Tennyson or Longfellow. One morning, Adams happened to be chatting in the studio of Hamilton Wilde,[33] when a middle-aged Englishman came in, evidently excited, and told of the shock he had just received, when riding near the Circus Maximus, at coming unexpectedly on the guillotine, where some criminal had been put to death an hour or two before. The sudden surprise had quite overcome him; and Adams, who seldom saw the point of a story till time had blunted it, listened sympathetically to learn what new form of grim horror had for the moment wiped out the memory of two thousand years of Roman bloodshed, or the consolation, derived from history and statistics, that most citizens of Rome seemed to be the better for guillotining. Only by slow degrees, he grappled the conviction that the victim of the shock was Robert Browning[34]; and, on the background of the Circus Maximus, the Christian martyrs flaming as torches, and the morning's murderer on the block, Browning seemed rather in place, as a middle-aged gentlemanly English Pippa Passes; while afterwards, in the light of Belgravia dinner-tables, he never made part of his background except by effacement. Browning might have sat with Gibbon, among the ruins, and few Romans would have smiled.

Yet Browning never revealed the poetic depths of Saint Francis[35]; William Story could not touch[36] the secret of Michael Angelo; and Mommsen[37] hardly said all that one felt by instinct in the lives of Cicero and Cæsar. They taught what, as a rule, needed no teaching, the lessons of a rather cheap imagination and cheaper politics. Rome was a bewildering complex of ideas, experiments, ambitions, energies; without her, the Western world was pointless and fragmentary; she gave heart and unity to it all; yet Gibbon might have gone on for the whole century, sitting among the ruins of the Capitol, and no one would have passed, capable of telling him what it meant. Perhaps it meant nothing.

So it ended; the happiest month of May that life had yet offered, fading behind the present, and probably beyond the past, somewhere into abstract time, grotesquely out of place with the Berlin scheme or a Boston future. Adams explained to himself that he was absorbing knowledge. He would have put it better had he said that knowledge was absorbing him. He was passive. In spite of swarming impressions he knew no more when he left Rome than he did when he entered it. As a marketable object, his value was less. His next step went far to convince him that accidental education, whatever its economical return might be, was prodigiously successful as an object in itself. Everything conspired to ruin his sound scheme of life, and to make him a vagrant as well as pauper. He went on to Naples, and there, in the hot June, heard rumors that Garibaldi and his thousand were about to attack Palermo.[38] Calling on the American Minister, Chandler[39] of Pennsylvania, he was kindly treated, not for his merit, but for his name, and Mr. Chandler amiably consented to send him to the seat of war as bearer of despatches to Captain Palmer[40] of the American sloop of war Iroquois. Young Adams seized the chance, and went to Palermo in a government transport filled with fleas, commanded by a charming Prince Caracciolo.[41]

He told all about it to the *Boston Courier*,[42] where the narrative probably exists to this day, unless the files of the *Courier* have wholly perished; but of its bearing on education the *Courier* did not speak. He himself would have much liked to know whether it had any bearing whatever, and what was its value as a postgraduate course. Quite apart from its value as life attained, realized, capitalized, it had also a certain value as a lesson in something, though Adams could never classify the branch of study. Loosely, the tourist called it knowledge of men, but it was just the reverse; it was knowledge of one's ignorance of men. Captain Palmer of the Iroquois, who was a friend of the young man's uncle, Sydney Brooks, took him with the officers of the ship to make an evening call on Garibaldi, whom they found in the Senate House towards sunset, at supper with his picturesque and piratic staff, in the full noise and color of the Palermo revolution. As a spectacle, it belonged to Rossini and the Italian opera, or to Alexandre Dumas[43] at the least, but the spectacle was not its educational side. Garibaldi left the table, and, sitting down at the window, had a few words of talk with Captain Palmer and young Adams. At that moment, in the summer of 1860, Garibaldi was certainly the most serious of the doubtful energies in the world; the most essential to gauge rightly. Even then society was dividing between banker and anarchist. One or the other, Garibaldi must serve. Himself a typical anarchist, sure to overshadow Europe and alarm empires bigger than Naples, his success depended on his mind; his energy was beyond doubt.

Adams had the chance to look this sphinx in the eyes, and,

for five minutes, to watch him like a wild animal, at the moment of his greatest achievement and most splendid action. One saw a quiet-featured, quiet-voiced man in a red flannel shirt; absolutely impervious; a type of which Adams knew nothing. Sympathetic it was, and one felt that it was simple; one suspected even that it might be childlike, but could form no guess of its intelligence. In his own eyes Garibaldi might be a Napoleon or a Spartacus[44]; in the hands of Cavour he might become a Condottiere[45]; in the eyes of history he might, like the rest of the world, be only the vigorous player in the game he did not understand. The student was none the wiser.

This compound nature of patriot and pirate had illumined Italian history from the beginning, and was no more intelligible to itself than to a young American who had no experience in double natures. In the end, if the "Autobiography" tells truth, Garibaldi saw and said that he had not understood his own acts; that he had been an instrument; that he had served the purposes of the class he least wanted to help; yet in 1860 he thought himself the revolution anarchic, Napoleonic, and his ambition was unbounded. What should a young Bostonian have made of a character like this, internally alive with childlike fancies, and externally quiet, simple, almost innocent; uttering with apparent conviction the usual commonplaces of popular politics that all politicians use as the small change of their intercourse with the public; but never betraying a thought?

Precisely this class of mind was to be the toughest problem of Adams's practical life, but he could never make anything of it. The lesson of Garibaldi, as education, seemed to teach the extreme complexity of extreme simplicity; but one could have learned this from a glow-worm. One did not need the vivid recollection of the low-voiced, simple-mannered, seafaring captain of Genoese adventurers and Sicilian brigands, supping in the July heat[46] and Sicilian dirt and revolutionary clamor, among the barricaded streets of insurgent Palermo, merely in order to remember that simplicity is complex.

Adams left the problem as he found it, and came north to stumble over others, less picturesque but nearer. He squandered two or three months on Paris. From the first he had avoided Paris, and had wanted no French influence in his education. He disapproved of France in the lump. A certain knowledge of the language one must have; enough to order dinner and buy a theatre ticket; but more he did not seek.[47] He disliked the Empire and the Emperor particularly, but this was a trifle; he disliked most the French mind. To save himself the trouble of drawing up a long list of all that he disliked, he disapproved of the whole, once for all, and shut them figuratively out of his life. France was not serious, and he was not serious in going there.

He did this in good faith, obeying the lessons his teachers had taught him; but the curious result followed that, being in no way responsible for the French and sincerely disapproving them, he felt quite at liberty to enjoy to the full everything he disapproved. Stated thus crudely, the idea sounds derisive; but, as a matter of fact, several thousand Americans passed much of their time there on this understanding. They sought to take share in every function that was open to approach, as they sought tickets to the opera, because they were not a part of it. Adams did like the rest. All thought of serious education had long vanished. He tried to acquire a few French idioms, without even aspiring to master a subjunctive, but he succeeded better in acquiring a modest taste for Bordeaux and Burgundy and one or two sauces; for the Trois Frères Provençaux and Voisin's and Philippe's and the Café Anglais; for the Palais Royal Theatre, and the Variétés and the Gymnase; for the Brohans and Bressant, Rose Chéri and Gil Perez, and other lights of the stage.[48] His friends were good to him. Life was amusing. Paris rapidly became familiar. In a month or six weeks he forgot even to disapprove of it; but he studied nothing, entered no society, and made no acquaintance. Accidental education went far in Paris, and one picked up a deal of knowledge that might become useful; perhaps, after all, the three months passed there might serve better purpose than the twenty-one months passed elsewhere; but he did not intend it — did not think it — and looked at it as a momentary and frivolous vacation before going home to fit himself for life. Therewith, after staying as long as he could and spending all the money he dared, he started with mixed emotions but no education, for home.

CHAPTER VII

Treason (1860–1861)

W HEN, forty years afterwards, Henry Adams looked back over his adventures in search of knowledge, he asked himself whether fortune or fate had ever dealt its cards quite so wildly to any of his known antecessors as when it led him to begin the study of law and to vote for Abraham Lincoln on the same day.

He dropped back on Quincy like a lump of lead; he rebounded like a football, tossed into space by an unknown energy which played with all his generation as a cat plays with mice. The simile is none too strong. Not one man in America wanted the Civil War, or expected or intended it. A small minority wanted secession. The vast majority wanted to go on with their occupations in peace. Not one, however clever or learned, guessed what happened. Possibly a few Southern loyalists in despair might dream it as an impossible chance; but none planned it.

As for Henry Adams, fresh from Europe and chaos of another sort, he plunged at once into a lurid atmosphere of politics, quite heedless of any education or forethought. His past melted away. The prodigal was welcomed home, but not even his father asked a malicious question about the Pandects.[1] At the utmost, he hinted at some shade of prodigality by quietly inviting his son to act as private secretary during the winter in Washington, as though any young man who could afford to throw away two winters on the Civil Law could afford to read Blackstone[2] for another winter without a master. The young man was beyond satire, and asked only a pretext for throwing all education to the east wind. November at best is sad, and November at Quincy had been from earliest childhood the least gay of seasons. Nowhere else does the uncharitable autumn wreak its spite so harshly on the frail

98

wreck of the grasshopper summer; yet even a Quincy November seemed temperate before the chill of a Boston January.

This was saying much, for the November of 1860 at Quincy stood apart from other memories as lurid beyond description. Although no one believed in civil war, the air reeked of it, and the Republicans organized their clubs and parades as Wide-Awakes[3] in a form military in all things except weapons. Henry reached home in time to see the last of these processions, stretching in ranks of torches along the hillside, file down through the November night to the Old House,[4] where Mr. Adams, their Member of Congress, received them, and, let them pretend what they liked, their air was not that of innocence.

Profoundly ignorant, anxious, and curious, the young man packed his modest trunk again, which had not yet time to be unpacked, and started for Washington with his family. Ten years had passed since his last visit, but very little had changed. As in 1800 and 1850, so in 1860, the same rude colony was camped in the same forest, with the same unfinished Greek temples for workrooms, and sloughs for roads. The Government had an air of social instability and incompleteness that went far to support the right of secession in theory as in fact; but right or wrong, secession was likely to be easy where there was so little to secede from. The Union was a sentiment, but not much more, and in December, 1860, the sentiment about the Capitol was chiefly hostile, so far as it made itself felt. John Adams was better off in Philadelphia in 1776[5] than his great-grandson Henry in 1860 in Washington.

Patriotism ended by throwing a halo over the Continental Congress, but over the close of the Thirty-sixth Congress in 1860–61, no halo could be thrown by any one who saw it. Of all the crowd swarming in Washington that winter, young Adams was surely among the most ignorant and helpless, but he saw plainly that the knowledge possessed by everybody about him was hardly greater than his own. Never in a long life did he seek to master a lesson so obscure. Mr. Sumner was given to saying after Oxenstiern:

"Quantula sapientia mundus regitur!"[6] Oxenstiern talked of a world that wanted wisdom; but Adams found himself seeking education in a world that seemed to him both unwise and ignorant. The Southern secessionists were certainly unbalanced in mind — fit for medical treatment, like other victims of hallucination — haunted by suspicion, by *idées fixes,*[7] by violent morbid excitement; but this was not all. They were stupendously ignorant of the world. As a class, the cotton-planters were mentally one-sided, ill-balanced, and provincial to a degree rarely known. They were a close society on whom the new fountains of power had poured a stream of wealth and slaves that acted like oil on flame. They showed a young student his first object-lesson of the way in which excess of power worked when held by inadequate hands.

This might be a commonplace of 1900, but in 1860 it was paradox. The Southern statesmen were regarded as standards of statesmanship, and such standards barred education. Charles Sumner's chief offence was his insistence on Southern ignorance, and he stood a living proof of it.[8] To this school, Henry Adams had come for a new education, and the school was seriously, honestly, taken by most of the world, including Europe, as proper for the purpose, although the Sioux Indians would have taught less mischief. From such contradictions among intelligent people, what was a young man to learn?

He could learn nothing but cross-purpose. The old and typical Southern gentleman developed as cotton-planter had nothing to teach or to give, except warning. Even as example to be avoided, he was too glaring in his defiance of reason, to help the education of a reasonable being. No one learned a useful lesson from the Confederate school except to keep away from it. Thus, at one sweep, the whole field of instruction south of the Potomac was shut off; it was overshadowed by the cotton planters, from whom one could learn nothing but bad temper, bad manners, poker, and treason.

Perforce, the student was thrown back on Northern precept and example; first of all, on his New England surroundings. Republican houses were few in Washington, and Mr. and Mrs. Adams aimed to create a social centre for New Englanders. They took a house on I Street, looking over Pennsylvania Avenue, well out towards Georgetown — the Markoe house — and there the private secretary began to learn his social duties, for the political were confined to committee-rooms and lobbies of the Capitol. He had little to do, and knew not how to do it rightly, but he knew of no one who knew more.

The Southern type was one to be avoided; the New England type was oneself. It had nothing to show except one's own features. Setting aside Charles Sumner, who stood quite alone and was the boy's oldest friend, all the New Englanders were sane and steady men, well-balanced, educated, and free from meanness or intrigue — men whom one liked to act with, and who, whether graduates or not, bore the stamp of Harvard College. Anson Burlingame was one exception, and perhaps Israel Washburn another;[9] but as a rule the New Englander's strength was his poise which almost amounted to a defect. He offered no more target for love than for hate; he attracted as little as he repelled; even as a machine, his motion seemed never accelerated. The character, with its force or feebleness, was familiar: one knew it to the core; one was it — had been run in the same mould.

There remained the Central and Western States, but there the choice of teachers was not large and in the end narrowed itself to Preston King, Henry Winter Davis, Owen Lovejoy, and a few other men born with social faculty.[10] Adams took most kindly to Henry J. Raymond, who came to view the field for the *New York Times*, and who was a man of the world. The average Congressman was civil enough, but had nothing to ask except offices, and nothing to offer but the views of his district. The average Senator was more reserved, but had not much more to say, being always, excepting one or two genial natures, handicapped by his own importance.

Study it as one might, the hope of education, till the arrival of the President-elect, narrowed itself to the possible influence of only two men — Sumner and Seward.

Sumner was then fifty years old. Since his election as Senator in 1851 he had passed beyond the reach of his boy friend, and, after his Brooks injuries, his nervous system never quite recovered its tone; but perhaps eight or ten years of solitary existence as Senator had most to do with his development. No man, however strong, can serve ten years as schoolmaster, priest, or Senator, and remain fit for anything else. All the dogmatic stations in life have the effect of fixing a certain stiffness of attitude forever, as though they mesmerized the subject. Yet even among Senators there were degrees in dogmatism, from the frank South Carolinian brutality, to that of Webster, Benton, Clay, or Sumner himself, until in extreme cases, like Conkling, it became Shakespearian and *bouffe* — as Godkin used to call it — like Malvolio. Sumner had become dogmatic like the rest, but he had at least the merit of qualities that warranted dogmatism. He justly thought, as Webster had thought before him, that his great services and sacrifices, his superiority in education, his oratorical power, his political experience, his representative character at the head of the whole New England contingent, and, above all, his knowledge of the world, made him the most important member of the Senate; and no Senator had ever saturated himself more thoroughly with the spirit and temper of the body.

Although the Senate is much given to admiring in its members a superiority less obvious or quite invisible to outsiders, one Senator seldom proclaims his own inferiority to another, and still more seldom likes to be told of it. Even the greatest Senators seemed to inspire little personal affection in each other, and betrayed none at all. Sumner had a number of rivals who held his judgment in no high esteem, and one of these was Senator Seward. The two men would have disliked each other by instinct had they lived in different planets. Each was created only for exasperating the other; the virtues of one were the faults of his rival, until no good quality seemed to remain of either. That the public service must suffer was certain, but what were the sufferings of the public service compared with the risks run by a young mosquito — a private secretary — trying to buzz admiration in the ears of each, and unaware that each would impatiently slap at him for belonging to the other? Innocent and unsuspicious beyond what was permitted even in a nursery, the private secretary courted both.

Private secretaries are servants of a rather low order, whose business is to serve sources of power. The first news of a professional kind, imparted to private secretary Adams on reaching Washington, was that the President-elect, Abraham Lincoln, had selected Mr. Seward for his Secretary of State, and that Seward was to be the medium for communicating his wishes to his followers. Every young man naturally accepted the wishes of Mr. Lincoln as orders, the more because he could see that the new President was likely to need all the help that several million young men would be able to give, if they counted on having any President at all to serve. Naturally one waited impatiently for the first meeting with the new Secretary of State.

Governor Seward was an old friend of the family. He professed to be a disciple and follower of John Quincy Adams. He had been Senator since 1849, when his responsibilities as leader had separated him from the Free Soil contingent, for, in the dry light of the first Free Soil faith, the ways of New York politics and of Thurlow Weed had not won favor; but the fierce heat which welded the Republican Party in 1856 melted many such barriers,[12] and when Mr. Adams came to Congress in December, 1859, Governor Seward instantly renewed his attitude of family friend, became a daily intimate in the household, and lost no chance of forcing his fresh ally to the front.

A few days after their arrival in December, 1860, the Governor, as he was always called, came to dinner, alone, as one of the family, and the private secretary had the chance he wanted to watch him as carefully as one generally watches men who dispose of one's future. A slouching, slender figure; a head like a wise macaw; a beaked nose; shaggy eyebrows; unorderly hair and clothes; hoarse voice; offhand manner; free talk, and perpetual cigar, offered a new type — of western New York — to fathom; a type in one way simple because it was only double — political and personal; but complex because the political had become na- ture, and no one could tell which was the mask and which the features. At table, among friends, Mr. Seward threw off restraint, or seemed to throw it off, in reality, while in the world he threw it off, like a politician, for effect. In both cases he chose to appear as a free talker, who loathed pomposity and enjoyed a joke; but how much was nature and how much was mask, he was himself too simple a nature to know. Underneath the surface he was conventional after the conventions of western New York and Albany. Politicians thought it unconventionality. Bostonians thought it provincial. Henry Adams thought it charming. From the first sight, he loved the Governor, who, though sixty years old, had the youth of his sympathies. He noticed that Mr. Seward was never petty or personal; his talk was large; he generalized; he never seemed to pose for statesmanship; he did not require an attitude of prayer. What was more unusual — almost sin- gular and quite eccentric — he had some means, unknown to other Senators, of producing the effect of unselfishness.

Superficially Mr. Seward and Mr. Adams were contrasts; es- sentially they were much alike. Mr. Adams was taken to be rigid, but the Puritan character in all its forms could be supple enough when it chose; and in Massachusetts all the Adamses had been attacked in succession as no better than political mercenaries. Mr. Hildreth,[13] in his standard history, went so far as to echo with approval the charge that treachery was hereditary in the family. Any Adams had at least to be thick-skinned, hardened to every contradictory epithet that virtue could supply, and, on the whole,

armed to return such attentions; but all must have admitted that
they had invariably subordinated local to national interests, and
would continue to do so, whenever forced to choose. C. F. Adams
was sure to do what his father had done, as his father had followed
the steps of John Adams, and no doubt thereby earned his epithets.

The inevitable followed, as a child fresh from the nursery
should have had the instinct to foresee, but the young man on
the edge of life never dreamed. What motives or emotions drove
his masters on their various paths he made no pretence of guessing; even at that age he preferred to admit his dislike for guessing motives; he knew only his own infantile ignorance, before
which he stood amazed, and his innocent good-faith, always
matter of simple-minded surprise. Critics who know ultimate
truth will pronounce judgment on history; all that Henry Adams
ever saw in man was a reflection of his own ignorance, and he never
saw quite so much of it as in the winter of 1860–61. Everyone
knows the story; everyone draws what conclusion suits his temper, and the conclusion matters now less than though it concerned
the merits of Adam and Eve in the Garden of Eden; but in 1861
the conclusion made the sharpest lesson of life; it was condensed
and concentrated education.[14]

Rightly or wrongly the new President and his chief advisers
in Washington decided that, before they could administer the
Government, they must make sure of a government to administer, and that this chance depended on the action of Virginia.
The whole ascendancy of the winter wavered between the effort
of the cotton States to drag Virginia out, and the effort of the
new President to keep Virginia in. Governor Seward representing the Administration in the Senate took the lead; Mr. Adams
took the lead in the House; and as far as a private secretary knew,
the party united on its tactics. In offering concessions to the
border States, they had to run the risk, or incur the certainty,
of dividing their own party, and they took this risk with open

eyes. As Seward himself, in his gruff way, said at dinner, after Mr. Adams and he had made their speeches: "If there's no secession now, you and I are ruined."

They won their game; this was their affair and the affair of the historians who tell their story; their private secretaries had nothing to do with it except to follow their orders. On that side a secretary learned nothing and had nothing to learn. The sudden arrival of Mr. Lincoln in Washington on February 23,[15] and the language of his inaugural address,[16] were the final term of the winter's tactics, and closed the private secretary's interest in the matter forever. Perhaps he felt, even then, a good deal more interest in the appearance of another private secretary, of his own age, a young man named John Hay,[17] who lighted on La Fayette Square at the same moment. Friends are born, not made, and Henry never mistook a friend except when in power. From the first slight meeting in February and March, 1861, he recognized Hay as a friend, and never lost sight of him at the future crossing of their paths; but, for the moment, his own task ended on March 4 when Hay's began. The winter's anxieties were shifted upon new shoulders, and Henry gladly turned back to Blackstone. He had tried to make himself useful, and had exerted energy that seemed to him portentous, acting in secret as newspaper correspondent, cultivating a large acquaintance and even haunting ballrooms where the simple, old-fashioned, Southern tone was pleasant even in the atmosphere of conspiracy and treason. The sum was next to nothing for education, because no one could teach; all were as ignorant as himself; none knew what should be done, or how to do it; all were trying to learn and were more bent on asking than on answering questions. The mass of ignorance in Washington was lighted up by no ray of knowledge. Society, from top to bottom, broke down.

From this law there was no exception, unless, perhaps, that of old General Winfield Scott,[18] who happened to be the only military figure that looked equal to the crisis. No one else either looked it, or was it, or could be it, by nature or training. Had young Adams been told that his life was to hang on the correctness of his estimate of the new President, he would have lost. He saw Mr. Lincoln but once; at the melancholy function called an Inaugural Ball. Of course he looked anxiously for a sign of character. He saw a long, awkward figure; a plain, ploughed face; a mind, absent in part, and in part evidently worried by white kid gloves; features that expressed neither self-satisfaction nor any other familiar Americanism, but rather the same painful sense of becoming educated and of needing education that tormented a private secretary; above all a lack of apparent force. Any private secretary in the least fit for his business would have thought, as Adams did, that no man living needed so much education as the new President but that all the education he could get would not be enough.

As far as a young man of anxious temperament could see, no one in Washington was fitted for his duties; or rather, no duties in March were fitted for the duties in April. The few people who thought they knew something were more in error than those who knew nothing. Education was matter of life and death, but all the education in the world would have helped nothing. Only one man in Adams's reach seemed to him supremely fitted by knowledge and experience to be an adviser and friend. This was Senator Sumner; and there, in fact, the young man's education began; there it ended.

Going over the experience again, long after all the great actors were dead, he struggled to see where he had blundered. In the effort to make acquaintances, he lost friends, but he would have liked much to know whether he could have helped it. He had necessarily followed Seward and his father; he took for granted that his business was obedience, discipline, and silence; he supposed the party to require it, and that the crisis overruled all personal doubts. He was thunderstruck to learn that Senator Sumner privately denounced the course, regarded Mr. Adams as betraying the principles of his life, and broke off relations with his family.[19]

Many a shock was Henry Adams to meet in the course of a long life passed chiefly near politics and politicians, but the profoundest lessons are not the lessons of reason; they are sudden strains that permanently warp the mind. He cared little or nothing about the point in discussion; he was even willing to admit that Sumner might be right, though in all great emergencies he commonly found that every one was more or less wrong; he liked lofty moral principle and cared little for political tactics; he felt a profound respect for Sumner himself; but the shock opened a chasm in life that never closed, and as long as life lasted, he found himself invariably taking for granted, as a political instinct, without waiting further experiment — as he took for granted that arsenic poisoned — the rule that a friend in power is a friend lost.

On his own score, he never admitted the rupture, and never exchanged a word with Mr. Sumner on the subject, then or afterwards, but his education — for good or bad — made an enormous stride. One has to deal with all sorts of unexpected morals in life, and, at this moment, he was looking at hundreds of Southern gentlemen who believed themselves singularly honest, but who seemed to him engaged in the plainest breach of faith and the blackest secret conspiracy, yet they did not disturb his education. History told of little else; and not one rebel defection — not even Robert E. Lee's — cost young Adams a personal pang; but Sumner's struck home.

This, then, was the result of the new attempt at education, down to March 4, 1861; this was all; and frankly, it seemed to him hardly what he wanted. The picture of Washington in March, 1861, offered education, but not the kind of education that led to good. The process that Matthew Arnold described as wandering between two worlds, one dead, the other powerless to be born, helps nothing.[20] Washington was a dismal school. Even before the traitors had flown, the vultures descended on it in swarms that darkened the ground, and tore the carrion of political patronage into fragments and gobbets of fat and lean, on the very steps of the White House. Not a man there knew what his task was to be, or was fitted for it; everyone without exception, Northern or Southern, was to learn his business at the cost of the public. Lincoln, Seward, Sumner, and the rest, could give no help to the young man seeking education; they knew less than he; within six weeks they were all to be taught their duties by the uprising of such as he, and their education was to cost a million lives and ten thousand million dollars, more or less, North and South, before the country could recover its balance and movement.[21] Henry was a helpless victim, and, like all the rest, he could only wait for he knew not what, to send him he knew not where.

With the close of the session, his own functions ended. Ceasing to be private secretary he knew not what else to do but return with his father and mother to Boston in the middle of March, and, with childlike docility, sit down at a desk in the law-office of Horace Gray[22] in Court Street, to begin again: "My Lords and Gentlemen";[23] dozing after a two o'clock dinner, or waking to discuss politics with the future Justice. There, in ordinary times, he would have remained for life, his attempt at education in treason having, like all the rest, disastrously failed.

CHAPTER VIII

Diplomacy (1861)

H ARDLY a week passed when the newspapers announced
that President Lincoln had selected Charles Francis
Adams as his Minister to England.¹ Once more, silently,
Henry put Blackstone back on its shelf. As Friar Bacon's head
sententiously announced many centuries before: Time had passed!²
The Civil Law lasted a brief day; the Common Law prolonged its
shadowy existence for a week. The law, altogether, as path of
education, vanished in April, 1861, leaving a million young men
planted in the mud of a lawless world, to begin a new life without education at all. They asked few questions, but if they had
asked millions they would have got no answers. No one could help.
Looking back on this moment of crisis, nearly fifty years afterwards, one could only shake one's white beard in silent horror. Mr.
Adams once more intimated that he thought himself entitled to
the services of one of his sons, and he indicated Henry as the only
one who could be spared from more serious duties. Henry packed
his trunk again without a word. He could offer no protest. Ridiculous as he knew himself about to be in his new rôle, he was less
ridiculous than his betters. He was at least no public official, like
the thousands of improvised secretaries and generals who crowded
their jealousies and intrigues on the President. He was not a vul-
ture of carrion-patronage. He knew that his father's appointment was the result of Governor Seward's personal friendship;
he did not then know that Senator Sumner had opposed it, or the
reasons which Sumner alleged for thinking it unfit; but he could
have supplied proofs enough had Sumner asked for them, the
strongest and most decisive being that, in his opinion, Mr. Adams
had chosen a private secretary far more unfit than his chief. That
Mr. Adams was unfit might well be, since it was hard to find a fit

appointment in the list of possible candidates, except Mr. Sumner himself; and no one knew so well as this experienced Senator that the weakest of all Mr. Adams's proofs of fitness was his consent to quit a safe seat in Congress for an exceedingly unsafe seat in London with no better support than Senator Sumner, at the head of the Foreign Relations Committee, was likely to give him. In the family history, its members had taken many a dangerous risk, but never before had they taken one so desperate.

The private secretary troubled himself not at all about the unfitness of anyone; he knew too little; and, in fact, no one, except perhaps Mr. Sumner, knew more. The President and Secretary of State[3] knew least of all. As Secretary of Legation the Executive appointed the editor of a Chicago newspaper who had applied for the Chicago Post Office; a good fellow, universally known as Charley Wilson,[4] who had not a thought of staying in the post, or of helping the Minister. The Assistant Secretary[5] was inherited from Buchanan's time, a hard worker, but socially useless. Mr. Adams made no effort to find efficient help; perhaps he knew no name to suggest; perhaps he knew too much of Washington; but he could hardly have hoped to find a staff of strength in his son.

The private secretary was more passive than his father, for he knew not where to turn. Sumner alone could have smoothed his path by giving him letters of introduction, but if Sumner wrote letters, it was not with the effect of smoothing paths. No one, at that moment, was engaged in smoothing either paths or people. The private secretary was no worse off than his neighbors except in being called earlier into service. On April 13[6] the storm burst and rolled several hundred thousand young men like Henry Adams into the surf of a wild ocean, all helpless like himself, to be beaten about for four years by the waves of war. Adams still had time to watch the regiments form ranks before Boston State House in the April evenings and march southward, quietly enough, with the air of business they wore from their cradles, but with few signs or sounds of excitement. He had time also to go down the harbor to see his brother Charles quartered in Fort Independence before being thrown, with a hundred thousand more, into the furnace of the Army of the Potomac to get educated in a fury of fire. Few things were for the moment so trivial in importance as the solitary private secretary crawling down to the wretched old Cunard steamer Niagara at East Boston to start again for Liverpool. This time the pitcher of education had gone to the fountain once too often; it was fairly broken; and the young man had got to meet a hostile world without defence — or arms.

The situation did not seem even comic, so ignorant was the world of its humors; yet Minister Adams sailed for England, May 1, 1861, with much the same outfit as Admiral Dupont[7] would have enjoyed if the Government had sent him to attack Port Royal with one cabin-boy in a rowboat. Luckily for the cabin-boy, he was alone. Had Secretary Seward and Senator Sumner given to Mr. Adams the rank of Ambassador and four times his salary, a palace in London, a staff of trained secretaries, and personal letters of introduction to the royal family and the whole peerage, the private secretary would have been cabin-boy still, with the extra burden of many masters; he was the most fortunate person in the party, having for master only his father who never fretted, never dictated, never disciplined, and whose idea of American diplomacy was that of the eighteenth century. Minister Adams remembered how his grandfather had sailed from Mount Wollaston in midwinter, 1778, on the little frigate Boston, taking his eleven-year-old son John Quincy with him, for secretary, on a diplomacy of adventure that had hardly a parallel for success[8]. He remembered how John Quincy, in 1809, had sailed for Russia, with himself, a baby of two years old, to cope with Napoleon and the Czar Alexander single-handed, almost as much of an adventurer as John Adams before him, and almost as successful. He thought it natural that the Government should send him out as an adventurer also, with a twenty-three-year-old son, and he did not even notice that he left not a friend behind him. No doubt he could depend on Seward, but on whom could Seward depend? Certainly not on the Chairman of the Committee of Foreign Relations. Minister Adams had no friend in the Senate; he could hope for no favors, and he asked none. He thought it right to play the adventurer as his father and grandfather had done before him, without a murmur. This was a lofty view, and for him answered his objects, but it bore hard on cabin-boys, and when, in time, the young man realized what had happened, he felt it as a betrayal. He modestly thought himself unfit for the career of adventurer, and judged his father to be less fit than himself. For the first time America was posing as the champion of legitimacy and order. Her representatives should know how to play their rôle; they should wear the costume; but, in the mission attached to Mr. Adams in 1861, the only rag of legitimacy or order was the private secretary, whose stature was not sufficient to impose awe on the Court and Parliament of Great Britain.

One inevitable effect of this lesson was to make a victim of the scholar and to turn him into a harsh judge of his masters. If they overlooked him, he could hardly overlook them, since they stood with their whole weight on his body. By way of teaching him quickly, they sent out their new Minister to Russia in the same ship. Secretary Seward had occasion to learn the merits of Cassius M. Clay[9] in the diplomatic service, but Mr. Seward's education profited less than the private secretary's, Cassius Clay as a teacher having no equal though possibly some rivals. No young man, not in Government pay, could be asked to draw, from such lessons, any confidence in himself, and it was notorious that, for the next two years, the persons were few indeed who felt, or had reason to feel, any sort of confidence in the Government; fewest of all among those who were in it. At home, for the most part, young men went to the war, grumbled and died; in England they might grumble or not; no one listened.

Above all, the private secretary could not grumble to his chief. He knew surprisingly little, but that much he did know. He never labored so hard to learn a language as he did to hold his tongue, and it affected him for life. The habit of reticence — of talking without meaning — is never effaced. He had to begin it at once. He was already an adept when the party landed at Liverpool, May 13, 1861, and went instantly up to London: a family of early Christian martyrs about to be flung into an arena of lions, under the glad eyes of Tiberius Palmerston.[10] Though Lord Palmerston would have laughed his peculiar Palmerston laugh at figuring as Tiberius, he would have seen only evident resemblance in the Christian martyrs, for he had already arranged the ceremony.

Of what they had to expect, the Minister knew no more than his son. What he or Mr. Seward or Mr. Sumner may have thought is the affair of history and their errors concern historians. The errors of a private secretary concerned no one but himself, and were a large part of his education. He thought on May 12 that he was going to a friendly Government and people, true to the anti-slavery principles which had been their steadiest profession. For a hundred years the chief effort of his family had aimed at bringing the Government of England into intelligent coöperation with the objects and interests of America. His father was about to make a new effort, and this time the chance of success was promising. The slave States had been the chief apparent obstacle to good understanding. As for the private secretary himself, he was, like all Bostonians, instinctively English. He could not conceive the idea of a hostile England. He supposed himself, as one of the members of a famous anti-slavery family, to be welcome everywhere in the British Islands.

On May 13, he met the official announcement that England recognized the belligerency of the Confederacy. This beginning of a new education tore up by the roots nearly all that was left of Harvard College and Germany. He had to learn — the sooner the better — that his ideas were the reverse of truth; that in May, 1861, no one in England — literally no one — doubted that Jefferson Davis[11] had made or would make a nation, and nearly all were glad of it, though not often saying so. They mostly imitated Palmerston, who, according to Mr. Gladstone,[12] "desired the severance as a diminution of a dangerous power, but prudently held his tongue." The sentiment of anti-slavery had disappeared. Lord John Russell,[13] as Foreign Secretary, had received the rebel emissaries, and had decided to recognize their belligerency before the arrival of Mr. Adams in order to fix the position of the British Government in advance. The recognition of independence would then become an understood policy; a matter of time and occasion.

Whatever Minister Adams may have felt, the first effect of this shock upon his son produced only a dullness of comprehension — a sort of hazy inability to grasp the missile or realize the blow. Yet he realized that to his father it was likely to be fatal. The chances were great that the whole family would turn round and go home within a few weeks. The horizon widened out in endless waves of confusion. When he thought over the subject in the long leisure of later life, he grew cold at the idea of his situation had his father then shown himself what Sumner thought him to be — unfit for his post. That the private secretary was unfit for his — trifling though it were — was proved by his unreflecting confidence in his father. It never entered his mind that his father might lose his nerve or his temper, and yet in a subsequent knowledge of statesmen and diplomats extending over several generations, he could not certainly point out another who could have stood such a shock without showing it. He passed this long day, and tedious journey to London, without once thinking of the possibility that his father might make a mistake. Whatever the Minister thought, and certainly his thought was not less active than his son's, he showed no trace of excitement. His manner was the same as ever; his mind and temper were as perfectly balanced; not a word escaped; not a nerve twitched.

The test was final, for no other shock so violent and sudden could possibly recur. The worst was in full sight. For once the private secretary knew his own business, which was to imitate his father as closely as possible and hold his tongue. Dumped thus into Maurigy's Hotel at the foot of Regent Street, in the midst of a London season, without a friend or even an acquaintance, he preferred to laugh at his father's bewilderment before the waiter's " 'amhandheggsir" for breakfast, rather than ask a question or express a doubt. His situation, if taken seriously, was too appalling to face. Had he known it better, he would only have thought it worse.

Politically or socially, the outlook was desperate, beyond retrieving or contesting. Socially, under the best of circumstances, a newcomer in London society needs years to establish a position, and Minister Adams had not a week or an hour to spare, while his son had not even a remote chance of beginning. Politically the prospect looked even worse, and for Secretary Seward and Senator Sumner it was so; but for the Minister, on the spot, as he came to realize exactly where he stood, the danger was not so imminent. Mr. Adams was always one of the luckiest of men, both in what he achieved and in what he escaped. The blow, which prostrated Seward and Sumner, passed over him. Lord John Russell had acted — had probably intended to act — kindly by him in forestalling his arrival. The blow must have fallen within three months, and would then have broken him down. The British Ministers were a little in doubt still — a little ashamed of themselves — and certain to wait the longer for their next step in proportion to the haste of their first.

This is not a story of the diplomatic adventures of Charles Francis Adams, but of his son Henry's adventures in search of an education, which, if not taken too seriously, tended to humor. The father's position in London was not altogether bad; the son's was absurd. Thanks to certain family associations, Charles Francis Adams naturally looked on all British Ministers as enemies; the only public occupation of all Adamses for a hundred and fifty years at least, in their brief intervals of quarrelling with State Street, had been to quarrel with Downing Street;[14] and the

British Government, well used to a liberal unpopularity abroad, even when officially rude liked to be personally civil. All diplomatic agents are liable to be put, so to speak, in a corner, and are none the worse for it. Minister Adams had nothing in especial to complain of; his position was good while it lasted, and he had only the chances of war to fear. The son had no such compensations. Brought over in order to help his father, he could conceive no way of rendering his father help, but he was clear that his father had got to help him. To him, the Legation was social ostracism, terrible beyond anything he had known. Entire solitude in the great society of London was doubly desperate because his duties as private secretary required him to know everybody and go with his father and mother everywhere they needed escort. He had no friend, or even enemy, to tell him to be patient. Had anyone done it, he would surely have broken out with the reply that patience was the last resource of fools as well as of sages; if he was to help his father at all, he must do it at once, for his father would never so much need help again. In fact he never gave his father the smallest help, unless it were as a footman, a clerk, or a companion for the younger children.

He found himself in a singular situation for one who was to be useful. As he came to see the situation closer, he began to doubt whether secretaries were meant to be useful. Wars were too common in diplomacy to disturb the habits of the diplomat. Most secretaries detested their chiefs, and wished to be anything but useful. At the St. James's Club, to which the Minister's son could go only as an invited guest, the most instructive conversation he ever heard among the young men of his own age who hung about the tables, more helpless than himself, was: "Quel chien de pays!" or, "Que tu es beau aujourd'hui, mon cher!"[15] No one wanted to discuss affairs; still less to give or get information. That was the affair of their chiefs, who were also slow to assume work not specially ordered from their Courts. If the American Minister was in trouble to-day, the Russian Ambassador was in trouble yesterday, and the Frenchman would be in trouble to-morrow. It would all come in the day's work. There was nothing professional in worry. Empires were always tumbling to pieces and diplomats were always picking them up.

This was his whole diplomatic education, except that he found rich veins of jealousy running between every chief and his staff. His social education was more barren still, and more trying to his vanity. His little mistakes in etiquette or address made him writhe with torture. He never forgot the first two or three social functions he attended: one an afternoon at Miss Burdett Coutts's[16] in Stratton Place, where he hid himself in the embrasure of a window and hoped that no one noticed him; another was a garden-party given by the old anti-slavery Duchess Dowager of Sutherland[17] at Chiswick, where the American Minister and Mrs. Adams were kept in conversation by the old Duchess till everyone else went away except the young Duke and his cousins, who set to playing leap-frog on the lawn. At intervals during the next thirty years Henry Adams continued to happen upon the Duke, who, singularly enough, was always playing leap-frog. Still another nightmare he suffered at a dance given by the old Duchess Dowager of Somerset, a terrible vision in castanets, who seized him and forced him to perform a Highland fling before the assembled nobility and gentry, with the daughter of the Turkish Ambassador for partner. This might seem humorous to some, but to him the world turned to ashes.

When the end of the season came, the private secretary had not yet won a private acquaintance, and he hugged himself in his solitude when the story of the battle of Bull Run appeared in the *Times*.[18] He felt only the wish to be more private than ever, for Bull Run was a worse diplomatic than military disaster. All this is history and can be read by public schools if they choose; but the curious and unexpected happened to the Legation, for the effect of Bull Run on them was almost strengthening. They no longer felt doubt. For the next year they went on only from week to week, ready to leave England at once, and never assuming more than three months for their limit. Europe was waiting to see them go. So certain was the end that no one cared to hurry it.

So far as a private secretary could see, this was all that saved his father. For many months he looked on himself as lost or finished in the character of private secretary; and as about to begin, without further experiment, a final education in the ranks of the Army of the Potomac where he would find most of his friends enjoying a much pleasanter life than his own. With this idea uppermost in his mind, he passed the summer and the autumn, and began the winter. Any winter in London is a severe trial; one's first winter is the most trying; but the month of December, 1861, in Mansfield Street, Portland Place,[19] would have gorged a glutton of gloom.

One afternoon when he was struggling to resist complete nervous depression in the solitude of Mansfield Street, during the absence of the Minister and Mrs. Adams on a country visit, Reuter's telegram[20] announcing the seizure of Mason and Slidell from a British mail-steamer was brought to the office. All three secretaries, public and private were there — nervous as wild beasts under the long strain on their endurance — and all three, though they knew it to be not merely their order of departure — not merely diplomatic rupture — but a declaration of war — broke into shouts of delight. They were glad to face the end. They saw it and cheered it! Since England was waiting only for its own moment to strike, they were eager to strike first.

They telegraphed the news to the Minister, who was staying with Monckton Milnes[21] at Fryston in Yorkshire. How Mr. Adams took it, is told in the "Lives" of Lord Houghton and William E. Forster who was one of the Fryston party.[22] The moment was for him the crisis of his diplomatic career; for the secretaries it was merely the beginning of another intolerable delay, as though they were a military outpost waiting orders to quit an abandoned position. At the moment of sharpest suspense, the Prince Consort sickened and died.[23] Portland Place at Christmas in a black fog was never a rosy landscape, but in 1861 the most hardened Londoner lost his ruddiness. The private secretary had one source of comfort denied to them — he should not be private secretary long.

He was mistaken — of course! He had been mistaken at every point of his education, and, on this point, he kept up the same mistake for nearly seven years longer, always deluded by the notion that the end was near. To him the Trent Affair[24] was nothing but one of many affairs which he had to copy in a delicate round hand into his books, yet it had one or two results personal to him which left no trace on the Legation records. One of these, and to him the most important, was to put an end forever to the idea of being "useful." Hitherto, as an independent and free citizen, not in the employ of the Government, he had kept up his relations with the American press. He had written pretty frequently to Henry J. Raymond, and Raymond had used his letters in the *New York Times*.[25] He had also become fairly intimate with the two or three friendly newspapers in London, the *Daily News*, the *Star*, the weekly *Spectator* ; and he had tried to give them news and views that should have a certain common character, and prevent clash. He had even gone down to Manchester to study the cotton famine, and wrote a long account of his visit which his brother Charles had published in the *Boston Courier*.[26] Unfortunately it was printed with his name, and instantly came back upon him in the most crushing shape possible — that of a long, satirical leader in the *London Times*.[27] Luckily the *Times* did not know its victim to be a part, though not an official, of the Legation, and lost the chance to make its satire fatal; but he instantly learned the narrowness of his escape from old Joe Parkes,[28] one of the traditional busy-bodies of politics, who had haunted London since 1830, and who, after rushing to the *Times* office, to tell them all they did not know about Henry Adams, rushed to the Legation to tell Adams all he did not want to know about the *Times*. For a moment Adams thought his "usefulness" at an end in other respects than in the press, but a day or two more taught him the value of obscurity. He was totally unknown; he had not even a club; London was empty; no one thought twice about the *Times* article; no one except Joe Parkes ever spoke of it; and the world had other persons — such as President Lincoln, Secretary Seward, and Commodore Wilkes [29] — for constant and favorite objects of ridicule. Henry Adams escaped, but he never tried to be useful again. [30] The Trent Affair dwarfed individual effort. His education at least had reached the point of seeing its own proportions. "Surtout point de zèle!" [31] Zeal was too hazardous a profession for a Minister's son to pursue, as a volunteer manipulator, among Trent Affairs and rebel cruisers. [32] He wrote no more letters and meddled with no more newspapers, but he was still young, and felt unkindly towards the editor of the *London Times*.

Mr. Delane [33] lost few opportunities of embittering him, and he felt little or no hope of repaying these attentions; but the Trent Affair passed like a snowstorm, leaving the Legation, to its surprise, still in place. Although the private secretary saw in this delay — which he attributed to Mr. Seward's good sense — no reason for changing his opinion about the views of the British Government, he had no choice but to sit down again at his table, and go on copying papers, filing letters, and reading newspaper accounts of the incapacity of Mr. Lincoln and the brutality of Mr. Seward — or *vice versa*. The heavy months dragged on and winter slowly turned to spring without improving his position or spirits. Socially he had but one relief; and, to the end of life, he never forgot the keen gratitude he owed for it. During this tedious winter and for many months afterwards, the only gleams of sunshine were on the days he passed at Walton-on-Thames as the guest of Mr. and Mrs. Russell Sturgis [34] at Mount Felix.

His education had unfortunately little to do with bankers, although old George Peabody and his partner, Junius Morgan, [35] were strong allies. Joshua Bates [36] was devoted, and no one could be

kinder than Thomas Baring,[37] whose little dinners in Upper Grosvenor Street were certainly the best in London; but none offered
a refuge to compare with Mount Felix, and, for the first time,
the refuge was a liberal education. Mrs. Russell Sturgis was one of
the women to whom an intelligent boy attaches himself as closely
as he can. Henry Adams was not a very intelligent boy, and he
had no knowledge of the world, but he knew enough to understand
that a cub needed shape. The kind of education he most required
was that of a charming woman, and Mrs. Russell Sturgis, a dozen
years older than himself, could have good-naturedly trained a
school of such, without an effort, and with infinite advantage to
them. Near her he half forgot the anxieties of Portland Place.
During two years of miserable solitude, she was in this social polar
winter, the single source of warmth and light.

Of course the Legation itself was home, and, under such pressure, life in it could be nothing but united. All the inmates made
common cause, but this was no education. One lived, but was
merely flayed alive. Yet, while this might be exactly true of the
younger members of the household, it was not quite so with the
Minister and Mrs. Adams. Very slowly, but quite steadily, they
gained foothold. For some reason partly connected with American sources, British society had begun with violent social prejudice against Lincoln, Seward, and all the Republican leaders
except Sumner. Familiar as the whole tribe of Adamses had been
for three generations with the impenetrable stupidity of the British mind, and weary of the long struggle to teach it its own interests, the fourth generation could still not quite persuade itself
that this new British prejudice was natural. The private secretary suspected that Americans in New York and Boston had something to do with it. The Copperhead was at home in Pall Mall.[38]
Naturally the Englishman was a coarse animal and liked coarseness. Had Lincoln and Seward been the ruffians supposed, the
average Englishman would have liked them the better. The exceedingly quiet manner and the unassailable social position of

Minister Adams in no way conciliated them. They chose to ignore him, since they could not ridicule him. Lord John Russell set the example. Personally the Minister was to be kindly treated; politically he was negligible; he was there to be put aside. London and Paris imitated Lord John. Everyone waited to see Lincoln and his hirelings disappear in one vast *débâcle*.[39] All conceived that the Washington Government would soon crumble, and that Minister Adams would vanish with the rest.

This situation made Minister Adams an exception among diplomats. European rulers for the most part fought and treated as members of one family, and rarely had in view the possibility of total extinction; but the Governments and society of Europe, for a year at least, regarded the Washington Government as dead, and its Ministers as nullities. Minister Adams was better received than most nullities because he made no noise. Little by little, in private, society took the habit of accepting him, not so much as a diplomat, but rather as a member of opposition, or an eminent counsel retained for a foreign Government. He was to be received and considered; to be cordially treated as, by birth and manners, one of themselves. This curiously English way of getting behind a stupidity gave the Minister every possible advantage over a European diplomat. Barriers of race, language, birth, habit, ceased to exist. Diplomacy held diplomats apart in order to save Governments, but Earl Russell could not hold Mr. Adams apart. He was undistinguishable from a Londoner. In society few Londoners were so widely at home. None had such double personality and corresponding double weight.

The singular luck that took him to Fryston to meet the shock of the Trent Affair under the sympathetic eyes of Monckton Milnes and William E. Forster never afterwards deserted him. Both Milnes and Forster needed support and were greatly relieved to be supported. They saw what the private secretary in May had overlooked, the hopeless position they were in if the American Minister made a mistake, and, since his strength was

theirs, they lost no time in expressing to all the world their estimate of the Minister's character. Between them the Minister was
almost safe.

One might discuss long whether, at that moment, Milnes or
Forster were the more valuable ally, since they were influences
of different kinds. Monckton Milnes was a social power in London,
possibly greater than Londoners themselves quite understood, for
in London society as elsewhere, the dull and the ignorant made a
large majority, and dull men always laughed at Monckton Milnes.
Every bore was used to talk familiarly about "Dicky Milnes,"
the "cool of the evening";[40] and of course he himself affected social
eccentricity, challenging ridicule with the indifference of one who
knew himself to be the first wit in London, and a maker of men —
of a great many men. A word from him went far. An invitation
to his breakfast-table went farther. Behind his almost Falstaffian
mask and laugh of Silenus,[41] he carried a fine, broad, and high
intelligence which no one questioned. As a young man he had
written verses, which some readers thought poetry, and which
were certainly not altogether prose. Later, in Parliament he made
speeches, chiefly criticized as too good for the place and too high
for the audience. Socially, he was one of two or three men who
went everywhere, knew everybody, talked of everything, and had
the ear of Ministers; but unlike most wits, he held a social position
of his own that ended in a peerage, and he had a house in Upper
Brook Street to which most clever people were exceedingly glad
of admission. His breakfasts were famous, and no one liked to
decline his invitations, for it was more dangerous to show timidity
than to risk a fray. He was a voracious reader, a strong critic,
an art connoisseur in certain directions, a collector of books, but
above all he was a man of the world by profession, and loved the
contacts — perhaps the collisions — of society. Not even Henry
Brougham[42] dared do the things he did, yet Brougham defied rebuff.
Milnes was the good-nature of London; the Gargantuan type of its
refinement and coarseness; the most universal figure of May Fair.[43]

Compared with him, figures like Hayward, or Delane, or Venables, or Henry Reeve[44] were quite secondary, but William E. Forster stood in a different class. Forster had nothing whatever to do with May Fair. Except in being a Yorkshireman he was quite the opposite of Milnes. He had at that time no social or political position; he never had a vestige of Milnes's wit or variety; he was a tall, rough, ungainly figure, affecting the singular form of self-defense which the Yorkshiremen and Lancashiremen seem to hold dear — the exterior roughness assumed to cover an internal, emotional, almost sentimental nature. Kindly he had to be, if only by his inheritance from a Quaker ancestry, but he was a Friend one degree removed. Sentimental and emotional he must have been, or he could never have persuaded a daughter of Dr. Arnold to marry him.[45] Pure gold, without a trace of base metal; honest, unselfish, practical; he took up the Union cause and made himself its champion, as a true Yorkshireman was sure to do, partly because of his Quaker anti-slavery convictions, and partly because it gave him a practical opening in the House. As a new member, he needed a field.

Diffidence was not one of Forster's weaknesses. His practical sense and his personal energy soon established him in leadership, and made him a powerful champion, not so much for ornament as for work. With such a manager, the friends of the Union in England began to take heart. Minister Adams had only to look on as his true champions, the heavy-weights, came into action, and even the private secretary caught now and then a stray gleam of encouragement as he saw the ring begin to clear for these burly Yorkshiremen to stand up in a prize-fight likely to be as brutal as ever England had known. Milnes and Forster were not exactly light-weights, but Bright and Cobden were the hardest hitters in England, and with them for champions the Minister could tackle even Lord Palmerston without much fear of foul play.

In society John Bright and Richard Cobden[46] were never seen, and even in Parliament they had no large following. They were classed as enemies of order—anarchists—and anarchists they were if hatred of the so-called established orders made them so. About them was no sort of political timidity. They took bluntly the side of the Union against Palmerston whom they hated. Strangers to London society, they were at home in the American Legation, delightful dinner-company, talking always with reckless freedom. Cobden was the milder and more persuasive; Bright was the more dangerous to approach; but the private secretary delighted in both, and nourished an ardent wish to see them talk the same language to Lord John Russell from the gangway[47] of the House.

With four such allies as these, Minister Adams stood no longer quite helpless. For the second time the British Ministry felt a little ashamed of itself after the Trent Affair, as well it might, and disposed to wait before moving again. Little by little, friends gathered about the Legation who were no fair-weather companions. The old anti-slavery, Exeter Hall, Shaftesbury clique turned out to be an annoying and troublesome enemy,[48] but the Duke of Argyll[49] was one of the most valuable friends the Minister found, both politically and socially, and the Duchess was as true as her mother. Even the private secretary shared faintly in the social profit of this relation, and never forgot dining one night at the Lodge, and finding himself after dinner engaged in instructing John Stuart Mill about the peculiar merits of an American protective system. In spite of all the probabilities, he convinced himself that it was not the Duke's claret which led him to this singular form of loquacity; he insisted that it was the fault of Mr. Mill himself who led him on by assenting to his point of view. Mr. Mill took no apparent pleasure in dispute, and in that respect the Duke would perhaps have done better; but the secretary had to admit that though at other periods of life he was sufficiently and even amply snubbed by Englishmen, he could never recall a single occasion during this trying year, when he had to complain of rudeness.

Friendliness he found here and there, but chiefly among his elders; not among fashionable or socially powerful people, either men or women; although not even this rule was quite exact, for Frederick Cavendish's[50] kindness and intimate relations made Devonshire House almost familiar, and Lyulph Stanley's[51] ardent Americanism created a certain cordiality with the Stanleys of Alderley whose house was one of the most frequented in London. Lorne,[52] too, the future Argyll, was always a friend. Yet the regular course of society led to more literary intimacies. Sir Charles Trevelyan's[53] house was one of the first to which young Adams was asked, and with which his friendly relations never ceased for near half a century, and then only when death stopped them. Sir Charles and Lady Lyell[54] were intimates. Tom Hughes[55] came into close alliance. By the time society began to reopen its doors after the death of the Prince Consort, even the private secretary occasionally saw a face he knew, although he made no more effort of any kind, but silently waited the end. Whatever might be the advantages of social relations to his father and mother, to him the whole business of diplomacy and society was futile. He meant to go home.

CHAPTER IX

Foes or Friends (1862)

O F the year 1862 Henry Adams could never think without a shudder. The war alone did not greatly distress him; already in his short life he was used to seeing people wade in blood, and he could plainly discern in history, that man from the beginning had found his chief amusement in bloodshed; but the ferocious joy of destruction at its best requires that one should kill what one hates, and young Adams neither hated nor wanted to kill his friends the rebels, while he wanted nothing so much as to wipe England off the earth. Never could any good come from that besotted race! He was feebly trying to save his own life. Every day the British Government deliberately crowded him one step further into the grave. He could see it; the Legation knew it; no one doubted it; no one thought of questioning it. The Trent Affair showed where Palmerston and Russell stood. The escape of the rebel cruisers from Liverpool was not, in a young man's eyes, the sign of hesitation, but the proof of their fixed intention to intervene. Lord Russell's replies to Mr. Adams's notes were discourteous in their indifference, and, to an irritable young private secretary of twenty-four, were insolent in their disregard of truth. Whatever forms of phrase were usual in public to modify the harshness of invective, in private no political opponent in England, and few political friends, hesitated to say brutally of Lord John Russell that he lied. This was no great reproach, for, more or less, every statesman lied, but the intensity of the private secretary's rage sprang from his belief that Russell's form of defence covered intent to kill. Not for an instant did the Legation draw a free breath. The suspense was hideous and unendurable.

The Minister, no doubt, endured it, but he had support and consideration, while his son had nothing to think about but his friends who were mostly dying under McClellan[2] in the swamps about Richmond, or his enemies who were exulting in Pall Mall[3]. He bore it as well as he could till midsummer, but, when the story of the second Bull Run[4] appeared, he could bear it no longer, and after a sleepless night, walking up and down his room without reflecting that his father was beneath him, he announced at breakfast his intention to go home into the army. His mother seemed to be less impressed by the announcement than by the walking over her head, which was so unlike her as to surprise her son. His father, too, received the announcement quietly. No doubt they expected it, and had taken their measures in advance. In those days, parents got used to all sorts of announcements from their children. Mr. Adams took his son's defection as quietly as he took Bull Run; but his son never got the chance to go. He found obstacles constantly rising in his path. The remonstrances of his brother Charles, who was himself in the Army of the Potomac[5], and whose opinion had always the greatest weight with Henry, had much to do with delaying action; but he felt, of his own accord, that if he deserted his post in London, and found the Capuan comforts[6] he expected in Virginia where he would have only bullets to wound him, he would never forgive himself for leaving his father and mother alone to be devoured by the wild beasts of the British amphitheatre. This reflection might not have stopped him, but his father's suggestion was decisive. The Minister pointed out that it was too late for him to take part in the actual campaign, and that long before next spring they would all go home together.

The young man had copied too many affidavits about rebel cruisers to miss the point of this argument, so he sat down again to copy some more. Consul Dudley[7] at Liverpool provided a continuous supply. Properly, the affidavits were no business of the private secretary, but practically the private secretary did a second secretary's work, and was glad to do it, if it would save Mr. Seward the trouble of sending more secretaries of his own selection to help the Minister. The work was nothing, and no one

The Education of Henry Adams

ever complained of it; not even Moran, the Secretary of Legation after the departure of Charley Wilson, though he might sit up all night to copy. Not the work, but the play exhausted. The effort of facing a hostile society was bad enough, but that of facing friends was worse. After terrific disasters like the seven days before Richmond and the second Bull Run, friends needed support; a tone of bluff would have been fatal, for the average mind sees quickest through a bluff; nothing answers but candor; yet private secretaries never feel candid, however much they feel the reverse, and therefore they must affect candor; not always a simple act when one is exasperated, furious, bitter, and choking with tears over the blunders and incapacity of one's Government. If one shed tears, they must be shed on one's pillow. Least of all, must one throw extra strain on the Minister, who had all he could carry without being fretted in his family. One must read one's *Times* every morning over one's muffin without reading aloud — "Another disastrous Federal Defeat"; and one might not even indulge in harmless profanity. Self-restraint among friends required much more effort than keeping a quiet face before enemies. Great men were the worst blunderers. One day the private secretary smiled, when standing with the crowd in the throne-room while the endless procession made bows to the royal family, at hearing, behind his shoulder, one Cabinet Minister remark gaily to another: "So the Federals have got another licking!" The point of the remark was its truth. Even a private secretary had learned to control his tones and guard his features and betray no joy over the "lickings" of an enemy — in the enemy's presence.

London was altogether beside itself on one point, in especial; it created a nightmare of its own, and gave it the shape of Abraham Lincoln. Behind this it placed another demon, if possible more devilish, and called it Mr. Seward. In regard to these two men, English society seemed demented. Defence was useless; explanation was vain; one could only let the passion exhaust itself. One's best friends were as unreasonable as enemies, for the belief in poor Mr. Lincoln's brutality and Seward's ferocity[8] became a dogma of popular faith. The last time Henry Adams saw Thackeray, before his sudden death at Christmas in 1863, was in entering the house of Sir Henry Holland[9] for an evening reception. Thackeray was pulling on his coat downstairs, laughing because, in his usual blind way, he had stumbled into the wrong house and not found it out till he shook hands with old Sir Henry, whom he knew very well, but who was not the host he expected. Then his tone changed as he spoke of his — and Adams's — friend, Mrs. Frank Hampton, of South Carolina, whom he had loved as Sally Baxter and painted as Ethel Newcome[10] Though he had never quite forgiven her marriage, his warmth of feeling revived when he heard that she had died of consumption at Columbia while her parents and sister were refused permission to pass through the lines to see her. In speaking of it, Thackeray's voice trembled and his eyes filled with tears. The coarse cruelty of Lincoln and his hirelings was notorious. He never doubted that the Federals made a business of harrowing the tenderest feelings of women — particularly of women — in order to punish their opponents. On quite insufficient evidence he burst into violent reproach. Had Adams carried in his pocket the proofs that the reproach was unjust, he would have gained nothing by showing them. At that moment Thackeray, and all London society with him, needed the nervous relief of expressing emotion; for if Mr. Lincoln was not what they said he was — what were they?

For like reason, the members of the Legation kept silence, even in private, under the boorish Scotch jibes of Carlyle[11] If Carlyle was wrong, his diatribes would give his true measure, and this measure would be a low one, for Carlyle was not likely to be more sincere or more sound in one thought than in another. The proof that a philosopher does not know what he is talking about is apt to sadden his followers before it reacts on himself. Demolition of one's idols is painful, and Carlyle had been an idol. Doubts cast on his stature spread far into general darkness like shadows of a setting sun. Not merely the idols fell, but also the habit of faith. If Carlyle, too, was a fraud, what were his scholars and school?

Society as a rule was civil, and one had no more reason to complain than every other diplomatist has had, in like conditions, but one's few friends in society were mere ornament. The Legation could not dream of contesting social control. The best they could do was to escape mortification, and by this time their relations were good enough to save the Minister's family from that annoyance. Now and then, the fact could not be wholly disguised that some one had refused to meet — or to receive — the Minister; but never an open insult, or any expression of which the Minister had to take notice. Diplomacy served as a buffer in times of irritation, and no diplomat who knew his business fretted at what every diplomat — and none more commonly than the English — had to expect; therefore Henry Adams, though not a diplomat and wholly unprotected, went his way peacefully enough, seeing clearly that society cared little to make his acquaintance, but seeing also no reason why society should discover charms in him of which he was himself unconscious. He went where he was asked; he was always courteously received; he was, on the whole, better treated than at Washington; and he held his tongue.

For a thousand reasons, the best diplomatic house in London was Lord Palmerston's, while Lord John Russell's was one of the worst. Of neither host could a private secretary expect to know anything. He might as well have expected to know the Grand Lama. Personally Lord Palmerston was the last man in London that a cautious private secretary wanted to know. Other Prime Ministers may perhaps have lived who inspired among diplomatists as much distrust as Palmerston, and yet between Palmerston's word and Russell's word, one hesitated to decide, and gave years of education to deciding, whether either could be trusted, or how far. The Queen herself in her famous memorandum of August 12, 1850, gave her opinion of Palmerston[12] in words that differed little from words used by Lord John Russell, and both the

Queen and Russell said in substance only what Cobden and Bright said in private. Every diplomatist agreed with them, yet the diplomatic standard of trust seemed to be other than the parliamentarian. No professional diplomatists worried about falsehoods. Words were with them forms of expression which varied with individuals, but falsehood was more or less necessary to all. The worst liars were the candid. What diplomatists wanted to know was the motive that lay beyond the expression. In the case of Palmerston they were unanimous in warning new colleagues that they might expect to be sacrificed by him to any momentary personal object. Every new Minister or Ambassador at the Court of St. James[13] received this preliminary lesson that he must, if possible, keep out of Palmerston's reach. The rule was not secret or merely diplomatic. The Queen herself had emphatically expressed the same opinion officially. If Palmerston had an object to gain, he would go down to the House of Commons and betray or misrepresent a foreign Minister, without concern for his victim. No one got back on him with a blow equally mischievous — not even the Queen — for, as old Baron Brunnow[14] described him: "C'est une peau de rhinocère!"[15] Having gained his point, he laughed, and his public laughed with him, for the usual British — or American — public likes to be amused, and thought it very amusing to see these beribboned and bestarred foreigners caught and tossed and gored on the horns of this jovial, slashing, devil-may-care British bull.

Diplomatists have no right to complain of mere lies; it is their own fault, if, educated as they are, the lies deceive them; but they complain bitterly of traps. Palmerston was believed to lay traps. He was the *enfant terrible*[16] of the British Government. On the other hand, Lady Palmerston[17] was believed to be good and loyal. All the diplomats and their wives seemed to think so, and took their troubles to her, believing that she would try to help them. For this reason among others, her evenings at home — Saturday Reviews, they were called — had great vogue. An ignorant young

American could not be expected to explain it. Cambridge House was no better for entertaining than a score of others. Lady Palmerston was no longer young or handsome, and could hardly at any age have been vivacious. The people one met there were never smart and seldom young; they were largely diplomatic, and diplomats are commonly dull; they were largely political, and politicians rarely decorate or beautify an evening party; they were sprinkled with literary people, who are notoriously unfashionable; the women were of course ill-dressed and middle-aged; the men looked mostly bored or out of place; yet, beyond a doubt, Cambridge House was the best, and perhaps the only political house in London, and its success was due to Lady Palmerston, who never seemed to make an effort beyond a friendly recognition. As a lesson in social education, Cambridge House gave much subject for thought. First or last, one was to know dozens of statesmen more powerful and more agreeable than Lord Palmerston; dozens of ladies more beautiful and more painstaking than Lady Palmerston; but no political house so successful as Cambridge House. The world never explains such riddles. The foreigners said only that Lady Palmerston was "sympathique."

The small fry of the Legations were admitted there, or tolerated, without a further effort to recognize their existence, but they were pleased because rarely tolerated anywhere else, and there they could at least stand in a corner and look at a bishop or even a duke. This was the social diversion of young Adams. No one knew him — not even the lackeys. The last Saturday evening he ever attended, he gave his name as usual at the foot of the staircase, and was rather disturbed to hear it shouted up as "Mr. Handrew Hadams!" He tried to correct it, and the footman shouted more loudly: "Mr. Hanthony Hadams!" With some temper he repeated the correction, and was finally announced as "Mr. Halexander Hadams," and under this name made his bow for the last time to Lord Palmerston who certainly knew no better.

Far down the staircase one heard Lord Palmerston's laugh as

he stood at the door receiving his guests, talking probably to one of his henchmen, Delane, Borthwick,[18] or Hayward, who were sure to be near. The laugh was singular, mechanical, wooden, and did not seem to disturb his features. "Ha!... Ha!... Ha!" Each was a slow, deliberate ejaculation, and all were in the same tone, as though he meant to say: "Yes!... Yes!... Yes!" by way of assurance. It was a laugh of 1810 and the Congress of Vienna.[19] Adams would have much liked to stop a moment and ask whether William Pitt and the Duke of Wellington[20] had laughed so; but young men attached to foreign Ministers asked no questions at all of Palmerston and their chiefs asked as few as possible. One made the usual bow and received the usual glance of civility; then passed on to Lady Palmerston, who was always kind in manner, but who wasted no remarks; and so to Lady Jocelyn[21] with her daughter, who commonly had something friendly to say; then went through the diplomatic corps, Brunnow, Musurus, Azeglio, Apponyi, Van de Weyer, Bille, Tricoupi,[22] and the rest, finally dropping into the hands of some literary accident as strange there as oneself. The routine varied little. There was no attempt at entertainment. Except for the desperate isolation of these two first seasons, even secretaries would have found the effort almost as mechanical as a levee at St. James's Palace.

Lord Palmerston was not Foreign Secretary; he was Prime Minister, but he loved foreign affairs and could no more resist scoring a point in diplomacy than in whist. Ministers of foreign powers, knowing his habits, tried to hold him at arms'-length, and, to do this, were obliged to court the actual Foreign Secretary, Lord John Russell, who, on July 30, 1861, was called up to the House of Lords as an earl. By some process of personal affiliation, Minister Adams succeeded in persuading himself that he could trust Lord Russell more safely than Lord Palmerston. His son, being young and ill-balanced in temper, thought there was nothing to choose. Englishmen saw little difference between them, and Americans were bound to follow English experience in English character. Minister

Adams had much to learn, although with him as well as with his son, the months of education began to count as æons.

Just as Brunnow predicted, Lord Palmerston made his rush at last, as unexpected as always, and more furiously than though still a private secretary of twenty-four.[23] Only a man who had been young with the battle of Trafalgar[24] could be fresh and jaunty to that point, but Minister Adams was not in a position to sympathize with octogenarian youth[25] and found himself in a danger as critical as that of his numerous predecessors. It was late one afternoon in June, 1862, as the private secretary returned, with the Minister, from some social function, that he saw his father pick up a note from his desk and read it in silence. Then he said curtly: "Palmerston wants a quarrel!" This was the point of the incident as he felt it. Palmerston wanted a quarrel; he must not be gratified; he must be stopped. The matter of quarrel was General Butler's famous woman-order at New Orleans,[26] but the motive was the belief in President Lincoln's brutality that had taken such deep root in the British mind. Knowing Palmerston's habits, the Minister took for granted that he meant to score a diplomatic point by producing this note in the House of Commons. If he did this at once, the Minister was lost; the quarrel was made; and one new victim to Palmerston's passion for popularity was sacrificed.

The moment was nervous — as far as the private secretary knew, quite the most critical moment in the records of American diplomacy — but the story belongs to history, not to education, and can be read there by anyone who cares to read it. As a part of Henry Adams's education it had a value distinct from history. That his father succeeded in muzzling Palmerston without a public scandal, was well enough for the Minister, but was not enough for a private secretary who liked going to Cambridge House, and was puzzled to reconcile contradictions. That Palmerston had wanted a quarrel was obvious; why, then, did he submit so tamely to being made the victim of the quarrel? The correspondence that followed his note was conducted feebly on his side, and he allowed the United States Minister to close it by a refusal to receive further communications from him except through Lord Russell. The step was excessively strong, for it broke off private relations as well as public, and cost even the private secretary his invitations to Cambridge House. Lady Palmerston tried her best, but the two ladies found no resource except tears. They had to do with an American Minister perplexed in the extreme. Not that Mr. Adams lost his temper, for he never felt such a weight of responsibility, and was never more cool; but he could conceive no other way of protecting his Government, not to speak of himself, than to force Lord Russell to interpose. He believed that Palmerston's submission and silence were due to Russell. Perhaps he was right; at the time, his son had no doubt of it, though afterwards he felt less sure. Palmerston wanted a quarrel; the motive seemed evident; yet when the quarrel was made, he backed out of it; for some reason it seemed that he did not want it — at least, not then. He never showed resentment against Mr. Adams at the time or afterwards. He never began another quarrel. Incredible as it seemed, he behaved like a well-bred gentleman who felt himself in the wrong. Possibly this change may have been due to Lord Russell's remonstrances, but the private secretary would have felt his education in politics more complete had he ever finally made up his mind whether Palmerston was more angry with General Butler, or more annoyed at himself, for committing what was in both cases an unpardonable *bêtise*.[27]

At the time, the question was hardly raised, for no one doubted Palmerston's attitude or his plans. The season was near its end, and Cambridge House was soon closed. The Legation had troubles enough without caring to publish more. The tide of English feeling ran so violently against it that one could only wait to see whether General McClellan would bring it relief. The year 1862 was a dark spot in Henry Adams's life, and the education it gave was mostly one that he gladly forgot. As far as he was aware, he made no friends; he could hardly make enemies; yet towards the

close of the year he was flattered by an invitation from Monckton Milnes to Fryston, and it was one of many acts of charity towards the young that gave Milnes immortality. Milnes made it
his business to be kind. Other people criticized him for his manner of doing it, but never imitated him. Naturally, a dispirited,
disheartened private secretary was exceedingly grateful, and never
forgot the kindness, but it was chiefly as education that this
first country visit had value. Commonly, country visits are much
alike, but Monckton Milnes was never like anybody, and his
country parties served his purpose of mixing strange elements.
Fryston was one of a class of houses that no one sought for its natural beauties, and the winter mists of Yorkshire were rather more
evident for the absence of the hostess on account of them, so that
the singular guests whom Milnes collected to enliven his December had nothing to do but astonish each other, if anything could
astonish such men. Of the five, Adams alone was tame; he alone
added nothing to the wit or humor, except as a listener; but they
needed a listener and he was useful. Of the remaining four, Milnes
was the oldest, and perhaps the sanest in spite of his superficial
eccentricities, for Yorkshire sanity was true to a standard of its
own, if not to other conventions; yet even Milnes startled a young
American whose Boston and Washington mind was still fresh.
He would not have been startled by the hard-drinking, horse-
racing Yorkshireman of whom he had read in books; but Milnes
required a knowledge of society and literature that only himself
possessed, if one were to try to keep pace with him. He had sought
contact with everybody and everything that Europe could offer.
He knew it all from several points of view, and chiefly as humorous.

The second of the party was also of a certain age; a quiet, well-
mannered, singularly agreeable gentleman of the literary class.
When Milnes showed Adams to his room to dress for dinner, he
stayed a moment to say a word about this guest, whom he called
Stirling of Keir.[28] His sketch closed with the hint that Stirling was

violent only on one point — hatred of Napoleon III. On that point, Adams was himself sensitive, which led him to wonder how bad the Scotch gentleman might be.[29] The third was a man of thirty or thereabouts, whom Adams had already met at Lady Palmerston's carrying his arm in a sling. His figure and bearing were sympathetic — almost pathetic — with a certain grave and gentle charm, a pleasant smile, and an interesting story. He was Laurence Oliphant,[30] just from Japan, where he had been wounded in the fanatics' attack on the British Legation. He seemed exceptionally sane and peculiarly suited for country houses, where every man would enjoy his company, and every woman would adore him. He had not then published "Piccadilly"; perhaps he was writing it; while, like all the young men about the Foreign Office, he contributed to *The Owl.*[31]

The fourth was a boy, or had the look of one, though in fact a year older than Adams himself. He resembled in action — and in this trait, was remotely followed, a generation later, by another famous young man, Robert Louis Stevenson[32] — a tropical bird, high-crested, long-beaked, quick-moving, with rapid utterance and screams of humor, quite unlike any English lark or nightingale. One could hardly call him a crimson macaw among owls, and yet no ordinary contrast availed. Milnes introduced him as Mr. Algernon Swinburne.[33] The name suggested nothing. Milnes was always unearthing new coins and trying to give them currency. He had unearthed Henry Adams who knew himself to be worthless and not current. When Milnes lingered a moment in Adams's room to add that Swinburne had written some poetry, not yet published, of really extraordinary merit, Adams only wondered what more Milnes would discover, and whether by chance he could discover merit in a private secretary. He was capable of it.

In due course this party of five men sat down to dinner with the usual club manners of ladyless dinner-tables, easy and formal at the same time. Conversation ran first to Oliphant who told his dramatic story simply, and from him the talk drifted off into other channels, until Milnes thought it time to bring Swinburne out. Then, at last, if never before, Adams acquired education. What he had sought so long, he found; but he was none the wiser; only the more astonished. For once, too, he felt at ease, for the others were no less astonished than himself, and their astonishment grew apace. For the rest of the evening Swinburne figured alone; the end of dinner made the monologue only freer, for in 1862, even when ladies were not in the house, smoking was forbidden, and guests usually smoked in the stables or the kitchen; but Monckton Milnes was a licensed libertine who let his guests smoke in Adams's bedroom, since Adams was an American-German barbarian[34] ignorant of manners; and there after dinner all sat — or lay — till far into the night, listening to the rush of Swinburne's talk. In a long experience, before or after, no one ever approached it; yet one had heard accounts of the best talking of the time, and read accounts of talkers in all time, among the rest, of Voltaire,[35] who seemed to approach nearest the pattern.

That Swinburne was altogether new to the three types of men-of-the-world before him; that he seemed to them quite original, wildly eccentric, astonishingly gifted, and convulsingly droll, Adams could see; but what more he was, even Milnes hardly dared say. They could not believe his incredible memory and knowledge of literature, classic, mediæval, and modern; his faculty of reciting a play of Sophocles or a play of Shakespeare, forward or backward, from end to beginning; or Dante, or Villon, or Victor Hugo.[36] They knew not what to make of his rhetorical recitation of his own unpublished ballads — "Faustine"; the "Four Boards of the Coffin Lid"; the "Ballad of Burdens" — which he declaimed as though they were books of the Iliad.[37] It was singular that his most appreciative listener[38] should have been the author only of pretty verses like "We wandered by the brook-side," and "She seemed to those that saw them meet"; and who never cared to write in any other tone; but Milnes took everything into his sympathies, including Americans like young Adams whose standards were stiffest of all, while Swinburne, though millions of ages far from them, united them by his humor even more than by his poetry. The story of his first day[39] as a member of Professor Stubbs's household was professionally clever farce, if not high comedy, in a young man who could write a Greek ode or a Provençal chanson as easily as an English quatrain.

Late at night when the symposium broke up, Stirling of Keir wanted to take with him to his chamber a copy of "Queen Rosamund,"[40] the only volume Swinburne had then published, which was on the library table, and Adams offered to light him down with his solitary bedroom candle. All the way, Stirling was ejaculating explosions of wonder, until at length, at the foot of the stairs and at the climax of his imagination, he paused, and burst out: "He's a cross between the devil and the Duke of Argyll!"[41]

To appreciate the full merit of this description, a judicious critic should have known both, and Henry Adams knew only one — at least in person — but he understood that to a Scotchman the likeness meant something quite portentous, beyond English experience, supernatural, and what the French call *moyenâgeux*,[42] or mediæval with a grotesque turn. That Stirling as well as Milnes should regard Swinburne as a prodigy greatly comforted Adams, who lost his balance of mind at first in trying to imagine that Swinburne was a natural product of Oxford, as muffins and pork-pies of London, at once the cause and effect of dyspepsia. The idea that one has actually met a real genius dawns slowly on a Boston mind, but it made entry at last.

Then came the sad reaction, not from Swinburne whose genius never was in doubt, but from the Boston mind which, in its uttermost flights, was never *moyenâgeux*. One felt the horror of Longfellow and Emerson, the doubts of Lowell and the humor of Holmes, at the wild Walpurgis-night[43] of Swinburne's talk. What could a shy young private secretary do about it? Perhaps, in his good nature, Milnes thought that Swinburne might find a friend in Stirling or Oliphant, but he could hardly have fancied Henry Adams rousing in him even an interest. Adams could no more interest Algernon Swinburne than he could interest Encke's comet.[44] To Swinburne he could be no more than a worm. The quality of genius was an education almost ultimate, for one touched there the limits of the human mind on that side; but one could only receive; one had nothing to give — nothing even to offer.

Swinburne tested him then and there by one of his favorite tests — Victor Hugo; for to him the test of Victor Hugo was the surest and quickest of standards. French poetry is at best a severe exercise for foreigners; it requires extraordinary knowledge of the language and rare refinement of ear to appreciate even the recitation of French verse; but unless a poet has both, he lacks something of poetry. Adams had neither. To the end of his life he never listened to a French recitation with pleasure, or felt a sense of majesty in French verse; but he did not care to proclaim his weakness, and he tried to evade Swinburne's vehement insistence by parading an affection for Alfred de Musset.[45] Swinburne would have none of it; de Musset was unequal; he did not sustain himself on the wing.

Adams would have given a world or two, if he owned one, to sustain himself on the wing like de Musset, or even like Hugo; but his education as well as his ear was at fault, and he succumbed. Swinburne tried him again on Walter Savage Landor.[46] In truth the test was the same, for Swinburne admired in Landor's English the qualities that he felt in Hugo's French; and Adams's failure was equally gross, for, when forced to despair, he had to admit that both Hugo and Landor bored him. Nothing more was needed. One who could feel neither Hugo nor Landor was lost.

The sentence was just and Adams never appealed from it. He knew his inferiority in taste as he might know it in smell. Keenly mortified by the dullness of his senses and instincts, he knew he was no companion for Swinburne; probably he could be only an annoyance; no number of centuries could ever educate him to Swinburne's level, even in technical appreciation; yet he often wondered whether there was nothing he had to offer that was worth the poet's acceptance. Certainly such mild homage as the American insect would have been only too happy to bring, had he known how, was hardly worth the acceptance of anyone. Only in France is the attitude of prayer possible; in England it became absurd. Even Monckton Milnes, who felt the splendors of Hugo and Landor, was almost as helpless as an American private secretary in personal contact with them. Ten years afterwards Adams met him at the Geneva Conference,[47] fresh from Paris, bubbling with delight at a call he had made on Hugo: "I was shown into a large room," he said, "with women and men seated in chairs against the walls, and Hugo at one end throned. No one spoke. At last Hugo raised his voice solemnly, and uttered the words: 'Quant à moi, je crois en Dieu!' Silence followed. Then a woman responded as if in deep meditation: 'Chose sublime! un Dieu qui croit en Dieu!'" [48]

With the best of will, one could not do this in London; the actors had not the instinct of the drama; and yet even a private secretary was not wholly wanting in instinct. As soon as he reached town he hurried to Pickering's[49] for a copy of "Queen Rosamund," and at that time, if Swinburne was not joking, Pickering had sold seven copies. When the "Poems and Ballads" came out, and met their great success and scandal, he sought one of the first copies from Moxon.[50] If he had sinned and doubted at all, he wholly repented and did penance before "Atalanta in Calydon," and would have offered Swinburne a solemn worship as Milnes's female offered Hugo, if it would have pleased the poet. Unfortunately it was worthless.

The three young men returned to London, and each went his own way. Adams's interest in making friends was something desperate, but "the London season," Milnes used to say, "is a season for making acquaintances and losing friends"; there was no intimate life. Of Swinburne he saw no more till Monckton

Milnes summoned his whole array of Frystonians to support him in presiding at the dinner of the Authors' Fund, when Adams found himself seated next to Swinburne, famous then, but no nearer. They never met again.[51] Oliphant he met oftener; all the world knew and loved him; but he too disappeared in the way that all the world knows.[52] Stirling of Keir, after one or two efforts, passed also from Adams's vision into Sir William Stirling-Maxwell. The only record of his wonderful visit to Fryston may perhaps exist still in the registers of the St. James's Club, for immediately afterwards Milnes proposed Henry Adams for membership, and unless his memory erred, the nomination was seconded by Tricoupi and endorsed by Laurence Oliphant and Evelyn Ashley.[53] The list was a little singular for variety, but on the whole it suggested that the private secretary was getting on.

CHAPTER X

Political Morality (1862)

ON Moran's promotion to be Secretary, Mr. Seward inquired whether Minister Adams would like the place of Assistant Secretary for his son. It was the first — and last — office ever offered him, if indeed he could claim what was offered in fact to his father. To them both, the change seemed useless. Any young man could make some sort of Assistant Secretary; only one, just at that moment, could make an Assistant Son. More than half his duties were domestic; they sometimes required long absences; they always required independence of the Government service. His position was abnormal. The British Government by courtesy allowed the son to go to Court as Attaché, though he was never attached, and after five or six years' toleration, the decision was declared irregular. In the Legation, as private secretary, he was liable to do Secretary's work. In society, when official, he was attached to the Minister; when unofficial, he was a young man without any position at all. As the years went on, he began to find advantages in having no position at all except that of young man. Gradually he aspired to become a gentleman; just a member of society like the rest. The position was irregular; at that time many positions were irregular; yet it lent itself to a sort of irregular education that seemed to be the only sort of education the young man was ever to get.

Such as it was, few young men had more. The spring and summer of 1863 saw a great change in Secretary Seward's management of foreign affairs. Under the stimulus of danger, he too got education. He felt, at last, that his official representatives abroad needed support. Officially he could give them nothing but despatches, which were of no great value to anyone; and at best the mere weight of an office had little to do with the public. Governments were made to deal with Governments, not with private individuals or with the opinions of foreign society. In order to affect European opinion, the weight of American opinion had to be brought to bear personally, and had to be backed by the weight of American interests. Mr. Seward set vigorously to work and sent over every important American on whom he could lay his hands. All came to the Legation more or less intimately, and Henry Adams had a chance to see them all, bankers or bishops, who did their work quietly and well, though, to the outsider, the work seemed wasted and the "influential classes" more indurated with prejudice than ever. The waste was only apparent; the work all told in the end, and meanwhile it helped education.

Two or three of these gentlemen were sent over to aid the Minister and to coöperate with him. The most interesting of these was Thurlow Weed, who came to do what the private secretary himself had attempted two years before, with boyish ignorance of his own powers. Mr. Weed took charge of the press, and began, to the amused astonishment of the secretaries, by making what the Legation had learned to accept as the invariable mistake of every amateur diplomat; he wrote letters to the *London Times*. Mistake or not, Mr. Weed soon got into his hands the threads of management, and did quietly and smoothly all that was to be done. With his work the private secretary had no connection; it was he that interested. Thurlow Weed was a complete American education in himself. His mind was naturally strong and beautifully balanced; his temper never seemed ruffled; his manners were carefully perfect in the style of benevolent simplicity, the tradition of Benjamin Franklin. He was the model of political management and patient address; but the trait that excited enthusiasm in a private secretary was his faculty of irresistibly conquering confidence. Of all flowers in the garden of education, confidence was becoming the rarest; but before Mr. Weed went away, young Adams followed him about not only obediently — for obedience had long since become a blind instinct — but rather with sympathy and affection, much like a little dog.

The sympathy was not due only to Mr. Weed's skill of management, although Adams never met another such master, or anyone who approached him; nor was the confidence due to any display of professions, either moral or social, by Mr. Weed. The trait that astounded and confounded cynicism was his apparent unselfishness. Never, in any man who wielded such power, did Adams meet anything like it. The effect of power and publicity on all men is the aggravation of self, a sort of tumor that ends by killing the victim's sympathies; a diseased appetite, like a passion for drink or perverted tastes; one can scarcely use expressions too strong to describe the violence of egotism it stimulates; and Thurlow Weed was one of the exceptions; a rare immune. He thought apparently not of himself, but of the person he was talking with. He held himself naturally in the background. He was not jealous. He grasped power, but not office. He distributed offices by handfuls without caring to take them. He had the instinct of empire: he gave, but he did not receive. This rare superiority to the politicians he controlled, a trait that private secretaries never met in the politicians themselves, excited Adams's wonder and curiosity, but when he tried to get behind it, and to educate himself from the stores of Mr. Weed's experience, he found the study still more fascinating. Management was an instinct with Mr. Weed; an object to be pursued for its own sake, as one plays cards; but he appeared to play with men as though they were only cards; he seemed incapable of feeling himself one of them. He took them and played them for their face-value; but once, when he had told, with his usual humor, some stories of his political experience which were strong even for the Albany lobby, the private secretary made bold to ask him outright: "Then, Mr. Weed, do you think that no politician can be trusted?" Mr. Weed hesitated for a moment; then said in his mild manner: "I never advise a young man to begin by thinking so."

This lesson, at the time, translated itself to Adams in a moral sense, as though Mr. Weed had said: "Youth needs illusions!"

As he grew older he rather thought that Mr. Weed looked on it as a question of how the game should be played. Young men most needed experience. They could not play well if they trusted to a general rule. Every card had a relative value. Principles had better be left aside; values were enough. Adams knew that he could never learn to play politics in so masterly a fashion as this: his education and his nervous system equally forbade it, although he admired all the more the impersonal faculty of the political master who could thus efface himself and his temper in the game. He noticed that most of the greatest politicians in history had seemed to regard men as counters. The lesson was the more interesting because another famous New Yorker came over at the same time who liked to discuss the same problem. Secretary Seward sent William M. Evarts[2] to London as law counsel, and Henry began an acquaintance with Mr. Evarts that soon became intimate. Evarts was as individual as Weed was impersonal; like most men, he cared little for the game, or how it was played, and much for the stakes, but he played it in a large and liberal way, like Daniel Webster, "a great advocate employed in politics." Evarts was also an economist of morals, but with him the question was rather how much morality one could afford. "The world can absorb only doses of truth," he said; "too much would kill it." One sought education in order to adjust the dose.

The teachings of Weed and Evarts were practical, and the private secretary's life turned on their value. England's power of absorbing truth was small. Englishmen, such as Palmerston, Russell, Bethell,[3] and the society represented by the *Times* and *Morning Post*, as well as the Tories represented by Disraeli,[4] Lord Robert Cecil,[5] and the *Standard*, offered a study in education that sickened a young student with anxiety. He had begun — contrary to Mr. Weed's advice — by taking their bad faith for granted. Was he wrong? To settle this point became the main object of the diplomatic education so laboriously pursued, at a cost already stupendous, and promising to become ruinous. Life changed front, according as one thought oneself dealing with honest men or with rogues.

Thus far, the private secretary felt officially sure of dishonesty. The reasons that satisfied him had not altogether satisfied his father, and of course his father's doubts gravely shook his own convictions, but, in practice, if only for safety, the Legation put little or no confidence in Ministers, and there the private secretary's diplomatic education began. The recognition of belligerency, the management of the Declaration of Paris,[6] the Trent Affair, all strengthened the belief that Lord Russell had started in May, 1861, with the assumption that the Confederacy was established; every step he had taken proved his persistence in the same idea; he never would consent to put obstacles in the way of recognition; and he was waiting only for the proper moment to interpose. All these points seemed so fixed — so self-evident — that no one in the Legation would have doubted or even discussed them except that Lord Russell obstinately denied the whole charge, and persisted in assuring Minister Adams of his honest and impartial neutrality.

With the insolence of youth and zeal, Henry Adams jumped at once to the conclusion that Earl Russell — like other statesmen — lied; and, although the Minister thought differently, he had to act as though Russell were false. Month by month the demonstration followed its mathematical stages; one of the most perfect educational courses in politics and diplomacy that a young man ever had a chance to pursue. The most costly tutors in the world were provided for him at public expense — Lord Palmerston, Lord Russell, Lord Westbury,[7] Lord Selborne,[8] Mr. Gladstone,[9] Lord Granville,[10] and their associates, paid by the British Government; William H. Seward, Charles Francis Adams, William Maxwell Evarts, Thurlow Weed, and other considerable professors employed by the American Government; but there was only one student to profit by this immense staff of teachers. The private secretary alone sought education.

To the end of his life he labored over the lessons then taught. Never was demonstration more tangled. Hegel's[11] metaphysical doctrine of the identity of opposites was simpler and easier to understand. Yet the stages of demonstration were clear. They began in June, 1862, after the escape of one rebel cruiser, by the remonstrances of the Minister against the escape of "No. 290," which was imminent. Lord Russell declined to act on the evidence. New evidence was sent in every few days, and with it, on July 24, was included Collier's[12] legal opinion: "It appears difficult to make out a stronger case of infringement of the Foreign Enlistment Act, which, if not enforced on this occasion, is little better than a dead letter." Such language implied almost a charge of collusion with the rebel agents — an intent to aid the Confederacy. In spite of the warning, Earl Russell let the ship, four days afterwards, escape.

Young Adams had nothing to do with law; that was business of his betters. His opinion of law hung on his opinion of lawyers. In spite of Thurlow Weed's advice, could one afford to trust human nature in politics? History said not. Sir Robert Collier seemed to hold that Law agreed with History.[13] For education the point was vital. If one could not trust a dozen of the most respected private characters in the world, composing the Queen's Ministry, one could trust no mortal man.

Lord Russell felt the force of this inference, and undertook to disprove it. His effort lasted till his death. At first he excused himself by throwing the blame on the law officers. This was a politician's practice, and the lawyers overruled it. Then he pleaded guilty to criminal negligence, and said in his "Recollections":[14] "I assent entirely to the opinion of the Lord Chief Justice of England that the Alabama ought to have been detained during the four days I was waiting for the opinion of the law officers. But I think that the fault was not that of the commissioners of customs, it was my fault as Secretary of State for Foreign Affairs." This concession brought all parties on common ground. Of course it was his fault! The true issue lay not in the question of his fault, but of his intent. To a young man, getting an education in politics, there could be no sense in history unless a constant course of faults implied a constant motive.

For his father the question was not so abstruse; it was a practical matter of business to be handled as Weed or Evarts handled their bargains and jobs. Minister Adams held the convenient belief that, in the main, Russell was true, and the theory answered his purposes so well that he died still holding it. His son was seeking education, and wanted to know whether he could, in politics, risk trusting anyone. Unfortunately no one could then decide; no one knew the facts. Minister Adams died without knowing them. Henry Adams was an older man than his father in 1862, before he learned a part of them. The most curious fact, even then, was that Russell believed in his own good faith and that Argyll believed in it also.

Argyll betrayed a taste for throwing the blame on Bethell, Lord Westbury, then Lord Chancellor, but this escape helped Adams not at all. On the contrary, it complicated the case of Russell. In England, one half of society enjoyed throwing stones at Lord Palmerston, while the other half delighted in flinging mud at Earl Russell, but everyone of every party united in pelting Westbury with every missile at hand. The private secretary had no doubts about him, for he never professed to be moral. He was the head and heart of the whole rebel contention, and his opinions on neutrality were as clear as they were on morality. The private secretary had nothing to do with him, and regretted it, for Lord Westbury's wit and wisdom were great; but as far as his authority went, he affirmed the law that in politics no man should be trusted.

Russell alone insisted on his honesty of intention and persuaded both the Duke and the Minister[16] to believe him. Everyone in the Legation accepted his assurances as the only assertions they could venture to trust. They knew he expected the rebels to win in the end, but they believed he would not actively interpose to decide it. On that — on nothing else — they rested their frail hopes of remaining a day longer in England. Minister Adams remained six years longer in England; then returned to America to lead a busy life till he died in 1886 still holding the same faith in Earl Russell, who had died in 1878. In 1889, Spencer Walpole published the official life of Earl Russell, and told a part of the story which had never been known to the Minister[17] and which astounded his son, who burned with curiosity to know what his father would have said of it.

The story was this: The Alabama escaped, by Russell's confessed negligence, on July 28, 1862. In America the Union armies had suffered great disasters before Richmond and at the second Bull Run, August 29–30, followed by Lee's invasion of Maryland, September 7, the news of which, arriving in England on September 14, roused the natural idea that the crisis was at hand. The next news was expected by the Confederates to announce the fall of Washington or Baltimore. Palmerston instantly, September 14, wrote to Russell: "If this should happen, would it not be time for us to consider whether in such a state of things England and France might not address the contending parties and recommend an arrangement on the basis of separation?"

This letter, quite in the line of Palmerston's supposed opinions, would have surprised no one, if it had been communicated to the Legation; and indeed, if Lee had captured Washington, no one could have blamed Palmerston for offering intervention. Not Palmerston's letter but Russell's reply, merited the painful attention of a young man seeking a moral standard for judging politicians: —

GOTHA, September, 17, 1862.

MY DEAR PALMERSTON: —

Whether the Federal army is destroyed or not, it is clear that it is driven back to Washington and has made no progress in subduing the insurgent States. Such being the case, I agree with you that the time is come for offering mediation to the United States Government with a view to the recognition of the independence of the Confederates. I agree further that in case of failure, we ought ourselves to recognize the Southern States as an independent State. For the purpose of taking so important a step, I think we must have a meeting of the Cabinet. The 23d or 30th would suit me for the meeting.

We ought then, if we agree on such a step, to propose it first to France, and then on the part of England and France, to Russia and other powers, as a measure decided upon by us.

We ought to make ourselves safe in Canada, not by sending more troops there, but by concentrating those we have in a few defensible posts before the winter sets in. . . .

Here, then, appeared in its fullest force, the practical difficulty in education which a mere student could never overcome; a difficulty not in theory, or knowledge, or even want of experience, but in the sheer chaos of human nature. Lord Russell's course had been consistent from the first, and had all the look of rigid determination to recognize the Southern Confederacy "with a view" to breaking up the Union. His letter of September 17 hung directly on his encouragement of the Alabama and his protection of the rebel navy; while the whole of his plan had its root in the Proclamation of Belligerency, May 13, 1861. The policy had every look of persistent forethought, but it took for granted the deliberate dishonesty of three famous men: Palmerston, Russell, and Gladstone. This dishonesty, as concerned Russell, was denied by Russell himself, and disbelieved by Argyll, Forster, and most of America's friends in England, as well as by Minister Adams. What the Minister would have thought had he seen this letter of September 17, his son would have greatly liked to know, but he would have liked still more to know what the Minister would have thought of Palmerston's answer, dated September 23: —

. . . It is evident that a great conflict is taking place to the northwest of Washington, and its issue must have a great effect on the state of affairs. If the Federals sustain a great defeat, they may be at once ready for mediation, and the iron should be struck while it is hot. If, on the other hand, they should have the best of it, we may wait awhile and see what may follow...

The rôles were reversed. Russell wrote what was expected from Palmerston, or even more violently; while Palmerston wrote what was expected from Russell, or even more temperately. The private secretary's view had been altogether wrong, which would not have much surprised even him, but he would have been greatly astonished to learn that the most confidential associates of these men knew little more about their intentions than was known in the Legation. The most trusted member of the Cabinet was Lord Granville, and to him Russell next wrote. Granville replied at once decidedly opposing recognition of the Confederacy, and Russell sent the reply to Palmerston, who returned it October 2, with the mere suggestion of waiting for further news from America. At the same time Granville wrote to another member of the Cabinet, Lord Stanley of Alderley, a letter published forty years afterwards in Granville's "Life"[18](I, 442) — to the private secretary altogether the most curious and instructive relic of the whole lesson in politics: —

... I have written to Johnny my reasons for thinking it decidedly premature. I, however, suspect you will settle to do so. Pam., Johnny, and Gladstone would be in favor of it, and probably Newcastle. I do not know about the others. It appears to me a great mistake. ...

Out of a Cabinet of a dozen members, Granville, the best informed of them all, could pick only three who would favor recognition. Even a private secretary thought he knew as much as this, or more. Ignorance was not confined to the young and insignificant, nor were they the only victims of blindness. Granville's letter made only one point clear. He knew of no fixed policy or conspiracy. If any existed, it was confined to Palmerston, Russell, Gladstone, and perhaps Newcastle. In truth, the Legation knew, then, all that was to be known, and the true fault of education was to suspect too much.

By that time, October 3, news of Antietam and of Lee's retreat into Virginia had reached London. The Emancipation Proclamation arrived.[19] Had the private secretary known all that Granville or Palmerston knew, he would surely have thought the danger past, at least for a time, and any man of common sense would have told him to stop worrying over phantoms. This healthy lesson would have been worth much for practical education, but it was quite upset by the sudden rush of a new actor upon the stage with a rhapsody that made Russell seem sane, and all education superfluous.

This new actor, as every one knows, was William Ewart Gladstone, then Chancellor of the Exchequer. If, in the domain of the world's politics, one point was fixed, one value ascertained, one element serious, it was the British Exchequer; and if one man lived who could be certainly counted as sane by overwhelming interest, it was the man who had in charge the finances of England. If education had the smallest value, it should have shown its force in Gladstone, who was educated beyond all record of English training. From him, if from no one else, the poor student could safely learn.

Here is what he learned! Palmerston notified Gladstone, September 24, of the proposed intervention: "If I am not mistaken, you would be inclined to approve such a course."[20]Gladstone replied the next day: "He was glad to learn what the Prime Minister had told him; and for two reasons especially he desired that the proceedings should be prompt: the first was the rapid progress of the Southern arms and the extension of the area of Southern feeling; the second was the risk of violent impatience in the cotton-towns of Lancashire such as would prejudice the dignity and disinterestedness of the proffered mediation."

Had the puzzled student seen this letter, he must have concluded from it that the best educated statesman England ever produced did not know what he was talking about, an assumption which all the world would think quite inadmissible from a private secretary — but this was a trifle. Gladstone having thus arranged, with Palmerston and Russell, for intervention in the American war, reflected on the subject for a fortnight from September 25 to October 7, when he was to speak on the occasion of a great dinner at Newcastle. He decided to announce the Government's policy with all the force his personal and official authority could give it. This decision was no sudden impulse; it was the result of deep reflection pursued to the last moment. On the morning of October 7, he entered in his diary: "Reflected further on what I should say about Lancashire and America, for both these subjects are critical." That evening at dinner, as the mature fruit of his long study, he deliberately pronounced the famous phrase: —

. . . We know quite well that the people of the Northern States have not yet drunk of the cup — they are still trying to hold it far from their lips — which all the rest of the world see they nevertheless must drink of. We may have our own opinions about slavery; we may be for or against the South; but there is no doubt that Jefferson Davis and other leaders of the South have made an army; they are making, it appears, a navy; and they have made, what is more than either, they have made a nation. . . .

Looking back, forty years afterwards, on this episode, one asked oneself painfully what sort of a lesson a young man should have drawn, for the purposes of his education, from this world-famous teaching of a very great master. In the heat of passion at the moment, one drew some harsh moral conclusions: Were they incorrect? Posed bluntly as rules of conduct, they led to the worst possible practices. As morals, one could detect no shade of difference between Gladstone and Napoleon except to the advantage of Napoleon. The private secretary saw none; he accepted the teacher in that sense; he took his lesson of political morality as learned, his notice to quit as duly served, and supposed his education to be finished.

Everyone thought so, and the whole City was in a turmoil. Any intelligent education ought to end when it is complete. One would then feel fewer hesitations and would handle a surer world. The old-fashioned logical drama required unity and sense; the actual drama is a pointless puzzle, without even an intrigue. When the curtain fell on Gladstone's speech, any student had the right to suppose the drama ended; none could have affirmed that it was about to begin; that one's painful lesson was thrown away.

Even after forty years, most people would refuse to believe it; they would still insist that Gladstone, Russell, and Palmerston were true villains of melodrama. The evidence against Gladstone in special seemed overwhelming. The word "must" can never be used by a responsible Minister of one Government towards another, as Gladstone used it. No one knew so well as he that he and his own officials and friends at Liverpool were alone "making" a rebel navy, and that Jefferson Davis had next to nothing to do with it. As Chancellor of the Exchequer he was the Minister most interested in knowing that Palmerston, Russell, and himself were banded together by mutual pledge to make the Confederacy a nation the next week, and that the Southern leaders had as yet no hope of "making a nation" but in them. Such thoughts occurred to everyone at the moment and time only added to their force. Never in the history of political turpitude had any brigand of modern civilization offered a worse example. The proof of it was that it outraged even Palmerston, who immediately put up Sir George Cornewall Lewis to repudiate the Chancellor of the Exchequer, against whom he turned his press at the same time. Palmerston had no notion of letting his hand be forced by Gladstone.

Russell did nothing of the kind; if he agreed with Palmerston, he followed Gladstone. Although he had just created a new evangel of non-intervention for Italy, and preached it like an apostle, he preached the gospel of intervention in America as though he were a mouthpiece of the Congress of Vienna. On October 13, he issued his call for the Cabinet to meet, on October 23, for discussion of the "duty of Europe to ask both parties, in the most friendly and conciliatory terms, to agree to a suspension of arms." Meanwhile Minister Adams, deeply perturbed and profoundly anxious, would betray no sign of alarm, and purposely delayed to ask explanation. The howl of anger against Gladstone became louder every day, for everyone knew that the Cabinet was called for October 23, and then could not fail to decide its policy about the United States. Lord Lyons put off his departure for America till October 25 expressly to share in the conclusions to be discussed on October 23. When Minister Adams at last requested an interview, Russell named October 23 as the day. To the last moment every act of Russell showed that, in his mind, the intervention was still in doubt.

When Minister Adams, at the interview, suggested that an explanation was due him, he watched Russell with natural interest, and reported thus: —

... His lordship took my allusion at once, though not without a slight indication of embarrassment. He said that Mr. Gladstone had been evidently much misunderstood. I must have seen in the newspapers the letters which contained his later explanations. That he had certain opinions in regard to the nature of the struggle in America, as on all public questions, just as other Englishmen had, was natural enough. And it was the fashion here for public men to express such as they held in their public addresses. Of course it was not for him to disavow anything on the part of Mr. Gladstone; but he had no idea that in saying what he had, there was a serious intention to justify any of the inferences that had been drawn from it of a disposition in the Government now to adopt a new policy. ...

A student trying to learn the processes of politics in a free government could not but ponder long on the moral to be drawn from this "explanation" of Mr. Gladstone by Earl Russell. The point set for study as the first condition of political life, was whether any politician could be believed or trusted. The question which a private secretary asked himself, in copying this despatch of October 24, 1862, was whether his father believed, or should believe, one word of Lord Russell's "embarrassment." The "truth" was not known for thirty years, but when published, seemed to be the reverse of Earl Russell's statement. Mr. Gladstone's speech had been drawn out by Russell's own policy of intervention and had no sense except to declare the "disposition in the Government now to adopt" that new policy. Earl Russell never disavowed Gladstone, although Lord Palmerston and Sir George Cornewall Lewis instantly did so. As far as the curious student could penetrate the mystery, Gladstone exactly expressed Earl Russell's intent.

As political education, this lesson was to be crucial; it would decide the law of life. All these gentlemen were superlatively honorable; if one could not believe them, Truth in politics might be ignored as a delusion. Therefore the student felt compelled to reach some sort of idea that should serve to bring the case within a general law. Minister Adams felt the same compulsion. He bluntly told Russell that while he was "willing to acquit" Gladstone of "any deliberate intention to bring on the worst effects," he was bound to say that Gladstone was doing it quite as certainly as if he had one; and to this charge, which struck more sharply at Russell's secret policy than at Gladstone's public defence of it, Russell replied as well as he could: —

. . . His lordship intimated as guardedly as possible that Lord Palmerston and other members of the Government regretted the speech, and Mr. Gladstone himself was not disinclined to correct, as far as he could, the misinterpretation which had been made of it. It was still their intention to adhere to the rule of perfect neutrality in the struggle, and to let it come to its natural end without the smallest interference, direct or otherwise. But he could not say what circumstances might happen from month to month in the future. I observed that the policy he mentioned was satisfactory to us, and asked if I was to understand him as saying that no change of it was now proposed. To which he gave his assent. . . .

Minister Adams never knew more. He retained his belief that Russell could be trusted, but that Palmerston could not. This was the diplomatic tradition, especially held by the Russian diplomats. Possibly it was sound, but it helped in no way the education of a private secretary. The cat's-paw theory[21] offered no safer clue, than the frank, old-fashioned, honest theory of villainy. Neither the one nor the other was reasonable.

No one ever told the Minister that Earl Russell, only a few hours before, had asked the Cabinet to intervene, and that the Cabinet had refused. The Minister was led to believe that the Cabinet meeting was not held, and that its decision was informal. Russell's biographer said that, "with this memorandum [of Russell's, dated October 13] the Cabinet assembled from all parts of the country on October 23; but . . . members of the Cabinet doubted the policy of moving, or moving at that time." The Duke of Newcastle and Sir George Grey[22] joined Granville in opposition. As far as known, Russell and Gladstone stood alone. "Considerations such as these prevented the matter being pursued any further."

Still no one has distinctly said that this decision was formal; perhaps the unanimity of opposition made the formal Cabinet unnecessary; but it is certain that, within an hour or two before or after this decision, "his lordship said [to the United States Minister] that the policy of the Government was to adhere to a strict neutrality and to leave this struggle to settle itself." When Mr. Adams, not satisfied even with this positive assurance, pressed for a categorical answer: "I asked him if I was to understand that policy as not now to be changed; he said: Yes!"

John Morley's comment on this matter, in the "Life of Gladstone," forty years afterwards, would have interested the Minister, as well as his private secretary: "If this relation be accurate," said Morley of a relation officially published at the time, and never questioned, "then the Foreign Secretary did not construe strict neutrality as excluding what diplomatists call good offices." For a vital lesson in politics, Earl Russell's construction of neutrality mattered little to the student, who asked only Russell's intent, and cared only to know whether his construction had any other object than to deceive the Minister.

In the grave one can afford to be lavish of charity, and possibly

Earl Russell may have been honestly glad to reassure his personal friend Mr. Adams; but to one who is still in the world even if not of it, doubts are as plenty as days. Earl Russell totally deceived the private secretary, whatever he may have done to the Minister. The policy of abstention was not settled on October 23. Only the next day, October 24, Gladstone circulated a rejoinder to G. C. Lewis, insisting on the duty of England, France, and Russia to intervene by representing, "with moral authority and force, the opinion of the civilized world upon the conditions of the case." Nothing had been decided. By some means, scarcely accidental, the French Emperor was led to think that his influence might turn the scale, and only ten days after Russell's categorical "Yes!" Napoleon officially invited him to say "No!"[23]He was more than ready to do so. Another Cabinet meeting was called for November 11, and this time Gladstone himself reports the debate: —

Nov. 11. We have had our Cabinet to-day and meet again to-morrow. I am afraid we shall do little or nothing in the business of America. But I will send you definite intelligence. Both Lords Palmerston and Russell are *right*.

Nov. 12. The United States affair has ended and not well. Lord Russell rather turned tail. He gave way without resolutely fighting out his battle. However, though we decline for the moment, the answer is put upon grounds and in terms which leave the matter very open for the future.

Nov. 13. I think the French will make our answer about America public; at least it is very possible. But I hope they may not take it as a positive refusal, or at any rate that they may themselves act in the matter. It will be clear that we concur with them, that the war should cease. Palmerston gave to Russell's proposal a feeble and half-hearted support.

Forty years afterwards, when everyone except himself, who looked on at this scene, was dead, the private secretary of 1862 read these lines with stupor, and hurried to discuss them with John Hay, who was more astounded than himself. All the world had been at cross-purposes, had misunderstood themselves and the situation, had followed wrong paths, drawn wrong conclusions, and had known none of the facts. One would have done better to draw no conclusions at all. One's diplomatic education was a long mistake.

These were the terms of this singular problem as they presented themselves to the student of diplomacy in 1862: Palmerston, on September 14, under the impression that the President was about to be driven from Washington and the Army of the Potomac dispersed, suggested to Russell that in such a case, intervention might be feasible. Russell instantly answered that, in any case, he wanted to intervene and should call a Cabinet for the purpose. Palmerston hesitated; Russell insisted; Granville protested. Meanwhile the rebel army was defeated at Antietam, September 17, and driven out of Maryland. Then Gladstone, October 7, tried to force Palmerston's hand by treating the intervention as a *fait accompli*.[24] Russell assented, but Palmerston put up Sir George Cornewall Lewis to contradict Gladstone and treated him sharply in the press, at the very moment when Russell was calling a Cabinet to make Gladstone's words good. On October 23, Russell assured Adams that no change in policy was now proposed. On the same day he had proposed it, and was voted down. Instantly Napoleon III appeared as the ally of Russell and Gladstone with a proposition which had no sense except as a bribe to Palmerston to replace[25] America, from pole to pole, in her old dependence on Europe, and to replace England in her old sovereignty of the seas, if Palmerston would support France in Mexico. The young student of diplomacy, knowing Palmerston, must have taken for granted that Palmerston inspired this motion and would support it; knowing Russell and his Whig antecedents, he would conceive that Russell must oppose it; knowing Gladstone and his lofty principles, he would not doubt that Gladstone violently denounced the scheme. If education was worth a straw, this was the only arrangement of persons that a trained student would imagine possible, and it was the arrangement actually assumed by nine men out of ten, as history. In truth, each valuation was false. Palmerston never showed favor to the scheme and gave it only "a feeble and half-hearted support." Russell gave way without resolutely fighting out "*his*" battle." The only resolute, vehement, conscientious champion of Russell, Napoleon, and Jefferson Davis was Gladstone.

Other people could afford to laugh at a young man's blunders, but to him the best part of life was thrown away if he learned such a lesson wrong. Henry James[26] had not yet taught the world to read a volume for the pleasure of seeing the lights of his burning-glass turned on alternate sides of the same figure. Psychological study was still simple, and at worst — or at best — English character was never subtle. Surely no one would believe that complexity was the trait that confused the student of Palmerston, Russell, and Gladstone. Under a very strong light human nature will always appear complex and full of contradictions, but the British statesman would appear, on the whole, among the least complex of men.

Complex these gentlemen were not. Disraeli alone might, by contrast, be called complex, but Palmerston, Russell, and Gladstone deceived only by their simplicity. Russell was the most interesting to a young man because his conduct seemed most statesmanlike. Every act of Russell, from April, 1861, to November, 1862, showed the clearest determination to break up the Union. The only point in Russell's character about which the student thought no doubt to be possible was its want of good faith. It was thoroughly dishonest, but strong. Habitually Russell said one thing and did another. He seemed unconscious of his own contradictions even when his opponents pointed them out, as they were much in the habit of doing, in the strongest language. As the student watched him deal with the Civil War in America, Russell alone showed persistence, even obstinacy, in a definite determination, which he supported, as was necessary, by the usual definite falsehoods. The young man did not complain of the falsehoods; on the contrary, he was vain of his own insight in detecting them; but he was wholly upset by the idea that Russell should think himself true.

Young Adams thought Earl Russell a statesman of the old school, clear about his objects and unscrupulous in his methods — dishonest but strong. Russell ardently asserted that he had no objects, and that though he might be weak he was above all else honest. Minister Adams leaned to Russell personally and thought him true, but officially, in practice, treated him as false. *Punch*,[27] before 1862, commonly drew Russell as a schoolboy telling lies, and afterwards as prematurely senile, at seventy. Education stopped there. No one, either in or out of England, ever offered a rational explanation of Earl Russell.

Palmerston was simple — so simple as to mislead the student altogether — but scarcely more consistent. The world thought him positive, decided, reckless; the record proved him to be cautious, careful, vacillating. Minister Adams took him for pugnacious and quarrelsome; the "Lives" of Russell, Gladstone, and Granville show him to have been good-tempered, conciliatory, avoiding quarrels. He surprised the Minister by refusing to pursue his attack on General Butler. He tried to check Russell. He scolded Gladstone. He discouraged Napoleon. Except Disraeli none of the English statesmen were so cautious as he in talking of America. Palmerston told no falsehoods; made no professions; concealed no opinions; was detected in no double-dealing. The most mortifying failure in Henry Adams's long education was that, after forty years of confirmed dislike, distrust, and detraction of Lord Palmerston, he was obliged at last to admit himself in error, and to consent in spirit — for by that time he was nearly as dead as any of them [28] — to beg his pardon.

Gladstone was quite another story, but with him a student's difficulties were less because they were shared by all the world including Gladstone himself. He was the sum of contradictions. The highest education could reach, in this analysis, only a reduction

to the absurd, but no absurdity that a young man could reach in
1862 would have approached the level that Mr. Gladstone admitted, avowed, proclaimed, in his confessions of 1896, which brought
all reason and all hope of education to a still-stand: —

I have yet to record an undoubted error, the most singular and
palpable, I may add the least excusable of them all, especially since
it was committed so late as in the year 1862 when I had outlived half
a century. . . . I declared in the heat of the American struggle that
Jefferson Davis had made a nation. . . . Strange to say, this declaration, most unwarrantable to be made by a Minister of the Crown
with no authority other than his own, was not due to any feeling of
partisanship for the South or hostility to the North. . . . I really,
though most strangely, believed that it was an act of friendliness to
all America to recognize that the struggle was virtually at an end. . . .
That my opinion was founded upon a false estimate of the facts was
the very least part of my fault. I did not perceive the gross impro-
priety of such an utterance from a Cabinet Minister of a power allied
in blood and language, and bound to loyal neutrality; the case being
further exaggerated by the fact that we were already, so to speak,
under indictment before the world for not (as was alleged) having
strictly enforced the laws of neutrality in the matter of the cruisers.
My offence was indeed only a mistake, but one of incredible grossness,
and with such consequences of offence and alarm attached to it, that
my failing to perceive them justly exposed me to very severe blame.
It illustrates vividly that incapacity which my mind so long retained,
and perhaps still exhibits, an incapacity of viewing subjects all
round. . . .

Long and patiently — more than patiently — sympathetically, did the private secretary, forty years afterwards in the
twilight of a life of study, read and re-read and reflect upon this
confession. Then, it seemed, he had seen nothing correctly at the
time. His whole theory of conspiracy — of policy — of logic and
connection in the affairs of man, resolved itself into "incredible
grossness." He felt no rancor, for he had won the game;[29] he forgave, since he must admit, the "incapacity of viewing subjects all
round" which had so nearly cost him his life and fortune; he was

willing even to believe. He noted, without irritation, that Mr. Gladstone, in his confession, had not alluded to the understanding between Russell, Palmerston, and himself; had even wholly left out his most "incredible" act, his ardent support of Napoleon's policy, a policy which even Palmerston and Russell had supported feebly, with only half a heart. All this was indifferent. Granting, in spite of evidence, that Gladstone had no set plan of breaking up the Union; that he was party to no conspiracy; that he saw none of the results of his acts which were clear to everyone else; granting in short what the English themselves seemed at last to conclude — that Gladstone was not quite sane; that Russell was verging on senility; and that Palmerston had lost his nerve — what sort of education should have been the result of it? How should it have affected one's future opinions and acts?

Politics cannot stop to study psychology. Its methods are rough; its judgments rougher still. All this knowledge would not have affected either the Minister or his son in 1862. The sum of the individuals would still have seemed, to the young man, one individual — a single will or intention — bent on breaking up the Union "as a diminution of a dangerous power." The Minister would still have found his interest in thinking Russell friendly and Palmerston hostile. The individual would still have been identical with the mass. The problem would have been the same; the answer equally obscure. Every student would, like the private secretary, answer for himself alone.

CHAPTER XI

The Battle of the Rams [1] *(1863)*

MINISTER ADAMS troubled himself little about what
he did not see of an enemy. His son, a nervous animal, made life a terror by seeing too much. Minister
Adams played his hand as it came, and seldom credited his opponents with greater intelligence than his own. Earl Russell suited
him; perhaps a certain personal sympathy united them; and indeed Henry Adams never saw Russell without being amused by
his droll likeness to John Quincy Adams. Apart from this shadowy personal relation, no doubt the Minister was diplomatically
right; he had nothing to lose and everything to gain by making a
friend of the Foreign Secretary, and whether Russell were true or
false mattered less, because, in either case, the American Legation could act only as though he were false. Had the Minister
known Russell's determined effort to betray and ruin him in October, 1862, [2] he could have scarcely used stronger expressions than
he did in 1863. Russell must have been greatly annoyed by Sir
Robert Collier's hint of collusion with the rebel agents in the
Alabama Case, but he hardened himself to hear the same innu-
endo repeated in nearly every note from the Legation. As time went
on, Russell was compelled, though slowly, to treat the American Minister as serious. He admitted nothing so unwillingly, for
the nullity or fatuity of the Washington Government was his
idée fixe; [3] but after the failure of his last effort for joint intervention on November 12, 1862, only one week elapsed before he received a note from Minister Adams repeating his charges about
the Alabama, and asking in very plain language for redress.
Perhaps Russell's mind was naturally slow to understand the force
of sudden attack, or perhaps age had affected it; this was one of
the points that greatly interested a student, but young men have

a passion for regarding their elders as senile, which was only in part warranted in this instance by observing that Russell's generation were mostly senile from youth. They had never got beyond 1815.[4] Both Palmerston and Russell were in this case. Their senility was congenital, like Gladstone's Oxford training and High Church illusions,[5] which caused wild eccentricities in his judgment. Russell could not conceive that he had misunderstood and mismanaged Minister Adams from the start, and when, after November 12, he found himself on the defensive, with Mr. Adams taking daily a stronger tone, he showed mere confusion and helplessness.

Thus, whatever the theory, the action of diplomacy had to be the same. Minister Adams was obliged to imply collusion between Russell and the rebels. He could not even stop at criminal negligence. If, by an excess of courtesy, the Minister were civil enough to admit that the escape of the Alabama had been due to criminal negligence, he could make no such concession in regard to the ironclad rams which the Lairds[6] were building; for no one could be so simple as to believe that two armored ships-of-war could be built publicly, under the eyes of the Government, and go to sea like the Alabama, without active and incessant collusion. The longer Earl Russell kept on his mask of assumed ignorance, the more violently, in the end, the Minister would have to tear it off. Whatever Mr. Adams might personally think of Earl Russell, he must take the greatest possible diplomatic liberties with him if this crisis were allowed to arrive.

As the spring of 1863 drew on, the vast field cleared itself for action. A campaign more beautiful — better suited for training the mind of a youth eager for training — has not often unrolled itself for study, from the beginning, before a young man perched in so commanding a position. Very slowly, indeed, after two years of solitude, one began to feel the first faint flush of new and imperial life. One was twenty-five years old, and quite ready to assert it; some of one's friends were wearing stars on their collars; some had won stars of a more enduring kind. At moments one's breath came quick. One began to dream the sensation of wielding unmeasured power. The sense came, like vertigo, for an instant, and passed, leaving the brain a little dazed, doubtful, shy. With an intensity more painful than that of any Shakespearean drama, men's eyes were fastened on the armies in the field. Little by little, at first only as a shadowy chance of what might be, if things could be rightly done, one began to feel that, somewhere behind the chaos in Washington power was taking shape; that it was massed and guided as it had not been before. Men seemed to have learned their business — at a cost that ruined — and perhaps too late. A private secretary knew better than most people how much of the new power was to be swung in London, and almost exactly when; but the diplomatic campaign had to wait for the military campaign to lead. The student could only study.

Life never could know more than a single such climax. In that form, education reached its limits. As the first great blows began to fall, one curled up in bed in the silence of night, to listen with incredulous hope. As the huge masses struck, one after another, with the precision of machinery, the opposing mass, the world shivered. Such development of power was unknown. The magnificent resistance and the return shocks heightened the suspense. During the July days Londoners were stupid with unbelief. They were learning from the Yankees how to fight.

An American saw in a flash what all this meant to England, for one's mind was working with the acceleration of the machine at home; but Englishmen were not quick to see their blunders. One had ample time to watch the process, and had even a little time to gloat over the repayment of old scores. News of Vicksburg[7] and Gettysburg[8] reached London one Sunday afternoon, and it happened that Henry Adams was asked for that evening to some small reception at the house of Monckton Milnes. He went early in order to exchange a word or two of congratulation before the rooms should fill, and on arriving he found only the ladies in the drawing-room; the gentlemen were still sitting over their wine. Presently they came in, and, as luck would have it, Delane of the *Times* came first. When Milnes caught sight of his young American friend, with a whoop of triumph he rushed to throw both arms about his neck and kiss him on both cheeks. Men of later birth who knew too little to realize the passions of 1863 —backed by those of 1813[9]—and reinforced by those of 1763 — might conceive that such publicity embarrassed a private secretary who came from Boston and called himself shy; but that evening, for the first time in his life, he happened not to be thinking of himself. He was thinking of Delane, whose eye caught his, at the moment of Milnes's embrace. Delane probably regarded it as a piece of Milnes's foolery; he had never heard of young Adams, and never dreamed of his resentment at being ridiculed in the *Times*;[10] he had no suspicion of the thought floating in the mind of the American Minister's son, for the British mind is the slowest of all minds, as the files of the *Times* proved,[11] and the capture of Vicksburg had not yet penetrated Delane's thick cortex of fixed ideas. Even if he had read Adams's thought, he would have felt for it only the usual amused British contempt for all that he had not been taught at school. It needed a whole generation for the *Times* to reach Milnes's standpoint.

Had the Minister's son carried out the thought, he would surely have sought an introduction to Delane on the spot, and assured him that he regarded his own personal score as cleared off — sufficiently settled, then and there — because his father had assumed the debt, and was going to deal with Mr. Delane himself. "You come next!" would have been the friendly warning. For nearly a year the private secretary had watched the board arranging itself for the collision between the Legation and Delane who stood behind the Palmerston Ministry. Mr. Adams had been steadily strengthened and reinforced from Washington in view of the final struggle. The situation had changed since the Trent Affair. The work was efficiently done; the organization was fairly complete. No doubt, the Legation itself was still as weakly manned and had as poor an outfit as the Legations of Guatemala or Portugal. Congress was always jealous of its diplomatic service, and the Chairman of the Committee of Foreign Relations was not likely to press assistance on the Minister to England. For the Legation not an additional clerk was offered or asked. The Secretary, the Assistant Secretary, and the private secretary did all the work that the Minister did not do. A clerk at five dollars a week would have done the work as well or better, but the Minister could trust no clerk; without express authority he could admit no one into the Legation; he strained a point already by admitting his son. Congress and its committees were the proper judges of what was best for the public service, and if the arrangement seemed good to them, it was satisfactory to a private secretary who profited by it more than they did. A great staff would have suppressed him. The whole Legation was a sort of improvised, volunteer service, and he was a volunteer with the rest. He was rather better off than the rest, because he was invisible and unknown. Better or worse, he did his work with the others, and if the secretaries made any remarks about Congress, they made no complaints, and knew that none would have received a moment's attention.

If they were not satisfied with Congress, they were satisfied with Secretary Seward. Without appropriations for the regular service, he had done great things for its support. If the Minister had no secretaries, he had a staff of active consuls; he had a well-organized press; efficient legal support; and a swarm of social allies permeating all classes. All he needed was a victory in the field, and Secretary Stanton[12] undertook that part of diplomacy. Vicksburg and Gettysburg cleared the board, and, at the end of July, 1863, Minister Adams was ready to deal with Earl Russell or Lord Palmerston or Mr. Gladstone or Mr. Delane, or anyone else who stood in his way; and by the necessity of the case, was obliged to deal with all of them shortly.

Even before the military climax at Vicksburg and Gettysburg, the Minister had been compelled to begin his attack; but this was history, and had nothing to do with education.[13] The private secretary copied the notes into his private books, and that was all the share he had in the matter, except to talk in private.

No more volunteer services were needed; the volunteers were in a manner sent to the rear; the movement was too serious for skirmishing. All that a secretary could hope to gain from the affair was experience and knowledge of politics. He had a chance to measure the motive forces of men; their qualities of character; their foresight; their tenacity of purpose.

In the Legation no great confidence was felt in stopping the rams. Whatever the reason, Russell seemed immovable. Had his efforts for intervention in September, 1862, been known to the Legation in September, 1863, the Minister must surely have admitted that Russell had, from the first, meant to force his plan of intervention on his colleagues. Every separate step since April, 1861, led to this final coercion. Although Russell's hostile activity of 1862 was still secret — and remained secret for some five-and-twenty years — his *animus*[14] seemed to be made clear by his steady refusal to stop the rebel armaments. Little by little, Minister Adams lost hope. With loss of hope came the raising of tone, until at last, after stripping Russell of every rag of defence and excuse, he closed by leaving him loaded with connivance in the rebel armaments, and ended by the famous sentence: "It would be superfluous in me to point out to your lordship that this is war!"[15]

What the Minister meant by this remark was his own affair; what the private secretary understood by it, was a part of his education. Had his father ordered him to draft an explanatory paragraph to expand the idea as he grasped it, he would have continued thus:—

"It would be superfluous: 1st. Because Earl Russell not only knows it already, but has meant it from the start. 2d. Because it is the only logical and necessary consequence of his unvarying action. 3d. Because Mr. Adams is not pointing out to *him* that 'this is war,' but is pointing it out to the world, to complete the record."

This would have been the matter-of-fact sense in which the private secretary copied into his books the matter-of-fact statement with which, without passion or excitement, the Minister announced that a state of war existed. To his copying eye, as clerk, the words, though on the extreme verge of diplomatic propriety, merely stated a fact, without novelty, fancy, or rhetoric. The fact had to be stated in order to make clear the issue. The war was Russell's war — Adams only accepted it.

Russell's reply to this note of September 5 reached the Legation on September 8, announcing at last to the anxious secretaries that "instructions have been issued which will prevent the departure of the two ironclad vessels from Liverpool." The members of the modest Legation in Portland Place accepted it as Grant had accepted the capitulation of Vicksburg. The private secretary conceived that, as Secretary Stanton had struck and crushed by superior weight the rebel left on the Mississippi, so Secretary Seward had struck and crushed the rebel right in England, and he never felt a doubt as to the nature of the battle. Though Minister Adams should stay in office till he were ninety, he would never fight another campaign of life and death like this; and though the private secretary should covet and attain every office in the gift of President or people, he would never again find education to compare with the life-and-death alternative of this two-year-and-a-half struggle in London, as it had racked and thumb-screwed him in its shifting phases; but its practical value as education turned on his correctness of judgment in measuring the men and their forces. He felt respect for Russell as for Palmerston because they represented traditional England and an English policy, respectable enough in itself, but which, for four generations, every Adams had fought and exploited as the chief source of his political fortunes.[16] As he understood it, Russell had followed this policy steadily, ably, even vigorously, and had brought it to the moment of execution. Then he had met wills stronger than his own, and, after persevering to the last possible instant, had been beaten. Lord North[17] and George Canning had a like experience. [18]

This was only the idea of a boy, but, as far as he ever knew, it was also the idea of his Government. For once, the volunteer secretary was satisfied with his Government. Commonly the self-respect of a secretary, private or public, depends on, and is proportional to, the severity of his criticism, but in this case the English campaign seemed to him as creditable to the State Department as the Vicksburg campaign to the War Department, and more decisive. It was well planned, well prepared, and well executed. He could never discover a mistake in it. Possibly he was biassed by personal interest, but his chief reason for trusting his own judgment was that he thought himself to be one of only half a dozen persons who knew something about it. When others criticised Mr. Seward, he was rather indifferent to their opinions because he thought they hardly knew what they were talking about, and could not be taught without living over again the London life of 1862. To him Secretary Seward seemed immensely strong and steady in leadership; but this was no discredit to Russell or Palmerston or Gladstone. They, too, had shown power, patience and steadiness of purpose. They had persisted for two years and a half in their plan for breaking up the Union, and had yielded at last only in the jaws of war. After a long and desperate struggle, the American Minister had trumped their best card and won the game.

Again and again, in after life, he went back over the ground to see whether he could detect error on either side. He found none. At every stage the steps were both probable and proved. All the more he was disconcerted that Russell should indignantly and with growing energy, to his dying day, deny and resent the axiom of Adams's whole contention, that from the first he meant to break up the Union. Russell affirmed that he meant nothing of the sort;

that he had meant nothing at all; that he meant to do right; that he did not know what he meant. Driven from one defence after another, he pleaded at last, like Gladstone, that he had no defence. Concealing all he could conceal — burying in profound secrecy his attempt to break up the Union in the autumn of 1862 — he affirmed the louder his scrupulous good faith. What was worse for the private secretary, to the total derision and despair of the lifelong effort for education, as the final result of combined practice, experience, and theory — he proved it.

Henry Adams had, as he thought, suffered too much from Russell to admit any plea in his favor; but he came to doubt whether this admission really favored him. Not until long after Earl Russell's death was the question reopened. Russell had quitted office in 1866; he died in 1878; the biography was published in 1889. During the Alabama controversy and the Geneva Conference in 1872,[19] his course as Foreign Secretary had been sharply criticised, and he had been compelled to see England pay more than £3,000,000 penalty for his errors. On the other hand, he brought forward — or his biographer for him — evidence tending to prove that he was not consciously dishonest, and that he had, in spite of appearances, acted without collusion, agreement, plan, or policy, as far as concerned the rebels. He had stood alone, as was his nature. Like Gladstone, he had thought himself right.

In the end, Russell entangled himself in a hopeless ball of admissions, denials, contradictions, and resentments which led even his old colleagues to drop his defence, as they dropped Gladstone's; but this was not enough for the student of diplomacy who had made a certain theory his law of life, and wanted to hold Russell up against himself; to show that he had foresight and persistence of which he was unaware. The effort became hopeless when the biography in 1889 published papers which upset all that Henry Adams had taken for diplomatic education; yet he sat down once more, when past sixty years old, to see whether he could unravel the skein.

Of the obstinate effort to bring about an armed intervention, on the lines marked out by Russell's letter to Palmerston from Gotha, 17 September, 1862, nothing could be said beyond Gladstone's plea in excuse for his speech in pursuance of the same effort, that it was "the most singular and palpable error," "the least excusable," "a mistake of incredible grossness," which passed defence; but while Gladstone threw himself on the mercy of the public for his speech, he attempted no excuse for Lord Russell who led him into the "incredible grossness" of announcing the Foreign Secretary's intent. Gladstone's offence, "singular and palpable," was not the speech alone, but its cause — the policy that inspired the speech. "I weakly supposed . . . I really, though most strangely, believed that it was an act of friendliness."[20]Whatever absurdity Gladstone supposed, Russell supposed nothing of the sort. Neither he nor Palmerston "most strangely believed" in any proposition so obviously and palpably absurd, nor did Napoleon delude himself with philanthropy. Gladstone, even in his confession, mixed up policy, speech, motives, and persons, as though he were trying to confuse chiefly himself.

There Gladstone's activity seems to have stopped. He did not reappear in the matter of the rams. The rebel influence shrank in 1863, as far as is known, to Lord Russell alone, who wrote on September 1[21] that he could not interfere in any way with those vessels, and thereby brought on himself Mr. Adams's declaration of war on September 5. A student held that, in this refusal, he was merely following his policy of September, 1862, and of every step he had taken since 1861.

The student was wrong. Russell proved that he had been feeble, timid, mistaken, senile, but not dishonest. The evidence is convincing. The Lairds had built these ships in reliance on the known opinion of the law-officers that the statute did not apply, and a jury would not convict. Minister Adams replied that, in this case, the statute should be amended, or the ships stopped by exercise of the political power. Bethell rejoined that this would be a violation of neutrality; one must preserve the *status quo*. Tacitly Russell connived with Laird, and, had he meant to interfere, he was bound to warn Laird that the defect of the statute would no longer protect him, but he allowed the builders to go on till the ships were ready for sea. Then, on September 3, two days before Mr. Adams's "superfluous" letter, he wrote to Lord Palmerston begging for help; "The conduct of the gentlemen who have contracted for the two ironclads at Birkenhead is so very suspicious," — he began, and this he actually wrote in good faith and deep confidence to Lord Palmerston, his chief, calling "the conduct" of the rebel agents "suspicious" when no one else in Europe or America felt any suspicion about it, because the whole question turned not on the rams, but on the technical scope of the Foreign Enlistment Act, — "that I have thought it necessary to direct that they should be detained," not, of course, under the statute, but on the ground urged by the American Minister, of international obligation above the statute. "The Solicitor General has been consulted and concurs in the measure as one of policy though not of strict law. We shall thus test the law, and, if we have to pay damages, we have satisfied the opinion which prevails here as well as in America that that kind of neutral hostility should not be allowed to go on without some attempt to stop it."[22]

For naïveté that would be unusual in an unpaid attaché of Legation, this sudden leap from his own to his opponent's ground, after two years and a half of dogged resistance, might have roused Palmerston to inhuman scorn, but instead of derision, well earned by Russell's old attacks on himself, Palmerston met the appeal with wonderful loyalty. "On consulting the law officers he found that there was no lawful ground for meddling with the ironclads," or, in unprofessional language, that he could trust neither his law officers nor a Liverpool jury; and therefore he suggested buying the ships for the British Navy. As proof of "criminal negligence" in the past, this suggestion seemed decisive, but Russell, by this time, was floundering in other troubles of negligence, for he had neglected to notify the American Minister. He should have done so at once, on September 3. Instead he waited till September 4, and then merely said that the matter was under "serious and anxious consideration." This note did not reach the Legation till three o'clock on the afternoon of September 5 — after the "superfluous" declaration of war had been sent. Thus, Lord Russell had sacrificed the Lairds: had cost his Ministry the price of two ironclads, besides the Alabama Claims — say, in round numbers, twenty million dollars — and had put himself in the position of appearing to yield only to a threat of war. Finally he wrote to the Admiralty a letter which, from the American point of view, would have sounded youthful from an Eton schoolboy: —

September 14, 1863.

MY DEAR DUKE: —
It is of the utmost importance and urgency that the ironclads building at Birkenhead should not go to America to break the blockade. They belong to Monsieur Bravay of Paris. If you will offer to buy them on the part of the Admiralty you will get money's worth if he accepts your offer; and if he does not, it will be presumptive proof that they are already bought by the Confederates. I should state that we have suggested to the Turkish Government to buy them; but you can easily settle that matter with the Turks. . . .

The hilarity of the secretaries in Portland Place would have been loud had they seen this letter and realized the muddle of difficulties into which Earl Russell had at last thrown himself under the impulse of the American Minister; but, nevertheless, these letters upset from top to bottom the results of the private secretary's diplomatic education forty years after he had supposed it complete. They made a picture different from anything he had conceived and rendered worthless his whole painful diplomatic experience.

To reconstruct, when past sixty, an education useful for any practical purpose, is no practical problem, and Adams saw no use in attacking it as only theoretical. He no longer cared whether he understood human nature or not; he understood quite as much of it as he wanted; but he found in the "Life of Gladstone" (ii, 464) a remark several times repeated that gave him matter for curious thought. "I *always* hold," said Mr. Gladstone, "that politicians are the men whom, as a rule, it is most difficult to comprehend"; and he added, by way of strengthening it: "For my own part, I never have thus understood, or thought I understood, *above one or two.*"

Earl Russell was certainly not one of the two.

Henry Adams thought he also had understood one or two; but the American type was more familiar. Perhaps this was the sufficient result of his diplomatic education; it seemed to be the whole.

CHAPTER XII

Eccentricity (1863)

KNOWLEDGE of human nature is the beginning and end of political education, but several years of arduous study in the neighborhood of Westminster[1] led Henry Adams to think that knowledge of English human nature had little or no value outside of England. In Paris, such a habit stood in one's way; in America, it roused all the instincts of native jealousy. The English mind was one-sided, eccentric, systematically unsystematic, and logically illogical. The less one knew of it, the better.

This heresy, which would scarcely have been allowed to penetrate a Boston mind — it would, indeed, have been shut out by instinct as a rather foolish exaggeration — rested on an experience which Henry Adams gravely thought he had a right to think conclusive — for him. That it should be conclusive for anyone else never occurred to him, since he had no thought of educating anybody else. For him — alone — the less English education he got, the better!

For several years, under the keenest incitement to watchfulness, he observed the English mind in contact with itself and other minds. Especially with the American the contact was interesting because the limits and defects of the American mind were one of the favorite topics of the European. From the old-world point of view, the American had no mind; he had an economic thinking-machine which could work only on a fixed line. The American mind exasperated the European as a buzz-saw might exasperate a pine forest. The English mind disliked the French mind because it was antagonistic, unreasonable, perhaps hostile, but recognized it as at least a thought. The American mind was not a thought at all; it was a convention, superficial, narrow, and ignorant; a mere cutting instrument, practical, economical, sharp, and direct.

The English themselves hardly conceived that their mind was either economical, sharp, or direct; but the defect that most struck an American was its enormous waste in eccentricity. Americans needed and used their whole energy, and applied it with close economy; but English society was eccentric by law and for sake of the eccentricity itself.

The commonest phrase overheard at an English club or dinner-table was that So-and-So "is quite mad." It was no offence to So-and-So; it hardly distinguished him from his fellows; and when applied to a public man, like Gladstone, it was qualified by epithets much more forcible. Eccentricity was so general as to become hereditary distinction. It made the chief charm of English society as well as its chief terror.

The American delighted in Thackeray as a satirist, but Thackeray quite justly maintained that he was not a satirist at all, and that his pictures of English society were exact and good-natured. The American, who could not believe it, fell back on Dickens, who, at all events, had the vice of exaggeration to extravagance, but Dickens's English audience thought the exaggeration rather in manner or style, than in types. Mr. Gladstone himself went to see Sothern act Dundreary,[2] and laughed till his face was distorted — not because Dundreary was exaggerated, but because he was ridiculously like the types that Gladstone had seen — or might have seen — in any club in Pall Mall. Society swarmed with exaggerated characters; it contained little else.

Often this eccentricity bore all the marks of strength; perhaps it was actual exuberance of force, a birthmark of genius. Boston thought so. The Bostonian called it national character — native vigor — robustness — honesty — courage. He respected and feared it. British self-assertion, bluff, brutal, blunt as it was, seemed to him a better and nobler thing than the acuteness of the Yankee or the polish of the Parisian. Perhaps he was right.

These questions of taste, of feeling, of inheritance, need no settlement. Every one carries his own inch-rule of taste, and amuses himself by applying it, triumphantly, wherever he travels. Whatever others thought, the cleverest Englishmen held that the national eccentricity needed correction, and were beginning to correct it. The savage satires of Dickens and the gentler ridicule of Matthew Arnold against the British middle class were but a part of the rebellion, for the middle class were no worse than their neighbors in the eyes of an American in 1863; they were even a very little better in the sense that one could appeal to their interests, while a university man, like Gladstone, stood outside of argument. From none of them could a young American afford to borrow ideas.

The private secretary, like every other Bostonian, began by regarding British eccentricity as a force. Contact with it, in the shape of Palmerston, Russell, and Gladstone, made him hesitate; he saw his own national type — his father, Weed, Evarts, for instance — deal with the British, and show itself certainly not the weaker; certainly sometimes the stronger. Biassed though he were, he could hardly be biassed to such a degree as to mistake the effects of force on others, and while — labor as he might — Earl Russell and his state papers seemed weak to a secretary, he could not see that they seemed strong to Russell's own followers. Russell might be dishonest or he might be merely obtuse — the English type might be brutal or might be only stupid — but strong, in either case, it was not, nor did it seem strong to Englishmen.

Eccentricity was not always a force; Americans were deeply interested in deciding whether it was always a weakness. Evidently, on the hustings or in Parliament, among eccentricities, eccentricity was at home; but in private society the question was not easy to answer. That English society was infinitely more amusing because of its eccentricities, no one denied. Barring the atrocious insolence and brutality which Englishmen and especially Englishwomen showed to each other — very rarely, indeed, to foreigners — English society was much more easy and tolerant than American.

One must expect to be treated with exquisite courtesy this week and be totally forgotten the next, but this was the way of the world, and education consisted in learning to turn one's back on others with the same unconscious indifference that others showed among themselves. The smart of wounded vanity lasted no long time with a young man about town who had little vanity to smart, and who, in his own country, would have found himself in no better position. He had nothing to complain of. No one was ever brutal to him. On the contrary, he was much better treated than ever he was likely to be in Boston — let alone New York or Washington — and if his reception varied inconceivably between extreme courtesy and extreme neglect, it merely proved that he had become, or was becoming, at home. Not from a sense of personal griefs or disappointments did he labor over this part of the social problem, but only because his education was becoming English, and the further it went, the less it promised.

By natural affinity the social eccentrics commonly sympathized with political eccentricity. The English mind took naturally to rebellion — when foreign — and it felt particular confidence in the Southern Confederacy because of its combined attributes — foreign rebellion of English blood — which came nearer ideal eccentricity than could be reached by Poles, Hungarians, Italians or Frenchmen. All the English eccentrics rushed into the ranks of rebel sympathizers, leaving few but well-balanced minds to attach themselves to the cause of the Union. None of the English leaders on the Northern side were marked eccentrics. William E. Forster was a practical, hard-headed Yorkshireman, whose chief ideals in politics took shape as working arrangements on an economical base. Cobden, considering the one-sided conditions of his life, was remarkably well balanced. John Bright was stronger in his expressions than either of them, but with all his self-assertion he stuck to his point, and his point was practical. He did not, like Gladstone, box the compass of thought, "furiously earnest," as Monckton Milnes said, "on both sides of every question"; he was rather, on the whole, a consistent conservative of the old Commonwealth[3] type, and seldom had to defend inconsistencies. Monckton Milnes himself was regarded as an eccentric, chiefly by those who did not know him, but his fancies and hobbies were only ideas a little in advance of the time; his manner was eccentric but not his mind, as anyone could see who read a page of his poetry. None of them, except Milnes, was a university man. As a rule, the Legation was troubled very little, if at all, by indiscretions, extravagances, or contradictions among its English friends. Their work was always judicious, practical, well considered, and almost too cautious. The "cranks" were all rebels, and the list was portentous. Perhaps it might be headed by old Lord Brougham,[4] who had the audacity to appear at a July 4th reception at the Legation, led by Joe Parkes, and claim his old credit as "Attorney General to Mr. Madison." The Church was rebel, but the dissenters were mostly with the Union.[5] The universities were rebel, but the university men who enjoyed most public confidence — like Lord Granville, Sir George Cornewall Lewis, Lord Stanley, Sir George Grey [6]— took infinite pains to be neutral for fear of being thought eccentric. To most observers, as well as to the *Times*, the *Morning Post*, and the *Standard*, a vast majority of the English people seemed to follow the professional eccentrics; even the emotional philanthropists took that direction; Lord Shaftesbury[7] and Carlisle,[8] Fowell Buxton,[9] and Gladstone, threw their sympathies on the side which they should naturally have opposed, and did so for no reason except their eccentricity; but the "canny" Scots and Yorkshiremen were cautious.

This eccentricity did not mean strength. The proof of it was the mismanagement of the rebel interests. No doubt the first cause of this trouble lay in the Richmond Government[10] itself. No one understood why Jefferson Davis chose Mr. Mason[11] as his agent for London at the same time that he made so good a choice as Mr. Slidell[12] for Paris. The Confederacy had plenty of excellent men to send to London, but few who were less fitted than Mason. Possibly Mason had a certain amount of common sense, but he seemed to have nothing else, and in London society he counted merely as one eccentric more. He enjoyed a great opportunity; he might even have figured as a new Benjamin Franklin with all society at his feet; he might have roared as lion of the season and made the social path of the American Minister almost impassable; but Mr. Adams had his usual luck in enemies, who were always his most valuable allies if his friends only let them alone.[13] Mason was his greatest diplomatic triumph. He had his collision with Palmerston; he drove Russell off the field; he swept the board before Cockburn[14]; he overbore Slidell; but he never lifted a finger against Mason, who became his bulwark of defence.

Possibly Jefferson Davis and Mr. Mason shared two defects in common which might have led them into this serious mistake. Neither could have had much knowledge of the world, and both must have been unconscious of humor. Yet at the same time with Mason, President Davis sent out Slidell to France and Mr. Lamar[15] to Russia. Some twenty years later, in the shifting search for the education he never found, Adams became closely intimate at Washington with Lamar, then Senator from Mississippi, who had grown to be one of the calmest, most reasonable and most amiable Union men in the United States, and quite unusual in social charm. In 1860 he passed for the worst of Southern fire-eaters, but he was an eccentric by environment, not by nature; above all his Southern eccentricities, he had tact and humor; and perhaps this was a reason why Mr. Davis sent him abroad with the others, on a futile mission to St. Petersburg. He would have done better in London, in place of Mason. London society would have delighted in him; his stories would have won success; his manners would have made him loved; his oratory would have swept every audience; even Monckton Milnes could never have resisted the temptation of having him to breakfast between Lord Shaftesbury and the Bishop of Oxford.[16]

Lamar liked to talk of his brief career in diplomacy, but he never spoke of Mason. He never alluded to Confederate management or criticised Jefferson Davis's administration. The subject that amused him was his English allies. At that moment — the early summer of 1863 — the rebel party in England were full of confidence, and felt strong enough to challenge the American Legation to a show of power. They knew better than the Legation what they could depend upon: that the law officers and commissioners of customs at Liverpool dared not prosecute the iron-clad ships; that Palmerston, Russell, and Gladstone were ready to recognize the Confederacy; that the Emperor Napoleon would offer them every inducement to do it. In a manner they owned Liverpool and especially the firm of Laird who were building their ships. The political member of the Laird firm was Lindsay,[17] about whom the whole web of rebel interests clung — rams, cruisers, munitions, and Confederate loan; social introductions and parliamentary tactics. The firm of Laird, with a certain dignity, claimed to be champion of England's navy; and public opinion, in the summer of 1863, still inclined towards them.

Never was there a moment when eccentricity, if it were a force, should have had more value to the rebel interest; and the managers must have thought so, for they adopted or accepted as their champion an eccentric of eccentrics; a type of 1820; a sort of Brougham of Sheffield,[18] notorious for poor judgment and worse temper. Mr. Roebuck[19] had been a tribune of the people, and, like tribunes of most other peoples, in growing old, had grown fatuous. He was regarded by the friends of the Union as rather a comical personage — a favorite subject for *Punch* to laugh at — with a bitter tongue and a mind enfeebled even more than common by the political epidemic of egotism. In all England they could have found no opponent better fitted to give away his own case. No American man of business would have paid him attention; yet the Lairds, who certainly knew their own affairs best, let Roebuck represent them and take charge of their interests.

With Roebuck's doings, the private secretary had no concern except that the Minister sent him down to the House of Commons on June 30, 1863, to report the result of Roebuck's motion to recognize the Southern Confederacy. The Legation felt no anxiety, having Vicksburg already in its pocket, and Bright and Forster to say so;[20] but the private secretary went down and was admitted under the gallery on the left, to listen, with great content, while John Bright, with astonishing force, caught and shook and tossed Roebuck, as a big mastiff shakes a wiry, ill-conditioned, toothless, bad-tempered Yorkshire terrier. The private secretary felt an artistic sympathy with Roebuck, for, from time to time, by way of practice, Bright in a friendly way was apt to shake him too, and he knew how it was done. The manner counted for more than the words. The scene was interesting, but the result was not in doubt.

All the more sharply he was excited, near the year 1879, in Washington, by hearing Lamar begin a story after dinner, which, little by little, became dramatic, recalling the scene in the House of Commons. The story, as well as one remembered, began with Lamar's failure to reach St. Petersburg at all, and his consequent detention in Paris waiting instructions. The motion to recognize the Confederacy was about to be made, and, in prospect of the debate, Mr. Lindsay collected a party at his villa on the Thames to bring the rebel agents into relations with Roebuck. Lamar was sent for, and came. After much conversation of a general sort, such as is the usual object or resource of the English Sunday, finding himself alone with Roebuck, Lamar, by way of showing interest, bethought himself of John Bright and asked Roebuck whether he expected Bright to take part in the debate: "No, sir!" said Roebuck sententiously; "Bright and I have met before. It was the old story — the story of the sword-fish and the whale! No, sir! Mr. Bright will not cross swords with me again!"

Thus assured, Lamar went with the more confidence to the House on the appointed evening, and was placed under the gallery, on the right, where he listened to Roebuck and followed the debate with such enjoyment as an experienced debater feels in these contests, until, as he said, he became aware that a man, with a singularly rich voice and imposing manner, had taken the floor, and was giving Roebuck the most deliberate and tremendous pounding he ever witnessed, "until at last," concluded Lamar, "it dawned on my mind that the sword-fish was getting the worst of it."

Lamar told the story in the spirit of a joke against himself rather than against Roebuck; but such jokes must have been unpleasantly common in the experience of the rebel agents. They were surrounded by cranks of the worst English species, who distorted their natural eccentricities and perverted their judgment. Roebuck may have been an extreme case, since he was actually in his dotage,[21] yet this did not prevent the Lairds from accepting his lead, or the House from taking him seriously. Extreme eccentricity was no bar, in England, to extreme confidence; sometimes it seemed a recommendation; and unless it caused financial loss, it rather helped popularity.

The question whether British eccentricity was ever strength weighed heavily in the balance of education. That Roebuck should mislead the rebel agents on so strange a point as that of Bright's courage was doubly characteristic because the Southern people themselves had this same barbaric weakness of attributing want of courage to opponents, and owed their ruin chiefly to such ignorance of the world. Bright's courage was almost as irrational as that of the rebels themselves. Everyone knew that he had the courage of a prize-fighter. He struck, in succession, pretty nearly every man in England that could be reached by a blow, and when he could not reach the individual he struck the class, or when the class was too small for him, the whole people of England. At times he had the whole country on his back. He could not act on the defensive; his mind required attack. Even among friends at the dinner-table he talked as though he were denouncing them, or some one else, on a platform; he measured his phrases, built his sentences, cumulated his effects, and pounded his opponents, real or imagined. His humor was glow, like iron at dull heat; his blow was elementary, like the thrash of a whale.

One day in early spring, March 26, 1863, the Minister requested his private secretary to attend a Trades Unions Meeting at St. James's Hall, which was the result of Professor Beesly's[22] patient efforts to unite Bright and the Trades Unions on an American platform. The secretary went to the meeting and made a report[23] which reposes somewhere on file in the State Department to this day, as harmless as such reports should be; but it contained no mention of what interested young Adams most — Bright's psychology. With singular skill and oratorical power, Bright managed at the outset, in his opening paragraph, to insult or outrage every class of Englishman commonly considered respectable, and, for fear of any escaping, he insulted them repeatedly under consecutive heads. The rhetorical effect was tremendous: —

"Privilege thinks it has a great interest in the American contest," he began in his massive, deliberate tones; "and every morning with blatant voice, it comes into our streets and curses the American Republic. Privilege has beheld an afflicting spectacle for many years past. It has beheld thirty million of men happy and prosperous, without emperors — without king (*cheers*) — without the surroundings of a court (*renewed cheers*) — without nobles, except such as are made by eminence in intellect and virtue — without State bishops and State priests, those vendors of the love that works salvation (*cheers*) — without great armies and great navies — without a great debt and great taxes — and Privilege has shuddered at what might happen to old Europe if this great experiment should succeed."[24]

An ingenious man, with an inventive mind, might have managed, in the same number of lines, to offend more Englishmen than Bright struck in this sentence; but he must have betrayed artifice and hurt his oratory. The audience cheered furiously, and the private secretary felt peace in his much troubled mind, for he knew how careful the Ministry would be, once they saw Bright talk republican principles before Trades Unions; but, while he did not, like Roebuck, see reason to doubt the courage of a man who, after quarrelling with the Trades Unions,[25] quarreled with all the world outside the Trades Unions, he did feel a doubt whether to class Bright as eccentric or conventional. Everyone called Bright "un-English," from Lord Palmerston to William E. Forster; but to an American he seemed more English than any of his critics. He was a liberal hater, and what he hated he reviled after the manner of Milton, but he was afraid of no one. He was almost the only man in England, or, for that matter, in Europe, who hated Palmerston and was not afraid of him, or of the press or the pulpit, the clubs or the bench, that stood behind him. He loathed the whole fabric of sham religion, sham loyalty, sham aristocracy, and sham socialism. He had the British weakness of believing only in himself and his own conventions. In all this, an American saw, if one may make the distinction, much racial eccentricity, but little that was personal. Bright was singularly well poised; but he used singularly strong language.

Long afterwards, in 1880, Adams happened to be living again in London for a season, when James Russell Lowell was transferred there as Minister;[26] and as Adams's relations with Lowell had become closer and more intimate with years, he wanted the new Minister to know some of his old friends. Bright was then in the Cabinet, and no longer the most radical member even there, but he was still a rare figure in society. He came to dinner, along with Sir Francis Doyle and Sir Robert Cunliffe,[27] and as usual did most of the talking. As usual also, he talked of the things most on his mind. Apparently it must have been some reform of the criminal law which the Judges opposed, that excited him, for at the end of dinner, over the wine, he took possession of the table in his old way, and ended with a superb denunciation of the Bench, spoken in his massive manner, as though every word were a hammer, smashing what it struck:—

"For two hundred years, the Judges of England sat on the Bench, condemning to the penalty of death every man, woman, and child who stole property to the value of five shillings; and, during all that time, not one Judge ever remonstrated against the law. We English are a nation of brutes, and ought to be exterminated to the last man."

As the party rose from table and passed into the drawing-room, Adams said to Lowell that Bright was very fine. "Yes!" replied Lowell; "but too violent!" [28]

Precisely this was the point that Adams doubted. Bright knew his Englishmen better than Lowell did — better than England did. He knew what amount of violence in language was necessary to drive an idea into a Lancashire or Yorkshire head. He knew that no violence was enough to affect a Somersetshire or Wiltshire peasant.[29] Bright kept his own head cool and clear. He was not excited; he never betrayed excitement. As for his denunciation of the English Bench, it was a very old story, not original with him. That the English were a nation of brutes was a commonplace generally admitted by Englishmen and universally accepted by foreigners; while the matter of their extermination could be treated only as unpractical, on their deserts, because they were probably not very much worse than their neighbors. Had Bright said that the French, Spaniards, Germans, or Russians were a nation of brutes and ought to be exterminated, no one would have found fault; the whole human race, according to the highest authority, has been exterminated once already for the same reason, and only the rainbow protects them from a repetition of it. What shocked Lowell was that he denounced his own people.

Adams felt no moral obligation to defend Judges, who, as far as he knew, were the only class of society specially adapted to defend themselves; but he was curious — even anxious — as a point of education, to decide for himself whether Bright's language was violent for its purpose. He thought not. Perhaps Cobden did better by persuasion, but that was another matter. Of course,

even Englishmen sometimes complained of being so constantly
told that they were brutes and hypocrites, although they were
told little else by their censors, and bore it, on the whole, meekly;
but the fact that it was true in the main troubled the ten-pound
voter[30] much less than it troubled Newman,[31] Gladstone, Ruskin,[32]
Carlyle, and Matthew Arnold. Bright was personally disliked by
his victims, but not distrusted. They never doubted what he
would do next, as they did with John Russell, Gladstone, and
Disraeli. He betrayed no one, and he never advanced an opinion
in practical matters which did not prove to be practical.

The class of Englishmen who set out to be the intellectual opposites of Bright, seemed to an American bystander the weakest and
most eccentric of all. These were the trimmers, the political economists, the anti-slavery and doctrinaire class, the followers of de
Tocqueville, and of John Stuart Mill. As a class, they were timid
— with good reason — and timidity, which is high wisdom in philosophy, sicklies the whole cast of thought[33] in action. Numbers of
these men haunted London society, all tending to free-thinking, but
never venturing much freedom of thought. Like the anti-slavery
doctrinaires of the forties and fifties, they became mute and useless
when slavery struck them in the face. For type of these eccentrics,
literature seems to have chosen Henry Reeve,[34] at least to the extent
of biography. He was a bulky figure in society, always friendly,
good-natured, obliging, and useful; almost as universal as Milnes[35]
and more busy. As editor of the *Edinburgh Review* he had authority and even power, although the *Review* and the whole Whig
doctrinaire school[36] had begun — as the French say — to date;
and of course the literary and artistic sharpshooters of 1867 —
like Frank Palgrave[37] frothed and foamed at the mere mention
of Reeve's name. Three-fourths of their fury was due only to his
ponderous manner. London society abused its rights of personal
criticism by fixing on every too conspicuous figure some word or
phrase that stuck to it. Everyone had heard of Mrs. Grote as
"the origin of the word grotesque." Everyone had laughed at

the story of Reeve approaching Mrs. Grote,[38] with his usual somewhat florid manner, asking in his literary dialect how her husband
the historian was: "And how is the learned Grotius?" "Pretty
well, thank you, Puffendorf!" One winced at the word, as though
it were a drawing of Forain.[39]

No one would have been more shocked than Reeve had he been
charged with want of moral courage. He proved his courage afterwards by publishing the "Greville Memoirs,"[40] braving the dis-
pleasure of the Queen. Yet the *Edinburgh Review* and its editor
avoided taking sides except where sides were already fixed. Americanism would have been bad form in the liberal *Edinburgh Review;*
it would have seemed eccentric even for a Scotchman, and Reeve
was a Saxon of Saxons. To an American this attitude of oscillat-
ing reserve seemed more eccentric than the reckless hostility of
Brougham or Carlyle, and more mischievous, for he never could be
sure what preposterous commonplace it might encourage.

The sum of these experiences in 1863 left the conviction that
eccentricity was weakness. The young American who should
adopt English thought was lost. From the facts, the conclusion
was correct, yet, as usual, the conclusion was wrong. The years
of Palmerston's last Cabinet, 1859 to 1865, were avowedly years
of truce — of arrested development. The British system like the
French, was in its last stage of decomposition. Never had the
British mind shown itself so *décousu* — so unravelled, at sea,
floundering in every sort of historical shipwreck. Eccentricities
had a free field. Contradictions swarmed in State and Church.
England devoted thirty years of arduous labor to clearing away
only a part of the *débris*. A young American in 1863 could see little or nothing of the future. He might dream, but he could not
foretell, the suddenness with which the old Europe, with England
in its wake, was to vanish in 1870. He was in dead-water, and
the parti-colored, fantastic cranks swam about his boat, as though
he were the ancient mariner, and they saurians of the prime.[41]

CHAPTER XIII

The Perfection of Human Society (1864)

MINISTER ADAMS'S success in stopping the rebel rams fixed his position once for all in English society. From that moment he could afford to drop the character of diplomatist, and assume what, for an American Minister in London, was an exclusive diplomatic advantage, the character of a kind of American Peer of the Realm.[1] The British never did things by halves. Once they recognized a man's right to social privileges, they accepted him as one of themselves. Much as Lord Derby and Mr. Disraeli were accepted as leaders of Her Majesty's domestic Opposition, Minister Adams had a rank of his own as a kind of leader of Her Majesty's American Opposition. Even the *Times* conceded it. The years of struggle were over, and Minister Adams rapidly gained a position which would have caused his father or grandfather to stare with incredulous envy.

This Anglo-American form of diplomacy was chiefly undiplomatic, and had the peculiar effect of teaching a habit of diplomacy useless or mischievous everywhere but in London. Nowhere else in the world could one expect to figure in a rôle so unprofessional. The young man knew no longer what character he bore. Private secretary in the morning, son in the afternoon, young man about town in the evening, the only character he never bore was that of diplomatist, except when he wanted a card to some great function. His diplomatic education was at an end; he seldom met a diplomat, and never had business with one; he could be of no use to them, or they to him; but he drifted inevitably into society, and, do what he might, his next education must be one of English social life. Tossed between the horns of successive dilemmas, he reached his twenty-sixth birthday without the power of earning five dollars in any occupation. His friends in the army were almost as badly off, but even army life ruined a young man less fatally than London society. Had he been rich, this form of ruin would have mattered nothing; but the young men of 1865 were none of them rich; all had to earn a living; yet they had reached high positions of responsibility and power in camps and Courts, without a dollar of their own and with no tenure of office.

Henry Adams had failed to acquire any useful education; he should at least have acquired social experience. Curiously enough, he failed here also. From the European or English point of view, he had no social experience, and never got it. Minister Adams happened on a political interregnum[2] owing to Lord Palmerston's personal influence from 1860 to 1865; but this political interregnum was less marked than the social still-stand during the same years. The Prince Consort was dead; the Queen had retired[3]; the Prince of Wales was still a boy. In its best days, Victorian society had never been "smart." During the forties, under the influence of Louis Philippe, Courts affected to be simple, serious and middle class; and they succeeded. The taste of Louis Philippe was *bourgeois* beyond any taste except that of Queen Victoria. Style lingered in the background with the powdered footman behind the yellow chariot, but speaking socially the Queen had no style save what she inherited. Balmoral[4] was a startling revelation of royal taste. Nothing could be worse than the toilettes at Court unless it were the way they were worn. One's eyes might be dazzled by jewels, but they were heirlooms, and if any lady appeared well dressed, she was either a foreigner or "fast." Fashion was not fashionable in London until the Americans and the Jews were let loose. The style of London toilette universal in 1864 was grotesque, like Monckton Milnes on horseback in Rotten Row.

Society of this sort might fit a young man in some degree for editing Shakespeare or Swift, but had little relation with the society of 1870, and none with that of 1900. Owing to other causes, young Adams never got the full training of such style as still existed. The embarrassments of his first few seasons socially ruined him. His own want of experience prevented his asking introductions to the ladies who ruled society; his want of friends prevented his knowing who these ladies were; and he had every reason to expect snubbing if he put himself in evidence. This sensitiveness was thrown away on English society, where men and women treated each others' advances much more brutally than those of strangers, but young Adams was son and private secretary too; he could not be as thick-skinned as an Englishman. He was not alone. Every young diplomat, and most of the old ones, felt awkward in an English house from a certainty that they were not precisely wanted there, and a possibility that they might be told so.

If there was in those days a country house in England which had a right to call itself broad in views and large in tastes, it was Bretton in Yorkshire; and if there was a hostess who had a right to consider herself fashionable as well as charming, it was Lady Margaret Beaumont; yet one morning at breakfast there, sitting by her side — not for his own merits — Henry Adams heard her say to herself in her languid and liberal way, with her rich voice and musing manner, looking into her tea-cup: "I don't think I care for foreigners!" Horror-stricken, not so much on his own account as on hers, the young man could only execute himself as gaily as he might: "But Lady Margaret, please make one small exception for me!" Of course she replied, what was evident, that she did not call him a foreigner, and her genial Irish charm made the slip of tongue a happy courtesy; but none the less she knew that, except for his momentary personal introduction, he was in fact a foreigner, and there was no imaginable reason why she should like him, or any other foreigner, unless it were because she was bored by natives. She seemed to feel that her indifference needed a reason to excuse itself in her own eyes, and she showed the subconscious sympathy of the Irish nature which never feels itself perfectly at home even in England. She, too, was some shadowy shade un-English.

Always conscious of this barrier, while the war lasted the private secretary hid himself among the herd of foreigners till he found his relations fixed and unchangeable. He never felt himself in society, and he never knew definitely what was meant as society by those who were in it. He saw far enough to note a score of societies which seemed quite independent of each other. The smartest was the smallest, and to him almost wholly strange. The largest was the sporting world, also unknown to him except through the talk of his acquaintances. Between or beyond these lay groups of nebulous societies. His lawyer friends, like Evarts, frequented legal circles where one still sat over the wine and told anecdotes of the bench and bar; but he himself never set eyes on a judge except when his father took him to call on old Lord Lyndhurst,[6] where they found old Lord Campbell,[7] both abusing old Lord Brougham. The Church and the Bishops formed several societies which no secretary ever saw except as an interloper. The Army; the Navy; the Indian Service; the medical and surgical professions; City people; artists; County families; the Scotch, and indefinite other subdivisions of society existed, which were as strange to each other as they were to Adams. At the end of eight or ten seasons in London society he professed to know less about it, or how to enter it, than he did when he made his first appearance at Miss Burdett Coutts's in May, 1861.

Sooner or later every young man dropped into a set or circle, and frequented the few houses that were willing to harbor him. An American who neither hunted nor raced, neither shot nor fished nor gambled, and was not marriageable, had no need to think of society at large. Ninety-nine houses in every hundred were useless to him, a greater bore to him than he to them. Thus the question of getting into — or getting out of — society which troubled young foreigners greatly, settled itself after three or four years of painful speculation. Society had no unity; one wandered about in it like a maggot in cheese; it was not a hansom cab, to be got into, or out of, at dinner-time.

Therefore he always professed himself ignorant of society; he never knew whether he had been in it or not, but from the accounts of his future friends, like General Dick Taylor[8] or George Smalley, and of various ladies who reigned in the seventies, he inclined to think that he knew very little about it. Certain great houses and certain great functions of course he attended, like everyone else who could get cards, but even of these the number was small that kept an interest or helped education. In seven years he could remember only two that seemed to have any meaning for him, and he never knew what that meaning was. Neither of the two was official; neither was English in interest; and both were scandals to the philosopher while they scarcely enlightened men of the world.

One was at Devonshire House,[9] an ordinary, unpremeditated evening reception. Naturally everyone went to Devonshire House if asked, and the rooms that night were fairly full of the usual people. The private secretary was standing among the rest, when Mme. de Castiglione entered,[10] the famous beauty of the Second Empire. How beautiful she may have been, or indeed what sort of beauty she was, Adams never knew, because the company, consisting of the most refined and aristocratic society in the world, instantly formed a lane, and stood in ranks to stare at her, while those behind mounted on chairs to look over their neighbors' heads; so that the lady walked through this polite mob, stared completely out of countenance, and fled the house at once. This was all!

The other strange spectacle was at Stafford House,[11] April 13, 1864, when, in a palace gallery that recalled Paolo Veronese's[12] pictures of Christ in his scenes of miracle, Garibaldi, in his gray capote over his red shirt, received all London, and three duchesses literally worshipped at his feet. Here, at all events, a private secretary had surely caught the last and highest touch of social experience; but what it meant — what social, moral, or mental development it pointed out to the searcher of truth — was not a matter to be treated fully by a leader in the *Morning Post* or even by a sermon in Westminster Abbey. Mme. de Castiglione and Garibaldi covered, between them, too much space for simple measurement; their curves were too complex for mere arithmetic. The task of bringing the two into any common relation with an ordered social system tending to orderly development — in London or elsewhere — was well fitted for Algernon Swinburne or Victor Hugo, but was beyond any process yet reached by the education of Henry Adams, who would probably, even then, have rejected, as superficial or supernatural, all the views taken by any of the company who looked on with him at these two interesting and perplexing sights.

From the Court, or Court society, a mere private secretary got nothing at all, or next to nothing, that could help him on his road through life. Royalty was in abeyance. One was tempted to think in these years, 1860–65, that the nicest distinction between the very best society and the second-best, was their attitude towards royalty. The one regarded royalty as a bore, and avoided it, or quietly said that the Queen had never been in society. The same thing might have been said of fully half the peerage. Adams never knew even the names of half the rest; he never exchanged ten words with any member of the royal family; he never knew any one in those years who showed interest in any member of the royal family, or who would have given five shillings for the opinion of any royal person on any subject; or cared to enter any royal or noble presence, unless the house was made attractive by as much social effort as would have been necessary in other countries where no rank existed. No doubt, as one of a swarm, young Adams slightly knew various gilded youth who frequented balls and led such dancing as was most in vogue, but they seemed to set no value on rank; their anxiety was only to know where to find the best partners before midnight, and the best supper after midnight. To the American, as to Arthur Pendennis or Barnes Newcome,[13] the value of social position and knowledge was evident enough; he valued it at rather more than it was worth to

199

him; but it was a shadowy thing which seemed to vary with every street corner; a thing which had shifting standards, and which no one could catch outright. The half-dozen leaders and beauties of his time, with great names and of the utmost fashion, made some of the poorest marriages, and the least showy careers.

Tired of looking on at society from the outside, Adams grew to loathe the sight of his Court dress; to groan at every announcement of a Court ball; and to dread every invitation to a formal dinner. The greatest social event gave not half the pleasure that one could buy for ten shillings at the opera when Patti sang Cherubino or Gretchen,[14] and not a fourth of the education. Yet this was not the opinion of the best judges. Lothrop Motley,[15] who stood among the very best, said to him early in his apprenticeship that the London dinner and the English country house were the perfection of human society. The young man meditated over it, uncertain of its meaning. Motley could not have thought the dinner itself perfect, since there was not then — outside of a few bankers or foreigners — a good cook or a good table in London, and nine out of ten of the dinners that Motley ate came from Gunter's,[16] and all were alike. Everyone, especially in young society, complained bitterly that Englishmen did not know a good dinner when they ate it, and could not order one if they were given *carte blanche*. Henry Adams was not a judge, and knew no more than they, but he heard the complaints, and he could not think that Motley meant to praise the English *cuisine*.

Equally little could Motley have meant that dinners were good to look at. Nothing could be worse than the toilettes; nothing less artistic than the appearance of the company. One's eyes might be dazzled by family diamonds, but, if an American woman were present, she was sure to make comments about the way the jewels were worn. If there was a well-dressed lady at table, she was either an American or "fast." She attracted as much notice as though she were on the stage. No one could possibly admire an English dinner-table.

Least of all did Motley mean that the taste or the manners were perfect. The manners of English society were notorious, and the taste was worse. Without exception every American woman rose in rebellion against English manners. In fact, the charm of London which made most impression on Americans was the violence of its contrasts; the extreme badness of the worst, making background for the distinction, refinement, or wit of a few, just as the extreme beauty of a few superb women was more effective against the plainness of the crowd. The result was mediæval, and amusing; sometimes coarse to a degree that might have startled a roustabout, and sometimes courteous and considerate to a degree that suggested King Arthur's Round Table; but this artistic contrast was surely not the perfection that Motley had in his mind. He meant something scholarly, worldly, and modern; he was thinking of his own tastes.

Probably he meant that, in his favorite houses, the tone was easy, the talk was good, and the standard of scholarship was high. Even there he would have been forced to qualify his adjectives. No German would have admitted that English scholarship was high, or that it was scholarship at all, or that any wish for scholarship existed in England. Nothing that seemed to smell of the shop or of the lecture-room was wanted. One might as well have talked of Renan's Christ[17] at the table of the Bishop of London, as talk of German philology at the table of an Oxford don. Society, if a small literary class could be called society, wanted to be amused in its old way. Sydney Smith, who had amused, was dead; so was Macaulay, who instructed if he did not amuse; Thackeray died at Christmas, 1863; Dickens[18] never felt at home, and seldom appeared, in society; Bulwer Lytton[19] was not sprightly; Tennyson[20] detested strangers; Carlyle was mostly detested by them; Darwin never came to town; the men of whom Motley must have been thinking were such as he might meet at Lord Houghton's breakfasts: Grote, Jowett, Milman, or Froude[21]; Browning, Matthew Arnold, or Swinburne; Bishop Wilberforce[22], Venables, or Hayward;

or perhaps Gladstone, Robert Lowe, or Lord Granville. A relatively small class, commonly isolated, suppressed, and lost at the usual London dinner, such society as this was fairly familiar even to a private secretary, but to the literary American it might well seem perfection since he could find nothing of the sort in America. Within the narrow limits of this class, the American Legation was fairly at home; possibly a score of houses, all liberal, and all literary, but perfect only in the eyes of a Harvard College historian.[23] They could teach little worth learning, for their tastes were antiquated and their knowledge was ignorance to the next generation. What was altogether fatal for future purposes, they were only English.

A social education in such a medium was bound to be useless in any other, yet Adams had to learn it to the bottom. The one thing needful for a private secretary, was that he should not only seem, but should actually be, at home. He studied carefully, and practised painfully, what seemed to be the favorite accomplishments of society. Perhaps his nervousness deceived him; perhaps he took for an ideal of others what was only his reflected image; but he conceived that the perfection of human society required that a man should enter a drawing-room where he was a total stranger, and place himself on the hearth-rug, his back to the fire, with an air of expectant benevolence, without curiosity, much as though he had dropped in at a charity concert, kindly disposed to applaud the performers and to overlook mistakes. This ideal rarely succeeded in youth, and towards thirty it took a form of modified insolence and offensive patronage; but about sixty it mellowed into courtesy, kindliness, and even deference to the young which had extraordinary charm both in women and in men. Unfortunately Adams could not wait till sixty for education; he had his living to earn; and the English air of patronage would earn no income for him anywhere else.

After five or six years of constant practice, anyone can acquire the habit of going from one strange company to another without thinking much of oneself or of them, as though silently reflecting that "in a world where we are all insects, no insect is alien; perhaps they are human in parts";[24] but the dreamy habit of mind which comes from solitude in crowds is not fitness for social success except in London. Everywhere else it is injury. England was a social kingdom whose social coinage had no currency elsewhere.

Englishwomen, from the educational point of view, could give nothing until they approached forty years old. Then they become very interesting — very charming — to the man of fifty. The young American was not worth the young Englishwoman's notice, and never received it. Neither understood the other. Only in the domestic relation, in the country — never in society at large — a young American might accidentally make friends with an Englishwoman of his own age, but it never happened to Henry Adams. His susceptible nature was left to the mercy of American girls, which was professional duty rather than education as long as diplomacy held its own.

Thus he found himself launched on waters where he had never meant to sail, and floating along a stream which carried him far from his port. His third season in London society saw the end of his diplomatic education, and began for him the social life of a young man who felt at home in England — more at home there than anywhere else. With this feeling, the mere habit of going to garden parties, dinners, receptions, and balls had nothing to do. One might go to scores without a sensation of home. One might stay in no end of country houses without forgetting that one was a total stranger and could never be anything else. One might bow to half the dukes and duchesses in England, and feel only the more strange. Hundreds of persons might pass with a nod and never come nearer. Close relation in a place like London is a personal mystery as profound as chemical affinity. Thousands pass, and one separates himself from the mass to attach himself to another, and so make, little by little, a group.

One morning, April 27, 1863, he was asked to breakfast with Sir Henry Holland, the old Court physician who had been acquainted with every American Minister since Edward Everett, and was a valuable social ally, who had the courage to try to be of use to everybody, and who, while asking the private secretary to breakfast one day, was too discreet to betray what he might have learned about rebel doings at his breakfast-table the day before. He had been friendly with the Legation, in the teeth of society, and was still bearing up against the weight of opinion, so that young Adams could not decline his invitations, although they obliged him to breakfast in Brook Street at nine o'clock in the morning, alternately with Mr. James M. Mason. Old Dr. Holland was himself as hale as a hawk, driving all day bare-headed about London, and eating Welsh rarebit every night before bed; he thought that any young man should be pleased to take his early muffin in Brook Street, and supply a few crumbs of war news for the daily peckings of eminent patients. Meekly, when summoned, the private secretary went, and on reaching the front door, this particular morning, he found there another young man in the act of rapping the knocker. They entered the breakfast-room together, where they were introduced to each other, and Adams learned that the other guest was a Cambridge undergraduate, Charles Milnes Gaskell, son of James Milnes Gaskell,[25] the Member for Wenlock; another of the Yorkshire Milneses, from Thornes[26] near Wakefield. Fate had fixed Adams to Yorkshire. By another chance it happened that young Milnes Gaskell was intimate at Cambridge with William Everett[27] who was also about to take his degree. A third chance inspired Mr. Evarts with a fancy for visiting Cambridge, and led William Everett to offer his services as host. Adams acted as courier to Mr. Evarts, and at the end of May they went down for a few days, when William Everett did the honors as host with a kindness and attention that made his cousin sorely conscious of his own social shortcomings. Cambridge was pretty, and the dons were kind. Mr. Evarts enjoyed his visit, but this was merely a part of the private secretary's day's work. What affected his whole life was the intimacy then begun with Milnes Gaskell and his circle of undergraduate friends, just about to enter the world.

Intimates are predestined. Adams met in England a thousand people, great and small; jostled against everyone, from royal princes to gin-shop loafers; attended endless official functions and private parties; visited every part of the United Kingdom and was not quite a stranger at the Legations in Paris and Rome; he knew the societies of certain country houses, and acquired habits of Sunday-afternoon calls; but all this gave him nothing to do, and was life wasted. For him nothing whatever could be gained by escorting American ladies to drawing-rooms or American gentlemen to levees at St. James's Palace, or bowing solemnly to people with great titles, at Court balls, or even by awkwardly jostling royalty at garden parties; all this was done for the Government, and neither President Lincoln nor Secretary Seward would ever know enough of their business to thank him for doing what they did not know how to get properly done by their own servants; but for Henry Adams — not private secretary — all the time taken up by such duties was wasted. On the other hand, his few personal intimacies concerned him alone, and the chance that made him almost a Yorkshireman was one that must have started under the Heptarchy.[28]

More than any other county in England, Yorkshire retained a sort of social independence of London. Scotland itself was hardly more distinct. The Yorkshire type[29] had always been the strongest of the British strains; the Norwegian and the Dane were a different race from the Saxon. Even Lancashire had not the mass and the cultivation of the West Riding. London could never quite absorb Yorkshire, which, in its turn had no great love for London and freely showed it. To a certain degree, evident enough to Yorkshiremen, Yorkshire was not English — or was all England, as they might choose to express it. This must have been the reason why young Adams was drawn there rather than elsewhere. Monckton Milnes alone took the trouble to draw him, and possibly Milnes was the only man in England with whom Henry Adams, at that moment, had a chance of calling out such an un-English effort. Neither Oxford nor Cambridge nor any region south of the Humber contained a considerable house where a young American would have been sought as a friend. Eccentricity alone did not account for it. Monckton Milnes was a singular type, but his distant cousin, James Milnes Gaskell, was another, quite as marked, in an opposite sense. Milnes never seemed willing to rest; Milnes Gaskell never seemed willing to move. In his youth one of a very famous group — Arthur Hallam,[30] Tennyson, Manning,[31] Gladstone, Francis Doyle — and regarded as one of the most promising; an adorer of George Canning; in Parliament since coming of age; married into the powerful connection of the Wynns of Wynstay;[32] rich according to Yorkshire standards; intimate with his political leaders; he was one of the numerous Englishmen who refuse office rather than make the effort of carrying it, and want power only to make it a source of indolence. He was a voracious reader and an admirable critic; he had forty years of parliamentary tradition on his memory; he liked to talk and to listen; he liked his dinner and, in spite of George Canning, his dry champagne; he liked wit and anecdote; but he belonged to the generation of 1830, a generation which could not survive the telegraph and railway, and which even Yorkshire could hardly produce again. To an American he was a character even more unusual and more fascinating than his distant cousin Lord Houghton.

Mr. Milnes Gaskell was kind to the young American whom his son brought to the house, and Mrs. Milnes Gaskell was kinder, for she thought the American perhaps a less dangerous friend than some Englishman might be, for her son, and she was probably right. The American had the sense to see that she was herself one of the most intelligent and sympathetic women in England; her sister, Miss Charlotte Wynn,[33] was another; and both were of an age and a position in society that made their friendship a compliment as well as a pleasure. Their consent and approval settled the matter. In England, the family is a serious fact; once admitted to it, one is there for life. London might utterly vanish from one's horizon, but as long as life lasted, Yorkshire lived for its friends.

In the year 1857, Mr. James Milnes Gaskell, who had sat for thirty years in Parliament as one of the Members for the borough of Wenlock in Shropshire, bought Wenlock Abbey[34] and the estate that included the old monastic buildings. This new, or old, plaything amused Mrs. Milnes Gaskell. The Prior's house, a charming specimen of fifteenth-century architecture, had been long left to decay as a farmhouse. She put it in order, and went there to spend a part of the autumn of 1864. Young Adams was one of her first guests, and drove about Wenlock Edge and the Wrekin[35] with her, learning the loveliness of this exquisite country, and its stores of curious antiquity. It was a new and charming existence; an experience greatly to be envied — ideal repose and rural Shakespearian peace — but a few years of it were likely to complete his education, and fit him to act a fairly useful part in life as an Englishman, an ecclesiastic, and a contemporary of Chaucer.

CHAPTER XIV

Dilettantism (1865–1866)

THE campaign of 1864 and the reëlection of Mr. Lincoln in November set the American Minister on so firm a footing that he could safely regard his own anxieties as over, and the anxieties of Earl Russell and the Emperor Napoleon as begun. With a few months more his own term of four years would come to an end, and even though the questions still under discussion with England should somewhat prolong his stay, he might look forward with some confidence to his return home in 1865. His son no longer fretted. The time for going into the army had passed. If he were to be useful at all, it must be as a son, and as a son he was treated with the widest indulgence and trust. He knew that he was doing himself no good by staying in London, but thus far in life he had done himself no good anywhere, and reached his twenty-seventh birthday without having advanced a step, that he could see, beyond his twenty-first. For the most part, his friends were worse off than he. The war was about to end and they were to be set adrift in a world they would find altogether strange.

At this point, as though to cut the last thread of relation, six months were suddenly dropped out of his life in England. The London climate had told on some of the family; the physicians prescribed a winter in Italy. Of course the private secretary was detached as their escort, since this was one of his professional functions; and he passed six months, gaining an education as Italian courier, while the Civil War came to its end. As far as other education went, he got none, but he was amused. Travelling in all possible luxury, at some one else's expense, with diplomatic privileges and position, was a form of travel hitherto untried. The Cornice in *vettura*[1] was delightful; Sorrento[2] in winter offered hills to climb and grottos to explore, and Naples near by to visit; Rome at Easter was an experience necessary for the education of every properly trained private secretary; the journey north by *vettura* through Perugia and Siena[3] was a dream; the Splügen Pass[4] if not equal to the Stelvio, was worth seeing; Paris had always something to show. The chances of accidental education were not so great as they had been, since one's field of experience had grown large; but perhaps a season at Baden Baden[5] in these later days of its brilliancy offered some chances of instruction, if it were only the sight of fashionable Europe and America on the race-course watching the Duke of Hamilton[6] in the middle, improving his social advantages by the conversation of Cora Pearl.[7]

The assassination of President Lincoln fell on the party while they were at Rome, where it seemed singularly fitting to that nursery of murderers and murdered, as though America were also getting educated. Again one went to meditate on the steps of the Santa Maria in Ara Cœli, but the lesson seemed as shallow as before. Nothing happened. The travellers changed no plan or movement. The Minister did not recall them to London. The season was over before they returned; and when the private secretary sat down again at his desk in Portland Place before a mass of copy in arrears, he saw before him a world so changed as to be beyond connection with the past. His identity, if one could call a bundle of disconnected memories an identity, seemed to remain; but his life was once more broken into separate pieces; he was a spider and had to spin a new web in some new place with a new attachment.

All his American friends and contemporaries who were still alive looked singularly commonplace without uniforms, and hastened to get married and retire into back streets and suburbs until they could find employment. Minister Adams, too, was going home "next fall," and when the fall came, he was going home "next spring," and when the spring came, President Andrew Johnson was at loggerheads with the Senate,[8] and found it best to keep things unchanged. After the usual manner of public servants who had acquired the habit of office and lost the faculty of will, the members of the Legation in London continued the daily routine of English society, which, after becoming a habit, threatened to become a vice. Had Henry Adams shared a single taste with the young Englishmen of his time, he would have been lost; but the custom of pounding up and down Rotten Row every day, on a hack, was not a taste, and yet was all the sport he shared. Evidently he must set to work; he must get a new education; he must begin a career of his own.

Nothing was easier to say, but even his father admitted two careers to be closed. For the law, diplomacy had unfitted him; for diplomacy he already knew too much. Anyone who had held, during the four most difficult years of American diplomacy, a position at the centre of action, with his hands actually touching the lever of power, could not beg a post of Secretary at Vienna or Madrid in order to bore himself doing nothing until the next President should do him the honor to turn him out. For once all his advisers agreed that diplomacy was not possible.

In any ordinary system he would have been called back to serve in the State Department, but, between the President and the Senate, service of any sort became a delusion. The choice of career was more difficult than the education which had proved impracticable. Adams saw no road; in fact there was none. All his friends were trying one path or another, but none went a way that he could have taken. John Hay passed through London in order to bury himself in second-rate Legations for years,[9] before he drifted home again to join Whitelaw Reid[10] and George Smalley[11] on the *Tribune*. Frank Barlow and Frank Bartlett[12] carried Major Generals' commissions into small law business. Miles[13] stayed in the army. Henry Higginson,[14] after a desperate struggle, was forced into State Street; Charles Adams wandered about, with brevet-brigadier rank, trying to find employment.[15] Scores of others tried experiments more or less unsuccessful. Henry Adams could see easy ways of making a hundred blunders; he could see no likely way of making a legitimate success. Such as it was, his so-called education was wanted nowhere.

One profession alone seemed possible—the Press. In 1860 he would have said that he was born to be an editor, like at least a thousand other young graduates from American colleges who entered the world every year enjoying the same conviction; but in 1866 the situation was altered; the possession of money had become doubly needful for success, and double energy was essential to get money. America had more than doubled her scale. Yet the press was still the last resource of the educated poor who could not be artists and would not be tutors. Any man who was fit for nothing else could write an editorial or a criticism. The enormous mass of misinformation accumulated in ten years of nomad life could always be worked off on a helpless public, in diluted doses, if one could but secure a table in the corner of a newspaper office. The press was an inferior pulpit; an anonymous schoolmaster; a cheap boarding-school; but it was still the nearest approach to a career for the literary survivor of a wrecked education. For the press, then, Henry Adams decided to fit himself, and since he could not go home to get practical training, he set to work to do what he could in London.

He knew, as well as any reporter on the *New York Herald*, that this was not an American way of beginning, and he knew a certain number of other drawbacks which the reporter could not see so clearly. Do what he might, he drew breath only in the atmosphere of English methods and thoughts; he could breathe none other. His mother — who should have been a competent judge, since her success and popularity in England exceeded that of her husband — averred that every woman who lived a certain time in England came to look and dress like an Englishwoman, no matter how she struggled. Henry Adams felt himself catching an English tone of mind and processes of thought,[16] though at heart more hostile to them than ever. As though to make him more helpless and wholly distort his life, England grew more and more agreeable and amusing. Minister Adams became, in 1866, almost a historical monument in London; he held a position altogether his own. His old opponents disappeared. Lord Palmerston died in October, 1865; Lord Russell tottered on six months longer, but then vanished from power;[17] and in July, 1866, the conservatives came into office. Traditionally the Tories were easier to deal with than the Whigs, and Minister Adams had no reason to regret the change. His personal relations were excellent and his personal weight increased year by year. On that score the private secretary had no cares, and not much copy. His own position was modest, but it was enough; the life he led was agreeable; his friends were all he wanted, and, except that he was at the mercy of politics, he felt much at ease. Of his daily life he had only to reckon so many breakfasts; so many dinners; so many receptions, balls, theatres, and country-parties; so many cards to be left; so many Americans to be escorted — the usual routine of every young American in a Legation; all counting for nothing in sum, because, even if it had been his official duty — which it was not — it was mere routine, a single, continuous, unbroken act, which led to nothing and nowhere except Portland Place[18] and the grave.

The path that led somewhere was the English habit of mind which deepened its ruts every day. The English mind was like the London drawing-room, a comfortable and easy spot, filled with bits and fragments of incoherent furnitures, which were never meant to go together, and could be arranged in any relation without making a whole, except by the square room. Philosophy might dispute about innate ideas[19] till the stars died out in the sky, but about innate tastes no one, except perhaps a collie dog, has the right to doubt; least of all, the Englishman, for his tastes are his being; he drifts after them as unconsciously as a honey-bee drifts after his flowers, and, in England, every one must drift with him. Most young Englishmen drifted to the race-course or the moors or the hunting-field; a few towards books; one or two followed some form of science; and a number took to what, for want of a better name, they called Art. Young Adams inherited a certain taste for the same pursuit from his father who insisted that he had it not, because he could not see what his son thought he saw in Turner.[20] The Minister, on the other hand, carried a sort of æsthetic rag-bag of his own, which he regarded as amusement, and never called art. So he would wander off on a Sunday to attend service successively in all the city churches built by Sir Christopher Wren;[21] or he would disappear from the Legation day after day to attend coin sales at Sotheby's,[22] where his son attended alternate sales of drawings, engravings, or water-colors. Neither knew enough to talk much about the other's tastes, but the only difference between them was a slight difference of direction. The Minister's mind like his writings showed a correctness of form and line that his son would have been well pleased had he inherited.

Of all supposed English tastes, that of art was the most alluring and treacherous. Once drawn into it, one had small chance of escape, for it had no centre or circumference, no beginning, middle, or end, no origin, no object, and no conceivable result as education. In London one met no corrective. The only American who came by, capable of teaching, was William Hunt,[23] who stopped to paint the portrait of the Minister which now completes the family series at Harvard College. Hunt talked constantly, and was, or afterwards became, a famous teacher, but Henry Adams did not know enough to learn. Perhaps, too, he had inherited or acquired a stock of tastes, as young men must, which he was slow to outgrow. Hunt had no time to sweep out the rubbish of Adams's mind. The portrait finished, he went.

As often as he could, Adams ran over to Paris, for sunshine, and there always sought out Richardson in his attic in the Rue du Bac,[24] or wherever he lived, and they went off to dine at the Palais Royal, and talk of whatever interested the students of the Beaux Arts.[25] Richardson, too, had much to say, but had not yet seized his style. Adams caught very little of what lay in his mind, and the less, because, to Adams, everything French was bad except the restaurants, while the continuous life in England made French art seem worst of all. This did not prove that English art, in 1866, was good; far from it; but it helped to make bric-a-brac of all art, after the manner of England.

Not in the Legation, or in London, but in Yorkshire at Thornes, Adams met the man that pushed him furthest in this English garden of innate disorder called taste. The older daughter of the Milnes Gaskells[26] had married Francis Turner Palgrave. Few Americans will ever ask whether anyone has described the Palgraves, but the family was one of the most describable in all England at that day. Old Sir Francis,[27] the father, had been much the greatest of all the historians of early England, the only one who was un-English; and the reason of his superiority lay in his name, which was Cohen, and his mind which was Cohen also, or at least not English. He changed his name to Palgrave in order to please his wife. They had a band of remarkable sons:[28] Francis Turner, Gifford, Reginald, Inglis; all of whom made their mark. Gifford was perhaps the most eccentric, but his "Travels" in Arabia were famous, even among the famous travels of that generation. Francis Turner — or, as he was commonly called, Frank Palgrave — unable to work off his restlessness in travel like Gifford, and stifled in the atmosphere of the Board of Education, became a critic. His art-criticisms helped to make the *Saturday Review* a terror to the British artist. His literary taste, condensed into the "Golden Treasury," helped Adams to more literary education than he ever got from any taste of his own. Palgrave himself held rank as one of the minor poets; his hymns had vogue. As an art-critic he was too ferocious to be liked; even Holman Hunt[29] found his temper humorous; among many rivals, he may perhaps have had a right to claim the much-disputed rank of being the most unpopular man in London; but he liked to teach, and asked only for a docile pupil. Adams was docile enough, for he knew nothing and liked to listen. Indeed, he had to listen, whether he liked or not, for Palgrave's voice was strident, and nothing could stop him. Literature, painting, sculpture, architecture were open fields for his attacks, which were always intelligent if not always kind, and when these failed, he readily descended to meaner levels. John Richard Green,[30] who was Palgrave's precise opposite, and whose Irish charm of touch and humor defended him from most assaults, used to tell with delight of Palgrave's call on him just after he had moved into his new Queen Anne house in Kensington Square: "Palgrave called yesterday, and the first thing he said was, 'I've counted three anachronisms on your front doorstep.'"

Another savage critic, also a poet, was Thomas Woolner,[31] a type almost more emphatic than Palgrave in a society which resounded with emphasis. Woolner's sculpture showed none of the rough assertion that Woolner himself showed, when he was not making supernatural effort to be courteous, but his busts were remarkable, and his work altogether was, in Palgrave's clamorous opinion, the best of his day. He took the matter of British art — or want of art — seriously, almost ferociously, as a personal grievance and torture; at times he was rather terrifying in the anarchistic wrath of his denunciation. As Henry Adams felt no responsibility for English art, and had no American art to offer for sacrifice, he listened with enjoyment to language much like Carlyle's, and accepted it without a qualm. On the other hand, as a third member of this critical group, he fell in with Stopford Brooke[32] whose tastes lay in the same direction, and whose expression was modified by clerical propriety. Among these men, one wandered off into paths of education much too devious and slippery for an American foot to follow. He would have done better to go on the race-track, as far as concerned a career.

Fortunately for him he knew too little ever to be an art-critic, still less an artist. For some things ignorance is good, and art is one of them. He knew he knew nothing, and had not the trained eye or the keen instinct that trusted itself; but he was curious, as he went on, to find out how much others knew. He took Palgrave's word as final about a drawing of Rembrandt or Michael Angelo, and he trusted Woolner implicitly about a Turner; but when he quoted their authority to any dealer, the dealer pooh-poohed it, and declared that it had no weight in the trade. If he went to a sale of drawings or paintings, at Sotheby's or Christie's,[33] an hour afterwards, he saw these same dealers watching Palgrave or Woolner for a point, and bidding over them. He rarely found two dealers agree in judgment. He once bought a water-color from the artist himself, out of his studio, and had it doubted an hour afterwards by the dealer to whose place he took it for framing. He was reduced to admit that he could not prove its authenticity; internal evidence was against it.

One morning in early July, 1867, Palgrave stopped at the Legation in Portland Place on his way downtown, and offered to take Adams to Sotheby's, where a small collection of old drawings was on show. The collection was rather a curious one, said to be that of Sir Anthony Westcomb,[34] from Liverpool, with an undisturbed record of a century, but with nothing to attract notice. Probably none but collectors or experts examined the portfolios. Some dozens of these were always on hand, following every sale, and especially on the lookout for old drawings, which became rarer every year. Turning rapidly over the numbers, Palgrave stopped at one containing several small drawings, one marked as Rembrandt, one as Rafael,[35] and putting his finger on the Rafael, after careful examination; "I should buy this," he said; "it looks to me like one of those things that sell for five shillings one day, and fifty pounds the next." Adams marked it for a bid, and the next morning came down to the auction. The numbers sold slowly, and at noon he thought he might safely go to lunch. When he came back, half an hour afterwards, the drawing was gone. Much annoyed at his own stupidity, since Palgrave had expressly said he wanted the drawing for himself if he had not in a manner given it to Adams, the culprit waited for the sale to close, and then asked the clerk for the name of the buyer. It was Holloway, the art dealer, near Covent Garden, whom he slightly knew. Going at once to the shop he waited till young Holloway came in, with his purchases under his arm, and without attempt at preface, he said: "You bought to-day, Mr. Holloway, a number that I wanted. Do you mind letting me have it?" Holloway took out the parcel, looked over the drawings, and said that he had bought the number for the sake of the Rembrandt, which he thought possibly genuine; taking that out, Adams might have the rest for the price he paid for the lot — twelve shillings.[36]

Thus, down to that moment, every expert in London had probably seen these drawings. Two of them — only two — had thought them worth buying at any price, and of these two, Palgrave chose the Rafael, Holloway the one marked as Rembrandt. Adams, the purchaser of the Rafael, knew nothing whatever on the subject, but thought he might credit himself with education to the value of twelve shillings, and call the drawing nothing. Such items of education commonly came higher.

He took the drawing to Palgrave. It was closely pasted to an old, rather thin, cardboard mount, and, on holding it up to the window, one could see lines on the reverse. "Take it down to Reed[37] at the British Museum," said Palgrave; "he is Curator of the drawings, and, if you ask him, he will have it taken off the mount." Adams amused himself for a day or two by searching Rafael's works for the figure, which he found at last in the Parnasso,[38] the figure of Horace,[39] of which, as it happened — though Adams did not know it — the British Museum owned a much finer drawing. At last he took the dirty, little, unfinished red-chalk sketch to Reed whom he found in the Curator's room, with some of the finest Rafael drawings in existence, hanging on the walls. "Yes!" said Mr. Reed; "I noticed this at the sale; but it's not Rafael!" Adams, feeling himself incompetent to discuss this subject, reported the result to Palgrave, who said that Reed knew nothing about it. Also this point lay beyond Adams's competence; but he noted that

Reed was in the employ of the British Museum as Curator of the best — or nearly the best — collection in the world, especially of Rafaels, and that he bought for the Museum. As expert he had rejected both the Rafael and the Rembrandt at first-sight, and after his attention was recalled to the Rafael for a further opinion he rejected it again.

A week later, Adams returned for the drawing, which Mr. Reed took out of his drawer and gave him, saying with what seemed a little doubt or hesitation: "I should tell you that the paper shows a water-mark, which I find the same as that of paper used by Marc Antonio."[40]A little taken aback by this method of studying art, a method which even a poor and ignorant American might use as well as Rafael himself, Adams asked stupidly: "Then you think it genuine?" "Possibly!" replied Reed; "but much overdrawn."

Here was expert opinion after a second revise, with help of water-marks! In Adams's opinion it was alone worth another twelve shillings as education; but this was not all. Reed continued: "The lines on the back seem to be writing, which I cannot read, but if you will take it down to the manuscript room, they will read it for you."

Adams took the sheet down to the keeper of the manuscripts and begged him to read the lines. The keeper, after a few minutes' study, very obligingly said he could not: "It is scratched with an artist's crayon, very rapidly, with many unusual abbreviations and old forms. If anyone in Europe can read it, it is the old man at the table yonder, Libri![41]Take it to him!"

This expert broke down on the alphabet! He could not even judge a manuscript; but Adams had no right to complain, for he had nothing to pay, not even twelve shillings, though he thought these experts worth more, at least for his education. Accordingly he carried his paper to Libri, a total stranger to him, and asked the old man, as deferentially as possible, to tell him whether the lines had any meaning. Had Adams not been an ignorant person he would have known all about Libri, but his ignorance was vast, and perhaps was for the best. Libri looked at the paper, and then looked again, and at last bade him sit down and wait. Half an hour passed before he called Adams back and showed him these lines: —

> "Or questo credo ben che una elleria
> Te offende tanto che te offese il core.
> Perche sei grande nol sei in tua volia;
> Tu vedi e gia non credi il tuo valore;
> Passate gia son tutte gelosie;
> Tu sei di sasso; non hai piu dolore."[42]

As far as Adams could afterwards recall it, this was Libri's reading, but he added that the abbreviations were many and unusual; that the writing was very ancient; and that the word he read as "elleria" in the first line was not Italian at all.

By this time, one had got too far beyond one's depth to ask questions. If Libri could not read Italian, very clearly Adams had better not offer to help him. He took the drawing, thanked everybody, and having exhausted the experts of the British Museum, took a cab to Woolner's studio, where he showed the figure and repeated Reed's opinion. Woolner snorted: "Reed's a fool!" he said; "he knows nothing about it; there may be a rotten line or two, but the drawing's all right."

For forty years Adams kept this drawing on his mantelpiece, partly for its own interest, but largely for curiosity to see whether any critic or artist would ever stop to look at it. None ever did, unless he knew the story. Adams himself never wanted to know more about it. He refused to seek further light. He never cared to learn whether the drawing was Rafael's, or whether the verses were Rafael's, or whether even the water-mark was Rafael's. The experts — some scores of them including the British Museum, — had affirmed that the drawing was worth a certain moiety of twelve shillings. On that point, also, Adams could offer no opinion, but he was clear that his education had profited by it to that extent — his amusement even more.

Art was a superb field for education, but at every turn he met the same old figure, like a battered and illegible signpost that ought to direct him to the next station but never did. There was no next station. All the art of a thousand — or ten thousand — years had brought England to stuff which Palgrave and Woolner brayed in their mortars; derided, tore in tatters, growled at, and howled at, and treated in terms beyond literary usage. Whistler[43] had not yet made his appearance in London, but the others did quite as well. What result could a student reach from it? Once, on returning to London, dining with Stopford Brooke, some one asked Adams what impression the Royal Academy Exhibition[44] made on him. With a little hesitation, he suggested that it was rather a chaos, which he meant for civility; but Stopford Brooke abruptly met it by asking whether chaos were not better than death. Truly the question was worth discussion. For his own part, Adams inclined to think that neither chaos nor death was an object to him as a searcher of knowledge — neither would have vogue in America — neither would help him to a career. Both of them led him away from his objects, into an English dilettante museum of scraps, with nothing but a wall-paper to unite them in any relation of sequence. Possibly English taste was one degree more fatal than English scholarship, but even this question was open to argument. Adams went to the sales and bought what he was told to buy; now a classical drawing by Rafael or Rubens[45]; now a water-color by Girtin or Cotman[46], if possible unfinished because it was more likely to be a sketch from nature; and he bought them not because they went together — on the contrary, they made rather awkward spots on the wall as they did on the mind — but because he could afford to buy those, and not others. Ten pounds did not go far to buy a Michael Angelo, but was a great deal of money to a private secretary. The effect was spotty, fragmentary, feeble; and the more so because the British mind was constructed in that way — boasted of it, and held it to be true philosophy as well as sound method.

What was worse, no one had a right to denounce the English as wrong. Artistically their mind was scrappy, and everyone knew it, but perhaps thought itself, history, and nature, were scrappy, and ought to be studied so. Turning from British art to British literature, one met the same dangers. The historical school was a playground of traps and pitfalls. Fatally one fell into the sink of history — antiquarianism. For one who nourished a natural weakness for what was called history, the whole of British literature in the nineteenth century was antiquarianism or anecdotage, for no one except Buckle[47] had tried to link it with ideas, and commonly Buckle was regarded as having failed. Macaulay was the English historian. Adams had the greatest admiration for Macaulay, but he felt that anyone who should even distantly imitate Macaulay would perish in self-contempt. One might as well imitate Shakespeare. Yet evidently something was wrong here, for the poet and the historian ought to have different methods, and Macaulay's method ought to be imitable if it were sound; yet the method was more doubtful than the style. He was a dramatist; a painter; a poet, like Carlyle. This was the English mind, method, genius, or whatever one might call it; but one never could quite admit that the method which ended in Froude and Kinglake[48] could be sound for America where passion and poetry were eccentricities. Both Froude and Kinglake, when one met them at dinner, were very agreeable, very intelligent; and perhaps the English method was right, and art fragmentary by essence. History, like everything else, might be a field of scraps, like the refuse about a Staffordshire iron-furnace.[49] One felt a little natural reluctance to decline and fall like Silas Wegg[50] on the golden dust-heap of British refuse; but if one must, one could at least expect a degree from Oxford and the respect of the Athenæum Club.

While drifting, after the war ended, many old American friends came abroad for a holiday, and among the rest, Dr. Palfrey, busy with his "History of New England." Of all the relics of childhood, Dr. Palfrey was the most sympathetic, and perhaps the more so

because he, too, had wandered into the pleasant meadows of antiquarianism, and had forgotten the world in his pursuit of the New
England Puritan. Although America seemed becoming more and
more indifferent to the Puritan except as a slightly rococo ornament, he was only the more amusing as a study for the Monk-
barns[51] of Boston Bay, and Dr. Palfrey took him seriously, as his
clerical education required. His work was rather an Apologia in
the Greek sense; a justification of the ways of God to Man, or,
what was much the same thing, of Puritans to other men; and the
task of justification was onerous enough to require the occasional
relief of a contrast or scapegoat. When Dr. Palfrey happened on
the picturesque but unpuritanic figure of Captain John Smith,[52]
he felt no call to beautify Smith's picture or to defend his moral
character; he became impartial and penetrating. The famous
story of Pocahontas roused his latent New England scepticism.
He suggested to Adams, who wanted to make a position for himself, that an article in the *North American Review* on Captain John
Smith's relations with Pocahontas would attract as much attention, and probably break as much glass, as any other stone that
could be thrown by a beginner. Adams could suggest nothing
better. The task seemed likely to be amusing. So he planted
himself in the British Museum and patiently worked over all the
material he could find, until, at last, after three or four months
of labor, he got it in shape and sent it to Charles Norton,[53] who
was then editing the *North American*. Mr. Norton very civilly
and even kindly accepted it. The article appeared in January,
1867.

Surely, here was something to ponder over, as a step in education; something that tended to stagger a sceptic! In spite of personal wishes, intentions, and prejudices; in spite of civil wars and
diplomatic education; in spite of determination to be actual,
daily, and practical, Henry Adams found himself, at twenty-eight,
still in English society, dragged on one side into English dilettantism, which of all dilettantism he held the most futile; and,

on the other, into American antiquarianism, which of all antiquarianism he held the most foolish. This was the result of five
years in London. Even then he knew it to be a false start. He had
wholly lost his way. If he were ever to amount to anything, he
must begin a new education, in a new place, with a new purpose.

CHAPTER XV

Darwinism (1867–1868)

POLITICS, diplomacy, law, art, and history had opened no outlet for future energy or effort, but a man must do something, even in Portland Place, when winter is dark and winter evenings are exceedingly long. At that moment Darwin was convulsing society. The geological champion of Darwin was Sir Charles Lyell, and the Lyells were intimate at the Legation. Sir Charles constantly said of Darwin, what Palgrave said of Tennyson, that the first time he came to town, Adams should be asked to meet him, but neither of them ever came to town, or ever cared to meet a young American, and one could not go to them because they were known to dislike intrusion. The only Americans who were not allowed to intrude were the half-dozen in the Legation. Adams was content to read Darwin, especially his "Origin of Species" and his "Voyage of the Beagle." [1] He was a Darwinist before the letter, [2] a predestined follower of the tide; but he was hardly trained to follow Darwin's evidences. Fragmentary the British mind might be, but in those days it was doing a great deal of work in a very un-English way, building up so many and such vast theories on such narrow foundations as to shock the conservative, and delight the frivolous. The atomic theory; the correlation and conservation of energy; the mechanical theory of the universe; the kinetic theory of gases, and Darwin's Law of Natural Selection, were examples of what a young man had to take on trust. Neither he nor anyone else knew enough to verify them; in his ignorance of mathematics, he was particularly helpless; but this never stood in his way. The ideas were new and seemed to lead somewhere — to some great generalization which would finish one's clamor to be educated. That a beginner should understand them all, or believe them all, no one could expect, still less exact. Henry Adams was Darwinist because it was easier than not, for his ignorance exceeded belief, and one must know something in order to contradict even such triflers as Tyndall[3] and Huxley.[4]

By rights, he should have been also a Marxist, but some narrow trait of the New England nature seemed to blight socialism, and he tried in vain to make himself a convert. He did the next best thing; he became a Comteist, within the limits of evolution. He was ready to become anything but quiet. As though the world had not been enough upset in his time, he was eager to see it upset more. He had his wish, but he lost his hold on the results by trying to understand them.

He never tried to understand Darwin; but he still fancied he might get the best part of Darwinism from the easier study of geology; a science which suited idle minds as well as though it were history. Every curate in England dabbled in geology and hunted for vestiges of Creation.[5] Darwin hunted only for vestiges of Natural Selection, and Adams followed him, although he cared nothing about Selection, unless perhaps for the indirect amusement of upsetting curates. He felt, like nine men in ten, an instinctive belief in Evolution, but he felt no more concern in Natural than in unnatural Selection, though he seized with greediness the new volume on the "Antiquity of Man" which Sir Charles Lyell published in 1863 in order to support Darwin by wrecking the Garden of Eden.[6] Sir Charles next brought out, in 1866, a new edition of his "Principles,"[7] then the highest text-book of geology; but here the Darwinian doctrine grew in stature. Natural Selection led back to Natural Evolution, and at last to Natural Uniformity. This was a vast stride. Unbroken Evolution under uniform conditions pleased everyone—except curates and bishops; it was the very best substitute for religion; a safe, conservative, practical, thoroughly Common-Law[8] deity. Such a working system for the universe suited a young man who had just helped to waste five or ten thousand million dollars and a million lives, more of less, to enforce unity and uniformity on people who objected to it; the idea was only too seductive in its perfection; it had the charm of art. Unity and Uniformity were the whole motive of philosophy, and if Darwin, like a true Englishman, preferred to back into it — to reach God *a posteriori*[9] — rather than start from it, like Spinoza,[10] the difference of method taught only the moral that the best way of reaching unity was to unite. Any road was good that arrived.

Life depended on it. One had been, from the first, dragged hither and thither like a French poodle on a string, following always the strongest pull, between one form of unity or centralization and another. The proof that one had acted wisely because of obeying the primordial habit of nature flattered one's self-esteem. Steady, uniform, unbroken evolution from lower to higher seemed easy. So, one day when Sir Charles came to the Legation to inquire about getting his "Principles" properly noticed in America, young Adams found nothing simpler than to suggest that he could do it himself if Sir Charles would tell him what to say. Youth risks such encounters with the universe before one succumbs to it, yet even he was surprised at Sir Charles's ready assent, and still more so at finding himself, after half an hour's conversation, sitting down to clear the minds of American geologists about the principles of their profession. This was getting on fast; Arthur Pendennis[11] had never gone so far.

The geologists were a hardy class, not likely to be much hurt by Adams's learning, nor did he throw away much concern on their account. He undertook the task chiefly to educate, not them, but himself, and if Sir Isaac Newton[12] had, like Sir Charles Lyell, asked him to explain for Americans his last edition of the "Principia," Adams would have jumped at the chance. Unfortunately the mere reading such works for amusement is quite a different matter from studying them for criticism. Ignorance must always begin at the beginning. Adams must inevitably have begun by asking Sir Isaac for an intelligible reason why the apple fell to the ground. He did not know enough to be satisfied with the fact. The Law of Gravitation was so-and-so, but what was Gravitation? and he would have been thrown quite off his base if Sir Isaac had answered that he did not know.

At the very outset Adams struck on Sir Charles's Glacial Theory or theories. He was ignorant enough to think that the glacial epoch looked like a chasm between him and a uniformitarian world. If the glacial period were uniformity, what was catastrophe? To him the two or three labored guesses that Sir Charles suggested or borrowed to explain glaciation were proof of nothing, and were quite unsolid as support for so immense a superstructure as geological uniformity. If one were at liberty to be as lax in science as in theology, and to assume unity from the start, one might better say so, as the Church did, and not invite attack by appearing weak in evidence. Naturally a young man, altogether ignorant, could not say this to Sir Charles Lyell or Sir Isaac Newton; but he was forced to state Sir Charles's views, which he thought weak as hypotheses and worthless as proofs. Sir Charles himself seemed shy of them. Adams hinted his heresies in vain. At last he resorted to what he thought the bold experiment of inserting a sentence in the text, intended to provoke correction. "The introduction [by Louis Agassiz] of this new geological agent seemed at first sight inconsistent with Sir Charles's argument, obliging him to allow that causes had in fact existed on the earth capable of producing more violent geological changes than would be possible in our own day." The hint produced no effect. Sir Charles said not a word; he let the paragraph stand; and Adams never knew whether the great Uniformitarian was strict or lax in his uniformitarian creed; but he doubted.

Objections fatal to one mind are futile to another, and as far as concerned the article, the matter ended there, although the glacial epoch remained a misty region in the young man's Darwinism. Had it been the only one, he would not have fretted about it; but uniformity often worked queerly and sometimes did not work as Natural Selection at all. Finding himself at a loss for some single figure to illustrate the Law of Natural Selection, Adams asked Sir Charles for the simplest case of uniformity on record. Much to his surprise Sir Charles told him that certain forms, like *Terebratula*,[13] appeared to be identical from the beginning to the end of geological time. Since this was altogether too much uniformity and much too little selection, Adams gave up the attempt to begin at the beginning, and tried starting at the end — himself. Taking for granted that the vertebrates would serve his purpose, he asked Sir Charles to introduce him to the first vertebrate. Infinitely to his bewilderment, Sir Charles informed him that the first vertebrate was a very respectable fish, among the earliest of all fossils, which had lived, and whose bones were still reposing, under Adams's own favorite Abbey on Wenlock Edge.

By this time, in 1867, Adams had learned to know Shropshire familiarly, and it was the part of his diplomatic education which he loved best. Like Catherine Olney in "Northanger Abbey,"[14] he yearned for nothing so keenly as to feel at home in a thirteenth-century Abbey, unless it were to haunt a fifteenth-century Prior's House, and both these joys were his at Wenlock. With companions or without, he never tired of it. Whether he rode about the Wrekin, or visited all the historical haunts from Ludlow Castle and Stokesay to Boscobel and Uriconium;[15] or followed the Roman road or scratched in the Abbey ruins, all was amusing and carried a flavor of its own like that of the Roman Campagna;[16] but perhaps he liked best to ramble over the Edge on a summer afternoon and look across the Marches[17] to the mountains of Wales. The peculiar flavor of the scenery had something to do with absence of evolution; it was better marked in Egypt: it was felt wherever time-sequences became interchangeable. One's instinct abhors time. As one lay on the slope of the Edge, looking sleepily through the summer haze towards Shrewsbury or Cader Idris or Caer Caradoc[18] or Uriconium, nothing suggested sequence. The Roman road was twin to the railroad; Uriconium, was well worth Shrewsbury; Wenlock and Buildwas were far superior to Bridgnorth.[19] The shepherds of Caractacus or Offa,[20] or the monks of Buildwas, had they approached where he lay in the grass, would have taken him only for another and tamer variety of Welsh thief. They would have seen little to surprise them in the modern landscape unless it were the steam of a distant railway. One might mix up the terms of time as one liked, or stuff the present anywhere into the past, measuring time by Falstaff's Shrewsbury clock,[21] without violent sense of wrong, as one could do it on the Pacific Ocean; but the triumph of all was to look south along the Edge to the abode of one's earliest ancestor and nearest relative, the ganoid fish, whose name, according to Professor Huxley, was *Pteraspis*, a cousin of the sturgeon, and whose kingdom, according to Sir Roderick Murchison,[22] was called Siluria. Life began and ended there. Behind that horizon lay only the Cambrian,[23] without vertebrates or any other organism except a few shell-fish. On the further verge of the Cambrian rose the crystalline rocks from which every trace of organic existence had been erased.

That here, on the Wenlock Edge of time, a young American, seeking only frivolous amusement, should find a legitimate parentage as modern as though just caught in the Severn[24] below, astonished him as much as though he had found Darwin himself. In the scale of evolution, one vertebrate was as good as another. For anything he, or any one else, knew, nine hundred and ninety-nine parts of evolution out of a thousand lay behind or below the *Pteraspis*. To an American in search of a father, it mattered nothing whether the father breathed through lungs, or walked on fins, or on feet. Evolution of mind was altogether another matter and belonged to another science, but whether one traced descent from the shark or the wolf was immaterial even in morals. This matter had been discussed for ages without scientific result. La Fontaine[25] and other fabulists maintained that the wolf, even in morals, stood higher than man; and in view of the late civil war, Adams had doubts of his own on the facts of moral evolution: —

"Tout bien considéré, je te soutiens en somme,
   Que scélérat pour scélérat,
Il vaut mieux être un loup qu'un homme." [26]

It might well be! At all events, it did not enter into the problem of *Pteraspis,* for it was quite certain that no complete proof of Natural Selection had occurred back to the time of *Pteraspis,* and that before *Pteraspis* was eternal void. No trace of any vertebrate had been found there; only starfish, shell-fish, polyps, or trilobites whose kindly descendants he had often bathed with, as a child on the shores of Quincy Bay.

That *Pteraspis* and shark were his cousins, great-uncles, or grandfathers, in no way troubled him, but that either or both of them should be older than evolution itself seemed to him perplexing; nor could he at all simplify the problem by taking the sudden back-somersault into Quincy Bay in search of the fascinating creature he had called a horseshoe, whose huge dome of shell and sharp spur of tail had so alarmed him as a child. In Siluria, he understood, Sir Roderick Murchison called the horseshoe a *Limulus,*[27] which helped nothing. Neither in the *Limulus* nor in the *Terebratula,* nor in the *Cestracion Philippi,*[28] any more than in the *Pteraspis,* could one conceive an ancestor, but, if one must, the choice mattered little. Cousinship had limits but no one knew enough to fix them. When the vertebrate vanished in Siluria, it disappeared instantly and forever. Neither vertebra nor scale nor print reappeared, nor any trace of ascent or descent to a lower type. The vertebrate began in the Ludlow shale, as complete as Adams himself — in some respects more so — at the top of the column of organic evolution: and geology offered no sort of proof that he had ever been anything else. Ponder over it as he might, Adams could see nothing in the theory of Sir Charles but pure inference, precisely like the inference of Paley,[29] that, if one found a watch, one inferred a maker. He could detect no more evolution in life since the *Pteraspis* than he could detect it in architecture since the Abbey. All he could prove was change. Coal-power alone asserted evolution — of power — and only by violence could be forced to assert selection of type.

All this seemed trivial to the true Darwinian, and to Sir Charles it was mere defect in the geological record. Sir Charles labored only to heap up the evidences of evolution; to cumulate them till the mass became irresistible. With that purpose, Adams gladly studied and tried to help Sir Charles, but, behind the lesson of the day, he was conscious that, in geology as in theology, he could prove only Evolution that did not evolve; Uniformity that was not uniform; and Selection that did not select. To other Darwinians — except Darwin — Natural Selection seemed a dogma to be put in the place of the Athanasian creed;[30] it was a form of religious hope; a promise of ultimate perfection. Adams wished no better; he warmly sympathized in the object; but when he came to ask himself what he truly thought, he felt that he had no Faith; that whenever the next new hobby should be brought out, he should surely drop off from Darwinism like a monkey from a perch; that the idea of one Form, Law, Order, or Sequence had no more value for him than the idea of none; that what he valued most was Motion, and that what attracted his mind was Change.

Psychology was to him a new study, and a dark corner of education. As he lay on Wenlock Edge, with the sheep nibbling the grass close about him as they or their betters had nibbled the grass — or whatever there was to nibble — in the Silurian kingdom of Pteraspis, he seemed to have fallen on an evolution far more wonderful than that of fishes. He did not like it; he could not account for it; and he determined to stop it. Never since the days of his *Limulus* ancestry had any of his ascendants thought thus. Their modes of thought might be many, but their thought was one. Out of his millions of millions of ancestors, back to the Cambrian mollusks, every one had probably lived and died in the illusion of Truths which did not amuse him, and which had never changed. Henry Adams was the first in an infinite series to discover and admit to himself that he really did not care whether truth was, or was not, true. He did not even care that it should be proved true, unless the process were new and amusing. He was a Darwinian for fun.

From the beginning of history, this attitude had been branded as criminal — worse than crime — sacrilege! Society punished it ferociously and justly, in self-defence. Mr. Adams, the father, looked on it as moral weakness; it annoyed him; but it did not annoy him nearly so much as it annoyed his son, who had no need to learn from Hamlet the fatal effect of the pale cast of thought on enterprises great or small.[31] He had no notion of letting the currents of his action be turned awry by this form of conscience. To him, the current of his time was to be his current, lead where it might. He put psychology under lock and key; he insisted on maintaining his absolute standards; on aiming at ultimate Unity. The mania for handling all the sides of every question, looking into every window, and opening every door, was, as Bluebeard[32] judiciously pointed out to his wives, fatal to their practical usefulness in society. One could not stop to chase doubts as though they were rabbits. One had no time to paint and putty the surface of Law, even though it were cracked and rotten. For the young men whose lives were cast in the generation between 1867 and 1900, Law should be Evolution from lower to higher, aggregation of the atom in the mass, concentration of multiplicity in unity, compulsion of anarchy in order; and he would force himself to follow wherever it led, though he should sacrifice five thousand millions more in money, and a million more lives.

As the path ultimately led, it sacrificed much more than this; but at the time, he thought the price he named a high one, and he could not foresee that science and society would desert him in paying it. He, at least, took his education as a Darwinian in good faith. The Church was gone, and Duty was dim, but Will should take its place, founded deeply in interest and law. This was the result of five or six years in England; a result so British as to be almost the equivalent of an Oxford degree.

Quite serious about it, he set to work at once. While confusing his ideas about geology to the apparent satisfaction of Sir Charles who left him his field-compass in token of it, Adams turned resolutely to business, and attacked the burning question of specie payments. His principles assured him that the honest way to resume payments was to restrict currency[33] He thought he might win a name among financiers and statesmen at home by showing how this task had been done by England, after the classical suspension of 1797–1821[34] Setting himself to the study of this perplexed period, he waded as well as he could through a morass of volumes, pamphlets, and debates, until he learned to his confusion that the Bank of England itself and all the best British financial writers held that restriction was a fatal mistake, and that the best treatment of a debased currency was to let it alone, as the Bank had in fact done. Time and patience were the remedies.

The shock of this discovery to his financial principles was serious; much more serious than the shock of the *Terebratula* and *Pteraspis* to his principles of geology. A mistake about Evolution was not fatal; a mistake about specie payments would destroy forever the last hope of employment in State Street. Six months of patient labor would be thrown away if he did not publish, and with it his whole scheme of making himself a position as a practical man-of-business. If he did publish, how could he tell virtuous bankers in State Street that moral and absolute principles of abstract truth[35] such as theirs, had nothing to do with the matter, and that they had better let it alone? Geologists, naturally a humble and helpless class, might not revenge impertinences offered to their science; but capitalists never forgot or forgave.

With labor and caution he made one long article on British Finance in 1816, and another on the Bank Restriction of 1797–1821, and, doing both up in one package, he sent it to the *North American* for choice. He knew that two heavy, technical, financial studies thus thrown at an editor's head, would probably return to crush the author; but the audacity of youth is more sympathetic

233

— when successful — than his ignorance. The editor accepted both.

When the post brought his letter, Adams looked at it as though he were a debtor who had begged for an extension. He read it with as much relief as the debtor, if it had brought him the loan. The letter gave the new writer literary rank. Henceforward he had the freedom of the press. These articles, following those on Pocahontas and Lyell, enrolled him on the permanent staff of the *North American Review*. Precisely what this rank was worth, no one could say; but, for fifty years the *North American Review* had been the stage coach which carried literary Bostonians to such distinction as they had achieved. Few writers had ideas which warranted thirty pages of development, but for such as thought they had, the *Review* alone offered space. An article was a small volume which required at least three months' work, and was paid, at best, five dollars a page. Not many men even in England or France could write a good thirty-page article, and practically no one in America read them; but a few score of people, mostly in search of items to steal, ran over the pages to extract an idea or a fact, which was a sort of wild game — a blue-fish or a teal — worth anywhere from fifty cents to five dollars. Newspaper writers had their eye on quarterly pickings. The circulation of the *Review* had never exceeded three or four hundred copies, and the *Review* had never paid its reasonable expenses. Yet it stood at the head of American literary periodicals; it was a source of suggestion to cheaper workers; it reached far into societies that never knew its existence; it was an organ worth playing on; and, in the fancy of Henry Adams, it led, in some indistinct future, to playing on a New York daily newspaper.

With the editor's letter under his eyes, Adams asked himself what better he could have done. On the whole, considering his helplessness, he thought he had done as well as his neighbors. No one could yet guess which of his contemporaries was most likely to play a part in the great world. A shrewd prophet in Wall Street might perhaps have set a mark on Pierpont Morgan, but hardly on the Rockefellers or William C. Whitney or Whitelaw Reid. No one would have picked out William McKinley or John Hay or Mark Hanna for great statesmen. Boston was ignorant of the careers in store for Alexander Agassiz and Henry Higginson. Phillips Brooks was unknown; Henry James was unheard; Howells was new; Richardson and LaFarge were struggling for a start.[36] Out of any score of names and reputations that should reach beyond the century, the thirty-years-old who were starting in the year 1867 could show none that was so far in advance as to warrant odds in its favor. The army men had for the most part fallen to the ranks. Had Adams foreseen the future exactly as it came, he would have been no wiser, and could have chosen no better path.

Thus it turned out that the last year in England was the pleasantest. He was already old in society, and belonged to the Silurian horizon. The Prince of Wales had come. Mr. Disraeli, Lord Stanley, and the future Lord Salisbury had thrown into the background the memories of Palmerston and Russell. Europe was moving rapidly, and the conduct of England during the American Civil War was the last thing that London liked to recall. The revolution since 1861 was nearly complete, and, for the first time in history, the American felt himself almost as strong as an Englishman. He had thirty years to wait before he should feel himself stronger. Meanwhile even a private secretary could afford to be happy. His old education was finished; his new one was not begun; he still loitered a year, feeling himself near the end of a very long, anxious, tempestuous, successful voyage, with another to follow, and a summer sea between.

He made what use he could of it. In February, 1868, he was back in Rome with his friend Milnes Gaskell. For another season he wandered on horseback over the campagna or on foot through the Rome of the middle ages, and sat once more on the steps of Ara Cœli, as had become with him almost a superstition, like the waters of the fountain of Trevi.[37] Rome was still tragic and solemn as ever, with its mediæval society, artistic, literary, and clerical, taking itself as seriously as in the days of Byron and Shelley.[38] The long ten years of accidental education had changed nothing for him there. He knew no more in 1868 than in 1858. He had learned nothing whatever that made Rome more intelligible to him, or made life easier to handle. The case was no better when he got back to London and went through his last season. London had become his vice. He loved his haunts, his houses, his habits, and even his hansom cabs. He loved growling like an Englishman, and going into society where he knew not a face, and cared not a straw. He lived deep into the lives and loves and disappointments of his friends. When at last he found himself back again at Liverpool, his heart wrenched by the act of parting, he moved mechanically, unstrung, but he had no more acquired education than when he first trod the steps of the Adelphi Hotel in November,[39] 1858. He could see only one great change, and this was wholly in years. Eaton Hall no longer impressed his imagination; even the architecture of Chester roused but a sleepy interest; he felt no sensation whatever in the atmosphere of the British peerage, but mainly an habitual dislike to most of the people who frequented their country houses; he had become English to the point of sharing their petty social divisions, their dislikes and prejudices against each other; he took England no longer with the awe of American youth, but with the habit of an old and rather worn suit of clothes. As far as he knew, this was all that Englishmen meant by social education, but in any case it was all the education he had gained from seven years in London.

CHAPTER XVI

The Press (1868)

A T ten o'clock of a July night, in heat that made the tropical rain-shower simmer, the Adams family and the Motley family clambered down the side of their Cunard steamer into the government tugboat, which set them ashore in black darkness at the end of some North River pier. Had they been Tyrian traders[1] of the year B.C. 1000, landing from a galley fresh from Gibraltar, they could hardly have been stranger on the shore of a world, so changed from what it had been ten years before. The historian of the Dutch, no longer historian but diplomatist, started up an unknown street, in company with the private secretary who had become private citizen, in search of carriages to convey the two parties to the Brevoort House.[2] The pursuit was arduous but successful. Towards midnight they found shelter once more in their native land.

How much its character had changed or was changing, they could not wholly know, and they could but partly feel. For that matter, the land itself knew no more than they. Society in America was always trying, almost as blindly as an earthworm, to realize and understand itself; to catch up with its own head, and to twist about in search of its tail. Society offered the profile of a long, straggling caravan, stretching loosely towards the prairies, its few score of leaders far in advance and its millions of immigrants, negroes, and Indians far in the rear, somewhere in archaic time. It enjoyed the vast advantage over Europe that all seemed, for the moment, to move in one direction, while Europe wasted most of its energy in trying several contradictory movements at once; but whenever Europe or Asia should be polarized or oriented towards the same point, America might easily lose her lead. Meanwhile each newcomer needed to slip into a place as near the head of the caravan as possible, and needed most to know where the leaders could be found.

One could divine pretty nearly where the force lay, since the last ten years had given to the great mechanical energies — coal, iron, steam — a distinct superiority in power over the old industrial elements — agriculture, handwork, and learning; but the result of this revolution on a survivor from the fifties resembled the action of the earthworm; he twisted about, in vain, to recover his starting-point; he could no longer see his own trail; he had become an estray; a flotsam or jetsam of wreckage; a belated reveller, or a scholar-gipsy like Matthew Arnold's.[3] His world was dead. Not a Polish Jew fresh from Warsaw or Cracow [4] — not a furtive Yacoob or Ysaac still reeking of the Ghetto, snarling a weird Yiddish to the officers of the customs — but had a keener instinct, an intenser energy, and a freer hand than he — American of Americans, with Heaven knew how many Puritans and Patriots behind him, and an education that had cost a civil war. He made no complaint and found no fault with his time; he was no worse off than the Indians or the buffalo who had been ejected from their heritage by his own people; but he vehemently insisted that he was not himself at fault. The defeat was not due to him, nor yet to any superiority of his rivals. He had been unfairly forced out of the track, and must get back into it as best he could.

One comfort he could enjoy to the full. Little as he might be fitted for the work that was before him, he had only to look at his father and Motley to see figures less fitted for it than he. All were equally survivals from the forties—bric-a-brac from the time of Louis Philippe; stylists; doctrinaires; ornaments that had been more or less suited to the colonial architecture, but which never had much value in Desbrosses Street or Fifth Avenue.[5] They could scarcely have earned five dollars a day in any modern industry. The men who commanded high pay were as a rule not ornamental. Even Commodore Vanderbilt and Jay Gould[6] lacked social charm. Doubtless the country needed ornament — needed it very badly indeed — but it needed energy still more, and capital most of all, for its supply was ridiculously out of proportion to its wants. On the new scale of power, merely to make the continent habitable for civilized people would require an immediate outlay that would have bankrupted the world. As yet, no portion of the world except a few narrow stretches of western Europe had ever been tolerably provided with the essentials of comfort and convenience; to fit out an entire continent with roads and the decencies of life would exhaust the credit of the entire planet. Such an estimate seemed outrageous to a Texan member of Congress who loved the simplicity of nature's noblemen; but the mere suggestion that a sun existed above him would outrage the self-respect of a deep-sea fish that carried a lantern on the end of its nose.[7] From the moment that railways were introduced, life took on extravagance.

Thus the belated reveller who landed in the dark at the Desbrosses Street ferry, found his energies exhausted in the effort to see his own length. The new Americans, of whom he was to be one, must, whether they were fit or unfit, create a world of their own, a science, a society, a philosophy, a universe, where they had not yet created a road or even learned to dig their own iron. They had no time for thought; they saw, and could see, nothing beyond their day's work; their attitude to the universe outside them was that of the deep-sea fish. Above all, they naturally and intensely disliked to be told what to do, and how to do it, by men who took their ideas and their methods from the abstract theories of history, philosophy, or theology. They knew enough to know that their world was one of energies quite new.

All this, the newcomer understood and accepted, since he could not help himself and saw that the American could help himself as little as the newcomer; but the fact remained that the more he knew, the less he was educated. Society knew as much as this, and seemed rather inclined to boast of it,[8] at least on the stump; but the leaders of industry betrayed no sentiment, popular or other. They used, without qualm, whatever instruments they found at hand. They had been obliged, in 1861, to turn aside and waste immense energy in settling what had been settled a thousand years before, and should never have been revived. At prodigious expense, by sheer force, they broke resistance down, leaving everything but the mere fact of power untouched, since nothing else had a solution. Race and thought were beyond reach. Having cleared its path so far, society went back to its work, and threw itself on that which stood first — its roads. The field was vast; altogether beyond its power to control offhand; and society dropped every thought of dealing with anything more than the single fraction called a railway system. This relatively small part of its task was still so big as to need the energies of a generation, for it required all the new machinery to be created — capital, banks, mines, furnaces, shops, power-houses, technical knowledge, mechanical population, together with a steady remodelling of social and political habits, ideas, and institutions to fit the new scale and suit the new conditions. The generation between 1865 and 1895 was already mortgaged to the railways, and no one knew it better than the generation itself.

Whether Henry Adams knew it or not, he knew enough to act as though he did. He reached Quincy once more, ready for the new start. His brother Charles had determined to strike for the railroads; Henry was to strike for the press; and they hoped to play into each other's hands. They had great need, for they found no one else to play with. After discovering the worthlessness of a so-called education, they had still to discover the worthlessness of so-called social connection. No young man had a larger acquaintance and relationship than Henry Adams, yet he knew no one who could help him. He was for sale, in the open market. So were many of his friends. All the world knew it, and knew too that they were cheap; to be bought at the price of a mechanic. There was no concealment, no delicacy, and no illusion about it. Neither he nor his friends complained; but he felt sometimes a little surprised that, as far as he knew, no one, seeking in the labor market, ever so much as inquired about their fitness. The want of solidarity between old and young seemed American. The young man was required to impose himself, by the usual business methods, as a necessity on his elders, in order to compel them to buy him as an investment. As Adams felt it, he was in a manner expected to blackmail. Many a young man complained to him in after life of the same experience, which became a matter of curious reflection as he grew old. The labor market of good society was ill-organized.

Boston seemed to offer no market for educated labor. A peculiar and perplexing amalgam Boston always was, and although it had changed much in ten years, it was not less perplexing. One no longer dined at two o'clock; one could no longer skate on Back Bay;[9] one heard talk of Bostonians worth five millions or more as something not incredible. Yet the place seemed still simple, and less restless-minded than ever before. In the line that Adams had chosen to follow, he needed more than all else the help of the press, but any shadow of hope on that side vanished instantly. The less one meddled with the Boston press, the better. All the newspapermen were clear on that point. The same was true of politics. Boston meant business. The Bostonians were building railways. Adams would have liked to help in building railways, but had no education. He was not fit.

He passed three or four months thus, visiting relations, renewing friendships, and studying the situation. At thirty years old, the man who has not yet got further than to study the situation, is lost, or near it. He could see nothing in the situation that could be of use to him. His friends had won no more from it than he. His brother Charles, after three years of civil life, was no better off than himself, except for being married and in greater need of income. His brother John had become a brilliant political leader on the wrong side.[10] No one had yet regained the lost ground of the war.

He went to Newport[11] and tried to be fashionable, but even in the simple life of 1868, he failed as fashion. All the style he had learned so painfully in London was worse than useless in America where every standard was different. Newport was charming, but it asked for no education and gave none. What it gave was much gayer and pleasanter, and one enjoyed it amazingly; but friendships in that society were a kind of social partnership, like the classes at college; not education but the subjects of education. All were doing the same thing, and asking the same question of the future. None could help. Society seemed founded on the law that all was for the best New Yorkers in the best of Newports, and that all young people were rich if they could waltz. It was a new version of the Ant and Grasshopper.[12]

At the end of three months, the only person, among the hundreds he had met, who had offered him a word of encouragement or had shown a sign of acquaintance with his doings, was Edward Atkinson.[13] Boston was cool towards sons, whether prodigals or other, and needed much time to make up its mind what to do for them — time which Adams, at thirty years old, could hardly spare. He had not the courage or self-confidence to hire an office in State Street, as so many of his friends did, and doze there alone, vacuity within and a snowstorm outside, waiting for Fortune to knock at the door, or hoping to find her asleep in the elevator; or on the staircase, since elevators were not yet in use. Whether this course would have offered his best chance he never knew; it was one of the points in practical education which most needed a clear understanding, and he could never reach it. His father and mother would have been glad to see him stay with them and begin reading Blackstone again, and he showed no very filial tenderness by abruptly breaking the tie that had lasted so long. After all, perhaps Beacon Street was as good as any other street for his objects in life; possibly his easiest and surest path was from Beacon Street to State Street and back again, all the days of his years. Who could tell? Even after life was over, the doubt could not be determined.

In thus sacrificing his heritage, he only followed the path that had led him from the beginning. Boston was full of his brothers. He had reckoned from childhood on outlawry as his peculiar birthright. The mere thought of beginning life again in Mount Vernon Street lowered the pulsations of his heart. This is a story of education — not a mere lesson of life — and, with education, temperament has in strictness nothing to do, although in practice they run close together. Neither by temperament nor by education was he fitted for Boston. He had drifted far away and behind his companions there; no one trusted his temperament or education; he had to go.

Since no other path seemed to offer itself, he stuck to his plan of joining the press, and selected Washington as the shortest road to New York, but, in 1868, Washington stood outside the social pale. No Bostonian had ever gone there.[14] One announced one's self as an adventurer and an office-seeker, a person of deplorably bad judgment, and the charges were true. The chances of ending in the gutter were, at best, even. The risk was the greater in Adams's case, because he had no very clear idea what to do when he got there. That he must educate himself over again, for objects quite new, in an air altogether hostile to his old educations, was the only certainty; but how he was to do it — how he was to convert the idler in Rotten Row into the lobbyist of the Capital — he had not an idea, and no one to teach him. The question of money is rarely serious for a young American unless he is married, and money never troubled Adams more than others; not because he had it, but because he could do without it, like most people in Washington who all lived on the income of bricklayers; but with or without money he met the difficulty that, after getting to Washington in order to go on the press, it was necessary to seek a press to go on. For large work he could count on the *North American Review*, but this was scarcely a press. For current discussion and correspondence, he could depend on the New York *Nation ;* but what he needed was a New York daily, and no

New York daily needed him. He lost his one chance by the death of Henry J. Raymond. The *Tribune* under Horace Greeley[15] was out of the question both for political and personal reasons, and because Whitelaw Reid had already undertaken that singularly venturesome position, amid difficulties that would have swamped Adams in four-and-twenty hours. Charles A. Dana[16] had made the *Sun* a very successful as well as a very amusing paper, but had hurt his own social position in doing it; and Adams knew himself well enough to know that he could never please himself and Dana too; with the best intentions, he must always fail as a black-guard, and at that time a strong dash of blackguardism was life to the *Sun*. As for the *New York Herald*, it was a despotic em-pire admitting no personality but that of Bennett.[17] Thus, for the moment, the New York daily press offered no field except the free-trade Holy Land of the *Evening Post* under William Cullen Bryant,[18] while beside it lay only the elevated plateau of the New Jerusalem occupied by Godkin and the *Nation*. Much as Adams liked Godkin, and glad as he was to creep under the shelter of the *Evening Post* and the *Nation*, he was well aware that he should find there only the same circle of readers that he reached in the *North American Review*.

The outlook was dim, but it was all he had, and at Washing-ton, except for the personal friendship of Mr. Evarts who was then Attorney-General and living there, he would stand in solitude much like that of London in 1861. Evarts did what no one in Boston seemed to care for doing; he held out a hand to the young man. Whether Boston, like Salem,[19] really shunned strangers, or whether Evarts was an exception even in New York, he had the social instinct which Boston had not. Generous by nature, prodi-gal in hospitality, fond of young people, and a born man-of-the-world, Evarts gave and took liberally, without scruple, and ac-cepted the world without fearing or abusing it. His wit was the least part of his social attraction. His talk was broad and free. He laughed where he could; he joked if a joke was possible; he was true to his friends, and never lost his temper or became ill-[20] natured. Like all New Yorkers he was decidedly not a Bostonian; but he was what one might call a transplanted New Englander, like General Sherman;[21] a variety, grown in ranker soil. In the course of life, and in widely different countries, Adams incurred heavy debts of gratitude to persons on whom he had no claim and to whom he could seldom make return; perhaps half-a-dozen such debts remained unpaid at last, although six is a large number as lives go; but kindness seldom came more happily than when Mr. Evarts took him to Washington in October, 1868.

Adams accepted the hospitality of the sleeper, with deep gratitude, the more because his first struggle with a sleeping-car made him doubt the value — to him — of a Pullman civilization; but he was even more grateful for the shelter of Mr. Evarts's house in H Street at the corner of Fourteenth, where he abode in safety and content till he found rooms in the roomless village. To him the village seemed unchanged. Had he not known that a great war and eight years of astonishing movement had passed over it, he would have noticed nothing that betrayed growth. As of old, houses were few; rooms fewer; even the men were the same. No one seemed to miss the usual comforts of civilization, and Adams was glad to get rid of them, for his best chance lay in the eighteenth century.

The first step, of course, was the making of acquaintance, and the first acquaintance was naturally the President, to whom an aspirant to the press officially paid respect. Evarts immediately took him to the White House and presented him to President Andrew Johnson.[22] The interview was brief and consisted in the stock remark common to monarchs and valets, that the young man looked even younger than he was. The young man felt even younger than he looked. He never saw the President again, and never felt a wish to see him, for Andrew Johnson was not the sort of man whom a young reformer of thirty, with two or three foreign educations, was likely to see with enthusiasm; yet, musing over the interview as a matter of education, long years afterwards, he could not help recalling the President's figure with a distinctness that surprised him. The old-fashioned Southern Senator and statesman sat in his chair at his desk with a look of self-esteem that had its value. None doubted. All were great men; some, no doubt, were greater than others; but all were statesmen and all were supported, lifted, inspired by the moral certainty of rightness. To them the universe was serious, even solemn, but it was their universe, a Southern conception of right. Lamar used to say that he never entertained a doubt of the soundness of the Southern system until he found that slavery could not stand a war. Slavery was only a part of the Southern system, and the life of it all — the vigor — the poetry — was its moral certainty of self. The Southerner could not doubt; and this self-assurance not only gave Andrew Johnson the look of a true President, but actually made him one. When Adams came to look back on it afterwards, he was surprised to realize how strong the Executive was in 1868 — perhaps the strongest he was ever to see. Certainly he never again found himself so well satisfied, or so much at home.

Seward was still Secretary of State. Hardly yet an old man, though showing marks of time and violence, Mr. Seward seemed little changed in these eight years. He was the same — with a difference. Perhaps he — unlike Henry Adams — had at last got an education, and all he wanted. Perhaps he had resigned himself to doing without it. Whatever the reason, although his manner was as roughly kind as ever, and his talk as free, he appeared to have closed his account with the public; he no longer seemed to care; he asked nothing, gave nothing, and invited no support; he talked little of himself or of others, and waited only for his discharge. Adams was well pleased to be near him in these last days of his power and fame, and went much to his house in the evenings when he was sure to be at his whist. At last, as the end drew near, wanting to feel that the great man — the only chief he ever served even as a volunteer — recognized some personal relation, he asked Mr. Seward to dine with him one evening in his rooms, and play his game of whist there, as he did every night in his own house. Mr. Seward came and had his whist, and Adams remembered his rough parting speech: "A very sensible entertainment!" It was the only favor he ever asked of Mr. Seward, and the only one he ever accepted.

Thus, as a teacher of wisdom, after twenty years of example, Governor Seward passed out of one's life, and Adams lost what should have been his firmest ally; but in truth the State Department had ceased to be the centre of his interest, and the Treasury had taken its place. The Secretary of the Treasury was a man new to politics — Hugh McCulloch[23] — not a person of much importance in the eyes of practical politicans such as young members of the press meant themselves to become, but they all liked Mr. McCulloch, though they thought him a stop-gap rather than a force. Had they known what sort of forces the Treasury was to offer them for support in the generation to come, they might have reflected a long while on their estimate of McCulloch. Adams was fated to watch the flittings of many more Secretaries than he ever cared to know, and he rather came back in the end to the idea that McCulloch was the best of them, although he seemed to represent everything that one liked least. He was no politician, he had no party, and no power. He was not fashionable or decorative. He was a banker, and towards bankers Adams felt the narrow prejudice which the serf feels to his overseer; for he knew he must obey, and he knew that the helpless showed only their helplessness when they tempered obedience by mockery. The world, after 1865, became a bankers' world, and no banker would ever trust one who had deserted State Street, and had gone to Washington with purposes of doubtful credit, or of no credit at all, for he could not have put up enough collateral to borrow five thousand dollars of any bank in America. The banker never would trust him, and he would never trust the banker. To him, the banking mind was obnoxious; and this antipathy caused him the more surprise at finding McCulloch the broadest, most liberal, most genial, and most practical public man in Washington.

There could be no doubt of it. The burden of the Treasury at that time was very great. The whole financial system was in chaos; every part of it required reform; the utmost experience, tact, and skill could not make the machine work smoothly. No one knew how well McCulloch did it until his successor took it in charge, and tried to correct his methods. Adams did not know enough to appreciate McCulloch's technical skill, but he was struck at his open and generous treatment of young men. Of all rare qualities, this was, in Adams's experience, the rarest. As a rule, officials dread interference. The strongest often resent it most. Any official who admits equality in discussion of his official course, feels it to be an act of virtue; after a few months or years he tires of the effort. Every friend in power is a friend lost. This rule is so nearly absolute that it may be taken in practice as admitting no exception. Apparent exceptions exist, and McCulloch was one of them.

McCulloch had been spared the gluttonous selfishness and infantile jealousy which are the commoner results of early political education. He had neither past nor future, and could afford to be careless of his company. Adams found him surrounded by all the active and intelligent young men in the country. Full of faith, greedy for work, eager for reform, energetic, confident, capable, quick of study, charmed with a fight, equally ready to defend or attack, they were unselfish, and even — as young men went — honest. They came mostly from the army, with the spirit of the volunteers. Frank Walker,[24] Frank Barlow, Frank Bartlett were types of the generation. Most of the press, and much of the public, especially in the West, shared their ideas. No one denied the need for reform. The whole government, from top to bottom, was rotten with the senility of what was antiquated and the instability of what was improvised. The currency was only one example; the tariff was another; but the whole fabric required reconstruction as much as in 1789, for the Constitution had become as antiquated as the Confederation. Sooner or later a shock must come, the more dangerous the longer postponed. The Civil War had made a new system in fact; the country would have to reorganize the machinery in practice and theory.

One might discuss indefinitely the question which branch of government needed reform most urgently; all needed it enough, but no one denied that the finances were a scandal, and a constant, universal nuisance. The tariff was worse, though more interests upheld it. McCulloch had the singular merit of facing reform with large good-nature and willing sympathy — outside of parties, jobs, bargains, corporations or intrigues — which Adams never was to meet again.

Chaos often breeds life, when order breeds habit. The Civil War had bred life. The army bred courage. Young men of the volunteer type were not always docile under control, but they were handy in a fight. Adams was greatly pleased to be admitted as one of them. He found himself much at home with them — more at home than he ever had been before, or was ever to be again — in the atmosphere of the Treasury. He had no strong party passion, and he felt as though he and his friends owned this administration, which, in its dying days, had neither friends nor future except in them.

These were not the only allies; the whole government in all its branches was alive with them. Just at that moment the Supreme Court was about to take up the Legal Tender cases where Judge Curtis[25] had been employed to argue against the constitutional power of the Government to make an artificial standard of value in time of peace. Evarts was anxious to fix on a line of argument that should have a chance of standing up against that of Judge Curtis, and was puzzled to do it. He did not know which foot to put forward. About to deal with Judge Curtis, the last of the strong jurists of Marshall's[26] school, he could risk no chances. In doubt, the quickest way to clear one's mind is to discuss, and Evarts deliberately forced discussion. Day after day, driving, dining, walking he provoked Adams to dispute his positions. He needed an anvil, he said, to hammer his ideas on.

Adams was flattered at being an anvil, which is, after all, more solid than the hammer; and he did not feel called on to treat Mr. Evarts's arguments with more respect than Mr. Evarts himself expressed for them; so he contradicted with freedom. Like most young men, he was much of a doctrinaire, and the question was, in any event, rather historical or political than legal. He could easily maintain, by way of argument, that the required power had never been given, and that no sound constitutional reason could possibly exist for authorizing the Government to overthrow the standard of value without necessity, in time of peace. The dispute itself had not much value for him, even as education, but it led to his seeking light from the Chief Justice[27] himself. Following up the subject for his letters to the *Nation* and his articles in the *North American Review*, Adams grew to be intimate with the Chief Justice, who, as one of the oldest and strongest leaders of the Free Soil Party, had claims to his personal regard; for the old Free Soilers were becoming few. Like all strong-willed and self-asserting men, Mr. Chase had the faults of his qualities. He was never easy to drive in harness, or light in hand. He saw vividly what was wrong, and did not always allow for what was relatively right. He loved power as though he were still a Senator. His position towards Legal Tender was awkward. As Secretary of the Treasury he had been its author; as Chief Justice he became its enemy. Legal Tender caused no great pleasure or pain in the sum of life to a newspaper correspondent, but it served as a subject for letters, and the Chief Justice was very willing to win an ally in the press who would tell his story as he wished it to be read. The intimacy in Mr. Chase's house grew rapidly, and the alliance was no small help to the comforts of a struggling newspaper adventurer in Washington. No matter what one might think of his politics or temper, Mr. Chase was a dramatic figure, of high senatorial rank, if also of certain senatorial faults; a valuable ally.

As was sure, sooner or later, to happen, Adams one day met Charles Sumner on the street, and instantly stopped to greet him. As though eight years of broken ties were the natural course of friendship, Sumner at once, after an exclamation of surprise, dropped back into the relation of hero to the school boy. Adams enjoyed accepting it. He was then thirty years old and Sumner was fifty-seven; he had seen more of the world than Sumner ever dreamed of, and he felt a sort of amused curiosity to be treated once more as a child. At best, the renewal of broken relations is a nervous matter, and in this case it bristled with thorns, for Sumner's quarrel with Mr. Adams had not been the most delicate of his ruptured relations, and he was liable to be sensitive in many ways that even Bostonians could hardly keep in constant mind; yet it interested and fascinated Henry Adams as a new study of political humanity. The younger man knew that the meeting would have to come, and was ready for it, if only as a newspaper need; but to Sumner it came as a surprise and a disagreeable one, as Adams conceived. He learned something — a piece of practical education worth the effort — by watching Sumner's behavior. He could see that many thoughts — mostly unpleasant — were passing through his mind, since he made no inquiry about any of Adams's family, or allusion to any of his friends or his residence abroad. He talked only of the present. To him, Adams in Washington should have seemed more or less of a critic, perhaps a spy, certainly an intriguer or adventurer like scores of others; a politician without party; a writer without principles; an office-seeker certain to beg for support. All this was, for his purposes, true. Adams could do him no good, and would be likely to do him all the harm in his power. Adams accepted it all; expected to be kept at arm's length; admitted that the reasons were just. He was the more surprised to see that

Sumner invited a renewal of old relations. He found himself treated almost confidentially. Not only was he asked to make a fourth at Sumner's pleasant little dinners in the house on La Fayette Square,[28] but he found himself admitted to the Senator's study and informed of his views, policy and purposes, which were sometimes even more astounding than his curious gaps or lapses of omniscience.

On the whole, the relation was the queerest that Henry Adams ever kept up. He liked and admired Sumner, but thought his mind a pathological study. At times he inclined to think that Sumner felt his solitude, and, in the political wilderness, craved educated society; but this hardly told the whole story. Sumner's mind had reached the calm of water which receives and reflects images without absorbing them; it contained nothing but itself. The images from without, the objects mechanically perceived by the senses, existed by courtesy until the mental surface was ruffled, but never became part of the thought. Henry Adams roused no emotion; if he had roused a disagreeable one, he would have ceased to exist. The mind would have mechanically rejected, as it had mechanically admitted him. Not that Sumner was more aggressively egoistic than other Senators — Conkling, for instance — but that with him the disease had affected the whole mind; it was chronic and absolute; while, with other Senators for the most part, it was still acute.

Perhaps for this very reason, Sumner was the more valuable acquaintance for a newspaper-man. Adams found him most useful; perhaps quite the most useful of all these great authorities who were the stock-in-trade of the newspaper business; the accumulated capital of a Silurian age. A few months or years more, and they were gone. In 1868, they were like the town itself, changing but not changed. La Fayette Square was society. Within a few hundred yards of Mr. Clark Mills's nursery monument[29] to the equestrian seat of Andrew Jackson, one found all one's acquaintance as well as hotels, banks, markets and national government. Beyond the Square the country began. No rich or fashionable stranger had yet discovered the town. No literary or scientific man, no artist, no gentleman without office or employment, had ever lived there. It was rural, and its society was primitive. Scarcely a person in it had ever known life in a great city. Mr. Evarts, Mr. Sam Hooper,[30] of Boston, and perhaps one or two of the diplomatists had alone mixed in that sort of world. The happy village was innocent of a club. The one-horse tram on F Street to the Capitol was ample for traffic. Every pleasant spring morning at the Pennsylvania Station, society met to bid good-bye to its friends going off on the single express. The State Department was lodged in an infant asylum far out on Fourteenth Street while Mr. Mullett was constructing his architectural infant asylum[31] next the White House. The value of real estate had not increased since 1800, and the pavements were more impassable than the mud. All this favored a young man who had come to make a name. In four-and-twenty hours he could know everybody; in two days everybody knew him.

After seven years' arduous and unsuccessful effort to explore the outskirts of London society, the Washington world offered an easy and delightful repose. When he looked round him, from the safe shelter of Mr. Evarts's roof, on the men he was to work with — or against — he had to admit that nine-tenths of his acquired education was useless, and the other tenth harmful. He would have to begin again from the beginning. He must learn to talk to the Western Congressman, and to hide his own antecedents. The task was amusing. He could see nothing to prevent him from enjoying it, with immoral unconcern for all that had gone before and for anything that might follow. The lobby offered a spectacle almost picturesque. Few figures on the Paris stage were more entertaining and dramatic than old Sam Ward,[32] who knew more of life than all the departments of the Government together, including the Senate and the Smithsonian.[33] Society had not much to give, but what it had, it gave with an open hand. For the moment, politics had ceased to disturb social relations. All parties were mixed up and jumbled together in a sort of tidal slack-water. The Government resembled Adams himself in the matter of education. All that had gone before was useless, and some of it was worse.

CHAPTER XVII

President Grant (1869)

THE first effect of this leap into the unknown was a fit of
low spirits new to the young man's education; due in
part to the overpowering beauty and sweetness of the
Maryland autumn, almost unendurable for its strain on one who
had toned his life down to the November grays and browns of
northern Europe. Life could not go on so beautiful and so sad.
Luckily, no one else felt it or knew it. He bore it as well as he
could, and when he picked himself up, winter had come, and he
was settled in bachelor's quarters, as modest as those of a clerk
in the Departments, far out on G Street, towards Georgetown,[1]
where an old Finn named Dohna, who had come out with the
Russian Minister Stoeckel long before, had bought or built a new
house. Congress had met. Two or three months remained to the
old administration, but all interest centered in the new one. The
town began to swarm with office-seekers, among whom a young
writer was lost. He drifted among them, unnoticed, glad to learn
his work under cover of the confusion. He never aspired to become a regular reporter; he knew he should fail in trying a career
so ambitious and energetic; but he picked up friends on the press
— Nordhoff, Murat Halstead, Henry Watterson, Sam Bowles
— all reformers,[2] and all mixed and jumbled together in a tidal
wave of expectation, waiting for General Grant to give orders.
No one seemed to know much about it. Even Senators had nothing
to say. One could only make notes and study finance.

In waiting, he amused himself as he could. In the amusements
of Washington, education had no part, but the simplicity of the
amusements proved the simplicity of everything else, ambitions,
interests, thoughts, and knowledge. Proverbially Washington
was a poor place for education, and of course young diplomats

avoided or disliked it, but, as a rule, diplomats disliked every place except Paris, and the world contained only one Paris. They abused London more violently than Washington; they praised no post under the sun; and they were merely describing three-fourths of their stations when they complained that there were no theatres, no restaurants, no *monde*, no *demi-monde*, no drives, no splendor, and, as Mme. de Struve used to say, no *grandezza*.[3] This was all true; Washington was a mere political camp, as transient and temporary as a camp-meeting for religious revival, but the diplomats had least reason to complain, since they were more sought for there than they would ever be elsewhere. For young men Washington was in one way paradise, since they were few, and greatly in demand. After watching the abject unimportance of the young diplomat in London society, Adams found himself a young duke in Washington. He had ten years of youth to make up, and a ravenous appetite. Washington was the easiest society he had ever seen, and even the Bostonian became simple, good-natured, almost genial, in the softness of a Washington spring. Society went on excellently well without houses, or carriages, or jewels, or toilettes, or pavements, or shops, or *grandezza* of any sort; and the market was excellent as well as cheap. One could not stay there a month without loving the shabby town. Even the Washington girl, who was neither rich nor well-dressed nor well-educated nor clever, had singular charm, and used it. According to Mr. Adams the father, this charm dated back as far as Monroe's administration,[4] to his personal knowledge.

Therefore, behind all the processes of political or financial or newspaper training, the social side of Washington was to be taken for granted as three-fourths of existence. Its details matter nothing. Life ceased to be strenuous, and the victim thanked God for it. Politics and reform became the detail, and waltzing the profession. Adams was not alone. Senator Sumner had as private secretary a young man named Moorfield Storey,[5] who became a dangerous example of frivolity. The new Attorney General,

E. R. Hoar, brought with him from Concord a son, Sam Hoar,[6] whose example rivalled that of Storey. Another impenitent was named Dewey,[7] a young naval officer. Adams came far down in the list. He wished he had been higher. He could have spared a world of superannuated history, science, or politics, to have reversed better in waltzing.

He had no adequate notion how little he knew, especially of women, and Washington offered no standard of comparison. All were profoundly ignorant together, and as indifferent as children to education. No one needed knowledge. Washington was happier without style. Certainly Adams was happier without it; happier than he had ever been before; happier than any one in the harsh world of strenuousness could dream of. This must be taken as background for such little education as he gained; but the life belonged to the eighteenth century, and in no way concerned education for the twentieth.

In such an atmosphere, one made no great pretence of hard work. If the world wants hard work, the world must pay for it; and, if it will not pay, it has no fault to find with the worker. Thus far, no one had made a suggestion of pay for any work that Adams had done or could do; if he worked at all, it was for social consideration, and social pleasure was his pay. For this he was willing to go on working, as an artist goes on painting when no one buys his pictures. Artists have done it from the beginning of time, and will do it after time has expired, since they cannot help themselves, and they find their return in the pride of their social superiority as they feel it. Society commonly abets them and encourages their attitude of contempt. The society of Washington was too simple and Southern as yet, to feel anarchistic longings, and it never read or saw what artists produced elsewhere, but it good-naturedly abetted them when it had the chance, and respected itself the more for the frailty. Adams found even the Government at his service, and everyone willing to answer his questions. He worked, after a fashion; not very hard, but as much as the Government would have required of him for nine hundred dollars a year; and his work defied frivolity. He got more pleasure from writing than the world ever got from reading him, for his work was not amusing, nor was he. One must not try to amuse money-lenders or investors, and this was the class to which he began by appealing. He gave three months to an article on the finances of the United States, just then a subject greatly needing treatment; and when he had finished it, he sent it to London to his friend Henry Reeve, the ponderous editor of the *Edinburgh Review*. Reeve probably thought it good; at all events, he said so; and he printed it in April. Of course it was reprinted in America, but in England such articles were still anonymous, and the author remained unknown.[8]

The author was not then asking for advertisement, and made no claim for credit. His object was literary. He wanted to win a place on the staff of the *Edinburgh Review*, under the vast shadow of Lord Macaulay; and, to a young American in 1868, such rank seemed colossal — the highest in the literary world — as it had been only five-and-twenty years before. Time and tide had flowed since then, but the position still flattered vanity, though it brought no other flattery or reward except the regular thirty pounds of pay — fifty dollars a month, measured in time and labor.

The Edinburgh article finished, he set himself to work on a scheme for the *North American Review*. In England, Lord Robert Cecil had invented for the *London Quarterly* an annual review of politics which he called the "Session." Adams stole the idea and the name — he thought he had been enough in Lord Robert's house, in days of his struggle with adversity, to excuse the theft — and began what he meant for a permanent series of annual political reviews which he hoped to make, in time, a political authority. With his sources of information, and his social intimacies at Washington, he could not help saying something that would command attention. He had the field to himself, and he meant to give himself a free hand, as he went on. Whether the newspapers liked it or not, they would have to reckon with him; for such a power, once established, was more effective than all the speeches in Congress or reports to the President that could be crammed into the Government presses.

The first of these "Sessions" appeared in April, but it could not be condensed into a single article, and had to be supplemented in October by another which bore the title of "Civil Service Reform," and was really a part of the same review.[9] A good deal of authentic history slipped into these papers. Whether anyone except his press associates ever read them, he never knew and never greatly cared. The difference is slight, to the influence of an author, whether he is read by five hundred readers, or by five hundred thousand; if he can select the five hundred, he reaches the five hundred thousand. The fateful year 1870[10] was near at hand, which was to mark the close of the literary epoch, when quarterlies gave way to monthlies; letter-press to illustration; volumes to pages. The outburst was brilliant. Bret Harte[11] led, and Robert Louis Stevenson followed. Guy de Maupassant[12] and Rudyard Kipling[13] brought up the rear, and dazzled the world. As usual, Adams found himself fifty years behind his time, but a number of belated wanderers kept him company, and they produced on each other the effect or illusion of a public opinion. They straggled apart, at longer and longer intervals, through the procession, but they were still within hearing distance of each other. The drift was still superficially conservative. Just as the Church spoke with apparent authority, so the quarterlies laid down an apparent law, and no one could surely say where the real authority, or the real law, lay. Science did not know. Truths *a priori* held their own against truths purely relative. According to Lowell, Right was forever on the Scaffold, Wrong was forever on the Throne;[14] and most people still thought they believed it. Adams was not the only relic of the eighteenth century, and he could still depend on a certain number of listeners — mostly respectable, and some rich.

Want of audience did not trouble him; he was well enough off in that respect, and would have succeeded in all his calculations if this had been his only hazard. Where he broke down was at a point where he always suffered wreck and where nine adventurers out of ten make their errors. One may be more or less certain of organized forces; one can never be certain of men. He belonged to the eighteenth century, and the eighteenth century upset all his plans. For the moment, America was more eighteenth century than himself; it reverted to the stone age.

As education — of a certain sort — the story had probably a certain value, though he could never see it. One seldom can see much education in the buck of a broncho; even less in the kick of a mule. The lesson it teaches is only that of getting out of the animal's way. This was the lesson that Henry Adams had learned over and over again in politics since 1860.

At least four-fifths of the American people — Adams among the rest [15] — had united in the election of General Grant to the Presidency, and probably had been more or less affected in their choice by the parallel they felt between Grant and Washington. Nothing could be more obvious. Grant represented order. He was a great soldier, and the soldier always represented order. He might be as partisan as he pleased, but a general who had organized and commanded half a million or a million men in the field, must know how to administer. Even Washington, who was, in education and experience, a mere cave-dweller,[16] had known how to organize a government, and had found Jeffersons and Hamiltons to organize his departments. The task of bringing the Government back to regular practices, and of restoring moral and mechanical order to administration, was not very difficult; it was ready to do it itself, with a little encouragement. No doubt the confusion, especially in the old slave States and in the currency, was considerable, but the general disposition was good, and everyone had echoed the famous phrase: "Let us have peace." [17]

Adams was young and easily deceived, in spite of his diplomatic adventures, but even at twice his age he could not see that this reliance on Grant was unreasonable. Had Grant been a Congressman one would have been on one's guard, for one knew the type. One never expected from a Congressman more than good intentions and public spirit. Newspaper-men as a rule had no great respect for the lower House; Senators had less; and Cabinet officers had none at all. Indeed, one day when Adams was pleading with a Cabinet officer for patience and tact in dealing with Representatives, the Secretary[18] impatiently broke out: "You can't use tact with a Congressman! A Congressman is a hog! You must take a stick and hit him on the snout!" Adams knew far too little, compared with the Secretary, to contradict him, though he thought the phrase somewhat harsh even as applied to the average Congressman of 1869 — he saw little or nothing of later ones — but he knew a shorter way of silencing criticism. He had but to ask: "If a Congressman is a hog, what is a Senator?" This innocent question, put in a candid spirit, petrified any executive officer that ever sat a week in his office. Even Adams admitted that Senators passed belief. The comic side of their egotism partly disguised its extravagance, but faction had gone so far under Andrew Johnson that at times the whole Senate seemed to catch hysterics of nervous bucking without apparent reason. Great leaders, like Sumner and Conkling, could not be burlesqued; they were more grotesque than ridicule could make them; even Grant, who rarely sparkled in epigram, became witty on their account; but their egotism and factiousness were no laughing matter. They did permanent and terrible mischief, as Garfield and Blaine, and even McKinley and John Hay, were to feel.[19] The most troublesome task of a reform President was that of bringing the Senate back to decency.

Therefore no one, and Henry Adams less than most, felt hope that any President chosen from the ranks of politics or politicians would raise the character of government; and by instinct if not by reason, all the world united on Grant. The Senate understood what the world expected, and waited in silence for a struggle with Grant more serious than that with Andrew Johnson. Newspaper-men were alive with eagerness to support the President against the Senate. The newspaper-man is, more than most men, a double personality; and his person feels best satisfied in its double instincts when writing in one sense and thinking in another. All newspaper-men, whatever they wrote, felt alike about the Senate. Adams floated with the stream. He was eager to join in the fight which he foresaw as sooner or later inevitable. He meant to support the Executive in attacking the Senate and taking away its two-thirds vote and power of confirmation, nor did he much care how it should be done, for he thought it safer to effect the revolution in 1870 than to wait till 1920.

With this thought in his mind, he went to the Capitol to hear the names announced which should reveal the carefully guarded secret of Grant's Cabinet. To the end of his life, he wondered at the suddenness of the revolution which actually, within five minutes, changed his intended future into an absurdity so laughable as to make him ashamed of it. He was to hear a long list of Cabinet announcements not much weaker or more futile than that of Grant, and none of them made him blush, while Grant's nominations had the singular effect of making the hearer ashamed, not so much of Grant, as of himself. He had made another total misconception of life — another inconceivable false start. Yet, unlikely as it seemed, he had missed his motive narrowly, and his intention had been more than sound, for the Senators made no secret of saying with senatorial frankness that Grant's nominations betrayed his intent as plainly as they betrayed his incompetence. A great soldier might be a baby politician.

Adams left the Capitol, much in the same misty mental condition that he recalled as marking his railway journey to London on May 13, 1861; he felt in himself what Gladstone bewailed so sadly, "the incapacity of viewing things all round."[20] He knew, without absolutely saying it, that Grant had cut short the life which Adams had laid out for himself in the future. After such a miscarriage, no thought of effectual reform could revive for at least one generation, and he had no fancy for ineffectual politics. What course could he sail next? He had tried so many, and society had barred them all! For the moment, he saw no hope but in following the stream on which he had launched himself. The new Cabinet, as individuals, were not hostile. Subsequently Grant made changes in the list which were mostly welcome to a Bostonian — or should have been — although fatal to Adams. The name of Hamilton Fish[21], as Secretary of State, suggested extreme conservatism and probable deference to Sumner. The name of George S. Boutwell, as Secretary of the Treasury, suggested only a somewhat lugubrious joke; Mr. Boutwell could be described only as the opposite of Mr. McCulloch, and meant inertia; or, in plain words, total extinction for anyone resembling Henry Adams. On the other hand, the name of Jacob D. Cox[22], as Secretary of the Interior, suggested help and comfort; while that of Judge Hoar, as Attorney-General, promised friendship. On the whole, the personal outlook, merely for literary purposes, seemed fairly cheerful, and the political outlook, though hazy, still depended on Grant himself. No one doubted that Grant's intention had been one of reform; that his aim had been to place his administration above politics; and until he should actually drive his supporters away, one might hope to support him. One's little lantern must therefore be turned on Grant. One seemed to know him so well, and really knew so little.

By chance it happened that Adam Badeau[23] took the lower suite of rooms at Dohna's, and, as it was convenient to have one table, the two men dined together and became intimate. Badeau was exceedingly social, though not in appearance imposing. He was stout; his face was red, and his habits were regularly irregular; but he was very intelligent, a good newspaper-man, and an excellent military historian. His life of Grant was no ordinary book. Unlike most newspaper-men, he was a friendly critic of Grant, as suited an officer who had been on the General's staff. As a rule, the newspaper correspondents in Washington were unfriendly, and the lobby sceptical. From that side one heard tales that made one's hair stand on end, and the old West Point army officers were no more flattering. All described him as vicious, narrow, dull, and vindictive. Badeau, who had come to Washington for a consulate which was slow to reach him, resorted more or less to whiskey for encouragement, and became irritable, besides being loquacious. He talked much about Grant, and showed a certain artistic feeling for analysis of character, as a true literary critic would naturally do. Loyal to Grant, and still more so to Mrs. Grant, who acted as his patroness, he said nothing, even when far gone, that was offensive about either, but he held that no one except himself and Rawlins[24] understood the General. To him, Grant appeared as an intermittent energy, immensely powerful when awake, but passive and plastic in repose. He said that neither he nor the rest of the staff knew why Grant succeeded; they believed in him because of his success. For stretches of time, his mind seemed torpid. Rawlins and the others would systematically talk their ideas into it, for weeks, not directly, but by discussion among themselves, in his presence. In the end, he would announce the idea as his own, without seeming conscious of the discussion; and would give the orders to carry it out with all the energy that belonged to his nature. They could never measure his character or be sure when he would act. They could never follow a mental process in his thought. They were not sure that he did think.

In all this, Adams took deep interest, for although he was not, like Badeau, waiting for Mrs. Grant's power of suggestion to act on the General's mind in order to germinate in a consulate or a legation, his portrait gallery of great men was becoming large, and it amused him to add an authentic likeness of the greatest general the world had seen since Napoleon. Badeau's analysis was rather delicate; infinitely superior to that of Sam Ward or Charles Nordhoff.

Badeau took Adams to the White House one evening and introduced him to the President and Mrs. Grant. First and last, he saw a dozen Presidents at the White House, and the most famous were by no means the most agreeable, but he found Grant the most curious object of study among them all. About no one did opinions differ so widely. Adams had no opinion, or occasion to make one. A single word with Grant satisfied him that, for his own good, the fewer words he risked, the better. Thus far in life he had met with but one man of the same intellectual or unintellectual type — Garibaldi. Of the two, Garibaldi seemed to him a trifle the more intellectual, but, in both, the intellect counted for nothing; only the energy counted. The type was pre-intellectual, archaic, and would have seemed so even to the cave-dwellers. Adam, according to legend, was such a man.[25]

In time one came to recognize the type in other men, with differences and variations, as normal; men whose energies were the greater, the less they wasted on thought; men who sprang from the soil to power; apt to be distrustful of themselves and of others; shy; jealous; sometimes vindictive; more or less dull in outward appearance; always needing stimulants, but for whom action was the highest stimulant — the instinct of fight. Such men were forces of nature, energies of the prime, like the *Pteraspis*, but they made short work of scholars. They had commanded thousands of such and saw no more in them than in others. The fact was certain; it crushed argument and intellect at once.

Adams did not feel Grant as a hostile force; like Badeau he saw only an uncertain one. When in action he was superb and safe to follow; only when torpid he was dangerous. To deal with him one must stand near, like Rawlins, and practice more or less sympathetic habits. Simple-minded beyond the experience of Wall Street or State Street, he resorted, like most men of the same intellectual calibre, to commonplaces when at a loss for expression: "Let us have peace!" or "The best way to treat a bad law is to execute it";[26] or a score of such reversible sentences generally to be gauged by their sententiousness; but sometimes he made one doubt his good faith; as when he seriously remarked to a particularly bright young woman that Venice would be a fine city if it were drained.[27] In Mark Twain, this suggestion would have taken rank among his best witticisms; in Grant it was a measure of simplicity not singular. Robert E. Lee betrayed the same intellectual commonplace, in a Virginian form, not to the same degree, but quite distinctly enough for one who knew the American. What worried Adams was not the commonplace; it was, as usual, his own education. Grant fretted and irritated him, like the *Terebratula,* as a defiance of first principles. He had no right to exist. He should have been extinct for ages. The idea that, as society grew older, it grew one-sided, upset evolution, and made of education a fraud. That, two thousand years after Alexander the Great and Julius Cæsar, a man like Grant should be called — and should actually and truly be — the highest product of the most advanced evolution, made evolution ludicrous. One must be as commonplace as Grant's own commonplaces to maintain such an absurdity. The progress of evolution from President Washington to President Grant, was alone evidence enough to upset Darwin.

Education became more perplexing at every phase. No theory was worth the pen that wrote it. America had no use for Adams because he was eighteenth-century, and yet it worshipped Grant because he was archaic and should have lived in a cave and worn skins. Darwinists ought to conclude that America was reverting to the stone age, but the theory of reversion was more absurd than that of evolution. Grant's administration reverted to nothing. One could not catch a trait of the past, still less of the future. It was not even sensibly American. Not an official in it, except perhaps Rawlins whom Adams never met, and who died in September, suggested an American idea.

Yet this administration, which upset Adams's whole life, was not unfriendly; it was made up largely of friends. Secretary Fish was almost kind; he kept the tradition of New York social values; he was human and took no pleasure in giving pain. Adams felt no prejudice whatever in his favor, and he had nothing in mind or person to attract regard; his social gifts were not remarkable; he was not in the least magnetic; he was far from young; but he won confidence from the start and remained a friend to the finish. As far as concerned Mr. Fish, one felt rather happily suited, and one was still better off in the Interior Department with J. D. Cox. Indeed, if Cox had been in the Treasury and Boutwell in the Interior, one would have been quite satisfied as far as personal relations went, while, in the Attorney-General's Office, Judge Hoar seemed to fill every possible ideal, both personal and political.

The difficulty was not the want of friends, and had the whole government been filled with them, it would have helped little without the President and the Treasury. Grant avowed from the start a policy of drift; and a policy of drift attaches only barnacles. At thirty, one has no interest in becoming a barnacle, but even in that character Henry Adams would have been ill-seen. His friends were reformers, critics, doubtful in party allegiance, and he was himself an object of suspicion. Grant had no objects, wanted no help, wished for no champions. The Executive asked only to be let alone. This was his meaning when he said: "Let us have peace!"

No one wanted to go into opposition. As for Adams, all his hopes of success in life turned on his finding an administration to support. He knew well enough the rules of self-interest. He was for sale. He wanted to be bought. His price was excessively cheap, for he did not even ask an office, and had his eye, not on the Government, but on New York.[28] All he wanted was something to support; something that would let itself be supported. Luck went dead against him. For once, he was fifty years in advance of his time.[29]

CHAPTER XVIII

Free Fight[1] *(1869–1870)*

THE old New Englander was apt to be a solitary animal, but the young New Englander was sometimes human. Judge Hoar brought his son Sam to Washington, and Sam Hoar loved largely and well. He taught Adams the charm of Washington spring. Education for education, none ever compared with the delight of this. The Potomac and its tributaries squandered beauty. Rock Creek was as wild as the Rocky Mountains. Here and there a negro log cabin alone disturbed the dogwood and the judas-tree, the azalea and the laurel. The tulip and the chestnut gave no sense of struggle against a stingy nature. The soft, full outlines of the landscape carried no hidden horror of glaciers in its bosom. The brooding heat of the profligate vegetation; the cool charm of the running water; the terrific splendor of the June thunder-gust in the deep and solitary woods, were all sensual, animal, elemental. No European spring had shown him the same intermixture of delicate grace and passionate depravity that marked the Maryland May.[2] He loved it too much, as though it were Greek and half human. He could not leave it, but loitered on into July, falling into the Southern ways of the summer village about La Fayette Square, as one whose rights of inheritance could not be questioned. Few Americans were so poor as to question them.

In spite of the fatal deception — or undeception — about Grant's political character, Adams's first winter in Washington had so much amused him that he had not a thought of change. He loved it too much to question its value. What did he know about its value, or what did anyone know? His father knew more about it than anyone else in Boston, and he was amused to find that his father, whose recollections went back to 1820, betrayed for Washington much the same sentimental weakness, and described the society about President Monroe much as his son felt the society about President Johnson. He feared its effect on young men, with some justice, since it had been fatal to two of his brothers;[3] but he understood the charm, and he knew that a life in Quincy or Boston was not likely to deaden it.

Henry was in a savage humor on the subject of Boston. He saw Boutwells at every counter. He found a personal grief in every tree. Fifteen or twenty years afterwards, Clarence King used to amuse him by mourning over the narrow escape that nature had made in attaining perfection. Except for two mistakes, the earth would have been a success. One of these errors was the inclination of the ecliptic;[4] the other was the differentiation of the sexes, and the saddest thought about the last was that it should have been so modern. Adams, in his splenetic temper, held that both these unnecessary evils had wreaked their worst on Boston. The climate made eternal war on society, and sex was a species of crime. The ecliptic had inclined itself beyond recovery till life was as thin as the elm trees. Of course he was in the wrong. The thinness was in himself, not in Boston; but this is a story of education, and Adams was struggling to shape himself to his time. Boston was trying to do the same thing. Everywhere, except in Washington, Americans were toiling for the same object. Everyone complained of surroundings, except where, as at Washington, there were no surroundings to complain of. Boston kept its head better than its neighbors did, and very little time was needed to prove it, even to Adams's confusion.

Before he got back to Quincy, the summer was already half over, and in another six weeks the effects of President Grant's character showed themselves. They were startling — astounding — terrifying. The mystery that shrouded the famous, classical attempt of Jay Gould[5] to corner gold in September, 1869, has never been cleared up — at least so far as to make it intelligible to Adams. Gould was led, by the change at Washington, into the belief that he could safely corner gold without interference from the Government. He took a number of precautions, which he admitted; and he spent a large sum of money, as he also testified, to obtain assurances which were not sufficient to have satisfied so astute a gambler; yet he made the venture. Any criminal lawyer must have begun investigation by insisting, rigorously, that no such man, in such a position, could be permitted to plead that he had taken, and pursued, such a course, without assurances which did satisfy him. The plea was professionally inadmissible.

This meant that any criminal lawyer would have been bound to start an investigation by insisting that Gould had assurances from the White House or the Treasury, since none other could have satisfied him. To young men wasting their summer at Quincy for want of some one to hire their services at three dollars a day, such a dramatic scandal was Heaven-sent. Charles and Henry Adams jumped at it like salmon at a fly, with as much voracity as Jay Gould, or his *âme damnée*[6] Jim Fisk,[7] had ever shown for Erie; and with as little fear of consequences. They risked something; no one could say what; but the people about the Erie office were not regarded as lambs.

The unravelling a skein so tangled as that of the Erie Railway was a task that might have given months of labor to the most efficient District Attorney, with all his official tools to work with. Charles took the railway history; Henry took the so-called Gold Conspiracy; and they went to New York to work it up. The surface was in full view. They had no trouble in Wall Street, and they paid their respects in person to the famous Jim Fisk in his Opera-House Palace; but the New York side of the story helped Henry little. He needed to penetrate the political mystery, and for this purpose he had to wait for Congress to meet. At first he feared that Congress would suppress the scandal, but the Congressional Investigation was ordered and took place. He soon knew all that was to be known; the material for his essay was furnished by the Government.

Material furnished by a government seldom satisfies critics or historians, for it lies always under suspicion. Here was a mystery, and as usual, the chief mystery was the means of making sure that any mystery existed. All Adams's great friends — Fish, Cox, Hoar, Evarts, Sumner, and their surroundings — were precisely the persons most mystified. They knew less than Adams did; they sought information, and frankly admitted that their relations with the White House and the Treasury were not confidential. No one volunteered advice. No one offered suggestion. One got no light, even from the press, although press agents expressed in private the most damning convictions with their usual cynical frankness. The Congressional Committee took a quantity of evidence which it dared not probe, and refused to analyze. Although the fault lay somewhere on the Administration, and could lie nowhere else, the trail always faded and died out at the point where any member of the Administration became visible. Everyone dreaded to press inquiry. Adams himself feared finding out too much. He found out too much already, when he saw in evidence that Jay Gould had actually succeeded in stretching his net over Grant's closest surroundings, and that Boutwell's[8] incompetence was the bottom of Gould's calculation. With the conventional air of assumed confidence, everyone in public assured everyone else that the President himself was the savior of the situation, and in private assured each other that if the President had not been caught this time, he was sure to be trapped the next, for the ways of Wall Street were dark and double. All this was wildly exciting to Adams. That Grant should have fallen, within six months, into such a morass — or should have let Boutwell drop him into it — rendered the outlook for the next four years — probably eight — possibly twelve — mysterious, or frankly opaque, to a young man who had hitched his wagon, as Emerson told him, to the star of reform.[9] The country might outlive it, but not he. The worst scandals of the eighteenth century were relatively harmless by the side of this, which smirched executive, judiciary, banks, corporate systems, professions, and people, all the great active forces of society, in one dirty cesspool of vulgar corruption. Only six months before, this innocent young man, fresh from the cynicism of European diplomacy, had expected to enter an honorable career in the press as the champion and confidant of a new Washington, and already he foresaw a life of wasted energy, sweeping the stables of American society clean of the endless corruption which his second Washington was quite certain to breed.

By vigorously shutting one's eyes, as though one were an Assistant Secretary, a writer for the press might ignore the Erie scandal, and still help his friends or allies in the Government who were doing their best to give it an air of decency; but a few weeks showed that the Erie scandal was a mere incident, a rather vulgar Wall Street trap, into which, according to one's point of view, Grant had been drawn by Jay Gould, or Jay Gould had been misled by Grant. One could hardly doubt that both of them were astonished and disgusted by the result; but neither Jay Gould nor any other astute American mind — still less the complex Jew [10] could ever have accustomed itself to the incredible and inexplicable lapses of Grant's intelligence; and perhaps, on the whole, Gould was the less mischievous victim, if victims they both were. The same laxity that led Gould into a trap which might easily have become the penitentiary, led the United States Senate, the Executive departments and the Judiciary into confusion, cross-purposes, and ill-temper that would have been scandalous in a boarding-school of girls. For satirists or comedians, the study was rich and endless, and they exploited its corners with happy results, but a young man fresh from the rustic simplicity of London noticed with horror that the grossest satires on the American Senator and politician never failed to excite the laughter and applause of every audience. Rich and poor joined in throwing contempt on their own representatives. Society laughed a vacant and meaningless derision over its own failure. Nothing remained for a young man without position or power except to laugh too.

Yet the spectacle was no laughing matter to him, whatever it might be to the public. Society is immoral and immortal; it can afford to commit any kind of folly, and indulge in any sort of vice; it cannot be killed, and the fragments that survive can always laugh at the dead; but a young man has only one chance, and brief time to seize it. Anyone in power above him can extinguish the chance. He is horribly at the mercy of fools and cowards. One dull administration can rapidly drive out every active subordinate. At Washington, in 1869–70, every intelligent man about the Government prepared to go. The people would have liked to go too, for they stood helpless before the chaos; some laughed and some raved; all were disgusted; but they had to content themselves by turning their backs and going to work harder than ever on their railroads and foundries. They were strong enough to carry even their politics. Only the helpless remained stranded in Washington.

The shrewdest statesman of all was Mr. Boutwell, who showed how he understood the situation by turning out of the Treasury everyone who could interfere with his repose, and then locking himself up in it, alone. What he did there, no one knew. His colleagues asked him in vain. Not a word could they get from him, either in the Cabinet or out of it, of suggestion or information on matters even of vital interest. The Treasury as an active influence ceased to exist. Mr. Boutwell waited with confidence for society to drag his department out of the mire, as it was sure to do if he waited long enough.

Warned by his friends in the Cabinet as well as in the Treasury that Mr. Boutwell meant to invite no support, and cared to receive none, Adams had only the State and Interior Departments left to serve. He wanted no better than to serve them. Opposition was his horror; pure waste of energy; a union with Northern Democrats and Southern rebels who never had much in common with any Adams, and had never shown any warm interest about them except to drive them from public life.[11] If Mr. Boutwell turned him out of the Treasury with the indifference or contempt that made even a beetle helpless, Mr. Fish opened the State Department freely, and seemed to talk with as much openness as any newspaper-man could ask. At all events, Adams could cling to this last plank of salvation, and make himself perhaps the recognized champion of Mr. Fish in the New York press. He never once thought of his disaster between Seward and Sumner in 1861.[12] Such an accident could not occur again. Fish and Sumner were inseparable, and their policy was sure to be safe enough for support. No mosquito could be so unlucky as to be caught a second time between a Secretary and a Senator who were both his friends.

This dream of security lasted hardly longer than that of 1861. Adams saw Sumner take possession of the Department, and he approved; he saw Sumner seize the British mission for Motley, and he was delighted; but when he renewed his relations with Sumner in the winter of 1869–70, he began slowly to grasp the idea that Sumner had a foreign policy of his own which he proposed also to force on the Department. This was not all. Secretary Fish seemed to have vanished. Besides the Department of State over which he nominally presided in the Infant Asylum[13] on Fourteenth Street, there had risen a Department of Foreign Relations over which Senator Sumner ruled with a high hand at the Capitol; and, finally, one clearly made out a third Foreign Office in the War Department, with President Grant himself for chief, pressing a policy of extension in the West Indies[14] which no Northeastern man ever approved. For his life, Adams could not learn where to place himself among all these forces. Officially he would have followed the responsible Secretary of State, but he could not find the Secretary. Fish seemed to be friendly towards Sumner, and docile towards Grant, but he asserted as yet no policy of his own. As for Grant's policy, Adams never had a chance to know fully what it was, but, as far as he did know, he was ready to give it ardent support. The difficulty came only when he heard Sumner's views, which, as he had reason to know, were always commands, to be disregarded only by traitors.

Little by little, Sumner unfolded his foreign policy, and Adams gasped with fresh astonishment at every new article of the creed. To his profound regret he heard Sumner begin by imposing his veto on all extension within the tropics; which cost the island of St. Thomas to the United States, besides the Bay of Samana as an alternative, and ruined Grant's policy.[15] Then he listened with incredulous stupor while Sumner unfolded his plan for concentrating and pressing every possible American claim against England, with a view of compelling the cession of Canada to the United States.[16]

Adams did not then know — in fact, he never knew, or could find anyone to tell him — what was going on behind the doors of the White House. He doubted whether Mr. Fish or Bancroft Davis[17] knew much more than he. The game of cross-purposes was as impenetrable in Foreign Affairs as in the Gold Conspiracy. President Grant let everyone go on, but whom he supported, Adams could not be expected to divine. One point alone seemed clear to a man — no longer so very young — who had lately come from a seven years' residence in London. He thought he knew as much as anyone in Washington about England, and he listened with the more perplexity to Mr. Sumner's talk, because it opened the gravest doubts of Sumner's sanity. If war was his object, and Canada were worth it, Sumner's scheme showed genius, and Adams was ready to treat it seriously; but if he thought he could obtain Canada from England as a voluntary set-off to the Alabama Claims, he drivelled. On the point of fact, Adams was as peremptory as Sumner on the point of policy, but he could only wonder whether Mr. Fish would dare say it. When at last Mr. Fish did say it, a year later, Sumner publicly cut his acquaintance.

Adams was the more puzzled because he could not believe Sumner so mad as to quarrel both with Fish and with Grant. A quarrel with Seward and Andrew Johnson was bad enough, and had profited no one; but a quarrel with General Grant was lunacy. Grant might be whatever one liked, as far as morals or temper or intellect were concerned, but he was not a man whom a light-weight cared to challenge for a fight; and Sumner, whether he knew it or not, was a very light weight in the Republican Party, if separated from his Committee of Foreign Relations. As a party manager he had not the weight of half-a-dozen men whose very names were unknown to him.

Between these great forces, where was the Administration and how was one to support it? One must first find it, and even then it was not easily caught. Grant's simplicity was more disconcerting than the complexity of a Talleyrand.[18] Mr. Fish afterwards told Adams, with the rather grim humor he sometimes indulged in, that Grant took a dislike to Motley[19] because he parted his hair in the middle. Adams repeated the story to Godkin, who made much play with it in the *Nation*, till it was denied. Adams saw no reason why it should be denied. Grant had as good a right to dislike the hair as the head, if the hair seemed to him a part of it. Very shrewd men have formed very sound judgments on less material than hair — on clothes, for example, according to Mr. Carlyle, or on a pen, according to Cardinal de Retz [20]— and nine men in ten could hardly give as good a reason as hair for their likes or dislikes. In truth, Grant disliked Motley at sight, because they had nothing in common; and for the same reason he disliked Sumner. For the same reason he would be sure to dislike Adams if Adams gave him a chance. Even Fish could not be quite sure of Grant, except for the powerful effect which wealth had, or appeared to have, on Grant's imagination.

The quarrel that lowered over the State Department did not break in storm till July, 1870,[21] after Adams had vanished, but another quarrel, almost as fatal to Adams as that between Fish and Sumner, worried him even more. Of all members of the Cabinet, the one whom he had most personal interest in cultivating was Attorney-General Hoar. The Legal Tender decision, which had been the first stumbling-block to Adams at Washington, grew in interest till it threatened to become something more serious than a block; it fell on one's head like a plaster ceiling, and could not be escaped. The impending battle between Fish and Sumner was nothing like so serious as the outbreak between Hoar and Chief Justice Chase. Adams had come to Washington hoping to support the Executive in a policy of breaking down the Senate, but he never dreamed that he would be required to help in breaking down the Supreme Court. Although, step by step, he had been driven, like the rest of the world, to admit that American society had outgrown most of its institutions, he still clung to the Supreme Court, much as a churchman clings to his bishops,[22] because they are his only symbol of unity; his last rag of Right. Between the Executive and the Legislature, citizens could have no Rights; they were at the mercy of Power. They had created the Court to protect them from unlimited Power, and it was little enough protection at best. Adams wanted to save the independence of the Court at least for his lifetime, and could not conceive that the Executive should wish to overthrow it.

Frank Walker shared this feeling, and, by way of helping the Court, he had promised Adams for the *North American Review* an article on the history of the Legal Tender Act, founded on a volume just then published by Spaulding,[23] the putative father of the legal-tender clause in 1861. Secretary Jacob D. Cox, who alone sympathized with reform, saved from Boutwell's decree of banishment such reformers as he could find place for, and he saved Walker for a time by giving him the Census of 1870. Walker was obliged to abandon his article for the *North American* in order to devote himself to the Census. He gave Adams his notes, and Adams completed the article.

He had not toiled in vain over the Bank of England Restriction. He knew enough about Legal Tender to leave it alone. If the banks and bankers wanted fiat money, fiat money was good enough for a newspaper-man; and if they changed about and wanted "intrinsic" value, gold and silver came equally welcome to a writer who was paid half the wages of an ordinary mechanic. He had no notion of attacking or defending Legal Tender; his object was to defend the Chief Justice and the Court. Walker argued that, whatever might afterwards have been the necessity for legal tender, there was no necessity for it at the time the Act was passed. With the help of the Chief Justice's recollections, Adams completed the article, which appeared in the April number of the *North American*. Its ferocity was Walker's, for Adams never cared to abandon the knife for the hatchet, but Walker reeked of the army and the *Springfield Republican*, and his energy ran away with Adams's restraint.[24] The unfortunate Spaulding complained loudly of this treatment, not without justice, but the article itself had serious historical value, for Walker demolished every shred of Spaulding's contention that legal tender was necessary at the time; and the Chief Justice told his part of the story with conviction. The Chief Justice seemed to be pleased. The Attorney-General, pleased or not, made no sign. The article had enough historical interest to induce Adams to reprint it in a volume of Essays twenty years afterwards; but its historical value was not its point in education. The point was that, in spite of the best intentions, the plainest self-interest, and the strongest wish to escape further trouble, the article threw Adams into opposition. Judge Hoar, like Boutwell, was implacable.

Hoar went on to demolish the Chief Justice; while Henry Adams went on, drifting further and further from the Administration. He did this in common with all the world, including Hoar himself.[25] Scarcely a newspaper in the country kept discipline. The *New York Tribune* was one of the most criminal.[26] Dissolution of ties in every direction marked the dissolution of temper, and the Senate Chamber became again a scene of irritated egotism that passed ridicule. Senators quarrelled with each other, and no one objected, but they picked quarrels also with the Executive and threw every Department into confusion. Among others they quarrelled with Hoar, and drove him from office.

That Sumner and Hoar, the two New Englanders in great position who happened to be the two persons most necessary for his success at Washington, should be the first victims of Grant's lax rule,[27] must have had some meaning for Adams's education, if Adams could only have understood what it was. He studied, but failed. Sympathy with him was not their weakness. Directly, in the form of help, he knew he could hope as little from them as from Boutwell. So far from inviting attachment they, like other New Englanders, blushed to own a friend. Not one of the whole delegation would ever, of his own accord, try to help Adams or any other young man who did not beg for it, but they would always accept whatever services they had not to pay for. The lesson of education was not there. The selfishness of politics was the earliest of all political education, and Adams had nothing to learn from its study; but the situation struck him as curious — so curious that he devoted years to reflecting upon it. His four most powerful friends had matched themselves, two and two, and were fighting in pairs to a finish; Sumner-Fish; Chase-Hoar; with foreign affairs and the judiciary as prizes! What value had the fight in education?

Adams was puzzled, and was not the only puzzled bystander. The stage-type of statesman was amusing, whether as Roscoe Conkling or Colonel Mulberry Sellers,[28] but what was his value? The statesmen of the old type, whether Sumners or Conklings or Hoars or Lamars, were personally as honest as human nature could produce. They trod with lofty contempt on other people's jobs, especially when there was good in them. Yet the public thought that Sumner and Conkling cost the country a hundred times more than all the jobs they ever trod on; just as Lamar and the old Southern statesmen, who were also honest in money-matters, cost the country a civil war. This painful moral doubt worried Adams less than it worried his friends and the public, but it affected the whole field of politics for twenty years. The newspapers discussed little else than the alleged moral laxity of Grant, Garfield, and Blaine. If the press were taken seriously, politics turned on jobs, and some of Adams's best friends, like Godkin, ruined their influence by their insistence on points of morals. Society hesitated, wavered, oscillated between harshness and laxity, pitilessly sacrificing the weak, and deferentially following the strong. In spite of all such criticism, the public nominated Grant, Garfield, and Blaine for the Presidency, and voted for them afterwards, not seeming to care for the question; until young men were forced to see that either some new standard must be created, or none could be upheld. The moral law had expired — like the Constitution.

Grant's administration outraged every rule of ordinary decency, but scores of promising men, whom the country could not well spare, were ruined in saying so. The world cared little for decency. What it wanted, it did not know; probably a system that would work, and men who could work it; but it found neither. Adams had tried his own little hands on it, and had failed. His friends had been driven out of Washington or had taken to fisticuffs. He himself sat down and stared helplessly into the future.

The result was a review of the Session for the July *North American* into which he crammed and condensed everything he thought he had observed and all he had been told. He thought it good history then, and he thought it better twenty years afterwards; he thought it even good enough to reprint. As it happened, in the process of his devious education, this "Session" of 1869–70 proved to be his last study in current politics, and his last dying testament as a humble member of the press. As such, he stood by it. He could have said no more, had he gone on reviewing every session in the rest of the century. The political dilemma was as clear in 1870 as it was likely to be in 1970. The system of 1789 had broken down, and with it the eighteenth-century fabric of *a priori*, or moral, principles. Politicians had tacitly given it up. Grant's administration marked the avowal. Nine-tenths of men's political energies must henceforth be wasted on expedients to piece out — to patch — or, in vulgar language, to tinker — the political machine as often as it broke down. Such a system, or want of system, might last centuries, if tempered by an occasional revolution or civil war; but as a machine, it was, or soon would be, the poorest in the world — the clumsiest — the most inefficient.

Here again was an education, but what it was worth he could not guess. Indeed, when he raised his eyes to the loftiest and most triumphant results of politics — to Mr. Boutwell, Mr. Conkling or even Mr. Sumner — he could not honestly say that such an education, even when it carried one up to these unattainable heights, was worth anything. There were men, as yet standing on lower levels — clever and amusing men like Garfield and Blaine — who took no little pleasure in making fun of the senatorial demi-gods, and who used language about Grant himself which the *North American Review* would not have admitted. One asked doubtfully what was likely to become of these men in their turn. What kind of political ambition was to result from this destructive political education?

Yet the sum of political life was, or should have been, the attainment of a working political system. Society needed to reach it. If moral standards broke down, and machinery stopped working, new morals and machinery of some sort had to be invented. An eternity of Grants, or even of Garfields or of Conklings or of Jay Goulds, refused to be conceived as possible. Practical Americans laughed, and went their way. Society paid them to be practical. Whenever society cared to pay Adams, he too would be practical, take his pay, and hold his tongue; but meanwhile he was driven to associate with Democratic Congressmen and educate them. He served David Wells[29] as an active assistant professor of revenue reform, and turned his rooms into a college. The Administration drove him, and thousands of other young men, into active enmity not only to Grant, but to the system or want of system, which took possession of the President. Every hope or thought which had brought Adams to Washington proved to be absurd. No one wanted him; no one wanted any of his friends in reform; the blackmailer alone was the normal product of politics as of business.

All this was excessively amusing. Adams never had been so busy, so interested, so much in the thick of the crowd. He knew Congressmen by scores and newspaper-men by the dozen. He wrote for his various organs all sorts of attacks and defences. He enjoyed the life enormously, and found himself as happy as Sam Ward or Sunset Cox,[30] much happier than his friends Fish or J. D. Cox, or Chief Justice Chase or Attorney-General Hoar or Charles Sumner. When spring came, he took to the woods, which were best of all, for after the first of April, what Maurice de Guérin[31] called "the vast maternity" of nature showed charms more voluptuous than the vast paternity of the United States Senate. Senators were less ornamental than the dogwood or even the judas-tree. They were, as a rule, less good company. Adams astonished himself by remarking what a purified charm was lent to the Capitol by the greatest possible distance, as one caught glimpses of the dome over miles of forest foliage. At such moments he pondered on the distant beauty of St. Peter's and the steps of Ara Cœli.

Yet he shortened his spring, for he needed to get back to London for the season. He had finished his New York "Gold Conspiracy," which he meant for his friend Henry Reeve and the *Edinburgh Review*. It was the best piece of work he had done, but this was not his reason for publishing it in England. The Erie scandal had provoked a sort of revolt among respectable New Yorkers, as well as among some who were not so respectable; and the attack on Erie was beginning to promise success. London was a sensitive spot for the Erie management, and it was thought well to strike them there, where they were socially and financially exposed. The tactics suited him in another way, for any expression about

America in an English review attracted ten times the attention in America that the same article would attract in the *North American*. Habitually the American dailies reprinted such articles in full. Adams wanted to escape the terrors of copyright; his highest ambition was to be pirated and advertised free of charge, since, in any case, his pay was nothing. Under the excitement of chase, he was becoming a pirate himself, and liked it.

CHAPTER XIX

Chaos (1870)

ONE fine May afternoon in 1870 Adams drove again up St.
James's Street wondering more than ever at the marvels
of life. Nine years had passed since the historic entrance
of May, 1861. Outwardly London was the same. Outwardly
Europe showed no great change. Palmerston and Russell were forgotten; but Disraeli and Gladstone were still much alive. One's
friends were more than ever prominent. John Bright was in the
Cabinet; W. E. Forster was about to enter it; reform ran riot.
Never had the sun of progress shone so fair. Evolution from lower
to higher raged like an epidemic. Darwin was the greatest of proph-
ets in the most evolutionary of worlds. Gladstone had overthrown the Irish Church; was overthrowing the Irish landlords;
was trying to pass an Education Act.[1] Improvement, prosperity,
power, were leaping and bounding over every country road.
Even America, with her Erie scandals and Alabama Claims, hardly
made a discordant note.

At the Legation, Motley ruled; the long Adams reign was forgotten; the rebellion had passed into history.[2] In society no one
cared to recall the years before the Prince of Wales.[3] The smart
set had come to their own. Half the houses that Adams had
frequented, from 1861 to 1865, were closed or closing in 1870.
Death had ravaged one's circle of friends. Mrs. Milnes Gaskell
and her sister Miss Charlotte Wynn were both dead, and Mr.
James Milnes Gaskell was no longer in Parliament. That field
of education seemed closed too.

One found oneself in a singular frame of mind—more eighteenth-century than ever — almost rococo — and unable to catch
anywhere the cog-wheels of evolution. Experience ceased to
educate. London taught less freely than of old. That one bad

style was leading to another — that the older men were more amusing than the younger — that Lord Houghton's breakfast-table showed gaps hard to fill — that there were fewer men one wanted to meet — these, and a hundred more such remarks, helped little towards a quicker and more intelligent activity. For English reforms, Adams cared nothing. The reforms were themselves mediæval. The Education Bill of his friend W. E. Forster seemed to him a guaranty against all education he had use for.[4] He resented change. He would have kept the Pope in the Vatican and the Queen at Windsor Castle as historical monuments. He did not care to Americanize Europe. The Bastille or the Ghetto[5] was a curiosity worth a great deal of money, if preserved; and so was a Bishop; so was Napoleon III. The tourist was the great conservative who hated novelty and adored dirt. Adams came back to London without a thought of revolution or restlessness or reform. He wanted amusement, quiet, and gaiety.

Had he not been born in 1838 under the shadow of Boston State House, and been brought up in the Early Victorian epoch, he would have cast off his old skin, and made his court to Marlborough House,[6] in partnership with the American woman and the Jew banker. Common-sense dictated it; but Adams and his friends were unfashionable by some law of Anglo-Saxon custom — some innate atrophy of mind. Figuring himself as already a man of action, and rather far up towards the front, he had no idea of making a new effort or catching up with a new world. He saw nothing ahead of him. The world was never more calm. He wanted to talk with Ministers about the Alabama Claims, because he looked on the Claims as his own special creation, discussed between him and his father long before they had been discussed by Government; he wanted to make notes for his next year's articles; but he had not a thought that, within three months, his world was to be upset, and he under it. Frank Palgrave came one day, more contentious, contemptuous, and paradoxical than ever, because Napoleon III seemed to be threatening war with Germany. Palgrave said that "Germany would beat France into scraps" if there was war. Adams thought not. The chances were always against catastrophes. No one else expected great changes in Europe. Palgrave was always extreme; his language was incautious — violent!

In this year of all years, Adams lost sight of education. Things began smoothly, and London glowed with the pleasant sense of familiarity and dinners. He sniffed with voluptuous delight the coal-smoke of Cheapside and revelled in the architecture of Oxford Street.[7] May Fair never shone so fair to Arthur Pendennis[8] as it did to the returned American. The country never smiled its velvet smile of trained and easy hostess as it did when he was so lucky as to be asked on a country visit. He loved it all — everything — had always loved it! He felt almost attached to the Royal Exchange.[9] He thought he owned the St. James's Club. He patronized the Legation.

The first shock came lightly, as though Nature were playing tricks on her spoiled child, though she had thus far not exerted herself to spoil him. Reeve refused the Gold Conspiracy. Adams had become used to the idea that he was free of the Quarterlies, and that his writing would be printed of course; but he was stunned by the reason of refusal. Reeve said it would bring half-a-dozen libel suits on him. One knew that the power of Erie[10] was almost as great in England as in America, but one was hardly prepared to find it controlling the Quarterlies. The English press professed to be shocked in 1870 by the Erie scandal, as it had professed in 1860 to be shocked by the scandal of slavery, but when invited to support those who were trying to abate these scandals, the English press said it was afraid. To Adams, Reeve's refusal seemed portentous. He and his brother and the *North American Review*[11] were running greater risks every day, and no one thought of fear. That a notorious story, taken bodily from an official document, should scare the *Edinburgh Review* into silence for fear of Jay Gould and Jim Fisk, passed even Adams's experience of English eccentricity, though it was large.

He gladly set down Reeve's refusal of the Gold Conspiracy to respectability and editorial law, but when he sent the manuscript on to the *Quarterly*, the editor of the *Quarterly* also refused it. The literary standard of the two Quarterlies was not so high as to suggest that the article was illiterate beyond the power of an active and willing editor to redeem it. Adams had no choice but to realize that he had to deal in 1870 with the same old English character of 1860, and the same inability in himself to understand it. As usual, when an ally was needed, the American was driven into the arms of the radicals. Respectability, everywhere and always, turned its back the moment one asked to do it a favor. Called suddenly away from England, he despatched the article, at the last moment, to the *Westminster Review* and heard no more about it for nearly six months.

He had been some weeks in London when he received a telegram from his brother-in-law at the Bagni di Lucca[12] telling him that his sister had been thrown from a cab and injured, and that he had better come on. He started that night, and reached the Bagni di Lucca on the second day. Tetanus had already set in.

The last lesson — the sum and term of education — began then. He had passed through thirty years of rather varied experience without having once felt the shell of custom broken. He had never seen Nature — only her surface — the sugar-coating that she shows to youth. Flung suddenly in his face, with the harsh brutality of chance, the terror of the blow stayed by him thenceforth for life, until repetition made it more than the will could struggle with; more than he could call on himself to bear. He found his sister,[13] a woman of forty, as gay and brilliant in the terrors of lockjaw as she had been in the careless fun of 1859, lying in bed in consequence of a miserable cab-accident that had bruised her foot. Hour by hour the muscles grew rigid, while the mind remained bright, until after ten days of fiendish torture she died in convulsions.

One had heard and read a great deal about death, and even seen a little of it, and knew by heart the thousand commonplaces of religion and poetry which seemed to deaden one's senses and veil the horror. Society being immortal, could put on immortality at will. Adams being mortal, felt only the mortality. Death took features altogether new to him, in these rich and sensuous surroundings. Nature enjoyed it, played with it, the horror added to her charm, she liked the torture, and smothered her victim with caresses. Never had one seen her so winning. The hot Italian summer brooded outside, over the market-place and the picturesque peasants, and, in the singular color of the Tuscan atmosphere, the hills and vineyards of the Apennines seemed bursting with midsummer blood. The sickroom itself glowed with the Italian joy of life; friends filled it; no harsh northern lights pierced the soft shadows; even the dying woman shared the sense of the Italian summer, the soft, velvet air, the humor, the courage, the sensual fulness of Nature and man. She faced death, as women mostly do, bravely and even gaily, racked slowly to unconsciousness, but yielding only to violence, as a soldier sabred in battle. For many thousands of years, on these hills and plains, Nature had gone on sabring men and women with the same air of sensual pleasure.

Impressions like these are not reasoned or catalogued in the mind; they are felt as part of violent emotion; and the mind that feels them is a different one from that which reasons; it is thought of a different power and a different person. The first serious consciousness of Nature's gesture — her attitude towards life — took form then as a phantasm, a nightmare, an insanity of force. For the first time, the stage-scenery of the senses collapsed; the human mind felt itself stripped naked, vibrating in a void of shapeless energies, with resistless mass, colliding, crushing, wasting, and destroying what these same energies had created and labored from eternity to perfect. Society became fantastic, a vision of pantomime with a mechanical motion; and its so-called thought merged in the mere sense of life, and pleasure in the sense. The usual anodynes of social medicine became evident artifice. Stoicism was perhaps the best; religion was the most human; but the idea that any personal deity could find pleasure or profit in torturing a poor woman, by accident, with a fiendish cruelty known to man only in perverted and insane temperaments, could not be held for a moment. For pure blasphemy, it made pure atheism a comfort. God might be, as the Church said, a Substance, but He could not be a Person.

With nerves strained for the first time beyond their power of tension, he slowly travelled northwards with his friends, and stopped for a few days at Ouchy [14] to recover his balance in a new world; for the fantastic mystery of coincidences had made the world, which he thought real, mimic and reproduce the distorted nightmare of his personal horror. He did not yet know it, and he was twenty years in finding it out; but he had need of all the beauty of the Lake below and of the Alps above, to restore the finite to its place. For the first time in his life, Mont Blanc for a moment looked to him what it was — a chaos of anarchic and purposeless forces — and he needed days of repose to see it clothe itself again with the illusions of his senses, the white purity of its snows, the splendor of its light, and the infinity of its heavenly peace. Nature was kind; Lake Geneva was beautiful beyond itself, and the Alps put on charms real as terrors; but man became chaotic, and before the illusions of Nature were wholly restored, the illusions of Europe suddenly vanished, leaving a new world to learn.

On July 4, all Europe had been in peace; on July 14, Europe was in full chaos of war. [15] One felt helpless and ignorant, but one might have been king or kaiser without feeling stronger to deal with the chaos. Mr. Gladstone was as much astounded as Adams; the Emperor Napoleon was nearly as stupefied as either, and Bismarck himself hardly knew how he did it. As education, the outbreak of the war was wholly lost on a man dealing with death hand-to-hand, who could not throw it aside to look at it across the Rhine. Only when he got up to Paris, he began to feel the approach of catastrophe. Providence set up no *affiches*[16] to announce the tragedy. Under one's eyes France cut herself adrift, and floated off, on an unknown stream, towards a less known ocean. Standing on the curb of the Boulevard, one could see as much as though one stood by the side of the Emperor or in command of an army corps. The effect was lurid. The public seemed to look on the war, as it had looked on the wars of Louis XIV and Francis I, as a branch of decorative art. The French, like true artists, always regarded war as one of the fine arts. Louis XIV practised it; Napoleon I perfected it; and Napoleon III had till then pursued it in the same spirit with singular success. In Paris, in July, 1870, the war was brought out like an opera of Meyerbeer.[17] One felt oneself a supernumerary hired to fill the scene. Every evening at the theatre the comedy was interrupted by order, and one stood up by order, to join in singing the *Marseillaise* to order. For nearly twenty years one had been forbidden to sing the *Marseillaise* under any circumstances, but at last regiment after regiment marched through the streets shouting "Marchons!" while the bystanders cared not enough to join. Patriotism seemed to have been brought out of the Government stores, and distributed by grammes *per capita*. One had seen one's own people dragged unwillingly into a war, and had watched one's own regiments march to the front without sign of enthusiasm; on the contrary, most serious, anxious, and conscious of the whole weight of the crisis; but in Paris everyone conspired to ignore the crisis, which everyone felt at hand. Here was education for the million, but the lesson was intricate. Superficially Napoleon and his Ministers and marshals were playing a game against Thiers and Gambetta.[18] A bystander knew almost as little as they did about the result. How could Adams prophesy that in another year or two, when he spoke of *his* Paris and its tastes, people would smile at his dotage?

As soon as he could, he fled to England and once more took refuge in the profound peace of Wenlock Abbey. Only the few remaining monks, undisturbed by the brutalities of Henry VIII —

three or four young Englishmen — survived there, with Milnes Gaskell acting as Prior. The August sun was warm; the calm of the Abbey was ten times secular;[19] not a discordant sound — hardly a sound of any sort except the cawing of the ancient rookery at sunset — broke the stillness; and, after the excitement of the last month, one felt a palpable haze of peace brooding over the Edge and the Welsh Marches. Since the reign of *Pteraspis*, nothing had greatly changed; nothing except the monks. Lying on the turf, the ground littered with newspapers, the monks studied the war correspondence. In one respect Adams had succeeded in educating himself; he had learned to follow a campaign.

While at Wenlock, he received a letter from President Eliot[20] inviting him to take an Assistant Professorship of History, to be created shortly at Harvard College. After waiting ten or a dozen years for some one to show consciousness of his existence, even a *Terebratula* would be pleased and grateful for a compliment which implied that the new President of Harvard College wanted his help; but Adams knew nothing about history, and much less about teaching, while he knew more than enough about Harvard College; and wrote at once to thank President Eliot, with much regret that the honor should be above his powers. His mind was full of other matters. The summer, from which he had expected only amusement and social relations with new people, had ended in the most intimate personal tragedy, and the most terrific political convulsion he had ever known or was likely to know. He had failed in every object of his trip. The Quarterlies had refused his best essay. He had made no acquaintances and hardly picked up the old ones. He sailed from Liverpool, on September 1, to begin again where he had started two years before, but with no longer a hope of attaching himself to a President or a party or a press. He was a free lance and no other career stood in sight or in mind. To that point education had brought him.

Yet he found, on reaching home, that he had not done quite so badly as he feared. His article on the Session in the July *North*

American had made a success. Though he could not quite see what partisan object it served, he heard with flattered astonishment that it had been reprinted by the Democratic National Committee and circulated as a campaign document by the hundred thousand copies. He was henceforth in opposition, do what he might; and a Massachusetts Democrat, say what he pleased; while his only reward or return for this partisan service consisted in being formally answered by Senator Timothy Howe, of Wisconsin, in a Republican campaign document, presumed to be also freely circulated, in which the Senator, besides refuting his opinions, did him the honor — most unusual and picturesque in a Senator's rhetoric — of likening him to a begonia.[21]

The begonia is, or then was, a plant of such senatorial qualities as to make the simile, in intention, most flattering. Far from charming in its refinement, the begonia was remarkable for curious and showy foliage; it was conspicuous; it seemed to have no useful purpose; and it insisted on standing always in the most prominent positions. Adams would have greatly liked to be a begonia in Washington, for this was rather his ideal of the successful statesman, and he thought about it still more when the *Westminster Review* for October brought him his article on the Gold Conspiracy, which was also instantly pirated on a great scale. Piratical he was himself henceforth driven to be, and he asked only to be pirated, for he was sure not to be paid; but the honors of piracy resemble the colors of the begonia; they are showy but not useful. Here was a *tour de force* he had never dreamed himself equal to performing: two long, dry, quarterly, thirty or forty page articles, appearing in quick succession, and pirated for audiences running well into the hundred thousands; and not one person, man or woman, offering him so much as a congratulation, except to call him a begonia.

Had this been all, life might have gone on very happily as before, but the ways of America to a young person of literary and political tastes were such as the so-called evolution of civilized man had not before evolved. No sooner had Adams made at Washington what he modestly hoped was a sufficient success, than his whole family set on him to drag him away. For the first time since 1861 his father interposed; his mother entreated; and his brother Charles argued and urged that he should come to Harvard College. Charles had views of further joint operations in a new field. He said that Henry had done at Washington all he could possibly do; that his position there wanted solidity; that he was, after all, an adventurer; that a few years in Cambridge would give him personal weight; that his chief function was not to be that of teacher, but that of editing the *North American Review* which was to be coupled with the professorship, and would lead to the daily press. In short, that he needed the university more than the university needed him.

Henry knew the university well enough to know that the department of history was controlled by one of the most astute and ideal administrators in the world — Professor Gurney [22] — and that it was Gurney who had established the new professorship, and had cast his net over Adams to carry the double load of mediæval history and the *Review*. He could see no relation whatever between himself and a professorship. He sought education; he did not sell it. He knew no history; he knew only a few historians; his ignorance was mischievous because it was literary, accidental, indifferent. On the other hand he knew Gurney, and felt much influenced by his advice. One cannot take oneself quite seriously in such matters; it could not much affect the sum of solar energies whether one went on dancing with girls in Washington, or began talking to boys at Cambridge. The good people who thought it did matter had a sort of right to guide. One could not reject their advice; still less disregard their wishes.

The sum of the matter was that Henry went out to Cambridge and had a few words with President Eliot which seemed to him almost as American as the talk about diplomacy with his father ten years before. [23] "But, Mr. President," urged Adams, "I know nothing about Mediæval History." With the courteous manner and bland smile so familiar for the next generation of Americans, Mr. Eliot mildly but firmly replied, "If you will point out to me any one who knows more, Mr. Adams, I will appoint him." The answer was neither logical nor convincing, but Adams could not meet it without overstepping his privileges. He could not say that, under the circumstances, the appointment of any professor at all seemed to him unnecessary.

So, at twenty-four hours' notice, he broke his life in halves again in order to begin a new education, on lines he had not chosen, in subjects for which he cared less than nothing; in a place he did not love, and before a future which repelled. Thousands of men have to do the same thing, but his case was peculiar because he had no need to do it. He did it because his best and wisest friends urged it, and he never could make up his mind whether they were right or not. To him this kind of education was always false. For himself he had no doubts. He thought it a mistake; but his opinion did not prove that it was one, since, in all probability, whatever he did would be more or less a mistake. He had reached cross-roads of education which all led astray. What he could gain at Harvard College he did not know, but in any case it was nothing he wanted. What he lost at Washington he could partly see, but in any case it was not fortune. Grant's administration wrecked men by thousands, but profited few. Perhaps Mr. Fish was the solitary exception. One might search the whole list of Congress, Judiciary, and Executive during the twenty-five years 1870 to 1895, and find little but damaged reputation. The period was poor in purpose and barren in results.

Henry Adams, if not the rose,[24] lived as near it as any politician, and knew, more or less, all the men in any way prominent at Washington, or knew all about them. Among them, in his opinion, the best equipped, the most active-minded, and most industrious was Abram Hewitt,[25] who sat in Congress for a dozen years, between 1874 and 1886, sometimes leading the House and always wielding influence second to none. With nobody did Adams form closer or longer relations than with Mr. Hewitt, whom he regarded as the most useful public man in Washington; and he was the more struck by Hewitt's saying, at the end of his laborious career as legislator, that he left behind him no permanent result except the Act consolidating the Surveys. Adams knew no other man who had done so much, unless Mr. Sherman's legislation is accepted [26] as an instance of success. Hewitt's nearest rival would probably have been Senator Pendleton who stood father to civil service reform in 1882, an attempt to correct a vice that should never have been allowed to be born. These were the men who succeeded.

The press stood in much the same light. No editor, no political writer, and no public administrator achieved enough good reputation to preserve his memory for twenty years. A number of them achieved bad reputations, or damaged good ones that had been gained in the Civil War. On the whole, even for Senators, diplomats, and Cabinet officers, the period was wearisome and stale.

None of Adams's generation profited by public activity unless it were William C. Whitney, and even he could not be induced to return to it. Such ambitions as these were out of one's reach, but supposing one tried for what was feasible, attached oneself closely to the Garfields, Arthurs, Frelinghuysens, Blaines, Bayards, or Whitneys, who happened to hold office[27]; and supposing one asked for the mission to Belgium or Portugal, and obtained it; supposing one served a term as Assistant Secretary or Chief of Bureau; or, finally, supposing one had gone as sub-editor on the *New York Tribune* or *Times* — how much more education would one have gained than by going to Harvard College? These questions seemed better worth an answer than most of the questions on examination papers at college or in the civil service; all the more because one never found an answer to them, then or afterwards, and because, to his mind, the value of American society altogether was mixed up with the value of Washington.

At first, the simple beginner, struggling with principles, wanted to throw off responsibility on the American people, whose bare

and toiling shoulders had to carry the load of every social or
political stupidity; but the American people had no more to do
with it than with the customs of Peking. American character
might perhaps account for it, but what accounted for American
character? All Boston, all New England, and all respectable New
York, including Charles Francis Adams the father and Charles
Francis Adams the son, agreed that Washington was no place for
a respectable young man. All Washington, including Presidents,
Cabinet officers, Judiciary, Senators, Congressmen, and clerks,
expressed the same opinion, and conspired to drive away every
young man who happened to be there, or tried to approach. Not
one young man of promise remained in the Government service.
All drifted into opposition. The Government did not want them
in Washington. Adams's case was perhaps the strongest because
he thought he had done well. He was forced to guess it, since he
knew no one who would have risked so extravagant a step as that
of encouraging a young man in a literary career, or even in a political one; society forbade it, as well as residence in a political
capital; but Harvard College must have seen some hope for him,
since it made him professor against his will; even the publishers
and editors of the *North American Review* must have felt a certain
amount of confidence in him, since they put the *Review* in his hands.
After all, the *Review* was the first literary power in America, even
though it paid almost as little in gold as the United States Treasury. The degree of Harvard College might bear a value as ephemeral as the commission of a President of the United States; but
the government of the college, measured by money alone, and
patronage, was a matter of more importance than that of some
branches of the national service. In social position, the college was
the superior of them all put together. In knowledge, she could
assert no superiority, since the Government made no claims,
and prided itself on ignorance. The service of Harvard College
was distinctly honorable; perhaps the most honorable in America;
and if Harvard College thought Henry Adams worth employing at

four dollars a day,[28] why should Washington decline his services when he asked nothing? Why should he be dragged from a career he liked in a place he loved, into a career he detested, in a place and climate he shunned? Was it enough to satisfy him, that all America should call Washington barren and dangerous? What made Washington more dangerous than New York?

The American character showed singular limitations which sometimes drove the student of civilized man to despair. Crushed by his own ignorance — lost in the darkness of his own gropings — the scholar finds himself jostled of a sudden by a crowd of men who seem to him ignorant that there is a thing called ignorance; who have forgotten how to amuse themselves; who cannot even understand that they are bored. The American thought of himself as a restless, pushing, energetic, ingenious person, always awake and trying to get ahead of his neighbors. Perhaps this idea of the national character might be correct for New York or Chicago; it was not correct for Washington. There the American showed himself, four times in five, as a quiet, peaceful, shy figure, rather in the mould of Abraham Lincoln, somewhat sad, sometimes pathetic, once tragic; or like Grant, inarticulate, uncertain, distrustful of himself, still more distrustful of others, and awed by money. That the American, by temperament, worked to excess, was true; work and whiskey were his stimulants; work was a form of vice; but he never cared much for money or power after he earned them. The amusement of the pursuit was all the amusement he got from it; he had no use for wealth. Jim Fisk alone seemed to know what he wanted; Jay Gould never did. At Washington one met mostly such true Americans, but if one wanted to know them better, one went to study them in Europe. Bored, patient, helpless; pathetically dependent on his wife and daughters; indulgent to excess; mostly a modest, decent, excellent, valuable citizen; the American was to be met at every railway station in Europe, carefully explaining to every listener that the happiest day of his life would be the day he should land on the pier at New York. He was ashamed to be amused; his mind no longer answered to the stimulus of variety; he could not face a new thought. All his immense strength, his intense nervous energy, his keen analytic perceptions, were oriented in one direction, and he could not change it. Congress was full of such men; in the Senate, Sumner was almost the only exception; in the Executive, Grant and Boutwell were varieties of the type — political specimens — pathetic in their helplessness to do anything with power when it came to them. They knew not how to amuse themselves; they could not conceive how other people were amused. Work, whiskey, and cards were life. The atmosphere of political Washington was theirs — or was supposed by the outside world to be in their control — and this was the reason why the outside world judged that Washington was fatal even for a young man of thirty-two, who had passed through the whole variety of temptations, in every capital of Europe, for a dozen years; who never played cards, and who loathed whiskey.

CHAPTER XX

Failure (1871)

FAR back in childhood, among its earliest memories, Henry Adams could recall his first visit to Harvard College. He must have been nine years old when on one of the singularly gloomy winter afternoons which beguiled Cambridgeport,[1] his mother drove him out to visit his aunt, Mrs. Everett. Edward Everett was then President of the college and lived in the old President's House on Harvard Square. The boy remembered the drawing-room, on the left of the hall door, in which Mrs. Everett received them. He remembered a marble greyhound in the corner. The house had an air of colonial self-respect that impressed even a nine-year-old child.

When Adams closed his interview with President Eliot, he asked the Bursar about his aunt's old drawing-room, for the house had been turned to base uses. The room and the deserted kitchen adjacent to it were to let. He took them. Above him, his brother Brooks, then a law student, had rooms, with a private staircase. Opposite was J. R. Dennett,[2] a young instructor almost as literary as Adams himself, and more rebellious to conventions. Inquiry revealed a boarding-table, somewhere in the neighborhood, also supposed to be superior in its class. Chauncey Wright, Francis Wharton, Dennett, John Fiske,[3] or their equivalents in learning and lecture, were seen there, among three or four law students like Brooks Adams. With these primitive arrangements, all of them had to be satisfied. The standard was below that of Washington, but it was, for the moment, the best.

For the next nine months the Assistant Professor had no time to waste on comforts or amusements. He exhausted all his strength in trying to keep one day ahead of his duties. Often the stint ran on, till night and sleep ran short. He could not stop to think whether he were doing the work rightly. He could not get it done to please him, rightly or wrongly, for he never could satisfy himself what to do.

The fault he had found with Harvard College as an undergraduate must have been more or less just, for the college was making a great effort to meet these self-criticisms, and had elected President Eliot in 1869 to carry out its reforms. Professor Gurney was one of the leading reformers, and had tried his hand on his own department of History. The two full Professors of History — Torrey [4] and Gurney, charming men both — could not cover the ground. Between Gurney's classical courses and Torrey's modern ones, lay a gap of a thousand years, which Adams was expected to fill. The students had already elected courses numbered 1, 2, and 3, without knowing what was to be taught or who was to teach. If their new professor had asked what idea was in their minds, they must have replied that nothing at all was in their minds, since their professor had nothing in his, and down to the moment he took his chair and looked his scholars in the face, he had given, as far as he could remember, an hour, more or less, to the Middle Ages.

Not that his ignorance troubled him! He knew enough to be ignorant. His course had led him through oceans of ignorance; he had tumbled from one ocean into another till he had learned to swim; but even to him education was a serious thing. A parent gives life, but as parent, gives no more. A murderer takes life, but his deed stops there. A teacher affects eternity; he can never tell where his influence stops. A teacher is expected to teach truth, and may perhaps flatter himself that he does so, if he stops with the alphabet or the multiplication table, as a mother teaches truth by making her child eat with a spoon; but morals are quite another truth and philosophy is more complex still. A teacher must either treat history as a catalogue, a record, a romance, or as an evolution; and whether he affirms or denies evolution, he falls into all the burning faggots of the pit. He makes of his scholars either priests or atheists, plutocrats or socialists, judges or anarchists, almost in spite of himself. In essence incoherent and immoral, history had either to be taught as such — or falsified.

Adams wanted to do neither. He had no theory of evolution to teach, and could not make the facts fit one. He had no fancy for telling agreeable tales to amuse sluggish-minded boys, in order to publish them afterwards as lectures. He could still less compel his students to learn the Anglo-Saxon Chronicle and the Venerable Bede by heart.[5] He saw no relation whatever between his students and the Middle Ages unless it were the Church, and there the ground was particularly dangerous. He knew better than though he were a professional historian that the man who should solve the riddle of the Middle Ages and bring them into the line of evolution from past to present, would be a greater man than Lamarck or Linnæus;[6] but history had nowhere broken down so pitiably, or avowed itself so hopelessly bankrupt, as there. Since Gibbon, the spectacle was almost a scandal. History had lost even the sense of shame. It was a hundred years behind the experimental sciences. For all serious purpose, it was less instructive than Walter Scott and Alexandre Dumas.

All this was without offence to Sir Henry Maine, Tylor, McLennan, Buckle, Auguste Comte, and the various philosophers who, from time to time, stirred the scandal, and made it more scandalous.[7] No doubt, a teacher might make some use of these writers or their theories; but Adams could fit them into no theory of his own. The college expected him to pass at least half his time in teaching the boys a few elementary dates and relations, that they might not be a disgrace to the university.[8] This was formal; and he could frankly tell the boys that, provided they passed their examinations, they might get their facts where they liked, and use the teacher only for questions. The only privilege a student had that was worth his claiming, was that of talking to the professor, and the professor was bound to encourage it. His only difficulty on that side was to get them to talk at all. He had to devise schemes to find what they were thinking about, and induce them to risk criticism from their fellows. Any large body of students stifles the student. No man can instruct more than half-a-dozen students at once. The whole problem of education is one of its cost in money.

The lecture system to classes of hundreds, which was very much that of the twelfth century, suited Adams not at all. Barred from philosophy and bored by facts, he wanted to teach his students something not wholly useless. The number of students whose minds were of an order above the average was, in his experience, barely one in ten; the rest could not be much stimulated by any inducements a teacher could suggest. All were respectable, and in seven years of contact, Adams never had cause to complain of one; but nine minds in ten take polish passively, like a hard surface; only the tenth sensibly reacts.

Adams thought that, as no one seemed to care what he did, he would try to cultivate this tenth mind, though necessarily at the expense of the other nine. He frankly acted on the rule that a teacher, who knew nothing of his subject, should not pretend to teach his scholars what he did not know, but should join them in trying to find the best way of learning it. The rather pretentious name of historical method was sometimes given to this process of instruction, but the name smacked of German pedagogy, and a young professor who respected neither history nor method, and whose sole object of interest was his students' minds, fell into trouble enough without adding to it a German parentage.

The task was doomed to failure for a reason which he could not control. Nothing is easier than to teach historical method, but, when learned, it has little use. History is a tangled skein that one may take up at any point, and break when one has unravelled enough; but complexity precedes evolution. The *Pteraspis* grins horribly from the closed entrance. One may not begin at the beginning, and one has but the loosest relative truths to follow up. Adams found himself obliged to force his material into some shape to which a method could be applied. He could think only of law as subject; the Law School as end; and he took, as victims of his experiment, half-a-dozen highly intelligent young men who seemed willing to work. The course began with the beginning, as far as the books showed a beginning in primitive man, and came down through the Salic Franks to the Norman English. Since no textbooks existed, the professor refused to profess, knowing no more than his students, and the students read what they pleased and compared their results. As pedagogy, nothing could be more triumphant. The boys worked like rabbits, and dug holes all over the field of archaic society; no difficulty stopped them; unknown languages yielded before their attack, and customary law became familiar as the police court; undoubtedly they learned, after a fashion, to chase an idea, like a hare, through as dense a thicket of obscure facts as they were likely to meet at the bar; but their teacher knew from his own experience that his wonderful method led nowhere, and they would have to exert themselves to get rid of it in the Law School even more than they exerted themselves to acquire it in the college. Their science had no system, and could have none, since its subject was merely antiquarian. Try as hard as he might, the professor could not make it actual.

What was the use of training an active mind to waste its energy? The experiments might in time train Adams as a professor, but this result was still less to his taste. He wanted to help the boys to a career, but not one of his many devices to stimulate the intellectual reaction of the student's mind satisfied either him or the students. For himself he was clear that the fault lay in the system, which could lead only to inertia. Such little knowledge of himself as he possessed warranted him in affirming that his mind required conflict, competition, contradiction even more than that of the student. He too wanted a rank-list to set his name upon. His reform of the system would have begun in the lecture-room at his own desk. He would have seated a rival assistant professor

opposite him, whose business should be strictly limited to expressing opposite views. Nothing short of this would ever interest
either the professor or the student; but of all university freaks,
no irregularity shocked the intellectual atmosphere so much as
contradiction or competition between teachers. In that respect
the thirteenth-century university system was worth the whole
teaching of the modern school.

All his pretty efforts to create conflicts of thought among his
students failed for want of system. None met the needs of instruction. In spite of President Eliot's reforms and his steady,
generous, liberal support, the system remained costly, clumsy and
futile. The university — as far as it was represented by Henry
Adams — produced at great waste of time and money results not
worth reaching.

He made use of his lost two years of German schooling to in-
flict their results on his students, and by a happy chance he was
in the full tide of fashion. The Germans were crowning their new
emperor at Versailles, and surrounding his head with a halo of
Pepins and Merwigs, Othos and Barbarossas.[9] James Bryce had
even discovered the Holy Roman Empire. Germany was never
so powerful, and the Assistant Professor of History had nothing
else as his stock in trade. He imposed Germany on his scholars
with a heavy hand. He was rejoiced; but he sometimes doubted
whether they should be grateful. On the whole, he was content
neither with what he had taught nor with the way he had taught
it. The seven years he passed in teaching seemed to him lost.

The uses of adversity are beyond measure strange. As a professor, he regarded himself as a failure. Without false modesty he
thought he knew what he meant. He had tried a great many experiments, and wholly succeeded in none. He had succumbed to
the weight of the system. He had accomplished nothing that he
tried to do. He regarded the system as wrong; more mischievous
to the teachers than to the students; fallacious from the beginning
to end. He quitted the university at last, in 1877, with a feeling,

that, if it had not been for the invariable courtesy and kindness shown by everyone in it, from the President to the injured students, he should be sore at his failure.

These were his own feelings, but they seemed not to be felt in the college. With the same perplexing impartiality that had so much disconcerted him in his undergraduate days, the college insisted on expressing an opposite view. John Fiske went so far in his notice of the family in "Appleton's Cyclopedia," as to say that Henry had left a great reputation at Harvard College; which was a proof of John Fiske's personal regard that Adams heartily returned; and set the kind expression down to *camaraderie*. The case was different when President Eliot himself hinted that Adams's services merited recognition. Adams could have wept on his shoulder in hysterics, so grateful was he for the rare good-will that inspired the compliment; but he could not allow the college to think that he esteemed himself entitled to distinction. He knew better, and his was among the failures which were respectable enough to deserve self-respect. Yet nothing in the vanity of life struck him as more humiliating than that Harvard College, which he had persistently criticised, abused, abandoned, and neglected, should alone have offered him a dollar, an office, an encouragement, or a kindness. Harvard College might have its faults, but at least it redeemed America, since it was true to its own.

The only part of education that the professor thought a success was the students. He found them excellent company. Cast more or less in the same mould, without violent emotions or sentiment, and, except for the veneer of American habits, ignorant of all that man had ever thought or hoped, their minds burst open like flowers at the sunlight of a suggestion. They were quick to respond; plastic to a mould; and incapable of fatigue. Their faith in education was so full of pathos that one dared not ask them what they thought they could do with education when they got it. Adams did put the question to one of them, and was surprised at the answer: "The degree of Harvard College is worth money to me in Chicago." This reply upset his experience; for the degree of Harvard College had been rather a drawback to a young man in Boston and Washington. So far as it went, the answer was good, and settled one's doubts. Adams knew no better, although he had given twenty years to pursuing the same education, and was no nearer a result than they. He still had to take for granted many things that they need not — among the rest, that his teaching did them more good than harm. In his own opinion the greatest good he could do them was to hold his tongue. They needed much faith then; they were likely to need more if they lived long.

He never knew whether his colleagues shared his doubts about their own utility. Unlike himself, they knew more or less their business. He could not tell his scholars that history glowed with social virtue; the Professor of Chemistry cared not a chemical atom whether society was virtuous or not. Adams could not pretend that mediæval society proved evolution; the Professor of Physics smiled at evolution. Adams was glad to dwell on the virtues of the Church and the triumphs of its art: the Professor of Political Economy had to treat them as waste of force. They knew what they had to teach; he did not. They might perhaps be frauds without knowing it; but he knew certainly nothing else of himself. He could teach his students nothing; he was only educating himself at their cost.

Education, like politics, is a rough affair, and every instructor has to shut his eyes and hold his tongue as though he were a priest. The students alone satisfied. They thought they gained something. Perhaps they did, for even in America and in the twentieth century, life could not be wholly industrial. Adams fervently hoped that they might remain content; but supposing twenty years more to pass, and they should turn on him as fiercely as he had turned on his old instructors — what answer could he make? The college had pleaded guilty, and tried to reform. He had pleaded guilty from the start, and his reforms had failed before those of the college.

The lecture-room was futile enough, but the faculty-room was worse. American society feared total wreck in the maelstrom of political and corporate administration, but it could not look for help to college dons. Adams knew, in that capacity, both Congressmen and professors, and he preferred Congressmen. The same failure marked the society of a college. Several score of the best-educated, most agreeable, and personally the most sociable people in America united in Cambridge to make a social desert that would have starved a polar bear. The liveliest and most agreeable of men — James Russell Lowell, Francis J. Child, Louis Agassiz, his son Alexander, Gurney, John Fiske, William James[10] and a dozen others, who would have made the joy of London or Paris — tried their best to break out and be like other men in Cambridge and Boston, but society called them professors, and professors they had to be. While all these brilliant men were greedy for companionship, all were famished for want of it. Society was a faculty-meeting without business. The elements were there; but society cannot be made up of elements — people who are expected to be silent unless they have observations to make — and all the elements are bound to remain apart if required to make observations.

Thus it turned out that of all his many educations, Adams thought that of school-teacher the thinnest. Yet he was forced to admit that the education of an editor, in some ways, was thinner still. The editor had barely time to edit; he had none to write. If copy fell short, he was obliged to scribble a book-review[11] on the virtues of the Anglo-Saxons or the vices of the Popes; for he knew more about Edward the Confessor or Boniface VIII[12] than he did about President Grant. For seven years he wrote nothing; the *Review* lived on his brother Charles's railway articles.[13] The editor could help others, but could do nothing for himself. As a writer, he was totally forgotten by the time he had been an editor for twelve months. As editor he could find no writer to take his place for politics and affairs of current concern. The *Review* became chiefly historical. Russell Lowell and Frank Palgrave helped him to keep it literary. The editor was a helpless drudge whose successes, if he made any, belonged to his writers; but whose failures might easily bankrupt himself. Such a Review may be made a sink of money with captivating ease. The secrets of success as an editor were easily learned; the highest was that of getting advertisements. Ten pages of advertising made an editor a success; five marked him as a failure. The merits or demerits of his literature had little to do with his results except when they led to adversity.

A year or two of education as editor satiated most of his appetite for that career as a profession. After a very slight experience, he said no more on the subject. He felt willing to let anyone edit, if he himself might write. Vulgarly speaking, it was a dog's life when it did not succeed, and little better when it did. A professor had at least the pleasure of associating with his students; an editor lived the life of an owl. A professor commonly became a pedagogue or a pedant; an editor became an authority on advertising. On the whole, Adams preferred his attic in Washington. He was educated enough. Ignorance paid better, for at least it earned fifty dollars a month.

With this result Henry Adams's education, at his entry into life, stopped, and his life began. He had to take that life as he best could, with such accidental education as luck had given him; but he held that it was wrong, and that, if he were to begin again, he would do it on a better system. He thought he knew nearly what system to pursue. At that time Alexander Agassiz had not yet got his head above water so far as to serve for a model, as he did twenty or thirty years afterwards; but the editorship of the *North American Review* had one solitary merit; it made the editor acquainted at a distance with almost everyone in the country who could write or who could be the cause of writing. Adams was vastly pleased to be received among these clever people as one of themselves, and felt always a little surprised at their treating him as an equal, for they all had education; but among them, only one stood out in extraordinary prominence as the type and model of what Adams would have liked to be, and of what the American, as he conceived, should have been and was not.

Thanks to the article on Sir Charles Lyell, Adams passed for a friend of geologists, and the extent of his knowledge mattered much less to them than the extent of his friendship, for geologists were as a class not much better off than himself, and friends were sorely few. One of his friends from earliest childhood, and nearest neighbor in Quincy, Frank Emmons,[14] had become a geologist and joined the Fortieth Parallel Survey under Government. At Washington in the winter of 1869–70, Emmons had invited Adams to go out with him on one of the field-parties in summer. Of course when Adams took the *Review* he put it at the service of the Survey, and regretted only that he could not do more. When the first year of professing and editing was at last over, and his July *North American* appeared, he drew a long breath of relief, and took the next train for the West. Of his year's work he was no judge. He had become a small spring in a large mechanism, and his work counted only in the sum; but he had been treated civilly by everybody, and he felt at home even in Boston. Putting in his pocket the July number of the *North American*, with a notice of the Fortieth Parallel Survey by Professor J. D. Whitney,[15] he started for the plains and the Rocky Mountains.

In the year 1871, the West was still fresh, and the Union Pacific was young.[16] Beyond the Missouri River, one felt the atmosphere of Indians and buffaloes. One saw the last vestiges of an old education, worth studying if one would; but it was not that which Adams sought; rather, he came out to spy upon the land of the future. The Survey occasionally borrowed troopers from the nearest station in case of happening on hostile Indians, but otherwise the topographers and geologists thought more about minerals than about Sioux. They held under their hammers a thousand miles of mineral country with all its riddles to solve, and its stores of possible wealth to mark. They felt the future in their hands.

Emmons's party was out of reach in the Uintahs, but Arnold Hague's had come in to Laramie[17] for supplies, and they took charge of Adams for a time. Their wanderings or adventures matter nothing to the story of education. They were all hardened mountaineers and surveyors who took everything for granted, and spared each other the most wearisome bore of English and Scotch life, the stories of the big game they killed. A bear was an occasional amusement; a wapiti[18] was a constant necessity; but the only wild animal dangerous to man was a rattlesnake or a skunk. One shot for amusement, but one had other matters to talk about.

Adams enjoyed killing big game, but loathed the labor of cutting it up; so that he rarely unslung the little carbine he was in a manner required to carry. On the other hand, he liked to wander off alone on his mule, and pass the day fishing a mountain stream or exploring a valley. One morning when the party was camped high above Estes Park,[19] on the flank of Long's Peak, he borrowed a rod, and rode down over a rough trail into Estes Park, for some trout. The day was fine, and hazy with the smoke of forest fires a thousand miles away; the park stretched its English beauties off to the base of its bordering mountains in natural landscape and archaic peace; the stream was just fishy enough to tempt lingering along its banks. Hour after hour the sun moved westward and the fish moved eastward, or disappeared altogether, until at last when the fisherman cinched his mule, sunset was nearer than he thought. Darkness caught him before he could catch his trail. Not caring to tumble into some fifty-foot hole, he "allowed" he was lost, and turned back. In half an hour he was out of the hills, and under the stars of Estes Park, but he saw no prospect of supper or of bed.

Estes Park was large enough to serve for a bed on a summer night for an army of professors, but the supper question offered difficulties. There was but one cabin in the Park, near its entrance, and he felt no great confidence in finding it, but he thought his mule cleverer than himself, and the dim lines of mountain crest against the stars fenced his range of error. The patient mule plodded on without other road than the gentle slope of the ground, and some two hours must have passed before a light showed in the distance. As the mule came up to the cabin door, two or three men came out to see the stranger.

One of these men was Clarence King[20] on his way up to the camp. Adams fell into his arms. As with most friendships, it was never a matter of growth or doubt. Friends are born in archaic horizons; they were shaped with the *Pteraspis* in Siluria; they have nothing to do with the accident of space. King had come up that day from Greeley in a light four-wheeled buggy, over a trail hardly fit for a commissariat mule, as Adams had reason to know since he went back in the buggy. In the cabin, luxury provided a room and one bed for guests. They shared the room and the bed, and talked till far towards dawn.

King had everything to interest and delight Adams. He knew more than Adams did of art and poetry; he knew America, especially west of the hundredth meridian, better than anyone; he knew the professor by heart, and he knew the Congressman better than he did the professor. He knew even women; even the American woman; even the New York woman, which is saying much. Incidentally he knew more practical geology than was good for him, and saw ahead at least one generation further than the textbooks. That he saw right was a different matter. Since the beginning of time no man has lived who is known to have seen right; the charm of King was that he saw what others did and a great deal more. His wit and humor; his bubbling energy which swept everyone into the current of his interest; his personal charm of youth and manners; his faculty of giving and taking, profusely, lavishly, whether in thought or in money as though he were Nature herself, marked him almost alone among Americans. He had in him something of the Greek — a touch of Alcibiades or Alexander.[21] One Clarence King only existed in the world.

A new friend is always a miracle, but at thirty-three years old, such a bird of paradise rising in the sage-brush was an avatar. One friend in a lifetime is much; two are many; three are hardly possible. Friendship needs a certain parallelism of life, a community of thought, a rivalry of aim. King, like Adams, and all their generation, was at that moment passing the critical point of his career. The one, coming from the west, saturated with the sunshine of the Sierras, met the other, drifting from the east, drenched in the fogs of London, and both had the same problems to handle — the same stock of implements — the same field to work in; above all, the same obstacles to overcome.

As a companion, King's charm was great, but this was not the quality that so much attracted Adams, nor could he affect even distant rivalry on this ground. Adams could never tell a story, chiefly because he always forgot it; and he was never guilty of a witticism, unless by accident. King and the Fortieth Parallel influenced him in a way far more vital. The lines of their lives converged, but King had moulded and directed his life logically, scientifically, as Adams thought American life should be directed. He had given himself education all of a piece, yet broad. Standing in the middle of his career, where their paths at last came together, he could look back and look forward on a straight line, with scientific knowledge for its base. Adams's life, past or future, was a succession of violent breaks or waves, with no base at all. King's abnormal energy had already won him great success. None of his contemporaries had done so much, single-handed, or were likely to leave so deep a trail. He had managed to induce Congress to adopt almost its first modern act of legislation. He had organized, as a civil — not military — measure, a Government Survey. He had paralleled the Continental Railway in Geology; a feat as yet unequalled by other governments which had as a rule no continents to survey. He was creating one of the classic scientific works of the century. The chances were great that he could, whenever he chose to quit the Government service, take the pick of the gold and silver, copper or coal, and build up his fortune as he pleased. Whatever prize he wanted lay ready for him — scientific, social, literary, political — and he knew how to take them in turn. With ordinary luck he would die at eighty the richest and most many-sided genius of his day.

So little egoistic he was that none of his friends felt envy of his extraordinary superiority, but rather grovelled before it, so that women were jealous of the power he had over men; but women were many and Kings were one. The men worshipped not so much their friend, as the ideal American they all wanted to be. The women were jealous because, at heart, King had no faith in the American woman; he loved types more robust.

The young men of the Fortieth Parallel had Californian instincts; they were brothers of Bret Harte. They felt no leanings towards the simple uniformities of Lyell and Darwin; they saw little proof of slight and imperceptible changes; to them, catastrophe was the law of change; they cared little for simplicity and much for complexity; but it was the complexity of Nature, not of New York or even of the Mississippi Valley. King loved paradox; he started them like rabbits, and cared for them no longer, when caught or lost; but they delighted Adams, for they helped, among other things, to persuade him that history was more amusing than science. The only question left open to doubt was their relative money value.

In Emmons's camp, far up in the Uintahs, these talks were continued till the frosts became sharp in the mountains. History and science spread out in personal horizons towards goals no longer far away. No more education was possible for either man. Such as they were, they had got to stand the chances of the world they lived in; and when Adams started back to Cambridge, to take up again the humble tasks of schoolmaster and editor he was harnessed to his cart. Education, systematic or accidental, had done its worst. Henceforth, he went on, submissive.

CHAPTER XXI

Twenty Years After (1892)[1]

ONCE more! this is a story of education, not of adventure! It is meant to help young men — or such as have intelligence enough to seek help — but it is not meant to amuse them. What one did — or did not do — with one's education, after getting it, need trouble the inquirer in no way; it is a personal matter which would only confuse him. Perhaps Henry Adams was not worth educating; most keen judges incline to think that barely one man in a hundred owns a mind capable of reacting to any purpose on the forces that surround him, and fully half of these react wrongly. The object of education for that mind should be the teaching itself how to react with vigor and economy. No doubt the world at large will always lag so far behind the active mind as to make a soft cushion of inertia to drop upon, as it did for Henry Adams; but education should try to lessen the obstacles, diminish the friction, invigorate the energy, and should train minds to react, not at haphazard, but by choice, on the lines of force that attract their world. What one knows is, in youth, of little moment; they know enough who know how to learn. Throughout human history the waste of mind has been appalling, and, as this story is meant to show, society has conspired to promote it. No doubt the teacher is the worst criminal, but the world stands behind him and drags the student from his course. The moral is stentorian. Only the most energetic, the most highly fitted, and the most favored have overcome the friction or the viscosity of inertia, and these were compelled to waste three-fourths of their energy in doing it.

Fit or unfit, Henry Adams stopped his own education in 1871, and began to apply it for practical uses, like his neighbors. At the end of twenty years, he found that he had finished, and could sum up the result. He had no complaint to make against man or woman. They had all treated him kindly; he had never met with ill-will, ill-temper, or even ill-manners, or known a quarrel. He had never seen serious dishonesty or ingratitude. He had found a readiness in the young to respond to suggestion that seemed to him far beyond all he had reason to expect. Considering the stock complaints against the world, he could not understand why he had nothing to complain of.

During these twenty years he had done as much work, in quantity, as his neighbors wanted; more than they would ever stop to look at, and more than his share. Merely in print, he thought altogether ridiculous the number of volumes he counted on the shelves of public libraries. He had no notion whether they served a useful purpose; he had worked in the dark; but so had most of his friends, even the artists, none of whom held any lofty opinion of their success in raising the standards of society, or felt profound respect for the methods or manners of their time, at home or abroad, but all of whom had tried, in a way, to hold the standard up. The effort had been, for the older generation, exhausting, as one could see in the Hunts;[2] but the generation after 1870 made more figure, not in proportion to public wealth or in the census, but in their own self-assertion. A fair number of the men who were born in the thirties had won names — Phillips Brooks; Bret Harte; Henry James; H. H. Richardson;[3] John La Farge; and the list might be made fairly long if it were worth while; but from their school had sprung others, like Augustus St. Gaudens, McKim, Stanford White,[4] and scores born in the forties, who counted as force even in the mental inertia of sixty or eighty million people. Among all these Clarence King, John Hay, and Henry Adams had led modest existences, trying to fill in the social gaps of a class which, as yet, showed but thin ranks and little cohesion. The combination offered no very glittering prizes, but they pursued it for twenty years with as much patience and effort as though it led to fame or power, until, at last, Henry Adams thought his own duties sufficiently performed and his account with society settled. He had enjoyed his life amazingly, and would not have exchanged it for any other that came in his way; he was, or thought he was, perfectly satisfied with it; but for reasons that had nothing to do with education,[5] he was tired; his nervous energy ran low; and, like a horse that wears out, he quitted the race-course, left the stable, and sought pastures as far as possible from the old. Education had ended in 1871; life was complete in 1890; the rest mattered so little!

As had happened so often, he found himself in London when the question of return imposed its verdict on him after much fruitless effort to rest elsewhere. The time was the month of January, 1892; he was alone, in hospital, in the gloom of midwinter.[6] He was close on his fifty-fourth birthday, and Pall Mall had forgotten him as completely as it had forgotten his elders. He had not seen London for a dozen years, and was rather amused to have only a bed for a world and a familiar black fog for horizon. The coal-fire smelt homelike; the fog had a fruity taste of youth; anything was better than being turned out into the wastes of Wigmore Street. He could always amuse himself by living over his youth, and driving once more down Oxford Street in 1858, with life before him to imagine far less amusing than it had turned out to be.

The future attracted him less. Lying there for a week he reflected on what he could do next. He had just come up from the South Seas with John La Farge,[7] who had reluctantly crawled away towards New York to resume the grinding routine of studio-work at an age when life runs low. Adams would rather, as choice, have gone back to the east, if it were only to sleep forever in the trade-winds under the southern stars, wandering over the dark purple ocean, with its purple sense of solitude and void. Not that he liked the sensation, but that it was the most unearthly he had felt. He had not yet happened on Rudyard Kipling's "Mandalay," but he knew the poetry before he knew the poem, like millions of wanderers, who have perhaps alone felt the world exactly as it is. Nothing attracted him less than the idea of beginning a new education. The old one had been poor enough; any new one could only add to its faults. Life had been cut in halves, and the old half had passed away, education and all, leaving no stock to graft on.

The new world he faced in Paris and London seemed to him fantastic. Willing to admit it real in the sense of having some kind of existence outside his own mind, he could not admit it reasonable. In Paris, his heart sank to mere pulp before the dismal ballets at the Grand Opera and the eternal vaudeville at the old Palais Royal; but, except for them, his own Paris of the Second Empire was as extinct as that of the first Napoleon. At the galleries and exhibitions, he was racked by the effort of art to be original, and when one day, after much reflection, John La Farge asked whether there might not still be room for something simple in art, Adams shook his head. As he saw the world, it was no longer simple and could not express itself simply. It should express what it was; and this was something that neither Adams nor La Farge understood.

Under the first blast of this furnace-heat, the lights seemed fairly to go out. He felt nothing in common with the world as it promised to be. He was ready to quit it, and the easiest path led back to the east; but he could not venture alone, and the rarest of animals is a companion. He must return to America to get one. Perhaps, while waiting, he might write more history, and on the chance as a last resource, he gave orders for copying everything he could reach in archives, but this was mere habit. He went home as a horse goes back to his stable, because he knew nowhere else to go.

Home was Washington. As soon as Grant's administration ended, in 1877, and Evarts became Secretary of State, Adams went back there, partly to write history, but chiefly because his seven years of laborious banishment, in Boston, convinced him that, as far as he had a function in life, it was as stable-companion to statesmen, whether they liked it or not. At about the same time, old George Bancroft[8] did the same thing, and presently John Hay came on to be Assistant Secretary of State for Mr. Evarts, and

317

stayed there to write the "Life" of Lincoln.[9] In 1884 Adams joined him in employing Richardson to build them adjoining houses on La Fayette Square. As far as Adams had a home this was it. To the house on La Fayette Square he must turn, for he had no other status — no position in the world.

Never did he make a decision more reluctantly than this of going back to his manger. His father and mother were dead. All his family led settled lives of their own. Except for two or three friends in Washington, who were themselves uncertain of stay, no one cared whether he came or went, and he cared least. There was nothing to care about. Everyone was busy; nearly everyone seemed contented. Since 1871 nothing had ruffled the surface of the American world, and even the progress of Europe in her sideway track to dis-Europeaning herself had ceased to be violent.

After a dreary January in Paris,[10] at last when no excuse could be persuaded to offer itself for further delay, he crossed the channel and passed a week with his old friend, Milnes Gaskell, at Thornes, in Yorkshire, while the westerly gales raved a warning against going home. Yorkshire in January is not an island in the South Seas. It has few points of resemblance to Tahiti; not many to Fiji or Samoa; but, as so often before, it was a rest between past and future, and Adams was grateful for it.

At last, on February 3, he drove, after a fashion, down the Irish Channel, on board the Teutonic. He had not crossed the Atlantic for a dozen years, and had never seen an ocean steamer of the new type. He had seen nothing new of any sort, or much changed in France or England. The railways made quicker time, but were no more comfortable. The scale was the same. The Channel service was hardly improved since 1858, or so little as to make no impression. Europe seemed to have been stationary for twenty years. To a man who had been stationary like Europe, the Teutonic was a marvel. That he should be able to eat his dinner through a week of howling winter gales was a miracle. That he should have a deck stateroom, with fresh air, and read all night, if he chose, by electric light, was matter for more wonder than life had yet supplied, in its old forms. Wonder may be double — even treble. Adams's wonder ran off into figures. As the Niagara was to the Teutonic — as 1860 was to 1890 — so the Teutonic and 1890 must be to the next term — and then? Apparently the question concerned only America. Western Europe offered no such conundrum. There one might double scale and speed indefinitely without passing bounds.

Fate was kind on that voyage. Rudyard Kipling, on his wedding trip to America, thanks to the mediation of Henry James, dashed over the passenger his exuberant fountain of gaiety and wit — as though playing a garden hose on a thirsty and faded begonia. Kipling could never know what peace of mind he gave, for he could hardly ever need it himself so much; and yet, in the full delight of his endless fun and variety, one felt the old conundrum repeat itself. Somehow, somewhere, Kipling and the American were not one, but two, and could not be glued together. The American felt that the defect, if defect it were, was in himself; he had felt it when he was with Swinburne, and, again, with Robert Louis Stevenson, even under the palms of Vailima;[11] but he did not carry self-abasement to the point of thinking himself singular. Whatever the defect might be, it was American; it belonged to the type; it lived in the blood. Whatever the quality might be that held him apart, it was English; it lived also in the blood; one felt it little if at all, with Celts, and one yearned reciprocally among Fiji cannibals.[12] Clarence King used to say that it was due to discord between the wave-lengths of the man-atoms; but the theory offered difficulties in measurement. Perhaps, after all, it was only that genius soars; but this theory, too, had its dark corners. All through life, one had seen the American on his literary knees to the European; and all through many lives back for some two centuries, one had seen the European snub or patronize the American; not always intentionally, but effectually. It was in the nature of things. Kipling neither snubbed nor patronized; he was all gaiety and good-nature; but he would have been first to feel what one meant. Genius has to pay itself that unwilling self-respect.

Towards the middle of February, 1892, Adams found himself again in Washington. In Paris and London he had seen nothing to make a return to life worth while; in Washington he saw plenty of reasons for staying dead. Changes had taken place there; improvements had been made; with time — much time — the city might become habitable according to some fashionable standard; but all one's friends had died or disappeared several times over, leaving one almost as strange as in Boston or London. Slowly, a certain society had built itself up about the Government; houses had been opened and there was much dining; much calling; much leaving of cards; but a solitary man counted for less than in 1868. Society seemed hardly more at home than he. Both Executive and Congress held it aloof. No one in society seemed to have the ear of anybody in Government. No one in Government knew any reason for consulting anyone in society. The world had ceased to be wholly political, but politics had become less social. A survivor of the Civil War — like George Bancroft, or John Hay — tried to keep footing, but without brilliant success. They were free to say or do what they liked, but no one took much notice of anything said or done.

A presidential election was to take place in November, and no one showed much interest in the result. The two candidates were singular persons, of whom it was the common saying that one of them had no friends; the other, only enemies. Calvin Brice,[13] who was at that time altogether the wittiest and cleverest member of the Senate, was in the habit of describing Mr. Cleveland[14] in glowing terms and at great length, as one of the loftiest natures and noblest characters of ancient or modern time; "but," he concluded, "in future I prefer to look on at his proceedings from the safe summit of some neighboring hill." The same remark applied to Mr. Harrison. In this respect, they were the greatest of Presidents, for, whatever harm they might do their enemies, was as nothing when compared to the mortality they inflicted on their friends. Men fled them as though they had the evil eye. To the American people, the two candidates and the two parties were so evenly balanced that the scales showed hardly a perceptible difference. Mr. Harrison[15] was an excellent President, a man of ability and force; perhaps the best President the Republican Party had put forward since Lincoln's death; yet, on the whole, Adams felt a shade of preference for President Cleveland, not so much personally as because the Democrats represented to him the last remnants of the eighteenth century; the survivors of Hosea Biglow's Cornwallis[16]; the sole remaining protestants against a banker's Olympus which had become, for five-and-twenty years, more and more despotic over Esop's frog-empire.[17] One might no longer croak except to vote for King Log, or — failing storks — for Grover Cleveland; and even then could not be sure where King Banker lurked behind. The costly education in politics had led to political torpor. Everyone did not share it. Clarence King and John Hay were loyal Republicans who never for a moment conceived that there could be merit in other ideals. With King, the feeling was chiefly love of archaic races;[18] sympathy with the negro and Indian and corresponding dislike of their enemies; but with Hay, party loyalty became a phase of being, a little like the loyalty of a highly cultivated churchman to his Church. He saw all the failings of the party, and still more keenly those of the partisans; but he could not live outside. To Adams a Western Democrat or a Western Republican, a city Democrat or a city Republican, a W. C. Whitney or a J. G. Blaine, were actually the same man, as far as their usefulness to the objects of King, Hay, or Adams was concerned. They graded themselves as friends or enemies, not as Republicans or Democrats. To Hay, the difference was that of being respectable or not.[19]

Since 1879, King, Hay, and Adams had been inseparable. Step by step, they had gone on in the closest sympathy, rather shunning than inviting public position, until, in 1892, none of them held any post at all. With great effort, in Hayes's administration, all King's friends, including Abram Hewitt and Carl Schurz,[20] had carried the bill for uniting the Surveys and had placed King at the head of the Bureau; but King waited only to organize the service, and then resigned, in order to seek his private fortune in the West. Hay, after serving as Assistant Secretary of State under Secretary Evarts during a part of Hayes's administration, then also insisted on going out, in order to write with Nicolay[21] the "Life" of Lincoln. Adams had held no office, and when his friends asked the reason, he could not go into long explanations, but preferred to answer simply that no President had ever invited him to fill one. The reason was good, and was also conveniently true, but left open an awkward doubt of his morals or capacity. Why had no President ever cared to employ him? The question needed a volume of intricate explanation. There never was a day when he would have refused to perform any duty that the Government imposed on him, but the American Government never to his knowledge imposed duties. The point was never raised with regard to him, or to anyone else. The Government required candidates to offer; the business of the Executive began and ended with the consent or refusal to confer. The social formula carried this passive attitude a shade further. Any public man who may for years have used some other man's house as his own, when promoted to a position of patronage commonly feels himself obliged to inquire, directly or indirectly, whether his friend wants anything; which is equivalent to a civil act of divorce, since he feels awkward in the old relation. The handsomest formula, in an impartial choice, was the grandly courteous Southern phrase of Lamar: "Of course Mr. Adams knows that anything in my power is at his service." *A la disposicion de Usted!*[22] The form must have been correct since it pleased both parties. He was right; Mr. Adams did know all about it; a bow and a conventional smile closed the subject forever, and everyone felt flattered.

Such an intimate, promoted to power, was always lost. His duties and cares absorbed him and affected his balance of mind. Unless his friend served some political purpose, friendship was an effort. Men who neither wrote for newspapers nor made campaign speeches, who rarely subscribed to the campaign fund, and who entered the White House as seldom as possible, placed themselves outside the sphere of usefulness, and did so with entirely adequate knowledge of what they were doing. They never expected the President to ask for their services, and saw no reason why he should do so. As for Henry Adams, in fifty years that he knew Washington, no one would have been more surprised than himself had any President ever asked him to perform so much of a service as to cross the square. Only Texan Congressmen imagined that the President needed their services in some remote consulate after worrying him for months to find one.

In Washington this law or custom is universally understood, and no one's character necessarily suffered because he held no office. No one took office unless he wanted it; and in turn the outsider was never asked to do work or subscribe money. Adams saw no office that he wanted, and he gravely thought that, from his point of view, in the long run, he was likely to be a more useful citizen without office. He could at least act as audience, and, in those days, a Washington audience seldom filled even a small theatre. He felt quite well satisfied to look on, and from time to time he thought he might risk a criticism of the players; but though he found his own position regular, he never quite understood that of John Hay. The Republican leaders treated Hay as one of themselves; they asked his services and took his money with a freedom that staggered even a hardened observer; but they never needed him in equivalent office. In Washington Hay was the only competent man in the party for diplomatic work. He corresponded in his powers of usefulness exactly with Lord Granville in London, who had been for forty years the saving grace of every Liberal administration in turn. Had usefulness to the public service been ever a question, Hay should have had a first-class mission under Hayes; should have been placed in the Cabinet by Garfield, and should have been restored to it by Harrison. These gentlemen were always using him; always invited his services, and always took his money.

Adams's opinion of politics and politicians, as he frankly admitted, lacked enthusiasm, although never, in his severest temper, did he apply to them the terms they freely applied to each other; and he explained everything by his old explanation of Grant's character as more or less a general type; but what roused in his mind more rebellion was the patience and good-nature with which Hay allowed himself to be used. The trait was not confined to politics. Hay seemed to like to be used, and this was one of his many charms; but in politics this sort of good-nature demands supernatural patience. Whatever astonishing lapses of social convention the politicians betrayed, Hay laughed equally heartily, and told the stories with constant amusement, at his own expense. Like most Americans, he liked to play at making Presidents, but, unlike most, he laughed not only at the Presidents he helped to make, but also at himself for laughing.

One must be rich, and come from Ohio or New York, to gratify an expensive taste like this. Other men, on both political flanks, did the same thing, and did it well, less for selfish objects than for the amusement of the game; but Hay alone lived in Washington and in the centre of the Ohio influences that ruled the Republican Party during thirty years. On the whole, these influences were respectable, and although Adams could not, under any circumstances, have had any value, even financially, for Ohio politicians, Hay might have much, as he showed, if they only knew enough to appreciate him. The American politician was occasionally an amusing object; Hay laughed, and, for want of other resource, Adams laughed too; but perhaps it was partly irritation at seeing how President Harrison dealt his cards that made Adams welcome President Cleveland back to the White House.

At all events, neither Hay nor King nor Adams had much to gain by reëlecting Mr. Harrison in 1892, or by defeating him, as far as he was concerned; and as far as concerned Mr. Cleveland, they seemed to have even less personal concern. The whole country, to outward appearance, stood in much the same frame of mind. Everywhere was slack-water. Hay himself was almost as languid and indifferent as Adams. Neither had occupation. Both had finished their literary work. The "Life" of Lincoln had been begun, completed, and published hand in hand with the "History" of Jefferson and Madison, so that between them they had written nearly all the American history there was to write. The intermediate period needed intermediate treatment; the gap between James Madison and Abraham Lincoln could not be judicially filled by either of them. Both were heartily tired of the subject, and America seemed as tired as they. What was worse, the redeeming energy of Americans which had generally served as the resource of minds otherwise vacant, the creation of new force, the application of expanding power, showed signs of check. Even the year before, in 1891, far off in the Pacific, one had met everywhere in the East a sort of stagnation — a creeping paralysis — complaints of shipping and producers — that spread throughout the whole southern hemisphere.[24] Questions of exchange and silver-production loomed large. Credit was shaken, and a change of party government might shake it even in Washington. The matter did not concern Adams, who had no credit, and was always richest when the rich were poor; but it helped to dull the vibration of society.

However they studied it, the balance of profit and loss, on the last twenty years, for the three friends, King, Hay, and Adams, was exceedingly obscure in 1892. They had lost twenty years, but what had they gained? They often discussed the question. Hay had a singular faculty for remembering faces, and would break off suddenly the thread of his talk, as he looked out of the window on La Fayette Square, to notice an old corps commander

or admiral of the Civil War, tottering along to the club for his
cards or his cocktail: "There is old Dash who broke the rebel
lines at Blankburg! Think of his having been a thunderbolt of
war!" Or what drew Adams's closer attention: "There goes
old Boutwell gambolling like the gambolling kid!" There they
went! Men who had swayed the course of empire as well as the
course of Hay, King, and Adams, less valued than the ephemeral
Congressman behind them, who could not have told whether the
general was a Boutwell or Boutwell a general. Theirs was the
highest known success, and one asked what it was worth to them.
Apart from personal vanity, what would they sell it for? Would
any one of them, from President downwards, refuse ten thousand
a year in place of all the consideration he received from the world
on account of his success?

Yet consideration had value, and at that time Adams enjoyed
lecturing Augustus St. Gaudens, in hours of depression, on its
economics: "Honestly you must admit that even if you don't pay
your expenses you get a certain amount of advantage from doing
the best work. Very likely some of the really successful Americans would be willing you should come to dinner sometimes, if you
did not come too often, while they would think twice about Hay,
and would never stand me." The forgotten statesman had no
value at all; the general and admiral not much; the historian but
little; on the whole, the artist stood best, and of course, wealth
rested outside the question, since it was acting as judge; but, in
the last resort, the judge certainly admitted that consideration
had some value as an asset, though hardly as much as ten — or
five — thousand a year.

Hay and Adams had the advantage of looking out of their windows on the antiquities of La Fayette Square, with the sense of
having all that anyone had; all that the world had to offer; all
that they wanted in life, including their names on scores of title-
pages and in one or two biographical dictionaries; but this had
nothing to do with consideration, and they knew no more than

Boutwell or St. Gaudens whether to call it success. Hay had passed ten years in writing the "Life" of Lincoln, and perhaps President Lincoln was the better for it, but what Hay got from it was not so easy to see, except the privilege of seeing popular book-makers steal from his book and cover the theft by abusing the author. Adams had given ten or a dozen years to Jefferson and Madison, with expenses which, in any mercantile business, could hardly have been reckoned at less than a hundred thousand dol-lars, on a salary of five thousand a year; and when he asked what return he got from this expenditure, rather more extravagant in proportion to his means than a racing-stable, he could see none whatever. Such works never return money. Even Frank Park-man[25] never printed a first edition of his relatively cheap and popu-lar volumes, numbering more than seven hundred copies, until quite at the end of his life. A thousand copies of a book that cost twenty dollars or more was as much as any author could expect; two thousand copies was a visionary estimate unless it were can-vassed for subscription. As far as Adams knew, he had but three serious readers — Abram Hewitt, Wayne McVeagh, and Hay himself.[26] He was amply satisfied with their consideration, and could dispense with that of the other fifty-nine million, nine hun-dred and ninety-nine thousand, nine hundred and ninety-seven; but neither he nor Hay was better off in any other respect, and their chief title to consideration was their right to look out of their windows on great men, alive or dead, in La Fayette Square, a privilege which had nothing to do with their writings.

The world was always good-natured; civil; glad to be amused; open-armed to anyone who amused it; patient with everyone who did not insist on putting himself in its way, or costing it money; but this was not consideration, still less power in any of its con-crete forms, and applied as well or better to a comic actor. Cer-tainly a rare soprano or tenor voice earned infinitely more applause as it gave infinitely more pleasure, even in America; but one does what one can with one's means, and casting up one's balance sheet, one expects only a reasonable return on one's capital. Hay and Adams had risked nothing and never played for high stakes. King had followed the ambitious course. He had played for many millions. He had more than once come close to a great success, but the result was still in doubt, and meanwhile he was passing the best years of his life underground.[27] For companionship he was mostly lost.

Thus, in 1892, neither Hay, King, nor Adams knew whether they had attained success, or how to estimate it, or what to call it; and the American people seemed to have no clearer idea than they. Indeed, the American people had no idea at all; they were wandering in a wilderness much more sandy than the Hebrews had ever trodden about Sinai; they had neither serpents nor golden calves to worship.[28] They had lost the sense of worship; for the idea that they worshipped money seemed a delusion. Worship of money was an old-world trait; a healthy appetite akin to worship of the Gods, or to worship of power in any concrete shape; but the American wasted money more recklessly than anyone ever did before; he spent more to less purpose than any extravagant court aristocracy; he had no sense of relative values, and knew not what to do with his money when he got it, except use it to make more, or throw it away. Probably, since human society began, it had seen no such curious spectacle as the houses of the San Francisco millionaires on Nob Hill.[29] Except for the railway system, the enormous wealth taken out of the ground since 1840, had disappeared.[30] West of the Alleghenies, the whole country might have been swept clean, and could have been replaced in better form within one or two years. The American mind had less respect for money than the European or Asiatic mind, and bore its loss more easily; but it had been deflected by its pursuit till it could turn in no other direction. It shunned, distrusted, disliked, the dangerous attraction of ideals, and stood alone in history for its ignorance of the past.

Personal contact brought this American trait close to Adams's

notice. His first step, on returning to Washington, took him out
to the cemetery known as Rock Creek, to see the bronze figure
which St. Gaudens had made for him in his absence.[31] Naturally
every detail interested him; every line; every touch of the artist;
every change of light and shade; every point of relation; every
possible doubt of St. Gaudens's correctness of taste or feeling;
so that, as the spring approached, he was apt to stop there often
to see what the figure had to tell him that was new; but, in all
that it had to say, he never once thought of questioning what it
meant. He supposed its meaning to be the one commonplace
about it — the oldest idea known to human thought. He knew
that if he asked an Asiatic its meaning, not a man, woman, or
child from Cairo to Kamchatka would have needed more than
a glance to reply. From the Egyptian Sphinx to the Kamakura
Daibuts; from Prometheus to Christ; from Michael Angelo to
Shelley, art had wrought on this eternal figure almost as though
it had nothing else to say.[32] The interest of the figure was not in
its meaning, but in the response of the observer. As Adams sat
there, numbers of people came, for the figure seemed to have become a tourist fashion, and all wanted to know its meaning. Most
took it for a portrait-statue, and the remnant were vacant-minded
in the absence of a personal guide. None felt what would have
been a nursery-instinct to a Hindu baby or a Japanese jinricksha-
runner. The only exceptions were the clergy, who taught a lesson
even deeper. One after another brought companions there, and,
apparently fascinated by their own reflection, broke out passionately against the expression they felt in the figure of despair, of
atheism, of denial. Like the others, the priest saw only what he
brought. Like all great artists, St. Gaudens held up the mirror
and no more. The American layman had lost sight of ideals; the
American priest had lost sight of faith. Both were more American than the old, half-witted soldiers who denounced the wasting, on a mere grave, of money which should have been given for
drink.

Landed, lost, and forgotten, in the centre of this vast plain of self-content, Adams could see but one active interest, to which all others were subservient, and which absorbed the energies of some sixty million people to the exclusion of every other force, real or imaginary. The power of the railway system had enormously increased since 1870. Already the coal output of 160,000,000 tons closely approached the 180,000,000 of the British Empire, and one held one's breath at the nearness of what one had never expected to see, the crossing of courses, and the lead of American energies. The moment was deeply exciting to a historian, but the railway system itself interested one less than in 1868, since it offered less chance for future profit. Adams had been born with the railway system; had grown up with it; had been over pretty nearly every mile of it with curious eyes, and knew as much about it as his neighbors; but not there could he look for a new education. Incomplete though it was, the system seemed on the whole to satisfy the wants of society better than any other part of the social machine, and society was content with its creation, for the time, and with itself for creating it. Nothing new was to be done or learned there, and the world hurried on to its telephones, bicycles, and electric trams. At past fifty, Adams solemnly and painfully learned to ride the bicycle.

Nothing else occurred to him as a means of new life. Nothing else offered itself, however carefully he sought. He looked for no change. He lingered in Washington till near July without noticing a new idea. Then he went back to England to pass his summer on the Deeside.[33] In October he returned to Washington and there awaited the reëlection of Mr. Cleveland, which led to no deeper thought than that of taking up some small notes that happened to be outstanding. He had seen enough of the world to be a coward, and above all he had an uneasy distrust of bankers. Even dead men allow themselves a few narrow prejudices.[34]

330

CHAPTER XXII

Chicago (1893)

RIFTING in the dead-water of the *fin-de-siècle*[1]— and during this last decade everyone talked, and seemed to feel *fin-de-siècle* — where not a breath stirred the idle air of education or fretted the mental torpor of self-content, one lived alone. Adams had long ceased going into society. For years he had not dined out of his own house, and in public his face was as unknown as that of an extinct statesman. He had often noticed that six months' oblivion amounts to newspaper-death, and that resurrection is rare. Nothing is easier, if a man wants it, than rest, profound as the grave.

His friends sometimes took pity on him, and came to share a meal or pass a night on their passage south or northwards, but existence was, on the whole, exceedingly solitary, or seemed so to him. Of the society favorites who made the life of every dinner-table and of the halls of Congress — Tom Reed, Bourke Cockran, Edward Wolcott[2]— he knew not one. Although Calvin Brice was his next neighbor for six years, entertaining lavishly as no one had ever entertained before in Washington, Adams never entered his house. W. C. Whitney rivalled Senator Brice in hospitality, and was besides an old acquaintance of the reforming era, but Adams saw him as little as he saw his chief, President Cleveland, or President Harrison or Secretary Bayard[3]or Blaine or Olney. One has no choice but to go everywhere or nowhere. No one may pick and choose between houses, or accept hospitality without returning it. He loved solitude as little as others did; but he was unfit for social work, and he sank under the surface.

Luckily for such helpless animals as solitary men, the world is not only good-natured but even friendly and generous; it loves to pardon if pardon is not demanded as a right. Adams's social offences were many, and no one was more sensitive to it than himself; but a few houses always remained which he could enter without being asked, and quit without being noticed. One was John Hay's; another was Cabot Lodge's; a third led to an intimacy which had the singular effect of educating him in knowledge of the very class of American politician who had done most to block his intended path in life. Senator Cameron[4] of Pennsylvania had married in 1880[5][1878] a young niece of Senator John Sherman of Ohio, thus making an alliance of dynastic importance in politics, and in society a reign of sixteen years, during which Mrs. Cameron and Mrs. Lodge[6] led a career, without precedent and without succession, as the dispensers of sunshine over Washington. Both of them had been kind to Adams, and a dozen years of this intimacy had made him one of their habitual household, as he was of Hay's. In a small society, such ties between houses become political and social force. Without intention or consciousness, they fix one's status in the world. Whatever one's preferences in politics might be, one's house was bound to the Republican interest when sandwiched between Senator Cameron, John Hay, and Cabot Lodge, with Theodore Roosevelt[7] equally at home in them all, and Cecil Spring Rice[8] to unite them by impartial variety. The relation was daily, and the alliance undisturbed by power or patronage, since Mr. Harrison, in those respects, showed little more taste than Mr. Cleveland for the society and interests of this particular band of followers, whose relations with the White House were sometimes comic, but never intimate.

In February, 1893, Senator Cameron took his family to South Carolina, where he had bought an old plantation at Coffin's Point on St. Helena Island, and Adams, as one of the family, was taken, with the rest, to open the new experience. From there he went on to Havana,[9] and came back to Coffin's Point to linger till near April. In May the Senator took his family to Chicago to see the Exposition, and Adams went with them. Early in June, all sailed for England together, and at last, in the middle of July, all found themselves in Switzerland, at Prangins, Chamounix, and Zermatt. On July 22 they drove across the Furka Pass and went down by rail to Lucerne.

Months of close contact teach character, if character has interest; and to Adams the Cameron type had keen interest, ever since it had shipwrecked his career in the person of President Grant. Perhaps it owed life to Scotch blood; perhaps to the blood of Adam and Eve, the primitive strain of man; perhaps only to the blood of the cottager working against the blood of the townsman; but whatever it was, one liked it for its simplicity. The Pennsylvania mind, as minds go, was not complex; it reasoned little and never talked; but in practical matters it was the steadiest of all American types; perhaps the most efficient; certainly the safest.

Adams had printed as much as this in his books,[10] but had never been able to find a type to describe, the two great historical Pennsylvanians having been, as everyone had so often heard, Benjamin Franklin of Boston and Albert Gallatin[11] of Geneva. Of Albert Gallatin, indeed, he had made a voluminous study and an elaborate picture, only to show that he was, if American at all, a New Yorker, with a Calvinistic strain — rather Connecticut than Pennsylvanian. The true Pennsylvanian was a narrower type; as narrow as the kirk; as shy of other people's narrowness as a Yankee; as self-limited as a Puritan farmer. To him, none but Pennsylvanians were white. Chinaman, negro, dago,[12] Italian, Englishman, Yankee — all was one in the depths of Pennsylvanian consciousness. The mental machine could run only on what it took for American lines. This was familiar, ever since one's study of President Grant in 1869; but in 1893, as then, the type was admirably strong and useful if one wanted only to run on the same lines. Practically the Pennsylvanian forgot his prejudices when he allied his interests. He then became supple in action and large in motive, whatever he thought of his colleagues. When he happened to be right — which was, of course, whenever one agreed with him — he was the strongest American in America. As an ally he was worth all the rest, because he understood his own class, who were always a majority; and knew how to deal with them as no New Englander could. If one wanted work done in Congress, one did wisely to avoid asking a New Englander to do it. A Pennsylvanian not only could do it, but did it willingly, practically, and intelligently.

Never in the range of human possibilities had a Cameron believed in an Adams — or an Adams in a Cameron — but they had curiously enough, almost always worked together. The Camerons had what the Adamses thought the political vice of reaching their objects without much regard to their methods. The loftiest virtue of the Pennsylvania machine had never been its scrupulous purity or sparkling professions. The machine worked by coarse means on coarse interests; but its practical success had been the most curious subject of study in American history. When one summed up the results of Pennsylvanian influence, one inclined to think that Pennsylvania set up the Government in 1789; saved it in 1861; created the American system; developed its iron and coal power; and invented its great railways. Following up the same line, in his studies of American character, Adams reached the result — to him altogether paradoxical — that Cameron's qualities and defects united in equal share to make him the most useful member of the Senate.

In the interest of studying, at last, a perfect and favorable specimen of this American type which had so persistently suppressed his own, Adams was slow to notice that Cameron strongly influenced him, but he could not see a trace of any influence which he exercised on Cameron. Not an opinion or a view of his on any subject was ever reflected back on him from Cameron's mind; not even an expression or a fact. Yet the difference in age was trifling, and in education slight. On the other hand, Cameron made deep impression on Adams, and in nothing so much as on the great subject of discussion that year — the question of silver.[13]

Adams had taken no interest in the matter, and knew nothing about it, except as a very tedious hobby of his friend Dana Horton;[14]

but inevitably, from the moment he was forced to choose sides, he was sure to choose silver. Every political idea and personal prejudice he ever dallied with held him to the silver standard, and made a barrier between him and gold. He knew well enough all that was to be said for the gold standard as economy, but he had never in his life taken politics for a pursuit of economy. One might have a political or an economical policy; one could not have both at the same time. This was heresy in the English school, but it had always been law in the American. Equally he knew all that was to be said on the moral side of the question, and he admitted that his interests were, as Boston maintained, wholly on the side of gold; but, had they been ten times as great as they were, he could not have helped his bankers or croupiers to load the dice and pack the cards to make sure his winning the stakes. At least he was bound to profess disapproval — or thought he was. From early childhood his moral principles had struggled blindly with his interests, but he was certain of one law that ruled all others — masses of men invariably follow interests in deciding morals. Morality is a private and costly luxury. The morality of the silver or gold standards was to be decided by popular vote, and the popular vote would be decided by interests; but on which side lay the larger interest? To him the interest was political; he thought it probably his last chance of standing up for his eighteenth-century principles, strict construction, limited powers, George Washington, John Adams, and the rest. He had, in a half-hearted way, struggled all his life against State Street, Banks, Capitalism altogether, as he knew it in old England or new England, and he was fated to make his last resistance behind the silver standard.

For him this result was clear, and if he erred, he erred in company with nine men out of ten in Washington, for there was little difference on the merits. Adams was sure to lean backwards, but the case seemed entirely different with Cameron, a typical Pennsylvanian, a practical politician, whom all the reformers, including all the Adamses, had abused for a lifetime for subservience to moneyed interests and political jobbery. He was sure to go with the banks and corporations which had made and sustained him. On the contrary, he stood out obstinately as the leading champion of silver in the East. The reformers, represented by the *Evening Post* and Godkin, whose personal interests lay with the gold standard, at once assumed that Senator Cameron had a personal interest in silver, and denounced his corruption as hotly as though he had been convicted of taking a bribe.

More than silver and gold, the moral standard interested Adams. His own interests were with gold, but he supported silver; the *Evening Post's* and Godkin's interests were with gold, and they frankly said so, yet they avowedly pursued their interests even into politics; Cameron's interests had always been with the corporations, yet he supported silver. Thus morality required that Adams should be condemned for going against his interests; that Godkin was virtuous in following his interests; and that Cameron was a scoundrel whatever he did.

Granting that one of the three was a moral idiot, which was it: — Adams or Godkin or Cameron? Until a Council or a Pope or a Congress or the newspapers or a popular election has decided a question of doubtful morality, individuals are apt to err, especially when putting money into their own pockets; but in democracies, the majority alone gives law. To anyone who knew the relative popularity of Cameron and Godkin, the idea of a popular vote between them seemed excessively humorous; yet the popular vote did in the end decide against Cameron, for Godkin.[15]

The Boston moralist and reformer went on, as always, like Dr. Johnson,[16] impatiently stamping his foot and following his interests, or his antipathies; but the true American, slow to grasp new and complicated ideas, groped in the dark to discover where his greater interest lay. As usual, the banks taught him. In the course of fifty years the banks taught one many wise lessons for which an insect had to be grateful whether it liked them or not; but of all the lessons Adams learned from them, none compared in dramatic effect with that of July 22, 1893, when, after talking silver all the morning with Senator Cameron on the top of their travelling-carriage crossing the Furka Pass, they reached Lucerne in the afternoon, where Adams found letters from his brothers requesting his immediate return to Boston because the community was bankrupt and he was probably a beggar.[17]

If he wanted education, he knew no quicker mode of learning a lesson than that of being struck on the head by it; and yet he was himself surprised at his own slowness to understand what had struck him. For several years a sufferer from insomnia, his first thought was of beggary of nerves, and he made ready to face a sleepless night, but although his mind tried to wrestle with the problem how any man could be ruined who had, months before, paid off every dollar of debt he knew himself to owe, he gave up that insoluble riddle in order to fall back on the larger principle that beggary could be no more for him than it was for others who were more valuable members of society, and, with that, he went to sleep like a good citizen, and the next day started for Quincy where he arrived August 7.

As a starting-point for a new education at fifty-five years old, the shock of finding oneself suspended, for several months, over the edge of bankruptcy, without knowing how one got there, or how to get away, is to be strongly recommended. By slow degrees the situation dawned on him that the banks had lent him, among others, some money—thousands or millions were—as bankruptcy—the same—for which he, among others, was responsible and of which he knew no more than they. The humor of this situation seemed to him so much more pointed than the terror, as to make him laugh at himself with a sincerity he had been long strange to. As far as he could comprehend, he had nothing to lose that he cared about, but the banks stood to lose their existence. Money mattered as little to him as to anybody, but money was their life. For the first time he had the banks in his power; he could afford to laugh; and the whole community was in the same position, though few laughed. All sat down on the banks and asked what the banks were going to do about it. To Adams the situation seemed farcical, but the more he saw of it, the less he understood it. He was quite sure that nobody understood it much better. Blindly some very powerful energy was at work, doing something that nobody wanted done. When Adams went to his bank to draw a hundred dollars of his own money on deposit, the cashier refused to let him have more than fifty, and Adams accepted the fifty without complaint because he was himself refusing to let the banks have some hundreds or thousands that belonged to them. Each wanted to help the other, yet both refused to pay their debts, and he could find no answer to the question which was responsible for getting the other into the situation, since lenders and borrowers were the same interest and socially the same person. Evidently the force was one; its operation was mechanical; its effect must be proportional to its power; but no one knew what it meant, and most people dismissed it as an emotion — a panic — that meant nothing.

Men died like flies under the strain, and Boston grew suddenly old, haggard, and thin. Adams alone waxed fat and was happy, for at last he had got hold of his world and could finish his education, interrupted for twenty years. He cared not whether it were worth finishing, if only it amused; but he seemed, for the first time since 1870, to feel that something new and curious was about to happen to the world. Great changes had taken place since 1870 in the forces at work; the old machine ran far behind its duty; somewhere — somehow — it was bound to break down, and if it happened to break precisely over one's head, it gave the better chance for study.

For the first time in several years he saw much of his brother Brooks in Quincy, and was surprised to find him absorbed in the same perplexities.[18] Brooks was then a man of forty-five years old; a strong writer and a vigorous thinker who irritated too many Boston conventions ever to suit the atmosphere; but the two brothers could talk to each other without atmosphere and were used to audiences of one. Brooks had discovered or developed a law of history that civilization followed the exchanges, and having worked it out for the Mediterranean was working it out for the Atlantic. Everything American, as well as most things European and Asiatic, became unstable by this law, seeking new equilibrium and compelled to find it. Loving paradox, Brooks, with the advantages of ten years' study, had swept away much rubbish in the effort to build up a new line of thought for himself, but he found that no paradox compared with that of daily events. The facts were constantly outrunning his thoughts. The instability was greater than he calculated; the speed of acceleration passed bounds. Among other general rules he laid down the paradox that, in the social disequilibrium between capital and labor, the logical outcome was not collectivism, but anarchism; and Henry made note of it for study.

By the time he got back to Washington on September 19, the storm having partly blown over, life had taken on a new face, and one so interesting that he set off to Chicago to study the Exposition again, and stayed there a fortnight absorbed in it. He found matter of study to fill a hundred years, and his education spread over chaos. Indeed, it seemed to him as though, this year, education went mad. The silver question, thorny as it was, fell into relations as simple as words of one syllable, compared with the problems of credit and exchange that came to complicate it; and when one sought rest at Chicago, educational game started like rabbits from every building, and ran out of sight among thousands of its kind before one could mark its burrow. The Exposition itself defied philosophy. One might find fault till the last gate closed, one could still explain nothing that needed explanation. As a scenic display, Paris had never approached it, but the inconceivable scenic display consisted in its being there at all — more surprising, as it was, than anything else on the continent, Niagara Falls, the Yellowstone Geysers, and the whole railway system thrown in, since these were all natural products in their place; while, since Noah's Ark, no such Babel of loose and ill-joined, such vague and ill-defined and unrelated thoughts and half-thoughts and experimental outcries as the Exposition, had ever ruffled the surface of the Lakes.

The first astonishment became greater every day. That the Exposition should be a natural growth and product of the North-west offered a step in evolution to startle Darwin; but that it should be anything else seemed an idea more startling still; and even granting it were not — admitting it to be a sort of industrial, speculative growth and product of the Beaux Arts [19] artistically induced to pass the summer on the shore of Lake Michigan — could it be made to seem at home there? Was the American made to seem at home in it? Honestly, he had the air of enjoying it as though it were all his own; he felt it was good; he was proud of it; for the most part, he acted as though he had passed his life in landscape gardening and architectural decoration. If he had not done it himself, he had known how to get it done to suit him, as he knew how to get his wives and daughters dressed at Worth's or Paquin's.[20] Perhaps he could not do it again; the next time he would want to do it himself and would show his own faults; but for the moment he seemed to have leaped directly from Corinth and Syracuse and Venice, over the heads of London and New York, to impose classical standards on plastic Chicago. Critics had no trouble in criticising the classicism, but all trading cities had always shown traders' taste, and, to the stern purist of religious faith, no art was thinner than Venetian Gothic. All traders' taste smelt of bric-a-brac; Chicago tried at least to give her taste a look of unity.

One sat down to ponder on the steps beneath Richard Hunt's dome[21] almost as deeply as on the steps of Ara Cœli, and much to the same purpose. Here was a breach of continuity — a rupture in historical sequence! Was it real, or only apparent? One's personal universe hung on the answer, for, if the rupture was real and the new American world could take this sharp and conscious twist towards ideals, one's personal friends would come in, at last, as winners in the great American chariot-race for fame. If the people of the Northwest actually knew what was good when they saw it, they would some day talk about Hunt and Richardson, La Farge and St. Gaudens, Burnham[22] and McKim, and Stanford White when their politicians and millionaires were otherwise forgotten. The artists and architects who had done the work offered little encouragement to hope it; they talked freely enough, but not in terms that one cared to quote; and to them the Northwest refused to look artistic. They talked as though they worked only for themselves; as though art, to the Western people, was a stage decoration; a diamond shirt-stud; a paper collar; but possibly the architects of Pæstum and Girgenti[23] had talked in the same way, and the Greek had said the same thing of Semitic Carthage[24] two thousand years ago.

Jostled by these hopes and doubts, one turned to the exhibits for help, and found it. The industrial schools tried to teach so much and so quickly that the instruction ran to waste. Some millions of other people felt the same helplessness, but few of them were seeking education, and to them helplessness seemed natural and normal, for they had grown up in the habit of thinking a steam-engine or a dynamo as natural as the sun, and expected to understand one as little as the other. For the historian alone the Exposition made a serious effort. Historical exhibits were common, but they never went far enough; none were thoroughly worked out. One of the best was that of the Cunard steamers, but still a student hungry for results found himself obliged to waste a pencil and several sheets of paper trying to calculate exactly when, according to the given increase of power, tonnage, and speed, the growth of the ocean steamer would reach its limits. His figures brought him, he thought, to the year 1927; another generation to spare before force, space, and time should meet. The ocean steamer ran the surest line of triangulation[25] into the future, because it was the nearest of man's products to a unity; railroads taught less because they seemed already finished except for mere increase in number; explosives taught most, but needed a tribe of chemists, physicists, and mathematicians to explain; the dynamo taught least because it had barely reached infancy, and, if its progress was to be constant at the rate of the last ten years, it would result in infinite costless energy within a generation. One lingered long among the dynamos, for they were new, and they gave to history a new phase. Men of science could never understand the ignorance and naïveté of the historian, who, when he came suddenly on a new power, asked naturally what it was; did it pull or did it push? Was it a screw or thrust? Did it flow or vibrate? Was it a wire or a mathematical line? And a score of such questions to which he expected answers and was astonished to get none.

Education ran riot at Chicago, at least for retarded minds which had never faced in concrete form so many matters of which they were ignorant. Men who knew nothing whatever — who had never run a steam-engine, the simplest of forces — who had never put their hands on a lever — had never touched an electric battery — never talked through a telephone, and had not the shadow of a notion what amount of force was meant by a *watt* or an *ampère* or an *erg*,[26] or any other term of measurement introduced within a hundred years — had no choice but to sit down on the steps and brood as they had never brooded on the benches of Harvard College, either as student or professor, aghast at what they had said and done in all these years, and still more ashamed of the childlike ignorance and babbling futility of the society that let them say and do it. The historical mind can think only in historical processes, and probably this was the first time since historians existed, that any of them had sat down helpless before a mechanical sequence. Before a metaphysical or a theological or a political sequence, most historians had felt helpless, but the single clue to which they had hitherto trusted was the unity of natural force.

Did he himself quite know what he meant? Certainly not! If he had known enough to state his problem, his education would have been complete at once. Chicago asked in 1893 for the first time the question whether the American people knew where they were driving. Adams answered, for one, that he did not know, but would try to find out. On reflecting sufficiently deeply, under the shadow of Richard Hunt's architecture, he decided that the American people probably knew no more than he did; but that they might still be driving or drifting unconsciously to some point in thought, as their solar system was said to be drifting towards some point in space; and that, possibly, if relations enough could be observed, this point might be fixed. Chicago was the first expression of American thought as a unity; one must start there.

Washington was the second. When he got back there, he fell headlong into the extra session of Congress called to repeal the Silver Act. The silver minority made an obstinate attempt to prevent it, and most of the majority had little heart in the creation of a single gold standard. The banks alone, and the dealers in exchange, insisted upon it; the political parties divided according to capitalistic geographical lines, Senator Cameron offering almost the only exception; but they mixed with unusual good-temper, and made liberal allowance for each others' actions and motives. The struggle was rather less irritable than such struggles generally were, and it ended like a comedy. On the evening of the final vote, Senator Cameron came back from the Capitol with Senator Brice, Senator Jones, Senator Lodge, and Moreton Frewen,[27] all in the gayest of humors as though they were rid of a heavy responsibility. Adams, too, in a bystander's spirit, felt light in mind.[28] He had stood up for his eighteenth century, his Constitution of 1789, his George Washington, his Harvard College, his Quincy, and his Plymouth Pilgrims, as long as anyone would stand up with him. He had said it was hopeless twenty years before, but he had kept on, in the same old attitude, by habit and taste, until he found himself altogether alone. He had hugged his antiquated dislike of bankers and capitalistic society until he had become little better than a crank. He had known for years that he must accept the régime, but he had known a great many other disagreeable certainties — like age, senility, and death — against which one made what little resistance one could. The matter was settled at last by the people. For a hundred years, between 1793 and 1893, the American people had hesitated, vacillated, swayed forward and back, between two forces, one simply industrial, the other capitalistic, centralizing, and mechanical. In 1893, the issue came on the single gold standard, and the majority at last declared itself, once for all, in favor of the capitalistic system with all its necessary machinery. All one's friends, all one's best citizens, reformers, churches, colleges, educated classes, had joined the banks to force submission to capitalism; a submission long foreseen by the mere law of mass. Of all forms of society or government, this was the one he liked least, but his likes or dislikes were as antiquated as the rebel doctrine of State rights. A capitalistic system had been adopted, and if it were to be run at all, it must be run by capital and by capitalistic methods; for nothing could surpass the nonsensity of trying to run so complex and so concentrated a machine by Southern and Western farmers in grotesque alliance with city day-laborers, as had been tried in 1800 and 1828, and had failed even under simple conditions.[29]

There, education in domestic politics stopped. The rest was question of gear; of running machinery; of economy; and involved no disputed principle. Once admitted that the machine must be efficient, society might dispute in what social interest it should be run, but in any case it must work concentration. Such great revolutions commonly leave some bitterness behind, but nothing in politics ever surprised Henry Adams more than the ease with which he and his silver friends slipped across the chasm, and alighted on the single gold standard and the capitalistic system with its methods; the protective tariff; the corporations and trusts; the trades-unions and socialistic paternalism which necessarily made their complement; the whole mechanical consolidation of force, which ruthlessly stamped out the life of the class into which Adams was born, but created monopolies capable of controlling the new energies that America adored.

Society rested, after sweeping into the ash-heap these cinders of a misdirected education. After this vigorous impulse, nothing remained for a historian but to ask — how long and how far!

CHAPTER XXIII

Silence (1894–1898)

THE convulsion of 1893 left its victims in dead-water, and closed much education. While the country braced itself up to an effort such as no one had thought within its powers, the individual crawled as he best could, through the wreck, and found many values of life upset. But for connecting the nineteenth and twentieth centuries, the four years, 1893 to 1897, had no value in the drama of education, and might be left out. Much that had made life pleasant between 1870 and 1890 perished in the ruin, and among the earliest wreckage had been the fortunes of Clarence King.[1] The lesson taught whatever the bystander chose to read in it; but to Adams it seemed singularly full of moral, if he could but understand it. In 1871 he had thought King's education ideal, and his personal fitness unrivalled. No other young American approached him for the combination of chances — physical energy, social standing, mental scope and training, wit, geniality, and science, that seemed superlatively American and irresistibly strong. His nearest rival was Alexander Agassiz, and, as far as their friends knew, no one else could be classed with them in the running. The result of twenty years' effort proved that the theory of scientific education failed where most theory fails — for want of money. Even Henry Adams, who kept himself, as he thought, quite outside of every possible financial risk, had been caught in the cogs, and held for months over the gulf of bankruptcy, saved only by the chance that the whole class of millionaires were more or less bankrupt too, and the banks were forced to let the mice escape with the rats;[2] but, in sum, education without capital could always be taken by the throat and forced to disgorge its gains, nor was it helped by the knowledge that no one intended it, but that all alike suffered.

Whether voluntary or mechanical the result for education was the same. The failure of the scientific scheme, without money to back it, was flagrant.

The scientific scheme in theory was alone sound, for science should be equivalent to money; in practice science was helpless without money. The weak holder was, in his own language, sure to be frozen out. Education must fit the complex conditions of a new society, always accelerating its movement, and its fitness could be known only from success. One looked about for examples of success among the educated of one's time — the men born in the thirties, and trained to professions. Within one's immediate acquaintance, three were typical: John Hay, Whitelaw Reid, and William C. Whitney; all of whom owed their free hand to marriage, education serving only for ornament, but among whom, in 1893, William C. Whitney was far and away the most popular type.[3]

Newspapers might prate about wealth till commonplace print was exhausted, but as matter of habit, few Americans envied the very rich for anything the most of them got out of money. New York might occasionally fear them, but more often laughed or sneered at them, and never showed them respect. Scarcely one of the very rich men held any position in society by virtue of his wealth, or could have been elected to an office, or even into a good club. Setting aside the few, like Pierpont Morgan, whose social position had little to do with greater or less wealth, riches were in New York no object of envy on account of the joys they brought in their train, and Whitney was not even one of the very rich; yet in his case the envy was palpable. There was reason for it. Already in 1893 Whitney had finished with politics after having gratified every ambition, and swung the country almost at his will; he had thrown away the usual objects of political ambition like the ashes of smoked cigarettes; had turned to other amusements, satiated every taste, gorged every appetite, won every object that New York afforded, and, not yet satisfied, had carried his field of activity abroad, until New York no longer knew what most to envy, his horses or his houses. He had succeeded precisely where Clarence King had failed.

Barely forty years had passed since all these men started in a bunch to race for power, and the results were fixed beyond reversal; but one knew no better in 1894 than in 1854 what an American education ought to be in order to count as success. Even granting that it counted as money, its value could not be called general. America contained scores of men worth five millions or upwards, whose lives were no more worth living than those of their cooks, and to whom the task of making money equivalent to education offered more difficulties than to Adams the task of making education equivalent to money. Social position seemed to have value still, while education counted for nothing. A mathematician, linguist, chemist, electrician, engineer, if fortunate, might average a value of ten dollars a day in the open market. An administrator, organizer, manager, with mediæval qualities of energy and will, but no education beyond his special branch, would probably be worth at least ten times as much.

Society had failed to discover what sort of education suited it best. Wealth valued social position and classical education as highly as either of these valued wealth, and the women still tended to keep the scales even. For anything Adams could see he was himself as contented as though he had been educated; while Clarence King, whose education was exactly suited to theory, had failed; and Whitney, who was no better educated than Adams, had achieved phenomenal success.

Had Adams in 1894 been starting in life as he did in 1854, he must have repeated that all he asked of education was the facile use of the four old tools: Mathematics, French, German, and Spanish. With these he could still make his way to any object within his vision, and would have a decisive advantage over nine rivals in ten. Statesman or lawyer, chemist or electrician, priest or professor, native or foreign, he would fear none.

King's breakdown, physical as well as financial, brought the

indirect gain to Adams that, on recovering strength, King induced him to go to Cuba, where, in January, 1894, they drifted
into the little town of Santiago. The picturesque Cuban society,
which King knew well, was more amusing than any other that
one had yet discovered in the whole broad world, but made no
profession of teaching anything unless it were Cuban Spanish or
the *danza;* and neither on his own nor on King's account did the
visitor ask any loftier study than that of the buzzards floating on
the trade-wind down the valley to Dos Bocas, or the colors of sea
and shore at sunrise from the height of the Gran Piedra; but, as
though they were still twenty years old and revolution were as
young as they, the decaying fabric, which had never been solid, fell
on their heads and drew them with it into an ocean of mischief.[4]
In the half-century between 1850 and 1900, empires were always
falling on one's head, and, of all lessons, these constant political
convulsions taught least. Since the time of Rameses,[5] revolutions
have raised more doubts than they solved, but they have sometimes the merit of changing one's point of view, and the Cuban
rebellion served to sever the last tie that attached Adams to a
Democratic administration. He thought that President Cleveland could have settled the Cuban question, without war, had he
chosen to do his duty, and this feeling, generally held by the Democratic Party, joined with the stress of economical needs and the
gold standard to break into bits the old organization and to leave
no choice between parties. The new American, whether consciously or not, had turned his back on the nineteenth century
before he was done with it; the gold standard, the protective system, and the laws of mass could have no other outcome, and, as
so often before, the movement, once accelerated by attempting
to impede it, had the additional, brutal consequence of crushing
equally the good and the bad that stood in its way.

The lesson was old — so old that it became tedious. One had
studied nothing else since childhood, and wearied of it. For yet
another year Adams lingered on these outskirts of the vortex,

among the picturesque, primitive types of a world which had never been fairly involved in the general motion, and were the more amusing for their torpor. After passing the winter with King in the West Indies, he passed the summer with Hay in the Yellowstone, and found there little to study. The Geysers were an old story; the Snake River posed no vital statistics except in its fordings; even the Tetons were as calm as they were lovely; while the wapiti and bear, innocent of strikes and corners, laid no traps. In return the party treated them with affection. Never did a band less bloody or bloodthirsty wander over the roof of the continent. Hay loved as little as Adams did, the labor of skinning and butchering big game; he had even outgrown the sedate, middle-aged, meditative joy of duck-shooting, and found the trout of the Yellowstone too easy a prey. Hallett Phillips[6] himself, who managed the party, loved to play Indian hunter without hunting so much as a field-mouse; Iddings[7] the geologist was reduced to shooting only for the table, and the guileless prattle of Billy Hofer alone taught the simple life. Compared with the Rockies of 1871, the sense of wildness had vanished; one saw no possible adventures except to break one's neck as in chasing an aniseed fox. Only the more intelligent ponies scented an occasional friendly and sociable bear.

When the party came out of the Yellowstone, Adams went on alone to Seattle and Vancouver to inspect the last American railway systems yet untried. They, too, offered little new learning, and no sooner had he finished this debauch of Northwestern geography than with desperate thirst for exhausting the American field, he set out for Mexico and the Gulf, making a sweep of the Caribbean and cleaning up, in these six or eight months, at least twenty thousand miles of American land and water.

He was beginning to think, when he got back to Washington in April, 1895, that he knew enough about the edges of life — tropical islands, mountain solitudes, archaic law, and retrograde types. Infinitely more amusing and incomparably more picturesque than civilization, they educated only artists, and, as one's sixtieth year approached, the artist began to die; only a certain intense cerebral restlessness survived which no longer responded to sensual stimulants; one was driven from beauty to beauty as though art were a trotting-match. For this, one was in some degree prepared, for the old man had been a stage-type since drama began; but one felt some perplexity to account for failure on the opposite or mechanical side, where nothing but cerebral action was needed.

Taking for granted that the alternative to art was arithmetic, he plunged deep into statistics, fancying that education would find the surest bottom there; and the study proved the easiest he had ever approached. Even the Government volunteered unlimited statistics, endless columns of figures, bottomless averages merely for the asking. At the Statistical Bureau, Worthington Ford[8] supplied any material that curiosity could imagine for filling the vast gaps of ignorance, and methods for applying the plasters of fact. One seemed for awhile to be winning ground, and one's averages projected themselves as laws into the future. Perhaps the most perplexing part of the study lay in the attitude of the statisticians, who showed no enthusiastic confidence in their own figures. They should have reached certainty, but they talked like other men who knew less. The method did not result in faith. Indeed, every increase of mass — of volume and velocity — seemed to bring in new elements, and, at last, a scholar, fresh in arithmetic and ignorant of algebra, fell into a superstitious terror of complexity as the sink of facts. Nothing came out as it should. In principle, according to figures, anyone could set up or pull down a society. One could frame no sort of satisfactory answer to the constructive doctrines of Adam Smith, or to the destructive criticisms of Karl Marx or to the anarchistic imprecations of Elisée Reclus.[9] One revelled at will in the ruin of every society in the past, and rejoiced in proving the prospective overthrow of every society that seemed possible in the future; but meanwhile these societies which violated every law, moral, arithmetical, and economical, not only propagated each other, but produced also fresh complexities with every propagation and developed mass with every complexity.

The human factor was worse still. Since the stupefying discovery of *Pteraspis* in 1867, nothing had so confused the student as the conduct of mankind in the *fin-de-siècle*. No one seemed very much concerned about this world or the future, unless it might be the anarchists, and they only because they disliked the present. Adams disliked the present as much as they did, and his interest in future society was becoming slight, yet he was kept alive by irritation at finding his life so thin and fruitless. Meanwhile he watched mankind march on, like a train of pack-horses on the Snake River, tumbling from one morass into another, and at short intervals, for no reason but temper, falling to butchery, like Cain. Since 1850, massacres had become so common that society scarcely noticed them unless they summed up hundreds of thousands, as in Armenia;[10] wars had been almost continuous, and were beginning again in Cuba, threatening in South Africa, and possible in Manchuria;[11] yet impartial judges thought them all not merely unnecessary, but foolish — induced by greed of the coarsest class, as though the Pharaohs or the Romans were still robbing their neighbors. The robbery might be natural and inevitable, but the murder seemed altogether archaic.

At one moment of perplexity to account for this trait of *Pteraspis*, or shark, which seemed to have survived every moral improvement of society, he took to study of the religious press. Possibly growth in human nature might show itself there. He found no need to speak unkindly of it; but, as an agent of motion, he preferred on the whole the vigor of the shark, with its chances of betterment; and he very gravely doubted, from his aching consciousness of religious void, whether any large fraction of society cared for a future life, or even for the present one, thirty years hence.[12] Not an act, or an expression, or an image, showed depth of faith or hope.

The object of education, therefore, was changed. For many years it had lost itself in studying what the world had ceased to care for; if it were to begin again, it must try to find out what the mass of mankind did care for, and why. Religion, politics, statistics, travel had thus far led to nothing. Even the Chicago Fair had only confused the roads. Accidental education could go no further, for one's mind was already littered and stuffed beyond hope with the millions of chance images stored away without order in the memory. One might as well try to educate a gravel-pit. The task was futile, which disturbed a student less than the discovery that, in pursuing it, he was becoming himself ridiculous. Nothing is more tiresome than a superannuated pedagogue.

For the moment he was rescued, as often before, by a woman. Towards midsummer, 1895, Mrs. Cabot Lodge bade him follow her to Europe with the Senator and her two sons. The study of history is useful to the historian by teaching him his ignorance of women; and the mass of this ignorance crushes one who is familiar enough with what are called historical sources to realize how few women have ever been known. The woman who is known only through a man is known wrong, and excepting one or two like Mme. de Sévigné,[13] no woman has pictured herself. The American woman of the nineteenth century will live only as the man saw her; probably she will be less known than the woman of the eighteenth; none of the female descendants of Abigail Adams[14] can ever be nearly so familiar as her letters have made her; and all this is pure loss to history, for the American woman of the nineteenth century was much better company than the American man; she was probably much better company than her grandmothers. With Mrs. Lodge and her husband, Senator since 1893, Adams's relations had been those of elder brother or uncle since 1871 when Cabot Lodge had left his examination-papers on Assistant Professor Adams's desk, and crossed the street to Christ Church in Cambridge to get married. With Lodge himself, as scholar, fellow instructor, co-editor of the *North American Review*, and political reformer from 1873 to 1878, he had worked intimately, but with him afterwards as politician he had not much relation; and since

Lodge had suffered what Adams thought the misfortune of becoming not only a Senator but a Senator from Massachusetts — a singular social relation which Adams had known only as fatal to friends — a superstitious student, intimate with the laws of historical fatality, would rather have recognized him only as an enemy; but apart from this accident he valued Lodge highly, and in the waste places of average humanity had been greatly dependent on his house. Senators can never be approached with safety, but a Senator who has a very superior wife and several superior children who feel no deference for Senators as such, may be approached at times with relative impunity while they keep him under restraint.

Where Mrs. Lodge summoned, one followed with gratitude, and so it chanced that in August one found oneself for the first time at Caen, Coutances, and Mont-Saint-Michel in Normandy.[15] If history had a chapter with which he thought himself familiar, it was the twelfth and thirteenth centuries; yet so little has labor to do with knowledge that these bare playgrounds of the lecture system turned into green and verdurous virgin forests merely through the medium of younger eyes and fresher minds. His German bias must have given his youth a terrible twist, for the Lodges saw at a glance what he had thought unessential because un-German. They breathed native air in the Normandy of 1200, a compliment which would have seemed to the Senator lacking in taste or even in sense when addressed to one of a class of men who passed life in trying to persuade themselves and the public that they breathed nothing less American than a blizzard; but this atmosphere, in the touch of a real emotion, betrayed the unconscious humor of the senatorial mind. In the thirteenth century, by an unusual chance, even a Senator became natural, simple, interested, cultivated, artistic, liberal — genial.

Through the Lodge eyes the old problem became new and personal; it threw off all association with the German lecture-room. One could not at first see what this novelty meant; it had the air of mere antiquarian emotion like Wenlock Abbey and *Pteraspis;* but it expelled archaic law and antiquarianism once for all, without seeming conscious of it; and Adams drifted back to Washington with a new sense of history. Again he wandered south, and in April returned to Mexico with the Camerons to study the charms of *pulque*[16] and Churriguerresque[17] architecture. In May he ran through Europe again with Hay, as far south as Ravenna.[18] There came the end of the passage. After thus covering once more, in 1896, many thousand miles of the old trails, Adams went home in October, with everyone else, to elect McKinley President and to start the world anew.[19]

For the old world of public men and measures since 1870, Adams wept no tears. Within or without, during or after it, as partisan or historian, he never saw anything to admire in it, or anything he wanted to save; and in this respect he reflected only the public mind which balanced itself so exactly between the unpopularity of both parties as to express no sympathy with either. Even among the most powerful men of that generation he knew none who had a good word to say for it. No period so thoroughly ordinary had been known in American politics since Christopher Columbus first disturbed the balance of American society; but the natural result of such lack of interest in public affairs, in a small society like that of Washington, led an idle bystander to depend abjectly on intimacy of private relation. One dragged oneself down the long vista of Pennsylvania Avenue, by leaning heavily on one's friends, and avoiding to look at anything else. Thus life had grown narrow with years, more and more concentrated on the circle of houses round La Fayette Square, which had no direct or personal share in power except in the case of Mr. Blaine, whose tumultuous struggle for existence held him apart. Suddenly Mr. McKinley entered the White House and laid his hand heavily on this special group. In a moment the whole nest, so slowly constructed, was torn to pieces and scattered over the world. Adams found himself alone. John Hay took his orders for London. Rockhill[20] departed to Athens. Cecil Spring Rice had been buried in Persia. Cameron refused to remain in public life either at home or abroad, and broke up his house on the Square. Only the Lodges and Roosevelts remained, but even they were at once absorbed in the interests of power. Since 1861, no such social convulsion had occurred.

Even this was not quite the worst. To one whose interests lay chiefly in foreign affairs, and who, at this moment, felt most strongly the nightmare of Cuban, Hawaiian, and Nicaraguan chaos,[21] the man in the State Department seemed more important than the man in the White House. Adams knew no one in the United States fit to manage these matters in the face of a hostile Europe,[22] and had no candidate to propose; but he was shocked beyond all restraints of expression to learn that the President meant to put Senator John Sherman in the State Department in order to make a place for Mr. Hanna in the Senate.[23] Grant himself had done nothing that seemed so bad as this to one who had lived long enough to distinguish between the ways of presidential jobbery, if not between the jobs. John Sherman, otherwise admirably fitted for the place, a friendly influence for nearly forty years, was notoriously feeble and quite senile, so that the intrigue seemed to Adams the betrayal of an old friend as well as of the State Department. One might have shrugged one's shoulders had the President named Mr. Hanna his Secretary of State, but Mr. Hanna was a man of force if not of experience, and selections much worse than this had often turned out well enough; but John Sherman must inevitably and tragically break down.

The prospect for once was not less vile than the men. One can bear coldly the jobbery of enemies, but not that of friends, and to Adams this kind of jobbery seemed always infinitely worse than all the petty money bribes ever exploited by the newspapers. Nor was the matter improved by hints that the President might call John Hay to the Department whenever John Sherman should retire. Indeed, had Hay been even unconsciously party to such an

intrigue,[24] he would have put an end, once for all, to further concern in public affairs on his friend's part; but even without this
last disaster, one felt that Washington had become no longer
habitable. Nothing was left there but solitary contemplation of
Mr. McKinley's ways which were not likely to be more amusing
than the ways of his predecessors; or of senatorial ways, which
offered no novelty of what the French language expressively calls
embêtement;[25] or of poor Mr. Sherman's ways which would surely
cause anguish to his friends. Once more, one must go!

Nothing was easier! On and off, one had done the same thing
since the year 1858, at frequent intervals, and had now reached
the month of March, 1897; yet, as the whole result of six years'
dogged effort to begin a new education, one could not recommend
it to the young. The outlook lacked hope. The object of travel had
become more and more dim, ever since the gibbering ghost of the
Civil Law had been locked in its dark closet, as far back as 1860.
Noah's dove[26] had not searched the earth for resting-places so carefully, or with so little success. Any spot on land or water satisfies a dove who wants and finds rest; but no perch suits a dove
of sixty years old, alone and uneducated, who has lost his taste
even for olives. To this, also, the young may be driven, as education, and the lesson fails in humor; but it may be worth knowing to
some of them that the planet offers hardly a dozen places where an
elderly man can pass a week alone without ennui, and none at all
where he can pass a year.

Irritated by such complaints, the world naturally answers that
no man of sixty should live, which is doubtless true, though not
original. The man of sixty, with a certain irritability proper to his
years, retorts that the world has no business to throw on him the
task of removing its carrion, and that while he remains he has a
right to require amusement — or at least education, since this costs
nothing to anyone—and that a world which cannot educate, will
not amuse, and is ugly besides, has even less right to exist than
he. Both views seem sound; but the world wearily objects to be

called by epithets what society always admits in practice; for no one likes to be told that he is a bore, or ignorant, or even ugly; and having nothing to say in its defence, it rejoins that, whatever license is pardonable in youth, the man of sixty who wishes consideration had better hold his tongue. This truth also has the defect of being too true. The rule holds equally for men of half that age. Only the very young have the right to betray their ignorance or ill-breeding. Elderly people commonly know enough not to betray themselves.

Exceptions are plenty on both sides, as the Senate knew to its acute suffering; but young or old, women or men, seemed agreed on one point with singular unanimity; each praised silence in others. Of all characteristics in human nature, this has been one of the most abiding. Mere superficial gleaning of what, in the long history of human expression, has been said by the fool or unsaid by the wise, shows that, for once, no difference of opinion has ever existed on this. "Even a fool," said the wisest of men,[27] "when he holdeth his peace, is counted wise," and still more often, the wisest of men, when he spoke the highest wisdom, has been counted a fool.[28] They agreed only on the merits of silence in others. Sophocles[29] made remarks in its favor, which should have struck the Athenians as new to them; but of late the repetition had grown tiresome. Thomas Carlyle vociferated his admiration of it.[30] Matthew Arnold[31] thought it the best form of expression; and Adams thought Matthew Arnold the best form of expression in his time. Algernon Swinburne called it the most noble to the end.[32] Alfred de Vigny's dying wolf remarked: —

> "A voir ce que l'on fut sur terre et ce qu'on laisse,
>   Seul le silence est grand; tout le reste est faiblesse." [33]

> "When one thinks what one leaves in the world when one dies,
>   Only silence is strong, — all the rest is but lies."

Even Byron, whom a more brilliant era of genius seemed to have

decided to be but an indifferent poet, had ventured to affirm
that —

> "The Alp's snow summit nearer heaven is seen
> Than the volcano's fierce eruptive crest;"

with other verses, to the effect that words are but a "temporary
torturing flame";[34] of which no one knew more than himself. The
evidence of the poets could not be more emphatic: —

> "Silent, while years engrave the brow!
> Silent, — the best are silent now!" [35]

Although none of these great geniuses had shown faith in silence
as a cure for their own ills or ignorance, all of them, and all philosophy after them, affirmed that no man, even at sixty, had ever
been known to attain knowledge; but that a very few were believed
to have attained ignorance, which was in result the same. More
than this, in every society worth the name, the man of sixty had
been encouraged to ride this hobby — the Pursuit of Ignorance
in Silence — as though it were the easiest way to get rid of him.
In America the silence was more oppressive than the ignorance;
but perhaps elsewhere the world might still hide some haunt of
futilitarian silence where content reigned — although long search
had not revealed it — and so the pilgrimage began anew!

The first step led to London where John Hay was to be established. One had seen so many American Ministers received in
London that the Lord Chamberlain himself scarcely knew more
about it; education could not be expected there; but there Adams
arrived, April 21, 1897, as though thirty-six years were so many
days, for Queen Victoria still reigned and one saw little change in
St. James's Street. True, Carlton House Terrace,[36] like the streets
of Rome, actually squeaked and gibbered with ghosts, till one felt
like Odysseus before the press of shadows, daunted by a "bloodless
fear";[37] but in spring London is pleasant, and it was more cheery
than ever in May, 1897, when everyone was welcoming the return

of life after the long winter since 1893. One's fortunes, or one's friends' fortunes, were again in flood.

This amusement could not be prolonged, for one found oneself the oldest Englishman in England, much too familiar with family jars better forgotten, and old traditions better unknown. No wrinkled Tannhäuser,[38] returning to the Wartburg, needed a wrinkled Venus to show him that he was no longer at home, and that even penitence was a sort of impertinence. He slipped away to Paris, and set up a household at St. Germain where he taught and learned French history for nieces who swarmed under the venerable cedars of the Pavillon d'Angoulême, and rode about the green forest-alleys of St. Germain and Marly.[39] From time to time Hay wrote humorous laments, but nothing occurred to break the summer-peace of the stranded Tannhäuser, who slowly began to feel at home in France as in other countries he had thought more homelike. At length, like other dead Americans, he went to Paris[40] because he could go nowhere else, and lingered there till the Hays came by, in January, 1898; and Mrs. Hay, who had been a staunch and strong ally for twenty years, bade him go with them to Egypt.

Adams cared little to see Egypt again, but he was glad to see Hay, and readily drifted after him to the Nile. What they saw and what they said had as little to do with education as possible, until one evening, as they were looking at the sun set across the Nile from Assouan, Spencer Eddy[41] brought them a telegram to announce the sinking of the Maine[42] in Havana Harbor. This was the greatest stride in education since 1865, but what did it teach? One leant on a fragment of column in the great hall at Karnak[43] and watched a jackal creep down the débris of ruin. The jackal's ancestors had surely crept up the same wall when it was building. What was his view about the value of silence? One lay in the sands and watched the expression of the Sphinx.[44] Brooks Adams had taught him that the relation between civilizations was that of trade. Henry wandered, or was storm-driven, down the coast. He tried to trace out the ancient harbor of Ephesus.[45] He went over to Athens, picked up Rockhill, and searched for the harbor of Tiryns;[46] together they went on to Constantinople and studied the great walls of Constantine and the greater domes of Justinian.[47] His hobby had turned into a camel, and he hoped, if he rode long enough in silence, that at last he might come on a city of thought along the great highways of exchange.

CHAPTER XXIV

Indian Summer (1898–1899)

THE summer of the Spanish War[1] began the Indian summer of life to one who had reached sixty years of age, and cared only to reap in peace such harvest as these sixty years had yielded. He had reason to be more than content with it. Since 1864 he had felt no such sense of power and momentum, and had seen no such number of personal friends wielding it. The sense of solidarity counts for much in one's contentment, but the sense of winning one's game[2] counts for more; and in London, in 1898, the scene was singularly interesting to the last survivor of the Legation of 1861. He thought himself perhaps the only person living who could get full enjoyment of the drama. He carried every scene of it, in a century and a half since the Stamp Act,[3] quite alive in his mind — all the interminable disputes of his disputatious ancestors as far back as the year 1750[4] — as well as his own insignificance in the Civil War, every step in which had the object of bringing England into an American system.[5] For this they had written libraries of argument and remonstrance, and had piled war on war, losing their tempers for life, and souring the gentle and patient Puritan nature of their descendants, until even their private secretaries at times used language almost intemperate; and suddenly, by pure chance, the blessing fell on Hay. After two hundred years of stupid and greedy blundering, which no argument and no violence affected, the people of England learned their lesson just at the moment when Hay would otherwise have faced a flood of the old anxieties. Hay himself scarcely knew how grateful he should be, for to him the change came almost of course. He saw only the necessary stages that had led to it, and to him they seemed natural; but to Adams, still living in the atmosphere of Palmerston and John Russell, the sudden appearance of Germany as the grizzly terror[6] which in twenty years effected what Adamses had tried for two hundred in vain — frightened England into America's arms — seemed as melodramatic as any plot of Napoleon the Great. He could feel only the sense of satisfaction at seeing the diplomatic triumph of all his family, since the breed existed, at last realized under his own eyes for the advantage of his oldest and closest ally.

This was history, not education, yet it taught something exceedingly serious, if not ultimate, could one trust the lesson. For the first time in his life, he felt a sense of possible purpose working itself out in history. Probably no one else on this earthly planet — not even Hay — could have come out on precisely such extreme personal satisfaction, but as he sat at Hay's table, listening to any member of the British Cabinet, for all were alike now, discuss the Philippines as a question of balance of power in the East, he could see that the family work of a hundred and fifty years fell at once into the grand perspective of true empire-building, which Hay's work set off with artistic skill. The roughness of the archaic foundations looked stronger and larger in scale for the refinement and certainty of the arcade. In the long list of famous American Ministers in London, none could have given the work quite the completeness, the harmony, the perfect ease of Hay.

Never before had Adams been able to discern the working of law in history, which was the reason of his failure in teaching it, for chaos cannot be taught; but he thought he had a personal property by inheritance in this proof of sequence and intelligence in the affairs of man — a property which no one else had right to dispute; and this personal triumph left him a little cold towards the other diplomatic results of the war. He knew that Porto Rico must be taken, but he would have been glad to escape the Philippines.[7] Apart from too intimate an acquaintance with the value of islands in the South Seas, he knew the West Indies well enough to be assured that, whatever the American people might think or say about it, they would sooner or later have to police those islands, not against Europe, but for Europe, and America too. Education on the outskirts of civilized life teaches not very much, but it taught this; and one felt no call to shoulder the load of archipelagoes in the antipodes when one was trying painfully to pluck up courage to face the labor of shouldering archipelagoes at home. The country decided otherwise, and one acquiesced readily enough, since the matter concerned only the public willingness to carry loads; in London, the balance of power in the East [8] came alone into discussion; and in every point of view one had as much reason to be gratified with the result as though one had shared in the danger, instead of being vigorously employed in looking on from a great distance. After all, friends had done the work, if not oneself, and he too serves a certain purpose who only stands and cheers.

In June, at the crisis of interest, the Camerons came over, and took the fine old house of Surrenden Dering in Kent which they made a sort of country house to the Embassy. Kent has charms rivalling those of Shropshire, and, even compared with the many beautiful places scattered along the Welsh border, few are nobler or more genial than Surrenden with its unbroken descent from the Saxons, its avenues, its terraces, its deer-park, its large repose on the Kentish hillside, and its broad outlook over what was once the forest of Anderida. Filled with a constant stream of guests, the house seemed to wait for the chance to show its charms to the American, with whose activity the whole world was resounding; and never since the battle of Hastings [9] could the little telegraph office of the Kentish village have done such work. There, on a hot July 4, 1898, to an expectant group under the shady trees, came the telegram announcing the destruction of the Spanish Armada, as it might have come to Queen Elizabeth in 1588; and there, later in the season, came the order summoning Hay to the State Department.

Hay had no wish to be Secretary of State. He much preferred to remain Ambassador, and his friends were quite as cold about it as he. No one knew so well what sort of strain falls on Secretaries

364

of State, or how little strength he had in reserve against it. Even at Surrenden he showed none too much endurance, and he would gladly have found a valid excuse for refusing. The discussion on both sides was earnest, but the decided voice of the conclave was that, though if he were a mere office-seeker he might certainly decline promotion, if he were a member of the Government he could not. No serious statesman could accept a favor[10] and refuse a service. Doubtless he might refuse, but in that case he must resign. The amusement of making Presidents has keen fascination for idle American hands, but these black arts have the old drawback of all deviltry; one must serve the spirit one evokes, even though the service were perdition to body and soul. For him, no doubt, the service, though hard, might bring some share of profit, but for the friends who gave this unselfish decision, all would prove loss. For one, Adams on that subject had become a little daft. No one in his experience had ever passed unscathed through that malarious marsh. In his fancy, office was poison; it killed — body and soul — physically and socially. Office was more poisonous than priestcraft or pedagogy in proportion as it held more power; but the poison he complained of was not ambition; he shared none of Cardinal Wolsey's[11] belated penitence for that healthy stimulant, as he had shared none of the fruits; his poison was that of the will — the distortion of sight — the warping of mind — the degradation of tissue — the coarsening of taste — the narrowing of sympathy to the emotions of a caged rat. Hay needed no office in order to wield influence. For him, influence lay about the streets, waiting for him to stoop to it; he enjoyed more than enough power without office; no one of his position, wealth, and political experience, living at the centre of politics in contact with the active party managers, could escape influence. His only ambition was to escape annoyance, and no one knew better than he that, at sixty years of age, sensitive to physical strain, still more sensitive to brutality, vindictiveness, or betrayal, he took office at cost of life.[12]

Neither he nor any of the Surrenden circle made pretence of gladness at the new dignity for, with all his gaiety of manner and lightness of wit, he took dark views of himself, none the lighter for their humor, and his obedience to the President's order was the gloomiest acquiescence he had ever smiled. Adams took dark views, too, not so much on Hay's account as on his own, for, while Hay had at least the honors of office, his friends would share only the ennuis of it; but, as usual with Hay, nothing was gained by taking such matters solemnly, and old habits of the Civil War[13] left their mark of military drill on everyone who lived through it. He shouldered his pack and started for home. Adams had no mind to lose his friend without a struggle, though he had never known such sort of struggle to avail. The chance was desperate, but he could not afford to throw it away; so, as soon as the Surrenden establishment broke up, on October 17, he prepared for return home, and on November 13, none too gladly, found himself again gazing into La Fayette Square.

He had made another false start and lost two years more of education; nor had he excuse; for, this time, neither politics nor society drew him away from his trail. He had nothing to do with Hay's politics at home or abroad,[14] and never affected agreement with his views or his methods, nor did Hay care whether his friends agreed or disagreed. They all united in trying to help each other to get along the best way they could, and all they tried to save was the personal relation. Even there, Adams would have been beaten had he not been helped by Mrs. Hay, who saw the necessity of distraction, and led her husband into the habit of stopping every afternoon to take his friend off for an hour's walk, followed by a cup of tea with Mrs. Hay afterwards, and a chat with anyone who called.

For the moment, therefore, the situation was saved, at least in outward appearance, and Adams could go back to his own pursuits which were slowly taking a direction. Perhaps they had no right to be called pursuits, for in truth one consciously pursued nothing, but drifted as attraction offered itself. The short session broke up the Washington circle, so that, on March 22, Adams was able to sail with the Lodges for Europe and to pass April in Sicily and Rome.

With the Lodges, education always began afresh. Forty years had left little of the Palermo that Garibaldi had shown to the boy of 1860, but Sicily in all ages seems to have taught only catastrophe and violence, running riot on that theme ever since Ulysses began its study on the eye of Cyclops.[15] For a lesson in anarchy, without a shade of sequence, Sicily stands alone and defies evolution. Syracuse[16] teaches more than Rome. Yet even Rome was not mute, and the church of Ara Cœli seemed more and more to draw all the threads of thought to a centre, for every new journey led back to its steps — Karnak, Ephesus, Delphi, Mycenæ, Constantinople, Syracuse — all lying on the road to the Capitol.[17] What they had to bring by way of intellectual riches could not yet be discerned, but they carried camel-loads of moral; and New York sent most of all, for, in forty years, America had made so vast a stride to empire that the world of 1860 stood already on a distant horizon somewhere on the same plane with the republic of Brutus[18] and Cato,[19] while schoolboys read of Abraham Lincoln as they did of Julius Cæsar. Vast swarms of Americans knew the Civil War only by school history, as they knew the story of Cromwell or Cicero,[20] and were as familiar with political assassination as though they had lived under Nero.[21] The climax of empire could be seen approaching, year after year, as though Sulla[22] were a President or McKinley a Consul.

Nothing annoyed Americans more than to be told this simple and obvious — in no way unpleasant — truth; therefore one sat silent as ever on the Capitol; but, by way of completing the lesson, the Lodges added a pilgrimage to Assisi and an interview with St. Francis,[23] whose solution of historical riddles seemed the most satisfactory — or sufficient — ever offered; worth fully forty years' more study, and better worth it than Gibbon himself, or even

St. Augustine, St. Ambrose, or St. Jerome.[24] The most bewildering effect of all these fresh cross-lights on the old Assistant Professor of 1874 was due to the astonishing contrast between what he had taught then and what he found himself confusedly trying to learn five-and-twenty years afterwards — between the twelfth century of his thirtieth and that of his sixtieth years. At Harvard College, weary of spirit in the wastes of Anglo-Saxon law, he had occasionally given way to outbursts of derision at shedding his life-blood for the sublime truths of Sac and Soc: —

> HIC JACET
> HOMUNCULUS SCRIPTOR
> DOCTOR BARBARICUS
> HENRICUS ADAMS
> ADAE FILIUS ET EVAE
> PRIMO EXPLICUIT
> SOCNAM [25]

The Latin was as twelfth-century as the law, and he meant as satire the claim that he had been first to explain the legal meaning of Sac and Soc, although any German professor would have scorned it as a shameless and presumptuous bid for immortality; but the whole point of view had vanished in 1900. Not he, but Sir Henry Maine and Rudolph Sohm,[26] were the parents or creators of Sac and Soc. Convinced that the clue of religion led to nothing, and that politics led to chaos, one had turned to the law, as one's scholars turned to the Law School, because one could see no other path to a profession.

The law had proved as futile as politics or religion, or any other single thread spun by the human spider; it offered no more continuity than architecture or coinage, and no more force of its own. St. Francis expressed supreme contempt for them all, and solved the whole problem by rejecting it altogether. Adams returned to Paris with a broken and contrite spirit, prepared to admit that his life had no meaning, and conscious that in any case it no longer mattered. He passed a summer of solitude contrasting sadly with the last at Surrenden; but the solitude did what the society did not — it forced and drove him into the study of his ignorance in silence. Here at last he entered the practice of his final profession. Hunted by ennui, he could no longer escape, and, by way of a summer school, he began a methodical survey — a triangulation — of the twelfth century. The pursuit had a singular French charm which France had long lost — a calmness, lucidity, simplicity of expression, vigor of action, complexity of local color, that made Paris flat. In the long summer days one found a sort of saturated green pleasure in the forests, and gray infinity of rest in the little twelfth-century churches that lined them, as unassuming as their own mosses, and as sure of their purpose as their round arches; but churches were many and summer was short, so that he was at last driven back to the quays and photographs.[27] For weeks he lived in silence.

His solitude was broken in November by the chance arrival of John La Farge. At that moment, contact with La Farge had a new value. Of all the men who had deeply affected their friends since 1850 John La Farge was certainly the foremost, and for Henry Adams, who had sat at his feet since 1872,[28] the question how much he owed to La Farge could be answered only by admitting that he had no standard to measure it by. Of all his friends La Farge alone owned a mind complex enough to contrast against the commonplaces of American uniformity, and in the process had vastly perplexed most Americans who came in contact with it. The American mind — the Bostonian as well as the Southern or Western — likes to walk straight up to its object, and assert or deny something that it takes for a fact; it has a conventional approach, a conventional analysis, and a conventional conclusion, as well as a conventional expression, all the time loudly asserting its unconventionality. The most disconcerting trait of John La Farge was his reversal of the process. His approach was quiet and indirect; he moved round an object, and never separated it from its surroundings; he prided himself on faithfulness to tradition and convention; he was never abrupt and abhorred dispute. His manners and attitude towards the universe were the same, whether tossing in the middle of the Pacific Ocean sketching the trade-wind from a whale-boat in the blast of sea-sickness, or drinking the *cha-no-yu* [29] in the formal rites of Japan, or sipping his cocoanut cup of kava in the ceremonial of Samoan chiefs, or reflecting under the sacred bo-tree at Anaradjpura. [30]

One was never quite sure of his whole meaning until too late to respond, for he had no difficulty in carrying different shades of contradiction in his mind. As he said of his friend Okakura, [31] his thought ran as a stream runs through grass, hidden perhaps but always there; and one felt often uncertain in what direction it flowed, for even a contradiction was to him only a shade of difference, a complementary color, about which no intelligent artist would dispute. Constantly he repulsed argument: "Adams, you reason too much!" was one of his standing reproaches even in the mild discussion of rice and mangoes in the warm night of Tahiti dinners. He should have blamed Adams for being born in Boston. The mind resorts to reason for want of training, and Adams had never met a perfectly trained mind.

To La Farge, eccentricity meant convention; a mind really eccentric never betrayed it. True eccentricity was a tone — a shade — a *nuance* — and the finer the tone, the truer the eccentricity. Of course all artists hold more or less the same point of view in their art, but few carry it into daily life, and often the contrast is excessive between their art and their talk. One evening Humphreys Johnston, [32] who was devoted to La Farge, asked him to meet Whistler at dinner. La Farge was ill — more ill than usual even for him — but he admired and liked Whistler, and insisted on going. By chance, Adams was so placed as to overhear the conversation of both, and had no choice but to hear that of Whistler, which engrossed the table. At that moment the Boer War [33] was raging, and, as everyone knows, on that subject Whistler raged worse than the Boers. For two hours he declaimed against England — witty, declamatory, extravagant, bitter, amusing, and noisy; but in substance what he said was not merely commonplace — it was true! That is to say, his hearers, including Adams and, as far as he knew, La Farge, agreed with it all, and mostly as a matter of course; yet La Farge was silent, and this difference of expression was a difference of art. Whistler in his art carried the sense of *nuance* and tone far beyond any point reached by La Farge, or even attempted; but in talk he showed, above or below his color-instinct, a willingness to seem eccentric where no real eccentricity, unless perhaps of temper, existed.

This vehemence, which Whistler never betrayed in his painting, La Farge seemed to lavish on his glass. With the relative value of La Farge's glass in the history of glass-decoration, Adams was too ignorant to meddle, and as a rule artists were if possible more ignorant than he; but whatever it was, it led him back to the twelfth century and to Chartres where La Farge not only felt at home, but felt a sort of ownership.[34] No other American had a right there, unless he too were a member of the Church and worked in glass. Adams himself was an interloper, but long habit led La Farge to resign himself to Adams as one who meant well, though deplorably Bostonian; while Adams, though near sixty years old before he knew anything either of glass or of Chartres, asked no better than to learn, and only La Farge could help him, for he knew enough at least to see that La Farge alone could use glass like a thirteenth-century artist. In Europe the art had been dead for centuries, and modern glass was pitiable. Even La Farge felt the early glass rather as a document than as a historical emotion, and in hundreds of windows at Chartres and Bourges[35] and Paris, Adams knew barely one or two that were meant to hold their own against a color-scheme so strong as his. In conversation La Farge's mind was opaline with infinite shades and refractions of light, and with color toned down to the finest gradations. In glass it was insubordinate; it was renaissance; it asserted his personal force with depth and vehemence of tone never before seen. He seemed bent on crushing rivalry.

Even the gloom of a Paris December at the Élysée Palace Hotel was somewhat relieved by this companionship, and education made a step backwards towards Chartres, but La Farge's health became more and more alarming, and Adams was glad to get him safely back to New York, January 15, 1900, while he himself went at once to Washington to find out what had become of Hay. Nothing good could be hoped, for Hay's troubles had begun, and were quite as great as he had foreseen. Adams saw as little encouragement as Hay himself did, though he dared not say so. He doubted Hay's endurance, the President's firmness in supporting him, and the loyalty of his party friends; but all this worry on Hay's account fretted him not nearly so much as the Boer War did on his own. Here was a problem in his political education that passed all experience since the Treason winter of 1860–61! Much to his astonishment, very few Americans seemed to share his point of view; their hostility to England seemed mere temper; but to Adams the war became almost a personal outrage. He had been taught from childhood, even in England, that his forbears and their associates in 1776 had settled, once for all, the liberties of the British free colonies, and he very strongly objected to being thrown on the defensive again, and forced to sit down, a hundred and fifty years after John Adams had begun the task, to prove, by appeal to law and fact, that George Washington was not a felon, whatever might be the case with George III.[36] For reasons still more personal, he declined peremptorily to entertain question of the felony of John Adams. He felt obliged to go even further, and avow the opinion that if at any time England should take towards Canada the position she took towards her Boer colonies, the United States would be bound, by their record, to interpose, and to insist on the application of the principles of 1776.[37] To him the attitude of Mr. Chamberlain[38] and his colleagues seemed exceedingly un-American, and terribly embarrassing to Hay.

Trained early, in the stress of civil war, to hold his tongue, and to help make the political machine run somehow, since it could never be made to run well, he would not bother Hay with theoretical objections which were every day fretting him in practical forms. Hay's chance lay in patience and good temper till the luck should turn, and to him the only object was time; but as political education the point seemed vital to Adams, who never liked shutting his eyes or denying an evident fact. Practical politics consists in ignoring facts, but education and politics are two different and often contradictory things. In this case, the contradiction seemed crude.

With Hay's politics, at home or abroad,[39] Adams had nothing whatever to do. Hay belonged to the New York school, like Abram Hewitt, Evarts, W. C. Whitney, Samuel J. Tilden — men who played the game for ambition or amusement, and played it, as a rule, much better than the professionals, but whose aims were considerably larger than those of the usual player, and who felt no great love for the cheap drudgery of the work. In return, the professionals felt no great love for them, and set them aside when they could. Only their control of money made them inevitable, and even this did not always carry their points. The story of Abram Hewitt would offer one type of this statesman series, and that of Hay another. President Cleveland set aside the one;[40] President Harrison set aside the other. "There is no politics in it," was his comment on Hay's appointment to office. Hay held a different opinion and turned to McKinley whose judgment of men was finer than common in Presidents. Mr. McKinley brought to the problem of American government a solution which lay very far outside of Henry Adams's education, but which seemed to be at least practical and American. He undertook to pool interests in a general trust into which every interest should be taken, more or less at its own valuation, and whose mass should, under his management, create efficiency. He achieved very remarkable results. How much they cost was another matter; if the public is ever driven to its last resources and the usual remedies of chaos, the result will probably cost more.

Himself a marvellous manager of men, McKinley found several manipulators to help him, almost as remarkable as himself, one of whom was Hay; but unfortunately Hay's strength was weakest and his task hardest. At home, interests could be easily combined by simply paying their price; but abroad whatever helped on one side, hurt him on another. Hay thought England must be brought first into the combine; but at that time Germany, Russia, and France were combining against England, and the Boer War helped them. For the moment Hay had no ally, abroad or at home, except Pauncefote,[41] and Adams always maintained that Pauncefote alone pulled him through.

Yet the difficulty abroad was far less troublesome than the obstacles at home. The Senate had grown more and more unmanageable, even since the time of Andrew Johnson, and this was less the fault of the Senate than of the system. "A treaty of peace, in any normal state of things," said Hay, "ought to be ratified with unanimity in twenty-four hours. They wasted six weeks in wrangling over this one, and ratified it with one vote to spare. We have five or six matters now demanding settlement. I can settle them all, honorably and advantageously to our own side; and I am assured by leading men in the Senate that not one of these treaties, if negotiated, will pass the Senate. I should have a majority in every case, but a malcontent third would certainly dish every one of them. To such monstrous shape has the original mistake of the Constitution grown in the evolution of our politics. You must understand, it is not merely *my* solution the Senate will reject. They will reject, for instance, any treaty, whatever, on any subject, with England. I doubt if they would accept any treaty of consequence with Russia or Germany. The recalcitrant third would be differently composed, but it would be on hand. So that the real duties of a Secretary of State seem to be three: to fight claims upon us by other States; to press more or less fraudulent claims of our own citizens upon other countries; to find offices for the friends of Senators when there are none. Is it worth while — for me — to keep up this useless labor?"[42]

To Adams, who, like Hay, had seen a dozen acquaintances struggling with the same enemies, the question had scarcely the interest of a new study. He had said all he had to say about it in a dozen or more volumes relating to the politics of a hundred years before.[43] To him, the spectacle was so familiar as to be humorous. The intrigue was too open to be interesting. The interference of the German and Russian legations, and of the Clan-na-Gael,[44] with the press and the Senate was innocently undisguised. The charming Russian Minister, Count Cassini,[45] the ideal of diplomatic manners and training, let few days pass without appealing through the press to the public against the government. The German Minister, Von Holleben,[46] more cautiously did the same thing, and of course every whisper of theirs was brought instantly to the Department. These three forces, acting with the regular opposition and the natural obstructionists, could always stop action in the Senate. The fathers had intended to neutralize the energy of government and had succeeded, but their machine was never meant to do the work of a twenty-million horse-power society in the twentieth century, where much work needed to be quickly and efficiently done. The only defence of the system was that, as Government did nothing well, it had best do nothing; but the Government, in truth, did perfectly well all it was given to do; and even if the charge were true, it applied equally to human society altogether, if one chose to treat mankind from that point of view. As a matter of mechanics, so much work must be done; bad machinery merely added to friction.

Always unselfish, generous, easy, patient, and loyal, Hay had treated the world as something to be taken in block without pulling it to pieces to get rid of its defects; he liked it all: he laughed and accepted; he had never known unhappiness and would have gladly lived his entire life over again exactly as it happened. In the whole New York school, one met a similar dash of humor and cynicism more or less pronounced but seldom bitter. Yet even the gayest of tempers succumbs at last to constant friction. The old friend was rapidly fading. The habit remained, but the easy intimacy, the careless gaiety, the casual humor, the equality of indifference, were sinking into the routine of office; the mind lingered in the Department; the thought failed to react; the wit and humor shrank within the blank walls of politics, and the irritations multiplied. To a head of bureau, the result seemed ennobling.[47]

Although, as education, this branch of study was more familiar and older than the twelfth century, the task of bringing the two periods into a common relation was new. Ignorance required that these political and social and scientific values of the twelfth and twentieth centuries should be correlated in some relation of movement that could be expressed in mathematics, nor did one care in the least that all the world said it could not be done, or that one knew not enough mathematics even to figure a formula beyond the schoolboy $s = \frac{gt^2}{2}$.[48] If Kepler and Newton[49] could take liberties with the sun and moon, an obscure person in a remote wilderness like La Fayette Square could take liberties with Congress, and venture to multiply half its attraction into the square of its time. He had only to find a value, even infinitesimal, for its attraction at any given time. A historical formula that should satisfy the conditions of the stellar universe weighed heavily on his mind; but a trifling matter like this was one in which he could look for no help from anybody — he could look only for derision at best.

All his associates in history condemned such an attempt as futile and almost immoral — certainly hostile to sound historical system. Adams tried it only because of its hostility to all that he had taught for history, since he started afresh from the new point that, whatever was right, all he had ever taught was wrong. He had pursued ignorance thus far with success, and had swept his mind clear of knowledge. In beginning again, from the starting point of Sir Isaac Newton, he looked about him in vain for a teacher. Few men in Washington cared to overstep the school conventions, and the most distinguished of them, Simon Newcomb,[50] was too sound a mathematician to treat such a scheme seriously. The greatest of Americans, judged by his rank in science, Willard Gibbs,[51] never came to Washington, and Adams never enjoyed a chance to meet him. After Gibbs, one of the most distinguished was Langley,[52] of the Smithsonian, who was more accessible, to whom Adams had been much in the habit of turning whenever he wanted an outlet for his vast reservoirs of ignorance. Langley listened with outward patience to his disputatious questionings; but he too nourished a scientific passion for doubt, and sentimental attachment for its avowal. He had the physicist's heinous fault of professing to know nothing between flashes of intense perception. Like so many other great observers, Langley was not a mathematician, and like most physicists, he believed in physics. Rigidly denying himself the amusement of philosophy, which consists chiefly in suggesting unintelligible answers to insoluble problems, he still knew the problems, and liked to wander past them in a courteous temper, even bowing to them distantly as though recognizing their existence, though doubting their respectability. He generously let others doubt what he felt obliged to affirm; and early put into Adams's hands the "Concepts of Modern Science," a volume by Judge Stallo,[53] which had been treated for a dozen years by the schools with a conspiracy of silence such as inevitably meets every revolutionary work that upsets the stock and machinery of instruction. Adams read and failed to understand; then he asked questions and failed to get answers.

Probably this was education. Perhaps it was the only scientific education open to a student sixty-odd years old, who asked to be as ignorant as an astronomer. For him the details of science meant nothing: he wanted to know its mass. Solar heat was not enough, or was too much. Kinetic atoms led only to motion; never to direction or progress. History had no use for multiplicity; it needed unity; it could study only motion, direction, attraction, relation. Everything must be made to move together; one must seek new worlds to measure; and so, like Rasselas,[54] Adams set out once more, and found himself on May 12 settled in rooms at the very door of the Trocadero.[55]

CHAPTER XXV

The Dynamo and the Virgin (1900)

UNTIL the Great Exposition of 1900[1] closed its doors in
November, Adams haunted it, aching to absorb knowledge, and helpless to find it. He would have liked to
know how much of it could have been grasped by the best-informed
man in the world. While he was thus meditating chaos, Langley
came by, and showed it to him. At Langley's behest, the Exhibition dropped its superfluous rags and stripped itself to the skin,
for Langley knew what to study, and why, and how; while Adams
might as well have stood outside in the night, staring at the Milky
Way. Yet Langley said nothing new, and taught nothing that one
might not have learned from Lord Bacon,[2] three hundred years
before; but though one should have known the "Advancement of
Science" as well as one knew the "Comedy of Errors,"[3] the literary knowledge counted for nothing until some teacher should show
how to apply it. Bacon took a vast deal of trouble in teaching
King James I[4] and his subjects, American or other, towards the
year 1620, that true science was the development or economy of
forces; yet an elderly American in 1900 knew neither the formula
nor the forces; or even so much as to say to himself that his historical business in the Exposition concerned only the economies
or developments of force since 1893, when he began the study at
Chicago.

Nothing in education is so astonishing as the amount of ignorance it accumulates in the form of inert facts. Adams had looked
at most of the accumulations of art in the storehouses called Art
Museums; yet he did not know how to look at the art exhibits of
1900.[5] He had studied Karl Marx and his doctrines of history with
profound attention, yet he could not apply them at Paris. Langley, with the ease of a great master of experiment, threw out of the

field every exhibit that did not reveal a new application of force, and naturally threw out, to begin with, almost the whole art exhibit. Equally, he ignored almost the whole industrial exhibit. He led his pupil directly to the forces. His chief interest was in new motors to make his airship feasible, and he taught Adams the astonishing complexities of the new Daimler[6] motor, and of the automobile, which, since 1893, had become a nightmare at a hundred kilometres an hour, almost as destructive as the electric tram which was only ten years older; and threatening to become as terrible as the locomotive steam-engine itself, which was almost exactly Adams's own age.[7]

Then he showed his scholar the great hall of dynamos,[8] and explained how little he knew about electricity or force of any kind, even of his own special sun, which spouted heat in inconceivable volume, but which, as far as he knew, might spout less or more, at any time, for all the certainty he felt in it. To him, the dynamo itself was but an ingenious channel for conveying somewhere the heat latent in a few tons of poor coal hidden in a dirty engine-house carefully kept out of sight; but to Adams the dynamo became a symbol of infinity. As he grew accustomed to the great gallery of machines, he began to feel the forty-foot dynamos as a moral force, much as the early Christians felt the Cross. The planet itself seemed less impressive, in its old-fashioned, deliberate, annual or daily revolution, than this huge wheel, revolving within arm's-length at some vertiginous speed, and barely murmuring — scarcely humming an audible warning to stand a hair's-breadth further for respect of power — while it would not wake the baby lying close against its frame. Before the end, one began to pray to it; inherited instinct taught the natural expression of man before silent and infinite force. Among the thousand symbols of ultimate energy, the dynamo was not so human as some, but it was the most expressive.

Yet the dynamo, next to the steam-engine, was the most familiar of exhibits. For Adams's objects its value lay chiefly in its occult mechanism. Between the dynamo in the gallery of machines and the engine-house outside, the break of continuity amounted to abysmal fracture for a historian's objects. No more relation could he discover between the steam and the electric current than between the Cross and the cathedral. The forces were interchangeable if not reversible, but he could see only an absolute *fiat* in electricity as in faith. Langley could not help him. Indeed, Langley seemed to be worried by the same trouble, for he constantly repeated that the new forces were anarchical, and especially that he was not responsible for the new rays, that were little short of parricidal in their wicked spirit towards science. His own rays,[9] with which he had doubled the solar spectrum, were altogether harmless and beneficent; but Radium denied its God [10] or, what was to Langley the same thing, denied the truths of his Science. The force was wholly new.

A historian who asked only to learn enough to be as futile as Langley or Kelvin,[11] made rapid progress under this teaching, and mixed himself up in the tangle of ideas until he achieved a sort of Paradise of ignorance vastly consoling to his fatigued senses. He wrapped himself in vibrations and rays which were new, and he would have hugged Marconi[12] and Branly[13] had he met them, as he hugged the dynamo; while he lost his arithmetic in trying to figure out the equation between the discoveries and the economies of force. The economies, like the discoveries, were absolute, supersensual, occult; incapable of expression in horse-power. What mathematical equivalent could he suggest as the value of a Branly coherer? Frozen air, or the electric furnace, had some scale of measurement, no doubt, if somebody could invent a thermometer adequate to the purpose; but X-rays[14] had played no part whatever in man's consciousness, and the atom itself had figured only as a fiction of thought. In these seven years man had translated himself into a new universe which had no common scale of measurement with the old. He had entered a supersensual world, in which he could measure nothing except by chance collisions of movements imperceptible to his senses, perhaps even imperceptible to his instruments, but perceptible to each other, and so to some known ray at the end of the scale. Langley seemed prepared for anything, even for an indeterminable number of universes interfused — physics stark mad in metaphysics.

Historians undertake to arrange sequences, — called stories, or histories — assuming in silence a relation of cause and effect. These assumptions, hidden in the depths of dusty libraries, have been astounding, but commonly unconscious and childlike; so much so, that if any captious critic were to drag them to light, historians would probably reply, with one voice, that they had never supposed themselves required to know what they were talking about. Adams, for one, had toiled in vain to find out what he meant. He had even published a dozen volumes of American history for no other purpose than to satisfy himself whether, by the severest process of stating, with the least possible comment, such facts as seemed sure, in such order as seemed rigorously consequent, he could fix for a familiar moment a necessary sequence of human movement. The result had satisfied him as little as at Harvard College. Where he saw sequence, other men saw something quite different, and no one saw the same unit of measure. He cared little about his experiments and less about his statesmen, who seemed to him quite as ignorant as himself and, as a rule, no more honest; but he insisted on a relation of sequence, and if he could not reach it by one method, he would try as many methods as science knew. Satisfied that the sequence of men led to nothing and that the sequence of their society could lead no further, while the mere sequence of time was artificial, and the sequence of thought was chaos, he turned at last to the sequence of force; and thus it happened that, after ten years' pursuit, he found himself lying in the Gallery of Machines at the Great Exposition of 1900, with his historical neck broken by the sudden irruption of forces totally new.

Since no one else showed much concern, an elderly person without other cares had no need to betray alarm. The year 1900 was not the first to upset schoolmasters. Copernicus and Galileo[15] had broken many professorial necks about 1600; Columbus had stood the world on its head towards 1500; but the nearest approach to the revolution of 1900 was that of 310, when Constantine[16] set up the Cross. The rays that Langley disowned, as well as those which he fathered, were occult, supersensual, irrational; they were a revelation of mysterious energy like that of the Cross; they were what, in terms of mediæval science, were called immediate modes of the divine substance.

The historian was thus reduced to his last resources. Clearly if he was bound to reduce all these forces to a common value, this common value could have no measure but that of their attraction on his own mind. He must treat them as they had been felt; as convertible, reversible, interchangeable attractions on thought. He made up his mind to venture it; he would risk translating rays into faith. Such a reversible process would vastly amuse a chemist, but the chemist could not deny that he, or some of his fellow physicists, could feel the force of both. When Adams was a boy in Boston, the best chemist[17] in the place had probably never heard of Venus except by way of scandal, or of the Virgin except as idolatry; neither had he heard of dynamos or automobiles or radium; yet his mind was ready to feel the force of all, though the rays were unborn and the women were dead.

Here opened another totally new education, which promised to be by far the most hazardous of all. The knife-edge along which he must crawl, like Sir Lancelot[18] in the twelfth century, divided two kingdoms of force which had nothing in common but attraction. They were as different as a magnet is from gravitation, supposing one knew what a magnet was, or gravitation, or love. The force of the Virgin was still felt at Lourdes,[19] and seemed to be as potent as X-rays; but in America neither Venus nor Virgin ever had value as force — at most as sentiment. No American had ever been truly afraid of either.

This problem in dynamics gravely perplexed an American historian. The Woman had once been supreme; in France she still seemed potent, not merely as a sentiment, but as a force. Why was she unknown in America? For evidently America was ashamed of her, and she was ashamed of herself, otherwise they would not have strewn fig-leaves so profusely all over her. When she was a true force, she was ignorant of fig-leaves, but the monthly-magazine-made American female had not a feature that would have been recognized by Adam. The trait was notorious, and often humorous, but anyone brought up among Puritans knew that sex was sin. In any previous age, sex was strength. Neither art nor beauty was needed. Everyone, even among Puritans, knew that neither Diana of the Ephesians [20] nor any of the Oriental goddesses was worshipped for her beauty. She was goddess because of her force; she was the animated dynamo; she was reproduction—the greatest and most mysterious of all energies; all she needed was to be fecund. Singularly enough, not one of Adams's many schools of education had ever drawn his attention to the opening lines of Lucretius, though they were perhaps the finest in all Latin literature, where the poet invoked Venus exactly as Dante invoked the Virgin:—

"Quae quoniam rerum naturam *sola* gubernas." [21]

The Venus of Epicurean philosophy survived in the Virgin of the Schools:—

"Donna, sei tanto grande, e tanto vali,
Che qual vuol grazia, e a te non ricorre,
Sua disianza vuol volar senz' ali." [22]

All this was to American thought as though it had never existed. The true American knew something of the facts, but nothing of the feelings; he read the letter, but he never felt the law. Before this historical chasm, a mind like that of Adams felt itself helpless; he turned from the Virgin to the Dynamo as though he were a Branly coherer. [23] On one side, at the Louvre and at Chartres, [24] as he knew by the record of work actually done and still before his eyes, was the highest energy ever known to man, the creator of four-fifths of his noblest art, exercising vastly more attraction over the human mind than all the steam-engines and dynamos ever dreamed of; and yet this energy was unknown to the American mind. An American Virgin would never dare command; an American Venus would never dare exist.

The question, which to any plain American of the nineteenth century seemed as remote as it did to Adams, drew him almost violently to study, once it was posed; and on this point Langleys were as useless as though they were Herbert Spencers[25] or dynamos. The idea survived only as art. There one turned as naturally as though the artist were himself a woman. Adams began to ponder, asking himself whether he knew of any American artist who had ever insisted on the power of sex, as every classic had always done; but he could think only of Walt Whitman;[26] Bret Harte,[27] as far as the magazines would let him venture; and one or two painters,[28] for the flesh-tones. All the rest had used sex for sentiment, never for force; to them, Eve was a tender flower, and Herodias[29] an unfeminine horror. American art, like the American language and American education, was as far as possible sexless.[30] Society regarded this victory over sex as its greatest triumph, and the historian readily admitted it, since the moral issue, for the moment, did not concern one who was studying the relations of unmoral force. He cared nothing for the sex of the dynamo until he could measure its energy.

Vaguely seeking a clue, he wandered through the art exhibit, and, in his stroll, stopped almost every day before St. Gaudens's General Sherman,[31] which had been given the central post of honor. St. Gaudens himself was in Paris, putting on the work his usual interminable last touches, and listening to the usual contradictory suggestions of brother sculptors. Of all the American artists who gave to American art whatever life it breathed in the seventies, St. Gaudens was perhaps the most sympathetic, but certainly the most inarticulate. General Grant or Don Cameron

had scarcely less instinct of rhetoric than he. All the others —
the Hunts, Richardson, John La Farge, Stanford White — were
exuberant; only St. Gaudens could never discuss or dilate on an
emotion, or suggest artistic arguments for giving to his work the
forms that he felt. He never laid down the law, or affected the
despot, or became brutalized like Whistler by the brutalities of
his world. He required no incense; he was no egoist; his simplicity of thought was excessive; he could not imitate, or give any
form but his own to the creations of his hand. No one felt more
strongly than he the strength of other men, but the idea that they
could affect him never stirred an image in his mind.

This summer his health was poor and his spirits were low. For
such a temper, Adams was not the best companion, since his own
gaiety was not *folle;*[32] but he risked going now and then to the
studio on Mont Parnasse to draw him out for a stroll in the Bois
de Boulogne,[33] or dinner as pleased his moods, and in return St.
Gaudens sometimes let Adams go about in his company.

Once St. Gaudens took him down to Amiens, with a party of
Frenchmen, to see the cathedral. Not until they found themselves actually studying the sculpture of the western portal, did
it dawn on Adams's mind that, for his purposes, St. Gaudens on
that spot had more interest to him than the cathedral itself. Great
men before great monuments express great truths, provided they
are not taken too solemnly. Adams never tired of quoting the
supreme phrase of his idol Gibbon, before the Gothic cathedrals:
"I darted a contemptuous look on the stately monuments of
superstition."[34] Even in the footnotes of his history, Gibbon had
never inserted a bit of humor more human than this, and one
would have paid largely for a photograph of the fat little historian,
on the background of Notre Dame of Amiens, trying to persuade
his readers — perhaps himself — that he was darting a contemptuous look on the stately monument, for which he felt in fact the
respect which every man of his vast study and active mind always
feels before objects worthy of it; but besides the humor, one felt

also the relation. Gibbon ignored the Virgin, because in 1789 religious monuments were out of fashion. In 1900 his remark sounded fresh and simple as the green fields to ears that had heard a hundred years of other remarks, mostly no more fresh and certainly less simple. Without malice, one might find it more instructive than a whole lecture of Ruskin. One sees what one brings, and at that moment Gibbon brought the French Revolution. Ruskin brought reaction against the Revolution. St. Gaudens had passed beyond all. He liked the stately monuments much more than he liked Gibbon or Ruskin; he loved their dignity; their unity; their scale; their lines; their lights and shadows; their decorative sculpture; but he was even less conscious than they of the force that created it all — the Virgin, the Woman — by whose genius "the stately monuments of superstition" were built, through which she was expressed. He would have seen more meaning in Isis [35] with the cow's horns, at Edfoo, who expressed the same thought. The art remained, but the energy was lost even upon the artist.

Yet in mind and person St. Gaudens was a survival of the 1500's; he bore the stamp of the Renaissance, and should have carried an image of the Virgin round his neck, or stuck in his hat, like Louis XI.[36] In mere time he was a lost soul that had strayed by chance into the twentieth century, and forgotten where it came from. He writhed and cursed at his ignorance, much as Adams did at his own, but in the opposite sense. St. Gaudens was a child of Benvenuto Cellini,[37] smothered in an American cradle. Adams was a quintessence of Boston, devoured by curiosity to think like Benvenuto. St. Gaudens's art was starved from birth, and Adams's instinct was blighted from babyhood. Each had but half of a nature, and when they came together before the Virgin of Amiens they ought both to have felt in her the force that made them one; but it was not so. To Adams she became more than ever a channel of force; to St. Gaudens she remained as before a channel of taste.

For a symbol of power, St. Gaudens instinctively preferred the horse, as was plain in his horse and Victory of the Sherman monument. Doubtless Sherman also felt it so. The attitude was so American that, for at least forty years, Adams had never realized that any other could be in sound taste. How many years had he taken to admit a notion of what Michael Angelo and Rubens [38] were driving at? He could not say; but he knew that only since 1895 had he begun to feel the Virgin or Venus as force, and not everywhere even so. At Chartres — perhaps at Lourdes — possibly at Cnidos [39] if one could still find there the divinely naked Aphrodite of Praxiteles — but otherwise one must look for force to the goddesses of Indian mythology. The idea died out long ago in the German and English stock. St. Gaudens at Amiens was hardly less sensitive to the force of the female energy than Matthew Arnold at the Grande Chartreuse. [40] Neither of them felt goddesses as power — only as reflected emotion, human expression, beauty, purity, taste, scarcely even as sympathy. They felt a railway train as power; yet they, and all other artists, constantly complained that the power embodied in a railway train could never be embodied in art. All the steam in the world could not, like the Virgin, build Chartres.

Yet in mechanics, whatever the mechanicians might think, both energies acted as interchangeable forces on man, and by action on man all known force may be measured. Indeed, few men of science measured force in any other way. After once admitting that a straight line was the shortest distance between two points, no serious mathematician cared to deny anything that suited his convenience, and rejected no symbol, unproved or unproveable, that helped him to accomplish work. The symbol was force, as a compass-needle or a triangle was force, as the mechanist might prove by losing it, and nothing could be gained by ignoring their value. Symbol or energy, the Virgin had acted as the greatest force the Western world ever felt, and had drawn man's activities to herself more strongly than any other power, natural or supernatural, had ever done; the historian's business was to follow the track of the energy; to find where it came from and where it went to; its complex source and shifting channels; its values, equivalents, conversions. It could scarcely be more complex than radium; it could hardly be deflected, diverted, polarized, absorbed more perplexingly than other radiant matter. Adams knew nothing about any of them, but as a mathematical problem of influence on human progress, though all were occult, all reacted on his mind, and he rather inclined to think the Virgin easiest to handle.

The pursuit turned out to be long and tortuous, leading at last into the vast forests of scholastic science. From Zeno[41] to Descartes, hand in hand with Thomas Aquinas,[42] Montaigne, and Pascal,[43] one stumbled as stupidly as though one were still a German student of 1860. Only with the instinct of despair could one force one's self into this old thicket of ignorance after having been repulsed at a score of entrances more promising and more popular. Thus far, no path had led anywhere, unless perhaps to an exceedingly modest living. Forty-five years of study had proved to be quite futile for the pursuit of power; one controlled no more force in 1900 than in 1850, although the amount of force controlled by society had enormously increased. The secret of education still hid itself somewhere behind ignorance, and one fumbled over it as feebly as ever. In such labyrinths, the staff is a force almost more necessary than the legs; the pen becomes a sort of blind-man's dog, to keep him from falling into the gutters. The pen works for itself, and acts like a hand, modelling the plastic material over and over again to the form that suits it best. The form is never arbitrary, but is a sort of growth like crystallization, as any artist knows too well; for often the pencil or pen runs into side-paths and shapelessness, loses its relations, stops or is bogged. Then it has to return on its trail, and recover, if it can, its line of force. The result of a year's work depends more on what is struck out than on what is left in; on the sequence of the main lines of thought, than on their play or variety. Compelled once more to lean heavily on this support, Adams covered more thousands of pages[44] with figures as formal as though they were algebra, laboriously striking out, altering, burning, experimenting, until the year had expired, the Exposition had long been closed, and winter drawing to its end, before he sailed from Cherbourg, on January 19, 1901, for home.

CHAPTER XXVI

Twilight (1901)

WHILE the world that thought itself frivolous, and submitted meekly to hearing itself decried as vain,[1] fluttered through the Paris Exposition, jogging the futilities of St. Gaudens, Rodin, and Besnard,[2] the world that thought itself serious, and showed other infallible marks of coming mental paroxysm, was engaged in weird doings at Peking and elsewhere such as startled even itself. Of all branches of education, the science of gauging people and events by their relative importance defies study most insolently. For three or four generations, society has united in withering with contempt and opprobrium the shameless futility of Mme. de Pompadour and Mme. du Barry;[3] yet, if one bid at an auction for some object that had been approved by the taste of either lady, one quickly found that it were better to buy half-a-dozen Napoleons or Frederics, or Maria Theresas,[4] or all the philosophy and science of their time, than to bid for a cane-bottomed chair that either of these two ladies had adorned. The same thing might be said, in a different sense, of Voltaire; while, as everyone knows, the money-value of any handstroke of Watteau or Hogarth, Nattier or Sir Joshua, is out of all proportion to the importance of the men.[5] Society seemed to delight in talking with solemn conviction about serious values, and in paying fantastic prices for nothing but the most futile. The drama acted at Peking,[6] in the summer of 1900, was, in the eyes of a student, the most serious that could be offered for his study, since it brought him suddenly to the inevitable struggle for the control of China, which, in his view, must decide the control of the world; yet, as a money-value, the fall of China was chiefly studied in Paris and London as a calamity to Chinese porcelain. The value of a Ming vase was more serious than universal war.[7]

The drama of the Legations interested the public much as though it were a novel of Alexandre Dumas, but the bearing of the drama on future history offered an interest vastly greater. Adams knew no more about it than though he were the best-informed statesman in Europe. Like them all, he took for granted that the Legations were massacred, and that John Hay, who alone championed China's "administrative entity," would be massacred too, since he must henceforth look on, in impotence, while Russia and Germany dismembered China, and shut up America at home. Nine statesmen out of ten, in Europe, accepted this result in advance, seeing no way to prevent it. Adams saw none, and laughed at Hay for his helplessness.

When Hay suddenly ignored European leadership, took the lead himself, rescued the Legations and saved China,[8] Adams looked on, as incredulous as Europe, though not quite so stupid, since, on that branch of education, he knew enough for his purpose. Nothing so meteoric had ever been done in American diplomacy. On returning to Washington, January 30, 1901, he found most of the world as astonished as himself, but less stupid than usual. For a moment, indeed, the world had been struck dumb at seeing Hay put Europe aside and set the Washington Government at the head of civilization so quietly that civilization submitted, by mere instinct of docility, to receive and obey his orders; but, after the first shock of silence, society felt the force of the stroke through its fineness, and burst into almost tumultuous applause. Instantly the diplomacy of the nineteenth century, with all its painful scuffles and struggles, was forgotten, and the American blushed to be told of his submissions in the past. History broke in halves.

Hay was too good an artist not to feel the artistic skill of his own work, and the success reacted on his health, giving him fresh life, for with him as with most men, success was a tonic, and depression a specific poison; but as usual, his troubles nested at home. Success doubles strain. President McKinley's diplomatic court had become the largest in the world, and the diplomatic relations required far more work than ever before, while the staff of the Department was little more efficient, and the friction in the Senate had become coagulated. Hay took to studying the "Diary" of John Quincy Adams eighty years before, and calculated that the resistance had increased about ten times, as measured by waste of days and increase of effort, although Secretary of State J. Q. Adams thought himself very hardly treated.[9] Hay cheerfully noted that it was killing him, and proved it, for the effort of the afternoon walk became sometimes painful.

For the moment, things were going fairly well, and Hay's unruly team were less fidgety, but Pauncefote still pulled the whole load and turned the dangerous corners safely, while Cassini and Holleben helped the Senate to make what trouble they could, without serious offence, and the Irish, after the genial Celtic nature, obstructed even themselves.[10] The fortunate Irish, thanks to their sympathetic qualities, never made lasting enmities; but the Germans seemed in a fair way to rouse ill-will and even ugly temper in the spirit of politics, which was by no means a part of Hay's plans. He had as much as he could do to overcome domestic friction, and felt no wish to alienate foreign powers. Yet so much could be said in favor of the foreigners that they commonly knew why they made trouble, and were steady to a motive. Cassini had for years pursued, in Peking as in Washington, a policy of his own, never disguised, and as little in harmony with his chief as with Hay;[11] he made his opposition on fixed lines for notorious objects; but Senators could seldom give a reason for obstruction. In every hundred men, a certain number obstruct by instinct, and try to invent reasons to explain it afterwards. The Senate was no worse than the board of a university; but incorporators as a rule have not made this class of men dictators on purpose to prevent action. In the Senate, a single vote commonly stopped legislation, or, in committee, stifled discussion.

Hay's policy of removing, one after another, all irritations, and closing all discussions with foreign countries, roused incessant obstruction, which could be overcome only by patience and bargaining in executive patronage, if indeed it could be overcome at all. The price actually paid was not very great except in the physical exhaustion of Hay and Pauncefote, Root[12] and McKinley. No serious bargaining of equivalents could be attempted; Senators would not sacrifice five dollars in their own States to gain five hundred thousand in another; but whenever a foreign country was willing to surrender an advantage without an equivalent, Hay had a chance to offer the Senate a treaty. In all such cases the price paid for the treaty was paid wholly to the Senate, and amounted to nothing very serious except in waste of time and wear of strength. "Life is so gay and horrid!" laughed Hay; "the Major will have promised all the consulates in the service; the Senators will all come to me and refuse to believe me dis-consulate; I shall see all my treaties slaughtered, one by one, by the thirty-four per cent of kickers and strikers; the only mitigation I can foresee is being sick a good part of the time; I am nearing my grand climacteric, and the great *culbute*[13] is approaching."

He was thinking of his friend Blaine, and might have thought of all his predecessors, for all had suffered alike, and to Adams as historian their sufferings had been a long delight — the solitary picturesque and tragic element in politics — incidentally requiring character-studies like Aaron Burr and William B. Giles, Calhoun and Webster and Sumner, with Sir Forcible Feebles like James M. Mason and stage exaggerations like Roscoe Conkling.[14] The Senate took the place of Shakespeare, and offered real Brutuses and Bolingbrokes, Jack Cades, Falstaffs, and Malvolios[15] — endless varieties of human nature nowhere else to be studied, and none the less amusing because they killed, or because they were like schoolboys in their simplicity. "Life is so gay and horrid!" Hay still felt the humor, though more and more rarely, but what he felt most was the enormous complexity and friction of the vast mass he was trying to guide. He bitterly complained that it had made him a bore — of all things the most senatorial, and to him the most obnoxious. The old friend was lost, and only the teacher remained, driven to madness by the complexities and multiplicities of his new world.

To one who, at past sixty years old, is still passionately seeking education, these small, or large, annoyances had no great value except as measures of mass and motion. For him the practical interest and the practical man were such as looked forward to the next election, or perhaps, in corporations, five or ten years. Scarcely half-a-dozen men in America could be named who were known to have looked a dozen years ahead; while any historian who means to keep his alignment with past and future must cover a horizon of two generations at least. If he seeks to align himself with the future, he must assume a condition of some sort for a world fifty years beyond his own. Every historian — sometimes unconsciously, but always inevitably — must have put to himself the question: How long could such-or-such an outworn system last? He can never give himself less than one generation to show the full effects of a changed condition. His object is to triangulate from the widest possible base to the furthest point he thinks he can see, which is always far beyond the curvature of the horizon.

To the practical man, such an attempt is idiotic, and probably the practical man is in the right to-day; but, whichever is right — if the question of right or wrong enters at all into the matter — the historian has no choice but to go on alone. Even in his own profession few companions offer help, and his walk soon becomes solitary, leading further and further into a wilderness where twilight is short and the shadows are dense. Already Hay literally staggered in his tracks for weariness. More worn than he, Clarence King dropped. One day in the spring he stopped an hour in Washington to bid good-bye, cheerily and simply telling how his doctors had condemned him to Arizona for his lungs. All three friends knew that they were nearing the end, and that if it were not the one it would be the other; but the affectation of readiness for death is a stage rôle, and stoicism is a stupid resource, though the only one. *Non dolet, Paete!* [16] One is ashamed of it even in the acting.

The sunshine of life had not been so dazzling of late but that a share of it flickered out for Adams and Hay when King disappeared from their lives; but Hay had still his family and ambition, while Adams could only blunder back alone, helplessly, wearily, his eyes rather dim with tears, to his vague trail across the darkening prairie of education, without a motive, big or small, except curiosity to reach, before he too should drop, some point that would give him a far look ahead. He was morbidly curious to see some light at the end of the passage, as though thirty years were a shadow, and he were again to fall into King's arms at the door of the last and only log cabin left in life. Time had become terribly short, and the sense of knowing so little when others knew so much, crushed out hope.

He knew not in what new direction to turn, and sat at his desk, idly pulling threads out of the tangled skein of science, to see whether or why they aligned themselves. The commonest and oldest toy he knew was the child's magnet, with which he had played since babyhood, the most familiar of puzzles. He covered his desk with magnets, and mapped out their lines of force by compass. Then he read all the books he could find, and tried in vain to makes his lines of force agree with theirs. The books confounded him. He could not credit his own understanding. Here was literally the most concrete fact in nature, next to gravitation which it defied; a force which must have radiated lines of energy without stop, since time began, if not longer, and which might probably go on radiating after the sun should fall into the earth, since no one knew why — or how — or what it radiated — or even whether it radiated at all. Perhaps the earliest known of all natural forces after the solar energies, it seemed to have suggested no idea to any one until some mariner bethought himself that it might serve for a pointer. Another thousand years passed when it taught some other intelligent man to use it as a pump, supply-pipe, sieve, or reservoir for collecting electricity, still without knowing how it worked or what it was. For a historian, the story of Faraday's [17] experiments and the invention of the dynamo passed belief; it revealed a condition of human ignorance and helplessness before the commonest forces, such as his mind refused to credit. He could not conceive but that some one, somewhere, could tell him all about the magnet, if one could but find the book — although he had been forced to admit the same helplessness in the face of gravitation, phosphorescence, and odors; and he could imagine no reason why society should treat radium as revolutionary in science when every infant, for ages past, had seen the magnet doing what radium did; for surely the kind of radiation mattered nothing compared with the energy that radiated and the matter supplied for radiation. He dared not venture into the complexities of chemistry, or microbes, so long as this child's toy offered complexities that befogged his mind beyond X-rays, and turned the atom into an endless variety of pumps endlessly pumping an endless variety of ethers. He wanted to ask Mme. Curie [18] to invent a motor attachable to her salt of radium, and pump its forces through it, as Faraday did with a magnet. He figured the human mind itself as another radiating matter through which man had always pumped a subtler fluid.

In all this futility, it was not the magnet or the rays or the microbes that troubled him, or even his helplessness before the forces. To that he was used from childhood. The magnet in its new relation staggered his new education by its evidence of growing complexity, and multiplicity, and even contradiction, in life. He could not escape it; politics or science, the lesson was the same, and at every step it blocked his path whichever way he turned. He found it in politics; he ran against it in science; he struck it in everyday life, as though he were still Adam in the Garden of Eden between God who was unity, and Satan who was complexity, with no means of deciding which was truth. The problem was the same for McKinley as for Adam, and for the

Senate as for Satan. Hay was going to wreck on it, like King and Adams.

All one's life, one had struggled for unity, and unity had always won. The National Government and the national unity had overcome every resistance, and the Darwinian evolutionists were triumphant over all the curates; yet the greater the unity and the momentum, the worse became the complexity and the friction. One had in vain bowed one's neck to railways, banks, corporations, trusts, and even to the popular will as far as one could understand it — or even further; the multiplicity of unity had steadily increased, was increasing, and threatened to increase beyond reason. He had surrendered all his favorite prejudices, and foresworn even the forms of criticism — except for his pet amusement, the Senate, which was a tonic or stimulant necessary to healthy life; he had accepted uniformity and *Pteraspis* and ice age and tramways and telephones; and now — just when he was ready to hang the crowning garland on the brow of a completed education — science itself warned him to begin it again from the beginning.

Maundering among the magnets he bethought himself that once, a full generation earlier, he had begun active life by writing a confession of geological faith at the bidding of Sir Charles Lyell, and that it might be worth looking at if only to steady his vision. He read it again, and thought it better than he could do at sixty-three; but elderly minds always work loose. He saw his doubts grown larger, and became curious to know what had been said about them since 1870. The Geological Survey supplied stacks of volumes, and reading for steady months; while, the longer he read, the more he wondered, pondered, doubted what his delightful old friend Sir Charles Lyell would have said about it.

Truly the animal that is to be trained to unity must be caught young. Unity is vision; it must have been part of the process of learning to see. The older the mind, the older its complexities, and the further it looks, the more it sees, until even the stars resolve themselves into multiples; yet the child will always see but one. Adams asked whether geology since 1867 had drifted towards unity or multiplicity, and he felt that the drift would depend on the age of the man who drifted.

Seeking some impersonal point for measure, he turned to see what had happened to his oldest friend and cousin the ganoid fish, the *Pteraspis* of Ludlow and Wenlock, with whom he had sported when geological life was young; as though they had all remained together in time to act the Mask of Comus[19] at Ludlow Castle, and repeat "how charming is divine philosophy!" He felt almost aggrieved to find Walcott[20] so vigorously acting the part of Comus as to have flung the ganoid all the way off to Colorado and far back into the Lower Trenton limestone, making the *Pteraspis* as modern as a Mississippi gar-pike by spawning an ancestry for him, indefinitely more remote, in the dawn of known organic life. A few thousand feet, more or less, of limestone were the liveliest amusement to the ganoid, but they buried the uniformitarian alive, under the weight of his own uniformity. Not for all the ganoid fish that ever swam, would a discreet historian dare to hazard even in secret an opinion about the value of Natural Selection by Minute Changes under Uniform Conditions, for he could know no more about it than most of his neighbors who knew nothing; but natural selection that did not select — evolution finished before it began — minute changes that refused to change anything during the whole geological record — survival of the highest order in a fauna which had no origin — uniformity under conditions which had disturbed everything else in creation — to an honest-meaning though ignorant student who needed to prove Natural Selection and not assume it, such sequence brought no peace. He wished to be shown that changes in form caused evolution in force; that chemical or mechanical energy had by natural selection and minute changes, under uniform conditions, converted itself into thought. The ganoid fish seemed to prove — to him — that it had selected neither new form nor new force, but that the curates were right in thinking that force could be increased in volume or raised in intensity only by help of outside force. To him, the ganoid was a huge perplexity, none the less because neither he nor the ganoid troubled Darwinians, but the more because it helped to reveal that Darwinism seemed to survive only in England. In vain he asked what sort of evolution had taken its place. Almost any doctrine seemed orthodox. Even sudden conversions due to mere vital force acting on its own lines quite beyond mechanical explanation, had cropped up again. A little more, and he would be driven back on the old independence of species.

What the ontologist thought about it was his own affair, like the theologist's views on theology, for complexity was nothing to them; but to the historian who sought only the direction of thought and had begun as the confident child of Darwin and Lyell in 1867, the matter of direction seemed vital. Then he had entered gaily the door of the glacial epoch, and had surveyed a universe of unities and uniformities. In 1900 he entered a far vaster universe, where all the old roads ran about in every direction, overrunning, dividing, subdividing, stopping abruptly, vanishing slowly, with side-paths that led nowhere, and sequences that could not be proved. The active geologists had mostly become specialists dealing with complexities far too technical for an amateur, but the old formulas still seemed to serve for beginners, as they had served when new.

So the cause of the glacial epoch remained at the mercy of Lyell and Croll,[21] although Geikie[22] had split up the period into half-a-dozen intermittent chills in recent geology and in the northern hemisphere alone, while no geologist had ventured to assert that the glaciation of the southern hemisphere could possibly be referred to a horizon more remote. Continents still rose wildly and wildly sank, though Professor Suess[23] of Vienna had written an epoch-making work, showing that continents were anchored like crystals, and only oceans rose and sank. Lyell's genial uniformity seemed genial still, for nothing had taken its place, though, in the interval, granite had grown young, nothing had been explained, and a bewildering system of huge overthrusts had upset geological mechanics. The textbooks refused even to discuss theories, frankly throwing up their hands and avowing that progress depended on studying each rock as a law to itself.

Adams had no more to do with the correctness of the science than the gar-pike or the Port Jackson shark, for its correctness in no way concerned him, and only impertinence could lead him to dispute or discuss the principles of any science; but the history of the mind concerned the historian alone, and the historian had no vital concern in anything else, for he found no change to record in the body. In thought the Schools, like the Church, raised ignorance to a faith and degraded dogma to heresy. Evolution survived like the trilobites without evolving, and yet the evolutionists held the whole field, and had even plucked up courage to rebel against the Cossack ukase of Lord Kelvin[24] forbidding them to ask more than twenty million years for their experiments. No doubt the geologists had always submitted sadly to this last and utmost violence inflicted on them by the Pontiff of Physical Religion in the effort to force unification of the universe; they had protested with mild conviction that they could not state the geological record in terms of time[25]; they had murmured *Ignoramus* under their breath; but they had never dared to assert the *Ignorabimus*[26] that lay on the tips of their tongues.

Yet the admission seemed close at hand. Evolution was becoming change of form broken by freaks of force, and warped at times by attractions affecting intelligence, twisted and tortured at other times by sheer violence, cosmic, chemical, solar, supersensual, electrolytic — who knew what? — defying science, if not denying known law; and the wisest of men could but imitate the Church, and invoke a "larger synthesis"[27] to unify the anarchy again. Historians have got into far too much trouble by following schools of theology in their efforts to enlarge their synthesis, that they should willingly repeat the process in science.

For human purposes a point must always be soon reached where larger synthesis is suicide.

Politics and geology pointed alike to the larger synthesis of rapidly increasing complexity; but still an elderly man knew that the change might be only in himself. The admission cost nothing. Any student, of any age, thinking only of a thought and not of his thought, should delight in turning about and trying the opposite motion, as he delights in the spring which brings even to a tired and irritated statesman the larger synthesis of peach-blooms, cherry-blossoms, and dogwood, to prove the folly of fret. Every schoolboy knows that this sum of all knowledge never saved him from whipping; mere years help nothing; King and Hay and Adams could neither of them escape floundering through the corridors of chaos that opened as they passed to the end; but they could at least float with the stream if they only knew which way the current ran. Adams would have liked to begin afresh with the *Limulus* and *Lepidosteus* in the waters of Braintree,[28] side by side with Adamses and Quincys and Harvard College, all unchanged and unchangeable since archaic time; but what purpose would it serve? A seeker of truth — or illusion — would be none the less restless, though a shark!

CHAPTER XXVII

Teufelsdröckh[1] (1901)

INEVITABLE Paris beckoned, and resistance became more and more futile as the store of years grew less; for the world contains no other spot than Paris where education can be pursued from every side. Even more vigorously than in the twelfth century, Paris taught in the twentieth, with no other school approaching it for variety of direction and energy of mind. Of the teaching in detail, a man who knew only what accident had taught him in the nineteenth century, could know next to nothing, since science had got quite beyond his horizon, and mathematics had become the only necessary language of thought; but one could play with the toys of childhood, including Ming porcelain, salons of painting, operas and theatres, beaux-arts and Gothic architecture, theology and anarchy, in any jumble of time; or totter about with Joe Stickney,[2] talking Greek philosophy or recent poetry, or studying "Louise"[3] at the Opéra Comique, or discussing the charm of youth and the Seine[4] with Bay Lodge and his exquisite young wife. Paris remained Parisian in spite of change, mistress of herself though China fell.[5] Scores of artists — sculptors and painters, poets and dramatists, workers in gems and metals, designers in stuffs and furniture — hundreds of chemists, physicists, even philosophers, philologists, physicians, and historians — were at work, a thousand times as actively as ever before, and the mass and originality of their product would have swamped any previous age, as it very nearly swamped its own; but the effect was one of chaos, and Adams stood as helpless before it as before the chaos of New York. His single thought was to keep in front of the movement, and, if necessary, lead it to chaos, but never fall behind. Only the young have time to linger in the rear.

The amusements of youth had to be abandoned, for not even

pugilism needs more staying-power than the labors of the pale-faced student of the Latin Quarter in the haunts of Montparnasse or Montmartre, where one must feel no fatigue at two o'clock in the morning in a beer-garden even after four hours of Mounet Sully at the Théatre Français.[6] In those branches, education might be called closed. Fashion, too, could no longer teach anything worth knowing to a man who, holding open the door into the next world, regarded himself as merely looking round to take a last glance of this. The glance was more amusing than any he had known in his active life, but it was more — infinitely more — chaotic and complex.

Still something remained to be done for education beyond the chaos, and as usual the woman helped. For thirty years or thereabouts, he had been repeating that he really must go to Baireuth. Suddenly Mrs. Lodge appeared on the horizon and bade him come. He joined them, parents and children, alert and eager and appreciative as ever, at the little old town of Rothenburg-on-the-Taube, and they went on to the Baireuth festival together.

Thirty years earlier, a Baireuth festival would have made an immense stride in education, and the spirit of the master would have opened a vast new world. In 1901 the effect was altogether different from the spirit of the master. In 1876 the rococo setting of Baireuth[7] seemed the correct atmosphere for Siegfried and Brünhilde, perhaps even for Parsifal. Baireuth was out of the world, calm, contemplative, and remote. In 1901 the world had altogether changed, and Wagner had become a part of it, as familiar as Shakespeare or Bret Harte. The rococo element jarred. Even the Hudson and the Susquehanna — perhaps the Potomac itself — had often risen to drown out the gods of Walhalla, and one could hardly listen to the "Götterdämmerung" in New York, among throngs of intense young enthusiasts, without paroxysms of nervous excitement that toned down to musical philistinism at Baireuth, as though the gods were Bavarian composers. New York or Paris might be whatever one pleased — venal, sordid, vulgar — but society nursed there, in the rottenness of its decay, certain anarchistic ferments, and thought them proof of art. Perhaps they were; and at all events, Wagner was chiefly responsible for them as artistic emotion. New York knew better than Baireuth what Wagner meant, and the frivolities of Paris had more than once included the rising of the Seine[8] to drown out the Etoile or Montmartre, as well as the sorcery of ambition that casts spells of enchantment on the hero. Paris still felt a subtile flattery in the thought that the last great tragedy of gods and men would surely happen there, while no one could conceive of its happening at Baireuth, or would care if it did. Paris coquetted with catastrophe as though it were an old mistress — faced it almost gaily as she had done so often, for they were acquainted since Rome began to ravage Europe; while New York met it with a glow of fascinated horror, like an inevitable earthquake, and heard Ternina[9] announce it with conviction that made nerves quiver and thrill as they had long ceased to do under the accents of popular oratory proclaiming popular virtue. Flattery had lost its charm, but the *Fluch-motif*[10] went home.

Adams had been carried with the tide till Brünhilde had become a habit and Ternina an ally. He too had played with anarchy; though not with socialism, which, to young men who nourished artistic emotions under the dome of the Pantheon,[11] seemed hopelessly bourgeois, and lowest middle-class. Bay Lodge and Joe Stickney had given birth to the wholly new and original party of Conservative Christian Anarchists, to restore true poetry under the inspiration of the "Götterdämmerung." Such a party saw no inspiration in Baireuth, where landscape, history, and audience were — relatively — stodgy, and where the only emotion was a musical dilettantism that the master had abhorred.

Yet Baireuth still amused even a conservative Christian anarchist who cared as little as "Grane, mein Ross,"[12] whether the singers sang false, and who came only to learn what Wagner had supposed himself to mean. This end attained as pleased Frau

Wagner and the Heiliger Geist,[13] he was ready to go on; and the Senator, yearning for sterner study, pointed to a haven at Moscow. For years Adams had taught American youth never to travel without a Senator who was useful even in America at times, but indispensable in Russia where, in 1901, anarchists, even though conservative and Christian, were ill-seen.

This wing of the anarchistic party consisted rigorously of but two members, Adams and Bay Lodge. The conservative Christian anarchist, as a party, drew life from Hegel and Schopenhauer[14] rightly understood. By the necessity of their philosophical descent, each member of the fraternity denounced the other as unequal to his lofty task and inadequate to grasp it. Of course, no third member could be so much as considered, since the great principle of contradiction[15] could be expressed only by opposites; and no agreement could be conceived, because anarchy, by definition, must be chaos and collision, as in the kinetic theory of a perfect gas.[16] Doubtless this law of contradiction was itself agreement, a restriction of personal liberty inconsistent with freedom; but the "larger synthesis" admitted a limited agreement provided it were strictly confined to the end of larger contradiction. Thus the great end of all philosophy — the "larger synthesis" — was attained, but the process was arduous, and while Adams, as the older member, assumed to declare the principle, Lodge necessarily denied both the assumption and the principle in order to assure its truth.

Adams proclaimed that in the last synthesis, order and anarchy were one, but that the unity was chaos. As anarchist, conservative and Christian, he had no motive or duty but to attain the end; and, to hasten it, he was bound to accelerate progress; to concentrate energy; to accumulate power; to multiply and intensify forces; to reduce friction, increase velocity and magnify momentum, partly because this was the mechanical law of the universe as science explained it; but partly also in order to get done with the present which artists and some others complained of; and finally — and chiefly — because a rigorous philosophy required it, in order to penetrate the beyond, and satisfy man's destiny by reaching the largest synthesis in its ultimate contradiction.

Of course the untaught critic instantly objected that this scheme was neither conservative, Christian, nor anarchic, but such objection meant only that the critic should begin his education in any infant school in order to learn that anarchy which should be logical would cease to be anarchic. To the conservative Christian anarchist, the amiable doctrines of Kropotkin[17] were sentimental ideas of Russian mental inertia covered with the name of anarchy merely to disguise their innocence; and the outpourings of Elisée Reclus were ideals of the French *ouvrier,*[18] diluted with absinthe, resulting in a bourgeois' dream of order and inertia. Neither made a pretence of anarchy except as a momentary stage towards order and unity. Neither of them had formed any other conception of the universe than what they had inherited from the priestly class to which their minds obviously belonged. With them, as with the socialist, communist, or collectivist, the mind that followed nature had no relation; if anarchists needed order, they must go back to the twelfth century where their thought had enjoyed its thousand years of reign. The conservative Christian anarchist could have no associate, no object, no faith except the nature of nature itself; and his "larger synthesis" had only the fault of being so supremely true that even the highest obligation of duty could scarcely oblige Lodge to deny it in order to prove it. Only the self-evident truth that no philosophy of order — except the Church — had ever satisfied the philosopher reconciled the conservative Christian anarchist to prove his own.

Naturally these ideas were so far in advance of the age that hardly more people could understand them than understood Wagner or Hegel; for that matter, since the time of Socrates, wise men have been mostly shy of claiming to understand anything; but such refinements were Greek or German, and affected the practical

American but little. He admitted that, for the moment, the darkness was dense. He could not affirm with confidence, even to himself, that his "largest synthesis" would certainly turn out to be chaos, since he would be equally obliged to deny the chaos. The poet groped blindly for an emotion. The play of thought for thought's sake had mostly ceased. The throb of fifty or a hundred million steam horse-power, doubling every ten years, and already more despotic than all the horses that ever lived, and all the riders they ever carried, drowned rhyme and reason. No one was to blame, for all were equally servants of the power, and worked merely to increase it; but the conservative Christian anarchist saw light.

Thus the student of Hegel prepared himself for a visit to Russia in order to enlarge his "synthesis" — and much he needed it! In America all were conservative Christian anarchists; the faith was national, racial, geographic. The true American had never seen such supreme virtue in any of the innumerable shades between social anarchy and social order as to mark it for exclusively human and his own. He never had known a complete union either in Church or State or Thought, and had never seen any need for it. The freedom gave him courage to meet any contradiction, and intelligence enough to ignore it. Exactly the opposite condition had marked Russian growth. The Czar's empire was a phase of conservative Christian anarchy more interesting to history than all the complex variety of American newspapers, schools, trusts, sects, frauds, and Congressmen. These were Nature — pure and anarchic as the conservative Christian anarchist saw Nature — active, vibrating, mostly unconscious, and quickly reacting on force; but, from the first glimpse one caught from the sleeping-car window, in the early morning, of the Polish Jew at the accidental railway station, in all his weird horror,[19] to the last vision of the Russian peasant, lighting his candle and kissing his ikon before the railway Virgin in the station at St. Petersburg, all was logical, conservative, Christian and anarchic. Russia had nothing in common with any ancient or modern world that history knew; she had been the oldest source of all civilization in Europe, and had kept none for herself; neither Europe nor Asia had ever known such a phase, which seemed to fall into no line of evolution whatever, and was as wonderful to the student of Gothic architecture in the twelfth century, as to the student of the dynamo in the twentieth. Studied in the dry light of conservative Christian anarchy, Russia became luminous like the salt of radium; but with a negative luminosity as though she were a substance whose energies had been sucked out — an inert residuum — with movement of pure inertia. From the car window one seemed to float past undulations of nomad life — herders deserted by their leaders and herds — wandering waves stopped in their wanderings — waiting for their winds or warriors to return and lead them westward; tribes that had camped, like Khirgis,[20] for the season, and had lost the means of motion without acquiring the habit of permanence. They waited and suffered. As they stood they were out of place, and could never have been normal. Their country acted as a sink of energy like the Caspian Sea, and its surface kept the uniformity of ice and snow. One Russian peasant kissing an ikon on a saint's day, in the Kremlin,[21] served for a hundred million. The student had no need to study Wallace, or re-read Tolstoi or Turgeniev or Dostoievski to refresh his memory of the most poignant analysis of human inertia ever put in words; Gorki was more than enough: Kropotkin answered every purpose.[22]

The Russian people could never have changed — could they ever be changed? Could inertia of race, on such a scale, be broken up, or take new form? Even in America, on an infinitely smaller scale, the question was old and unanswered. All the so-called primitive races, and some nearer survivals, had raised doubts which persisted against the most obstinate convictions of evolution. The Senator himself shook his head, and after surveying Warsaw and Moscow to his content, went on to St. Petersburg to ask questions of Mr. de Witte and Prince Khilkoff.[23] Their conversation added new doubts; for their efforts had been immense, their expenditure enormous, and their results on the people seemed to be uncertain as yet, even to themselves. Ten or fifteen years of violent stimulus seemed resulting in nothing, for, since 1898, Russia lagged.

The tourist-student, having duly reflected, asked the Senator whether he should allow three generations, or more, to swing the Russian people into the Western movement. The Senator seemed disposed to ask for more. The student had nothing to say. For him, all opinion founded on fact must be error, because the facts can never be complete, and their relations must be always infinite. Very likely, Russia would instantly become the most brilliant constellation of human progress through all the ordered stages of good; but meanwhile one might give a value as movement of inertia to the mass, and assume a slow acceleration that would, at the end of a generation, leave the gap between east and west relatively the same.

This result reached, the Lodges thought their moral improvement required a visit to Berlin; but forty years of varied emotions had not deadened Adams's memories of Berlin, and he preferred, at any cost, to escape new ones. When the Lodges started for Germany, Adams took steamer for Sweden and landed happily, in a day or two, at Stockholm.

Until the student is fairly sure that his problem is soluble, he gains little by obstinately insisting on solving it. One might doubt whether Mr. de Witte himself, or Prince Khilkoff, or any Grand Duke, or the Emperor, knew much more about it than their neighbors; and Adams was quite sure that, even in America, he should listen with uncertain confidence to the views of any Secretary of the Treasury, or railway president, or President of the United States whom he had ever known, that should concern the America of the next generation. The mere fact that any man should dare to offer them would prove his incompetence to judge. Yet Russia was too vast a force to be treated as an object of unconcern. As inertia, if in no other way, she represented three-fourths of the human race, and her movement might be the true movement of the future, against the hasty and unsure acceleration of America. No one could yet know what would best suit humanity, and the tourist who carried his La Fontaine[24] in mind, caught himself talking as bear or as monkey according to the mirror he held before him. "Am I satisfied?" he asked:—

> "Moi? pourquoi non?
> N'ai-je pas quatre pieds aussi bien que les autres?
> Mon portrait jusqu'ici ne m'a rien reproché;
> Mais pour mon frère l'ours, on ne l'a qu'ébauché;
> Jamais, s'il me veut croire, il ne se fera peindre."[25]

Granting that his brother the bear lacked perfection in details, his own figure as monkey was not necessarily ideal or decorative, nor was he in the least sure what form it might take even in one generation. He had himself never ventured to dream of three. No man could guess what the Daimler[26] motor and X-rays would do to him; but so much was sure; the monkey and motor were terribly afraid of the bear; how much, only a man close to their foreign departments knew. As the monkey looked back across the Baltic from the safe battlements of Stockholm, Russia looked more portentous than from the Kremlin.

The image was that of the retreating ice-cap — a wall of archaic glacier, as fixed, as ancient, as eternal, as the wall of archaic ice that blocked the ocean a few hundred miles to the northward, and more likely to advance. Scandinavia had been ever at its mercy. Europe had never changed. The imaginary line that crossed the level continent from the Baltic to the Black Sea, merely extended the northern barrier-line. The Hungarians and Poles on one side still struggled against the Russian inertia of race, and retained their own energies under the same conditions that caused inertia across the frontier. Race ruled the conditions; conditions hardly affected race; and yet no one could tell the patient tourist what race was, or how it should be known. History offered a feeble and delusive smile at the sound of the word; evolutionists and ethnologists disputed its very existence; no one knew what to make of it; yet, without the clue, history was a nursery tale.

The Germans, Scandinavians, Poles and Hungarians, energetic as they were, had never held their own against the heterogeneous mass of inertia called Russia, and trembled with terror whenever Russia moved. From Stockholm one looked back on it as though it were an ice-sheet, and so had Stockholm watched it for centuries. In contrast with the dreary forests of Russia and the stern streets of St. Petersburg, Stockholm seemed a southern vision, and Sweden lured the tourist on. Through a cheerful New England landscape and bright autumn, he rambled northwards till he found himself at Trondhjem and discovered Norway. Education crowded upon him in immense masses as he triangulated these vast surfaces of history about which he had lectured and read for a life-time. When the historian fully realizes his ignorance — which sometimes happens to Americans — he becomes even more tiresome to himself than to others, because his *naïveté* is irrepressible. Adams could not get over his astonishment, though he had preached the Norse doctrine[27] all his life against the stupid and beer-swilling Saxon boors whom Freeman[28] loved, and who, to the despair of science, produced Shakespeare. Mere contact with Norway started voyages of thought, and, under their illusions, he took the mail steamer to the north, and on September 14, reached Hammerfest.

Frivolous amusement was hardly what one saw, through the equinoctial twilight, peering at the flying tourist, down the deep fiords, from dim patches of snow, where the last Laps and reindeer were watching the mail steamer thread the intricate channels outside, as their ancestors had watched the first Norse fishermen learn them in the succession of time; but it was not the Laps, or the snow, or the arctic gloom, that impressed the tourist, so much as the lights of an electro-magnetic civilization and the stupefying contrast with Russia, which more and more insisted on taking the first place in historical interest. Nowhere had the new forces

so vigorously corrected the errors of the old, or so effectively re-
dressed the balance of the ecliptic. As one approached the end—
the spot where, seventy years before,[29] a futile Carlylean Teufelsdröckh had stopped to ask futile questions of the silent infinite
— the infinite seemed to have become loquacious, not to say
familiar, chattering gossip in one's ear. An installation of electric
lighting and telephones led tourists close up to the polar ice-cap,
beyond the level of the magnetic pole; and there the newer Teufelsdröckh sat dumb with surprise, and glared at the permanent
electric lights of Hammerfest.

He had good reason — better than the Teufelsdröckh of 1830, in
his liveliest Scotch imagination,[30] ever dreamed, or mortal man had
ever told. At best, a week in these dim Northern seas, without
means of speech, within the Arctic circle, at the equinox, lent
itself to gravity if not to gloom; but only a week before, break-
fasting in the restaurant at Stockholm, his eye had caught, across
the neighboring table, a headline in a Swedish newspaper, announcing an attempt on the life of President McKinley,[31] and from
Stockholm to Trondhjem, and so up the coast to Hammerfest, day
after day the news came, telling of the President's condition, and
the doings and sayings of Hay and Roosevelt, until at last a little
journal was cried on reaching some dim haven, announcing the
President's death a few hours before. To Adams the death of
McKinley and the advent of Roosevelt were not wholly void of
personal emotion, but this was little in comparison with his depth
of wonder at hearing hourly reports from his most intimate friends,
sent to him far within the realm of night, not to please him, but to
correct the faults of the solar system.[32] The electro-dynamo-social
universe worked better than the sun.

No such strange chance had ever happened to a historian before,
and it upset for the moment his whole philosophy of conservative
anarchy. The acceleration was marvellous, and wholly in the lines
of unity. To recover his grasp of chaos, he must look back across
the gulf to Russia, and the gap seemed to have suddenly become

an abyss. Russia was infinitely distant. Yet the nightmare of the glacial ice-cap still pressed down on him from the hills, in full vision, and no one could look out on the dusky and oily sea that lapped these spectral islands without consciousness that only a day's steaming to the northward would bring him to the ice-barrier, ready at any moment to advance, which obliged tourists to stop where Laps and reindeer and Norse fishermen had stopped so long ago that memory of their very origin was lost. Adams had never before met a *ne plus ultra*,[33] and knew not what to make of it; but he felt at least the emotion of his Norwegian fishermen ancestors, doubtless numbering hundreds of thousands, jammed with their faces to the sea, the ice on the north, the ice-cap of Russian inertia pressing from behind, and the ice a trifling danger compared with the inertia. From the day they first followed the retreating ice-cap round the North Cape, down to the present moment, their problem was the same.

The new Teufelsdröckh, though considerably older than the old one, saw no clearer into past or future, but he was fully as much perplexed. From the archaic ice-barrier to the Caspian Sea, a long line of division, permanent since ice and inertia first took possession, divided his lines of force, with no relation to climate or geography or soil.

The less a tourist knows, the fewer mistakes he need make, for he will not expect himself to explain ignorance. A century ago he carried letters and sought knowledge; to-day he knows that no one knows; he needs too much and ignorance is learning. He wandered south again, and came out at Kiel, Hamburg, Bremen, and Cologne. A mere glance showed him that here was a Germany new to mankind. Hamburg was almost as American as St. Louis. In forty years, the green rusticity of Düsseldorf had taken on the sooty grime of Birmingham. The Rhine in 1900 resembled the Rhine of 1858 much as it resembled the Rhine of the Salic Franks. Cologne was a railway centre that had completed its cathedral[34] which bore an absent-minded air of a cathedral of Chicago. The thirteenth century, carefully strained-off, catalogued, and locked up, was visible to tourists as a kind of Neanderthal, cave-dwelling, curiosity. The Rhine was more modern than the Hudson, as might well be, since it produced far more coal; but all this counted for little beside the radical change in the lines of force.

In 1858[35] the whole plain of northern Europe, as well as the Danube in the south, bore evident marks of being still the prehistoric highway between Asia and the ocean. The trade-route followed the old routes of invasion, and Cologne was a resting-place between Warsaw and Flanders. Throughout northern Germany, Russia was felt even more powerfully than France. In 1901 Russia had vanished, and not even France was felt; hardly England or America. Coal alone was felt — its stamp alone pervaded the Rhine district and persisted to Picardy[36] — and the stamp was the same as that of Birmingham and Pittsburgh. The Rhine produced the same power, and the power produced the same people — the same mind — the same impulse. For a man sixty-three years old who had no hope of earning a living, these three months of education were the most arduous he ever attempted, and Russia was the most indigestible morsel he ever met; but the sum of it, viewed from Cologne, seemed reasonable. From Hammerfest to Cherbourg on one shore of the ocean — from Halifax to Norfolk on the other — one great empire was ruled by one great emperor — Coal.[37] Political and human jealousies might tear it apart or divide it, but the power and the empire were one. Unity had gained that ground. Beyond lay Russia, and there an older, perhaps a surer, power, resting on the eternal law of inertia, held its own.

As a personal matter, the relative value of the two powers became more interesting every year; for the mass of Russian inertia was moving irresistibly over China, and John Hay stood in its path. As long as de Witte ruled, Hay was safe. Should de Witte fall, Hay would totter. One could only sit down and watch the doings of Mr. de Witte and Mr. de Plehve.[38]

CHAPTER XXVIII

The Height of Knowledge (1902)

AMERICA has always taken tragedy lightly. Too busy to stop the activity of their twenty-million-horse-power society, Americans ignore tragic motives that would have overshadowed the Middle Ages; and the world learns to regard assassination as a form of hysteria, and death as neurosis, to be treated by a rest-cure. Three hideous political murders,[1] that would have fattened the Eumenides[2] with horror, have thrown scarcely a shadow on the White House.

The year 1901 was a year of tragedy that seemed to Hay to centre on himself. First came, in summer, the accidental death of his son, Del Hay.[3] Close on the tragedy of his son, followed that of his chief, "all the more hideous that we were so sure of his recovery." The world turned suddenly into a graveyard. "I have acquired the funeral habit." "Nicolay is dying. I went to see him yesterday, and he did not know me." Among the letters of condolence showered upon him was one from Clarence King at Pasadena, "heart-breaking in grace and tenderness — the old King manner"; and King himself "simply waiting till nature and the foe have done their struggle." The tragedy of King impressed him intensely: "There you have it in the face!" he said — "the best and brightest man of his generation, with talents immeasurably beyond any of his contemporaries; with industry that has often sickened me to witness it; with everything in his favor but blind luck; hounded by disaster from his cradle, with none of the joy of life to which he was entitled, dying at last, with nameless suffering, alone and uncared-for, in a California tavern. *Ça vous amuse, la vie?*"[4]

The first summons that met Adams, before he had even landed on the pier at New York, December 29, was to Clarence King's funeral, and from the funeral service he had no gayer road to travel

416

than that which led to Washington, where a revolution had occurred[5] that must in any case have made the men of his age instantly old, but which, besides hurrying to the front the generation that till then he had regarded as boys, could not fail to break the social ties that had till then held them all together.

Ça vous amuse, la vie? Honestly, the lessons of education were becoming too trite. Hay himself, probably for the first time, felt half glad that Roosevelt should want him to stay in office, if only to save himself the trouble of quitting; but to Adams all was pure loss. On that side, his education had been finished at school. His friends in power were lost, and he knew life too well to risk total wreck by trying to save them.

As far as concerned Roosevelt, the chance was hopeless. To them at sixty-three, Roosevelt at forty-three could not be taken seriously in his old character, and could not be recovered in his new one. Power when wielded by abnormal energy is the most serious of facts, and all Roosevelt's friends know that his restless and combative energy was more than abnormal. Roosevelt, more than any other man living within the range of notoriety, showed the singular primitive quality that belongs to ultimate matter — the quality that mediæval theology assigned to God[6] — he was pure act. With him wielding unmeasured power with immeasurable energy, in the White House, the relation of age to youth — of teacher to pupil — was altogether out of place; and no other was possible. Even Hay's relation[7] was a false one, while Adams's ceased of itself. History's truths are little valuable now; but human nature retains a few of its archaic, proverbial laws, and the wisest courtier that ever lived — Lucius Seneca[8] himself — must have remained in some shade of doubt what advantage he should get from the power of his friend and pupil Nero Claudius,[9] until, as a gentleman past sixty, he received Nero's filial invitation to kill himself. Seneca closed the vast circle of his knowledge by learning that a friend in power was a friend lost — a fact very much worth insisting upon — while the gray-headed moth that had fluttered through many moth-administrations and had singed his wings more or less in them all, though he now slept nine months out of the twelve, acquired an instinct of self-preservation that kept him to the north side of La Fayette Square,[10] and, after a sufficient habitude of Presidents and Senators, deterred him from hovering between them.

Those who seek education in the paths of duty are always deceived by the illusion that power in the hands of friends is an advantage to them. As far as Adams could teach experience, he was bound to warn them that he had found it an invariable disaster. Power is poison.[11] Its effect on Presidents had been always tragic, chiefly as an almost insane excitement at first, and a worse reaction afterwards; but also because no mind is so well balanced as to bear the strain of seizing unlimited force without habit or knowledge of it; and finding it disputed with him by hungry packs of wolves and hounds whose lives depend on snatching the carrion. Roosevelt enjoyed a singularly direct nature and honest intent, but he lived naturally in restless agitation that would have worn out most tempers in a month, and his first year of Presidency showed chronic excitement that made a friend tremble. The effect of unlimited power on limited mind is worth noting in Presidents because it must represent the same process in society, and the power of self-control must have limit somewhere in face of the control of the infinite.

Here, education seemed to see its first and last lesson, but this is a matter of psychology which lies far down in the depths of history and of science; it will recur in other forms. The personal lesson is different. Roosevelt was lost, but this seemed no reason why Hay and Lodge should also be lost, yet the result was mathematically certain. With Hay, it was only the steady decline of strength, and the necessary economy of force; but with Lodge[12] it was law of politics. He could not help himself, for his position as the President's friend and independent statesman at once was false, and he must be unsure in both relations.

To a student, the importance of Cabot Lodge was great — much greater than that of the usual Senator — but it hung on his position in Massachusetts rather than on his control of Executive patronage; and his standing in Massachusetts was highly insecure. Nowhere in America was society so complex or change so rapid. No doubt the Bostonian had always been noted for a certain chronic irritability—a sort of Bostonitis which, in its primitive Puritan forms, seemed due to knowing too much of his neighbors, and thinking too much of himself. Many years earlier William M. Evarts had pointed out to Adams the impossibility of uniting New England behind a New England leader. The trait led to good ends — such as admiration of Abraham Lincoln and George Washington—but the virtue was exacting; for New England standards were various, scarcely reconcilable with each other, and constantly multiplying in number, until balance between them threatened to become impossible. The old ones were quite difficult enough — State Street and the banks exacted one stamp; the old Congregational clergy another; Harvard College, poor in votes, but rich in social influence, a third; the foreign element, especially the Irish, held aloof, and seldom consented to approve anyone; the new socialist class, rapidly growing, promised to become more exclusive than the Irish. New power was disintegrating society, and setting independent centres of force to work, until money had all it could do to hold the machine together. No one could represent it faithfully as a whole.

Naturally, Adams's sympathies lay strongly with Lodge, but the task of appreciation was much more difficult in his case than in that of his chief friend and scholar, the President. As a type for study, or a standard for education, Lodge was the more interesting of the two. Roosevelts are born and never can be taught; but Lodge was a creature of teaching — Boston incarnate — the child of his local parentage; and while his ambition led him to be more, the intent, though virtuous, was — as Adams admitted in his own case — restless. An excellent talker, a voracious reader, a ready wit, an accomplished orator, with a clear mind and a powerful memory, he could never feel perfectly at ease whatever leg he stood on, but shifted, sometimes with painful strain of temper, from one sensitive muscle to another, uncertain whether to pose as an uncompromising Yankee; or a pure American; or a patriot in the still purer atmosphere of Irish, Germans, or Jews; or a scholar and historian of Harvard College. English to the last fibre of his thought — saturated with English literature, English tradition, English taste — revolted by every vice and by most virtues of Frenchmen and Germans, or any other Continental standards, but at home and happy among the vices and extravagances of Shakespeare — standing first on the social, then on the political foot; now worshipping, now banning; shocked by the wanton display of immorality, but practising the license of political usage; sometimes bitter, often genial, always intelligent — Lodge had the singular merit of interesting. The usual statesmen flocked in swarms like crows, black and monotonous. Lodge's plumage was varied, and, like his flight, harked back to race. He betrayed the consciousness that he and his people had a past, if they dared but avow it, and might have a future, if they could but divine it.

Adams, too, was Bostonian, and the Bostonian's uncertainty of attitude was as natural to him as to Lodge. Only Bostonians can understand Bostonians and thoroughly sympathize with the inconsequences of the Boston mind. His theory and practice were also at variance. He professed in theory equal distrust of English thought, and called it a huge rag-bag of bric-a-brac, sometimes precious but never sure. For him, only the Greek, the Italian or the French standards had claims to respect, and the barbarism of Shakespeare was as flagrant as to Voltaire; but his theory never affected his practice. He knew that his artistic standard was the illusion of his own mind; that English disorder approached nearer to truth, if truth existed, than French measure[13] or Italian line, or German logic; he read his Shakespeare as the Evangel of conservative Christian anarchy, neither very conservative nor very Christian, but stupendously anarchistic. He loved the atrocities of English art and society, as he loved Charles Dickens and Miss Austen,[14] not because of their example, but because of their humor. He made no scruple of defying sequence and denying consistency — but he was not a Senator.

Double standards are inspiration to men of letters, but they are apt to be fatal to politicians. Adams had no reason to care whether his standards were popular or not, and no one else cared more than he; but Roosevelt and Lodge were playing a game in which they were always liable to find the shifty sands of American opinion yield suddenly under their feet. With this game an elderly friend had long before carried acquaintance as far as he wished. There was nothing in it for him but the amusement of the pugilist or acrobat. The larger study was lost in the division of interests and the ambitions of fifth-rate men; but foreign affairs dealt only with large units, and made personal relation possible with Hay which could not be maintained with Roosevelt or Lodge. As an affair of pure education the point is worth notice from young men who are drawn into politics. The work of domestic progress is done by masses of mechanical power — steam, electric, furnace, or other — which have to be controlled by a score or two of individuals who have shown capacity to manage it. The work of internal government has become the task of controlling these men, who are socially as remote as heathen gods, alone worth knowing, but never known, and who could tell nothing of political value if one skinned them alive. Most of them have nothing to tell, but are forces as dumb as their dynamos, absorbed in the development or economy of power. They are trustees for the public, and whenever society assumes the property, it must confer on them that title; but the power will remain as before, whoever manages it, and will then control society without appeal, as it controls its stokers and pit-men. Modern politics is, at bottom, a struggle not of men but of forces. The men become every year more and more creatures of force, massed about central power-houses. The conflict is no longer between the men, but between the motors that drive the men, and the men tend to succumb to their own motive forces.

This is a moral that man strongly objects to admit, especially in mediæval pursuits like politics and poetry, nor is it worth while for a teacher to insist upon it. What he insists upon is only that, in domestic politics, everyone works for an immediate object, commonly for some private job, and invariably in a near horizon, while in foreign affairs the outlook is far ahead, over a field as wide as the world. There the merest scholar could see what he was doing. For history, international relations are the only sure standards of movement; the only foundation for a map. For this reason, Adams had always insisted that international relation was the only sure base for a chart of history.

He cared little to convince anyone of the correctness of his view, but as teacher he was bound to explain it, and as friend he found it convenient. The Secretary of State has always stood as much alone as the historian. Required to look far ahead and round him, he measures forces unknown to party managers, and has found Congress more or less hostile ever since Congress first sat. The Secretary of State exists only to recognize the existence of a world which Congress would rather ignore; of obligations which Congress repudiates whenever it can; of bargains which Congress distrusts and tries to turn to its advantage or to reject. Since the first day the Senate existed, it has always intrigued against the Secretary of State whenever the Secretary has been obliged to extend his functions beyond the appointment of Consuls in Senators' service.

This is a matter of history which anyone may approve or dispute as he will; but as education it gave new resources to an old scholar, for it made of Hay the best schoolmaster since 1865. Hay had become the most imposing figure ever known in the office. He had an influence that no other Secretary of State ever possessed, as he had a nation behind him such as history had never imagined. He needed to write no state papers; he wanted no help, and he stood far above counsel or advice; but he could instruct an attentive scholar as no other teacher in the world could do; and Adams sought only instruction — wanted only to chart the international channel for fifty years to come; to triangulate the future; to obtain his dimension, and fix the acceleration of movement in politics since the year 1200, as he was trying to fix it in philosophy and physics; in finance and force.

Hay had been so long at the head of foreign affairs that at last the stream of events favored him. With infinite effort he had achieved the astonishing diplomatic feat of inducing the Senate, with only six negative votes, to permit Great Britain to renounce, without equivalent, treaty rights which she had for fifty years defended tooth and nail.[15] This unprecedented triumph in his negotiations with the Senate enabled him to carry one step further his measures for general peace. About England the Senate could make no further effective opposition, for England was won, and Canada alone could give trouble.[16] The next difficulty was with France, and there the Senate blocked advance, but England assumed the task, and, owing to political changes in France, effected the object — a combination which, as late as 1901, had been visionary.[17] The next, and far more difficult step, was to bring Germany into the combine; while, at the end of the vista, most unmanageable of all, Russia remained to be satisfied and disarmed. This was the instinct of what might be named McKinleyism; the system of combinations, consolidations, trusts, realized at home, and realizable abroad.

With the system, a student nurtured in ideas of the eighteenth century had nothing to do, and made not the least pretence of meddling; but nothing forbade him to study, and he noticed to his astonishment that this capitalistic scheme of combining governments, like railways or furnaces, was in effect precisely the socialist scheme of Jaurès and Bebel.[18] That John Hay, of all men, should adopt a socialist policy seemed an idea more absurd than conservative Christian anarchy, but paradox had become the only orthodoxy in politics as in science. When one saw the field, one realized that Hay could not help himself, nor could Bebel. Either Germany must destroy England and France to create the next inevitable unification as a system of continent against continent — or she must pool interests. Both schemes in turn were attributed to the Kaiser;[19] one or the other he would have to choose; opinion was balanced doubtfully on their merits; but, granting both to be feasible, Hay's and McKinley's statesmanship turned on the point of persuading the Kaiser to join what might be called the Coal-power combination, rather than build up the only possible alternative, a Gun-power combination by merging Germany in Russia. Thus Bebel and Jaurès, McKinley and Hay, were partners.

The problem was pretty — even fascinating — and, to an old Civil-War private soldier in diplomacy, as rigorous as a geometrical demonstration. As the last possible lesson in life, it had all sorts of ultimate values. Unless education marches on both feet — theory and practice — it risks going astray; and Hay was probably the most accomplished master of both then living. He knew not only the forces but also the men, and he had no other thought than his policy.

Probably this was the moment of highest knowledge that a scholar could ever reach. He had under his eyes the whole educational staff of the Government at a time when the Government had just reached the heights of highest activity and influence. Since 1860, education had done its worst, under the greatest masters and at enormous expense to the world, to train these two minds to catch and comprehend every spring of international action, not to speak of personal influence; and the entire machinery of politics in several great countries had little to do but supply the last and best information. Education could be carried no further.

With its effects on Hay, Adams had nothing to do; but its effects on himself were grotesque. Never had the proportions of his ignorance looked so appalling. He seemed to know nothing —

to be groping in darkness — to be falling forever in space; and the worst depth consisted in the assurance, incredible as it seemed, that no one knew more. He had, at least, the mechanical assurance of certain values to guide him — like the relative intensities of his Coal-powers, and relative inertia of his Gun-powers — but he conceived that had he known, besides the mechanics, every relative value of persons, as well as he knew the inmost thoughts of his own Government — had the Czar and the Kaiser and the Mikado[20] turned schoolmasters, like Hay, and taught him all they knew, he would still have known nothing. They knew nothing themselves. Only by comparison of their ignorance could the student measure his own.

CHAPTER XXIX

The Abyss of Ignorance (1902)

THE years hurried past, and gave hardly time to note their work. Three or four months, though big with change, come to an end before the mind can catch up with it. Winter vanished; spring burst into flower; and again Paris opened its arms, though not for long. Mr. Cameron came over, and took the castle of Inverlochy[1] for three months, which he summoned his friends to garrison. Lochaber seldom laughs, except for its children, such as Camerons, McDonalds, Campbells[2] and other products of the mist; but in the summer of 1902 Scotland put on fewer airs of coquetry than usual. Since the terrible harvest of 1879 which one had watched sprouting on its stalks on the Shropshire hillsides, nothing had equalled the gloom. Even when the victims fled to Switzerland, they found the Lake of Geneva and the Rhine not much gayer, and Carlsruhe no more restful than Paris; until at last, in desperation, one drifted back to the Avenue of the Bois de Boulogne, and, like the Cuckoo,[3] dropped into the nest of a better citizen. Diplomacy has its uses. Reynolds Hitt,[4] transferred to Berlin, abandoned his attic to Adams, and there, for long summers to come, he hid in ignorance and silence.

Life at last managed of its own accord to settle itself into a working arrangement. After so many years of effort to find one's drift, the drift found the seeker, and slowly swept him forward and back, with a steady progress oceanwards. Such lessons as summer taught, winter tested, and one had only to watch the apparent movement of the stars in order to guess one's declination. The process is possible only for men who have exhausted auto-motion. Adams never knew why, knowing nothing of Faraday, he began to mimic Faraday's trick of seeing lines of force all about him, where he had always seen lines of will. Perhaps the effect of knowing no mathematics is to leave the mind to imagine figures — images — phantoms; one's mind is a watery mirror at best; but, once conceived, the image became rapidly simple, and the lines of force presented themselves as lines of attraction. Repulsions counted only as battle of attractions. By this path, the mind stepped into the mechanical theory of the universe before knowing it, and entered a distinct new phase of education.

This was the work of the dynamo and the Virgin of Chartres. Like his masters, since thought began, he was handicapped by the eternal mystery of Force — the sink of all science. For thousands of years in history, he found that Force had been felt as occult attraction — love of God and lust for power in a future life. After 1500, when this attraction began to decline, philosophers fell back on some *vis a tergo* — instinct of danger from behind, like Darwin's survival of the fittest; and one of the greatest minds, between Descartes and Newton — Pascal — saw the master-motor of man in *ennui*,[5] which was also scientific: "I have often said that all the troubles of man come from his not knowing how to sit still." Mere restlessness forces action. "So passes the whole of life. We combat obstacles in order to get repose, and, when got, the repose is insupportable; for we think either of the troubles we have, or of those that threaten us; and even if we felt safe on every side, *ennui* would of its own accord spring up from the depths of the heart where it is rooted by nature, and would fill the mind with its venom."[6]

"If goodness lead him not, yet weariness
May toss him to My breast."[7]

Ennui, like Natural Selection, accounted for change, but failed to account for direction of change. For that, an attractive force was essential; a force from outside; a shaping influence. Pascal and all the old philosophies called this outside force God or Gods. Caring but little for the name, and fixed only on tracing the Force, Adams had gone straight to the Virgin at Chartres, and asked her

to show him God, face to face, as she did for St. Bernard.[8] She
replied, kindly as ever, as though she were still the young mother
of to-day, with a sort of patient pity for masculine dulness: "My
dear outcast, what is it you seek? This is the Church of Christ!
If you seek him through me, you are welcome, sinner or saint;
but he and I are one. We are Love! We have little or nothing to
do with God's other energies which are infinite, and concern us the
less because our interest is only in man, and the infinite is not know-
able to man. Yet if you are troubled by your ignorance, you see
how I am surrounded by the masters of the Schools! Ask them!"

The answer sounded singularly like the usual answer of British
science which had repeated since Bacon that one must not try to
know the unknowable, though one was quite powerless to ignore
it; but the Virgin carried more conviction, for her feminine lack of
interest in all perfections except her own was honester than the
formal phrase of science; since nothing was easier than to follow her
advice, and turn to Thomas Aquinas,[9] who, unlike modern physicists, answered at once and plainly: "To me," said St. Thomas,
"Christ and the Mother are one Force — Love — simple, single,
and sufficient for all human wants; but Love is a human interest
which acts even on man so partially that you and I, as philosophers,
need expect no share in it. Therefore we turn to Christ and the
Schools who represent all other Force. We deal with Multiplicity
and call it God. After the Virgin has redeemed by her personal
Force as Love all that is redeemable in man, the Schools embrace
the rest, and give it Form, Unity, and Motive."

This chart of Force was more easily studied than any other possible scheme, for one had but to do what the Church was always
promising to do — abolish in one flash of lightning not only
man, but also the Church itself, the earth, the other planets, and
the sun, in order to clear the air; without affecting mediæval
science. The student felt warranted in doing what the Church
threatened — abolishing his solar system altogether — in order
to look at God as actual; continuous movement, universal cause,

and interchangeable force. This was pantheism, but the Schools were pantheist; at least as pantheistic as the *Energetik*[10] of the Germans; and their deity was the ultimate energy, whose thought and act were one.

Rid of man and his mind, the universe of Thomas Aquinas seemed rather more scientific than that of Haeckel or Ernst Mach.[11] Contradiction for contradiction, Attraction for attraction, Energy for energy, St. Thomas's idea of God had merits. Modern science offered not a vestige of proof, or a theory of connection between its forces, or any scheme of reconciliation between thought and mechanics; while St. Thomas at least linked together the joints of his machine. As far as a superficial student could follow, the thirteenth century supposed mind to be a mode of force directly derived from the intelligent prime motor, and the cause of all form and sequence in the universe — therefore the only proof of unity. Without thought in the unit, there could be no unity; without unity no orderly sequence or ordered society. Thought alone was Form. Mind and Unity flourished or perished together.

This education startled even a man who had dabbled in fifty educations all over the world; for, if he were obliged to insist on a Universe, he seemed driven to the Church. Modern science guaranteed no unity. The student seemed to feel himself, like all his predecessors, caught, trapped, meshed in this eternal drag-net of religion.

In practice the student escapes this dilemma in two ways: the first is that of ignoring it, as one escapes most dilemmas; the second is that the Church rejects pantheism as worse than atheism, and will have nothing to do with the pantheist at any price. In wandering through the forests of ignorance, one necessarily fell upon the famous old bear that scared children at play;[12] but, even had the animal shown more logic than its victim, one had learned from Socrates[13] to distrust, above all other traps, the trap of logic — the mirror of the mind. Yet the search for a unit of force led into catacombs of thought where hundreds of thou-

sands of educations had found their end. Generation after generation of painful and honest-minded scholars had been content to
stay in these labyrinths forever, pursuing ignorance in silence, in
company with the most famous teachers of all time.[14] Not one of
them had ever found a logical highroad of escape.

Adams cared little whether he escaped or not, but he felt clear
that he could not stop there, even to enjoy the society of Spinoza
and Thomas Aquinas. True, the Church alone had asserted unity
with any conviction, and the historian alone knew what oceans
of blood and treasure the assertion had cost; but the only honest
alternative to affirming unity was to deny it; and the denial would
require a new education. At sixty-five years old a new education
promised hardly more than the old.

Possibly the modern legislator or magistrate might no longer
know enough to treat as the Church did the man who denied unity,
unless the denial took the form of a bomb; but no teacher would
know how to explain what he thought he meant by denying unity.
Society would certainly punish the denial if ever anyone learned
enough to understand it. Philosophers, as a rule, cared little what
principles society affirmed or denied, since the philosopher commonly held that though he might sometimes be right by good
luck on some one point, no complex of individual opinions could
possibly be anything but wrong; yet, supposing society to be ignored, the philosopher was no further forward. Nihilism[15] had no
bottom. For thousands of years every philosopher had stood on
the shore of this sunless sea, diving for pearls and never finding
them. All had seen that, since they could not find bottom, they
must assume it. The Church claimed to have found it, but, since
1450,[16] motives for agreeing on some new assumption of Unity,
broader and deeper than that of the Church, had doubled in force
until even the universities and schools, like the Church and State,
seemed about to be driven into an attempt to educate, though
specially forbidden to do it.

Like most of his generation, Adams had taken the word of science that the new unit was as good as found. It would not be an intelligence — probably not even a consciousness — but it would serve. He passed sixty years waiting for it, and at the end of that time, on reviewing the ground, he was led to think that the final synthesis of science and its ultimate triumph was the kinetic theory of gases; which seemed to cover all motion in space, and to furnish the measure of time.[17] So far as he understood it, the theory asserted that any portion of space is occupied by molecules of gas, flying in right lines at velocities varying up to a mile in a second, and colliding with each other at intervals varying up to 17,750,000 times in a second. To this analysis — if one understood it right — all matter whatever was reducible, and the only difference of opinion in science regarded the doubt whether a still deeper analysis would reduce the atom of gas to pure motion.

Thus, unless one mistook the meaning of motion, which might well be, the scientific synthesis commonly called Unity was the scientific analysis commonly called Multiplicity. The two things were the same, all forms being shifting phases of motion. Granting this ocean of colliding atoms, the last hope of humanity, what happened if one dropped the sounder into the abyss — let it go — frankly gave up Unity altogether? What was Unity? Why was one to be forced to affirm it?

Here everybody flatly refused help. Science seemed content with its old phrase of "larger synthesis," which was well enough for science, but meant chaos for man. One would have been glad to stop and ask no more, but the anarchist bomb bade one go on, and the bomb is a powerful persuader. One could not stop, even to enjoy the charms of a perfect gas colliding seventeen million times in a second, much like an automobile in Paris. Science itself had been crowded so close to the edge of the abyss that its attempts to escape were as metaphysical as the leap, while an ignorant old man felt no motive for trying to escape, seeing that the only escape possible lay in the form of *vis a tergo* commonly called Death. He got out his Descartes again; dipped into his Hume and Berkeley;[18] wrestled anew with his Kant; pondered solemnly over his Hegel and Schopenhauer and Hartmann;[19] strayed gaily away with his Greeks — all merely to ask what Unity meant, and what happened when one denied it.

Apparently one never denied it. Every philosopher, whether sane or insane, naturally affirmed it. The utmost flight of anarchy seemed to have stopped with the assertion of two principles, and even these fitted into each other, like good and evil, light and darkness. Pessimism itself, black as it might be painted, had been content to turn the universe of contradictions into the human thought as one Will, and treat it as representation. Metaphysics insisted on treating the universe as one thought or treating thought as one universe; and philosophers agreed, like a kinetic gas, that the universe could be known only as motion of mind, and therefore as unity. One could know it only as oneself; it was psychology.

Of all forms of pessimism, the metaphysical form was, for a historian, the least enticing. Of all studies, the one he would rather have avoided was that of his own mind. He knew no tragedy so heartrending as introspection, and the more, because — as Mephistopheles said of Marguerite[20] — he was not the first. Nearly all the highest intelligence known to history had drowned itself in the reflection of its own thought, and the bovine survivors had rudely told the truth about it, without affecting the intelligent. One's own time had not been exempt. Even since 1870 friends by scores had fallen victims to it. Within five-and-twenty years, a new library had grown out of it.[21] Harvard College was a focus of the study; France supported hospitals for it; England published magazines of it. Nothing was easier than to take one's mind in one's hand, and ask one's psychological friends what they made of it, and the more because it mattered so little to either party, since their minds, whatever they were, had pretty nearly ceased to reflect, and let them do what they liked with the small remnant, they could scarcely do anything very new with it. All one asked was to learn what they hoped to do.

Unfortunately the pursuit of ignorance in silence had, by this time, led the weary pilgrim into such mountains of ignorance that he could no longer see any path whatever, and could not even understand a signpost. He failed to fathom the depths of the new psychology, which proved to him that, on that side as on the mathematical side, his power of thought was atrophied, if, indeed, it ever existed. Since he could not fathom the science, he could only ask the simplest of questions: Did the new psychology hold that the ψυχή [22] — soul or mind — was or was not a unit? He gathered from the books that the psychologists had, in a few cases, distinguished several personalities in the same mind, each conscious and constant, individual and exclusive. The fact seemed scarcely surprising, since it had been a habit of mind from earliest recorded time, and equally familiar to the last acquaintance who had taken a drug or caught a fever, or eaten a Welsh rarebit [23] before bed; for surely no one could follow the action of a vivid dream, and still need to be told that the actors evoked by his mind were not himself, but quite unknown to all he had ever recognized as self. The new psychology went further, and seemed convinced that it had actually split personality not only into dualism, but also into complex groups, like telephonic centres and systems, that might be isolated and called up at will, and whose physical action might be occult in the sense of strangeness to any known form of force. Dualism seemed to have become as common as binary stars. [24] Alternating personalities turned up constantly, even among one's friends. The facts seemed certain, or at least as certain as other facts; all they needed was explanation.

This was not the business of the searcher of ignorance, who felt himself in no way responsible for causes. To his mind, the compound ψυχή took at once the form of a bicycle-rider, mechanically balancing himself by inhibiting all his inferior personalities, and sure to fall into the sub-conscious chaos below, if one of his inferior personalities got on top. The only absolute truth was the sub-conscious chaos below, which everyone could feel when he sought it.

433

Whether the psychologists admitted it or not, mattered little to the student who, by the law of his profession, was engaged in studying his own mind. On him, the effect was surprising. He woke up with a shudder as though he had himself fallen off his bicycle. If his mind were really this sort of magnet, mechanically dispersing its lines of force when it went to sleep, and mechanically orienting them when it woke up — which was normal, the dispersion or orientation? The mind, like the body, kept its unity unless it happened to lose balance, but the professor of physics, who slipped on a pavement and hurt himself, knew no more than an idiot what knocked him down, though he did know — what the idiot could hardly do — that his normal condition was idiocy, or want of balance, and that his sanity was unstable artifice. His normal thought was dispersion, sleep, dream, inconsequence; the simultaneous action of different thought-centres without central control. His artificial balance was acquired habit. He was an acrobat, with a dwarf on his back, crossing a chasm on a slack-rope, and commonly breaking his neck.

By that path of newest science, one saw no unity ahead — nothing but a dissolving mind — and the historian felt himself driven back on thought as one continuous Force, without Race, Sex, School, Country, or Church. This has been always the fate of rigorous thinkers, and has always succeeded in making them famous, as it did Gibbon, Buckle, and Auguste Comte.[25] Their method made what progress the science of history knew, which was little enough, but they did at last fix the law that, if history ever meant to correct the errors she made in detail, she must agree on a scale for the whole. Every local historian might defy this law till history ended, but its necessity would be the same for man as for space or time or force, and without it the historian would always remain a child in science.

Any schoolboy could see that man as a force must be measured by motion, from a fixed point. Psychology helped here by suggesting a unit — the point of history when man held the highest idea of himself as a unit in a unified universe. Eight or ten years of study had led Adams to think he might use the century 1150–1250, expressed in Amiens Cathedral and the works of Thomas Aquinas, as the unit from which he might measure motion down to his own time, without assuming anything as true or untrue, except relation. The movement might be studied at once in philosophy and mechanics. Setting himself to the task, he began a volume which he mentally knew as "Mont-Saint-Michel and Chartres: a Study of Thirteenth-Century Unity." From that point he proposed to fix a position for himself,[26] which he could label: "The Education of Henry Adams: a Study of Twentieth-Century Multiplicity." With the help of these two points of relation, he hoped to project his lines forward and backward indefinitely, subject to correction from anyone who should know better. Thereupon, he sailed for home.

CHAPTER XXX

Vis Inertiae[1] (1903)

WASHINGTON was always amusing, but in 1900, as in 1800, its chief interest lay in its distance from New York. The movement of New York had become planetary — beyond control — while the task of Washington, in 1900 as in 1800, was to control it. The success of Washington in the past century promised ill for its success in the next.

To a student who had passed the best years of his life in pondering over the political philosophy of Jefferson, Gallatin, and Madison,[2] the problem that Roosevelt took in hand seemed alive with historical interest, but it would need at least another half-century to show its results. As yet, one could not measure the forces or their arrangement; the forces had not even aligned themselves except in foreign affairs; and there one turned to seek the channel of wisdom as naturally as though Washington did not exist. The President could do nothing effectual in foreign affairs, but at least he could see something of the field.

Hay had reached the summit of his career, and saw himself on the edge of wreck. Committed to the task of keeping China "open," he saw China about to be shut. Almost alone in the world, he represented the "open door," and could not escape being crushed by it. Yet luck had been with him in full tide. Though Sir Julian Pauncefote had died in May, 1902, after carrying out tasks that filled an ex-private secretary of 1861 with open-mouthed astonishment, Hay had been helped by the appointment of Michael Herbert[3] as his successor, who counted for double the value of an ordinary diplomat. To reduce friction is the chief use of friendship, and in politics the loss by friction is outrageous. To Herbert and his wife, the small knot of houses that seemed to give a vague unity to foreign affairs opened their doors and their hearts, for the Herberts

were already at home there; and this personal sympathy prolonged
Hay's life, for it not only eased the effort of endurance, but it also
led directly to a revolution in Germany. Down to that moment,
the Kaiser, rightly or wrongly, had counted as the ally of the Czar
in all matters relating to the East. Holleben and Cassini were
taken to be a single force in Eastern affairs, and this supposed alliance gave Hay no little anxiety and some trouble. Suddenly
Holleben, who seemed to have had no thought but to obey with
almost agonized anxiety the least hint of the Kaiser's will, received a telegram ordering him to pretext illness and come home,
which he obeyed within four-and-twenty hours. The ways of the
German Foreign Office had been always abrupt, not to say ruthless, towards its agents, and yet commonly some discontent had
been shown as excuse; but, in this case, no cause was guessed for
Holleben's disgrace except the Kaiser's wish to have a personal
representative at Washington. Breaking down all precedent, he
sent Speck von Sternburg[4] to counterbalance Herbert.

Welcome as Speck was in the same social intimacy, and valuable
as his presence was to Hay, the personal gain was trifling compared
with the political. Of Hay's official tasks, one knew no more than
any newspaper reporter did,[5] but of one's own diplomatic education
the successive steps had become strides. The scholar was studying,
not on Hay's account, but on his own. He had seen Hay, in 1898,
bring England into his combine; he had seen the steady movement
which was to bring France back into an Atlantic system; and now
he saw suddenly the dramatic swing of Germany towards the West
— the movement of all others nearest mathematical certainty.
Whether the Kaiser meant it or not, he gave the effect of meaning
to assert his independence of Russia, and to Hay this change of
front had enormous value. The least was that it seemed to isolate
Cassini, and unmask the Russian movement which became more
threatening every month as the Manchurian scheme had to be
revealed.

Of course the student saw whole continents of study opened to

him by the Kaiser's *coup d'état.* Carefully as he had tried to follow
the Kaiser's career, he had never suspected such refinement of
policy, which raised his opinion of the Kaiser's ability to the
highest point, and altogether upset the centre of statesmanship.
That Germany could be so quickly detached from separate objects
and brought into an Atlantic system seemed a paradox more paradoxical than any that one's education had yet offered, though it
had offered little but paradox. If Germany could be held there, a
century of friction would be saved. No price would be too great
for such an object; although no price could probably be wrung out
of Congress as equivalent for it. The Kaiser, by one personal act
of energy, freed Hay's hands so completely that he saw his problems simplified to Russia alone.[6]

Naturally Russia was a problem ten times as difficult. The history of Europe for two hundred years had accomplished little but
to state one or two sides of the Russian problem. One's year of
Berlin in youth, though it taught no Civil Law, had opened one's
eyes to the Russian enigma, and both German and French historians had labored over its proportions with a sort of fascinated
horror. Germany, of all countries, was most vitally concerned in
it; but even a cave-dweller in La Fayette Square, seeking only a
measure of motion since the Crusades, saw before his eyes, in the
spring of 1903, a survey of future order or anarchy that would
exhaust the power of his telescopes and defy the accuracy of his
theodolites.

The drama had become passionately interesting and grew every
day more Byzantine; for the Russian Government itself showed
clear signs of dislocation, and the orders of Lamsdorf and de Witte[7]
were reversed when applied in Manchuria. Historians and students should have no sympathies or antipathies, but Adams had
private reasons for wishing well to the Czar and his people. At
much length, in several labored chapters of history, he had told
how the personal friendliness of the Czar Alexander I, in 1810,
saved the fortunes of J. Q. Adams,[8] and opened to him the brilliant

diplomatic career that ended in the White House. Even in his own effaced existence he had reasons, not altogether trivial, for gratitude to the Czar Alexander II, whose firm neutrality had saved him some terribly anxious days and nights in 1862[9]; while he had seen enough of Russia to sympathize warmly with Prince Khilkoff's railways and de Witte's industries. The last and highest triumph of history would, to his mind, be the bringing of Russia into the Atlantic combine, and the just and fair allotment of the whole world among the regulated activities of the universe. At the rate of unification since 1840,[10] this end should be possible within another sixty years; and, in foresight of that point, Adams could already finish — provisionally — his chart of international unity; but, for the moment, the gravest doubts and ignorance covered the whole field. No one — Czar or diplomat, Kaiser or Mikado — seemed to know anything. Through individual Russians one could always see with ease, for their diplomacy never suggested depth; and perhaps Hay protected Cassini[11] for the very reason that Cassini could not disguise an emotion, and never failed to betray that, in setting the enormous bulk of Russian inertia to roll over China, he regretted infinitely that he should have to roll it over Hay too. He would almost rather have rolled it over de Witte and Lamsdorf. His political philosophy, like that of all Russians, seemed fixed in the single idea that Russia must fatally roll — must, by her irresistible inertia, crush whatever stood in her way.

For Hay and his pooling policy, inherited from McKinley, the fatalism of Russian inertia meant the failure of American intensity. When Russia rolled over a neighboring people, she absorbed their energies in her own movement of custom and race which neither Czar nor peasant could convert, or wished to convert, into any Western equivalent. In 1903 Hay saw Russia knocking away the last blocks that held back the launch of this huge mass into the China Sea. The vast force of inertia known as China was to be united with the huge bulk of Russia in a single mass which no amount of new force could henceforward deflect. Had the Russian

Government, with the sharpest sense of enlightenment, employed scores of de Wittes and Khilkoffs, and borrowed all the resources of Europe, it could not have lifted such a weight; and had no idea of trying.

These were the positions charted on the map of political unity by an insect in Washington in the spring of 1903; and they seemed to him fixed. Russia held Europe and America in her grasp, and Cassini held Hay in his. The Siberian Railway offered checkmate to all possible opposition. Japan must make the best terms she could; England must go on receding; America and Germany would look on at the avalanche. The wall of Russian inertia that barred Europe across the Baltic, would bar America across the Pacific; and Hay's policy of the open door would infallibly fail.

Thus the game seemed lost, in spite of the Kaiser's brilliant stroke, and the movement of Russia eastward must drag Germany after it by its mere mass. To the humble student, the loss of Hay's game affected only Hay; for himself, the game — not the stakes — was the chief interest; and though want of habit made him object to read his newspapers blackened [12] — since he liked to blacken them himself — he was in any case condemned to pass but a short space of time either in Siberia or in Paris, and could balance his endless columns of calculation equally in either place. The figures, not the facts, concerned his chart, and he mused deeply over his next equation. The Atlantic would have to deal with a vast continental mass of inert motion, like a glacier, which moved, and consciously moved, by mechanical gravitation alone. Russia saw herself so, and so must an American see her; he had no more to do than measure, if he could, the mass. Was volume or intensity the stronger? What and where was the *vis nova* [13] that could hold its own before this prodigious ice-cap of *vis inertiae?* What was movement of inertia, and what its laws?

Naturally a student knew nothing about mechanical laws, but he took for granted that he could learn, and went to his books to ask. He found that the force of inertia had troubled wiser men than he. The dictionary said that inertia was a property of matter, by which matter tends, when at rest, to remain so, and, when in motion, to move on in a straight line. Finding that his mind refused to imagine itself at rest or in a straight line, he was forced, as usual, to let it imagine something else; and since the question concerned the mind, and not matter, he decided from personal experience that his mind was never at rest, but moved — when normal — about something it called a motive, and never moved without motives to move it.[14] So long as these motives were habitual, and their attraction regular, the consequent result might, for convenience, be called movement of inertia, to distinguish it from movement caused by newer or higher attraction; but the greater the bulk to move, the greater must be the force to accelerate or deflect it.

This seemed simple as running water; but simplicity is the most deceitful mistress that ever betrayed man. For years the student and the professor had gone on complaining that minds were unequally inert. The inequalities amounted to contrasts. One class of minds responded only to habit; another only to novelty. Race classified thought. Class-lists classified mind. No two men thought alike, and no woman thought like a man.

Race-inertia seemed to be fairly constant, and made the chief trouble in the Russian future. History looked doubtful when asked whether race-inertia had ever been overcome without destroying the race in order to reconstruct it; but surely sex-inertia had never been overcome at all. Of all movements of inertia, maternity and reproduction are the most typical, and women's property of moving in a constant line forever is ultimate, uniting history in its only unbroken and unbreakable sequence. Whatever else stops, the woman must go on reproducing, as she did in the Siluria of *Pteraspis;* sex is a vital condition, and race only a local one. If the laws of inertia are to be sought anywhere with certainty, it is in the feminine mind. The American always ostentatiously ignored sex, and American history mentioned hardly the name of a woman,

441

while English history handled them as timidly as though they were a new and undescribed species; but if the problem of inertia summed up the difficulties of the race question, it involved that of sex far more deeply, and to Americans vitally. The task of accelerating or deflecting the movement of the American woman had interest infinitely greater than that of any race whatever, Russian or Chinese, Asiatic or African.

On this subject, as on the Senate and the banks, Adams was conscious of having been born an eighteenth-century remainder. As he grew older, he found that Early Institutions lost their interest, but that Early Women became a passion. Without understanding movement of sex, history seemed to him mere pedantry. So insistent had he become on this side of his subject that with women he talked of little else, and — because women's thought is mostly subconscious and particularly sensitive to suggestion — he tried tricks and devices to disclose it. The woman seldom knows her own thought; she is as curious to understand herself as the man to understand her, and responds far more quickly than the man to a sudden idea. Sometimes, at dinner, one might wait till talk flagged, and then, as mildly as possible, ask one's liveliest neighbor whether she could explain why the American woman was a failure. Without an instant's hesitation, she was sure to answer: "Because the American man is a failure!" She meant it.

Adams owed more to the American woman than to all the American men he ever heard of, and felt not the smallest call to defend his sex who seemed able to take care of themselves; but from the point of view of sex he felt much curiosity to know how far the woman was right, and, in pursuing this inquiry, he caught the trick of affirming that the woman was the superior. Apart from truth, he owed her at least that compliment. The habit led sometimes to perilous personalities in the sudden give-and-take of table-talk. This spring, just before sailing for Europe in May, 1903, he had a message from his sister-in-law, Mrs. Brooks Adams, to say that she and her sister, Mrs. Lodge, and the Senator were coming to dinner by way of farewell; Bay Lodge and his lovely young wife sent word to the same effect; Mrs. Roosevelt joined the party; and Michael Herbert shyly slipped down to escape the solitude of his wife's absence. The party were too intimate for reserve, and they soon fell on Adams's hobby with derision which stung him to pungent rejoinder: "The American man is a failure! You are all failures!" he said. "Has not my sister[15] here more sense than my brother Brooks? Is not Bessie[16] worth two of Bay? Would n't we all elect Mrs. Lodge Senator against Cabot? Would the President have a ghost of a chance if Mrs. Roosevelt[17] ran against him? Do you want to stop at the Embassy, on your way home, and ask which would run it best — Herbert or his wife?"[18] The men laughed a little — not much! Each probably made allowance for his own wife as an unusually superior woman. Some one afterwards remarked that these half-dozen women were not a fair average. Adams replied that the half-dozen men were above all possible average; he could not lay his hands on another half-dozen their equals.

Gay or serious, the question never failed to stir feeling. The cleverer the woman, the less she denied the failure. She was bitter at heart about it. She had failed even to hold the family together, and her children ran away like chickens with their first feathers; the family was extinct like chivalry. She had failed not only to create a new society that satisfied her, but even to hold her own in the old society of Church or State; and was left, for the most part, with no place but the theatre or streets to decorate. She might glitter with historical diamonds and sparkle with wit as brilliant as the gems, in rooms as splendid as any in Rome at its best; but she saw no one except her own sex who knew enough to be worth dazzling, or was competent to pay her intelligent homage. She might have her own way, without restraint or limit, but she knew not what to do with herself when free. Never had the world known a more capable or devoted mother, but at forty her task was over, and she was left with no stage except that of her old duties, or of Washington society where she had enjoyed for a hundred years every advantage, but had created only a medley where nine men out of ten refused her request to be civilized, and the tenth bored her.

On most subjects, one's opinions must defer to science, but on this, the opinion of a Senator or a Professor, a chairman of a State Central Committee or a Railway President, is worth less than that of any woman on Fifth Avenue. The inferiority of man on this, the most important of all social subjects, is manifest. Adams had here no occasion to deprecate scientific opinion, since no woman in the world would have paid the smallest respect to the opinions of all professors since the serpent.[19] His own object had little to do with theirs. He was studying the laws of motion, and had struck two large questions of vital importance to America — inertia of race and inertia of sex. He had seen Mr. de Witte and Prince Khilkoff turn artificial energy to the value of three thousand million dollars, more or less, upon Russian inertia, in the last twenty years, and he needed to get some idea of the effects. He had seen artificial energy to the amount of twenty or five-and-twenty million steam horse-power created in America since 1840, and as much more economized, which had been socially turned over to the American woman, she being the chief object of social expenditure, and the household the only considerable object of American extravagance. According to scientific notions of inertia and force, what ought to be the result?

In Russia, because of race and bulk, no result had yet shown itself, but in America the results were evident and undisputed. The woman had been set free — volatilized like Clerk Maxwell's perfect gas;[20] almost brought to the point of explosion, like steam. One had but to pass a week in Florida, or on any of a hundred huge ocean steamers, or walk through the Place Vendôme,[21] or join a party of Cook's tourists[22] to Jerusalem, to see that the woman had been set free; but these swarms were ephemeral like clouds of butterflies in season, blown away and lost, while the reproductive sources lay hidden. At Washington, one saw other swarms as grave gatherings of Dames or Daughters,[23] taking themselves seriously, or brides fluttering fresh pinions; but all these shifting visions, unknown before 1840, touched the true problem slightly and superficially. Behind them, in every city, town, and farmhouse, were myriads of new types—or type-writers—telephone and telegraphgirls, shop-clerks, factory-hands, running into millions on millions, and, as classes, unknown to themselves as to historians. Even the schoolmistresses were inarticulate. All these new women had been created since 1840; all were to show their meaning before 1940.

Whatever they were, they were not content, as the ephemera[24] proved; and they were hungry for illusions as ever in the fourth century of the Church; but this was probably survival, and gave no hint of the future. The problem remained — to find out whether movement of inertia, inherent in function, could take direction except in lines of inertia. This problem needed to be solved in one generation of American women, and was the most vital of all problems of force.

The American woman at her best — like most other women — exerted great charm on the man, but not the charm of a primitive type. She appeared as the result of a long series of discards, and her chief interest lay in what she had discarded. When closely watched, she seemed making a violent effort to follow the man, who had turned his mind and hand to mechanics. The typical American man had his hand on a lever and his eye on a curve in his road; his living depended on keeping up an average speed of forty miles an hour, tending always to become sixty, eighty, or a hundred, and he could not admit emotions or anxieties or subconscious distractions, more than he could admit whiskey or drugs, without breaking his neck. He could not run his machine and a woman too; he must leave her, even though his wife, to find her own way, and all the world saw her trying to find her way by imitating him.

The result was often tragic, but that was no new thing in feminine history. Tragedy had been woman's lot since Eve. Her problem had been always one of physical strength and it was as physical perfection of force that her Venus had governed nature. The woman's force had counted as inertia of rotation, and her axis of rotation had been the cradle and the family. The idea that she was weak revolted all history; it was a palæontological falsehood that even an Eocene[25] female monkey would have laughed at; but it was surely true that, if her force were to be diverted from its axis, it must find a new field, and the family must pay for it. So far as she succeeded, she must become sexless like the bees, and must leave the old energy of inertia to carry on the race.

The story was not new. For thousands of years women had rebelled. They had made a fortress of religion — had buried themselves in the cloister, in self-sacrifice, in good works — or even in bad. One's studies in the twelfth century, like one's studies in the fourth, as in Homeric[26] and archaic time, showed her always busy in the illusions of heaven or of hell — ambition, intrigue, jealousy, magic — but the American woman had no illusions or ambitions or new resources, and nothing to rebel against, except her own maternity; yet the rebels increased by millions from year to year till they blocked the path of rebellion. Even her field of good works was narrower than in the twelfth century. Socialism, communism, collectivism, philosophical anarchism, which promised paradise on earth for every male, cut off the few avenues of escape which capitalism had opened to the woman, and she saw before her only the future reserved for machine-made, collectivist females.

From the male, she could look for no help; his instinct of power was blind. The Church had known more about women than science will ever know, and the historian who studied the sources of Christianity felt sometimes convinced that the Church had been made by the woman chiefly as her protest against man. At times, the historian would have been almost willing to maintain that the man had overthrown the Church chiefly because it was feminine. After the overthrow of the Church, the woman had no refuge

446

except such as the man created for himself. She was free; she had no illusions; she was sexless; she had discarded all that the male disliked; and although she secretly regretted the discard, she knew that she could not go backward. She must, like the man, marry machinery. Already the American man sometimes felt surprise at finding himself regarded as sexless; the American woman was oftener surprised at finding herself regarded as sexual.

No honest historian can take part with — or against — the forces he has to study. To him even the extinction of the human race should be merely a fact to be grouped with other vital statistics. No doubt everyone in society discussed the subject, impelled by President Roosevelt if by nothing else, and the surface current of social opinion seemed set as strongly in one direction as the silent undercurrent of social action ran in the other; but the truth lay somewhere unconscious in the woman's breast. An elderly man, trying only to learn the law of social inertia and the limits of social divergence could not compel the Superintendent of the Census to ask every young woman whether she wanted children, and how many; he could not even require of an octogenarian Senate the passage of a law obliging every woman, married or not, to bear one baby — at the expense of the Treasury — before she was thirty years old, under penalty of solitary confinement for life; yet these were vital statistics in more senses than all that bore the name, and tended more directly to the foundation of a serious society in the future. He could draw no conclusions whatever except from the birth-rate. He could not frankly discuss the matter with the young women themselves, although they would have gladly discussed it, because Faust was helpless in the tragedy of woman. He could suggest nothing. The Marguerite[27] of the future could alone decide whether she were better off than the Marguerite of the past; whether she would rather be victim to a man, a church, or a machine.

Between these various forms of inevitable inertia — sex and race — the student of multiplicity felt inclined to admit that —

ignorance against ignorance — the Russian problem seemed to him somewhat easier of treatment than the American. Inertia of race and bulk would require an immense force to overcome it, but in time it might perhaps be partially overcome. Inertia of sex could not be overcome without extinguishing the race, yet an immense force, doubling every few years, was working irresistibly to overcome it. One gazed mute before this ocean of darkest ignorance that had already engulfed society. Few centres of great energy lived in illusion more complete or archaic than Washington with its simple-minded standards of the field and farm, its Southern and Western habits of life and manners, its assumptions of ethics and history; but even in Washington, society was uneasy enough to need no further fretting. One was almost glad to act the part of horseshoe crab in Quincy Bay, and admit that all was uniform — that nothing ever changed — and that the woman would swim about the ocean of future time, as she had swum in the past, with the gar-fish and the shark, unable to change.

CHAPTER XXXI

The Grammar of Science (1903)

O F all the travels made by man since the voyages of Dante,[1] this new exploration along the shores of Multiplicity and Complexity promised to be the longest, though as yet it had barely touched two familiar regions — race and sex. Even within these narrow seas the navigator lost his bearings and followed the winds as they blew. By chance it happened that Raphael Pumpelly helped the winds; for, being in Washington on his way to Central Asia he fell to talking with Adams about these matters, and said that Wolcott Gibbs[2] thought he got most help from a book called the "Grammar of Science," by Karl Pearson.[3] To Adams's vision, Wolcott stood on the same plane with the three or four greatest minds of his century—the more so because in his ignorance he confounded him with another great mind, his rival Willard Gibbs,[4] and the idea that a man so incomparably superior should find help anywhere filled him with wonder. He sent for the volume and read it. From the time he sailed for Europe and reached his den on the Avenue du Bois until he took his return steamer at Cherbourg on December 26, he did little but try to find out what Karl Pearson could have taught Wolcott Gibbs.

Here came in, more than ever, the fatal handicap of ignorance in mathematics. Not so much the actual tool was needed, as the right to judge the product of the tool. Ignorant as one was of the finer values of French or German, and often deceived by the intricacies of thought hidden in the muddiness of the medium, one could sometimes catch a tendency to intelligible meaning even in Kant or Hegel; but one had not the right to a suspicion of error where the tool of thought was algebra. Adams could see in such parts of the "Grammar" as he could understand, little more than an enlargement of Stallo's book already twenty years old. He never found out what it could have taught a master like Wolcott Gibbs.

Yet the book had a historical value out of all proportion to its science. No such stride had any Englishman before taken in the lines of English thought. The progress of science was measured by the success of the "Grammar," when, for twenty years past, Stallo had been deliberately ignored under the usual conspiracy of silence inevitable to all thought which demands new thought-machinery. Science needs time to reconstruct its instruments, to follow a revolution in space; a certain lag is inevitable; the most active mind cannot instantly swerve from its path; but such revolutions are portentous, and the fall or rise of half-a-dozen empires interested a student of history less than the rise of the "Grammar of Science," the more pressingly because, under the silent influence of Langley, he was prepared to expect it.

For a number of years Langley had published in his Smithsonian Reports the revolutionary papers that foretold the overthrow of nineteenth-century dogma, and among the first was the famous address of Sir William Crookes on psychical research,[5] followed by a series of papers on Roentgen and Curie, which had steadily driven the scientific lawgivers of Unity into the open; but Karl Pearson was the first to pen them up for slaughter in the schools. The phrase is not stronger than that with which the "Grammar of Science" challenged the fight: "Anything more hopelessly illogical than the statements with regard to Force and Matter current in elementary textbooks of science, it is difficult to imagine,"[6] opened Mr. Pearson, and the responsible author of the "elementary textbook," as he went on to explain, was Lord Kelvin himself. Pearson shut out of science everything which the nineteenth century had brought into it. He told his scholars that they must put up with a fraction of the universe, and a very small fraction at that — the circle reached by the senses, where sequence could be taken for granted — much as the deep-sea fish takes for granted the circle of light which he generates. "Order and reason, beauty and benevolence, are characteristics and conceptions which we find solely associated with the mind of man." The assertion, as a broad truth, left one's mind in some doubt of its bearing, for order and beauty seemed to be associated also in the mind of a crystal, if one's senses were to be admitted as judge; but the historian had no interest in the universal truth of Pearson's or Kelvin's or Newton's laws; he sought only their relative drift or direction, and Pearson went on to say that these conceptions must stop: "Into the chaos beyond sense-impressions we cannot scientifically project them." We cannot even infer them: "In the chaos behind sensations, in the 'beyond' of sense-impressions, we cannot infer necessity, order or routine, for these are concepts formed by the mind of man on this side of sense-impressions"; but we must infer chaos: "Briefly chaos is all that science can logically assert of the supersensuous." The kinetic theory of gas is an assertion of ultimate chaos. In plain words, Chaos was the law of nature; Order was the dream of man.

No one means all he says, and yet very few say all they mean, for words are slippery and thought is viscous; but since Bacon and Newton, English thought had gone on impatiently protesting that no one must try to know the unknowable at the same time that everyone went on thinking about it. The result was as chaotic as kinetic gas; but with the thought a historian had nothing to do. He sought only its direction. For himself he knew, that, in spite of all the Englishmen that ever lived, he would be forced to enter supersensual chaos if he meant to find out what became of British science — or indeed of any other science. From Pythagoras[7] to Herbert Spencer, everyone had done it, although commonly science had explored an ocean which it preferred to regard as Unity or a Universe, and called Order. Even Hegel, who taught that every notion included its own negation, used the negation only to reach a "larger synthesis," till he reached the universal which thinks itself, contradiction and all. The Church alone had constantly protested that anarchy was not order, that Satan was not God, that pantheism was worse than atheism, and that Unity[8] could not be proved as a contradiction. Karl Pearson seemed to agree with the Church, but everyone else, including Newton, Darwin and Clerk Maxwell,[9] had sailed gaily into the supersensual, calling it:—

> "One God, one Law, one Element,
> And one far-off, divine event,
> To which the whole creation moves." [10]

Suddenly, in 1900, science raised its head and denied.

Yet, perhaps, after all, the change had not been so sudden as it seemed. Real and actual, it certainly was, and every newspaper betrayed it, but sequence could scarcely be denied by one who had watched its steady approach, thinking the change far more interesting to history than the thought. When he reflected about it, he recalled that the flow of tide had shown itself at least twenty years before; that it had become marked as early as 1893;[11] and that the man of science must have been sleepy indeed who did not jump from his chair like a scared dog when, in 1898, Mme. Curie threw on his desk the metaphysical bomb she called radium.[12] There remained no hole to hide in. Even metaphysics swept back over science with the green water of the deep-sea ocean and no one could longer hope to bar out the unknowable, for the unknowable was known.

The fact was admitted that the uniformitarians of one's youth had wound about their universe a tangle of contradictions meant only for temporary support to be merged in "larger synthesis," and had waited for the larger synthesis in silence and in vain. They had refused to hear Stallo. They had betrayed little interest in Crookes. At last their universe had been wrecked by rays, and Karl Pearson undertook to cut the wreck loose with an axe, leaving science adrift on a sensual raft in the midst of a supersensual chaos. The confusion seemed, to a mere passenger, worse than that of 1600 when the astronomers upset the world;[13] it resembled rather the convulsion of 310 when the *Civitas Dei* cut itself loose from the *Civitas Romae*,[14] and the Cross took the place of the legions; but the historian accepted it all alike; he knew that his opinion was worthless; only, in this case, he found himself on the raft, personally and economically concerned in its drift.

English thought had always been chaos and multiplicity itself, in which the new step of Karl Pearson marked only a consistent progress; but German thought had affected system, unity, and abstract truth, to a point that fretted the most patient foreigner, and to Germany the voyager in strange seas of thought alone[15] might resort with confident hope of renewing his youth. Turning his back on Karl Pearson and England, he plunged into Germany, and had scarcely crossed the Rhine when he fell into libraries of new works bearing the names of Ostwald, Ernst Mach, Ernst Haeckel,[16] and others less familiar, among whom Haeckel was easiest to approach, not only because of being the oldest and clearest and steadiest spokesman of nineteenth-century mechanical convictions, but also because in 1902 he had published a vehement renewal of his faith. The volume contained only one paragraph that concerned a historian; it was that in which Haeckel sank his voice almost to a religious whisper in avowing with evident effort, that the "proper essence of substance appeared to him more and more marvellous and enigmatic as he penetrated further into the knowledge of its attributes — matter and energy — and as he learned to know their innumerable phenomena and their evolution." Since Haeckel seemed to have begun the voyage into multiplicity that Pearson had forbidden to Englishmen, he should have been a safe pilot to the point, at least, of a "proper essence of substance" in its attributes of matter and energy; but Ernst Mach seemed to go yet one step further, for he rejected matter altogether, and admitted but two processes in nature — change of place and interconversion of forms. Matter was Motion — Motion was Matter — the thing moved.

A student of history had no need to understand these scientific ideas of very great men; he sought only the relation with the ideas of their grandfathers, and their common direction towards the ideas of their grandsons. He had long ago reached, with Hegel, the limits of contradiction; and Ernst Mach scarcely added a shade of variety to the identity of opposites; but both of them seemed to be in agreement with Karl Pearson on the facts of the supersensual universe which could be known only as unknowable.

With a deep sigh of relief, the traveller turned back to France. There he felt safe. No Frenchman except Rabelais[17] and Montaigne had ever taught anarchy other than as path to order. Chaos would be unity in Paris even if child of the guillotine. To make this assurance mathematically sure, the highest scientific authority in France was a great mathematician, M. Poincaré[18] of the Institut, who published in 1902 a small volume called "La Science et l'Hypothèse," which purported to be relatively readable. Trusting to its external appearance, the traveller timidly bought it, and greedily devoured it, without understanding a single consecutive page, but catching here and there a period that startled him to the depths of his ignorance, for they seemed to show that M. Poincaré was troubled by the same historical landmarks which guided or deluded Adams himself: "[In science] we are led," said M. Poincaré, "to act as though a simple law, when other things were equal, must be more probable than a complicated law. Half a century ago one frankly confessed it, and proclaimed that nature loves simplicity. She has since given us too often the lie. To-day this tendency is no longer avowed, and only as much of it is preserved as is indispensable so that science shall not become impossible."[19]

Here at last was a fixed point beyond the chance of confusion with self-suggestion. History and mathematics agreed. Had M. Poincaré shown anarchistic tastes, his evidence would have weighed less heavily; but he seemed to be the only authority in science who felt what a historian felt so strongly — the need of unity in a universe. "Considering everything we have made some approach towards unity. We have not gone as fast as we hoped fifty years ago; we have not always taken the intended road; but definitely we have gained much ground."[20] This was the most clear and con-

vincing evidence of progress yet offered to the navigator of ignorance; but suddenly he fell on another view which seemed to him
quite irreconcilable with the first: "Doubtless if our means of investigation should become more and more penetrating, we should
discover the simple under the complex; then the complex under
the simple; then anew the simple under the complex; and so on
without ever being able to foresee the last term."[21]

A mathematical paradise of endless displacement promised eternal bliss to the mathematician, but turned the historian green
with horror. Made miserable by the thought that he knew no
mathematics, he burned to ask whether M. Poincaré knew any
history, since he began by begging the historical question altogether, and assuming that the past showed alternating phases of
simple and complex — the precise point that Adams, after fifty
years of effort, found himself forced to surrender; and then going
on to assume alternating phases for the future which, for the weary
Titan of Unity, differed in nothing essential from the kinetic
theory of a perfect gas.

Since monkeys first began to chatter in trees, neither man nor
beast had ever denied or doubted Multiplicity, Diversity, Complexity, Anarchy, Chaos. Always and everywhere the Complex had
been true and the Contradiction had been certain. Thought started
by it. Mathematics itself began by counting one — two — three;
then imagining their continuity, which M. Poincaré was still exhausting his wits to explain or defend; and this was his explanation:
"In short, the mind has the faculty of creating symbols, and it is
thus that it has constructed mathematical continuity which is
only a particular system of symbols."[22] With the same light touch,
more destructive in its artistic measure than the heaviest-handed
brutality of Englishmen or Germans, he went on to upset relative
truth itself: "How should I answer the question whether Euclidian
Geometry is true? It has no sense! . . . Euclidian Geometry is, and
will remain, the most convenient."[23]

Chaos was a primary fact even in Paris — especially in Paris —

as it was in the Book of Genesis; but every thinking being in Paris or out of it had exhausted thought in the effort to prove Unity, Continuity, Purpose, Order, Law, Truth, the Universe, God, after having begun by taking it for granted, and discovering, to their profound dismay, that some minds denied it. The direction of mind, as a single force of nature, had been constant since history began. Its own unity had created a universe the essence of which was abstract Truth; the Absolute; God! To Thomas Aquinas, the universe was still a person; to Spinoza, a substance; to Kant, Truth was the essence of the "I"; an innate conviction; a categorical imperative; to Poincaré, it was a convenience; and to Karl Pearson, a medium of exchange.[24]

The historian never stopped repeating to himself that he knew nothing about it; that he was a mere instrument of measure, a barometer, pedometer, radiometer; and that his whole share in the matter was restricted to the measurement of thought-motion as marked by the accepted thinkers. He took their facts for granted. He knew no more than a firefly about rays — or about race — or sex — or ennui — or a bar of music — or a pang of love — or a grain of musk—or of phosphorus—or conscience—or duty — or the force of Euclidian geometry — or non-Euclidian — or heat—or light—or osmosis—or electrolysis—or the magnet — or ether — or *vis inertiae* — or gravitation — or cohesion—or elasticity — or surface tension — or capillary attraction — or Brownian motion—or of some scores, or thousands, or millions of chemical attractions, repulsions or indifferences which were busy within and without him; or, in brief, of Force itself, which, he was credibly informed, bore some dozen definitions in the textbooks, mostly contradictory, and all, as he was assured, beyond his intelligence; but summed up in the dictum of the last and highest science, that Motion seems to be Matter and Matter seems to be Motion, yet "we are probably incapable of discovering" what either is. History had no need to ask what either might be; all it needed to know was the admission of ignorance; the mere fact of multiplicity baffling science. Even as to the fact, science disputed, but radium happened to radiate something that seemed to explode the scientific magazine, bringing thought, for the time, to a standstill; though, in the line of thought-movement in history, radium was merely the next position, familiar and inexplicable since Zeno and his arrow:[25] continuous from the beginning of time, and discontinuous at each successive point. History set it down on the record — pricked its position on the chart — and waited to be led, or misled, once more.

The historian must not try to know what is truth, if he values his honesty; for, if he cares for his truths, he is certain to falsify his facts. The laws of history only repeat the lines of force or thought. Yet though his will be iron, he cannot help now and then resuming his humanity or simianity in face of a fear. The motion of thought had the same value as the motion of a cannonball seen approaching the observer on a direct line through the air. One could watch its curve for five thousand years. Its first violent acceleration in historical times had ended in the catastrophe of 310.[26] The next swerve of direction occurred towards 1500.[27] Galileo and Bacon[28] gave a still newer curve to it, which altered its values; but all these changes had never altered the continuity. Only in 1900, the continuity snapped.

Vaguely conscious of the cataclysm, the world sometimes dated it from 1893, by the Roentgen rays, or from 1898, by the Curies' radium; but in 1904, Arthur Balfour announced[29] on the part of British science that the human race without exception had lived and died in a world of illusion until the last year of the century. The date was convenient, and convenience was truth.

The child born in 1900 would, then, be born into a new world which would not be a unity but a multiple. Adams tried to imagine it, and an education that would fit it. He found himself in a land where no one had ever penetrated before; where order was an accidental relation obnoxious to nature; artificial compulsion imposed on motion; against which every free energy of the universe revolted; and which, being merely occasional, resolved itself back into anarchy at last. He could not deny that the law of the new multiverse explained much that had been most obscure, especially the persistently fiendish treatment of man by man; the perpetual effort of society to establish law, and the perpetual revolt of society against the law it had established; the perpetual building up of authority by force, and the perpetual appeal to force to overthrow it; the perpetual symbolism of a higher law, and the perpetual relapse to a lower one; the perpetual victory of the principles of freedom, and their perpetual conversion into principles of power; but the staggering problem was the outlook ahead into the despotism of artificial order which nature abhorred. The physicists had a phrase for it, unintelligible to the vulgar: "All that we win is a battle — lost in advance — with the irreversible phenomena in the background of nature." [30]

All that a historian won was a vehement wish to escape. He saw his education complete, and was sorry he ever began it. As a matter of taste, he greatly preferred his eighteenth-century education when God was a father and nature a mother, and all was for the best in a scientific universe. He repudiated all share in the world as it was to be, and yet he could not detect the point where his responsibility began or ended.

As history unveiled itself in the new order, man's mind had behaved like a young pearl oyster, secreting its universe to suit its conditions until it had built up a shell of *nacre*[31] that embodied all its notions of the perfect. Man knew it was true because he made it, and he loved it for the same reason. He sacrificed millions of lives to acquire his unity, but he achieved it, and justly thought it a work of art. The woman especially did great things, creating her deities on a higher level than the male, and, in the end, compelling the man to accept the Virgin as guardian of the man's God. The man's part in his Universe was secondary, but the woman was at home there, and sacrificed herself without limit to make it habitable, when man permitted it, as sometimes happened for brief intervals of war and famine; but she could not provide protection against forces of nature. She did not think of her universe as a raft to which the limpets stuck for life in the surge of a supersensual chaos; she conceived herself and her family as the centre and flower of an ordered universe which she knew to be unity because she had made it after the image of her own fecundity; and this creation of hers was surrounded by beauties and perfections which she knew to be real because she herself had imagined them.

Even the masculine philosopher admired and loved and celebrated her triumph, and the greatest of them sang it in the noblest of his verses: —

> "Alma Venus, coeli subter labentia signa
> Quae mare navigerum, quae terras frugiferenteis
> Concelebras . . . .
> Quae quoniam rerum naturam sola gubernas,
> Nec sine te quidquam dias in luminis oras
> Exoritur, neque fit laetum neque amabile quidquam;
> Te sociam studeo!" [32]

Neither man nor woman ever wanted to quit this Eden of their own invention, and could no more have done it of their own accord than the pearl oyster could quit its shell; but although the oyster might perhaps assimilate or embalm a grain of sand forced into its aperture, it could only perish in face of the cyclonic hurricane or the volcanic upheaval of its bed. Her supersensual chaos killed her.

Such seemed the theory of history to be imposed by science on the generation born after 1900. For this theory, Adams felt himself in no way responsible. Even as historian he had made it his duty always to speak with respect of everything that had ever been thought respectable — except an occasional statesman; but he had submitted to force all his life, and he meant to accept it for the future as for the past. All his efforts had been turned only to the search for its channel. He never invented his facts; they

459

were furnished him by the only authorities he could find. As for himself, according to Helmholz,[33] Ernst Mach, and Arthur Balfour, he was henceforth to be a conscious ball of vibrating motions, traversed in every direction by infinite lines of rotation or vibration, rolling at the feet of the Virgin at Chartres or of M. Poincaré in an attic at Paris, a centre of supersensual chaos. The discovery did not distress him. A solitary man of sixty-five years or more, alone in a Gothic cathedral or a Paris apartment, need fret himself little about a few illusions more or less. He should have learned his lesson fifty years earlier; the times had long passed when a student could stop before chaos or order; he had no choice but to march with his world.

Nevertheless, he could not pretend that his mind felt flattered by this scientific outlook. Every fabulist has told how the human mind has always struggled like a frightened bird to escape the chaos which caged it; how — appearing suddenly and inexplicably out of some unknown and unimaginable void; passing half its known life in the mental chaos of sleep; victim even when awake, to its own ill-adjustment, to disease, to age, to external suggestion, to nature's compulsion; doubting its sensations, and, in the last resort, trusting only to instruments and averages — after sixty or seventy years of growing astonishment, the mind wakes to find itself looking blankly into the void of death. That it should profess itself pleased by this performance was all that the highest rules of good breeding could ask; but that it should actually be satisfied would prove that it existed only as idiocy.

Satisfied, the future generation could scarcely think itself, for even when the mind existed in a universe of its own creation, it had never been quite at ease. As far as one ventured to interpret actual science, the mind had thus far adjusted itself by an infinite series of infinitely delicate adjustments forced on it by the infinite motion of an infinite chaos of motion; dragged at one moment into the unknowable and unthinkable, then trying to scramble back within its senses and to bar the chaos out, but always assimilating bits of it, until at last, in 1900, a new avalanche of unknown forces had fallen on it, which required new mental powers to control. If this view was correct, the mind could gain nothing by flight or by fight; it must merge in its supersensual multiverse, or succumb to it.

CHAPTER XXXII

Vis Nova[1] (1903–1904)

PARIS after midsummer is a place where only the industrious poor remain, unless they can get away; but Adams knew no spot where history would be better off, and the calm of the Champs Elysées[2] was so deep that when Mr. de Witte was promoted to a powerless dignity, no one whispered that the promotion was disgrace, while one might have supposed, from the silence, that the Viceroy Alexeieff[3] had reoccupied Manchuria as a fulfilment of treaty-obligation. For once, the conspiracy of silence became crime. Never had so modern and so vital a riddle been put before Western society, but society shut its eyes. Manchuria knew every step into war; Japan had completed every preparation; Alexeieff had collected his army and fleet at Port Arthur, mounting his siege guns and laying in enormous stores, ready for the expected attack; from Yokohama to Irkutsk, the whole East was under war conditions; but Europe knew nothing. The banks would allow no disturbance; the press said not a word, and even the embassies were silent. Every anarchist in Europe buzzed excitement and began to collect in groups, but the Hotel Ritz[4] was calm, and the Grand Dukes who swarmed there professed to know directly from the Winter Palace[5] that there would be no war.

As usual, Adams felt as ignorant as the best-informed statesman, and though the sense was familiar, for once he could see that the ignorance was assumed. After nearly fifty years of experience, he could not understand how the comedy could be so well acted. Even as late as November, diplomats were gravely asking every passer-by for his opinion, and avowed none of their own except what was directly authorized at St. Petersburg. He could make nothing of it. He found himself in face of his new problem — the workings of Russian inertia — and he could conceive no way of forming an opinion how much was real and how much was comedy had he been in the Winter Palace himself. At times he doubted whether the Grand Dukes or the Czar knew, but old diplomatic training forbade him to admit such innocence.

This was the situation at Christmas when he left Paris. On January 6, 1904, he reached Washington, where the contrast of atmosphere astonished him, for he had never before seen his country think as a world-power. No doubt, Japanese diplomacy had much to do with this alertness, but the immense superiority of Japanese diplomacy should have been more evident in Europe than in America, and in any case, could not account for the total disappearance of Russian diplomacy. A government by inertia greatly disconcerted study. One was led to suspect that Cassini never heard from his Government, and that Lamsdorf knew nothing of his own department; yet no such suspicion could be admitted. Cassini resorted to transparent *blague*[6]: " Japan seemed infatuated even to the point of war! But what can the Japanese do? As usual, sit on their heels and pray to Buddha!" One of the oldest and most accomplished diplomatists in the service could never show his hand so empty as this if he held a card to play; but he never betrayed stronger resource behind. "If any Japanese succeed in entering Manchuria, they will never get out of it alive." The inertia of Cassini, who was naturally the most energetic of diplomatists, deeply interested a student of race-inertia, whose mind had lost itself in the attempt to invent scales of force.

The air of official Russia seemed most dramatic in the air of the White House, by contrast with the outspoken candor of the President. Reticence had no place there. Everyone in America saw that, whether Russia or Japan were victim, one of the decisive struggles in American history was pending, and any pretence of secrecy or indifference was absurd. Interest was acute, and curiosity intense, for no one knew what the Russian Government meant or wanted, while war had become a question of days. To an impartial student who gravely doubted whether the Czar him-self acted as a conscious force or an inert weight, the straight-forward avowals of Roosevelt had singular value as a standard of measure. By chance it happened that Adams was obliged to take the place of his brother Brooks[7] at the Diplomatic Reception im-mediately after his return home, and the part of proxy included his supping at the President's table, with Secretary Root on one side, the President opposite, and Miss Chamberlain[8] between them. Naturally the President talked and the guests listened; which seemed, to one who had just escaped from the European conspiracy of silence, like drawing a free breath after stifling. Roosevelt, as everyone knew, was always an amusing talker, and had the reputation of being indiscreet beyond any other man of great importance in the world, except the Kaiser Wilhelm and Mr. Joseph Chamberlain,[9] the father of his guest at table; and this evening he spared none. With the usual abuse of the *quos ego*,[10] common to vigorous statesmen, he said all that he thought about Russians and Japanese, as well as about Boers and British,[11] with-out restraint, in full hearing of twenty people, to the entire satis-faction of his listener; and concluded by declaring that war was imminent; that it ought to be stopped; that it could be stopped: "I could do it myself; I could stop it to-morrow!" and he went on to explain his reasons for restraint.

That he was right, and that, within another generation, his suc-cessor would do what he would have liked to do, made no shadow of doubt in the mind of his hearer, though it would have been folly when he last supped at the White House in the dynasty of President Hayes; but the listener cared less for the assertion of power, than for the vigor of view. The truth was evident enough, ordinary, even commonplace if one liked, but it was not a truth of inertia, nor was the method to be mistaken for inert.

Nor could the force of Japan be mistaken for a moment as a force of inertia, although its aggressive was taken as methodi-cally — as mathematically — as a demonstration of Euclid, and

Adams thought that as against any but Russians it would have lost its opening. Each day counted as a measure of relative energy on the historical scale, and the whole story made a Grammar of new Science quite as instructive as that of Pearson.

The forces thus launched were bound to reach some new equilibrium which would prove the problem in one sense or another, and the war had no personal value for Adams except that it gave Hay his last great triumph. He had carried on his long contest with Cassini so skillfully that no one knew enough to understand the diplomatic perfection of his work, which contained no error; but such success is complete only when it is invisible, and his victory at last was victory of judgment, not of act. He could do nothing, and the whole country would have sprung on him had he tried. Japan and England saved his "open door"[12] and fought his battle. All that remained for him was to make the peace, and Adams set his heart on getting the peace quickly in hand, for Hay's sake as well as for that of Russia. He thought then that it could be done in one campaign, for he knew that, in a military sense, the fall of Port Arthur must lead to negotiation, and everyone felt that Hay would inevitably direct it; but the race was close, and while the war grew every day in proportions, Hay's strength every day declined.

St. Gaudens came on to model his head, and Sargent[13] painted his portrait, two steps essential to immortality which he bore with a certain degree of resignation, but he grumbled when the President made him go to St. Louis to address some gathering at the Exposition; and Mrs. Hay bade Adams go with them, for whatever use he could suppose himself to serve. He professed the religion of World's Fairs, without which he held education to be a blind impossibility; and obeyed Mrs. Hay's bidding the more readily because it united his two educations in one; but theory and practice were put to equally severe test at St. Louis. Ten years had passed since he last crossed the Mississippi, and he found everything new. In this great region from Pittsburgh through

Ohio and Indiana, agriculture had made way for steam; tall chimneys reeked smoke on every horizon, and dirty suburbs filled with scrap-iron, scrap-paper and cinders, formed the setting of every town. Evidently, cleanliness was not to be the birthmark of the new American, but this matter of discards concerned the measure of force little, while the chimneys and cinders concerned it so much that Adams thought the Secretary of State should have rushed to the platform at every station to ask who were the people; for the American of the prime seemed to be extinct with the Shawnee[14] and the buffalo.

The subject grew quickly delicate. History told little about these millions of Germans and Slavs, or whatever their race-names, who had overflowed these regions as though the Rhine and the Danube had turned their floods into the Ohio. John Hay was as strange to the Mississippi River as though he had not been bred on its shores,[15] and the city of St. Louis had turned its back on the noblest work of nature, leaving it bankrupt between its own banks. The new American showed his parentage proudly; he was the child of steam and the brother of the dynamo, and already, within less than thirty years, this mass of mixed humanities, brought together by steam, was squeezed and welded into approach to shape; a product of so much mechanical power, and bearing no distinctive marks but that of its pressure. The new American, like the new European, was the servant of the power-house, as the European of the twelfth century was the servant of the Church, and the features would follow the parentage.

The St. Louis Exposition was its first creation in the twentieth century, and, for that reason, acutely interesting. One saw here a third-rate town[16] of half-a-million people without history, education, unity, or art, and with little capital — without even an element of natural interest except the river which it studiously ignored — but doing what London, Paris, or New York would have shrunk from attempting. This new social conglomerate, with no tie but its steam-power and not much of that, threw away thirty or forty million dollars on a pageant as ephemeral as a stage flat. The world had never witnessed so marvellous a phantasm; by night Arabia's crimson sands had never returned a glow half so astonishing, as one wandered among long lines of white palaces, exquisitely lighted by thousands on thousands of electric candles, soft, rich, shadowy, palpable in their sensuous depths; all in deep silence, profound solitude, listening for a voice or a foot-fall or the plash of an oar, as though the Emir Mirza[17] were displaying the beauties of this City of Brass,[18] which could show nothing half so beautiful as this illumination, with its vast, white, monumental solitude, bathed in the pure light of setting suns. One enjoyed it with iniquitous rapture, not because of exhibits but rather because of their want. Here was a paradox like the stellar universe that fitted one's mental faults. Had there been no exhibits at all, and no visitors, one would have enjoyed it only the more.

Here education found new forage. That the power was wasted, the art indifferent, the economic failure complete,[19] added just so much to the interest. The chaos of education approached a dream. One asked oneself whether this extravagance reflected the past or imaged the future; whether it was a creation of the old American or a promise of the new one. No prophet could be believed, but a pilgrim of power, without constituency to flatter, might allow himself to hope. The prospect from the Exposition was pleasant; one seemed to see almost an adequate motive for power; almost a scheme for progress. In another half-century, the people of the central valleys should have hundreds of millions to throw away more easily than in 1900 they could throw away tens; and by that time they might know what they wanted. Possibly they might even have learned how to reach it.

This was an optimist's hope, shared by few except pilgrims of World's Fairs, and frankly dropped by the multitude, for, east of the Mississippi, the St. Louis Exposition met a deliberate conspiracy of silence,[20] discouraging, beyond measure, to an optimistic dream of future strength in American expression. The party got back to Washington on May 24, and before sailing for Europe, Adams went over, one warm evening, to bid good-bye on the garden-porch of the White House. He found himself the first person who urged Mrs. Roosevelt to visit the Exposition for its beauty, and, as far as he ever knew, the last.

He left St. Louis May 22, 1904, and on Sunday, June 5, found himself again in the town of Coutances, where the people of Normandy had built, towards the year 1250, an Exposition which architects still admired and tourists visited, for it was thought singularly expressive of force as well as of grace in the Virgin.[21] On this Sunday, the Norman world was celebrating a pretty church-feast — the Fête Dieu[22] — and the streets were filled with altars to the Virgin, covered with flowers and foliage; the pavements strewn with paths of leaves and the spring handiwork of nature; the cathedral densely thronged at mass. The scene was graceful. The Virgin did not shut her costly Exposition on Sunday, or any other day, even to American senators who had shut the St. Louis Exposition to her — or for her; and a historical tramp would gladly have offered a candle, or even a candle-stick in her honor, if she would have taught him her relation with the deity of the Senators. The power of the Virgin had been plainly One, embracing all human activity; while the power of the Senate, or its deity, seemed — might one say — to be more or less ashamed of man and his work. The matter had no great interest as far as it concerned the somewhat obscure mental processes of Senators who could probably have given no clearer idea than priests of the deity they supposed themselves to honor — if that was indeed their purpose; but it interested a student of force, curious to measure its manifestations. Apparently the Virgin — or her Son — had no longer the force to build expositions that one cared to visit, but had the force to close them. The force was still real, serious, and, at St. Louis, had been anxiously measured in actual money-value.[23]

That it was actual and serious in France as in the Senate Cham-

ber at Washington, proved itself at once by forcing Adams to
buy an automobile, which was a supreme demonstration because
this was the form of force which Adams most abominated. He
had set aside the summer for study of the Virgin, not as a sentiment but as a motive power, which had left monuments widely
scattered and not easily reached. The automobile alone could
unite them in any reasonable sequence, and although the force of
the automobile, for the purposes of a commercial traveller, seemed
to have no relation whatever to the force that inspired a Gothic
cathedral, the Virgin in the twelfth century would have guided
and controlled both bag-man[24] and architect, as she controlled the
seeker of history. In his mind the problem offered itself as to
Newton; it was a matter of mutual attraction, and he knew it,
in his own case, to be a formula as precise as $s = \frac{gt^2}{2}$, if he could
but experimentally prove it.[25] Of the attraction he needed no proof
on his own account; the costs of his automobile were more than
sufficient: but as teacher he needed to speak for others than himself. For him, the Virgin was an adorable mistress, who led the
automobile and its owner where she would, to her wonderful palaces and châteaux, from Chartres to Rouen, and thence to Amiens
and Laon, and a score of others, kindly receiving, amusing, charming and dazzling her lover, as though she were Aphrodite herself,
worth all else that man ever dreamed. He never doubted her
force, since he felt it to the last fibre of his being, and could no
more dispute its mastery than he could dispute the force of gravitation of which he knew nothing but the formula. He was only
too glad to yield himself entirely, not to her charm or to any
sentimentality of religion, but to her mental and physical energy
of creation which had built up these World's Fairs of thirteenth-
century force that turned Chicago and St. Louis pale.

"Both were faiths and both are gone,"[26] said Matthew Arnold of
the Greek and Norse divinities; but the business of a student was
to ask where they had gone. The Virgin had not even altogether

gone; her fading away had been excessively slow. Her adorer had pursued her too long, too far, and into too many manifestations of her power, to admit that she had any equivalent either of quantity or kind, in the actual world, but he could still less admit her annihilation as energy.

So he went on wooing, happy in the thought that at last he had found a mistress who could see no difference in the age of her lovers. Her own age had no time-measure. For years past, incited by John La Farge, Adams had devoted his summer schooling to the study of her glass at Chartres and elsewhere, and if the automobile had one *vitesse*[27] more useful than another, it was that of a century a minute; that of passing from one century to another without break. The centuries dropped like autumn leaves in one's road, and one was not fined for running over them too fast. When the thirteenth lost breath, the fourteenth caught on, and the sixteenth ran close ahead. The hunt for the Virgin's glass opened rich preserves. Especially the sixteenth century ran riot in sensuous worship. Then the ocean of religion, which had flooded France, broke into Shelley's light dissolved in star-showers thrown,[28] which had left every remote village strewn with fragments that flashed like jewels, and were tossed into hidden clefts of peace and forgetfulness. One dared not pass a parish church in Champagne or Touraine without stopping to look for its window of fragments, where one's glass[29] discovered the Christ-child in his manger, nursed by the head of a fragmentary donkey, with a Cupid playing into its long ears from the balustrade of a Venetian palace, guarded by a legless Flemish *leibwache*,[30] standing on his head with a broken halbert; all invoked in prayer by remnants of the donors and their children that might have been drawn by Fouquet or Pinturicchio,[31] in colors as fresh and living as the day they were burned in, and with feeling that still consoled the faithful for the paradise they had paid for and lost. France abounds in sixteenth-century glass. Paris alone contains acres of it, and the neighborhood within fifty miles contains scores of churches where the student may still imagine himself three hundred years old, kneeling before the Virgin's window in the silent solitude of an empty faith, crying his culp,[32] beating his breast, confessing his historical sins, weighed down by the rubbish of sixty-six years' education, and still desperately hoping to understand.

He understood a little, though not much. The sixteenth century had a value of its own, as though the ONE had become several, and Unity had counted more than Three,[33] though the Multiple still showed modest numbers. The glass had gone back to the Roman Empire and forward to the American continent;[34] it betrayed sympathy with Montaigne and Shakespeare; but the Virgin was still supreme. At Beauvais in the Church of St. Stephen was a superb tree of Jesse, famous as the work of Engrand le Prince, about 1570 or 1580, in whose branches, among the fourteen ancestors of the Virgin, three-fourths bore features of the Kings of France, among them Francis I and Henry II, who were hardly more edifying than Kings of Israel, and at least unusual as sources of divine purity.[35] Compared with the still more famous Tree of Jesse at Chartres, dating from 1150 or thereabouts, must one declare that Engrand le Prince proved progress? and in what direction? Complexity, Multiplicity, even a step towards Anarchy, it might suggest, but what step towards perfection?

One late afternoon, at midsummer, the Virgin's pilgrim was wandering through the streets of Troyes in close and intimate conversation with Thibaut of Champagne and his highly intelligent seneschal, the Sieur de Joinville,[36] when he noticed one or two men looking at a bit of paper stuck in a window. Approaching, he read that M. de Plehve had been assassinated at St. Petersburg.[37] The mad mixture of Russia and the Crusades, of the Hippodrome[38] and the Renaissance, drove him for refuge into the fascinating Church of St. Pantaleon near by. Martyrs, murderers, Cæsars, saints and assassins — half in glass and half in telegram; chaos of time, place, morals, forces and motive — gave him vertigo. Had one sat all one's life on the steps of Ara Cœli for this?

Was assassination forever to be the last word of Progress? No one in the street had shown a sign of protest; he himself felt none; the charming Church with its delightful windows, in its exquisite absence of other tourists, took a keener expression of celestial peace than could have been given it by any contrast short of explosive murder; the conservative Christian anarchist had come to his own, but which was he — the murderer or the murdered?

The Virgin herself never looked so winning — so One — as in this scandalous failure of her Grace. To what purpose had she existed, if, after nineteen hundred years, the world was bloodier than when she was born? The stupendous failure of Christianity tortured history. The effort for Unity could not be a partial success; even alternating Unity resolved itself into meaningless motion at last. To the tired student, the idea that he must give it up seemed sheer senility. As long as he could whisper, he would go on as he had begun, bluntly refusing to meet his creator with the admission that the creation had taught him nothing except that the square of the hypothenuse of a right-angled triangle might for convenience be taken as equal to something else.[39] Every man with self-respect enough to become effective, if only as a machine, has had to account to himself for himself somehow, and to invent a formula of his own for his universe, if the standard formulas failed. There, whether finished or not, education stopped. The formula, once made, could be but verified.

The effort must begin at once, for time pressed. The old formulas had failed, and a new one had to be made, but, after all, the object was not extravagant or eccentric. One sought no absolute truth. One sought only a spool on which to wind the thread of history without breaking it. Among indefinite possible orbits, one sought the orbit which would best satisfy the observed movement of the runaway star Groombridge,[40] 1838, commonly called Henry Adams. As term of a nineteenth-century education, one sought a common factor for certain definite historical fractions.

Any schoolboy could work out the problem if he were given the right to state it in his own terms.

Therefore, when the fogs and frosts stopped his slaughter of the centuries, and shut him up again in his garret, he sat down as though he were again a boy at school to shape after his own needs the values of a Dynamic Theory of History.

CHAPTER XXXIII

A *Dynamic Theory of History (1904)*

A DYNAMIC theory, like most theories, begins by begging the question: it defines Progress as the development and economy of Forces. Further, it defines force as anything that does, or helps to do work. Man is a force; so is the sun; so is a mathematical point, though without dimensions or known existence.

Man commonly begs the question again by taking for granted that he captures the forces. A dynamic theory, assigning attractive force to opposing bodies in proportion to the law of mass, takes for granted that the forces of nature capture man. The sum of force attracts; the feeble atom or molecule called man is attracted; he suffers education or growth; he is the sum of the forces that attract him; his body and his thought are alike their product; the movement of the forces controls the progress of his mind, since he can know nothing but the motions which impinge on his senses, whose sum makes education.

For convenience as an image, the theory may liken man to a spider in its web, watching for chance prey. Forces of nature dance like flies before the net, and the spider pounces on them when it can; but it makes many fatal mistakes, though its theory of force is sound. The spider-mind acquires a faculty of memory, and, with it, a singular skill of analysis and synthesis, taking apart and putting together in different relations the meshes of its trap. Man had in the beginning no power of analysis or synthesis approaching that of the spider, or even of the honey-bee; but he had acute sensibility to the higher forces. Fire taught him secrets that no other animal could learn; running water probably taught him even more, especially in his first lessons of mechanics; the animals helped to educate him, thrusting themselves into his hands merely for the sake of their food, and carrying his burdens or supplying his clothing; the grasses and grains were academies of study. With little or no effort on his part, all these forces formed his thought, induced his action, and even shaped his figure.

Long before history began, his education was complete, for the record could not have been started until he had been taught to record. The universe that had formed him took shape in his mind as a reflection of his own unity, containing all forces except himself. Either separately, or in groups, or as a whole, these forces never ceased to act on him, enlarging his mind as they enlarged the surface foliage of a vegetable, and the mind needed only to respond, as the forests did, to these attractions. Susceptibility to the highest forces is the highest genius; selection between them is the highest science; their mass is the highest educator. Man always made, and still makes, grotesque blunders in selecting and measuring forces, taken at random from the heap, but he never made a mistake in the value he set on the whole, which he symbolized as unity and worshipped as God. To this day, his attitude towards it has never changed, though science can no longer give to force a name.

Man's function as a force of nature was to assimilate other forces as he assimilated food. He called it the love of power. He felt his own feebleness, and he sought for an ass or a camel, a bow or a sling, to widen his range of power, as he sought a fetish or a planet in the world beyond. He cared little to know its immediate use, but he could afford to throw nothing away which he could conceive to have possible value in this or any other existence. He waited for the object to teach him its use, or want of use, and the process was slow. He may have gone on for hundreds of thousands of years, waiting for Nature to tell him her secrets; and, to his rivals among the monkeys, Nature has taught no more than at their start; but certain lines of force were capable of acting on individual apes, and mechanically selecting types of race or sources of variation. The individual that responded or reacted to lines of

475

new force then was possibly the same individual that reacts on it now, and his conception of the unity seems never to have changed in spite of the increasing diversity of forces; but the theory of variation is an affair of other science than history, and matters nothing to dynamics. The individual or the race would be educated on the same lines of illusion, which, according to Arthur Balfour, had not essentially varied down to the year 1900.[1]

To the highest attractive energy, man gave the name of divine, and for its control he invented the science called Religion, a word which meant, and still means, cultivation of occult force whether in detail or mass. Unable to define Force as a unity, man symbolized it and pursued it, both in himself, and in the infinite, as philosophy and theology; the mind is itself the subtlest of all known forces, and its self-introspection necessarily created a science which had the singular value of lifting his education, at the start, to the finest, subtlest, and broadest training both in analysis and synthesis, so that, if language is a test, he must have reached his highest powers early in his history; while the mere motive remained as simple an appetite for power as the tribal greed which led him to trap an elephant. Hunger, whether for food or for the infinite, sets in motion multiplicity and infinity of thought, and the sure hope of gaining a share of infinite power in eternal life would lift most minds to effort.

He had reached this completeness five thousand years ago, and added nothing to his stock of known forces for a very long time. The mass of nature exercised on him so feeble an attraction that one can scarcely account for his apparent motion. Only a historian of very exceptional knowledge would venture to say at what date between 3000 B.C. and 1000 A.D., the momentum of Europe was greatest; but such progress as the world made consisted in economies of energy rather than in its development; it was proved in mathematics, measured by names like Archimedes, Aristarchus, Ptolemy, and Euclid;[2] or in Civil Law, measured by a number of names which Adams had begun life by failing to learn; or in coinage, which was most beautiful near its beginning, and most barbarous at its close;[3] or it was shown in roads, or the size of ships, or harbors; or by the use of metals, instruments, and writing; all of them economies of force, sometimes more forceful than the forces they helped; but the roads were still travelled by the horse, the ass, the camel, or the slave; the ships were still propelled by sails or oars; the lever, the spring, and the screw bounded the region of applied mechanics. Even the metals were old.

Much the same thing could be said of religious or supernatural forces. Down to the year 300 of the Christian era they were little changed, and in spite of Plato and the sceptics were more apparently chaotic than ever. The experience of three thousand years had educated society to feel the vastness of Nature, and the infinity of her resources of power, but even this increase of attraction had not yet caused economies in its methods of pursuit.

There the Western world stood till the year A.D. 305, when the Emperor Diocletian[4] abdicated; and there it was that Adams broke down on the steps of Ara Cœli, his path blocked by the scandalous failure of civilization at the moment it had achieved complete success. In the year 305 the empire had solved the problems of Europe more completely than they have ever been solved since. The Pax Romana, the Civil Law, and Free Trade[5] should, in four hundred years, have put Europe far in advance of the point reached by modern society in the four hundred years since 1500, when conditions were less simple.

The efforts to explain, or explain away, this scandal had been incessant, but none suited Adams unless it were the economic theory of adverse exchanges and exhaustion of minerals; but nations are not ruined beyond a certain point by adverse exchanges, and Rome had by no means exhausted her resources. On the contrary, the empire developed resources and energies quite astounding. No other four hundred years of history before A.D. 1800 knew anything like it; and although some of these developments, like the Civil Law, the roads, aqueducts, and harbors, were rather

477

economies than force, yet in northwestern Europe alone the empire had developed three energies—France, England, and Germany[6]—competent to master the world. The trouble seemed rather to be that the empire developed too much energy, and too fast.

A dynamic law requires that two masses — nature and man — must go on, reacting upon each other, without stop, as the sun and a comet react on each other, and that any appearance of stoppage is illusive. The theory seems to exact excess, rather than deficiency, of action and reaction to account for the dissolution of the Roman Empire, which should, as a problem of mechanics, have been torn to pieces by acceleration. If the student means to try the experiment of framing a dynamic law, he must assign values to the forces of attraction that caused the trouble; and in this case he has them in plain evidence. With the relentless logic that stamped Roman thought, the empire, which had established unity on earth, could not help establishing unity in heaven. It was induced by its dynamic necessities to economize the gods.

The Church has never ceased to protest against the charge that Christianity ruined the empire,[7] and, with its usual force, has pointed out that its reforms alone saved the State. Any dynamic theory gladly admits it. All it asks is to find and follow the force that attracts. The Church points out this force in the Cross, and history needs only to follow it. The empire loudly asserted its motive. Good taste forbids saying that Constantine the Great speculated as audaciously as a modern stock-broker on values of which he knew at the utmost only the volume; or that he merged all uncertain forces into a single trust, which he enormously overcapitalized, and forced on the market; but this is the substance of what Constantine himself said in his Edict of Milan in the year 313, which admitted Christianity into the Trust of State Religions. Regarded as an Act of Congress, it runs: "We have resolved to grant to Christians as well as all others the liberty to practise the religion they prefer, in order that whatever exists of divinity or celestial power may help and favor us and all who are under our government." The empire pursued power — not merely spiritual but physical — in the sense in which Constantine issued his army order the year before, at the battle of the Milvian Bridge: *In hoc signo vinces!* [8] using the Cross as a train of artillery, which, to his mind, it was. Society accepted it in the same character. Eighty years afterwards, Theodosius[9] marched against his rival Eugene with the Cross for physical champion; and Eugene raised the image of Hercules[10] to fight for the pagans; while society on both sides looked on, as though it were a boxing-match, to decide a final test of force between the divine powers. The Church was powerless to raise the ideal. What is now known as religion affected the mind of old society but little. The laity, the people, the million, almost to a man, bet on the gods as they bet on a horse.

No doubt the Church did all it could to purify the process, but society was almost wholly pagan in its point of view, and was drawn to the Cross because, in its system of physics, the Cross had absorbed all the old occult or fetish-power. The symbol represented the sum of nature — the Energy of modern science — and society believed it to be as real as X-rays; perhaps it was! The emperors used it like gunpowder in politics; the physicians used it like rays in medicine; the dying clung to it as the quintessence of force, to protect them from the forces of evil on their road to the next life.

Throughout these four centuries the empire knew that religion disturbed economy, for even the cost of heathen incense affected the exchanges; but no one could afford to buy or construct a costly and complicated machine when he could hire an occult force at trifling expense. Fetish-power was cheap and satisfactory, down to a certain point. Turgot and Auguste Comte[11] long ago fixed this stage of economy as a necessary phase of social education, and historians seem now to accept it as the only gain yet made towards scientific history. Great numbers of educated people — perhaps a majority — cling to the method still, and practise it more or less strictly; but, until quite recently, no other was known.

The only occult power at man's disposal was fetish. Against it, no mechanical force could compete except within narrow limits.

Outside of occult or fetish-power, the Roman world was incredibly poor. It knew but one productive energy resembling a modern machine — the slave. No artificial force of serious value was applied to production or transportation, and when society developed itself so rapidly in political and social lines, it had no other means of keeping its economy on the same level than to extend its slave-system and its fetish-system to the utmost.

The result might have been stated in a mathematical formula as early as the time of Archimedes, six hundred years before Rome fell. The economic needs of a violently centralizing society forced the empire to enlarge its slave-system until the slave-system consumed itself and the empire too, leaving society no resource but further enlargement of its religious system in order to compensate for the losses and horrors of the failure. For a vicious circle, its mathematical completeness approached perfection. The dynamic law of attraction and reaction needed only a Newton to fix it in algebraic form.

At last, in 410, Alaric sacked Rome, and the slave-ridden, agricultural, uncommercial Western Empire — the poorer and less Christianized half — went to pieces. Society, though terribly shocked by the horrors of Alaric's [12] storm, felt still more deeply the disappointment in its new power, the Cross, which had failed to protect its Church. The outcry against the Cross became so loud among Christians that its literary champion, Bishop Augustine of Hippo [13] — a town between Algiers and Tunis — was led to write a famous treatise in defence of the Cross, familiar still to every scholar, in which he defended feebly the mechanical value of the symbol — arguing only that pagan symbols equally failed — but insisted on its spiritual value in the *Civitas Dei* which had taken the place of the *Civitas Romae* in human interest. "Granted that we have lost all we had! Have we lost faith? Have we lost piety? Have we lost the wealth of the inner man who is rich before God? These are the wealth of Christians!" The *Civitas Dei*, in its turn, became the sum of attraction for the Western world, though it also showed the same weakness in mechanics that had wrecked the *Civitas Romae*. St. Augustine and his people perished at Hippo towards 430, leaving society in appearance dull to new attraction.

Yet the attraction remained constant. The delight of experimenting on occult force of every kind is such as to absorb all the free thought of the human race. The gods did their work; history has no quarrel with them; they led, educated, enlarged the mind; taught knowledge; betrayed ignorance; stimulated effort. So little is known about the mind — whether social, racial, sexual or heritable; whether material or spiritual; whether animal, vegetable or mineral — that history is inclined to avoid it altogether; but nothing forbids one to admit, for convenience, that it may assimilate food like the body, storing new force and growing, like a forest, with the storage. The brain has not yet revealed its mysterious mechanism of gray matter. Never has Nature offered it so violent a stimulant as when she opened to it the possibility of sharing infinite power in eternal life, and it might well need a thousand years of prolonged and intense experiment to prove the value of the motive. During these so-called Middle Ages, the Western mind reacted in many forms, on many sides, expressing its motives in modes, such as Romanesque and Gothic architecture, glass windows and mosaic walls, sculpture and poetry, war and love, which still affect some people as the noblest work of man, so that, even to-day, great masses of idle and ignorant tourists travel from far countries to look at Ravenna and San Marco, Palermo and Pisa, Assisi, Cordova, Chartres,[14] with vague notions about the force that created them, but with a certain surprise that a social mind of such singular energy and unity should still lurk in their shadows.

The tourist more rarely visits Constantinople or studies the architecture of Sancta Sofia,[15] but when he does, he is distinctly conscious of forces not quite the same. Justinian has not the simplicity of Charlemagne.[16] The Eastern Empire showed an activity and variety of forces that classical Europe had never possessed. The navy of Nicephoras Phocas[17] in the tenth century would have annihilated in half an hour any navy that Carthage or Athens or Rome ever set afloat. The dynamic scheme began by asserting rather recklessly that between the Pyramids (B.C. 3000), and the Cross (A.D. 300), no new force affected Western progress, and antiquarians may easily dispute the fact; but in any case the motive influence, old or new, which raised both Pyramids and Cross was the same attraction of power in a future life that raised the dome of Sancta Sofia and the Cathedral at Amiens, however much it was altered, enlarged, or removed to distance in space. Therefore, no single event has more puzzled historians than the sudden, unexplained appearance of at least two new natural forces[18] of the highest educational value in mechanics, for the first time within record of history. Literally, these two forces seemed to drop from the sky at the precise moment when the Cross on one side and the Crescent[19] on the other, proclaimed the complete triumph of the *Civitas Dei*.[20] Had the Manichean doctrine[21] of Good and Evil as rival deities been orthodox, it would alone have accounted for this simultaneous victory of hostile powers.

Of the compass, as a step towards demonstration of the dynamic law, one may confidently say that it proved, better than any other force, the widening scope of the mind, since it widened immensely the range of contact between nature and thought. The compass educated. This must prove itself as needing no proof.

Of Greek fire and gunpowder, the same thing cannot certainly be said, for they have the air of accidents due to the attraction of religious motives. They belong to the spiritual world; or to the doubtful ground of Magic which lay between Good and Evil. They were chemical forces, mostly explosives, which acted and still act as the most violent educators ever known to man, but they were justly feared as diabolic, and whatever insolence man may have risked towards the milder teachers of his infancy, he was an abject pupil towards explosives. The Sieur de Joinville left a record of the energy with which the relatively harmless Greek fire educated and enlarged the French mind in a single night in the year 1249, when the crusaders were trying to advance on Cairo. The good king St. Louis and all his staff dropped on their knees at every fiery flame that flew by, praying — "God have pity on us!" and never had man more reason to call on his gods than they, for the battle of religion between Christian and Saracen was trifling compared with that of education between gunpowder and the Cross.

The fiction that society educated itself, or aimed at a conscious purpose, was upset by the compass and gunpowder which dragged and drove Europe at will through frightful bogs of learning. At first, the apparent lag for want of volume in the new energies lasted one or two centuries, which closed the great epochs of emotion by the Gothic cathedrals and scholastic theology. The moment had Greek beauty and more than Greek unity, but it was brief; and for another century or two, Western society seemed to float in space without apparent motion. Yet the attractive mass of nature's energy continued to attract, and education became more rapid than ever before. Society began to resist, but the individual showed greater and greater insistence, without realizing what he was doing. When the Crescent drove the Cross in ignominy from Constantinople in 1453, Gutenberg and Fust[22] were printing their first Bible at Mainz under the impression that they were helping the Cross. When Columbus discovered the West Indies in 1492, the Church looked on it as a victory of the Cross. When Luther and Calvin[23] upset Europe half a century later, they were trying, like St. Augustine, to substitute the *Civitas Dei* for the *Civitas Romae*. When the Puritans set out for New England in 1620, they too were looking to found a *Civitas Dei* in State Street;[24] and when Bunyan[25] made his Pilgrimage in 1678, he repeated St. Jerome.[26] Even when, after centuries of license, the Church reformed its discipline, and, to prove it, burned Giordano Bruno[27] in 1600, besides condemning Galileo in 1630 — as science goes on repeating to us every day — it condemned anarchists, not atheists. None of the astronomers were irreligious men; all of them made a point of magnifying God through his works; a form of science which did their religion no credit. Neither Galileo nor Kepler, neither Spinoza nor Descartes, neither Leibnitz[28] nor Newton, any more than Constantine the Great — if so much — doubted Unity. The utmost range of their heresies reached only its personality.

This persistence of thought-inertia is the leading idea of modern history. Except as reflected in himself, man has no reason for assuming unity in the universe, or an ultimate substance, or a prime-motor. The *a priori* insistence on this unity ended by fatiguing the more active — or reactive — minds; and Lord Bacon[29] tried to stop it. He urged society to lay aside the idea of evolving the universe from a thought, and to try evolving thought from the universe. The mind should observe and register forces — take them apart and put them together — without assuming unity at all. "Nature, to be commanded, must be obeyed." "The imagination must be given not wings but weights."[30] As Galileo reversed the action of earth and sun, Bacon reversed the relation of thought to force. The mind was thenceforth to follow the movement of matter, and unity must be left to shift for itself.

The revolution in attitude seemed voluntary, but in fact was as mechanical as the fall of a feather. Man created nothing. After 1500, the speed of progress so rapidly surpassed man's gait as to alarm everyone, as though it were the acceleration of a falling body which the dynamic theory takes it to be. Lord Bacon was as much astonished by it as the Church was, and with reason. Suddenly society felt itself dragged into situations altogether new and anarchic — situations which it could not affect, but which painfully affected it. Instinct taught it that the universe in its thought must be in danger when its reflection lost itself in space. The danger was all the greater because men of science covered it with "larger synthesis,"[31] and poets called the undevout astronomer mad. Society knew better. Yet the telescope held it rigidly standing on its head; the microscope revealed a universe that defied the senses; gunpowder killed whole races that lagged behind; the compass coerced the most imbruted mariner to act on the impossible idea that the earth was round; the press drenched Europe with anarchism. Europe saw itself, violently resisting, wrenched into false positions, drawn along new lines as a fish that is caught on a hook; but unable to understand by what force it was controlled. The resistance was often bloody, sometimes humorous, always constant. Its contortions in the eighteenth century are best studied in the wit of Voltaire,[32] but all history and all philosophy from Montaigne and Pascal to Schopenhauer and Nietzsche deal with nothing else; and still, throughout it all, the Baconian law held good; thought did not evolve nature, but nature evolved thought. Not one considerable man of science dared face the stream of thought; and the whole number of those who acted, like Franklin, as electric conductors of the new forces from nature to man, down to the year 1800, did not exceed a few score, confined to a few towns in western Europe. Asia refused to be touched by the stream, and America, except for Franklin, stood outside.

Very slowly the accretion of these new forces, chemical and mechanical, grew in volume until they acquired sufficient mass to take the place of the old religious science, substituting their attraction for the attractions of the *Civitas Dei*, but the process remained the same. Nature, not mind, did the work that the sun does on the planets. Man depended more and more absolutely on forces other than his own, and on instruments which superseded his senses. Bacon foretold it: "Neither the naked hand nor the understanding, left to itself, can effect much. It is by instruments and helps that the work is done."[33] Once done, the mind resumed its illusion, and society forgot its impotence; but no one better than Bacon knew its tricks, and for his true followers science always meant self-restraint, obedience, sensitiveness to impulse from without. "Non fingendum aut excogitandum sed inveniendum quid Natura faciat aut ferat." [34]

The success of this method staggers belief, and even to-day can be treated by history only as a miracle of growth, like the sports of nature. Evidently a new variety of mind had appeared. Certain men merely held out their hands — like Newton, watched an apple; like Franklin, flew a kite; like Watt, played with a tea-kettle [35] — and great forces of nature stuck to them as though she were playing ball. Governments did almost nothing but resist. Even gunpowder and ordnance, the great weapon of government, showed little development between 1400 and 1800. Society was hostile or indifferent, as Priestley and Jenner, and even Fulton, [36] with reason complained in the most advanced societies in the world, while its resistance became acute wherever the Church held control; until all mankind seemed to draw itself out in a long series of groups, dragged on by an attractive power in advance, which even the leaders obeyed without understanding, as the planets obeyed gravity, or the trees obeyed heat and light.

The influx of new force was nearly spontaneous. The reaction of mind on the mass of nature seemed not greater than that of a comet on the sun; and had the spontaneous influx of force stopped in Europe, society must have stood still, or gone backward, as in Asia or Africa. Then only economies of process would have counted as new force, and society would have been better pleased; for the idea that new force must be in itself a good is only an animal or vegetable instinct. As Nature developed her hidden energies, they tended to become destructive. Thought itself became tortured, suffering reluctantly, impatiently, painfully, the coercion of new method. Easy thought had always been movement of inertia, and mostly mere sentiment; but even the processes of mathematics measured feebly the needs of force.

The stupendous acceleration after 1800 ended in 1900 with the appearance of the new class of supersensual forces, before which the man of science stood at first as bewildered and helpless as, in the fourth century, a priest of Isis[37] before the Cross of Christ.

This, then, or something like this, would be a dynamic formula of history. Any schoolboy knows enough to object at once that it is the oldest and most universal of all theories. Church and State, theology and philosophy, have always preached it, differing only in the allotment of energy between nature and man. Whether the attractive energy has been called God or Nature, the mechanism has been always the same, and history is not obliged to decide whether the Ultimate tends to a purpose or not, or whether ultimate energy is one or many. Everyone admits that the will is a free force, habitually decided by motives. No one denies that motives exist adequate to decide the will; even though it may not always be conscious of them. Science has proved that forces, sensible and occult, physical and metaphysical, simple and complex, surround, traverse, vibrate, rotate, repel, attract, without stop; that man's senses are conscious of few, and only in a partial degree; but that, from the beginning of organic existence, his consciousness has been induced, expanded, trained in the lines of his sensitiveness; and that the rise of his faculties from a lower power to a higher, or from a narrower to a wider field, may be due to the function of assimilating and storing outside force or forces. There is nothing unscientific in the idea that, beyond the lines of force felt by the senses, the universe may be — as it has always been — either a supersensuous chaos or a divine unity, which irresistibly attracts, and is either life or death to penetrate. Thus far, religion, philosophy, and science seem to go hand in hand. The schools begin their vital battle only there. In the earlier stages of progress, the forces to be assimilated were simple and easy to absorb, but, as the mind of man enlarged its range, it enlarged the field of complexity, and must continue to do so, even into chaos, until the reservoirs of sensuous or supersensuous energies are exhausted, or cease to affect him, or until he succumbs to their excess.

For past history, this way of grouping its sequences may answer for a chart of relations, although any serious student would need to invent another, to compare or correct its errors; but past history is only a value of relation to the future, and this value is wholly one of convenience, which can be tested only by experiment. Any law of movement must include, to make it a convenience, some mechanical formula of acceleration.

CHAPTER XXXIV

A *Law of Acceleration (1904)*

IMAGES are not arguments, rarely even lead to proof, but the mind craves them, and, of late more than ever, the keenest experimenters find twenty images better than one, especially if contradictory; since the human mind has already learned to deal in contradictions.

The image needed here is that of a new centre, or preponderating mass, artificially introduced on earth in the midst of a system of attractive forces that previously made their own equilibrium, and constantly induced to accelerate its motion till it shall establish a new equilibrium. A dynamic theory would begin by assuming that all history, terrestrial or cosmic, mechanical or intellectual, would be reducible to this formula if we knew the facts.

For convenience, the most familiar image should come first; and this is probably that of the comet, or meteoric streams, like the Leonids and Perseids,[1] a complex of minute mechanical agencies, reacting within and without, and guided by the sum of forces attracting or deflecting it. Nothing forbids one to assume that the man-meteorite might grow, as an acorn does, absorbing light, heat, electricity — or thought; for, in recent times, such transference of energy has become a familiar idea; but the simplest figure, at first, is that of a perfect comet — say that of 1843[2] — which drops from space, in a straight line, at the regular acceleration of speed, directly into the sun, and after wheeling sharply about it, in heat that ought to dissipate any known substance, turns back unharmed, in defiance of law, by the path on which it came. The mind, by analogy, may figure as such a comet, the better because it also defies law.

Motion is the ultimate object of science, and measures of motion are many; but with thought as with matter, the true measure is mass in its astronomic sense — the sum or difference of attractive forces. Science has quite enough trouble in measuring its material motions without volunteering help to the historian, but the historian needs not much help to measure some kinds of social movement; and especially in the nineteenth century, society by common accord agreed in measuring its progress by the coal-output. The ratio of increase in the volume of coal-power may serve as dynamometer.

The coal-output of the world, speaking roughly, doubled every ten years between 1840 and 1900, in the form of utilized power, for the ton of coal yielded three or four times as much power in 1900 as in 1840. Rapid as this rate of acceleration in volume seems, it may be tested in a thousand ways without greatly reducing it. Perhaps the ocean steamer is nearest unity and easiest to measure, for anyone might hire, in 1905, for a small sum of money, the use of 30,000 steam-horse-power^3 to cross the ocean, and by halving this figure every ten years, he got back to 234 horse-power for 1835, which was accuracy enough for his purposes. In truth, his chief trouble came not from the ratio in volume of heat, but from the intensity, since he could get no basis for a ratio there. All ages of history have known high intensities, like the iron-furnace, the burning-glass, the blow-pipe; but no society has ever used high intensities on any large scale till now, nor can a mere bystander decide what range of temperature is now in common use. Loosely guessing that science controls habitually the whole range from absolute zero to 3000° Centigrade, one might assume, for convenience, that the ten-year ratio for volume could be used temporarily for intensity; and still there remained a ratio to be guessed for other forces than heat. Since 1800 scores of new forces had been discovered; old forces had been raised to higher powers, as could be measured in the navy-gun; great regions of chemistry had been opened up, and connected with other regions of physics. Within ten years a new universe of force had been revealed in radiation. Complexity had extended itself on immense horizons, and arithmetical ratios were useless for any attempt at accuracy. The force evolved seemed more like explosion than gravitation, and followed closely the curve of steam[4]; but, at all events, the ten-year ratio seemed carefully conservative. Unless the calculator was prepared to be instantly overwhelmed by physical force and mental complexity, he must stop there.

Thus, taking the year 1900 as the starting point for carrying back the series, nothing was easier than to assume a ten-year period of retardation as far back as 1820, but beyond that point the statistician failed, and only the mathematician could help. Laplace[5] would have found it child's-play to fix a ratio of progression in mathematical science between Descartes, Leibnitz, Newton, and himself. Watt could have given in pounds the increase of power between Newcomen's[6] engines and his own. Volta[7] and Benjamin Franklin would have stated their progress as absolute creation of power. Dalton[8] could have measured minutely his advance on Boerhaave.[9] Napoleon I must have had a distinct notion of his own numerical relation to Louis XIV.[10] No one in 1789 doubted the progress of force, least of all those who were to lose their heads by it.

Pending agreement between these authorities, theory may assume what it likes — say a fifty, or even a five-and-twenty-year period of reduplication for the eighteenth century, for the period matters little until the acceleration itself is admitted. The subject is even more amusing in the seventeenth than in the eighteenth century, because Galileo and Kepler, Descartes, Huygens,[11] and Isaac Newton took vast pains to fix the laws of acceleration for moving bodies, while Lord Bacon and William Harvey[12] were content with showing experimentally the fact of acceleration in knowledge; but from their combined results a historian might be tempted to maintain a similar rate of movement back to 1600, subject to correction from the historians of mathematics.

The mathematicians might carry their calculations back as far as the fourteenth century when algebra seems to have become for the first time the standard measure of mechanical progress in western Europe; for not only Copernicus and Tycho Brahe,[13] but even artists like Leonardo,[14] Michael Angelo, and Albert Dürer[15] worked by mathematical processes, and their testimony would probably give results more exact than that of Montaigne or Shakespeare; but, to save trouble, one might tentatively carry back the same ratio of acceleration, or retardation, to the year 1400, with the help of Columbus and Gutenberg, so taking a uniform rate during the whole four centuries (1400–1800), and leaving to statisticians the task of correcting it.

Or better, one might, for convenience, use the formula of squares to serve for a law of mind. Any other formula would do as well, either of chemical explosion, or electrolysis, or vegetable growth, or of expansion or contraction in innumerable forms; but this happens to be simple and convenient. Its force increases in the direct ratio of its squares. As the human meteoroid approached the sun or centre of attractive force, the attraction of one century squared itself to give the measure of attraction in the next.

Behind the year 1400, the process certainly went on, but the progress became so slight as to be hardly measurable. What was gained in the east or elsewhere, cannot be known; but forces, called loosely Greek fire and gunpowder, came into use in the west in the thirteenth century, as well as instruments like the compass, the blow-pipe, clocks and spectacles, and materials like paper; Arabic notation and algebra were introduced, while metaphysics and theology acted as violent stimulants to mind. An architect might detect a sequence between the Church of St. Peter's at Rome, the Amiens Cathedral, the Duomo at Pisa, San Marco at Venice, Sancta Sofia at Constantinople and the churches at Ravenna. All the historian dares affirm is that a sequence is manifestly there, and he has a right to carry back his ratio, to represent the fact, without assuming its numerical correctness. On the human mind as a moving body, the break in acceleration in the Middle Ages is only apparent; the attraction worked through shifting forms of force, as the sun works by light or heat, electricity, gravitation, or what not, on different organs with different sensibilities, but with invariable law.

The science of prehistoric man has no value except to prove that the law went back into indefinite antiquity. A stone arrowhead is as convincing as a steam-engine. The values were as clear a hundred thousand years ago as now, and extended equally over the whole world. The motion at last became infinitely slight, but[16] cannot be proved to have stopped. The motion of Newton's comet at aphelion may be equally slight. To evolutionists may be left the processes of evolution; to historians the single interest is the law of reaction between force and force — between mind and nature — the law of progress.

The great division of history into phases by Turgot and Comte first affirmed this law in its outlines by asserting the unity of progress, for a mere phase interrupts no growth, and nature shows innumerable such phases. The development of coal-power in the nineteenth century furnished the first means of assigning closer values to the elements; and the appearance of supersensual forces towards 1900 made this calculation a pressing necessity; since the next step became infinitely serious.

A law of acceleration, definite and constant as any law of mechanics, cannot be supposed to relax its energy to suit the convenience of man. No one is likely to suggest a theory that man's convenience has been consulted by Nature at any time, or that Nature has consulted the convenience of any of her creations, except perhaps the *Terebratula*. In every age man has bitterly and justly complained that Nature hurried and hustled him, for inertia almost invariably has ended in tragedy. Resistance is its law, and resistance to superior mass is futile and fatal.

Fifty years ago, science took for granted that the rate of acceleration could not last. The world forgets quickly, but even today the habit remains of founding statistics on the faith that consumption will continue nearly stationary. Two generations, with John Stuart Mill, talked of this stationary period, which was to follow the explosion of new power. All the men who were elderly in the forties died in this faith, and other men grew old nursing the same conviction, and happy in it; while science, for fifty years, permitted, or encouraged, society to think that force would prove to be limited in supply. This mental inertia of science lasted through the eighties before showing signs of breaking up; and nothing short of radium fairly wakened men to the fact, long since evident, that force was inexhaustible. Even then the scientific authorities vehemently resisted.

Nothing so revolutionary had happened since the year 300. Thought had more than once been upset, but never caught and whirled about in the vortex of infinite forces. Power leaped from every atom, and enough of it to supply the stellar universe showed itself running to waste at every pore of matter. Man could no longer hold it off. Forces grasped his wrists and flung him about as though he had hold of a live wire or a runaway automobile; which was very nearly the exact truth for the purposes of an elderly and timid single gentleman in Paris, who never drove down the Champs Elysées without expecting an accident, and commonly witnessing one; or found himself in the neighborhood of an official without calculating the chances of a bomb: So long as the rates of progress held good, these bombs would double in force and number every ten years.

Impossibilities no longer stood in the way. One's life had fattened on impossibilities. Before the boy was six years old, he had seen four impossibilities made actual — the ocean-steamer, the railway, the electric telegraph, and the Daguerreotype;[17] nor could he ever learn which of the four had most hurried others to come. He had seen the coal-output of the United States grow from nothing to three hundred million tons or more. What was far more serious, he had seen the number of minds, engaged in pursuing force — the truest measure of its attraction — increase from a few scores or hundreds, in 1838, to many thousands in 1905, trained to sharpness never before reached, and armed with instruments amounting to new senses of indefinite power and accuracy, while they chased force into hiding-places where Nature herself had never known it to be, making analyses that contradicted being, and syntheses that endangered the elements. No one could say that the social mind now failed to respond to new force, even when the new force annoyed it horribly. Every day Nature violently revolted, causing so-called accidents with enormous destruction of property and life, while plainly laughing at man, who helplessly groaned and shrieked and shuddered, but never for a single instant could stop. The railways alone approached the carnage of war; automobiles and fire-arms ravaged society, until an earthquake became almost a nervous relaxation. An immense volume of force had detached itself from the unknown universe of energy, while still vaster reservoirs, supposed to be infinite, steadily revealed themselves, attracting mankind with more compulsive course than all the Pontic Seas[18] or Gods or Gold that ever existed, and feeling still less of retiring ebb.

In 1850, science would have smiled at such a romance as this, but, in 1900, as far as history could learn, few men of science thought it a laughing matter. If a perplexed but laborious follower could venture to guess their drift, it seemed in their minds a toss-up between anarchy and order. Unless they should be more honest with themselves in the future than ever they were in the past, they would be more astonished than their followers when they reached the end. If Karl Pearson's notions of the universe were sound, men like Galileo, Descartes, Leibnitz, and Newton should have stopped the progress of science before 1700, supposing them to have been honest in the religious convictions they expressed. In 1900 they were plainly forced back on faith in a unity unproved and an order they had themselves disproved. They had reduced their universe to a series of relations to themselves. They had reduced themselves to motion in a universe of motions, with an acceleration, in their own case, of vertiginous violence.

With the correctness of their science, history had no right to meddle, since their science now lay in a plane where scarcely one or two hundred minds in the world could follow its mathematical processes; but bombs educate vigorously, and even wireless telegraphy or airships might require the reconstruction of society. If any analogy whatever existed between the human mind, on one side, and the laws of motion, on the other, the mind had already entered a field of attraction so violent that it must immediately pass beyond, into new equilibrium, like the Comet of Newton, or suffer dissipation altogether, like meteoroids in the earth's atmosphere. If it behaved like an explosive, it must rapidly recover equilibrium; if it behaved like a vegetable, it must reach its limits of growth; and even if it acted like the earlier creations of energy — the saurians and sharks — it must have nearly reached the limits of its expansion. If science were to go on doubling or quadrupling its complexities every ten years, even mathematics would soon succumb. An average mind had succumbed already in 1850; it could no longer understand the problem in 1900.

Fortunately, a student of history had no responsibility for the problem; he took it as science gave it, and waited only to be taught. With science or with society, he had no quarrel and claimed no share of authority. He had never been able to acquire knowledge, still less to impart it; and if he had, at times, felt serious differences with the American of the nineteenth century, he felt none with the American of the twentieth. For this new creation, born since 1900, a historian asked no longer to be teacher or even friend; he asked only to be a pupil, and promised to be docile, for once, even though trodden under foot; for he could see that the new American — the child of incalculable coal-power, chemical power, electric power, and radiating energy, as well as of new forces yet undetermined — must be a sort of God compared with any former creation of nature. At the rate of progress since 1800, every American who lived to the year 2000 would know how to control unlimited power. He would think in complexities unimaginable to an earlier mind. He would deal with problems altogether beyond the range of earlier society. To him the nineteenth century would stand on the same plane with the fourth — equally childlike — and he would only wonder how both of them, knowing so little, and so weak in force, should have done so much. Perhaps even he might go back, in 1964, to sit with Gibbon on the steps of Ara Cœli.

Meanwhile he was getting education. With that, a teacher who had failed to educate even the generation of 1870, dared not interfere. The new forces would educate. History saw few lessons in the past that would be useful in the future; but one, at least, it did see. The attempt of the American of 1800 to educate the American of 1900 had not often been surpassed for folly; and since 1800 the forces and their complications had increased a thousand times or more. The attempt of the American of 1900 to educate the American of 2000, must be even blinder than that of the Congressman of 1800, except so far as he had learned his ignorance. During a million or two of years, every generation in turn had toiled with endless agony to attain and apply power, all the while betraying the deepest alarm and horror at the power they created. The teacher of 1900, if foolhardy, might stimulate; if foolish, might resist; if intelligent, might balance, as wise and foolish have often tried to do from the beginning; but the forces would continue to educate, and the mind would continue to react. All the teacher could hope was to teach it reaction.

Even there his difficulty was extreme. The most elementary books of science betrayed the inadequacy of old implements of thought. Chapter after chapter closed with phrases such as one never met in older literature: "The cause of this phenomenon is not understood"; "science no longer ventures to explain causes"; "the first step towards a causal explanation still remains to be taken"; "opinions are very much divided"; "in spite of the contradictions involved"; "science gets on only by adopting different theories, sometimes contradictory." Evidently the new American would need to think in contradictions, and instead of Kant's famous four antinomies,[19] the new universe would know no law that could not be proved by its anti-law.

To educate—oneself to begin with—had been the effort of one's life for sixty years; and the difficulties of education had gone on doubling with the coal-output, until the prospect of waiting another ten years, in order to face a seventh doubling of complexities, allured one's imagination but slightly. The law of acceleration was definite, and did not require ten years more study except to show whether it held good. No scheme could be suggested to the new American, and no fault needed to be found, or complaint made; but the next great influx of new forces seemed near at hand, and its style of education promised to be violently coercive. The movement from unity into multiplicity, between 1200 and 1900, was unbroken in sequence, and rapid in acceleration. Prolonged one generation longer, it would require a new social mind. As though thought were common salt in indefinite solution it must enter a new phase subject to new laws. Thus far, since five or ten thousand years, the mind had successfully reacted, and nothing yet proved that it would fail to react — but it would need to jump.

CHAPTER XXXV

Nunc Age[1] *(1905)*

NEARLY forty years had passed since the ex-private secretary landed at New York with the ex-Ministers Adams and Motley, when they saw American society as a long caravan stretching out towards the plains. As he came up the bay again, November 5, 1904, an older man than either his father or Motley in 1868, he found the approach more striking than ever — wonderful — unlike anything man had ever seen — and like nothing he had ever much cared to see. The outline of the city became frantic in its effort to explain something that defied meaning. Power seemed to have outgrown its servitude and to have asserted its freedom. The cylinder had exploded, and thrown great masses of stone and steam against the sky. The city had the air and movement of hysteria, and the citizens were crying, in every accent of anger and alarm, that the new forces must at any cost be brought under control. Prosperity never before imagined, power never yet wielded by man, speed never reached by anything but a meteor, had made the world irritable, nervous, querulous, unreasonable and afraid. All New York was demanding new men, and all the new forces, condensed into corporations, were demanding a new type of man — a man with ten times the endurance, energy, will and mind of the old type — for whom they were ready to pay millions at sight. As one jolted over the pavements or read the last week's newspapers, the new man seemed close at hand, for the old one had plainly reached the end of his strength, and his failure had become catastrophic. Everyone saw it, and every municipal election shrieked chaos. A traveller in the highways of history looked out of the club window on the turmoil of Fifth Avenue, and felt himself in Rome, under Diocletian, witnessing the anarchy, conscious of the compulsion, eager for the solution, but unable to conceive whence the next impulse was to come or how it was to act. The two-thousand-years failure of Christianity roared upward from Broadway, and no Constantine the Great was in sight.

Having nothing else to do, the traveller went on to Washington to wait the end. There Roosevelt was training Constantines and battling Trusts[2] a student of mechanics felt entire sympathy, not merely as a matter of politics or society, but also as a measure of motion. The Trusts and Corporations stood for the larger part of the new power that had been created since 1840, and were obnoxious because of their vigorous and unscrupulous energy. They were revolutionary, troubling all the old conventions and values, as the screws of ocean steamers must trouble a school of herring. They tore society to pieces and trampled it under foot. As one of their earliest victims, a citizen of Quincy, born in 1838, had learned submission and silence, for he knew that, under the laws of mechanics, any change, within the range of the forces, must make his situation only worse; but he was beyond measure curious to see whether the conflict of forces would produce the new man, since no other energies seemed left on earth to breed. The new man could be only a child born of contact between the new and the old energies.

Both had been familiar since childhood, as the story has shown, and neither had warped the umpire's judgment by its favors. If ever judge had reason to be impartial, it was he. The sole object of his interest and sympathy was the new man, and the longer one watched, the less could be seen of him. Of the forces behind the Trusts, one could see something; they owned a complete organization, with schools, training, wealth and purpose; but of the forces behind Roosevelt one knew little; their cohesion was slight; their training irregular; their objects vague. The public had no idea what practical system it could aim at, or what sort of men could manage it. The single problem before it was not so much to control the Trusts as to create the society that could manage the

Trusts. The new American must be either the child of the new forces or a chance sport of nature. The attraction of mechanical power had already wrenched the American mind into a crab-like process which Roosevelt was making heroic efforts to restore to even action, and he had every right to active support and sympathy from all the world, especially from the Trusts themselves so far as they were human; but the doubt persisted whether the force that educated was really man or nature — mind or motion. The mechanical theory, mostly accepted by science, seemed to require that the law of mass should rule. In that case, progress would continue as before.

In that, or any other case, a nineteenth-century education was as useless or misleading as an eighteenth-century education had been to the child of 1838; but Adams had a better reason for holding his tongue. For his dynamic theory of history he cared no more than for the kinetic theory of gas; but, if it were an approach to measurement of motion, it would verify or disprove itself within thirty years. At the calculated acceleration, the head of the meteor-stream must very soon pass perihelion. Therefore, dispute was idle, discussion was futile, and silence, next to good-temper, was the mark of sense. If the acceleration, measured by the development and economy of forces, were to continue at its rate since 1800, the mathematician of 1950 should be able to plot the past and future orbit of the human race as accurately as that of the November meteoroids.

Naturally such an attitude annoyed the players in the game, as the attitude of the umpire is apt to infuriate the spectators. Above all, it was profoundly unmoral, and tended to discourage effort. On the other hand, it tended to encourage foresight and to economize waste of mind. If it was not itself education, it pointed out the economies necessary for the education of the new American. There, the duty stopped.

There, too, life stopped. Nature has educated herself to a singular sympathy for death. On the antarctic glacier, nearly five thousand feet above sea-level, Captain Scott[3] found carcasses of seals, where the animals had laboriously flopped up, to die in peace. "Unless we had actually found these remains, it would have been past believing that a dying seal could have transported itself over fifty miles of rough, steep, glacier-surface," but "the seal seems often to crawl to the shore or the ice to die, probably from its instinctive dread of its marine enemies." In India, Purun Dass,[4] at the end of statesmanship, sought solitude, and died in sanctity among the deer and monkeys, rather than remain with man. Even in America, the Indian Summer of life should be a little sunny and a little sad, like the season, and infinite in wealth and depth of tone — but never hustled. For that reason, one's own passive obscurity seemed sometimes nearer nature than John Hay's exposure. To the normal animal the instinct of sport is innate, and historians themselves were not exempt from the passion of baiting their bears; but in its turn even the seal dislikes to be worried to death in age by creatures that have not the strength or the teeth to kill him outright.

On reaching Washington, November 14, 1904, Adams saw at a glance that Hay must have rest. Already Mrs. Hay had bade him prepare to help in taking her husband to Europe as soon as the Session should be over, and although Hay protested that the idea could not even be discussed, his strength failed so rapidly that he could not effectually discuss it, and ended by yielding without struggle. He would equally have resigned office and retired, like Purun Dass, had not the President and the press protested; but he often debated the subject, and his friends could throw no light on it. Adams himself, who had set his heart on seeing Hay close his career by making peace in the East, could only urge that vanity for vanity, the crown of peacemaker was worth the cross of martyrdom; but the cross was full in sight, while the crown was still uncertain. Adams found his formula for Russian inertia exasperatingly correct. He thought that Russia should have negotiated instantly on the fall of Port Arthur, January 1, 1905; he found that she had not the energy, but meant to wait till her navy should be destroyed.[5] The delay measured precisely the time that Hay had to spare.[6]

The close of the Session on March 4 left him barely the strength to crawl on board ship, March 18, and before his steamer had reached half her course, he had revived, almost as gay as when he first lighted on the Markoe house in I Street forty-four years earlier. The clouds that gather round the setting sun do not always take a sober coloring from eyes that have kept watch on mortality;[7] or, at least, the sobriety is sometimes scarcely sad. One walks with one's friends squarely up to the portal of life, and bids good-bye with a smile. One has done it so often! Hay could scarcely pace the deck; he nourished no illusions; he was convinced that he should never return to his work, and he talked lightly of the death-sentence that he might any day expect, but he threw off the coloring of office and mortality together, and the malaria of power left its only trace in the sense of tasks incomplete.

One could honestly help him there. Laughing frankly at his dozen treaties hung up in the Senate Committee-room[8] like lambs in a butcher's shop, one could still remind him of what was solidly completed. In his eight years of office he had solved nearly every old problem of American statesmanship,[9] and had left little or nothing to annoy his successor. He had brought the great Atlantic powers into a working system, and even Russia seemed about to be dragged into a combine of intelligent equilibrium based on an intelligent allotment of activities. For the first time in fifteen hundred years a true Roman *pax*[10] was in sight, and would, if it succeeded, owe its virtues to him. Except for making peace in Manchuria, he could do no more; and if the worst should happen, setting continent against continent in arms — the only apparent alternative to his scheme — he need not repine at missing the catastrophe.

This rosy view served to soothe disgusts which every parting statesman feels, and commonly with reason. One had no need to get out one's notebook in order to jot down the exact figures on either side. Why add up the elements of resistance and anarchy? The Kaiser supplied him with these figures, just as the Cretic approached Morocco. Everyone was doing it, and seemed in a panic about it. The chaos waited only for his landing.

Arrived at Genoa, the party hid itself for a fortnight at Nervi,[11] and he gained strength rapidly as long as he made no effort and heard no call for action. Then they all went on to Nauheim[12] without relapse. There, after a few days, Adams left him for the regular treatment, and came up to Paris. The medical reports promised well, and Hay's letters were as humorous and light-handed as ever. To the last he wrote cheerfully of his progress, and amusingly, with his usual light scepticism, of his various doctors; but when the treatment ended, three weeks later, and he came on to Paris, he showed, at the first glance, that he had lost strength, and the return to affairs and interviews wore him rapidly out. He was conscious of it, and in his last talk before starting for London and Liverpool he took the end of his activity for granted. "You must hold out for the peace negotiations," was the remonstrance. "I've not time!" he replied. "You'll need little time!" was the rejoinder. Each was correct.

There it ended! Shakespeare himself could use no more than the commonplace to express what is incapable of expression. "The rest is silence!"[13] The few familiar words, among the simplest in the language, conveying an idea trite beyond rivalry, served Shakespeare, and, as yet, no one has said more. A few weeks afterwards, one warm evening in early July, as Adams was strolling down to dine under the trees at Armenonville,[14] he learned that Hay was dead. He expected it; on Hay's account, he was even satisfied to have his friend die, as we would all die if we could, in full fame, at home and abroad, universally regretted, and wielding his power to the last. One had seen scores of emperors and heroes fade into cheap obscurity even when alive; and now, at least, one had not that to fear for one's friend. It was not even the suddenness of the shock, or the sense of void, that threw Adams into the depths of

Hamlet's Shakespearean silence in the full flare of Paris frivolity in its favorite haunt where worldly vanity reached its most futile climax in human history; it was only the quiet summons to follow — the assent to dismissal. It was time to go. The three friends had begun life together; and the last of the three had no motive — no attraction — to carry it on after the others had gone. Education had ended for all three, and only beyond some remoter horizon could its values be fixed or renewed. Perhaps some day — say 1938, their centenary — they might be allowed to return together for a holiday, to see the mistakes of their own lives made clear in the light of the mistakes of their successors; and perhaps then, for the first time since man began his education among the carnivores, they would find a world that sensitive and timid natures could regard without a shudder.

Appendix A

Excerpts from letters of Henry Adams explaining the aims and purposes of the *Education*.

TO CHARLES FRANCIS ADAMS

Washington, 20 February, 1907.

I am sending you a volume which contains a certain number of personal allusions which you can identify from the index. Will you oblige me by glancing over them, and in case you object to any phrase or expression, will you please draw your pen through it, and, at the end, return me the volume.

(Ford, II, 472)

TO CHARLES MILNES GASKELL

Washington, 4 March, 1907.

. . I have to ask your permission for certain reminiscences which are taking shape in my mind, and which are meant as my closing lectures to undergraduates in the instruction abandoned and broken off in 1877. . . .

(Ford, II, 472)

TO HENRY CABOT LODGE

Washington, 5 March, 1907.

I send you a volume, in the nature of proof-sheets, which contains allusions to you and yours which I wish you would glance at, and after running your pen through anything that seems to you personally objectionable return the volume to me.

Yrs truly   Henry Adams
(Cater, p. 591)

TO THEODORE ROOSEVELT

Washington, 11 March, 1907.

. . Having passed your censorship, and Cabot's, and Speck's, I have a greater than you all to face—Charles Eliot's! I am still trembling before him as though I were always an undergraduate, while the thunders and lightnings of my own family are as gentle cooing of doves. If they scold or sneer, I can happily suppress the whole thing, as is my wont; but Charles Eliot's sentence will be damnation forever.

(Ford, II, 473)

TO ELIZABETH CAMERON

Washington, 13 March, 1907.

. . . .

Mr. Cameron writes me a note granting the *imprimatur*, and the President and Cabot have also passed the permission; but I am far from willing to publish, and am driven to it only as defence against the pressure to write a memoir of Hay, which I will not do, not on my account but on his. All memoirs lower the man in estimation. Such a side light is alone artistic. Yet I would gladly wipe out all that is said about his friends and contemporaries if it were possible to keep an atmosphere without it. If any of them from the President and Cabot and your husband downwards would hint a wish to be left out, I would do it gladly; and still more gladly would omit myself. To gibbet myself for a friend's sake is no agreeable thing, and must be disguised by all sorts of ornaments and flourishes, landscape backgrounds, and weeping Magdalens.

Thus far, no one has objected, not even my brother Charles as yet, or Brooks, though I expect protests from them, not so much on their account as on mine. They will certainly point out to me what I am pointing out to you, —that my art fails of its effect. In that case I can still suppress the whole thing, and stand ready to do so at a moment's notice. Cabot is the worst treated, but is lamblike, and John [Lodge] weeps that I have spoiled it all, and hopelessly ruined its good discipline for him, by concluding that he 'interests.' . . .

(Ford, II, 473)

TO CHARLES MILNES GASKELL

Paris, 10 May, 1907.

. . . .

Before sailing, I mailed to you the volume I had already announced, as my last Will and Testament, which is intended for you to strike out whatever you find objectionable, and return to me. As I have to ask the same favor of everyone else mentioned by name in the volume, the process is slow; but as the volume is wholly due to piety on account of my father and John Hay (the rest being thrown in to make mass), I am wholly indifferent about what shall be struck out, and almost equally so what shall be left in. You may lop liberally at your will. Indeed I am only waiting for the smallest objection from any one of my family—or of Hay's—to suppress it all. Thus far they have not dared squeak. Even the President and Cabot Lodge bow the neck in submission. As my experience leads me to think that no one any longer cares or even knows what is said or printed, and that one's audience in history and literature has shrunk to a mere band of survivors, not exceeding a thousand people in the entire world, I am in hopes a kind of esoteric literary art may survive, the freer and happier for the sense of privacy and *abandon*. Therefore I stop at no apparent *naiveté*. . . .

(Ford, II, 476)

TO CHARLES MILNES GASKELL

Paris, May 15, 1907.

If you consent to pass the volume with only proof-corrections, you relieve me of the fear of responsibility to anyone any more. Only the scientific people remain to alarm me, and they are, I think, as much alarmed as I. This being the case, you need not bother yourself about returning the volume. I had meant to call them all back, expecting large changes or omissions; but thus far, no changes of any consequence have been asked, and no omissions. The President tells me that he means to keep the volume, whatever I say; and the various ladies not only refuse to return it, but clamor for more copies. Even Cabot Lodge sends only one or two corrections of proofreading. My brother Charles threatens notes and comments, but Brooks and Mrs. Quincy refuse to bite me. Mrs. Hay and her children have suggested no change. Therefore it will not much matter whether the present volume is withdrawn or not. It will not make a scandal even if generally read.

Anyway it will remain where it is until we can get the Hay's 'Letters' published; and even then I prefer to publish the *Mt.-St.-Michel and Chartres* before this last volume. Then I shall have survived, buried and praised my friends, and shall go to sleep myself. *It is time.* . . .

(Ford, II, 477)

TO WILLIAM JAMES

Washington, 9 December, 1907.

Of course you have a right to the volume you want. In fact it was printed only for communication to you and a few others who were to help me—I fondly hoped—to file it into shape.

Appendix A

If I did not send it to you at once, as I did to Charles Eliot, it was because I feared your judgment more than his, but since, now, I must, let me explain.

Weary of my own imbecility, I tried to clean off a bit of the surface of my mind, in 1904, by printing a volume on the twelfth century, where I could hide, in the last hundred pages, a sort of anchor in history. I knew that not a hundred people in America would understand what I meant, and these were all taught in Jesuit schools, where I should be a hell-born scorpion. I need not publish when no one would read or understand.

Then I undertook,—always to clean my own mind,—a companion study of the twentieth century, where I could hide—in a stack of rubbish meant only to feed the foolish—a hundred more pages meant to complete the first hundred of 1904. No one would take the smallest interest in these. I knew they were safe. So was I.

Unless, indeed, you got hold of them! In that case, I was rather inclined to weep and wail in advance, for I knew your views better than my own.

With this I send the volume, which, as personal to me, is all in the last chapter. . . .

(Ford, II, 485)

TO MARGARET CHANLER

Washington, [January] 30, [1908].

. . . .

The *Education* I feel more timid about. It is meant only for revision, suggestion, correction, and general condemnation. It undertakes to offer itself for blame, contempt and refusal. It hobbles on its knees, asking to be raised and educated. It is a picture of my aphorism that it is impossible to underrate human intelligence—beginning with one's own. I am ashamed of it, and send it out into the world only to be whipped. . . .

(Cater, p. 611)

TO RICHARD OLNEY

Washington, [January] 30, [1908].

Of course I will send you the volume—today—and with much pleasure.

Nothing annoys me more than to appear self-conscious or captious, but I cannot help explaining that the volume as it stands is merely a proof sent out for revision to persons interested, and to no one else. You invite the task of proof reader, and it is assumed that you will score the margin with corrections, cross out pages and chapters which you find superfluous, and after the most thorough revision, will send me back the volume that I may adopt your changes in case the book should ever be published.

For this purpose alone I have gone to the expense of printing a few copies, and unless I attain my object—revision— I shall be at a great loss to know what next to do with the book—unless to throw it into the fire like half a dozen of its predecessors. It has at least served one purpose—that of educating *me*.

(Cater, p. 610)

TO WILLIAM JAMES

Washington, 11 February, 1908.

You are as kind as possible, to write me a long letter. I am grateful, for I can find no man to play with. The American is a singularly unsocial animal. For social purposes,—as far as I have read the records of society,—he is the most complete failure ever known; and I am the champion failer of all.

As for the volume [*Education*], it interests me chiefly as a literary experiment, hitherto, as far as I know, never tried or never successful. Your brother Harry tries such experiments in literary art daily, and would know instantly what I mean; but I doubt whether a dozen people in America— except architects or decorators—would know or care.

I care little myself, and have put too many such *tours-de-force* into the fire, to bother about explanation. This will probably follow the others, for I have got it so far into shape that I can see the impossibility of success. It is the old story of an American drama. You can't get your contrasts and backgrounds. . . .

(Ford, II, 490)

TO WILLIAM JAMES

Washington, 17 February, 1908.
. . . .
Did you ever read the Confessions of St. Augustine, or of Cardinal de Retz, or of Rousseau, or of Benvenuto Cellini, or even of my dear Gibbon? Of them all, I think St. Augustine alone has an idea of literary form,—a notion of writing a story with an end and object, not for the sake of the object, but for the form, like a romance. I have worked ten years to satisfy myself that the thing cannot be done today. The world does not furnish the contrasts or the emotion. If you will read my *Chartres*,—the last chapter is the only thing I ever wrote that I almost think good,—you will see why I knew my *Education* to be rotten.

(Ford, II, 490)

Appendix A

TO EDITH MORTON EUSTIS

[Washington], [February] 28, 1908.

A thousand thanks. If you knew how helpless I feel before the wicked, you would appreciate my gratitude.

Thanks for the return of the volume. Your honesty is singular for I cannot recover my loans from the usual borrower.

Between artists, or people trying to be artists the sole interest is that of form. Whether one builds a house, or paints a picture, or tells a story, our point of vision regards only the form—not the matter. The two volumes have not been done in order to teach others, but to educate myself in the possibilities of literary form. The arrangement, the construction, the composition, the art of climax are our only serious study. Now that I have the stuff before me—in clay—I can see where the form fails, but I cannot see how to correct the failures. I believe the scheme impossible.

If you are curious to study the literary problem, send for the *Confessions* of St. Augustine, my literary model, and ask him why he failed too, as artist.

(Cater, p. 614)

TO JAMES FORD RHODES

Washington, March 16, 1908.

. . . .

If you can imagine a centipede moving along in twenty little sections (each with a mathematical formula carefully concealed in his stomach) to the bottom of a hill; and then laboriously climbing in fifteen sections more (each with a new mathematical problem carefully concealed in its stomach) till it can get up on a hill an inch or two high, so as to see ahead a half inch or so, you will understand in advance all that the "Education" has to say.

(Adams Papers)

TO HENRY JAMES

Paris, 6 May, 1908.

Mea culpa! Peccavi! Parce, frater! It is but a form and a phrase, yet this volume is supposed to be lent out only for correction, suggestion and amendment, so that you are invited to return it, with your marginal comments whenever you have done with it. I need hardly tell *you* that my own marginal comment is broader than that of any reader, and precludes publication altogether. The volume is a mere shield of protection in the grave. I advise you to take your own life in the same way, in order to prevent biographers from taking it in theirs.

Also—you being a literary artist, and therefore worth the trouble of forewarning—I note for your exclusive use the intent of the literary artist— *c'est moi!*—to make this volume a completion and mathematical conclusion from the previous volume about the Thirteenth Century,—the three concluding chapters of this being only a working out to Q.E.D. of the three concluding chapters of that. This is only for my own horizon; not for your confusion. . . .

(Ford, II, 495)

TO WHITELAW REID

Paris, 9 Sept. 1908.

. . . .

I will send you the volume promptly since you wish it, instead of waiting until you have time to think about it; but pray do not forget that it is what it avows:—a story of how an average American education, in spite of the most favorable conditions ran down hill, for twenty years, into the bog labelled Failure; and how it had to be started again, under every disadvantage, and the blindest fumblings, to crawl uphill a little way in order at least to get a little view ahead of the field it should have begun by occupying.

Of course the path is sugar-coated in order to induce anyone to follow it. The nearer we can come to romance the more chance that somebody will read—and understand. But not one reader in a thousand ever understands. . . .

TO WHITELAW REID

Paris, Sept. 13, 1908.

I trust the *Education* will arrive all right, and, as for dissent, if you will kindly draw a pen through all you can, without too much fatigue, you will save me much trouble. An experiment like this volume, is hazardous, not as history, but as art. To write a heavy dissertation on modern education, and fill up the back-ground with moving figures that will carry the load is a literary *tour-de-force* that cannot wholly succeed even in the hands of St. Augustine or Rousseau. The only doubt is whether it wholly fails, and I want my extra two years to give me the perspective to decide whether or not I will pass the pen through it all. The volume on Chartres is involved in the same doubt, for both go together, the three last chapters of the *Education* being Q.E.D. of the three last chapters of Chartres. Two years hence, if I can keep my balance, I shall decide whether to put both in the fire,—or what. . . .

(Cater, p. 622)

TO BARRETT WENDELL

Washington, 12 March, 1909.

. . . .

My dispute, or rather my defense against self-criticism, is that our failures are really not due to ourselves alone. Society has a great share in it. When I read St. Augustine's *Confessions*, or Rousseau's, I feel certain that their faults, as literary artists, are worse than mine. We have all three undertaken to do what cannot be successfully done—mix narrative and didactic purpose and style. The charm of the effort is not in winning the game but in playing it. We all enjoy the failure. St. Augustine's narrative subsides at last into the dry sands of metaphysical theology. Rousseau's narrative fails wholly in didactic result; it subsides into still less artistic egoism. And I found that a narrative style was so incompatible with a didactic or scientific style, that I had to write a long supplementary chapter to explain in scientific terms what I could not put into narration without ruining the narrative. The game was singularly simple in that sense, but never played out successfully by any artist however great. Even allegory, as in Bunyan, remains only a relative success. The *Roman de la Rose* (the first part) is the best popular triumph ever won.

Yet I contend that the failure would be proportional (other things being equal) to the atmosphere, or setting. With St. Augustine's background, or Benvenuto's, or Saint-Simon's, the failure would be less perceptible than mine. Do what we please, the *tour-de-force* of writing drama with what is essentially undramatic, must always be unpleasantly evident. . . .

(Cater, p. 644)

TO HENRY OSBORN TAYLOR

Paris, 22 November, 1909.

. . . .

I have written you before—have I not?—that I aspire to be bound up with St. Augustine. Or rather, I would have aspired to it, if it were artistically possible to build another fourth-century church. It cannot be. The *Leit motif* is flat. One can get one's artistic effects only by flattening everything to a level. Perhaps that is why I so love flattery.

As for the readers whom you suggest, I would gladly encourage them to read, if I had the impudence to think anything worth reading. As for

514

Sherman Evarts, he has a right to the volume anyway, and has only to send for it; since it was put in print only to enable the persons named in it, to object or reject or correct whatever concerned them. Any person whose name is mentioned in it, has a right to it. Thus far, no one has objected, or has made any objection that has come to my ears, but I still hold myself ready to strike out whatever is objected to, by anyone authorized to object.

Really nothing matters. No one cares. In another generation, the proportion of *us* to all, will be as unity to infinity. I am satisfied that it is immaterial whether one man or a thousand or a hundred thousand read one's books. The author is as safe as the seventeenth-century clergyman who printed his Sermon on Righteousness,—his pet sermon, that his congregation so much admired!

Thus far I have never given a copy of the *Education* to anyone. Occasionally some bandit, like Theodore Roosevelt, has told me that I need never expect to see his copy again, but this is piracy—and *force majeure*. Theoretically all the copies are to be recalled, for the corrections, or, as time goes on, I doubt more and more whether the volume is even worth correcting. It served its only purpose by educating *me*. . . .

(Ford, II, 525)

Letter prefatory to "The Rule of Phase Applied to History"

(TO PROFESSOR . . .)

Washington, D.C.
January 1, 1909

My dear Sir

Many thanks for the favor you have done me by reading the *Education*. It is ponderous and it is private; two qualities which enhance the favor; but it has a certain excuse for both. Especially the privacy is vital to it. Every ward politician teaches us the first lesson of politics, that only direct, personal contact exerts influence; and since the distances which separate us make personal contact impossible, we can only fall back on the archaic resource of letter-writing; like Cadmus, whose date I have tried in vain to fix, but who, somewhat like myself, probably stole the idea. The volume sent you was meant as a letter; garrulous, intimate, confidential, as is permitted in order to serve a social purpose, but would sound a false note for the public ear. In truth, for the occasion, I am frankly a conspirator; I want to invite private confidence, and the public is my worst enemy.

To dismiss the Ego for a moment! Perhaps you have read the volume with enough attention to notice that it professes to have an object;—even insists on its object, from the first page to the last, till it risks routing its readers, for nine readers in ten run from an idea like a hare from a hound. No doubt they are right in running; few ideas are worth their study; but they make the teacher's task impossible. Sugar-coat his idea an inch thick, or disguise it as he will, the teacher cannot force it down unwilling throats; still less induce passive stomachs to digest it; unless the patient has some personal motive, some chance of profit or pleasure to incite his action. This is my apology for appealing directly, personally, to the dozen or two of possible readers who have a personal interest in the subject;—and to no one else.

The volume starts, as usual, with the commonplace that the subject of it, the lay-figure, the manikin, had no education, since the Universities of his time were a hundred years behind the level of his needs, and the technical schools at least fifty; but that the technical schools had the advantage of unity and energy of purpose. After illustrating this statement in a great variety of ways, through some four hundred pages, the book closes by a belabored effort to state the problem, for its special domain of history, in a scientific formula, which affects the terms of astronomy merely because every child is supposed to know the so-called law, as well as the fact, of gravitation.

In order not to exasperate the reader too much, the volume stopped there. The next step required an effort of thought on the reader's part, for it was clear that, if he knew a little,—the very little he should have been compelled to know,—of science, he would of his own accord go on to apply the same law in the terms of other branches of study than astronomy, not to prove its truth, but to prove its convenience. The statement in one set of terms implies that it can be made equally well in all. If he found that this translation was easy, he would incline to ask whether it was practical; and, last of all, he would have to decide whether it would become necessary.

Here the field enlarges itself. The chemical professor might at any moment invade the domain of history, and oust the historical professor from his throne; but the historical professor could still more easily invade the chemical laboratory, and demonstrate his laws of Röntgen—or any other—rays. The fact that the problem might be stated in terms of astronomical mass proved that it might even more readily be illustrated by the laboratory experiments on electric mass; and the demonstration was easy, for, within the possible error of a few technical terms, the law was mathematically definite. The professor of history would lecture to the students of chemistry in their own familiar formulas:—

"The human mind," he may say, "can be conveniently treated as a group of electric ions, each charged on a mathematical corpuscle, and obeying the law of electric mass. Viewed thus, as an electric charge, distributed on particles of gas in a vacuum tube traversed by an electric current, the acceleration will be as the volume of the current, increasing to infinity by the usual law of squares, according to the curve given in any recent text book. History then becomes an application of logarithms. You have assumed a numerical value of 1,000 for the past century. The law of astronomical mass gives you a certain value for the eighteenth century. The law of chemical mass will give you a value represented by 32. For the seventeenth century, it gives a value of 5.66; for the sixteenth, of 2.38; for the fifteenth, of 1.54; and thence, in a nearly straight line, like that of the comet, back to infinity. The curve is familiar, and only of academic interest as regards the past; but as regards the future, its interest is practical and immediate, since the acceleration for our actual century has the value of 1,000,000, and therefore approaches infinity. The similar problem of a comet likely to strike the earth, is much less vital. The most pressing concern of science, as well as of history, law and legislation, is to ascertain what effect such an acceleration will have on the ion of mind."

You can test this formula on your colleague, the Professor of Electro-chemistry, if you are anxious to find a *corpus vile;* but unless you wish to challenge his ridicule, you will not ask whether it is true. He knows no more about the truth of his formulas than we do; but he may know something,—though not much,—about its scientific convenience. Even this is a secondary matter for our purposes. Convenient or not, it is too obvious not to be soon used, and it is only surprising that some Gustave Le Bon, or Haeckel, or Ernst Mach, or Karl Pearson, has not advanced it already. Perhaps they have; certainly they have advanced much that is less scientific. Anyone can write a quarto volume about it, who will hire a chemical or mechanical student to give it a smattering of mathematics and electro-chemistry; and can do it with the utmost assurance if he starts by showing that, for the purposes of a teacher, the formula is convenient.

In any case, the problem is almost certain to take this dynamic form for us, as it did for Galileo and Newton, as well as for Clerk Maxwell, Helmholz, Hertz and Kelvin. You will probably have to play, in your professorial character, the rôle of Urban VIII, and either acquit or condemn it. To me, the answer is immaterial; I care not whether the earth moves or not, for my age exempts me from service. My task is limited to private suggestion, and I will under no circumstances cast my glove again into the ring; yet, old as I am, and weary of turning round and round in an endless ring of repetition, it is evident that I should not make so strenuous an effort to suggest, unless the suggestion seemed to me to be sorely needed. I presume that no competent teacher now ventures to teach any doctrine or formula as true; he teaches it only as a provisional step to the next synthesis. It will go hard with our Universities if they prove their incapacity to take their next step to a new synthesis. They need to polarise their lines of thought and force;

to coordinate their curves; to intensify their currents; to throw off their incumbrances; and, as far as I can see, the only channel wide enough to effect this coordination and contain this current, is, and ought to be, the department of history.

In order to make my meaning and method somewhat clearer, I have ventured to put it in shape, as well as I know how. For this purpose I have written the following essay on the Rule of Phase Applied to History. The student or professor who is properly trained, or who is naturally fit for study, will read it as though it were a mathematical formula suggested for the solution of a certain class of problems. He will not be concerned with the question whether it is true, which has no meaning to him; but he will be curious to test its convenience or its scope. If he should find it convenient for his own purposes of instruction, he will ask whether its usefulness may not be wider, and, at last, whether it might not serve as a universal formula for reconstructing and rearranging the whole scheme of University instruction so that it shall occupy a field of definite limits, distinct from the technical. In that case, he will conceive of the University as a system of education grouped about History; a main current of thought branching out, like a tree, into endless forms of activity, in regular development, according to the laws of physics; and to be studied as a single stream, not as now by a multiversal, but by a universal law; not as a scientific but as a historical unity; not as a practice of technical handling, but as a process of mental evolution in history, controlled, like the evolution of any series of chemical or electric equilibria, by one general formula. University education organised on this scheme, would begin by ceasing to compete with technical education, and would found all its instruction on historical method.

In this suggestion of a possible means of introducing order and idea into the chaos of University education, I am inclined to think that only the defects of my old University training prevent my success in making myself intelligible. The same defects are likely to prevent other University men from following me. The human mind perpetuates its own multiplicity, and perhaps does well. Chaos may suit it best, and history tends to show that all its numerous efforts to think in Universals or Universities have failed. Even in that case the attempt to reduce universals to one general formula of physics is only a natural and appropriate mode of University education which connects closely with the theory and practice of the middle-ages; it is a return to first principles.

With this introduction I venture to offer the Essay for your notice.

(*Henry Adams and His Friends*, ed. Harold Dean Cater
[Boston, 1947], pp. 781 f.)

Appendix B

TABLE 1

List of substantive revisions and corrections made by Henry Adams in the two copies of the 1907 printing of the *Education* which were used in the preparation of the 1918 edition published by the Massachusetts Historical Society and Houghton Mifflin Company. These changes have been adopted in the present edition. Nearly all were entered in the so-called "Thayer" copy, the one lent to William Roscoe Thayer as explained in the Textual Note. A few come from the "Abernethy" copy, the one originally delivered to Lodge, and are so identified below. The parallel passages are given by page and line. The pagination of the present edition corresponds exactly with that of the 1918 edition.

1907 *1973*

CHAPTER I

8.6 Vassal

11.9 Vassall

14.21–22 [Abernethy copy] sugar-bowl and cream-jug, which came afterwards to him and still exist [deletion not marked in Thayer copy]

18.28–29 sugar-bowl and cream-jug, which still exist

CHAPTER II

31.14–15 [Abernethy copy] meant. There was not a trout stream on the coast and no fly-fishing. Sport [deletion not marked in Thayer copy]

38.33–34 meant. Sport

CHAPTER III

43.30 He know not even

53.18 He knew not even

CHAPTER IV

47.25 Dozens of United States Senators

58.4 Dozens of eminent statesmen

47.26 in the Senate

58.5 in the legislature [cap. reduced by eds.]

CHAPTER V

64.4–5 Mr. Robert Abthorp of Boston

76.31–32 Mr. Robert Apthorp, of Boston [spelling correction appears in all subsequent references]

Appendix B

1907	1973

CHAPTER VI

1907	1973
78.32 could not teach	93.11 could not touch
81.3 grubworm	95.29 glow-worm

CHAPTER VII

1907	1973
85.32 on K Street [also corrected in Abernethy copy]	101.5 on I Street [also corrected in subsequent references]
89.15–16 epithets. The reproach came always from State Street.	105.5–6 epithets. [sentence cancelled]

CHAPTER VIII

1907	1973
106.19–21 "cool of the evening"; his appetite, his cayenne pepper, his teeth and his breakfasts; and of course [also corrected in Abernethy]	124.11 "cool of the evening"; and of course
106.24 further	124.15 farther

CHAPTER IX

1907	1973
112.27 Seaward	130.31 Seward
113.4 Ethel Newcomb	131.11 Ethel Newcome [similarly corrected in subsequent references]
117.29 The moment was nervous but	136.23–25 The moment was nervous—as far as the private secretary knew, quite the most critical moment in the records of American diplomacy—but

CHAPTER X

1907	1973
128.17 Bethel	148.27 Bethell [similarly corrected in subsequent references]
136.10–12 followed Gladstone. Although he must have known that the Cabinet would offer much opposition to his scheme, he persisted, and, on October 13 issued his call	157.27–31 followed Gladstone. Although he had just created a new evangel of non-intervention for Italy, and preached it like an apostle, he preached the gospel of intervention in America as though he were a mouthpiece of the Congress of Vienna. On October 13, he issued his call

Table 1

<table>
<tr><td align="center">*1907*</td><td align="center">*1973*</td></tr>
</table>

CHAPTER XI

147.25–26 was always meanly jealous	171.4 was always jealous

CHAPTER XII

160.22–23 The active member	186.14 The political member
163.2 Beesley's	189.6 Beesly's

CHAPTER XIII

179.21–22 In the year 1864, just as this new intimacy was forming, Mr. James Milnes Gaskell, who	207.7 In the year 1857, Mr. James Milnes Gaskell, who
179.28 part of the autumn. Young Adams	207.14 part of the autumn of 1864. Young Adams

CHAPTER XIV

183.16 His mother averred	211.29–31 His mother—who should have been a competent judge, since her success and popularity in England exceeded that of her husband—averred

CHAPTER XV

199.19–20 that no evolution worth treating as proof of the principle, had occurred	230.5–6 that no complete proof of Natural Selection had occurred
203.31–32 James McKinley	235.3 William McKinley

CHAPTER XVIII

242.16–17 demolish the Supreme Court, and struck its independence a blow from which it never could recover; while Henry	278.28 demolish the Chief Justice; while Henry
243.21 moral laxity	280.4 alleged moral laxity
243.27–28 to care for their morals; until	280.12 to care for the question; until
244.32–34 political education? The problem never was solved—had no solution. Garfield and Blaine	281.21 political education? [The two following sentences omitted at this point]

1907	1973
followed the failures of Grant and Sumner.	
244.36–37 If morals broke down	281.23–24 If moral standards broke down

CHAPTER XIX

256.15 few. One might	294.23–24 few. Perhaps Mr. Fish was the solitary exception. One might
256.17 [Abernethy copy: "excepting for Hamilton Fish, one would" is inserted after "years 1870–1895, and,"]	
256.30 so much. Hewitt's nearest rival	295.6–7 so much, unless Mr. Sherman's legislation is accepted as an instance of success. Hewitt's nearest rival

CHAPTER XX

262.11 La Marck	301.15 Lamarck

CHAPTER XXI

276.11 his betters. He	316.14 his elders. He
281.9 1877	321.32 1879

CHAPTER XXII

289.14 Burke	331.15 Bourke

CHAPTER XXIV

319.12 Woolsey	365.21 Wolsey
329.34–35 by the schools, much as Wolcott Gibbs himself was treated, with	377.25 by the schools with

[In the Abernethy copy the phrase was not marked for deletion but "Wolcott" was cancelled and in the margin Adams wrote "Willard." See Appendix B, Table 2, for Adams's explanatory interpolation, adopted in this edition.]

CHAPTER XXV

340.28 sailed from Cherburg	390.5 sailed from Cherbourg

CHAPTER XXVI

345.2 must put	395.15 must have put

Table 1

1907	1973
345.7–8 the horizon. He measures time by motion and space by mass.	395.20 of the horizon. [Sentence deleted]
345.10–11 to-day, since mass and motion have been so enormously increased; but	395.22 to-day; but
346.24 of gravitation;—and	397.9–10 of gravitation, phosphorescence, and odors; and

CHAPTER XXVII

354.10 as it had done	405.13 as she had done
355.28 the untaught and futile critic	407.5 the untaught critic
356.33–35 geographic. The attitude of expectation, optimism, bluff, had characterised the popular mind from far back, so that society was ready for any phase, and confident in making money out of it. The true	408.16 geographic. The true

XXVIII

371.7; 371.21 Jaurez [corrected in Abernethy copy]	423.32; 424.12 Jaurès
371.23 as vigorous as a geometrical	424.14 as rigorous as a geometrical

XXIX

374.30–31 was absolutely essential	427.30 was essential
376.3–4 Saint Thomas's God	429.8 St. Thomas's idea of God

XXXI

394.1–3 twenty years old. As usual, he was struck chiefly by the familiar, crying faults of the English mind, chaotic and fragmentary by essence. He never	449.28 twenty years old. He never
394.3 taught a great master	449.29 taught a master [correction from Abernethy copy]
394.4–5 Gibbs, and for practical results he saw no moral except the	449.29–450.1 Gibbs. Yet

1907	*1973*

general English commandment: "Thou shalt experiment!" Yet

394.7	any Englishman ever before	450.2	any Englishman before
394.10	deliberately ignored, and Wolcott Gibbs himself smothered under	450.5	deliberately ignored under

[In the Abernethy copy the words "and Wolcott Gibbs himself smothered" were marked for deletion (adopted by editors in 1918); in the Thayer copy the words "ignored and Wolcott Gibbs himself" were marked for deletion]

394.35–36	light at the end of his own nose	450.32	light which he generates.
395.32	that God could not be proved	451.33–34	that Unity could not be proved
397.23	the scientific ideas	453.31–32	these scientific ideas
399.33–400.2	He knew no more about rays than about race,—or sex,—or ennui,—or a bar of music, or a pang of love,—or a grain of musk,—or conscience,—or duty,— or the force of Euclidian geometry, —or non-Euclidian,—or heat,—or light,—or electrolysis,—or the magnet,—or ether,—or *vis inertiae,*—or gravitation,—or surface tension,—or capillary attraction,— or Brownian motion,—	456.18–25	He knew no more [than a firefly] about rays—[or] about race—or sex—or ennui—or a bar of music—or a pang of love—or a grain of musk—[or of phosphorus]—or conscience—or duty —or the force of Euclidian geometry—or non-Euclidian—or heat —or light—[or osmosis]—or electrolysis—or the magnet—or ether —or *vis inertiae*—or gravitation —[or cohesion—or elasticity]—or surface tension—or capillary attraction—or Brownian motion—
400.13–14	to radiate heat, and thus exploded the scientific magazine	457.2–3	to radiate something that seemed to explode the scientific magazine
402.33	to be nothing but a conscious ball	460.3	to be a conscious ball
403.5–8	fifty years before. Possibly Galileo, Descartes and Newton, if they believed the religious unity they professed, might have refused to go on with a science which led them into the arms of Helmholz and Haeckel; but the times	460.10	fifty years earlier; the times

Table 1

1907	*1973*
403.12–13 which caged it. Appearing	460.16 which caged it; how—appearing
403.21–22 would prove beyond all possible dispute that	460.26 would prove that

XXXII

408.3 born on its shores	466.15–16 bred on its shores
411.6 gone; for energy cannot perish. The Virgin	469.34 gone. The Virgin
411.11 annihilation as force	470.5 annihilation as energy

XXXIII

415.25 its exact use	475.25–26 its immediate use
415.28–29 He must have	475.29 He may have
415.31–32 acted on certain individual apes, and mechanically selected	475.32–33 were capable of acting on individual apes, and mechanically selecting
416.2 has been educated	476.5 would be educated
416.3 had not varied	476.6–7 had not essentially varied
416.8 theology, creating	476.13–14 theology; the mind is itself the subtlest of all known forces, and its self-introspection necessarily created
416.10 to the highest, finest	476.16 to the finest
416.15–16 certainty of gaining	476.22 sure hope of gaining
416.23 the mass and momentum of Europe were	476.29 the momentum of Europe was
416.24 as was made	476.30 as the world made
416.24–25 economies rather than in development of energy	476.30–31 economies of energy rather than in its development
417.2 more chaotic	477.11–12 more apparently chaotic
417.21 No four hundred	477.32 No other four hundred
418.26 for champion	479.7 for physical champion
419.27 four hundred years	480.11 six hundred years
421.10 Europe never possessed	482.3 Europe had never possessed
421.23 moment that	482.18 moment when
421.33 [no paragraph]	482.29 [new paragraph]
421.33 cannot be said	482.29–30 cannot certainly be said
422.19 more than Greek pathos	483.19 more than Greek unity
422.24–25 in shameful ignominy	483.25 in ignominy

525

1907	1973
423.13 unity from multiplicity	484.17–18 thought from the universe
423.20 The change of attitude	484.25 The revolution in attitude
423.20–21 mechanical as gravitation	484.26 mechanical as the fall of a feather
423.21–22 the revolution in forces	484.27 the speed of progress
423.23 were the approach of storm, or the acceleration	484.28 were the acceleration
423.24 body. Lord Bacon	484.29 body which the dynamic theory takes it to be. Lord Bacon
424.8 science ever dared face	485.17 science dared face
424.8–9 thought; but the	485.17–18 thought; and the
424.11 score, and these were confined	485.20 score, confined
424.12 by new force	485.21 by the stream
424.26 from without	486.1–3 from without. "Non fingendum aut excogitandum sed inveniendum quid Natura faciat aut ferat."
425.7–8 planet on the sun	486.22 comet on the sun
425.20 stood as bewildered	487.1 stood at first as bewildered
426.10–11 mind enlarged	487.31 mind of man enlarged

XXXIV

427.23 in defiance of every law of thermo-dynamics, by the path	489.25 in defiance of law, by the path
428.2–3 mass,—the sum of	490.1 mass in its astronomic sense —the sum or difference of
428.34 gravitation; but	491.2–3 gravitation, and followed closely the curve of steam; but
429.3 1800	491.9 1820
429.14 likes,—say a twenty-five year	491.22–23 likes—say a fifty, or even a five-and-twenty-year
429.22 the same rate	491.31 a similar rate
429.35 In other words, one	492.11 Or better, one
429.35–36 formula of terrestrial gravitation	492.11–12 formula of squares
430.1 chemical explosion or vegetable growth	492.13–14 chemical explosion, or electrolysis, or vegetable growth
430.2 but gravitation happens	492.14–15 but this happens

Table 2

1907	*1973*
430.3 convenient. As	492.15–16 convenient. Its force increases in the direct ratio of its squares. As
430.4–5 force, it may be supposed to have doubled its speed and energy every five-and-twenty years.	492.17–18 force, the attraction of one century squared itself to give the measure of attraction in the next.
430.9 west, as	492.22–23 west in the thirteenth century, as
430.9–10 the compass and blowpipe; while	492.23–25 the compass, the blowpipe, clocks and spectacles, and materials like paper; Arabic notation and algebra were introduced, while
430.25 infinitely small	493.8 infinitely slight
430.26 stopped. To	493.9–10 stopped. The motion of Newton's comet at aphelion may be equally slight. To
431.30 and generally witnessing	494.20–21 and commonly witnessing
431.31–32 the invariable law of progress	494.22–23 the rates of progress
432.5 force, increase	494.33 force—the truest measure of its attraction—increase
432.33–34 [paragraph]	495.30 [no paragraph]
433.32 to the year	496.33 into the year
435.7 mind. Thus	498.17–18 mind. As though thought were common salt in indefinite solution it must enter a new phase subject to new laws. Thus

TABLE 2

Corrections indicated by Adams but not adopted by the editors in 1918.

1907	*1973*
293.21 to learn backwards	316.14 to lean backwards [as corrected in Thayer copy]
393.11 To Adams's vision, Wolcott Gibbs stood on the same plane	449.11 To Adams's vision, Wolcott Gibbs stood on the same plane

Appendix B

1907	1973
with the three or four greatest minds of his century, and the idea that a man so incomparably superior	with the three or four greatest minds of his century—the more so because in his ignorance he confounded him with another great mind, his rival Willard Gibbs, and the idea that a man so incomparably superior [as corrected in Thayer copy]

In the Abernethy copy (See "Textual Note") he simply struck out the misleading words so as to make the sentence read as follows: "To Adams's vision, Wolcott Gibbs stood on the same plane with the great minds of his century, and the idea that a man so superior . . ." It should be pointed out that in neither copy did he replace the name of Wolcott Gibbs with that of Willard Gibbs except as noted above in Table 1 in the Abernethy copy at line 329.34–35 where he had obviously recalled that it was Willard Gibbs who had met "a conspiracy of silence." The editors in 1918 avoided the complications introduced by Adams's confession of error by simply changing all mentions of Wolcott Gibbs to Willard Gibbs, thus in most instances doing violence to Adams's second thoughts. As Adams neglected to recast the sentence (329.17, [377.4–6]) near the end of Chapter XXIV—"The greatest of Americans, judged by his rank in science, Wolcott Gibbs, never came to Washington . . ."—to make it accord with his correction in the opening paragraph of Chapter XXXI, "Willard Gibbs" has been substituted as in the 1918 edition to avoid confusion.

TABLE 3

List of substantive corrections made by the 1918 editors on their own authority and retained in this edition in those cases in which they correct obvious errors of fact or diction or establish consistency of typographical style or emphasis.

1907		1973	
2.3	Mount Vernon and	3.25	Mount Vernon Street and
8.10	Louis XVI,—	11.13	Louis Seize
11.15	he eat	15.4	he ate
20.11	enough the year	25.19	enough to the year
23.14	1848–1854	29.10	1848 to 1854
45.23	1854–1861	55.23	1854 to 1861

Table 3

1907		1973	
61.11	structure	73.20	structures
61.11	was	73.21	were
101.26	turned ashes	118.24–25	turned to ashes
106.24	further	124.15	farther
107.22	Yorkshiremen	125.16	Yorkshireman
114.20	memoranda	132.32	memorandum
120.17	capable	139.31	capable of it
132.19	view to	153.17	view" to
132.29	to knew	153.28	to know
152.21	1860	176.27	1861
159.32	Mr. Slidell	185.18	Slidell
166.35	1859–1865	193.21	1859 to 1865
171.23	wondered	197.32	wandered
173.31	eat	200.19	ate
173.33	eat	200.22	ate
180.20	Italy; of	208.22	Italy. Of
184.18	art	213.5	Art
196.7	in a string	226.10	on a string
198.17	Bridgenorth	229.1	Bridgnorth
211.8	and could	242.26	and he could
214.1	keep recalling	246.2	help recalling
219.14	that Mr. Sumner	252.10–11	that Sumner
220.12	Mullet	253.13	Mullett
221.18	Halsted	255.20	Halstead
254.3	made success	292.1	made a success
256.17	1870–1895	294.25–26	1870 to 1895
272.19	know	313.2	knew
275.26	M'Kim	315.26	McKim
279.6	Vaiala	319.20	Vailima
284.6	that was to write	325.11	there was to write
289.14	Burke	331.15	Bourke
300.9	that	342.23	than
302.5	1893–97	346.6–7	1893 to 1897
309.4	desk, to take the train for Washington to get married.	353.30–31	desk, and crossed the street to Christ Church in Cambridge to get married. [The correction indicates that Lodge took an active part in the editing]
311.21	State, but Mr. Hanna	356.24	State, for Mr. Hanna
319.12	Woolsey's	365.21	Wolsey's

	1907		*1973*
321.7	Sylla	367.26	Sulla
326.33	at that time both Germany	374.9	at that time Germany
329.17	Wolcott Gibbs	377.5–6	Willard Gibbs [See above, Table 2]
360.31	fisherman	412.29	fishermen
362.1	fisherman	414.7	fishermen
368.3	statesman	420.16	statesmen
383.16–17	Speck Sternburg	437.17	Speck von Sternburg
409.18	May 22	462.1	May 24
422.25	Faust	483.26	Fust
428.10	between 1800 and 1900	490.10	between 1840 and 1900

TABLE 4

List of 1907 readings restored in the present edition because of errors, mis-readings or altered emphasis in the 1918 edition.

	1907 restored readings	*1973*	*1918 rejected readings*
30.13	was herded with	37.27	was here with
33.35	were going	42.3	was going
46.32	these Virginians	57.5	the Virginians
51.6	standards	62.2	standard
58.6	grandfather ever achieved	70.6	grandfather achieved
59.30	would	71.31	could
61.17	return	73.27	turn
65.3	looking out at	78.3	looking at
75.28	which	89.24	while
94.19–20	carrion-patronage	110.22	carrion—patronage
100.26	a clerk	117.20	clerk
132.35	awhile	153.36	a while
139.32	conclusions and had	162.2–3	conclusions, had
143.8	him his life	165.36	him life
145.14	excess	168.15	access
145.21	violently,	168.23	violently
155.9	would scarcely	180.10	scarcely would
158.21	thought,	183.33	thought;
158.31	always	184.10	largely
159.6	Carlisle	184.24	Carlyle
163.1	Trades Unions	189.5	Trades-Union

Table 5

1907 restored readings	1973	*1918 rejected readings*
170.20 replied,	196.24	replied
171.10 County	197.18	county
189.2 taken aback	218.11	taken back
190.13 verses	219.28	verse
198.12 had	228.28	has
213.32 The young man	245.30	The younger man
242.36 but	279.15	although
253.36–37 sight or in mind	291.31	sight or mind
274.5 matter which would only confuse	314.6	matter only which would confuse
282.4 pleased	322.31	released
294.11 vote did in the end	336.26	vote in the end did
295.5–6 thousands or millions	337.25	thousands of millions
306.28 cleaning	350.28	clearing
313.10 Sophocles	358.20	Socrates
326.33 were combining	374.9	were all combining
329.31 though doubting	377.21	while doubting
334.20 1900, with his historical	382.31	1900, his historical
355.14–15 principle, Lodge	406.23	principle Bay Lodge
356.11 oblige Lodge	407.26	oblige Bay Lodge
357.3 Thought	408.20	thought
390.6 millions on millions	445.7	millions of millions
393.8 Wolcott Gibbs	449.9	Willard Gibbs
393.10 Wolcott Gibbs	449.11	Willard Gibbs
393.16 Wolcott Gibbs	449.18	Willard Gibbs
394.4 Wolcott Gibbs	449.29	Willard Gibbs
410.34 could no more	469.25	could not more
415.1 thrusting	474.29	trusting
431.2 has	493.25	had
433.10 Newton, or suffer dissipation	496.10	Newton, to suffer dissipation
441 [blank]	505	THE END

TABLE 5

Corrections in the Athenaeum copy. Where the identical correction was indicated in the Thayer copy, only the page and line number are supplied. (These corrections may be examined, with one exception as noted, in Table 1 where the corresponding pages in the present edition are given.) The remaining entries list by page and line those corrections which did not appear in the Thayer copy (nor the Abernethy copy) and which were therefore not included in either the 1918 or the present edition. The figures in brackets indicate the pages and lines in the present edition where the corrections would have appeared had Adams adopted them in the subsequent revisions.

1907 Athenaeum

203.31–32

293.21   [Table 2]

319.12

329.17 [377.5]   "Wolcott" cancelled; "Willard" to be substituted.

329.34 [377.25]   "Wolcott" cancelled

345.2; 345.7–8; 345.10–11

356.33–35

373 [426]   Chapter heading inserted: "A Kinetic Theory of History"

374.18–19 [427.17]   "which was also scientific" cancelled. Insertion: "a sort of kinetic theory of progress: which Auguste Comte long afterwards enrolled in the service of his Positive Philosophy"

375 [428]   (top) "The Abyss of Ignorance" cancelled; "A Kinetic Theory of History" to be substituted.

378.4 [431.18]   To be inserted after "phases of motion": "This offered a kinetic theory of history, without clue to unity or direction, which might have suited Pascal."

386.36 [441.18]   To be inserted before "The inequalities": "Profoundly ignorant of physics, they had still fallen upon the identical difficulty which so much troubled the physicists in trying to induce the gases to obey a mathematical formula. The molecules positively refused to move with the same speeds."

394.10–12 [450.5]   Marked for deletion: "and Wolcott Gibbs himself smothered under the usual conspiracy of silence inevitable to all thought which demands new thought-machinery."

399.27 [456.11]   "convenient symbol" to be substituted for "convenience."

399.34 [456.19]   "or color—or line" to be inserted [exact point not clearly indicated]

400.2 [456.24]   To be inserted: "or elasticity, or cohesion" [point not clearly indicated]

400.5 [456.27]   "Energy" to replace "Force."

408.3

409.18   "May 22" to be corrected to "May 24."

415.15 [475.14]   To be inserted: "The history of magic is a long illustration of this law."

416.14 [476.20]   To be inserted after "trap an elephant": "The theory and practice of divination and magic rested on the human appetite for power, and became probably the largest and most complex branch of science."

417.21   Insert of "other" is preceded by "?."

Table 6

418.20 [479.1]   To be inserted after "under our government": "In spite of all that has been, or can be, said about the superstitions of the Church, one can hardly deny that pagan society was more superstitious still, and devoted its resources on a still larger scale to raising itself to the level of the Gods, or to drawing the Gods to its own level. This was the object of Constantine as it had been the object of his predecessors even in their persecution of Christianity."

418.22 [479.3]   "the year before" cancelled; "in 312" to be substituted.

418.29 [479.10]   Cancelled: "The Church was powerless to raise the ideal."

419.27

426.13 [487.34]   "him" cancelled; "man" to be substituted.

427.23 [489.25]   Cancelled: "in defiance of every law of thermo-dynamics"

427.25 [489.27]   To be inserted: "In another analogy it might figure as a current of electrons governed by the laws of electric mass: 'In liquids and gases, every current may be explained by regarding it as consisting of *ions* which transport, with finite speeds, the electric charges they carry from one electrode to the other.' "

434.35 [498.7]   "or an eighth" to be inserted after "a seventh."

TABLE 6

List of Adams's annotations supplying supporting documentation. Those in the Athenaeum copy are identified by the letter A followed by the page number. Those in the Thayer copy are identified by the letter T followed by the page number. There were none in the Abernethy copy. The left hand column indicates the page and line number in the present edition at which the annotation begins. Each is transcribed as written.

227.5   Lapparent, 1055 (Ed. 1906) [A. 196]

228.5   Gaudry. Essai etc. p. 195 [A. 197]

229.12   Owens Paleontology p. 144 [T. 198]

229.15   Dé Peret, Transformations, p. 95, 107 [T. 198]

229.21   Gaudry, Essay de Paléontologie Scientifique 1896, p. 47
The Ganoid is classed by Vaillant in the Australian genus (Galtung) Ceradobus now living. [A. 199]

229.34   Friedrich Ratzel in Oswald's Annalen II, 1 Dec. 1902 [A. 199]

230.4   J. Reinke, Einleitung in die Theoretische Biologie (1901), 500–503 [A. 199]

230.24   Déperet, 97, 98 [T. 200]

230.33   Owens, Paleontology, 175. [T. 200]

358.20   Antigone 334, 375 [T. 313]

381.3   L'Evolution des Forces, Gustave Le Bon, 131, 132 [A. 332]

396.30   Lucien Poincaré, L'Electricité, 23, 46, 59, 61, 65, 74 [A. 346]

397.2 Bouty, La Verité Scientifique, 248–9. Life & Letters of Faraday, Vol. 2. Ch. 7. [A. 346]

397.2 Lodge, Modern Views, etc. p. 320–321, 314, for the pump and for phosphorescence [T. 346]

397.12 L'Evolution des Forces, Gustave LeBon. 129, 131 [A. 346]

397.18 Lucien Poincaré, La Physique Moderne, 274, 275 [A. 346]

397.28 Emile Ricard, quoted by Gustave Le Bon, Forces, 5 [A. 347]

400.1 Brunhes. La Degradation de l'Energie, 1908. p. 169 [A. 349]

400.7 Lapparent, 724 [A. 349]

400.13 Der Richtungsbegriff und seine Bedeutung fur die Philosophie. Von Goldscheid. Annalen der Naturphilosophie VI, 1, April, 1907 [A. 349]

400.22 Von Zittel au Congrès de Zürich (See Déperet, Transformations, 120) [A. 349]

426.28 Life of Faraday, II, 362 [A. 374]

427.19 Martineau, II, 152. [Annotates the proposed insertion listed in Table 5 at page 374, lines 18–19] [A. 374]

427.30 André Lalande, La Dissolution opposée a l'Evolution. 1899. p. 102, 104, 382 [A. 374]

429.5 Duhem, L'Evolution de la Méchanique. Chapter V. pp. 32–42 [A. 376]

429.9 Houlleirgue. Du Laboratoire etc., 264. [A. 376]

431.4 Poincaré. La Valeur de la Science, 270. [A. 377]

431.5 Lodge, Modern Views, etc. 336. [T. 377]

431.7 Bouty, La Verité Scientifique, 289, 298. [A. 377]

431.10 Le Bon. Forces, 59 [T. 377]

433.9 Camille Sabatier, Revue Générale, 15 mai, 1908, 362. [A. 379]

441.1 Poincaré. La Science et l'Hypothèse, 113, 115. [A. 386]

441.3 Poincaré. La Science et l'Hypothèse, 113 [T. 386]

441.3 Gustave Le Bon, L'Evolution des Forces, 24 [A. 386]

452.8 L. Poincaré. La Physique Moderne, 304 [A. 396]

452.18 Id. 12 Poincaré [A. 396]

454.21 Faraday's Life, II, 380 [A. 398]

454.24 Poincaré. La Valeur de la Science, 180 [A. 398]

455.11 Bouty, La Verité Scientifique, 128, 198 [A. 398]

455.32 L. Houlleirgue. Du Laboratoire à l'Usine, 299 [A. 399]

456.5 Lalande, Dissolution, 373 [A. 399]

456.23 Gustave Le Bon, Forces, 348ff. [A. 400]

456.32 "This word is failure" Kelvin, Jubilee Address, 1904 [A. 400]

457.2 Poincaré. La Valeur de la Science, 198–199 [A. 400]

457.29 "On arrive ainsi à la preuve qu'il existe au moins deux Univers." Kapteyn and Eddington on the stellar universe, 1908. [A. 401]

458.13 Bouty. La Verité Scientifique, 285 [A. 401]

Table 6

460.22   H. Poincaré. La Valeur de la Science, 276 [A. 403]

474.11   Gustave le Bon, Evolution des Forces p. 58° 74.

°"All forces of nature" (e.g. Thought) "are engendered by the perturbations of equilibrium in ether or matter, and disappear when the troubled equilibriums are reestablished." [A. 414]

475.14   Hubert, p. 144 [Annotates the proposed insertion listed in Table 5 at page 415, line 14] [A. 415]

476.8   "Le polythéisme et le fétichisme n'offrent encore que des formations embryonnaires des pluralismes en travail de monisme." Roberty. La Recherche de l'Unité. Paris, 1894 [A. 416]

484.16   Illa domum scientia ceteris est praestantior quae intellectum humanum minimum multiplicitate onerat. De Dignitate, III, 4 [A. 423]

487.23   Bouty. La Verité Scientifique, 205 [A. 426]

489.19   Bouty. La Verité Scientifique. 205 [A. 427]

489.19   Le Bon. Forces, 222 [T. 427]

489.25   Manville. Les Découvertes Moderne, 1908. 176. [Annotates the proposed insertion given in Table 5 at page 427, line 25] [A. 427]

490.1   For Mass, see Poincaré, Science et l'Hypothèse, 120–125. Le Bon, Evolution des Forces. 28–29. [T. 428]

493.31   Bouty. La Verité Scientifique. 35. [A. 431]

496.18   Poincaré. La Valeur de la Science, 276.

Bouty, La Verité Scientifique. 54, 176. [A. 433]

Selected Bibliography

PRINCIPAL WRITINGS OF HENRY ADAMS

The Life of Albert Gallatin. Philadelphia, 1879.
Democracy. An American Novel. (anonymous) New York, 1880.
John Randolph. Boston, 1882.
Esther. A Novel. (pseudonym, Frances Snow Compton) New York, 1884.
History of the United States of America during the Administrations of Jefferson and Madison. 9 vols. New York, 1889–91.
Historical Essays. New York, 1891.
Memoirs of Marau Taaroa Last Queen of Tahiti. Privately printed, Washington, 1893. Revised as *Memoirs of Arii Taimai*. Privately printed, Washington, 1901.
Mont-Saint-Michel and Chartres. Privately printed, Washington, 1904. Boston, 1913.
The Education of Henry Adams. Privately printed, Washington, 1907. Boston, 1918.
A Letter to American Teachers of History. Privately printed, Baltimore, 1910.
The Life of George Cabot Lodge. Boston, 1911.
The Degradation of the Democratic Dogma. Ed. by Brooks Adams. Boston, 1919.
A Cycle of Adams Letters. 2 vols. Ed. by Worthington Chauncey Ford. Boston, 1920.
Letters of Henry Adams 1858–1891. Ed. by Worthington Chauncey Ford. Boston, 1930. [cited elsewhere in this volume as Ford, I]
Letters of Henry Adams 1892–1918. Ed. by Worthington Chauncey Ford. Boston, 1938. [cited elsewhere in this volume as Ford, II]
Henry Adams and His Friends. Letters edited with introduction by Harold Dean Cater. Boston, 1947. [cited elsewhere in this volume as Cater]
For a complete list of Adams's writings see Samuels I, 313–21; II, 423–26; III, 591–94.

SELECTED LIST OF SECONDARY WORKS

Adams, James Truslow. *The Adams Family*. New York, 1930.
Baym, Max I. *The French Education of Henry Adams*. New York, 1951.

Bibliography

Beringause, Arthur F. *Brooks Adams*. New York, 1955.

Chanler, Margaret. *Roman Spring*. Boston, 1935.

Conder, John J. *A Formula of His Own*. Chicago, 1970.

Dennett, Tyler. *John Hay: From Poetry to Politics*. New York, 1933.

Duberman, Martin B. *Charles Francis Adams 1807–1886*. Boston, 1960.

Garraty, John A. *Henry Cabot Lodge*. New York, 1953.

Greenslet, Ferris. *Under the Bridge*. Boston, 1943.

Gwynn, Stephen. *The Letters and Friendships of Sir Cecil Spring Rice*. Boston, 1929.

Hay, John. *Letters of John Hay and Extracts from Diary*. Washington, 1908.

Hochfield, George. *Henry Adams: An Introduction and Interpretation*. New York, 1962.

Hume, Robert A. *Runaway Star: An Appreciation of Henry Adams*. Ithaca, 1951.

Jordy, William. *Henry Adams: Scientific Historian*. New Haven, 1952. [includes an extensive annotated bibliography of books and articles]

King, Clarence. *Clarence King Memoirs*. New York, 1904.

La Farge, John. *Reminiscences of the South Seas*. Garden City, N.Y., 1912.

Levenson, J. C. *The Mind and Art of Henry Adams*. Boston, 1957.

Lyon, Melvin. *Symbol and Idea in Henry Adams*. Lincoln, 1970.

Mane, Robert. *Henry Adams on the Road to Chartres*. Cambridge, Mass., 1971.

Samuels, Ernest. *The Young Henry Adams*. Cambridge, Mass., 1948. *Henry Adams: The Middle Years*. Cambridge, Mass., 1958. *Henry Adams: The Major Phase*. Cambridge, Mass., 1964. [cited elsewhere in this volume as Samuels I, II, and III]

Stevenson, Elizabeth. *Henry Adams*. New York, 1955.

Thayer, William Roscoe. *John Hay*. Boston, 1915.

Thoron, Ward (ed.). *The Letters of Mrs. Henry Adams*. Boston, 1936.

Wagner, Vern. *The Suspension of Henry Adams: A Study of Manner and Matter*. Detroit, 1969.

Wasser, Henry. *The Scientific Thought of Henry Adams*. Thessaloniki, 1956.

Wharton, Edith. *A Backward Glance*. New York, 1934.

Wilkins, Thurman. *Clarence King*. New York, 1958.

BIBLIOGRAPHICAL ESSAYS

Harbert, Earl N. "Henry Adams," *Fifteen American Authors before 1900* (eds.) Robert A. Rees and Earl N. Harbert. Madison, 1971.

Vandersee, Charles A. "Henry Adams," *American Literary Realism 1870–1910*, II, 2 (Summer, 1969).

Notes

The following frequently cited works are abbreviated as follows: *Letters of Henry Adams 1858–1891* and *Letters of Henry Adams 1892–1918*, both collections edited by Worthington Chauncey Ford, as Ford I and Ford II; Ernest Samuels, *The Young Henry Adams; Henry Adams: The Middle Years; Henry Adams: The Major Phase*, as Samuels I, Samuels II, and Samuels III.

The identification of a person may be located in the Notes by consulting the note to the first or, in a few instances, to a subsequent page reference in the Index.

Where an annotation does not identify all the persons in a passage, consult the Index entry for the person about whom information is desired.

PRELIMINARIES

iv 1 The original private printing, which was dated at Washington, carried no notice of copyright. He made a gift of the valuable copyright to the Massachusetts Historical Society, with which he had long been associated as a corresponding member.

v 2 The 1907 printing did not contain a table of contents. It was supplied by Adams for the posthumous edition of 1918. In the 1907 printing only the dates appeared as chapter titles.

xxvii 3 One learns from his letters that the actual writing was already underway in 1903. The manuscript was nearly completed by December, 1905; Adams continued to work on it in Washington and Paris during 1906. Forty copies were originally printed by Furst and Company of Baltimore toward the close of 1906, but the "Author's Preface" had yet to be run off and the books bound. The work was finally completed early in 1907 as indicated by the date of the Author's Preface (p. xxx). Adams sent out the first copy in the middle of February, 1907. Sixty additional copies were subsequently printed to meet the demand for copies from his friends. Copies were sent to persons significantly mentioned in the text, e.g. Theodore Roosevelt, Henry Cabot Lodge, Brooks and Charles Adams, Charles Milnes Gaskell, Henry James, and many others with the request that they return them with their corrections. Only a very few returned their copies or sug-

539

gested corrections. For the response to Adams's gift, see Samuels, III, 332 ff.

4   To a large degree this explanation is a rationalization of the process of composition. Although Adams had thought about writing some sort of autobiographical commentary as far back as the early nineties, the *Education* grew out of the earlier book and was not planned simultaneously with it. For an account of its composition see Samuels, III, 310 ff.

5   By Furst and Company of Baltimore. Copyright January 7, 1905, by Henry Adams.

6   For Adams's appreciative reading of St. Augustine's *Confessions* and the influence of the book upon him, see Samuels, III, 340 ff. Cf. Adams to Henry James, February 17, 1908 (Ford, II, 490):

> Did you ever read the *Confessions* of St. Augustine, or of Cardinal de Retz, or of Rousseau, or of Benevenuto Cellini, or even of my dear Gibbon? Of them all, I think St. Augustine alone has an idea of literary form,—a notion of writing a story with an end and object, not for the sake of the object, but for the form, like a romance.

See also Koretz, "Augustine's *Confessions* and *The Education of Henry Adams*," *Comparative Literature*, 12 (Summer 1960), 193–206.

xxviii 7   For his own extended commentary on his intention, see the draft letter in Appendix A, which he had planned to send to his fellow historians to accompany the philosophic essay "The Rule of Phase Applied to History," an essay published in revised form posthumously in 1919 in *The Degradation of the Democratic Dogma*. The forty-five page essay was written in 1908, but Adams set it aside as unsatisfactory and replaced it with *A Letter to American Teachers of History*, the full title of the book referred to in the "Editor's Preface."

8   He suffered a cerebral thrombosis on April 24, 1912, accompanied by a partial paralysis which lasted for several months. He recovered sufficiently to resume his annual sojourns in France until the outbreak of World War I. Although he continued to carry on his extensive correspondence in his own hand and by dictation to the very end and occupied himself with research in medieval *chansons*, he wrote nothing further for publication. However, he did help Father Sigourney Fay during World War I with an article highly critical of the German character, "The Genesis of the Super-German," *Dublin Review*, April 1918, pp. 224–233.

9   Ralph Adams Cram persuaded Adams to allow the publication of the revised version of the *Chartres*. Adams gave the copyright to the

Institute with the request that the royalties be used to provide copies of the work to impecunious architects. The royalties proved sufficiently large to enable the Institute to commission a stained glass window for Chartres Cathedral.

10   A characteristic example of Adams's pose of Socratic humility. He did, in fact, resist editor Greenslet's efforts to have the book published in his lifetime.

11   The date of the beginning of World War I, which seemed to Adams the Q.E.D. of all his pessimistic demonstrations.

12   Since this statement was written *before* the volume came into the hands of the actual editors in 1918 it fails to take account of the many changes they felt obliged to make in preparing the trade edition. See the "Textual Note" for the circumstances of editing and publication and Appendix B, Tables 1 and 3, for the editorial changes. In the "Editor's Preface" laid into the volume sent to Lodge in 1916 Adams mistakenly referred to Chapters XXXIX and XL of the *Education*. This was corrected by the editors to Chapters XXXIII and XXXIV. In the last paragraph, however, the editors changed Adams's phrase "has now decided to publish" to "now publishes." Adams's phrase has been restored.

13   The signature by Henry Cabot Lodge and the date of September, 1918, represent a kind of private joke upon posterity, for the "Editor's Preface" was written by Henry Adams himself in 1916 as explained in the following letter to Henry Cabot Lodge, March 1, 1916:

> I send you herewith a sealed packet containing a copy of my *Education*, corrected and prepared for publication. Should the question arise at any future time, I wish that you, on behalf of the Historical Society, would take charge of the matter, and see that the volume is printed as I leave it. With this view I have written a so-called Editor's Preface, which you have read, and which I have taken the liberty, subject to your assent, to stamp with your initials. Also, may I beg that you will bar the introduction of all illustrations of any sort. You know that I do not consider illustrations as my work, or having part in any correct rendering of my ideas. Least of all do I wish portraits. I have always followed the rule of making the reader think only of the text, and I do not want to abandon it here.

Lodge did assent to the deception, solacing his conscience with the belief that people who read the preface "would have no sort of doubt I had written it." Quoted in Samuels, III, 560.

xxix   14   The translation appears to be Adams's own.

15 Franklin's unfinished *Autobiography*, which was begun in 1771 and first published in English in a garbled edition in 1818, quickly became an American classic, admired both for its literary style and its moral inspiration.

16 An allusion to St. Augustine.

xxx 17 A characteristic hyperbole. As an avid reader of diaries and autobiographies, Adams was familiar with almost all of the significant memoirs of his time, including those of figures like Carlyle, Darwin, Huxley, Mill, Newman, Ruskin, Spencer, and Trollope. He was obviously influenced by them, but none of them had systematically imposed upon their personal experience a philosophic and historical thesis like his, a thesis in which terms like "education" and "useful" took on very special meanings.

18 Adams seems here to wish to justify his own reticent omissions and the third-person detachment of his narrative. In this respect the statement is a piece of wishful thinking, as the whole drift of autobiography as of psychology at the turn of the century was toward greater introspection and egocentricity.

19 In his reference to the manikin-persona and the imagery of the tailor, Adams here recalls the "clothes philosophy" of Carlyle's *Sartor Resartus,* a favorite book of Adams's young manhood. For the pervasive influence of that book, see the Carlyle entries in the Index and note especially Ch. XXVII, which bears the title of Carlyle's pilgrim hero. For an analysis of the Carlylean aspects of the *Education,* see Samuels, III, 347–353.

20 His sixty-ninth birthday. His deliberately dating the preface as of his birthday suggests that he intended the book to serve as a kind of ceremonial birthday message to his friends and acquaintances. Since he dispatched a bound copy to his brother Charles on February 20, only four days after the printed date of the preface, it is probable that the preface was written some weeks earlier as the printer in Baltimore had to set up the type of the preface, run off the sheets, and bind the initial forty copies. Adams used a similar symbolic dating of the preface of his *Letter to American Teachers of History* in 1910 on the occasion of his seventy-second birthday.

CHAPTER I *Quincy* (*1838–1848*)

3 1 John Hancock (1737–93), the first signer of the Declaration of Independence and first governor of the state of Massachusetts.

2   His uncle, Nathaniel Langdon Frothingham (1793–1870), pastor of the First Church, 1818–50. His wife, Ann Brooks, and Adams's mother, Abigail, were sisters. Adams discontinued the use of his middle name, Brooks, in 1870, when he became editor of the *North American Review.*

3   The Temple in Jerusalem, built by King Solomon in Biblical times, was the religious center of the Jewish people. It was part of an elaborate complex of buildings which also included the royal palace. The physical analogy is rather fanciful since the Temple itself was the house of worship or synagogue of Jerusalem. The religious rite of circumcision was performed on all Jewish male infants. The anachronism, in the hypothetical case—since the Temple had been destroyed in antiquity—points up the unfortunate vein of anti-Semitism that marked Adams's thinking in his later years. "Israel Cohen" serves here as the most typical Jewish name imaginable. By the time Adams began to write the *Education,* the immigrant Jew and the Jewish banker had become for him twin symbols of the social and economic disintegration of American life, and his private letters are filled with his denunciations of them; hence the special relevance of the comparison. A characteristic outburst appears soon after the Panic of 1893 in a letter to an English friend (Ford, II, 35): "I am myself more than ever at odds with my time. I detest it, and everything that belongs to it, and live only in the wish to see the end of it, with all its infernal Jewry. I want to put every money-lender to death, and to sink Lombard Street and Wall Street under the ocean." A few years later he exclaimed to another friend: "The Jew has got into the soul. I see him—or her—now everywhere, and wherever he—or she—goes, there must remain a taint in the blood forever." (Adams Papers, Adams to Phillips, July 26, 1896). See also n. 4, Ch. XVI. Note his return to the theme in Ch. XVI, p. 238. For an account of this anti-Semitic obsession which was shared by many persons of his acquaintance, see Samuels, III, Index, "Anti-Semitism," "Jews."

4   4   This fabulous exploit of the vengeful giant is recounted in Book I, Ch. XVII of Rabelais' *Gargantua and Pantagruel* (1552). Napoleon and Bismarck were, of course, giants in a quite different sense, Napoleon as the conqueror of Europe at the beginning of the nineteenth century and Bismarck as the shaper of imperial Germany at its end. ". . . must bear his own universe" is an allusion to the mythical Atlas.

5   5   ". . . on the doctrine of chances," according to the so-called laws of probability.

6   The railroad was extended to Quincy from Boston in 1846.

543

7   The steamship *Britannia* inaugurated regular service in 1840. The first crossing under steam power alone took place in 1838.

8   During the crisis his father kept a day and night vigil at his bedside, and when the noted Dr. Bigelow and his learned consultant Dr. Jackson decided to prescribe smelling salts, the father recorded in his Diary: "Oh, how my heart was in my throat in all this and how utterly did I feel the vanity of trusting to medical help in this moment of agonizing trial" (Adams Papers, December 11, 1841).

6   9   As recorded in his father's Diary, the move to 57 Mount Vernon Street occurred January 12, a providentially mild winter's day. An entry for January 20 reads: "My boy Henry is now recovering the use of his limbs and appears gradually to be returning to health."

10   According to Darwin's theory of evolution, natural selection occurred through the "survival of the fittest" (Herbert Spencer's phrase).

11   John Quincy Adams II (1833–94); Charles Francis Adams Jr. (1835–1915).

7   12   Edith Squires married in England the first Henry Adams, who emigrated with her to the Massachusetts Bay Colony about 1633. The allusions are to the recurring struggles of the colony against the authority of the British Crown and against the short-lived dictatorship of Oliver Cromwell (1599–1658), the English Puritan leader who deposed Charles I in 1647.

8   13   The family moved to Quincy each summer, usually residing there from mid-spring to late autumn. Their house was near the "Mansion" of grandfather John Quincy Adams. Henry's father commuted to his office in Boston during the summer and regularly passed an hour or so each evening with his aged parents at the Mansion.

9   14   The symbolic center of old Boston on which stands the state capitol.

15   The financial center of Boston.

11   16   John Adams returned from London in 1789, after four years' service as American minister to England. However, he had already served twice in France on diplomatic missions: the first time in 1778; the second from 1779 to 1783 when he helped negotiate the Treaty of Paris, signed in 1783, ending the Revolutionary War. When President, he appointed his son John Quincy Adams minister to Berlin, recalling him in 1801 when Jefferson succeeded to the Presidency. In 1817 John Quincy Adams returned to the United States, after having helped negotiate the Treaty of Ghent in 1814 and having thereafter served as minister to England. John Adams negotiated the purchase

of the house on the County Highway, now Adams Street, from Leonard Vassall, while still in London. The deed, dated September 26, 1787, shows that he paid 600 pounds for seven parcels of land. "The first of these, a seven acre tract, was the 'Old House' [Adams National Historic Site] with its adjoining farmland." It had been built by Leonard Vassall's grandfather, Major Leonard Vassall Borland in 1731. The house was subsequently much altered. (W. C. Edwards, *Historic Quincy Massachusetts* [Quincy, Mass., 1957], pp. 39–41, 348.)

17 Actually Grandfather Brooks died on January 1, 1849.

12   18 Genesis IV, 16. The Lord's curse condemned Cain to be a wandering outlaw on earth for having killed his brother Abel. When Cain protested the harshness of his punishment, the Lord put a mark on his forehead to protect him from earthly vengeance. In his fanciful adaptation of the legend, Adams simultaneously identifies himself with the murdered younger brother and with Cain who felt himself the victim of arbitrary authority.

13   19 Henry was not alone in his dislike for summer schooling. His father noted in his Diary (June 29, 1844):

> Kept school all morning for my children who are on the whole not very willing scholars and who try my patience a good deal.

In the preceding summer he had placed two of the older children with a schoolmaster in Hingham and afterwards wrote in his Diary (October 21, 1843):

> I have been on the whole very well satisfied with the care taken of the children by him, but as a schoolmaster I should very much doubt whether his course of instruction would profit them much. In the summer children should recruit their physical powers rather than be sedentary, and they make better progress for it in the winter.

20 John Quincy Adams bitterly opposed Polk for his Southern expansionist policy. When he learned of Polk's election he wrote in his Diary, "It is the victory of the slavery element in the Constitution" (*Diary of John Quincy Adams*, ed. Allan Nevins [New York, 1969], Nov. 8, 1844).

14   21 Geologizing became one of Henry Adams's hobbies. It should also be noted that the Quincy quarries were famous for their granite.

15   22 John Quincy Adams refused to submit to party discipline, most notably when he rebelled against the Federalist leadership and supported Jefferson. In spite of his intransigence he achieved the highest distinction as a statesman, serving as a United States senator, minister

to Russia, secretary of state, and finally President of the United States. He became most famous, perhaps, for his courageous return to Congress as an ex-President where he was the most formidable spokesman for the antislavery cause and earned the sobriquet "Old Man Eloquent."

23 Josiah Quincy (1772–1864), a noted Federalist leader, president of Harvard College from 1829 to 1845. He was, in fact, only five years younger than John Quincy Adams.

16 24 In the rare sense of "uncertainty."

25 *Adventures of Peregrine Pickle* (1751) by Tobias Smollett (1721–71); *The History of Tom Jones* (1749) by Henry Fielding (1707–54); Hannah More (1745–1833), a famous English religious writer.

17 26 The small central district of London which was governed by its own council. The Tower of London is the ancient fortress on the east side of the City, repository of the Crown Jewels and much visited by tourists.

27 George Romney (1734–1802), a favorite painter of the British aristocracy. His portraits of women are full of grace and sweetness and warmth of coloring.

28 Abigail Smith Adams (1744–1818), one of the earliest American advocates of rights for women. She has been a favorite subject for biographers. Her inimitable letters were edited in two volumes by her grandson, Henry Adams's father.

18 29 Federalist President John Adams, a conservative, was defeated for re-election by Thomas Jefferson, a member of the popular Republican party, in a bitterly contested election for the Presidency. In 1796 Washington appointed John Quincy Adams Minister to Portugal but before he could leave, his father became President and sent him to Berlin.

30 The "hundred days" from March 20, 1815, to June 28, 1815, comprised the brief period of Napoleon's return to power in France after his exile in the island of Elba. He was defeated at Waterloo on June 18, 1815.

31 The Prince of Wales (1762–1830) ruled as Prince Regent for nine years after his father, George III (1738–1820), became permanently deranged in 1811. On his father's death in 1820 he became George IV.

32 The date is erroneous. John Quincy Adams was elected in 1830 to the Twenty-second Congress and took his seat in 1831. See Ford, II, 491.

19 33 Louisa Catherine Adams's adventurous career had a special

fascination for her grandson Henry. In 1869 he worked on her volu-
minous Memoirs with a view to their publication in several volumes.
The project was abandoned when he became a teacher at Harvard.
His meticulous transcripts are preserved at the Houghton Library,
Harvard University.

34 "primal sin," as rhymed in the Puritan *New England Primer,* "In
Adams's fall/We sinnèd all"; "fall from grace," the expulsion of Adam
and Eve from Eden; "curse of Abel," the allusion is to the curse originally laid upon Abel's father, Adam, which Abel as well as Cain inherited, namely, the sinful and disobedient nature which became
Adam's lot with his fall from grace and loss of innocence.

35 It would be more accurate to say that Henry's father was one-
quarter Marylander by birth and Henry himself, one-eighth, in view
of the fact that Henry's grandmother, Louisa Catherine, was herself
only half Marylander as *her* mother was of an English London family.

20 36 The date was November 20, 1846, when the old man suffered a
slight stroke (cerebral hemorrhage) while walking with Dr. George
Parkman (1790–1849) and fell to his knees on the pavement. He was
back in his seat in Congress on February 12, 1847. His deformed
handwriting in the remaining fragmentary entries in his Diary reflected
the partial paralysis. He returned to Congress in November, 1847,
and in spite of his enfeebled condition he was regular in attendance
and vigilant to oppose the pro-slavery measures which were offered in
the House. His second stroke, on the floor of the House, occurred
Feb. 21, 1848. He died on the 23rd. (Samuel F. Bemis, *John Quincy
Adams and the Union* [New York, 1956].)

37 Probably the Dr. George Parkman of n.36 who donated the site
for a new building for the Harvard Medical College. He was an uncle
of Francis Parkman (1823–93), the famed historian of the Oregon
Trail and of the French presence on the American continent. Francis
Parkman was a second cousin of Henry Adams.

38 Peter P. F. Degrand (d. 1855), originally a Philadelphia banker.
In J. Q. Adams's Diary he is depicted as an inveterate job seeker.
(Bemis, *op. cit.*, pp. 22, 137.)

39 Gilbert Stuart (1755–1828), an American portrait painter, best
known for his portraits of George Washington. He painted portraits
of both John Adams and John Quincy Adams.

40 Rev. William Parsons Lunt (1805–57). He delivered the funeral
oration at the commemorative services for John Quincy Adams on
March 11, 1848.

41   Joseph Stevens Buckminster (1784–1812), one of the first Unitarian ministers in Boston and a noted founder of Biblical scholarship in the United States.

42   William Ellery Channing (1780–1842), the most influential spokesman of the Unitarian movement, famous for his epochal sermon delivered in 1820, "The Moral Argument against Calvinism."

21   43   Henry Adams's great-grandfather, President John Adams (1735–1826), was buried in the crypt of the First Parish church as was also his wife Abigail (Smith) Adams (1744–1818).

44   Edward Everett (1794–1865), brother-in-law of Henry Adams's mother. Famous Unitarian preacher and statesman-congressman, minister to England, president of Harvard from 1846 to 1849. Much admired for his florid orations.

45   Sam[uel] Adams's father, Samuel Adams (1689–1748), was a first cousin of President John Adams's father, John Adams (1691–1761), and hence Sam Adams was a second cousin of President John Adams.

46   State Street, the financial center of Boston and chief support of the most conservative elements in the Federalist party.

47   This rather highly colored summary of Boston history alludes to such affairs as the popular revolt against the royal governor, Sir Edmund Andros, in 1689; the struggles of patriots like John Adams and his second cousin, the more radical Sam Adams, with the Tories before the Revolution; the expropriation of the property of fugitive Tories during the Revolution; the Federalist opposition to Jefferson's embargo measures which led to the Essex Junto Conspiracy; and finally to the pro-English Hartford Convention of Federalists opposed to continuation of the War of 1812 and favoring a New England federation detached from the Union. John Quincy Adams deplored the divisive tactics of his party and deserted it. In 1877 Henry Adams published *Documents Relating to New England Federalism 1800–1815*, which justified his grandfather's political reversal on the grounds of national loyalty. The reference to Florence recalls the prolonged and savage struggles of the Guelphs, the papal faction, and the Ghibellines, the faction supporting the German emperor, during the Middle Ages and the three hundred years of wars and intrigues of the Medici dynasty whose rule endured until 1737.

22   48   In the parable of the Prodigal Son (Luke xv, 11–32), the father forgave the young man who had wasted his portion in "riotous living" and welcomed him home with a feast for which a fatted calf was

killed. Grandfather Brooks was reputedly the wealthiest man in New England. Having early made his fortune as a merchant, he turned to real estate and mortgage loans. It was said of him that he never asked for more than 6 percent interest. He represented to his grandson the power and influence of the commercial interests of Boston. At the same time the grandson could not help being partially indebted to the old man for his own affluence since his mother was "amply provided for" in Grandfather Brooks's will. The Suffolk Bank was the arch-representative of financial monopoly.

CHAPTER II   *Boston (1848–1854)*

23   1   Louisa Catherine Adams (m. Charles Kuhn, 1854) was born August 13, 1831, not 1830. She died July 13, 1870. The other children besides Henry Adams were: John Quincy (1833–94), Charles Francis (1835–1915), Arthur (1841–46), Mary (1846–1928), Brooks (1848–1927). That Brooks played a significant role in Henry's re-education is indicated in the *Education*, pp. 339 and 360. The intellectual collaboration of the two brothers is analyzed in Arthur F. Beringause, *Brooks Adams* (New York, 1955) and in Samuels, III, Ch.IV, "Brothers in Prophecy."

24   2   The satirical term recalls the fact that Henry's grandfather had been denied a second term as President by the election of Andrew Jackson in a campaign marked by the utmost scurrility. In the election of 1824 Jackson had received the larger popular vote but he lost out to Adams in the electoral college. The ensuing political feud hamstrung the Administration and polarized the factions into the conservative National Republicans (Adams)—the predecessor of the Whig party—and the Jacksonian Democrats, a division that permanently marked American politics.

3   Cf. n. 46, Ch. I. Quincy, the ancestral home of the Adamses, symbolized the political principles of the family which now included the strongest moral opposition to the pro-slavery attitude of the conservative leaders of the State Street financial district. The complicated political quarrels included most notably John Adams's break with his fellow Federalist Alexander Hamilton, which in effect cost him reelection in 1800, and John Quincy Adams's disputes with the Federalist leadership in Boston.

4   Henry's father was well known as a writer on problems of the currency, being an advocate of "sound money," and he was for a time president of the Mt. Wollaston bank.

25   5 Daniel Webster (1782–1852), senator from Massachusetts after 1827; with Senator Henry Clay of Kentucky formed the Whig party in 1834 out of the National Republican followers of John Quincy Adams and the Democrats opposed to Jackson's abolition of the National Bank. They were joined by the southern States Rights leader John C. Calhoun. The new coalition included not only eastern capitalists and western farmers but southern plantation owners. The pressure toward compromise with slavery by the "Cotton" Whig faction led "Conscience Whigs" like Henry Adams's father to desert and help form the Free Soil party in 1848. Their candidates obtained no votes in the Electoral College. Webster's apostasy was completed in his famous Seventh of March address supporting the Compromise of 1850 which contained a strengthened Fugitive Slave law. William Henry Seward (1801–72), senator from New York widely known for his strong antislavery attitude who nevertheless supported the Whig compromise candidates for President in 1848 and 1852. His pragmatism in politics during these years was uncongenial to the Adamses, but by 1860 Henry's father was willing to follow Seward, who had become the leader of the new Republican party and who, though committed to antislavery, was equally committed to maintenance of the Union.

6 "Puritan politics," as Adams means to imply, had its roots in the English Puritan movement which aimed to purge the established Church of England of its worldly abuses and to obtain freedom of religious worship, a movement which culminated in the overthrow and execution of Charles I under the leadership of the Puritan general Oliver Cromwell. The Puritans were noted for their refusal to compromise their principles whether in religion or politics and they carried this zeal to America with them. The moral opposition that came to a head as a result of the bitter controversy over the Wilmot Proviso (relating to the future status of the territories wrested from Mexico) marked a polarization in American politics as significant in its way as that of 1776 when John Adams took his stand with the American Revolutionists against England.

26   7 "*a priori* thought," ideas and principles which are believed not to stand in need of proof, as in the Declaration of Independence: "We hold these truths to be self-evident: That all men are created equal . . ." etc.

8 Chiefly in connection with the biography of their father written by Charles Francis Adams, Henry's elder brother (*Charles Francis Adams,* Boston, 1900). For details of that discussion see Samuels, III, 152 ff.

27 9 All of these clergymen were influential in the great growth of the denomination between 1800 and 1835. The first Unitarian congregation in the United States was established in 1782 in King's Chapel in Boston. It discarded such orthodox dogmas of Calvinism as the Trinity, original sin, predestination, eternal damnation, vicarious atonement, and the divinity of Jesus. Dr. Palfrey, John Gorham Palfrey (1796–1881), a family friend of the Adamses, served in Congress and was famous as a New England historian. As editor of the *North American Review* he encouraged Henry Adams to write his first article for that quarterly. President John Walker (1794–1874), professor of religion at Harvard, president of Harvard after 1853. Ralph Waldo Emerson (1803–82), whose great *Essays* established him as the foremost writer of New England. He became the leading spokesman of the Transcendentalist movement which in pursuit of pure spirituality abandoned all traditional Christian observances such as the Lord's Supper which still survived in the Unitarian Church of the time.

10 Theodore Parker (1810–60), left the Unitarian church and founded the Congregational Society of Boston where he expounded Transcendentalism and used his pulpit to advance radical social and political reform; Brook Farm, from 1841 to 1847 an experiment in cooperative community living near West Roxbury, Massachusetts; "philosophy of Concord," the philosophic and literary movement which flourished from 1836 to 1860 in Concord, Massachusetts under the leadership of Ralph Waldo Emerson, whose inspiring essays and addresses—"Nature," "The American Scholar," "The Divinity School Address," "Self-Reliance," etc.—became the bible of the new movement. The group included Henry David Thoreau (*Walden*, 1854), Margaret Fuller, and others, and embraced a wide variety of intuitive speculation based on German transcendentalism, Platonic thought, and Oriental religious classics.

11 George Ticknor (1791–1871), First Smith Professor of French and Spanish literature at Harvard, author of a monumental history of Spanish literature; William Hickling Prescott (1796–1859), most noted for his histories of the conquest of Mexico and of Peru; Henry Wadsworth Longfellow (1807–82), the most popular American poet of the nineteenth century, author of *Hiawatha* (1855) and the *Courtship of Miles Standish* (1858); John Lothrop Motley (1814–77), historian (*Rise of the Dutch Republic*, 1856) and minister to Austria and to England; Oliver Wendell Holmes (1809–94), father of Justice Holmes, a leading Boston literary figure, novelist, poet, and author of the famous *Autocrat of the Breakfast Table* (1858).

28   12   Though Henry was his father's favorite son, his estimate of his father is not exaggerated. It is amply supported by Martin Duberman, *Charles Francis Adams 1807–1886* (Boston, 1960).

29   13   Robert Charles Winthrop (1804–94), descendant of the first governor of Massachusetts Bay Colony, speaker of the Thirtieth Congress, 1847–49, appointed United States senator to succeed Webster who had been appointed secretary of state. He was a conservative on the slavery issue and was defeated in the 1851 election by Charles Sumner, who was supported by a Free Soil coalition.

14   William Lloyd Garrison (1805–79), fiery editor of the abolitionist paper the *Liberator,* attacked the Constitution as a slaveholders' document and advocated division of the Union and immediate emancipation of slaves; Wendell Phillips (1811–84), prominent Boston Abolitionist and ardent supporter of Garrison; Edmund Quincy (1808–77), member of a distinguished New England family, reformer and author, closely associated with William Lloyd Garrison and a frequent contributor to antislavery publications.

15   To be taken in a somewhat ironical sense. Henry's father could not reconcile himself to the coalitionist tactics of the various factions among the Free Soilers, the Whigs, and the Republicans, all of whom courted his support, and as a result he periodically chose to go into political retirement, making his influence felt through an extensive correspondence and his connection with the *Boston Daily Whig* of which he was the principal editor from June, 1846, until August, 1848. Although the Free Soil party was not his creation he played an important role in its organization and in the behind-the-scenes maneuvering.

16   According to Duberman (*op. cit.,* p. 177) the group of intimates in the political discussions also included Anson Burlingame (1820–70), a prominent Boston lawyer who subsequently helped organize the Republican party in Massachusetts and who was rewarded by President Lincoln with appointment as minister to China, and Stephen C. Phillips (1801–57), congressman and the unsuccessful Free Soil candidate for governor in 1848. He retired from public life in 1849. Richard H. Dana, Jr. (1815–82), Boston lawyer and author (*Two Years before the Mast,* 1840), was active in Free Soil politics and defender without fee of fugitive slaves. Charles Sumner (1811–74), elected to the U.S. Senate from Massachusetts on the Free Soil ticket, became the eloquent leader of the New England opposition to the "Slave Power." He early favored emancipation and equal rights for slaves, and as a leader of the Radical Republicans opposed concilia-

tory policies toward the former Confederate states. He was active in the impeachment proceedings against President Andrew Johnson.

17 "Athenaeum Club," Pall Mall, London, founded by Sir Walter Scott and Thomas Moore in 1824 as a gathering place for men distinguished in literature, science, and the arts, and for patrons of the arts; "Combination Room at Trinity," the Commons Room at Trinity College, Oxford.

18 William M. Evarts (1818–1901), Boston-born lawyer, active in Republican politics, served as attorney general of the United States from July 1868 to March 1869 and as secretary of state under Hayes from 1877 to 1881. Henry Adams's intimacy with him began in 1863 when he was sent to London to serve as a legal adviser to Henry's father.

19 "Woolsack," the name given to the seat of the Lord Chancellor in the House of Lords.

30 20 Edmund Burke (1729–97), a British statesman of Irish birth and one of the greatest political orators in the House of Commons. His speech on conciliation with the American colonies (1775) became a classic of the literature of oratory. His political theory was deeply conservative as evidenced in his notable *Reflections on the French Revolution* (1790). He was long admired in America as the great spokesman of conservative principles.

21 Sumner like Everett was a man of great learning and scholarship. Both men had studied abroad for years. Webster was far less cosmopolitan, having entered early on the practice of law and then after a few years achieved fame as a remarkable political orator. Webster's politics also were more pragmatic than those of Everett, who was more of a humanitarian than Webster.

22 An allusion to Sumner's great Fourth of July oration, "The True Grandeur of Nations," given in Boston in 1845.

23 The heart of fashionable Boston. It descended down Beacon Hill from the State House.

24 George Ticknor (1791–1871). A distinguished scholar and man of the world. Ticknor was one of the first of a line of Harvard professors who prepared themselves to teach modern foreign languages by extended study in Europe. In fact in 1815 he crossed on the same vessel with Edward Everett, who was also seeking higher education abroad. After his retirement from Harvard he led a life of scholarship and social elegance. As a scholar he was most noted for his pioneer *History of Spanish Literature* (1849).

25 George R. Russell (1816–90), a Free Soil leader, an aspirant to Congress, who unselfishly withdrew from the race in 1858 to insure the nomination of Henry Adams's father.

31   26 John Ellerton Lodge (1807–62), a Boston merchant, father of Henry Cabot Lodge, for whom see index entry.

27 The *Boston Daily Whig*, which began publication only six months before his father became the editor and one of the proprietors of the paper. The other financial contributors were Dr. John Gorham Palfrey and Stephen C. Phillips. Neither Sumner nor Dana could afford to put any money into the venture. The initial circulation numbered only 212 but the paper appears to have been influential in Boston in helping to mobilize public opinion against slavery.

28 *The Works of John Adams*, 10 vols. (Boston, 1850–56), edited by Charles Francis Adams, who also wrote the *Life* contained in Vol. 1.

29 *Novanglus* was the pseudonym with which John Adams signed his controversial articles in the *Boston Gazette* replying to the loyalist essays signed *Massachusettensis* (author: Daniel Leonard of Taunton). The controversy ended abruptly when hostilities began at Lexington.

32   30 Cicero (106–43 B.C.) was the famous Roman orator and philosopher whose works were commonly studied in the required Latin classes at Harvard. The allusion is to *de Republica,* a dialogue on the best form of government.

31 Peter Harvey (1810–77), Whig politician. Cf. *Education,* p. 49. The contributors represent wealthy families of Boston, manufacturers, bankers, merchants, and entrepreneurs in the lucrative China trade.

32 See n. 13 above. Sumner had tried for a seat in Congress as a "Conscience" Whig in 1848 but was defeated by Winthrop.

33   33 Louis Philippe (1773–1850), king of France, 1830–48, a pseudo-liberal monarch who initially posed as a democrat but increasingly catered to the *bourgeoisie;* Francois Guizot (1787–1874), historian and premier of France, opposed parliamentary reform and extolled the virtues of acquiring wealth; Count Alexis de Tocqueville (1805–59), author of the celebrated *Democracy in America* (1835, 1840). Distressed by the Revolution of 1830 in France he came to America to see whether democracy was feasible. Although as a conservative he saw many disadvantages and dangers in the American system he also clearly recognized the advantages, especially the freedom and general prosperity of the people.

34 Robert Peel (1788–1850), prime minister of England, 1834–35. A member of the Tory party, he spoke for the business interests of

England and skillfully adhered to conservative financial policies. Thomas Macaulay (1800–59), historian and member of parliament, famous for his masterly *History of England* (1849–61). A liberal in politics, he had eloquently supported the Reform Bill for broadening the suffrage. He was not, however, a social reformer. He accepted middle class material values and like Guizot hoped for their spread. John Stuart Mill (1806–73), English philosopher and economist. His great essay *On Liberty* (1859) has remained the classic statement of the middle class liberal. He was an early advocate of rights for women and supported all of the humanitarian reforms of his day.

35 Thomas Carlyle (1795–1881), famed author of *Sartor Resartus,* (1836) which called for the spiritual regeneration of society, and *Heroes and Hero Worship* (1841), which called for great leaders. He became a friend of Ralph Waldo Emerson, the "sage of Concord," and carried on an extensive correspondence with him.

36 The passage is typical of Adams's metaphorical treatment of historical events. Seen in proper historical perspective, events for Adams reflect the working out of great tendencies or forces. The allusion here is to such developments as the formation of the first German federal parliament at Frankfort and the movement in Italy toward national unity and a republican government. In both instances the old order of small semi-feudal independent states was being overthrown as a result of complex impulses and pressures, economic, social, racial, and political.

37 The series of revolutionary outbreaks which swept Europe from Ireland to Austria in 1848 varied considerably in character. In France it was a working class attack on the bourgeoisie, its rationale being the *Communist Manifesto* of 1848. In Central Europe it was principally a revolt of the Liberal and popular elements against the autocratic monarchies whose guiding spirit was Prince Metternich. The success of the democratic movements was short-lived, however, in the face of racial rivalries, and the old order of antidemocratic states was soon reestablished by the imperial armies after much bloodshed. The Communist risings were a small part of the general movement and were totally suppressed.

38 Karl Marx (1818–83), chief political philosopher of the Communist movement, author with Friedrich Engels of the *Communist Manifesto* (1848), best known for his great critique of the capitalist system, *Capital,* first issued in German in 1867.

39 A fundamental tenet of Unitarianism as expressed in Channing's "Moral Argument against Calvinism," 1820.

40   An allusion to the great influence of the Massachusetts-born educational reformer Horace Mann (1796–1859), a noted humanitarian and believer in the indefinite perfectibility of man through education.

41   From Longfellow's poem "The Arsenal at Springfield," published in the *Belfry of Bruges and Other Poems* in 1845.

34   42   His father, who was devoutly religious, was aware of this falling off and recorded in his Diary in 1870 on the occasion of the death of his daughter Louisa that his chief shortcoming was that he had not interested his children sufficiently "into the sentiment of religion." "The Unitarian faith," he wrote, "is not warm enough to supply a want of many natures which if neglected brings an indifference."

35   43   Webster supported the Compromise of 1850, but the small Free Soil party did protest against it.

44   Octavius Frothingham (1822–95), at first a Unitarian minister, later became an independent clergyman, author of *Transcendentalism in New England: A History* (1876). Though deeply religious, he was even more unorthodox in his Christianity than Theodore Parker. His rejection of even the limited residue of Christian traditions retained by the Unitarian church of that period may well have been regarded by the Rev. Nathaniel Frothingham as "skepticism."

45   Emerson did not devise a systematic philosophical or theological system as was traditional among learned European philosophers. His method tended to be inspirational and literary.

46   The protagonist of James Russell Lowell's *Bigelow Papers,* First Series (1848), whose rhymed "Epistles" in upcountry New England dialect satirized the war with Mexico and the evils of slavery.

37   47   "a brand escaped from the burning," Old Testament, Zechariah III, 2.

48   For the details of his early schooling see Samuels, I, 4 ff.

38   49   For a fascinating account of the natural history of the neighborhood of Concord see *Walden* by Henry David Thoreau.

39   50   Historical novels by Sir Walter Scott (1771–1832).

CHAPTER III   *Washington (1850–1854)*

40   1   "bad taste of Queen Victoria and Louis Philippe," explained in *Education,* p. 195.

41   2   Charles attended the famous Boston Latin School whereas Henry, because the School Committee now required parents to be tax-paying residents, had to attend the private Latin School of Epes S. Dixwell.

3 Henry Lee Higginson (1834–1919), became a leading Boston financier and philanthropist. Note that a "slungshot" differs from a "slingshot"; it resembles a blackjack, a small bludgeon with a flexible handle.

4 James Savage (1832–63), son of the historian and antiquarian of the same name.

42 5 Noted soldiers. Turenne (1611–75) fought under Richelieu and Mazarin and in 1660 became Marshal General of France; Henri IV as a young man was forced to abjure his Protestantism. He subsequently escaped from the French court and joined the rebels against Henri III.

6 James Savage died of battle wounds at Charlottesville, Virginia, on October 22, 1863. Marvin was incorrectly identified in the 1918 Index as William Theophilus Rogers Marvin (1832–1913). One Thomas Marvin, Ninth Infantry, was killed at Gaines Mill, Va., June, 1862.

7 The Fugitive Slave Law, passed as part of the Compromise of 1850, provided for exclusive Federal jurisdiction over runaway slaves. The passage of the Kansas-Nebraska Bill on May 25, 1854, which in effect repealed the Missouri Compromise of 1820 as well as that of 1850, gave Southerners new confidence in their right to extend slavery while it outraged many Northerners, especially in New England. The day after its passage on May 26 a large Boston mob tried to rescue Anthony Burns, a runaway slave. They failed and Burns was taken to the wharf with the aid of a battalion of U.S. artillery, four platoons of marines, and a sheriff's posse. The hostile crowd was held back by twenty-two companies of state militia. This was the scene witnessed by young Henry Adams.

43 8 The Stamp Tax of 1765, requiring revenue stamps to be attached to all manner of documents and papers, was the first Act of Parliament to assert the right to tax American commodities directly for revenue purposes. The Tea Tax levied an import duty on tea and led to the famous Boston Tea Party of 1773, when demonstrators disguised as Indians dumped three tea cargoes into the harbor. The Boston Massacre occurred March 5, 1770, when British soldiers fired on a mob which was baiting them. Four persons were killed and several wounded by the volley. Captain Preston and the soldiers were charged with murder. John Adams was prevailed upon to defend them and secured an acquittal from the jury. These episodes helped precipitate the American Revolutionary War.

44 9 The Washington monument. Begun in 1848, it was not completed until 1884.

45   10   The north wing of the Capitol was the Senate wing until 1860 when the Supreme Court moved into it and the Senate moved into its present quarters. Subsequently the Supreme Court acquired its own imposing building.

11   Henry Clay (1777–1852), Virginia-born statesman who moved to Kentucky, a moderate on the slavery issue and a leading figure in the passage of the Missouri Compromise of 1820 and the Compromise of 1850; John Caldwell Calhoun (1782–1850), the South Carolina statesman who served as Vice President under President John Quincy Adams and was the leading political philosopher of the Southern states. He advocated the principle of dual sovereignty in his *Disquisition on Government* in *Works* (1853–5). Adams's recollection of seeing Calhoun is in error. Calhoun died late in March, two months before young Henry Adams got to Washington.

46   12   Refers to the manner of Roscoe Conkling (1829–88), a senator from New York, 1867–81. See Index for various references to him. Henry's father's Diary (June 3, 1850) records their visiting the floor of the House of Representatives and the *gallery* of the Senate chamber.

13   The "sacred codfish" carved in wood which hangs in the House of Representatives is symbolic of the first source of commercial prosperity of the Bay Colony. Henry's father served several terms in the Massachusetts legislature.

14   The call on President Zachary Taylor (1784–1850) took place on June 4, a month before he died. Charles Francis Adams noted in his Diary (June 4, 1850) that only two or three persons were there. They spent a half hour with the President, who, the Diary records, is "not a showman, still less a President yet there is a simplicity and modesty about him which is very taking." Henry's account of the rundown condition of things is borne out by his father's detailed Diary account which he probably consulted when preparing the *Education*.

15   The Free Soil ticket of Martin Van Buren and Charles Francis Adams did not carry a single state, but their candidacies split the Democratic party's vote in New York, thus giving the state's entire electoral vote to the Whig candidate, General Zachary Taylor.

16   Nathaniel Gorham (1738–96), president of the Continental Congress, 1786. He was the grandfather of Henry Adams's mother on her mother's side.

47   17   The date of the visit, June 13. Part of his father's Diary notation on that date: "pest of slavery visible everywhere," "sluggish and antiquated habits of the people."

18 John Marshall (1755–1835), Chief Justice of the Supreme Court, 1801–35, and shaper of its role as interpreter of the Constitution.

48 19 A recently hatched herring.

49 20 Peter Harvey (1810–77), a wealthy Boston merchant, served in both houses of the Massachusetts legislature; intimate friend of Daniel Webster.

21 Thurlow Weed (1797–1882), publisher of the *Albany Journal*, 1830–63. Supported Whigs and then Republicans. One of the most influential antislavery editors and politicians in the Northeast.

22 Henry Wilson (1812–75), Vice President under President Grant, 1873–75; John Bassett Alley (1817–96), congressman from Massachusetts, 1859–67; Anson Burlingame (1820–70), congressman from Massachusetts, 1855–61, minister to China, 1861–67. For the interesting details of the whole episode, see Duberman, *op. cit.*, pp. 170 ff.

23 George Sewall Boutwell (1818–1905), governor of Massachusetts from 1851 to 1852, secretary of the treasury under Grant, 1869–73.

50 24 Caleb Cushing (1800–79). First a Whig and then a Democrat, he presided over the Democratic convention in 1860 and then joined the seceding pro-slavery delegates to nominate John C. Breckinridge. However, he supported the administration during the Civil War and in 1873 Grant nominated him for Chief Justice of the Supreme Court but his pre-war record prevented confirmation. Cushing's exact expression was "one-ideaed abolition agitator." (Claude Fuess, *The Life of Caleb Cushing*, II [New York, 1923], 103)

CHAPTER IV *Harvard College (1854–1858)*

54 1 Criticism of the intellectual quality of Harvard education was habitual in the Adams family as one of its members was always serving on examining committees or on the Board of Overseers. Henry's father deplored the decline in English composition as did Henry's elder brother Charles. Interestingly enough, Charles Darwin, who regularly corresponded with Professor Asa Gray, the distinguished botanist at Harvard when Henry Adams was a student, envied Gray the company of so many brilliant colleagues. For a corrective to Adam's sardonic recollections see the account of his years at Harvard in Samuels, I, 8 ff.

55 2 Alexander Agassiz (1835–1910), class of 1855, son of the great Swiss geologist who taught at Harvard. Young Agassiz became a

highly successful geologist and mining engineer. He discovered and helped develop the fabulous Calumet and Hecla copper mines in Upper Michigan. Author of the monumental *Coral Reefs of the Tropical Pacific* (1903). Phillips Brooks (1835–93), class of 1855, the noted rector of Trinity church in Boston, 1869–91. He was a second cousin of Henry Adams. Henry Hobson Richardson (1838–86), class of 1859, distinguished American architect, noted for his adaptation of the Romanesque style. Oliver Wendell Holmes (1841–1935), class of 1861, son of Oliver Wendell Holmes, the American literary figure, author of the epochal *Common Law* (1881), justice of the U.S. Supreme Court, 1902–25.

57   3 William "Roony" Henry Fitzhugh Lee (1837–91).

     4 Benjamin D. M. Jones and James May (1837–1876).

     5 Nicholas Longworth Anderson (1838–92). Rose to become a Union Brevet Major General at the close of the Civil War. The Longworths, one of the most prominent and wealthy families in Cincinnati since the early years of the nineteenth century.

     6 Henry Lee (1756–1818), American Revolutionary hero.

58   7 *bos primigenius*, literally, "original ox."

59   8 Winfield Scott (1786–1866), commanding general of the United States Army, 1841–61. The expedition of 1500 soldiers was sent to Utah to reestablish Federal control of the territory and protect non-Mormons from violence. The Mormons made a token submission to Federal authority but the issues were not resolved for many years.

     9 A highly characteristic exaggeration. His courses in history though hard were very popular and a number of his distinguished students recalled his teaching with great admiration. See Samuels, I, 211 ff.

60 10 Another slip of Adams's satire. Volume I of Karl Marx's *Capital* was initially published in German in 1867, nine years after Adams was graduated from Harvard. The first English translation appeared in 1886. Adams's own copy is dated 1887.

    11 Auguste Comte (1798–1857), author of the very influential *Positive Philosophy* (6 vols., 1830–42), a pioneer work in sociology. The first English translation was published in London in 1853. It was popularized in England and America by John Stuart Mill's *Auguste Comte and Positivism* (1865). Professor Bowen, one of Adams's teachers at Harvard, relegated Comte to a footnote in his philosophy textbook. In the year that Adams entered Harvard Bowen wrote a sarcastic review of a translation of Comte in the *North American Review,* a magazine which was household reading in the Adams family.

12   Louis Agassiz (1807–73). It is useful to note for its bearing on Adams's attitude toward Darwinism that Agassiz was the chief opponent in America of Darwin's theory of evolution and of uniformitarian theories of geological development.

13   Cf. the following entry in the Diary of Henry's father, December 21, 1838: "What is the knowledge got at College? A negative quantity I say."

61   14   James Russell Lowell (1819–91), succeeded Longfellow as professor of belles-lettres and as leading Cambridge (Mass.) poet— *Vision of Sir Launfal, A Fable for Critics, The Biglow Papers;* later he became U.S. minister to Spain and to England.

15   Carlyle wrote a life of Schiller and translated Goethe's enormously popular *Wilhelm Meister* (1795–96). Matthew Arnold (1822–88), most famous for *Culture and Anarchy* (1869), shared the great enthusiasm for Goethe and showed his influence in his writings. His report to the British government on the state of higher education on the Continent particularly praised the high level of German scholarship and the thoroughness of instruction at the universities in contrast to the disorganized work at the British universities. Ernest Renan (1823–90), French philosopher and historian, whose writings were deeply influenced by German culture. Through his friendship with Carlyle, Emerson became intimately acquainted with the German idealist philosophers whom he adapted to his own version of Transcendentalism.

16   Honoré de Balzac (1799–1850), one of the greatest French novelists, noted for the powerful series of novels brought together as part of his *Comédie Humaine.*

17   Second Empire, 1852–70, autocratically ruled by Napoleon III, collapsed with the disastrous defeat of France in the Franco-German War of 1870, a war which for many seemed to prove the superiority of German culture.

62   18   Johann Wolfgang von Goethe (1749–1804), German poet (*Faust* I, 1808; II, 1833), novelist (*Wilhelm Meister,* 1795–96), philosopher, and statesman, regarded as a universal genius.

19   Immanuel Kant (1724–1804), Germany's most important philosopher whose critical system opened a new epoch in philosophical thought. His best-known works: *Critique of Pure Reason* (1781); *Critique of Practical Reason* (1788).

20   "Concord faith," Emersonian transcendentalism, a philosophy of

intuition and moral idealism which asserted that the true reality was spiritual.

21 "dark days of 1856," time of bitter controversy over the extension of slavery, marked especially by warfare in Kansas in which John Brown took part.

63 22 Adams changes Emerson's emphasis. See Emerson's essay *Nature*, Ch. VI: "A noble doubt perpetually suggests itself . . . whether nature outwardly exists. . . . Whether nature enjoy a substantial existence without, or is only in the apocalypse of the mind, it is alike useful and alike venerable to me."

23 objective, existing independent of the knower's mind; subjective, reality as perceived only by the mind.

64 24 James Walker (1794–1874), notable Unitarian minister, president of Harvard, 1853–60; Cornelius Felton (1807–62), professor of Greek, president of Harvard, 1860–62.

25 John LaFarge (1835–1910), New York artist, famous for his mural paintings and stained glass windows—Trinity Church, Boston; Minnesota State Capitol, etc.; Augustus St. Gaudens (1848–1907), American sculptor, figures significantly in later chapters (see Index); Clarence King (1842–1901), geologist and mining engineer (see *Education*, p. 311 for vivid characterization); John Hay (1838–1905), American author and diplomat, Adams's closest friend among men, appears frequently in later chapters.

65 26 Oxford, England's oldest university and traditionally aristocratic in its education.

68 27 Its highminded criticism of materialistic success rankled some conservatives. An editorial in the *Springfield Republican* in 1869 recalled that the oration was distinguished for little except its "irony and cynicism." Its high idealism, however, had pleased his father and his friends. See Samuels, I, 51.

69 28 Council of Trent, 1563, supreme meeting of the Roman Catholic church which condemned the doctrines of the Protestant Reformation.

29 Sir Anthony Absolute, character in *The Rivals* (1775) of Richard Brinsley Sheridan (1751–1816), a part played by Adams; Dr. Ollapod, a character in George Colman's (1732–94) *Poor Gentleman* (1801), in which Adams played the role of Sir Robert. Membership in the exclusive Hasty Pudding Club, whose main activity was theatricals, was much sought after.

30 For a documented account of Adams's career at Harvard based on contemporary records, see Samuels, I, 8–52.

CHAPTER V   *Berlin (1858–1859)*

71   1   The system of Roman law descending from the *Institutes* of the Emperor Justinian upon which the Continental legal systems were based. The intimate family friend, Senator Charles Sumner, whom young Henry Adams idolized, was a noted scholar not only of English and American Common Law but of Continental jurisprudence as well. Adams's great-grandfather had also been a student of Justinian's *Institutes* and believed that the Civil Law ought to be studied by Americans. See Samuels, I, 53 ff.

2   He sailed from New York on September 29 (not in November) with a few college classmates, arriving at Liverpool eleven days later and reaching Berlin October 22, as noted in the journal of his friend Benjamin Crowninshield (*A Private Journal 1856–58*, privately printed [Cambridge, Mass., 1941]).

3   *pons asinorum*, literally "the bridge of asses," term applied to the proposition in plane geometry that the base angles of an isosceles triangle are equal, so named from the difficulty experienced by beginners in mastering it.

4   George Paine Rainsford James (1799–1860), a popular British novelist, parodied by Thackeray.

72   5   Eaton Hall, four miles south of Chester, on the River Dee. According to the guidebooks this immense Gothic mansion, the original seat of the Grosvenor family, is one of the chief attractions of the area. A descendant of the family became Marquess of Westminster in 1831.

6   Oliver Twist, child character in Dickens's novel of that name (1837–38); Little Nell, child character in Dickens's *Old Curiosity Shop* (1841).

7   Charles I (1600–49). The royal army under Sir Marmaduke Langdale was defeated on Rowton Heath, September 24, 1645, by the Parliamentary forces which also repulsed a sortie of the king's troops from besieged Chester. The first Civil War ended with the surrender of the king's troops at Harlech Castle, March 13, 1647. Charles took refuge with the Scots army, but when he declined to meet their terms for a religious settlement they abandoned him on January 30, 1647. Charles was then seized by Cromwell's New Model army which soon thereafter overpowered Parliament. Charles rejected the settlement proposed by Cromwell's army and was finally tried for treason and beheaded January 30, 1649.

8 "Black District" (also known as "The Black Country") lay northwest of Birmingham, the chief manufacturing center of England, dotted with coal mines and iron foundries.

9 Francis Bowen (1811–90), philosopher and political economist, a hostile critic of positivism and socialism.

10 Mill was a leading advocate of free trade and laissez faire economics along with Cobden and Bright of the so-called Manchester school of economics. He was a Liberal reformer in British politics and a popularizer of scientific positivism. Since his reform ideas were popular with the working classes of the Black District, conservatives and Tories might well regard him as a Satan figuratively ruling in the inferno-like flames of the industrial centers and threatening their capitalist Eden.

73 11 The Strand, at that period a fashionable main thoroughfare in central London running from Charing Cross at Trafalgar Square (Nelson's monument and the National Gallery) to Fleet Street, the London newspaper center.

12 Samuel Johnson (1709–84), subject of Boswell's great *Life* (1791), literary critic, poet, lexicographer, and newspaper writer.

13 Allusion to the Vanity Fair of Bunyan's moralistic *Pilgrim's Progress* (1678), set up by Beelzebub and company and stocked with all manner of vain things, honors, kingdoms, and material delights; also the title of Thackeray's satirical novel of British life.

14 Piccadilly, then the great fashionable thoroughfare of London; part of its length borders Green Park.

15 November, 1858. See n. 2, above.

74 16 Adrian Van Ostade (1610–85), a Dutch painter; David Teniers (1610–90), a Flemish painter. Both were delineators of humble life and rural scenes.

17 Duke of Alva (1508–82), Spanish governor of occupied Netherlands, feared and hated for his despotic cruelty.

18 Peter Paul Rubens (1577–1640), the celebrated and prolific Flemish painter who made his home in Antwerp. His "Descent from the Cross," hanging in Antwerp Cathedral, is generally regarded as his masterpiece. Churches, which like Antwerp Cathedral were dedicated to the Virgin Mary, took on a special meaning when Adams began his researches for *Mont-Saint-Michel and Chartres*.

19 Malmsey, a sweet Madeira wine, popular in England.

76 20 Heinrich Heine (1799–1856), famous German Romantic lyric poet of Jewish descent.

21 Unter den Linden, until the destructive bombing raids of World War II, the broad showplace avenue of palaces, museums, embassies, government ministries, the opera, and university buildings.

22 During Sumner's Senate speech on May 22, 1856, denouncing the Kansas-Nebraska Bill, Preston S. Brooks, a South Carolina congressman suddenly confronted Sumner, charged him with libeling his state and one of the authors of the bill, and beat him unconscious.

23 Opera (1829) by Gioacchino Rossini (1792–1868) based on the play by Johann Schiller.

24 Robert East Apthorp (d. 1882), a prominent Bostonian, father of William Apthorp, Boston musical authority and critic.

77 25 *Gymnasium,* German name for a secondary school. Adams wrote an essay on his experience, published posthumously in *American Historical Review,* LIII (October 1947), 59–74, "Two Letters on a Prussian Gymnasium."

26 "Ober-tertia," the upper-third form or class.

27 The population was then about a half-million. It was part of the province of Brandenburg and did not become a separate administrative district until 1881. It was notorious as being one of the least sanitary cities of Europe, with open sewers, public pumps, and basement slum dwellings. Victory in the Franco-Prussian War in 1870–71 and the creation of the German Empire with Berlin the imperial capital initiated the rapid transformation of Berlin into a great modern city.

78 28 Wilhelm I (1797–1888); Friedrich Wilhelm IV (1795–1861), king of Prussia, 1849–58. Wilhelm I became regent in 1858 and king in 1861.

29 Adams was obviously familiar with the quixotic and impulsive episodes in the life of the rebellious poet. Heine spent a year at the University of Bonn, neglecting the study of law for literature, then attended briefly the University of Göttingen where he was repelled by the pedantic atmosphere.

79 30 "Berliner-kinder," real children of Berlin.

31 Heine's conversion to Christianity was recognized as a mere social gesture and not a denial of his origin. In 1831 he permanently settled in Paris where he wittily satirized the figures of the old order in Germany.

80 32 "Sinfonie," the German spelling.

33 "Haus-frauen," housewives.

81 34 Adams had first heard Wagner's "romantic opera" *Tannhäuser* during his stay in Berlin in the winter of 1858–59. The *Götterdäm-*

merung (*The Twilight of the Gods*), the third and concluding music drama of Wagner's epic cycle *The Ring of the Nibelung*, was a work of the composer's maturity. Its grandiose form tended to over-power the listener. Adams had attended an entire week of the Wagner festival at Bayreuth in July, 1901, dutifully attending one uncut ver-sion after another of the parts of the "Ring." *Parsifal*, Wagner's last work, impressed him as "a mass of German sentimentality which passes patience." (Ford II, 335.)

35 See n. 19, Ch. IV. Kant's idealism was essentially dualistic, op-posing spirit to nature, subject to object, phenomena to noumena. Georg Hegel (1770–1831) in his *Phenomenology of the Spirit* (1807) tries to unify nature and spirit by arguing that all things and their opposites are united in intelligence, that all contradictions are resolved by successively higher syntheses.

36 Johann Schiller (1759–1805), German dramatist and lyric poet, best known for his romantic drama *The Robbers* (1781) and his his-tory of *The Thirty Years War* (1789–93).

37 "best of Germanies," one of many of Adams's echoes of the famous line of Leibnitz as satirized by Voltaire in *Candide:* "All is for the best in the best of all possible worlds."

38 The Thüringian Forest was a 70-mile range of low wooded moun-tains in central Germany.

CHAPTER VI *Rome* (1859–1860)

82 1 Adams foreshortens the time. In actuality the tramp lasted two and a half days. See Samuels, I, 62 f.

2 John Chandler Bancroft (1835–1901), son of the historian George Bancroft and cousin of Adams's future wife, Marian Hooper; James J. Higginson (1836–1911), a classmate of Henry Adams's brother Charles and Henry's chief companion in Berlin; Benjamin Crownin-shield (1837–92), Henry's classmate and one of the "deputation" of gilded youths from Harvard who had crossed to Liverpool with Adams.

3 From Goethe's poem "Wanderer's Nightsong," written Septem-ber 6, 1780, in Goethe's hand on the wall of a small shooting lodge on the Gichelhahn, the highest of the hills around Ilmenau:

. . . Just wait! Soon
Thou too shall rest.

4 The so-called Sistine Madonna by Raphael (1483–1520), one of the very greatest painters of the Italian Renaissance; Correggio (1489–

1534), celebrated head of the school of painting at Parma in Italy. The Dresden gallery owned at least four of his paintings.

83 5 See reference to Matthew Arnold in *Education*, p. 108 and note.

6 As part of the settlement at the Congress of Vienna in 1815 the large Italian provinces of Lombardy and Venetia had been given to Austria. In 1858 Napoleon III (Charles Louis Napoleon Bonaparte, 1808–73) and Count Cavour of Italy, premier under King Victor Emmanuel, secretly agreed to provoke war with Austria in order to liberate the two provinces and establish an Italian confederacy. Napoleon III was a nephew of Napoleon I, who had once occupied Leipsic [Leipzig] during one of his campaigns in 1813. The meaning intended seems to be: "one looked on the return of [a] Napoleon as the most likely thing in the world."

84 7 A highly figurative allusion to the recurring invasions of the Italian peninsula of the Roman Empire which were begun in the fourth century A.D. by the "barbarian" peoples from the north like the Huns, the Vandals, the Visigoths, and the Franks. The identification of these peoples with contemporary France and Austria is a characteristic example of Adams's historical license.

8 "Guelphs and Ghibellines." Cf. n. 47, Ch. 1.

85 9 Niccolo Machiavelli (1649–1527), stateman and political philosopher in the service of the Medicis of Florence. His most famous work, *The Prince* (1513), is a treatise on how most efficiently to rule by putting aside considerations of ordinary morality or mercy. The moral dilemmas of politics and statecraft, the conflict between expediency and morality, constitute a chief theme of the *Education;* see especially Chs. X, XVII, and XVIII and Adams's novel *Democracy* (1880).

10 Louisa Catherine, seven years older than Henry and first-born of the children. She was married in 1854 to Charles Kuhn, member of a prominent Philadelphia family.

86 11 Stelvio Pass, on the borders of Tyrol and Italy, the loftiest carriage route in Europe, with a summit of 9055 feet; Valtellina, a mountain valley district in Lombardy corresponding to the Italian province of Sondrio. The party crossed late in August.

12 Garibaldi's "Cacciatori delle Alpi," literally Alpine hunters, a volunteer force of 3000 men organized in March and April, 1859, by Giuseppe Garibaldi (1807–82), the Italian patriot leader and one-time military adventurer in Brazil. The treaty of Villafranca, formally ending the war, was signed July 11, 1859.

13 "charming patriot," Mrs. Kuhn.

14 Austrian Jägers, Austrian riflemen and soldiers, originally formed from huntsmen who carried their own weapons.

15 Ortler Spitze, the highest peak (12,793 feet) in the Ortler Mountains of northeast Lombardy.

87 16 "eternal woman," an echo of the conclusion of Goethe's *Faust*, Part II. The symbolic idea was most fully embodied by Adams in 1904 in the Virgin of his *Mont-Saint-Michel and Chartres*. See especially *Education*, p. 196.

17 Frau Hofräthin von Reichenbach, wife of the botanist-geologist Heinrich Reichenbach (1793–1879).

18 "The Initials," a romance in the mode of Sir Walter Scott concerning a young Englishman who comes to Germany to learn the language and customs of the country and who is baffled by German society. Published in 1850 by an expatriated Englishwoman, Baroness Tautphoesus.

19 Raphael Pumpelly (1837–1923), a longtime friend of Adams, geologist and explorer who in 1859 took charge of the development of silver mines in Arizona, then Apache territory; Clarence King (1842–1901), who became one of Adams's closest intimates, was actually a student in the Sheffield Scientific School at Yale at this time. His observation of the primitive Digger Indians occurred in 1864 when he was with the geological survey of California.

20 "All experience . . . to build upon," adaptation of the following passage from Tennyson's "Ulysses" (1842): "Yet all experience is an arch wherethrough/Gleams that untraveled world . . ."

89 21 Henry's father was astonished and pleased by the broad popular support that made his election in the fall of 1859 a genuine triumph, for his hope of public office had been repeatedly dashed. The thirty-sixth Congress convened on December 9, 1859.

22 The six letters from Italy, signed H. B. A., were published in the *Boston Courier*, April 30, May 9, June 1, July 6, July 10, and July 13, 1860.

90 23 Palais Royal, in Paris, the palace opposite the Louvre built by Richelieu in 1629–34. The houses and galleries contained museums, shops, and a café on the garden terrace. The southwest angle housed the Théâtre Francais.

91 24 The Roman Forum, the political center first of Republican and then of Imperial Rome, a relatively small area, less than a hundred yards in length, surrounded by governmental structures, pagan temples, and monuments; allowed to fall into ruin after the collapse of

the empire at the beginning of the fourth century. Vatican, the area in Rome across the Tiber from the ruins of the Roman Forum, containing St. Peter's Cathedral and the Vatican Palace, the residence of the Pope and the administrative center of the Roman Catholic Church. Adams here uses the Forum and the Vatican with characteristic freedom as symbols of two great efforts in the Western world to create a lasting world order, efforts which had equally failed. In the ancient world, Rome of the Forum had attempted under the Republic and under the emperors to establish a Pax Romana, a Roman peace, in a universal secular state, for the old pagan religion had become moribund. That order had finally collapsed before the onslaught of the northern barbarians. Christianity, made the state religion by Constantine, had attempted to subordinate the secular state to the City of God, the *Civitas Dei,* as Augustine called it, but this effort in the end could not save Rome, and when in later centuries the Vatican asserted supremacy over the secular members of the Holy Roman Empire it too failed in its object of establishing a universal order. Cf. the theme of Ch. XXXIII.

25   Cola di Rienzi (1313–54), popular leader who overthrew the aristocracy in 1347 but became himself a tyrant and was murdered by the Roman mob; Tiberius Gracchus (163–133 B.C.), a popular tribune who sponsored important land reforms on behalf of small farmers, a work carried on by his brother Gaius. The senatorial opposition murdered him and three hundred of his followers during an election riot. Gaius met a similar fate. Aurelian (212–275), a Roman emperor, called the Restorer of the Roman Empire. He was murdered by an officer cabal. Note that in the arrangement of the names Adams himself avoids a chronological sequence.

26   "religion of history," i.e., a belief in the validity of chronologically linked events. Evolution illustrates the principle in explaining through cause and effect the successive stages in time of the origin and development of species. "The old religion . . . the same doctrine," presumably the illusion of growth and inevitable progress of Christianity from its founding by St. Peter. Adams suggests that the advocates of Evolution ignored the gaps and anomalies in the biological record as the Church historians glossed over the anarchic record of the Papacy and the moral contradictions within organized Christianity.

27   Edward Gibbon (1737–94), English historian. The famous passage from the "Autobiography" or "Memoirs of My Life" describing the inception of the *Decline and Fall* is from the first printed version of the unfinished autobiography, a copy of which Adams owned. The passage actually quoted in Murray's *Handbook,* but not followed by

Adams, came from a passage in Gibbon's *Journal* which his editor inserted in the *Memoirs*. It read: "It was at Rome on the fifteenth of October 1764, as I sat musing amidst the ruins of the Capitol while the barefooted friars were singing Vespers in the temple of Jupiter. . . ." (Edward Gibbon, *Autobiography*, Everyman's Library, p. 124.)

28 "Ara Coeli," altar of Heaven; church built on the site of the pagan temple of Juno where according to legend Augustus Caesar had announced the birth of Christ.

29 "Two great experiments." See n. 24 above.

92 30 Tacitus (A.D. 55–117), historian of Rome during its Imperial successes, noted for his pithy and incisive style; Michelangelo Buonarroti (1475–1564), greatest of Italian Renaissance painters and sculptors, whose "Last Judgment" and "Creation" in the Sistine Chapel in the Vatican exhibit the epic sweep of his imagination.

31 Count Camillo Cavour (1810–61), Italian premier, friend of Garibaldi.

32 Henry Temple Palmerston (1784–1865), prime minister of England from 1855. Adams disliked him for his vacillating behavior toward the North during the American Civil War. See Index for subsequent references to him. Tennyson and Longfellow, the most popular poets of their century, were, like Palmerston in politics, figures who fell short of true greatness of vision.

33 Hamilton Wilde (1827–84), expatriate Boston portraitist and genre painter.

93 34 Robert Browning (1812–89), English poet with whom Adams subsequently became acquainted; "Pippa Passes," a dramatic poem by Browning, in which the sweetly pious Pippa awakens the conscience of sinners; Belgravia, a fashionable district in London.

35 Saint Francis of Assisi (1182–1226), ascetic mystic and poet, founder of the Franciscan order, much admired by Adams as the exemplar of the unselfish life of intuitive faith. See esp. the chapter "The Mystics" in *Mont-Saint Michel and Chartres* in which Adams translates the "Cantico del Sole."

36 William Wetmore Story (1819–95), expatriate New England sculptor of neo-classical tastes whose studio was a favorite meeting place for distinguished Anglo-Americans, including among many others Browning, Hawthorne (cf. *The Marble Faun* [1860]), and Henry James (*William Wetmore Story and His Friends* [1903]).

37 Theodor Mommsen (1817–1903), German historian and archaeologist, professor of ancient history at Berlin, the meticulously learned

author of a 3-volume history of Rome and of authoritative technical studies of Roman inscriptions and coins; Cicero (106–43 B.C.), celebrated Roman orator, philosopher, and statesman; Caesar, presumably Julius Caesar (100–44 B.C.), general, statesman, and writer, subject of Shakespeare's tragic drama of that name. "They taught . . ."; i.e., Browning, Story, and Mommsen.

94   38   "Garibaldi and his thousand were about to attack Palermo," the greatest exploit in Garibaldi's career in which he placed himself at the head of a motley brigade of 1070 volunteers, swept from one triumph to another over the Bourbon armies, and proclaimed himself dictator of Sicily. Adams misdates the episode. Palermo was attacked on May 25, 1860, and not in June, and the Toledo with its 20,000 defenders capitulated May 30.

39   Joseph Ripley Chandler (1792–1880).

40   James Shedden Palmer (1810–67), subsequently served under Admiral Farragut during the Civil War.

41   "Prince Caracciolo," a humorous appellation recalling the gallant revolutionist Prince Francesco Caracciolo (1752–99), an admiral under Ferdinand IV of Naples who tried to prevent the landing of the British and Sicilian fleet in 1799 and who was as a result hanged by order of Admiral Nelson. In his travel letter to the *Boston Courier* (June 6, 1860) Adams described Captain Marino Caracciolo of the transport *Capri* to be "as jolly a little fellow as I ever saw, flying about and chatting all the time like a whirligig."

42   The two letters to the *Boston Courier* from Palermo (June 9) and Naples (June 15), have been reprinted in the *American Historical Review*, 25 (January 1920), 241–255.

43   Alexandre Dumas (1802–70), French author of highly popular historical novels of derring-do—*Count of Monte Cristo, The Three Musketeers.*

95   44   Spartacus (d. 71 B.C.), Roman slave, leader in the unsuccessful gladiatorial rebellion against Rome. For a time his guerrilla force brilliantly outwitted and defeated the Roman legions.

45   Condottiere, Italian term for the leader of mercenary soldiers who were hired by the Italian states in the wars of the fourteenth to sixteenth centuries.

46   "July heat" should read "June heat." By July 1 Adams had already established himself in Paris.

96   47   "but more he did not seek," another example of habitual exaggeration. He had studied French at Harvard and had been tutored in

it by his father. From Paris he wrote a number of long letters in fairly fluent French to his family.

48 The list indicates that Adams dined at some of the best restaurants in Paris, attended the theatres famous for comedies and vaudeville, and made a careful note of the chief actors, singers, and dancers.

CHAPTER VII *Treason* (*1860–1861*)

98 1 Pandects of Justinian were compiled for the emperor Justinian in the sixth century and consisted of fifty books of legal decisions. These were given the force of law by the emperor and thereafter constituted the most important body of Roman civil law.

2 Sir William Blackstone (1723–80). His *Commentaries on the Laws of England* (1765–68) was for a long time the most important introduction to the study of the Common Law in England and America.

99 3 Supporters of President Lincoln banded together into Wide-Awake Clubs to organize militant processions. The clubs were soon absorbed into regiments of volunteers.

4 Old House, the Adams mansion in Quincy. See n. 16, Ch. 1.

5 John Adams as a delegate to the Second Continental Congress in Philadelphia found himself in a community united by the desire for independence.

100 6 Count Axel Gustafsson Oxenstiern (1583–1654), Swedish statesman. "Quantula . . . regitur!" The whole phrase begins "Nescis, mi fili," "Behold, my sons, with how little wisdom the world is directed."

7 *idées fixes*, obsessions.

8 He still showed the effects of the physical assault on him by Preston Brooks on the floor of the Senate.

101 9 Anson Burlingame, see n. 16, Ch. II; Israel Washburn (1813–83), representative from Maine, was a key figure in the organization of the Republican party in 1854.

10 Preston King (1806–65), Republican senator from New York; Henry Winter Davis (1817–65), Baltimore lawyer and independent political leader, representative in Congress, 1855–61, as an anti-Secessionist vigorously supported compromise during the winter of 1860–61; Owen Lovejoy (1811–64), clergyman and antislavery congressman from Illinois, 1857–64, brother of Elijah Lovejoy who was lynched in 1837 by a pro-slavery mob at Alton, Illinois; Henry J. Raymond (1820–69), editor and co-founder of the *New York Times*, 1851, political leader in New York (lieutenant governor, 1855–57),

key figure with Thurlow Weed and William H. Seward in the Republican party.

102   11   Thomas Hart Benton (1782–1858), senator and congressman from Missouri, Democratic leader in Congress, ardent supporter of Andrew Jackson and influential spokesman for westward exploration and expansion; Henry Clay (1772–1852), important Southern statesman, a moderate on the slavery issue, originated the Compromise of 1850, remembered for his remark, "I would rather be right than President" when he was warned that his attack on Abolitionism might injure his career; Roscoe Conkling (1831–1902), congressman from New York and a Republican machine politician, an eloquent speaker, aggressive and flamboyant in manner, who became particularly obnoxious to Adams in the 1870's and 80's for his hostility to civil service reform for which Adams had become a strong advocate as an ally of Congressman James Garfield; *bouffe*, farcical; Edwin Lawrence Godkin (1831–1902), Irish-born journalist, edited the *Nation* from its founding in 1865 as a vehicle of political reform; Malvolio, the conceited and self-important steward of Olivia in Shakespeare's *Twelfth Night* whose vanity makes him the victim of absurd stratagems.

103   12   In 1856 Henry's father attended the Republican national convention in Philadelphia as an active delegate and was satisfied with the antislavery platform and with the candidate, Fremont, though originally he had preferred Seward. See Duberman, *op. cit.*, p. 207.

104   13   Richard Hildreth (1807–65), Boston historian and Whig politician, author of *History of the United States* (6 vols., 1849–56). Nonetheless, young Adams was friendly with Hildreth and wrote long letters to him urging support of his father's policies during the Secession winter. In vol. III, p. 80 of the *History* Hildreth commented that John Quincy Adams's sudden changes of party "exposed him to the charge of having acted the part of a political mercenary" and led the Federalists who had regarded John Adams's "negotiation with France as a piece of treachery to the party, [to] now exclaim that treachery was hereditary in the family."

105   14   Once again Adams chooses to depreciate his knowledge and his role in public affairs. In a letter to his brother from Washington December 9, 1860, he wrote: ". . . it's a great life; just what I wanted; and as I always feel that I am of real use here and can take an active part in it all, it never tires" (Ford, I, 62). During the session he contributed seventeen letters, December 4 to February 7, to the Boston *Daily Advertiser* as its anonymous Washington correspondent and prepared an article "The Great Secession Winter 1860–61," published

posthumously. (*Proceedings* of the Massachusetts Historical Society, 43 [1909–10], 656–687).

106 15 Because of threats against Lincoln's life, plans for his travel were changed and he was taken secretly to Washington by night.

16 Lincoln proposed to "hold, occupy, and possess" all property and places belonging to the Federal government, thus challenging the actions of the seceding states.

17 John Hay (1838–1905), studied law in Lincoln's office, was admitted to the bar in 1861, came to Washington to serve as assistant private secretary to the President, his friend John Nicolay having been appointed private secretary.

18 General Winfield Scott (1786–1866), the aged and ailing commander-in-chief of the U.S. army who retired in November, 1861. General Scott had experienced every military crisis since the War of 1812, including the war with England, with Mexico, and the wars with the Indians.

108 19 According to Henry's letter to his brother Charles on February 5, 1861, "His vanity has been hurt. . . . The difficulty was a miserably small one and not worth the noise it has made" (Ford, I, 85). The quarrel proved deeper than Henry realized and seems to have been brewing for some time, as Sumner resented the elder Adams's leadership of the Massachusetts delegation.

20 "wandering between two worlds . . .", from Matthew Arnold's "Stanzas from the Grand Chartreuse." The image became a favorite one with Adams as symbolizing his own predicament.

109 21 The passage illustrates the widening embrace of the metaphor of "education." Education becomes an omnibus term for knowledge of cause and effect in every area of human experience, especially history and politics. Note the frequent recurrence for rhetorical emphasis of the Socratic pose of ignorance, but an ignorance which at the same time is always less than that of other persons, even, as here, of Lincoln, Seward, and Sumner. Inasmuch as Adams has already pointed out in the chapter the limitations of these leaders, limitations of which he feels he was aware at the time, he can take the position that they knew less than he because they were unaware of their own ignorance. The implication seems to be that the soldiers, North and South, would by their actions on the battlefields show these leaders what really was at stake and what needed to be done.

22 Horace Gray (1828–1902), prominent Boston lawyer, a Free Soiler and Republican, and friend of the family. He rose from the

Massachusetts judiciary to the Supreme Court of the United States in 1881.

23 "My Lords and Gentlemen." In his introductory lecture in the *Commentaries* Blackstone stressed the importance of "lords and gentlemen" having a knowledge of English law.

CHAPTER VIII   *Diplomacy* (*1861*)

110   1   Charles Francis Adams was commissioned Minister to England on March 20, 1861.

2   A comic episode in Robert Greene's play, *The Honorable History of Friar Bacon and Friar Bungay*, acted in 1594. The magic head of brass is taught to speak and after a long vigil utters the words "Time is." The watching servant neglects to wake Friar Bacon. The head then says "Time was" and finally, not being heeded, concludes "Time is past" and falls down and breaks.

111   3   William H. Seward served as secretary of state from 1861 to 1870.

4   Charles Lush Wilson (d. 1878), editor of the *Chicago Daily Journal*.

5   The Assistant Secretary, Benjamin Moran (1820–86). His journal, kept from 1857 to 1874, reveals that he did not approve of young Adams's social ambitions and resented the private secretary's closeness to the Minister.

6   Fort Sumter surrendered to the Confederates on April 13.

112   7   Samuel Francis Dupont (1803–65), commander of the South Atlantic blockading squadron, 1861–63. Successfully attacked Port Royal, S.C., in November, 1861.

8   On the 1778 mission to France John Adams found he could accomplish little, as the affairs of the American commission were confused. He was sent back to France a year and a half later as a peace negotiator and imprudently quarreled with Benjamin Franklin, who as minister outranked him. However, by 1782 he succeeded singlehanded in getting Holland to give diplomatic recognition to the United States, and in 1783 he played an important part in negotiating the treaty of peace at Paris, especially in securing recognition of American fishing rights off the Newfoundland banks. John Quincy Adams was sent as Minister to Russia in 1809, and when the czar subsequently offered to arbitrate the War of 1812 three commissioners were sent out to act with Adams. England, however, declined the offer; hence it was not until 1814 that peace negotiations were opened with John Quincy Adams serving as head of the five American com-

575

missioners. After protracted and humiliating delays for the Americans the Treaty of Ghent was finally concluded and though practically nothing was gained, at least no right previously recognized (for example, to the Newfoundland fisheries) was surrendered.

113   9   Cassius Marcellus Clay (1810–1903), a liberal Kentucky statesman active in the antislavery movement. Henry Adams's mother thought him the vainest man she had ever known. He embarrassed Minister Adams by public denunciations of British policy. Henry Adams privately referred to him and the equally meddlesome Anson Burlingame as "noisy jackasses."

114   10   Henry John Temple (Viscount Palmerston) (1784–1865), prime minister, 1855–58, 1859–65. The British arrogance of Palmerston is here likened to that of the notorious emperor Tiberius Claudius Nero (42 B.C.–A.D. 37). The allusion is apparently to the Christians who were executed as scapegoats after the great fire at Rome, A.D. 64.

      11   Jefferson Davis (1808–89), president of the Confederate States of America, 1861–65.

115   12   William Ewart Gladstone (1809–98), British statesman, chancellor of the exchequer, 1855, 1859–66, subsequently prime minister for a number of terms. The quotation is from Lord Morley's *The Life of William Ewart Gladstone*, which Adams read in 1903 (II [New York, 1903], 75–86).

      13   Lord John Russell (1792–1878), a leading British statesman in England who entered the Whig [Liberal] ministry of Palmerston in 1860 as Foreign Secretary and was created an earl in 1861.

116   14   10 Downing Street, the official residence in London of the Prime Minister, traditionally regarded as the symbolic center of the government.

117   15   "St. James's Club," diplomatic and social club founded in 1857. Adams became a member in March, 1863. "Quel chien de pays!", "What a beastly country!" "Que tu es beau aujourd'hui, mon cher!", "How handsome you are today, my dear fellow."

118   16   Miss Burdett-Coutts (1814–1906), an immensely wealthy spinster who did not marry until she was sixty-seven. She was noted for her generous philanthropies and her remarkable social influence. She was created a baroness in 1871.

      17   Harriet Elizabeth Georgiana Leveson-Gower, Duchess of Sutherland (1806–68), mistress of the wardrobe and intimate friend of Queen Victoria, whose great London residence, Stafford House, St. James's Place, was an important center of society. Here the famed

protest of English ladies against American slavery was issued in 1853. Though the duchess was still in her mid-fifties, she evidently seemed old in young Henry Adams's eyes and grew no younger in his recollection forty years later. The young duke was George Granville William Sutherland Leveson-Gower (1828–82).

18   The first battle of Bull Run fought July 21, 1861, scarcely more than thirty miles from Washington, became a rout of the inexperienced Union volunteers who fled in panic across the Potomac. The city was saved only because the Confederates were too disorganized and exhausted to maintain the pursuit.

119   19   Initially located in 1861 at 7 Duke Street, the Legation was successively removed to 17 St. George Place, 5 Mansfield Street, and finally in April 1862 to palatial quarters at No. 5, Upper Portland Place.

20   A telegram from the newly organized Reuters Telegraph Agency (predecessor of the Reuters New Agency) whose telegraph facilities from Cork, Ireland, enabled it to beat the news from the ships arriving at Liverpool by several hours. Captain Charles Wilkes of the U.S.S. *San Jacinto* stopped the British mail ship *Trent* on November 8, 1861, and removed from it two Confederate agents, James Murray Mason and James Slidell, one on his way to London, the other to Paris. The furor in England over the boarding of a neutral ship died down when the U.S. released the agents on December 26, 1861, and disavowed the seizure.

21   Monckton Milnes, Baron Houghton (1809–85), member of Parliament, poet, socialite and literary patron, biographer of Keats. Fryston Hall was the family home.

22   William Edward Forster (1818–86), woolen manufacturer, member of Parliament, a strong liberal, associated with John Bright and William Cobden in support of the North and in opposition to recognition of the Confederacy. In the *Life of the Right Honourable William Edward Forster* (London, 1888) and *The Life, Letters, and Friendships of Richard Monckton Milnes* (London, 1890), both by T. Wemyss Reid, Adams is described as receiving the news with cool calmness.

120   23   Prince Albert (b. 1819) of the German duchy of Saxe-Coburg-Gotha, married Queen Victoria in 1840. His death on December 14, 1861, plunged the Queen into the deepest mourning.

24   Trent Affair. See n. 20 above.

25   The *New York Times* published 32 letters, June 7, 1861, to January 4, 1862.

26 December 16, 1861, reprinted in *American Historical Review,* LI (October 1945), 74–89.

27 The *Times* editorial was followed the next day by an even more sarcastic editorial in the *London Examiner.* Adams made himself particularly vulnerable by his patronizing comments on British social conventions.

28 Joseph Parkes (1796–1865), a Birmingham lawyer-politician who had acted as an intermediary between the Whigs and the Radicals during the agitation over the Reform Bill and who later became a Parliamentary solicitor in London and hence friendly with all factions.

121 29 Charles Wilkes (1798–1877), commander of the *San Jacinto,* was subsequently commissioned a commodore in July 1862.

30 A slight exaggeration, for though he stopped his newspaper correspondence, he did continue to try to influence people like Thurlow Weed in his private correspondence.

31 "Surtout point de zèle!", "Above all, beware of zeal!"

32 See *Education,* pp. *128* and *150* ff.

33 John Thaddeus Delane (1817–79), influential editor of the London *Times.*

34 Russell Sturgis (1805–1887), Massachusetts-born banker, a senior partner of Baring Brothers, leading London bankers, taken into the firm by Joshua Bates. (See n. 36 below.)

35 George Peabody (1795–1869), born in Massachusetts, made his fortune as a merchant, moved to England in 1837 and became a London banker, noted for his immense benefactions to American educational institutions; Junius Spencer Morgan (1813–90), native of Boston, international banker, partner 1854–64 in the international banking firm of George Peabody & Company, 1864–90 headed firm under name of J. S. Morgan & Co., father of the great American financier, John Pierpont Morgan (1837–1913), whose descendants continued the family leadership in international finance.

36 Joshua Bates (1788–1864), Massachusetts-born head of the London firm of Baring Brothers. Adams felt a strong partiality toward the firm as it had helped the United States at the time of the War of 1812.

122 37 Thomas Baring (1799–1873), member of the financial house and member of Parliament, 1833–37 and 1844–73.

38 Copperhead, derogatory epithet applied to Northern sympathizers with the Confederacy, derived from the deadly copperhead

snake which strikes without warning; Pall Mall, fashionable street in London frequented by high society, which was generally hostile to the North.

123   39   *débâcle,* a complete collapse. The disasters at the first and the second Bull Run and the succession of military miscalculations which followed seemed to spell defeat for the North.

124   40   Moncton Milnes once appeared at a dull party on a hot summer's evening and from the moment of his arrival the party became lively and refreshed, leading the noted wit Sydney Smith (See n. 18, Ch. XIII.) to call out it's the "cool of the evening."

These late breakfasts were in effect luncheons. Later in Washington Adams adopted the practice himself of sociable "breakfasts" at noon.

41   Falstaff, the convivial and robust comic character in Shakespeare's *Henry IV, Henry V,* and *The Merry Wives of Windsor;* Silenus, in Greek mythology the satyr-like companion of Dionysus whose worship was marked with orgiastic revels, whose laughter was presumably that of a merry sensualist.

42   Henry Brougham (1778–1868), lawyer, one of the founders and a frequent and slashing contributor to the authoritative *Edinburgh Review,* member of Parliament, lord chancellor, 1830–34, a commanding figure in public life, famed for his boundless energy and picturesque volubility in debate.

43   May Fair, [Mayfair], fashionable residential area of London, adjoining Hyde Park and Green Park.

125   44   Abraham Hayward (1801–84), essayist, contributor to leading periodicals of the day; George Stovin Venables (1810–80), barrister and writer, contributor of many articles to the *Saturday Review,* noted for the force and charm of his personality; Henry Reeve (1813–95), man-of-letters and editor of the *Edinburgh Review,* 1855–95.

45   In 1850 Forster, then 32, married Jane Martha Arnold (1821–99), sister of Matthew Arnold, the famous poet-essayist, and daughter of Dr. Thomas Arnold, the learned Anglican priest who as headmaster at Rugby made it one of the greatest private schools in England. Dr. Arnold later became Regius Professor of History at Oxford.

46   John Bright (1811–89), orator, statesman, defender of the manufacturers against the landed proprietors, leader of the Anti-Corn [Br. Wheat] Law League, member of Parliament, 1843–89, advocate of Parliamentary reform and free trade; Richard Cobden (1804–65), member of Parliament off and on from 1841 to 1865, strong advocate of free trade and low tariffs.

126   47   gangway of the House, the broad aisle in the House of Commons that separates the government and the opposition benches.

48   Anthony Ashley Cooper, seventh Earl of Shaftesbury (1801–85), philanthropist and social reformer. Many of the upper middle class and aristocratic social reformers did not believe that slavery was the real issue of the Civil War, particularly because it was not stated at the beginning as a war aim of the North. Moreover, there was a widespread conviction that the North could not subdue the South and that the terrible slaughter was futile and should be stopped. It should be noted that the Emancipation Proclamation was not issued by President Lincoln until 1863 and then largely as a military and political expedient.

49   George Douglas Campbell, Duke of Argyll (1823–1900), member of the House of Lords, prominent in the Liberal party, an independent and outspoken writer on public questions; Elizabeth Leveson-Gower (1824–78), married the Duke of Argyll in 1844. Concerning her mother, the Duchess of Sutherland, see n. 17 above.

127   50   Lord Frederick Charles Cavendish (1836–82), private secretary to Lord Granville, the president of the privy council, and nephew by marriage of the Duchess of Sutherland. He was assassinated by political terrorists the day he took office as chief secretary of Ireland. Devonshire House was the family home of the Cavendishes.

51   Edward Lyulph Stanley (1839–1929), a member of the historic family of landed aristocrats whose great wealth was augmented by industrial fortunes, and younger son of Lady Stanley of Alderly (the barony of Alderly was created in 1839). He became a Liberal politician, active in educational reform. Lady Stanley was a strenuous worker for higher education for women and helped to establish a number of schools and colleges for women.

52   Marquis of Lorne, John Douglas Sutherland Campbell (1845–1914), son of the eighth Duke of Carlyle.

53   Sir Charles Edward Trevelyan (1806–86), governor of Madras, 1859–60, finance minister of India, 1862–65, known for his social reform measures and as a philanthropist. Adams's greatest intimacy at the Trevelyan's was with the son George Otto Trevelyan (1838–1928), who was just Adams's age. George Otto Trevelyan was to become famous as the biographer of his uncle Lord Macaulay and as a historian. The allusion "only when death stopped them" remains obscure because Adams continued to be friendly with Sir Edward's son after Sir Edward's death and both the son and the son's wife outlived Adams.

54 Sir Charles Lyell (1797–1875), the leading English geologist, sympathetic to the United States during the Civil War, and a frequent visitor at the American Legation. He figures importantly in Ch. XV of the *Education*.

55 Thomas Hughes (1822–96), English reformer and politician, active in the Christian Socialist movement and a strong supporter of the North in the Civil War, author of the popular *Tom Brown's School Days* (1857), a didactic novel laid at Rugby under Dr. Arnold's head mastership. Its depiction of schoolboy cruelties opened the eyes of Englishmen to abuses in the great private schools.

CHAPTER IX *Foes or Friends* (1862)

128 1 The Confederates contracted in England for the building of commerce raiders. The *Florida* (under the name "Oreto") got away under British registry in March, 1862, and took on armament sent out from England on another ship and then raised the Confederate flag. The second cruiser, the *Alabama* (known as "No. 290"), got away in July, 1862. See *Education*, p. 150.

129 2 General George Brinton McClellan (1826–85) was made general-in-chief of the Union armies by Lincoln in November, 1861, but on March 11, 1862, because of Lincoln's waning confidence in him he was limited to the command of the Army of the Potomac. The "Peninsula Campaign" under McClellan to capture Richmond, Virginia, the Confederate capital, was waged from April to July, 1862, with a force of more than a hundred thousand men, but the campaign was finally abandoned after reaching to within a few miles of Richmond and the army returned to the Potomac River. In the Seven Days' Battle before Richmond the Union losses (killed, wounded, and missing) were nearly 16,000 men out of 91,000 engaged, the Confederate losses nearly 21,000 out of 95,000 engaged. McClellan was discredited for his failure to take Richmond, but whether the failure was owing to him or to others remains a matter of controversy.

3 Pall Mall, street frequented by high society, which was generally hostile to the North.

4 second Bull Run, fought August 29–31, 1862, a disastrous defeat which cancelled all the gains made by the Union armies in the Virginia theater of war during an entire year of fighting. Union casualties (15,000) were double those of the Confederates.

5 Charles was commissioned a first lieutenant in the First Massachusetts Cavalry in December, 1861, and was sent to Port Royal Is-

land, S.C., and then to Hilton Head, S.C., on occupation duty. In August, 1862, he was transferred to the Army of the Potomac and saw active service as a captain at Antietam, Gettysburg, and other battles. He rose to be colonel of the Fifth Massachusetts Cavalry, a Negro regiment, and after three and a half years' service was mustered out a brevet brigadier general.

6 "Capuan comforts": Capua was an ancient city of Italy traditionally noted for its luxury.

7 Thomas Haines Dudley (1819–93), U.S. consul at Liverpool from 1861 to 1872. Dudley asserted in the *Pennsylvania Magazine of History*, XVII (1893), that he reported 130 steamers which left England to run the Union blockade.

131 8 President Lincoln's assumption of dictatorial powers early in the war led to many abuses by over-zealous and frightened military officers who acted under them to arrest persons on suspicion and hold them without trial. Secretary of State Seward was heartily distrusted in England when the contents of one of his belligerently anti-British memoranda to the President on April 1 was somehow leaked to the British press. Adams's recollection gives a misleading impression at this point. He too was frightened by Seward's "crazy despatch" as he called it and wrote his brother at the time that if their father had "obeyed it literally, he would have made a war [against England] in five minutes. . . ." (Ford, I, 17.) Seward was thereafter induced to moderate greatly his "ferocity" of language.

9 Sir Henry Holland (1788–1873), distinguished physician and author, physician in ordinary to Queen Victoria, friend and adviser to almost every man of note in the first half of the century.

10 Sarah Baxter Hampton (1833–62). Thackeray met her in New York in 1852. She married Frank Hampton and moved to Charleston S.C. She died at Columbia, S.C. Ethel Newcome was the heroine of *The Newcomes* (1853–55).

11 "boorish Scotch gibes of Carlyle," probably an allusion to Carlyle's "The American Iliad in a Nutshell," a short fictional dialogue published in *Macmillan's Magazine*, VIII (August 1863), 301. Carlyle had no faith in democracy, which he regarded as rule by the mob and he was therefore hostile to the American system, a hostility most strongly expressed in "Shooting Niagara: and After" (1867). Adams himself became in his later years severely critical of democracy in America and reread Carlyle's *Sartor Resartus* (1836) with a keen appreciation of its relevance as a metaphor of his own moral quest as the allusions in the *Education* indicate.

132   12 The Queen specifically demanded of Palmerston that measures to which she had given her sanction "not be arbitrarily altered or modified by the minister."

133   13 Court of St. James, more strictly spelled Court of St. James's, after St. James's Palace which was formerly the royal residence.

        14 Philipp Brunnow (1797–1875), Russia's permanent ambassador to Great Britain, 1840–54, returned to London in 1858.

        15 C'est une peau de rhinocère!", "He has the skin of a rhinoceros."

        16 *enfant terrible,* one who has the manners of a rude child.

        17 Lady Palmerston (1787–1869), born Emily Mary Lamb. She married Palmerston in 1839 at the age of 52, two years after the death of her first husband. Their residence at 94 Piccadilly, Cambridge House, had so many visitors that a second gate was cut in the wall to allow the carriages to stream through.

135   18 Sir Algernon Borthwick (1830–1908), proprietor of the *Morning Post.*

        19 Perhaps an allusion to the duplicitous negotiations which Napoleon allowed to go on with England in 1810 concerning the independence of Holland when he had already resolved to occupy Holland. The Congress of Vienna assembled in 1814 at the close of the Napoleonic Wars to reorganize and repartition Europe after the dislocations of Napoleon's conquests. It became the symbol of cynical and unscrupulous statecraft.

        20 William Pitt (1759–1806), one of England's most brilliant prime ministers; Arthur Wellesley, Duke of Wellington (1769–1852), known as the "Iron Duke," one of England's greatest generals, best remembered for his series of victories in Spain against the French armies and for his decisive part in the defeat of Napoleon at Waterloo near Brussels in June, 1815. The prestige of his victories made him one of the most influential men in Europe.

        21 Lady Frances Elizabeth Jocelyn, born in 1819, youngest daughter of Lady Palmerston by her first husband; married Lord Jocelyn in 1841.

        22 All ministers to England: Constantine Musurus (1807–91), Turkish Minister; Emmanuel Vittorio Tapparelli, Marchese d'Azeglio (1816–90), Italian Minister; Rodolph Apponyi (1812–76), Austrian Minister; Silvain Van de Weyer (1802–74), Minister of Belgium; Torben van Bille, Danish Minister; Spyridon Tricoupi (1788–1873), Greek Minister.

136 23 The biographies of Palmerston reveal that rather than being a private secretary at 24 he was already a member of Parliament for Newton, Isle of Wight, having been elected in 1807 at the age of 23. Just previous to his election he had served as a junior lord of the admiralty. He delivered his maiden speech in Parliament at the age of 24. In the following year he was named Secretary for War.

24 Battle of Trafalgar, October 21, 1805, greatest British naval victory in the Napoleonic wars, fought off Cape Trafalgar, Spain. Lord Nelson, the admiral of the fleet, died heroically on the deck of his flagship.

25 "octogenarian youth," a slight rhetorical exaggeration suggesting the irresponsibility of second childhood; more accurately, at 77, Palmerston was a *septuagenarian.*

26 Benjamin Franklin Butler (1818–93), Union military commander in New Orleans after its surrender, from May to December, 1862. After much provocation from Southern ladies, he ordered that women who publicly insulted United States officers should be treated as common prostitutes, whereupon the President of the Confederacy, Jefferson Davis, decreed that if General Butler should ever be captured he was to be hanged as a felon. The moment might well have seemed the most crucial in American diplomacy, for if Palmerston's note signalled the intention of England to give diplomatic recognition to the Confederacy, the North would have recalled Adams and adopted Seward's original proposal, which had once been rejected by Lincoln, that he insist that the Powers reject the Confederacy or be faced with war with the United States.

137 27 *bêtise,* a piece of stupidity.

138 28 Stirling of Keir, Sir William Stirling-Maxwell (1818–78), Spanish scholar, historian and virtuoso, Lord Rector of St. Andrew, member of Parliament, succeeded to the baronetcy in 1865, adding the name Maxwell.

139 29 An ironic touch, as hatred of Napoleon III was not common to upperclass Englishmen or Scotsmen and might make them suspect to their acquaintances. Adams was "sensitive" about the French Emperor because for a time Napoleon III entertained the idea of recognizing the Confederacy in concert with England.

30 Laurence Oliphant (1829–88), first secretary of the British legation in Japan, 1861. His witty and satirical novel *Piccadilly* (1870) won a popular success. He was also known as a writer of pleasant travel books and subsequently of grandiose pseudo-philosophical works. For some years he was a member of an ascetic religious com-

munity in the U.S. In spite of eccentricities he was a brilliant personage in society. See also n. 52 below.

31 *The Owl,* founded by Sir Algernon Borthwick of the *Morning
Post* and a few other collaborators, did not begin publication until
1864, two years after this gathering. The writers dealt freely and
anonymously with private and personal matters.

32 Robert Louis Stevenson (1850–94), Scottish novelist, essayist,
and poet, author of *Treasure Island,* "The Strange Case of Dr. Jekyll
and Mr. Hyde," *Kidnapped,* and other writings. In 1890 Adams met
Stevenson in Samoa, where Stevenson spent his few remaining years,
and he sent home picturesque and unflattering descriptions of Stevenson and his American wife. For Adams's meeting with Stevenson see
Samuels, III, 28 ff.

33 Algernon Swinburne (1837–1909), a master of sensuous verse
forms, often censured for the pagan spirit of his poetry. *Atalanta in
Calydon* (1865), his first great success, a lyrical tragedy, is noted for
its melodious choruses.

140 34 "American-German barbarian," a picturesque linking of the ster-
eotype of the innocent American abroad with the primitive Teutonic
invaders of ancient Britain.

35 Jean Francois Arouet Voltaire (1694–1778), famous French
writer and skeptic whose satirical *Candide* (1758) was a favorite of
Adams.

36 Dante Alighieri (1265–1321), chief poet of Italy, author of *Vita
Nuova* and *Divina Commedia* (Inferno, Purgatory, Paradise) in which
his transfigured love, Beatrice, appears; Francois Villon (1431–63),
French lyric poet who celebrated the joys and sorrows of his poor and
roisterous student companions of the Latin Quarter ("Where Are the
Snows of Last Year Gone"); Victor Hugo (1802–85), French poet
and novelist and leader of the French Romantic movement in literature (his greatest novels: *Notre Dame of Paris, Les Miserables, Toilers
of the Sea;* his greatest poem: *La Légende des Siècles*); Sophocles
(495–406 B.C.), one of the three chief dramatists of ancient Greece
(*Oedipus Rex*).

37 "Faustine" and "Four Boards of the Coffin Lid" were first printed
in the *Spectator* in 1862. With the "Ballad of Burdens" they appeared
in *Poems and Ballads* (1866). The study in the original Greek of
Homer's *Iliad,* the epic of the Trojan War, was then a part of every
university education.

38 Richard Monckton Milnes (1809–85). The verses are slightly
misquoted. They should read: "I wandered by the brookside," "They

seemed to those that saw them meet" (Lord Houghton, *A Selection from the Works of Lord Houghton* [London, 1868], pp. 8, 47).

141 39 During Swinburne's third year at Oxford he was sent to read modern history with Professor William Stubbs (1825–1901), who was then also a clergyman. Swinburne's first day at Stubbs's country parsonage was a Sunday and Swinburne was excused from church to rest after his trip. As it was a fine day Swinburne arrayed himself in a scarlet dressing gown with slippers to match and watched the parishioners going to church. They, however, gathered to stare at him and the church remained empty until Stubbs rang the bell a second time.

40 *The Queen Mother, Rosamond* [misspelled *Rosamund* in 1907 and 1918]. *Two Plays* (1860).

41 George Douglas Campbell (1823–1900), Scottish statesman and writer on ecclesiastical questions; Lord Privy Seal, 1859–66; an eloquent speaker with a dominating personality, noted for his pungent and colorful language, a strong partisan of the North during the Civil War, known as the "Radical Duke."

42 Defined by Adams with characteristic feeling for nuance.

43 Walpurgis-night, the night preceding the pagan festival of May Day when according to old German superstition witches kept their annual rendezvous at the place of pagan sacrifices and frolicked with their master, the Devil; named after a medieval German nun whose relics were believed to provide protection against magic arts. "Walpurgis-Night" is a dramatic scene in Goethe's *Faust* Part I.

142 44 The remarkable comet whose orbit was first calculated by Johann Franz Encke (1791–1865), a German astronomer. Encke's star maps were used by Adams in pursuit of his interest in astronomy.

45 Alfred de Musset (1810–57), celebrated French lyric poet and playwright, regarded by many as the greatest French love poet and the type of the Romantic temperament.

46 Walter Savage Landor (1775–1864), English author, whose poetry and prose have been admired for their elaborate and sculptured style and their romantic treatment of historical and exotic themes as in *Imaginary Conversations* (prose), *Gebir* (epic poem).

143 47 See *"Alabama Claims"* in Index. Claims for indemnity against England for damage to American shipping by the Confederate raider *Alabama* (No. 290) which had been allowed to leave England during the Civil War. The arbitration was held at Geneva, Switzerland, principally during 1872; Henry Adams's father represented the United

States. The award to the United States of $15,000,000, an extremely large sum for that period, was regarded as a triumph of Adams's negotiating skill.

48 "Quant à moi, je crois en Dieu!", "As for me, I believe in God!" "Chose sublime! un Dieu qui croit en Dieu!", "How sublime! a God who believes in God!"

49 Basil Montagu Pickering (1836–78), Swinburne's first publisher (*The Queen Mother. Rosamond. Two Plays*, 1860).

50 *Poems and Ballads* (1866) was published by the firm (J.B. Payne and Arthur Moxon) which took over the business of Edward Moxon (1801–58), British poet and publisher, retaining his name. Many readers were scandalized by what was then regarded as indecently sensuous themes and imagery.

144 51 The recollection is erroneous. They met one more time at a breakfast party at Monckton Milnes's house in July, 1864. The hostess had not fled the "winter mists" though she may have left the men to themselves. See James Pope-Hennessy, *Monckton Milnes*, II (London, 1951), 141.

52 Oliphant came under the influence of an American mystic, Thomas Lake Harris, resigned his seat in Parliament in 1868, followed Harris to New York State, and entered his "Brotherhood of the New Life" and lived there as a farm laborer. Although he finally broke with Harris and travelled and wrote, he never returned to public life.

53 Anthony Evelyn Ashley (1836–1907), English biographer of Lord Palmerston.

CHAPTER X *Political Morality* (1862)

146 1 Benjamin Franklin (1706–90), served as the agent representative in England for the colony of Pennsylvania and became famous for his masterly protest against the Stamp Act in his examination before the House of Commons. Subsequently, as minister to France, through his urbanity and common sense he achieved a very great popular success in promoting American interests.

148 2 William Maxwell Evarts (1818–1901), a leading New York lawyer, chairman of the New York delegation to the Republican convention in 1860 but failed to win election as senator from New York in 1861; he later served as U.S. attorney general, counsel in the "Alabama Claims" arbitration, and secretary of state, 1877–81. He was famous as an orator; hence the parallel with Daniel Webster. As "law counsel" he acted as legal adviser to assist Minister Adams in

the proceedings in England against the building and outfitting of ships for the Confederacy.

3   Richard Bethell (1800–73), First Lord Westbury, became Baron Westbury of Westbury in 1861 and lord chancellor, and in that office presided over the House of Lords and headed the British judicial system. He was consequently a leading member of Palmerston's cabinet. He was generally conservative and strongly believed in the value of a landed aristocracy. He has been called the boldest judge who ever sat on an English bench.

4   Benjamin Disraeli (1804–81), a leading statesman and distinguished political novelist, whose works had been avidly read by the young Henry Adams. In Parliament he was a Tory critic of Lord Russell's foreign policy during the Civil War. Subsequently he served twice as prime minister and was created first Earl of Beaconsfield in 1876. He was a great favorite of Queen Victoria, whom he caused to be made Empress of India.

5   Robert Arthur Talbot Gascoyne Cecil (1830–1903), statesman and political writer, member of Parliament and opponent of Palmerston's government, critical of Gladstone's financial measures, influential writer on finance for the *Quarterly Review,* became Viscount Cranborne in 1865, and on death of his father, Lord Salisbury in 1868.

149   6   Declaration of Paris, adopted in 1856 at the conclusion of the Treaty of Paris, the treaty which ended the Crimean War involving England and France against Russia. The Declaration attempted to settle the maritime rights of nations in time of war, particularly the rights of neutral commerce (except for contraband of war) and the conditions for a binding blockade. Somewhat belatedly the United States, through Secretary of State Seward, moved in 1861 to subscribe to the Declaration as many other powers had already done. The involved negotiation broke down when England proposed that the ban against privateering in the Declaration should not be applicable to the Confederates on the ground that the war was an internal dispute.

7   See n. 3 above.

8   Roundell Palmer (1812–95), became solicitor general of England in 1861, was knighted that year, became attorney general in 1863, and subsequently was created first Earl of Selborne in 1872.

9   William Ewart Gladstone (1809–98), a leading statesman and writer; chancellor of the exchequer under Lord Palmerston, 1859–66, and one of the most powerful figures in his administration, became prime minister for the first time in 1868.

10 Granville George Leveson-Gower (1815–91), became second Earl of Granville in 1846 on the death of his father; diplomat and statesman, leader of the House of Lords during Liberal ministries after 1855; sometime president of the privy council.

150 11 Georg Wilhelm Friedrich Hegel (1770–1831), famous German philosopher, inventor of the Hegelian dialectic which rejects the syllogistic analysis of thought in favor of a system in which thought—and being—move in an endless continuum of thesis, antithesis, and synthesis, from an original tendency or state to its opposite and the unification of both into a new movement in which the opposites merge into an identity which was, so to speak, latent in them. Adams liked to apply the idea in a highly provisional way to the paradoxes and contradictions which he saw in human affairs. See Index for further allusions to Hegel.

12 Robert Porrett Collier (1817–86), counsel to the Admiralty, 1859; solicitor general, 1863–66; attorney general, 1868–71; writer of law treatises; created Baron Monkswell, 1885.

13 A characteristic kind of ellipsis in Adams's style. Collier's opinion, taken as representative of Law or the spirit of Law, seemed to prove, in effect, that Earl Russell was not to be trusted to do what he was obligated to do. This one legal demonstration agreed with what History repeatedly taught, namely, that men in politics were commonly untrustworthy.

14 (Earl Russell, *Recollections and Suggestions*, 1813–1873 [London, 1875], p. 407.) The passage from Earl Russell's book is not copied exactly: "opinion" should read "opinions"; "four days I was waiting" should read "four days in which I was waiting."

151 15 Duke of Argyll, a loyal friend and supporter of Minister Adams. See n. 49, Ch. VIII.

16 Duke of Argyll and Minister Adams.

152 17 Spencer Walpole, *The Life of Lord John Russell*, II (London, 1889), 360 ff. Cf. Adams's letter to his brother Charles, February 2, 1896: "The double-dyed rascality and duplicity of Lord Russell, which our father did not and could not believe, and which I only suspected, has since been proved by his own biography, in part, but in a worse form than I had supposed possible" (Ford, II, 95).

154 18 Lord Edward Fitzmaurice, *The Life of Granville George Leveson Gower, Second Earl Granville 1815–1891*, I (London, 1905), 442. An exclamation mark should follow "suspect you will settle to do so" giving a slightly different emphasis to the sentence.

155   19   The Preliminary Emancipation Proclamation announced by Lincoln to his Cabinet on September 22, 1862, five days after the Battle of Antietam, was to take effect on January 1, 1863.

20   This and the following items are quoted from John Morley, *The Life of William Ewart Gladstone*, II (New York, 1903), 77 ff.

159   21   "catspaw theory," based on the fable of the monkey who used a cat's paw to draw chestnuts from the fire. The meaning seems to be that Palmerston was the monkey and used Russell to save the situation precipitated by Gladstone.

160   22   Sir George Grey (1799–1882), home secretary under Palmerston and Russell.

161   23   Morley, *Gladstone*, II, 84; "In November (1862) the French Emperor renewed proposals of joint mediation," proposals which of course would be inconsistent with the policy of strict neutrality previously affirmed by Russell.

162   24   *fait accompli*, an accomplished fact.

25   "replace," in the sense of "restore."

163   26   Henry James (1843–1916), American novelist and friend of Adams noted for the extreme subtlety of his psychological analysis, especially in such later novels as *The Wings of the Dove* (1902) and *The Ambassadors* (1903).

164   27   *Punch*, a satirical illustrated London weekly magazine, founded 1841.

28   At the time of writing this Adams was about sixty-seven and though vigorous for his years he enjoyed posing as a used-up old man for whom life was practically over. He maintained the pose until his death at eighty in 1918.

165   29   "won the game," a recurring expression of Adams's signifying that the objectives for which he or his side had worked had been achieved, in this instance the winning of the Civil War and the successful prosecution by his father of the Alabama Claims. That British and European intervention would have driven the Adamses back to America is clear; that consequent defeat of the North would have cost Adams his "life and fortune" would seem unduly pessimistic.

CHAPTER XI   *The Battle of the Rams (1863)*

167   1   "Rams," ironclad warships with heavy prows for piercing an enemy ship.

2   By proposing mediation and diplomatic recognition of the Confederacy. See *Education*, pp. 161 ff.

3 *idée fixe,* obsessive idea.

168 4 1815, date of the Congress of Vienna which represented the success of Old World statecraft in restoring the status quo through the arbitrary arrangements of a few powerful statesmen. The senility lay in their inability to recognize in the United States the emergence of a new and independent world power.

5 Allusions to the aristocratic atmosphere and traditionalism of Oxford University. What Adams means by "High Church illusions" is perhaps suggested in the following from Lord Morley's biography of Gladstone: "The reader will have surmised that amidst all the press and the strain in affairs of state, Mr. Gladstone's intensity of interest in affairs of the [Established] church never for an intant slackened." Morley also quoted Gladstone's own description of his aims: "The whole of my public life with respect to matters ecclesiastical, for twenty years or more, has been a continuing effort . . . to extricate [the church] in some degree from entangled relations without shock or violence" (II, 158).

6 William Laird and Son, shipbuilders at Birkenhead, the seaport of Liverpool. The two ships were contracted for by the Confederate naval agent James D. Bullough.

169 7 Vicksburg, the chief city on the Mississippi between Memphis and New Orleans, of great strategic importance during the Civil War. The siege of the heavily fortified city began under U.S. Grant on May 18, 1863, and on July 4 the garrison of 37,000 Confederate soldiers surrendered.

8 Gettysburg, the decisive battle of the Civil War, July 1–3, 1863, in which the Federals under General Meade defeated General Lee with both sides suffering enormous casualties—the Federals, 23,000 killed and wounded; the Confederates, 31,000. It was here that General Pickett's gallant and futile charge took place.

170 9 1813, fifty years earlier, opened with Americans flushed by a series of brilliant morale-boosting naval victories over the British. In the autumn Captain Oliver Perry defeated a British squadron on Lake Erie. On land, however, the American forces were repeatedly thwarted. 1763, an additional fifty years earlier, marked a far more important turning point in American history. The Treaty of Paris, 1763, ended the Seven Years' War, the American phase being the French and Indian War, and eliminated France as a threat to the American colonies. At the same time it initiated the struggle between the American colonies and England for control of colonial trade and taxes.

10 Cf. *Education*, p. 120.

11 Charles Francis Adams and his son Henry in their letters of the period repeatedly remark the unwillingness of the *Times* to report news which ran contrary to its hopes and prejudices. Henry complained, for example, that even down to the last moment the *Times* declared the siege of Vicksburg was becoming "more and more hopeless each day."

171 12 Edwin McMasters Stanton (1814–69), secretary of war under President Lincoln. The more pacific title, secretary of defense, was given to the department in 1947, under President Harry Truman.

172 13 The offhand disclaimer is more rhetorical than real as Adams has in the preceding pages actually indicated all the historically significant actions of the minister, including his response to the threat of intervention and recognition and his protests against the repeated breeches of neutrality by British merchants to which the government closed its eyes.

14 *animus,* basic intention as it might be ascertained in a judicial proceeding.

15 The famous remark was contained in a note that C. F. Adams wrote to Earl Russell on September 5, 1863, as a culmination to a succession of protests. Most ironically the minister's statement was superfluous because Russell on September 2 had already ordered the ships detained. However, because of his uneasiness about the government's liability in the case, he appears to have delayed notifying the American minister of that fact until after Adams dispatched his note. Martin B. Duberman, C. F. Adams's biographer, says (*op. cit.*, p. 313), "The final decision to seize the ironclads was certainly taken before the receipt of Adams's famous 'this is war dispatch.'" To the same effect, Morison and Commager, *Growth of the American Republic, I* (New York, 1942), 70 n. In reviewing the episode Henry Adams took for granted that the apparent chronology of the dispatches coincided with the facts. The true chronology is revealed in the Layard Papers in the British Museum.

173 16 The "four" seems a verbal slip for "three," unless he means to imply that he regarded his work as private secretary at that time as the basis of a political career, an implication that is not supported by the facts. The notables of the three generations were: John Adams as Revolutionary leader against England and envoy to the peace negotiations; John Quincy Adams, as a negotiator of the Treaty of Ghent ending the War of 1812; Charles Francis Adams (Henry's father), as minister to England. Henry Adams was himself a member of the

fourth generation. The careers of his brothers at this period were unconnected with England.

174 17 Frederick North, second Earl of Guilford (1732–92), prime minister under George III, offered a conciliatory peace proposal in November, 1777, which might well have been accepted but it came too late as the American alliance with France had already been concluded and full independence seemed assured. After Burgoyne's surrender with his entire army at Saratoga on October 17, 1777, Lord North felt obliged to resign.

18 George Canning (1770–1827), British foreign secretary, 1807–09, whose intransigence in 1809 helped push the two nations toward war, learned to his regret, as he told the British minister to the United States after the war, that the hardest responsibility with respect to the United States was "not what to do, but what to bear."

175 19 Geneva Conference of 1872, at which Charles Francis Adams was the American arbitrator. The humiliating award amounted to $15,000,000 in gold, the equivalent of possibly $100,000,000 a century later.

176 20 The letter is quoted at length on page 165 of the *Education*.

21 It is now known, as indicated in n. 15 above, that Russell was greatly worried about the possible costly legal consequences of detaining the rams but still shrank from telling the American minister of the steps he was already taking to prevent the actual sailing of the ships. Russell's intentions were therefore far less clearly defined than Adams believed. Like much diplomacy, the British policy was opportunist, dictated by what was believed to be most advantageous for British imperial interests, and hence it was greatly dependent on the changes of fortune in the Civil War.

177 22 These letters and that on page 178 of the *Education* appear in Walpole, *op. cit.,* p. 371. The fact of the matter was that when Laird defended his building the ships the House of Commons cheered him and Palmerston, as Duberman (*op. cit.,* p. 303) reports: "instead of voicing disapproval of attempts to evade the Enlistment Act, as Russell had privately advised him to do, [Palmerston] defended the government's actions in the *Alabama* case." Duberman's account is a good corrective to the much oversimplified one of Henry Adams. As a contemporary observer of the affair in England at the time, young Henry Adams showed that he was quite aware of the complex predicament of law and policy in which Lord Russell found himself. See for example his letter to his brother September 16, 1863, Ford, II, 79–84.

180   1   Westminster, that part of central London which includes most of the important buildings, palaces, museums, and greatest residences and which legally constitutes the City of Westminster.

181   2   Edward Askew Sothern (1826–81), English comic actor, famous in England and America for his portrayal of the inane and fatuous Lord Dundreary in the comedy *Our American Cousin.* The long Dundreary side whiskers set a male fashion for many years. Sothern declared that he borrowed every trait of the characterization from people whom he knew.

184   3   The Puritan Commonwealth, 1649–60, represented the rise to power of the sober, moralistic, and God-fearing middle class in England, under the leadership of Oliver Cromwell.

4   Lord Henry Peter Brougham (1778–1868). A reference to his sustained attack in Parliament against the notorious Orders in Council which were a main cause of the War of 1812. The Orders, issued in retaliation against Napoleon's decrees, severely restricted neutral commerce. James Madison (1751–1836) was then secretary of state under President Jefferson.

5   "rebel," i.e., Confederates; "dissenters," Protestant sects outside the Anglican communion.

6   Edward George Geoffrey Smith Stanley, Earl of Derby (1815–91); Sir George Grey (1799–1882), home secretary under Lord Palmerston.

7   Anthony Ashley Cooper Shaftesbury (1801–85), seventh Earl of Shaftesbury, noted for his efforts in behalf of the poor and of factory and mine workers.

8   George W. F. Howard (1802–64), seventh Earl of Carlisle, a noted English reformer and philanthropist.

9   Sir Thomas Fowell Buxton (1837–1915) did not enter Parliament until 1865; he served until 1868. His grandfather had been a prominent antislavery leader in England succeeding William Wilberforce as head of the antislavery movement, and he himself was to become the president of the English antislavery league. At this time, however, Adams must have known him only as a young politician.

10   Richmond, Virginia, was the capital of the Confederate States of America.

11   James Murry Mason (1798–1871), Confederate commissioner to England from 1861 to 1863 when his commission was withdrawn. He had been a U.S. senator, 1848–61, an ardent supporter of slavery and

author of the Fugitive Slave Act of 1850. He chaired the Senate committee to investigate John Brown's Raid at Harper's Ferry and was one of the strongest advocates of secession in Virginia.

12 John Slidell (1793–1871), Confederate commissioner to France, 1862–65; U.S. senator from Louisiana, 1853–61, and an influential member of important committees.

185 13 Cf. remark attributed to Voltaire: "May God defend me from my friends; I can defend myself from my enemies."

14 Sir Alexander James Edmund Cockburn (1802–80), chief justice of the Queen's Bench, represented the British government in the Alabama Claims arbitration. His bad temper turned the neutral arbitrators against him, and his dissenting opinion was widely criticized. Minister Adams's vigorous protests rendered Slidell largely ineffective in England.

15 Lucius Quintus Cincinnatus Lamar (1825–93), congressman from Mississippi, 1857–61. He never got beyond Paris because the Confederate Senate refused to confirm his appointment. He was appointed a justice of the United States Supreme Court in 1888.

16 Shaftesbury (n. 7 above and n. 48, Ch. VIII) was a Confederate sympathizer. The Bishop of Oxford, Samuel Wilberforce (1805–73), son and biographer of the famous antislavery leader William Wilberforce.

186 17 William Schaw Lindsay (1816–77), member of Parliament for Sunderland. John Laird, who had been a managing partner of Laird's, became a member of Parliament in 1861, turning over his interest in the firm to his sons. The firm had designed the first ironclads and was the chief producer of them.

18 Brougham, see *Education,* p. 184 and n. 42, Ch. VIII. Sheffield, the steel-making center represented by Roebuck in Parliament.

19 John Arthur Roebuck (1801–79), member of Parliament for Sheffield for 30 years, introduced a motion proposing that England enter into negotiations with the great powers (principally France) to recognize the Confederacy as it was known that France desired a weakened U.S. so as to be able to extend French influence into Mexico.

187 20 John Bright refuted Roebuck's fears as "miserable jealousy," declared that Napoleon III could not be trusted and that England could not condone the evils of slavery. William E. Forster alluded to Vicksburg as evidence that the North was hardly conquered as Roebuck alleged and pointed out that recognition would lead to war with the

United States. Roebuck's motion was continued to July 13, 1863, and then discharged. (*Hansard's Parliamentary Debates*, 3rd ser., 171, 1771–1842.)

188 21 More figuratively than actually. Roebuck was then 62, which to the 25-year-old Adams apparently seemed the extreme of old age, especially since he was a violently outspoken champion of the Southern slaveholder. Roebuck continued active in politics for many years thereafter, dying in 1879 at the age of 78.

189 22 Professor Edward Spencer Beesly (1831–1915), professor of history in University College, London. He wrote a series of "Letters to the Working Class."

23 The report was published in the *New England Quarterly*, December, 1942.

24 Adams's transcript is not strictly accurate. The passage quoted is the sixth and not the opening paragraph of Bright's speech, and Adams introduces a few insignificant changes. One change, however, alters the sense: "vendors of love that works salvation" should read "vendors of lore which works salvation." (G. M. Trevelyan, *Life of John Bright* [London, 1913], p. 307.)

190 25 Though he vigorously supported political and civil rights for all, he opposed unions on the ground that they restricted free trade.

26 From his post as minister to Spain.

27 Sir Francis Hastings Charles Doyle (1810–88), poet and professor of poetry at Oxford; Sir Robert Alfred Cunliffe (1839–1905), baronet, active in Liberal Unionist politics, one of Adams's oldest English friends and a favorite companion.

191 28 This episode like many others recorded in the *Education* is obviously based on a contemporary entry in Adams's journal. Though he destroyed the college years portion of his journal in the 1880's, he continued to keep a journal as is clear from a surviving portion covering a few years of the late 1880's. (See Samuels, II, 327 ff.) Presumably he destroyed the remainder of his journals upon completing the *Education*, as no trace of them has ever been found. The subject of crime and punishment was much on Bright's mind at this moment as on the evening previous to the dinner he had lectured at the University College Debating Society on "Capital Punishment," arguing that the "country could be governed without . . . the penalty of hanging."

29 Lancashire, densely populated working class district, including the great manufacturing town of Manchester and the trading port of Liverpool; Yorkshire, in northeast England, populated at this period

largely by farmers, mine and quarry workers, and factory hands in the woolen factories and in the Sheffield iron and steel works. Somersetshire in the southwest and Wiltshire also in the southwest were both noted somewhat more for agriculture and sheep-raising than for manufacturing.

192 30 A qualification for voting for those who did not own real estate, admitting to the vote those paying an annual rent of at least £10, equivalent to $50 in U.S. coin of the period. This provision largely excluded the working classes.

31 John Henry Newman (1801–90), left the Anglican priesthood for the Roman Church and became a cardinal in 1879. He was an influential writer on educational and moral questions and author of the famous autobiography *Apologia Pro Vita Sua.*

32 John Ruskin (1819–1900), most famous for his books on art but also important for his writings on social questions.

33 *Hamlet* III. i. 85.: "Is sicklied o'er with the pale cast of thought."

34 Henry Reeve (1813–95), editor of the *Edinburgh Review,* 1855–95.

35 Richard Monckton Milnes, Lord Houghton.

36 The middle class party which arose at the end of the 17th century in opposition to the more conservative Tory party. Its main strength lay in the towns, whereas the landed gentry were likely to be Tory. The Whigs supported the supremacy of Parliament against the king and worked for electoral reform. They were succeeded at this period by the broader-based Liberal party which advocated more far-reaching social and economic reforms.

37 Francis Turner Palgrave (1824–97), art and literary critic and poet. He and his family are characterized at some length on page 214 of the *Education.*

193 38 Mrs. Harriet Grote (1792–1878), notorious for her love of brightly colored clothing. On seeing her with a rose-colored turban, the writer Sydney Smith remarked, "Now I know the meaning of grotesque" (M. L. Clarke, *George Grote: A Biography* [London, 1962], p. 24). George Grote, her husband (1794–1871), a friend and disciple of John Stuart Mill, was a famous historian of Greece. The facetious allusion and the sharp rejoinder play upon the men's names and personalities with a certain historical aptness. Hugo Grotius (1583–1645) was a statesman and jurist of vast learning. The German Samuel Pufendorf (1632–94), rarely spelled "Puffendorff," was the most noted student of the work of Grotius on international law and author of im-

portant treatises on law and history. Adams let the unusual spelling stand in the corrected copies of the 1907 edition, perhaps for the punning effect. It was retained in 1918.

39 Jean Louis Forain (1852–1931), famous for his satirical etchings of the French bourgeoisie.

40 Charles Cavendish Fulke Greville (1794–1865), while clerk of the privy council, had kept an insider's diary of English political life which he bequeathed to Reeve. When the first section was published, covering 1814–37, to the accession of Queen Victoria, the Queen accused Greville of "indiscretion, indelicacy, ingratitude towards friends, betrayal of confidence, and shameful disloyalty towards his sovereign" and declared Reeve's part in the publication was in "disgracefully bad taste," in spite of the fact that the "memoirs" had been heavily expurgated (*The Greville Memoirs,* ed. Lytton Strachey and Roger Fulford [London, 1938], pp. vi–ix).

41 An echoing allusion to Samuel Taylor Coleridge's poem "The Rime of the Ancient Mariner" (1797–1798); "saurians of the prime," extinct primeval lizard-like monsters.

CHAPTER XIII *The Perfection of Human Society (1864)*

194 1 In the British peerage a nobleman of one of the following ranks: duke, marquess, earl, viscount, baron. As private secretary to the minister, Henry Adams became intimately familiar with the gradations and order of precedence as well as the complicated inter-relationships and the titles of the nobility. His letters indicate that he took considerable pleasure as a young man in the ritual pageantry as when he was presented at court in full regalia of naval blue coat, white knee breeches, sword, and cocked hat.

195 2 The conservative administration which had preceded that of Palmerston had not had a majority in Parliament and had remained in office only because of the discord among the other parties. It went out of office when it lost a vote of confidence during the debate on an electoral reform bill. With much difficulty Palmerston was able to bring together representatives of the warring factions in the Liberal party. As his own conservatism reassured the Opposition, his administration presided over a kind of political truce which insured stability and a minimum of political controversy.

3 The husband of Queen Victoria, Prince Albert Francis Charles Augustus Emmanuel (1819–61) of the German House of Saxe-Coburg-Gotha, had been a principal advisor of the Queen. On his death in

November 1861, she went into prolonged mourning and thus cast a pall over Court society. Prince of Wales, eldest son of Queen Victoria, the future Edward VII, was born in 1841.

4 Balmoral, a figured woolen petticoat looped in front.

196 5 Lady Margaret de Burgh Canning (d. 1888), first wife of Wentworth Blackett Beaumont (created Baron Allendale in 1906). Adams continued his friendly acquaintance with the Beaumonts into the 1900's and mentioned visiting the second Mrs. Beaumont in 1906.

197 6 John Singleton Copley, Baron Lyndhurst (1772–1863), British jurist and statesman, son of the famous American-born painter John Singleton Copley. One-time member of Parliament, he served as attorney general and a number of terms as lord chancellor.

7 John Campbell, Baron Campbell (1779–1861), member of Parliament, became chief justice of the Queen's Bench and was lord chancellor, 1859–61. It should be noted that though the chapter title is dated 1864 the events and impressions given in this chapter range across the entire period of· 1861–65. See date given in *Education*, p. 199.

198 8 Richard Taylor (1826–79), son of President Zachary Taylor, served as a Confederate general in the Civil War, thereafter settled in Washington, published the unrepentant *Destruction and Reconstruction* (1879); George Smalley (1833–1916), see n. 11, Ch. XIV.

9 Devonshire House in Piccadilly, London, palatial residence of the Duke of Devonshire. See *Education*, p. 127 and n. 50, Ch. VIII.

10 Virginia Verases, Contessa di Castiglione (1835–99). Descended from a noble Tuscan family, she married in 1854 Conte Francesco di Castiglione, a household officer of Victor Emmanuel, King of Sardinia. In Paris after 1856 she exercised great influence at the splendid court of Napoleon III, who had become emperor of the Second French Empire in 1852; he was deposed in 1870 with the fall of the empire in the Franco-Prussian war.

11 Stafford House, London residence of Duke and Duchess of Sutherland: George Granville William Sutherland Leveson-Gower (1828–92).

12 Paolo Veronese (1528–88), a leading painter of the Venetian school. One of his most sumptuous paintings, "Marriage of Cana," at the Louvre in Paris, celebrates the first of Christ's miracles, the water changed into wine for the wedding feast (John II. 1–11).

199 13 Arthur Pendennis, the semi-aristocratic hero of Thackeray's *The History of Pendennis* (1848–50); Barnes Newcome, the unpleasant snob in Thackeray's novel *The Newcomes* (1853–55).

200   14   Adelina Patti (1843–1919), coloratura soprano who made her London debut at Covent Garden and became the idol of opera-goers; Cherubino, Count Almaviva's page in Mozart's *The Marriage of Figaro;* Gretchen, the familiar German diminutive of Margaret, Faust's beloved in Goethe's *Faust,* called Marguerite in Gounod's opera *Faust* in which Adelina Patti sang the role at Covent Garden, London, in 1863.

15   John Lothrop Motley (1814–77), Boston-bred historian (*Rise of the Dutch Republic*), minister to England, 1869–70, resided in England after 1868. Note the curious repetition in the next paragraph of phrases on p. 195 of *Education.*

16   Gunter's, a fashionable restaurant caterer.

201   17   Joseph Ernest Renan (1823–92), noted French historian and philosopher. His *Life of Jesus* (1863), which rejected the claim for the divinity of Jesus, was widely denounced.

18   Sydney Smith (1771–1845), writer on religious questions and a famous wit. Charles Dickens (1812–70), English novelist (*David Copperfield, Oliver Twist,* etc.). Contrast the tone of the following letter from Henry Adams to his brother Charles, June 18, 1863: "Yesterday we had a pleasant dinner at which Charles Dickens, John Forster [historian] . . . Louis Blanc [French economist], and other distinguished individuals were present; and a very jolly dinner it was" (Ford, II, 34).

19   Edward George Earle Lytton (1803–73), prolific English novelist, member of Parliament, raised to peerage in 1866.

20   Charles Darwin (1809–82), biologist (*Origin of Species,* 1859).

21   Benjamin Jowett (1817–93), professor of Greek at Oxford, famous for his translation of the *Dialogues of Plato;* Henry Hart Milman (1791–1868), English clergyman, professor of poetry at Oxford, noted for his *History of the Jews* (1830), and his *History of Christianity under the Empire* (1840); James Anthony Froude (1818–94), noted writer on English history, author of *Life of Thomas Carlyle* (1882).

22   Bishop Samuel Wilberforce (1805–73), son of the great antislavery leader William Wilberforce; he was dramatically routed at the 1860 meeting of the British Association for the Advancement of Science by Thomas Huxley when he attacked Darwin's *Origin of Species.*

202   23   Motley was educated at Harvard.

203   24   No source has been found for this epigram.

204   25   Charles Milnes Gaskell (1842–1919), author and politician, member of Parliament, 1885–92, became one of the closest of Adams's

lifelong English friends; James Milnes Gaskell (1810–73), member of Parliament for Wenlock, 1832–68, a lord of the treasury, 1841–46.

26 "Thornes," should read "Thorne," a small market town near the Don River; Wakefield, the chief agricultural town in the West Riding of Yorkshire.

27 William Everett (1839–1910), the son of Edward Everett and thus Adams's cousin; Harvard, 1859; Trinity College, Cambridge, 1863; taught Latin at Harvard during the same years that Henry Adams taught history; U.S. congressman, 1893–95.

205 28 Heptarchy, the period of the early English kingdoms, once erroneously thought to number seven, from the coming of the Anglo-Saxons in 449 and the union of the kingdoms in 829.

29 A highly impressionistic summary of the complex ethnic history of these English counties which were overrun by numerous successive waves of invaders and immigrants from prehistoric times to the Norman Conquest in 1066.

206 30 Arthur Henry Hallam (1811–33), youthful essayist, intimate friend of Tennyson who commemorated him in *In Memoriam* (1850).

31 Henry Edward Manning (1808–92), prominent member of the Oxford Movement until his conversion to the Roman Catholic church, became Archbishop of Westminster in 1865 and a cardinal in 1875.

32 Charles Watkins Wynn (1775–1850), politician, second son of Sir Watkin William Wynn, fourth baronet of Wynnstay, a lifelong friend of the poet Southey, member of Parliament 1831–50, called "Father of Parliament" for his long service. His younger brother Sir Henry Wynn (1783–1856), a diplomatist, was private secretary in 1801 to the then Lord Granville of the Foreign Office.

207 33 Miss Charlotte Wynn (1807–69), diarist, eldest daughter of Charles Watkins Wynn, close friend of the German minister, Christian Bunsen, of Thomas Carlyle, and of Frederick D. Maurice, the noted religious reformer.

34 Wenlock Abbey, the remains of the great abbey of the monastic order of the Cluniac Benedictines, founded by Roger de Montgomery in 1017. Much of the priory, which was dissolved under Henry VIII, remains. The picturesque Norman Gothic prior's house in the midst of the ruins continued to be inhabited and was owned by the Gaskells. Adams visited the abbey the first week in October, 1864. He then wrote: "My visit to Wenlock was very enjoyable. God only knows how old the Abbot's House is, in which they are as it were picknicking before going to their Yorkshire place for the winter. Such a cu-

rious edifice I never saw, and the winds of heaven permeated freely."
(Ford, II, 201.)

35 "Wenlock Edge and the Wrekin," in Shropshire about 150 miles
northwest of London. To the southwest of Much Wenlock rises the
sharp ridge of Wenlock Edge and to the north the isolated hill of the
Wrekin, one of the most striking remnants of an ancient pre-Cambrian
geologic formation, much frequented by amateur geologists like Henry
Adams. The Wrekin also designates the remains of the ancient forest
in that vicinity.

CHAPTER XIV *Dilettantism* (*1865–1866*)

208 1 The various Corniche roads cut spectacularly along the cliffs above
the Mediterranean French and Italian Rivieras. A *vettura* was a carriage drawn by horses.

2 Sorrento, a favorite seaside resort town. The most famous of the
grottoes was the Blue Grotto on the nearby isle of Capri, entered by
rowboat.

209 3 Perugia, one of the great art cities of Umbria; Siena (misspelled
in 1907 and 1918 editions), celebrated for its superb cathedral and
art treasures.

4 Splügen Pass, 6946 feet, on the carriage road from Lake Como in
Italy to Thusis in eastern Switzerland. The route took them down the
headwaters of the Rhine toward Lake Constance.

5 Baden Baden, located in southern Germany, one of the most
famous watering places in Europe, popular for its hot medicinal baths
and notorious for its luxurious gambling casinos (closed down in
1872).

6 Duke of Hamilton, presumably the young duke (1845–95) who
devoted himself to horse racing, yachting, and high living. His father,
the eleventh duke (1811–63), died in Paris at the notorious Maison
Dorée reportedly from a fall after supper.

7 Cora Pearl (1842–86), whose real name was Emma Elizabeth
Crouch. She was a famous courtesan of Napoleon III's Second Empire
and died in Paris in poverty.

210 8 "at loggerheads with the Senate," over Reconstruction policy.
Johnson wished to carry out the moderate policy of Lincoln but ran
head-on into the bitter opposition of the Radical Republicans under
Thaddeus Stevens who pushed through a Civil Rights bill early in
1866 over Johnson's veto.

9 Paris, 1865–67; Vienna, 1867–69; Madrid, 1869–70. Presumably Adams considered only London first-rate.

10 Whitelaw Reid (1837–1912), war correspondent for the Cincinnati *Gazette;* journalist for the *New York Tribune,* 1869, editor-in-chief, 1872; subsequently minister to France.

11 George Washburn Smalley (1833–1916), war correspondent for the *New York Tribune,* famous for first-hand reports of the Civil War and later of the Austro-Prussian War and Franco-Prussian War. Author of several books furthering Anglo-American friendship.

12 Frank Barlow, Francis Channing Barlow (1834–96), a brigadier general in the Civil War, wounded hero at Gettysburg, classmate of Henry Adams at Harvard, studied law and as attorney general of New York, 1872–73, directed the prosecution of the Tweed Ring; Frank Bartlett, William Francis Bartlett (1840–76), lost a leg in battle, returned to graduate with his Harvard class in 1862. Reenlisted and twice wounded, he became a legend with both sides; as a recklessly brave colonel he was so admired for courage that Confederates ordered their sharpshooters not to aim at him. Brevetted brigadier general, his remaining years were clouded by financial troubles.

13 Nelson Appleton Miles (1839–1925), became a noted Indian fighter against the Sioux, Nez Perce, and the Apaches, commanding general of the United States Army, 1895; played prominent role in Spanish-American war.

14 Henry Lee Higginson (1834–1919), prominent Boston investment banker, founded Boston Symphony Orchestra, 1881.

15 Charles Francis Adams, Jr., one of Henry's older brothers, spent a year in European travel after the Civil War to recover his health which had been impaired during the fighting. He surveyed the field of public opportunities, fixed on the developing railroads, began to write articles on them, was appointed to the Massachusetts Railroad Commission, and then became president of the financially troubled Union Pacific Railroad. His unsuccessful war with Wall Street and his disgust with high finance is told in his *Autobiography* (1915).

211 16 Also an English tone of speech and manner. He acquired "an English cut to his jib." (Henry Watterson, *'Marse Henry,'* II [New York, 1919], 33.)

212 17 Lord John Russell became prime minister on the death of Palmerston and resigned in 1866 when the Conservatives (Tories) came to power. Shortly after the 1830's the name Tory gave way to Conservative and similarly the name Whig to Liberal. In some circles, however, the old names still remained in use as convenient epithets.

Notes

18   No. 54 Portland Place was the residence of the American Minister during the later years of their stay. Earlier they resided at nearby No. 5 Upper Portland Place.

19   "dispute about innate ideas," an allusion to the idea prevalent in the 17th century, Descartes being its most prominent exponent, that certain ideas, for example, those of God, perfection and infinity, were part of the innate constitution of the mind, actually or potentially. The doctrine was effectively combatted by John Locke (1632–1704), the English philosopher who argued that the mind was a *tabula rasa*, a blank tablet, at birth and acquired ideas through sensations and experience.

213   20   Joseph M. Turner (1775–1851), the famous English landscape painter best known for his later canvases suffused with swirling light and color, especially in his seascapes. Adams greatly admired Turner and later acquired two of his works, one a watercolor he veiled each night with a piece of Chinese brocade.

21   Sir Christopher Wren (1631–1723), the most famous of English architects; his most celebrated structure, St. Paul's Cathedral. The Great Fire of London of 1666 provided much opportunity for rebuilding. Wren reputedly built fifty-two London churches.

22   Sotheby's, the famous London dealer in art objects. Coin collecting was his father's chief hobby. His fine collection was added to by Henry Adams who bequeathed it to the Massachusetts Historical Society.

23   William Morris Hunt (1824–79), an American painter, follower of the French artist Millet, noted for his genre pictures. Adams's friends Henry and William James, the novelist and the psychologist, both studied with Hunt at Newport shortly before the Civil War.

24   Rue du Bac, a street in the heart of the Latin Quarter.

25   Ecole des Beaux-Arts, on the Rue Bonaparte, the chief art school in France.

214   26   Cecil Milnes Gaskell. "Thornes" should read "Thorne."

27   "Old Sir Francis," Sir Francis Palgrave (1788–1861), English historian, son of Meyer Cohen, a Jew, became a Christian convert in 1823, author of the monumental *History of Normandy and England* (1851–64).

28   Francis Turner Palgrave (1824–97), editor of the *Golden Treasury of Songs and Lyrics* (1864); William Gifford Palgrave (1826–1888), became a Jesuit missionary in Syria and Arabia, left Jesuits in 1865, published a *Narrative of a Year's Journey through Central and*

604

Eastern Arabia (1865); Sir Reginald Palgrave (1829–1904), authority on banking and economics; Sir Robert Harry Inglis Palgrave (b. 1827), authority on banking and economics.

29   William Holman Hunt (1827–1910), English painter, one of the leaders of the Pre-Raphaelite school of artists and writers, especially noted for portrait of Dante Gabriel Rossetti.

215   30   John Richard Green (1837–83), historian, celebrated for his readable *Short History of the English People* (1874). He was a London clergyman in the 1860's, subsequently became librarian at Lambeth Palace of the archbishop of Canterbury. He and his wife became favorites of Adams and his wife after Henry Adams's marriage in 1872 to Marian Hooper (1844–85) and their wedding journey to England in that year.

31   Thomas Woolner (1825–92), English poet and sculptor, member of the so-called Pre-Raphaelite Brotherhood, a band of artists formed in 1848 in protest against academic dogma. The Brotherhood advocated a direct study of nature by artists and poets liberated from the rules developed under Raphael during the Italian Renaissance.

32   Stopford August Brooke (1832–1916), English clergyman, *Primer of English Literature* (1876); *A History of English Literature* (1892).

216   33   "Sotheby's or Christie's," leading art dealers and auction houses.

34   Sir Anthony Westcombe (d. 1752), so spelled in the Sotheby catalogue, one of the first collectors of drawings in England. He bequeathed his collection to the Bernard Granville family, which sold them in 1857. The Sotheby Sale Catalogue of drawings (mostly from the Westcombe collection) for July 5, 1867, lists two drawings by Rembrandt but none by Raphael. Presumably the drawing attributed to Raphael was in one of the two lots listed under "Miscellaneous."

35   Rembrandt van Rijn (1606–69), most noted of Dutch painters; Rafael Sanzio (1483–1520), commonly in English "Raphael," one of the greatest of Italian painters. The drawing is at the Adams Mansion House in Quincy and so mounted that the poem is visible.

217   36   About $2.40.

37   George W. Reed (1819–87), Keeper of Prints and Manuscripts and expert on Italian engravers of fifteenth century.

38   Parnasso, a reference to the fresco in one of the Raphael rooms in the Vatican (Stanza della Segnatura) representing a crowd of poets and musicians on Mount Parnassus, the legendary haunt of Apollo and the Muses.

39   Horace (65–8 B.C.), Roman author famous for lyrical and satir-

ical poems. The identification of Horace as the subject is no longer accepted and the figure is referred to as the "so-called Horace." Wölfflin, a leading art historian, suggests that the figure probably represents the Italian poet Sannazaro.

218　40　Marcantonio Raimondi (1475–1534), one of the chief Italian engravers of the Renaissance, made engravings of works of Raphael, Dürer, and others.

41　Guglielmo Libri (1803–69), mathematician, historian of Italian mathematics, and bibliographer, published a catalogue of books on Italy. He was a political refugee from Italy, sentenced in absentia as an anti-monarchist.

219　42　Now this I well believe that an (elleria?)
Offends you so much that it has affected your heart.
Because you are great you have not your wish;
You see and you no longer believe in your valor.
All jealousies have already passed:
You are of stone: and you no longer suffer pain.
Translation by Professor Joseph Fucilla of Northwestern University.

220　43　James Abbott McNeill Whistler (1834–1903), American expatriate painter, subject of much controversy for his revolutionary freedom of line and color.

44　Annual exhibitions of paintings and sculpture sponsored by the Royal Academy of Arts in London. The exhibition was held at the National Gallery and included nearly 3,000 items, an understandably overwhelming display.

45　Peter Paul Rubens (1577–1640), one of the most prolific painters of the Flemish school.

46　Thomas Girtin (1775–1802), English landscape painter, rated second to Turner, one of the founders of the English water color school; John Sell Cotman (1782–1842), English landscape painter, also noted for his architectural drawings.

221　47　Henry Thomas Buckle (1821–62), British historian, pioneer in the use of statistical and sociological data for the purpose of historical prediction, held that climate, soil, food and natural environment were determining factors in human history; author of *History of Civilization in England* (1857–61).

48　Alexander William Kinglake (1809–91), travel writer and historian, wrote an eight-volume history of the Crimean war.

49　"Staffordshire iron-furnace," in the smoky "Black Country" around Birmingham.

50   Silas Wegg, a rascally character in Dickens's *Our Mutual Friend* (1865) who is employed by the uneducated Mr. Boffin to read to him out of the "old familiar Decline-and-Fall-off-the-Rooshan-Empire."

222   51   Presumably the theological seminaries.

52   Captain John Smith (1579–1631), English adventurer, colonizer, and writer, president of the colony of Virginia, 1608–09. Adams's article disproving Smith's account of his rescue by Pocahontas outraged many patriotic Virginians.

53   Charles Eliot Norton (1827–1908), American author and famed professor of the history of art at Harvard University, 1874–98, edited the *North American Review* with James Russell Lowell, 1864–68.

CHAPTER XV   *Darwinism (1867–1868)*

224   1   *On the Origin of Species by Means of Natural Selection, or the Preservation of Favored Races in the Struggle for Life* (1859); *Journal of Researches into the Geology and Natural History of the various countries visited by H.M.S. Beagle* (1839).

2   "Darwinist before the letter," the implication being that he was in a sense a Darwinist before the term was invented, i.e. by natural inclination. See n. 7 below.

225   3   John Tyndall (1820–93), important English scientist. Known for a variety of discoveries in the physical sciences, his greatest reputation came as a popular lecturer on science. He was engaged for a long time in a controversy with James Thomson and other scientists over his theory of the nature of glacier motion. He lost out when the great Helmholtz adopted Thomson's thermodynamic explanation. Adams's epithet "trifler" probably alludes to this controversy and suggests as well a distaste for popularizers of science.

4   Thomas Henry Huxley (1825–95), distinguished English biologist and paleontologist, ardent advocate of the application of scientific method to all questions, leading supporter and popularizer of Darwin's theory. His relish for public controversy evidently lowered him in Adams's estimation.

5   An activity stimulated by the book *Vestiges of Creation* published anonymously in 1844 by Robert Chambers (1802–71) when the scientific study of the evolution of the earth was then highly controversial.

6   Lyell disproved the Biblical account of the origin of mankind by citing the extreme antiquity of flint implements in post-Pliocene strata. In the same work he gave his initial support to Darwin's theory.

7   Sir Charles Lyell (1797–1875), *Principles of Geology*, 10th ed. (1866); in this edition Lyell incorporated Darwin's theory of evolution. Adams's somewhat skeptical attitude toward Darwin at this date may be gathered in part from the remark in his essay-review in the *North American Review*, CVII (October 1868), following his summary of the arguments which led Lyell "to adopt opinions which many excellent men consider revolting." Adams added: "a more tangible objection than this repulsiveness. . . . is, that Mr. Darwin has, after all, announced only a theory . . . in its nature *incapable of proof*" [italics added]. By contrast an important British review in the *London Review* (April 1869) commended Lyell for accepting Darwin and enthusiastically supported the new theory as well as Lyell's theory that geological changes of the earth's surface could be explained "by reference to causes now in operation" rather than by the theory of primeval geological catastrophes as maintained by Louis Agassiz, Adams's teacher at Harvard.

8   The Common Law of England, the body of law slowly accumulated through the centuries based on judicial decisions, as opposed to royal fiat or enacted statutes.

226   9   *a posteriori*, after the fact; also a punning allusion to the Latin *posteriora*, hinder parts.

10   Benedict Spinoza (1632–77), famous Dutch philosopher of Portuguese Jewish origin, who conceived of God as one "infinite substance, of which finite existences are modes or limitations," and as the immanent or indwelling cause of the universe.

11   Arthur Pendennis, the hero of Thackeray's *History of Arthur Pendennis* (1848–50), who begins his career as an idle and conceited young man at the university and only slowly reforms his ways.

12   Sir Isaac Newton (1642–1727), mathematician and philosopher, author of the abstruse *Philosophiae Naturalis Principia Mathematica* (1686–87), noted for his formulation of the laws of motion and of universal gravitation.

228   13   *Terebratula*, a genus of brachiopods (molluscoida) which includes many living and a few fossil species.

14   "Northanger Abbey," a novel published in 1818 by Jane Austen (1775–1817). Adams evidently means to refer to Catherine Morland, the heroine of the novel who is won by Henry Tilney. There are no Olneys in the novel.

15   Ludlow Castle, a magnificent twelfth century ruin in the town of Ludlow, Shropshire; Stokesay, crenelated castle near Shrewsbury in

Shropshire, which is the finest and best preserved of its type in the county; Boscobel, mansion house near Shifnal in Shropshire famed as the house in a secret chamber of which Charles II took refuge in 1651; Urinconium, a rich Roman city near Wrekin Hill whose considerable ruins were being uncovered.

16   Roman Campagna, the undulating plain surrounding Rome in ancient times covered with towns and villas, now the site of such superb ruins as Hadrian's villa and Ostia Antica.

17   Marches, the border regions of England and Wales.

18   Cader Idris, a mountain in northwestern Wales; Caer Caradoc, a mountain in Shropshire.

229   19   Buildwas, a Cistercian abbey, now a great ruin; Bridgnorth, another castle ruin.

20   Caractacus, a king of ancient Britain, ca. A.D. 50; Offa, king of Mercia, ca. 757–796.

21   Falstaff, the fat, witty and cowardly braggart in Shakespeare's *Henry IV*, Part I. In Act V, sc. iv, during the battle of Shrewsbury Falstaff tries to take credit for the death of Hotspur by pretending to Prince Hal that Prince Hal's sword thrust had not been fatal, that Hotspur had risen again to fight with Falstaff "a long hour by the Shrewsbury clock." Such a clock, like Falstaff's, would run to suit one's feelings or convenience without regard for historical time sequence.

22   Sir Roderick Murchison (1792–1871), a Scottish geologist, associated with Lyell, author of *The Silurian System* (1838), which established the Silurian horizon of the Paleozoic era and described the corresponding system of rocks.

23   Cambrian, the earliest geological period of the Paleozoic era.

24   Severn, the second longest river in England, rises in Wales and crosses the plain of Shrewsbury in Shropshire.

25   Jean de la Fontaine (1621–95), French poet and dramatist, best remembered for his *Fables*.

230   26   From the dedicatory poem-fable to the Duke of Burgundy, "The Companions of Ulysses":

> Everything considered, I maintain in conclusion
>   That villain for villain
> It is better to be a wolf than a man.

27   *Limulus*, the horseshoe crab.

28   *Cestracion Philippi*, the so-called Port Jackson shark; similar forms of the genus occur as fossils in early strata, though the fossil

forms are much larger. For recent discussion of the genetic problems which perplexed Adams at this time (ca. 1905) as forty years earlier, the student might consult George G. Simpson, *Tempo and Mode in Evolution* (1944), and for a differing view, Richard Goldschmidt, *The Material Basis of Evolution* (1940). For an admirable summary of the conflicting views on the subject see William Jordy, *Henry Adams: Scientific Historian* (New Haven, 1952), pp. 190–198.

29 William Paley (1743–1805), English theologian. This famous analogy of God as the inferred watch maker occurs in his *Natural Theology or Evidences of the Existence and Attributes of the Deity collected from the Appearances of Nature* (1802).

231 30 Athanasian creed, the credal affirmation attributed to Athanasius (296–373) used in the Greek, Roman, and Anglican churches.

232 31   Thus conscience does make cowards of us all;
      And thus the native hue of resolution
      Is sicklied o'er with the pale cast of thought,
      And enterprises of great pith and moment
      With this regard their currents turn awry,
      And lose the name of action. (*Hamlet* III. i. 83–88.)

32 Bluebeard, a popular story from the French of Perrault, translated into English about 1729. There are parallels in many other languages. The wicked rich man, his face disfigured by a blue beard, obtains the hand of Fatima. Called away on business, he leaves the keys to his treasures but forbids her to look. Curiosity gets the better of her; she opens a closet and discovers the bodies of his previous wives. Bluebeard sees the blood-stained key on his return and orders her death as he had ordered the deaths of the others. She, however, is rescued.

233 33 As a war measure in 1862 the U.S. government had issued paper money, treasury notes ("greenbacks") not redeemable in specie, i.e. gold coin. As the notes were made legal tender for the payment of obligations they were in effect fiat money. Several hundred million dollars' worth were issued. At their lowest point they dropped to 35¢ (in gold) on the dollar. They were not redeemable in specie until 1879.

34 During this period the Napoleonic wars and the War of 1812 placed a heavy financial drain upon England. As a result the bank of England had suspended payment in specie on its notes in order to conserve its gold reserves.

35 An ironic allusion to the belief of the banking community that it was in the highest degree immoral for government to manipulate the currency; that morality required the issuance of notes, i.e. paper cur-

rency, worth in gold exactly what was stated on the face of the note and which the United States Treasury must redeem in gold on demand.

235　36　Note that these were all about the same age as Henry Adams. John Pierpont Morgan (1837–1913), a leading American international banker. See also n. 35, Ch. VIII, on the banking house of Morgan. John D. Rockefeller (1839–1937), founder of the Standard Oil Company, was one of America's richest capitalists; in his last years he became the foremost philanthropist in the country. William Collins Whitney (1841–1904), highly successful New York lawyer turned financier, secretary of the navy, 1885–89, social leader and sportsman. William McKinley (1843–1901), governor of Ohio, President of the U.S., 1895–1901. Alexander Agassiz (1835–1910), naturalist, geologist, developer of Calumet & Hecla copper mines which made him rich. Henry Lee Higginson (1834–1919), became prominent Boston banker and philanthropist. Henry James (1843–1916), American novelist. William Dean Howells (1837–1919), novelist and important editor and literary critic. Henry Hobson Richardson (1838–86), noted American architect. John LaFarge (1835–1910), American artist and noted muralist, revived art of stained glass windows.

37　fountain of Trevi, a large and beautiful monument in Rome, presided over by the figure of Neptune, a favorite resort of tourists who regard it as a wishing well and throw coins into the water.

236　38　George Gordon, Lord Byron (1788–1824), English poet; his *Childe Harold's Pilgrimage* (1811) contains a famous passage on Rome. Percy Bysshe Shelley (1792–1822), English poet, travelled in Italy with Byron, drowned near La Spezia; he was buried in the Protestant cemetery at Rome.

39　Actually October.

CHAPTER XVI　*The Press* (1868)

237　1　From Tyre, ancient capital of Phoenecia at the eastern end of the Mediterranean.

2　Brevoort House, a fashionable New York hotel.

238　3　A reference to two poems by Matthew Arnold: "The Strayed Reveller" (1849) and "The Scholar-Gypsy" (1853). In the latter poem occur these famous lines appropriate to Adams's mood:

> . . . this strange disease of modern life,
> With its sick hurry, and divided aims.

4   The comparison is anachronistic, being more appropriate to 1900 than to 1868. In 1868 Jewish immigration from Russian Poland was negligible. However, the murderous pogroms in scores of cities in Russia and Russian Poland which began in 1881 inspired wholesale emigration of impoverished Jews fleeing from officially countenanced outrages which from time to time ravaged the ghettoes. Adams's violently anti-Semitic opinions, scarcely hinted at in the *Education*, though pervasive in his correspondence, date from his exposure in Paris to the virulent French anti-Semitic movement of the 1890's which culminated in the infamous Dreyfus case when Dreyfus, a Jewish officer in the French army, was falsely accused of treason, convicted and sent to Devil's Island in 1894. He was not vindicated and pardoned until 1906. Adams like many members of his conservative Paris circle allied himself with those who regarded the effort to free Dreyfus as a conspiracy against law and order in France. Adams made a brief stopover in Warsaw where the conspicuousness of the Jewish population led him to write: "My only merit as a curio is antiquity, but the Jew is also a curiosity. He makes me creep." (Ford, II, 338.) Cf. the allusion to Israel Cohen on the first page of the *Education*. See Samuels, III, 356, for the Jew as symbol and scapegoat.

5   Desbrosses Street, a commercial street leading to a New York ferry; Fifth Avenue, at this date and later, the street in New York with the most palatial and fashionable town residences in America.

6   Cornelius Vanderbilt (1794–1877), began life as a boatman, rose to being a steamship and railroad magnate and immensely wealthy Wall Street financier; Jay Gould (1836–92), from humble beginnings rose to affluence almost as great as that of Vanderbilt. He became notorious for his acquisition and manipulation of railroads. It was he who managed to force out Henry Adams's brother Charles from the presidency of the Union Pacific.

239   7   A reference to the extraordinary phenomenon in many deep-sea species of phosphorescent organs that produce illumination with a lantern-like effect. Southern congressmen objected to lavish subsidies of railroad lines linking the East and West coasts as prejudicial to the economic development of their section.

8   The strain of anti-intellectualism here alluded to is explored with much clarity and at length in Richard Hofstadter, *Anti-Intellectualism in American Life* (New York, 1963).

241   9   The reclamation of land in the inner harbor was begun in 1856 and the vast project completed in 1886.

10   John Quincy Adams II was elected to the Massachusetts legislature in 1869 on the Democratic ticket and became the leader of the party in a state largely controlled by the Republican party. He was an unsuccessful candidate for governor in 1870 and 1871, and at a splinter convention in 1872 he was nominated for Vice President of the U.S. but received only one electoral vote.

11   Newport, Rhode Island, at this period the most fashionable watering place or summer resort in the U.S.

242   12   The initial poem in the *Fables* (1668) of Jean de la Fontaine, a moral fable of the industrious ant who laid up provision for the winter and the improvident grasshopper who sang all summer.

13   Edward Atkinson (1827–1905), prominent Boston businessman (insurance executive) and liberal economist, writer on social and economic reform.

243   14   That is, as a young man of an established family to begin a career outside of government or politics.

244   15   Horace Greeley (1811–72), journalist, author, and politician, founded the *New York Tribune* in 1841.

16   Charles Anderson Dana (1819–97), journalist and writer, assistant secretary of war. 1863–64; became editor and part-owner of the *New York Sun* in 1868, bringing a popular style into journalism.

17   James Gordon Bennett (1795–1872), founded the *New York Herald* in 1835. His son, James Gordon Bennett, Jr., sent Stanley in 1869 on the spectacular African expedition to find Livingston.

18   William Cullen Bryant (1794–1878), popular American poet and journalist, became editor and part-owner of the *Evening Post* in 1829. It should be noted that Adams did in fact contribute a number of pieces to the *Nation* and to the *Evening Post*. See Samuels, I, 317 ff.

19   The allusion to Salem would appear to be Adams's recollection of Nathaniel Hawthorne's reference to Salem, Massachusetts, in "The Custom House" introductory to *The Scarlet Letter*, as having "the chillist of social atmospheres." The tradition of Boston society's suspicion of strangers and narrow provinciality which is a recurring subject of complaint in Adams's letters is amusingly satirized in Cleveland Amory's *The Proper Bostonians* (1947).

245   20   William M. Evarts was born in Boston in 1818, went to Yale, and began the practice of law in New York in 1841.

21   William Tecumseh Sherman (1820–91), born in Ohio, famous in the Civil War for his daring "march to the sea" from Atlanta to

Savannah, Georgia, in 1864. He was descended from one of the earliest Massachusetts families. His younger brother became a prominent U.S. senator with whom Adams subsequently became acquainted.

22   Andrew Johnson (1808–75), succeeded to the Presidency on the assassination of Lincoln in 1865. A self-taught and self-made man who began life as a tailor in a mountain village in Tennessee, he was no cosmopolitan figure. He was under sharp criticism almost from the beginning from New England for his supposed indulgence toward the defeated Rebels. Though the impeachment proceedings against him early in 1868 failed, his administration was already discredited when Adams met him. He had opposed secession, but his sympathies were essentially Southern, and hence alien to Adams.

247   23   Hugh McCulloch (1808–95).

248   24   Francis Amasa Walker (1840–97), born in Boston, a statistician and political economist, at this time superintendent of the 1870 census, subsequently president of the Massachusetts Institute of Technology.

249   25   Benjamin R. Curtis (1809–1874), associate justice of the U.S. Supreme Court, 1851–57.

26   John Marshall (1755–1835), Chief Justice of the U.S. Supreme Court, 1801–35, established the supremacy of the Court on constitutional questions. The "greenbacks" were not legal tender for all purposes and their market value varied greatly with the activity of speculators who gambled on the likelihood that they might one day be made redeemable in gold coin. Businessmen were understandably reluctant to be forced to accept greenbacks at their face value as legal tender when they were being sold at a discount. The government was of course committed to maintaining the notes as legal tender. Though prices rose, debtors found it easier to pay off their mortgages in the depreciated currency. At the end of the first trial (1871) the Supreme Court held that the Civil War greenbacks were unconstitutional and hence not legal tender. In the second legal tender decision later in 1871 after two new justices were appointed to fill vacancies, the Court reversed itself and sustained the greenbacks as legal tender.

250   27   "Chief Justice," Salmon Portland Chase (1808–73), secretary of the treasury, 1861–64; Chief Justice of the Supreme Court, 1864–73.

252   28   Lafayette Square, the park just across Pennsylvania Avenue from the White House, with a heroic-sized statue of President Andrew Jackson in the center and one of the French general Lafayette, a hero of the Revolutionary War, in one of the corners.

614

29   Clark Mills (1815–83), American sculptor. His statue of Andrew Jackson on a horse reared up on its hind legs, adapted from a model of a rearing horse by the Italian sculptor Bernini, was a novelty in American sculpture. Displaying more "spirit than sophistication," in art critic Oliver Larkin's words (*Art and Life in America* [New York, 1949], p. 184), the enormous bronze which Adams contemplated for two decades from his front window overlooking Lafayette Square made him think of the prancing wooden horses often found in the nursery.

253   30   Samuel Hooper (1808–75), prominent merchant, congressman (1861–75), important ally of Secretary of the Treasury Chase during the Civil War.

31   A. B. Mullett (1834–93), American architect much influenced by the ornamental architecture that furbished the new straight avenues of Napoleon III's Paris; he designed the State, War, and Navy Building, a colossal version of a French chateau whose façade was a vast array of pilasters and columns and which still remains as a monument to the dangers of architectural imitation. Just west of the White House, it is now an Executive Office building.

32   Samuel Ward (1814–84), socialite, financier, and influential lobbyist whose sobriquet was "King of the Lobby," intimate of statesmen and writers. (Robert Steele, *Sam Ward: King of the Lobby* [Boston, 1965].)

33   Smithsonian Institution, the scientific and historical museum, originally consisting of the red brick castle-like structure on the south side of the Mall in Washington; founded in 1846 as a result of a gift of $500,000 by Englishman James Smithson. As chairman of two committees in Congress after he left the Presidency and returned to Congress, John Quincy Adams labored for eight years to establish the scientific and historical museum in Washington and finally saw his efforts succeed. He was noted for his love of science and his intense desire to see it fostered in the United States. See James Truslow Adams, *The Adams Family* (New York, 1930), pp. 224 ff.

CHAPTER XVII   *President Grant* (1869)

255   1   The house, at the present site of George Washington University, was about two miles distant from the Capitol.

2   Charles Nordhoff (1830–1901), American journalist and author, managing editor of *New York Evening Post;* Murat Halstead (1829–1908), editor and publisher of *Cincinnati Commercial;* Henry Watter-

son (1840–1921), editor of the newly merged (1868) *Louisville Courier-Journal;* Samuel Bowles (1826–78), prominent editor and publisher of the *Springfield* (Mass.) *Republican.*

256   3   *monde,* fashionable society; *demi-monde,* the fringe society of fashionable mistresses and courtesans; *grandezza,* literally, greatness, eminence in the great world.

4   James Monroe (1758–1831), President of the U.S., 1817–25.

5   Moorfield Storey (1845–1929), Massachusetts lawyer and writer on legal and social reform. He became co-editor of the *American Law Review* with Sam Hoar in 1873. He had served as a law clerk until his admission to the Bar in 1869 and then became assistant district attorney, 1869–71, in Boston.

257   6   Ebenezer Rockwood Hoar (1816–95), former judge of the Massachusetts Supreme Court. Sam Hoar (1845–1904), Civil War veteran; 1868, pardon clerk in office of U.S. Attorney General William M. Evarts; Harvard Law School, 1870; became one of the most successful lawyers in Boston.

7   George Dewey (1837–1917), at this period a lieutenant commander in the navy; in 1898 became "the hero of Manila Bay" when as admiral of the Asiatic Squadron he destroyed the Spanish fleet off Cavité in the Philippines.

258   8   He had hoped, however, that the authorship would be "leaked" to the press, as was usual, and, as he wrote his brother, "would make me unpopular" (Ford, I, 153), in the right quarters, of course. The article "American Finance, 1865–1869" appeared in the *Edinburgh Review,* CXXIX (April 1869), 504–533.

259   9   "The Session," "Civil Service Reform," *North American Review,* CVIII (April 1869), 610–40; CIX (October 1869), 443–476.

10   A rhetorical flourish, as the change had already begun with the founding of the *Atlantic Monthly* (1858), the *Nation* (1865), and *Harper's Weekly* (1857). The date probably had an ironic significance for Adams as in that year he became editor of the *North American Review* which was then a quarterly magazine continually struggling to make both ends meet. A year after he resigned the editorship in 1877 the magazine was moved from Boston to New York and issued monthly.

11   Bret Harte (1836–1902), famous for his local color stories of the Far West ("The Outcasts of Poker Flat," etc.) which appeared in the newly founded *Overland Monthly* (San Francisco, 1868) during

his editorship, and led to his triumphal reception in the East and a $10,000 contract with the *Atlantic Monthly*.

12 Guy de Maupassant (1850–93), one of the greatest and most daring of the French naturalistic novelists. His great success began with the publication in 1880 of his short story "Boule de Suif" ("A Ball of Tallow") in a French periodical.

13 Rudyard Kipling (1865–1936), British author whose stories of India, which appeared in a Lahore, India, periodical of which he was a youthful editor, made him famous when they were collected as *Plain Tales from the Hills* (1887) and launched him on a distinguished career as a novelist and poet.

14 A slightly altered line from James Russell Lowell's poem "The Present Crisis" (1845): in the original, "Truth forever on the scaffold, Wrong forever on the throne."

260 15 Henry Adams's father voted for Grant, though with some fear of the probable "extravagances" of Republican rule (Duberman, *op. cit.*, p. 495, n. 4). Henry Adams left the family residence in Boston for Washington some weeks before the November election.

16 George Washington (1732–99) had a rather desultory elementary education and left school at the age of fifteen. He became proficient in mathematics and served for a time as a public surveyor. His experience thereafter alternated between military service and the management of the Mount Vernon plantation. As a prominent Virginia planter he was repeatedly elected to the House of Burgesses. Thomas Jefferson (1743–1826), who served as secretary of state under Washington, was college educated, highly intellectual, and before entering Washington's cabinet had served as governor of Virginia and as minister to France. Alexander Hamilton (1757–1804) had a rather irregular education, though he managed to spend two years in college before the Revolution broke out. He served on Washington's staff and thereafter practiced law and entered politics and was one of the contributors to the great *Federalist Papers* which advocated the adoption of the Federal Constitution. He became secretary of the treasury in Washington's cabinet and wrote the epochal *Report on Manufactures* (1791).

17 The phrase used by Ulysses S. Grant (1822–85) when accepting the nomination for the Presidency, May 29, 1868.

261 18 The Secretary in question may well have been Adams's friend, Secretary of the Interior Jacob Dolson Cox. He and Attorney General Hoar were generally regarded as the only strong men in the cabinet. Both were energetic advocates of civil service reform, a reform strongly

resisted by congressmen devoted to the Spoils System. Of course the irascible attorney general was equally capable of the remark.

19   The allusion has a wide range of implication from the extremism in foreign policy and Reconstruction of Senator Charles Sumner of Massachusetts to the corrupt political practices of the notorious Senator Roscoe Conkling of New York. As chairman of the Senate Foreign Relations Committee Sumner defeated the arbitration treaty with England in 1869 by demanding not only money damages for England's violations of neutrality during the Civil War (see index for "Alabama, claims") but also the cession of Canada to the United States (see *Education*, p. 275), thus leaving a residue of suspicion of American foreign policy among British statesmen as well as a legacy of senatorial obstruction that was to becloud the treaty negotiations of Secretary of State John Hay under President William McKinley. Senator Conkling, one of the great political bosses who dominated the alliance between special business interests and government in the post-Civil War period, successfully frustrated the efforts of Congressman— and subsequently President—James Abram Garfield to overthrow the "Spoils system" through reform of the Federal civil service. It should be noted that though Sumner was hostile to Grant, the flamboyant Conkling was a great friend of the Grants, having promoted Grant's candidacy and election. Grant, who was irritated by Sumner's vanity, was heard to say when someone remarked that Sumner did not believe in the Bible, "Oh no, he wouldn't, he didn't write it" (W. E. Woodward, *Meet General Grant* [New York, 1928], p. 446). Grant's witticisms on Conkling appear to be lost. Adams includes Senator James G. Blaine's name probably because Blaine as secretary of state under President Benjamin Harrison found his proposals for reciprocal trade agreements frustrated by the Senate. Perhaps Adams also felt that Blaine's bitter controversy with England over sealing rights in the Bering Sea (1891) was another legacy of anti-British attitudes of the Senate Foreign Relations Committee.

262   20   Cf. *Education*, p. 165.

263   21   Hamilton Fish (1808–93), governor of New York, 1848–50; U.S. senator, 1851–57; secretary of state, 1869–77.

22   Jacob Dolson Cox (1827–1900), governor of Ohio, 1866–68; secretary of the interior, 1869–70; a progressive ally of Congressman Garfield; introduced the merit system in his department which led to his resignation in 1870 under pressure of corrupt politicians.

23   Adam Badeau (1831–95), author, soldier, diplomat; military secretary of General Grant until March, 1869; appointed secretary of

London legation, 1869, and shortly thereafter consul general at London; wrote *Military History of Ulysses S. Grant* (1885); *Grant in Peace* (1887).

264   24   John Aaron Rawlins (1831–69), army chief of staff under Grant; secretary of war, March to September, 1869.

265   25   Adams's ironic reading of Genesis wherein Adam unthinkingly eats of the forbidden fruit proffered by Eve.

      26   "The best way to treat a bad law is to execute it" appears to be a paraphrase of the following from Grant's inaugural address in 1869: "I know no method to secure repeal of bad or obnoxious laws so effectual as their strict execution."

266   27   Another version reported in the press in April, 1878, when Grant visited Venice on his world tour was: "Venice would be a pretty city if it were only drained."

267   28   That is, a career as a journalist and publicist. Cf. his letter to his brother Charles, May 21, 1869: "I will not go down into the rough-and-tumble, nor mix with the crowd, nor write anonymously, except for mere literary practice . . . I have told you before that I mean to be unpopular. . . . You work for power. I work for my own satisfaction . . ." (Ford, I, 160).

      29   A foreshadowing of the opportunities that would open up as a result of the consolidation of Federal power under President McKinley and of the establishment of a global foreign policy (as he came to believe) under Secretary of State John Hay.

CHAPTER XVIII   *Free Fight* (1869–1870)

268   1   Cf. Adams's letter to his English friend, C. M. Gaskell, March 28, 1870: "Such a coil as there is here now! . . . a universal free fight, with everyone abusing everyone else . . ." (Ford, I, 184).

      2   Verbal echoes of the foregoing passage occur in T. S. Eliot's "Gerontion" (1920).

269   3   Henry Adams's unstable uncle George committed suicide in 1829; his improvident uncle John died after a long illness in 1834. Their father, John Quincy Adams, had of course lived in Washington from 1817 to 1825 as secretary of state under Monroe and from 1825 to 1829 as President, and retained his residence in Washington while a congressman until his death in 1848.

      4   An allusion to the 23° tilt of the axis of the earth to the plane of the earth's orbit around the sun, a tilting which accounts for the

changes in the seasons in the northern and southern hemispheres and the differences in climate.

5 Jay Gould (1836–92), an American capitalist who became president of the Erie railroad, the stock of which he manipulated in his notorious financial manipulations. He attempted to purchase the available gold coin and bullion on the American market so as to command a monopoly price from persons whose contracts required payment in gold, especially contracts in international trade. The "corner" was belatedly broken when Grant finally ordered Secretary of the Treasury Boutwell to release $4,000,000 in government-owned gold and sell it on the market. The implication is that Gould had somehow received assurances that the government would keep out of the market. At the height of the panic the price of the gold dollar (⅟₂₀ of an ounce of pure gold) rose to $1.65 in paper "greenback" currency which was not redeemable in specie. Forewarned of the action of the government Gould sold while Fisk frantically bought. See n. 7 below.

270 6 *âme damnée*, a soul damned to hell, as souls owned by Satan.

7 James Fisk (1834–72), financier, associate of Gould in financial piracies. Though apparently "betrayed" by Gould in the conspiracy, Fisk suffered no loss in the bankruptcy of the Erie railroad stockbrokers as he had persuaded them to buy gold at their own risk.

271 8 George Sewall Boutwell, secretary of the treasury; see index.

9 "Hitch your wagon to a star," Ralph Waldo Emerson, in the essay "Civilization," *Society and Solitude* (1870).

272 10 For Adams's highly ambivalent attitude toward Jews, see Samuels, III, Index, "Jews." As a historian he early developed his interest in anthropology to embrace an impressionistic scheme of ethnic, national, and sectional characteristics and types which reflected in the main the prejudices of his class. In London in the 1890's he commonly sought out the Jewish bankers in Lombard street for information on financial trends in spite of his dislike of them as a class, as he regarded them as the most knowledgeable. The allusion seems also to invoke the circumstance that Gould was partly of Jewish descent.

274 11 As in the case of John Adams, who was defeated for re-election by Thomas Jefferson of Virginia, and John Quincy Adams, who was defeated for re-election by Andrew Jackson of Tennessee.

12 See *Education*, p. 107.

13 The former City Orphan Asylum housed the State Department from 1866 to 1875. Demolished in 1940's.

14 The treaty for the annexation of Santo Domingo which was sponsored by President Grant was rejected by the Senate on June 30, under the leadership of Senator Sumner. The day after the adverse vote Grant angrily ordered Secretary Fish to recall Minister Motley, who was Sumner's protégé.

275 15 In the preceding term Secretary Seward had begun negotiations for the purchase of the Danish West Indies (now the U.S. Virgin Islands) of which St. Thomas was the largest; it was finally acquired by the U.S. in 1917 for $25,000,000. The Bay of Samana is located in the island of Santo Domingo.

16 For Sumner's proposal concerning Canada, see n. 19, Ch. XVII.

17 John Chandler Bancroft Davis (1822–1907), diplomatist and legal authority, assistant secretary of state at this period.

276 18 Charles Maurice de Talleyrand (1754–1838), French statesman who served as minister of foreign affairs under Napoleon, then helped restore the Bourbon dynasty; famous for skill in diplomacy.

19 He was recalled from London by President Grant in July 1870 and failing to resign he was summarily dismissed in December. Adams made fictional use of the incident in his anonymous novel *Democracy* (1880) in the portrayal of Nathan Gore.

20 A reference to Carlyle's ironical "Clothes Philosophy" in *Sartor Resartus,* a work whose influence can be seen throughout the *Education. Cardinal de Retz* (1614–79). His vivid *Memoirs* which depicted the court and courtiers of Louis XIV was one of Adams's favorite books. The allusion to de Retz's forming a judgment about a newly-elected pope from the fact that the pope-elect had used the same pen for two years was one that Adams used before in his *History* (I, Ch. 7).

21 When Grant lost his temper over Sumner's check to his foreign policy and ordered Secretary Fish to recall Motley from London.

277 22 As a member of the highest order of hierarchy a bishop in the Roman Catholic Church is the peer even of the pope and has administrative and legal jurisdiction over the lower clergy and the property of the Church, powers which enable him to serve as a protector of the diocese. A bishop has a similar role in the Anglican and other churches.

23 Elbridge Gerry Spaulding (1809–97), banker and congressman. After the New York banks stopped payment in gold in 1862, he introduced a bill for the issuance of irredeemable treasury notes ("greenbacks") which would be legal tender for the payment of debts.

Adopted as a desperate war measure in 1862, it led to the authorization of $450,000,000 in greenbacks. The just-published volume: *A Resource of War . . . History of the Legal Tender Paper Money . . .* (1869).

278   24 The self-deprecation gives a misleading impression of Adams's role in this complicated episode. Judge Hoar, that is to say, Attorney General Hoar, argued in support of the constitutionality of the Legal Tender Act of 1862 in *Hepburn vs. Griswold*. Chief Justice Chase, speaking for the majority (in the 4 to 3 decision) on February 7, 1870, held the act unconstitutional. On the same day Grant, possibly anticipating an adverse decision, had added two justices to the Supreme Court restoring the number to nine. Walker's appointment occurred on the same day, whereupon he turned over his notes to Adams. Adams not only wished to support the narrow majority but as a "sound money" man to teach the principle that the Legal Tender Act violated laws of economics that were "deeper than statute or than constitutional law." (See Samuels, I, 192–195.) Attorney General Hoar pressed for a reversal of the decision and therefore attacked the Chief Justice's opinion. On May 1, 1871, the Court in a 5 to 4 decision reversed itself and held the Legal Tender Act to be constitutional.

25 Grant requested Hoar's resignation as attorney general in June, 1870, much to Hoar's surprise and to the dismay of the liberal press, especially since only six months earlier Grant had nominated Hoar to the Supreme Court, a nomination which the Senate rejected. Senator Simon Cameron, chairman of the Committee on Foreign Relations, remarked: "What could you expect from a man who had snubbed seventy senators?" (E. S. Bradley, *Simon Cameron: Lincoln's Secretary of War* [Philadelphia, 1966], p. 315).

26 Under its editor Horace Greeley the paper made common cause with Western farmers in demanding expansion of the use of the irredeemable "greenback" currency in order to put more money into circulation and raise farm prices. His other sin, in the eyes of tariff reformers like Adams, was to support energetically the demand of manufacturers for higher tariffs, arguing that free trade and low tariffs were part of a British scheme to cripple American industry with resulting injury to American workingmen. To Adams these notions were dangerous heresies.

279   27 Hoar had himself recognized that it was unusual to have two men from the same state in the Cabinet (Secretary of the Treasury Boutwell was also from Massachusetts), and when the Senate rejected his nomination to the Supreme Court he informed Grant that he was

prepared to resign. When Grant tried to get senatorial support for his San Domingo treaty, Southern senators pointed out to Grant that the South had no representation in the Cabinet. Grant yielded to the pressure. Hoar was ignorant of this horse-trading. As for Sumner, Grant, angered by Sumner's successful obstruction of the treaty, managed to have him deposed from the chairmanship of the Senate Foreign Relations Committee when the new Congress met in March, 1871.

28 Colonel Mulberry Sellers was the preposterously self-deluded character in the dramatization of the satirical novel *The Gilded Age: A Tale of To-day* (1873) by Mark Twain and C. D. Warner.

281 29 David Ames Wells (1828–98), a noted economist, U.S. commissioner of revenue, 1866–70.

282 30 Samuel Sullivan Cox (1824–89), at that period a popular Democratic congressman from New York, who as a Columbus, Ohio, editor had earned his nickname by an extremely florid description of a sunset.

31 Maurice de Guérin (1810–39), a French Romantic poet and writer of poetic prose (*Centaur*, 1845), noted for his intense feeling for nature. Matthew Arnold in his essay on the poet renders the phrase "le vaste sein de la terre" which concludes the *Centaur* as the "vast bosom of Earth." Adams's freer rendering of the particular phrase would appear to be based on his reading of Arnold's essay in which it is cited.

CHAPTER XIX   *Chaos* (1870)

284 1 Gladstone became prime minister in December, 1868, and he procured the passage in the following July of a bill disestablishing the Irish Church and withdrawing all subsidies. In 1870 his Irish Land Act provided protection of tenants against arbitrary evictions. In the following session of Parliament religious tests in the universities were abolished. In 1873, however, his plan to establish an Irish university acceptable both to Catholics and Protestants failed of adoption.

2 John Lothrop Motley succeeded Charles Francis Adams as minister to England in 1869. See also notes 14, 19, Ch. XVIII. The "rebellion" refers to the Civil War.

3 The Prince of Wales (later became Edward VII) was the second child of Queen Victoria and Prince Consort Albert. Albert died in 1861, his death marking the end of a chapter of social history. The young Prince of Wales married Princess Alexandra of Denmark in 1863.

285   4   Forster's Elementary Education Act, which was finally adopted in 1870, proved to be a complicated compromise which left standing the system of state-aided parochial elementary schools alongside a new system of tax-supported public schools in which non-denominational Christian religious instruction was authorized. School attendance was not made compulsory until 1876.

5   The Bastille was the notorious royal prison in Paris which was captured and razed to the ground by the Paris revolutionists in 1789. The Ghetto, a long-surviving relic of the Middle Ages, was the small, crowded, and noisome slum of the large European cities where Jews were required to live.

6   Marlborough House, the London residence of the Prince of Wales, where for want of other occupation the prince devoted himself largely to a life of pleasure. His favorite sport was horse racing. The allusions would seem to be a covert thrust at the Prince's attractiveness to rich American women and his penchant for running up gambling debts. Although he did not succeed to the throne until the death of Queen Victoria in 1901 when he was sixty years of age, the prince was much before the public as a popular speaker in behalf of worthy causes, and though not active in politics he effectively advanced the public relations of the crown, if not always in a dignified manner.

286   7   Cheapside, an important business street near St. Paul's Church; Oxford Street, a main thoroughfare adjacent to fashionable London of the West End.

8   Arthur Pendennis, the poet-dandy who is the hero of the novel (1850) named for him by William Makepeace Thackeray.

9   Royal Exchange, the London stock exchange, near the Bank of England.

10   "Power of Erie," the Erie Railroad management in New York City.

11   *North American Review,* an allusion to the exposé type articles contributed by the two brothers in 1869 and 1870, particularly Charles Francis's outspoken "Chapters of Erie" and Henry's "Sessions" articles and "The Legal Tender Act."

287   12   Bagni di Lucca, a famous health spa some 60 miles northeast of Pisa in the mountainous section of northwestern Tuscany in Italy.

13   Louisa Catherine (Adams) Kuhn. See *Education,* pp. 23, 35, 88, 287.

289   14   Ouchy, the port of Lausanne on Lake Geneva in Switzerland.

15   The struggle for domination of Europe between Prussia under Bismarck and the French Empire under Napoleon III came to a head over the nomination of rival candidates for the throne of Spain by France and Prussia. Bismarck, unwilling to appear the aggressor, succeeded through a trick in provoking the French to declare war, a step which the sixty-two year old French emperor and the war party favored to advance the imperial foreign policy and to put an end to the strikes and the incipient socialist revolution in France. Sedan capitulated on September 1, 1870, and the French emperor surrendered with his army of 84,000 to the Germans. A revolutionary government set itself up in Paris and carried on the war. Paris capitulated at the end of January, 1871, and a humiliating peace was signed. The Third Republic was thereupon established and the Revolutionary Commune in Paris was ruthlessly suppressed by the new government in a six-week siege from which the German army held aloof. The isolated outrages of the revolutionary terrorists were avenged a hundredfold over by the massacre of some 20 or 30 thousand Parisian defenders. These latter events occurred in the year following Adams's visit.

290   16   *affiches,* posters.

17   Giacomo Meyerbeer (1791–1864), German composer noted for his gorgeously staged operas.

18   Louis Adolphe Thiers (1797–1877), French statesman and historian, leader of the Liberal opposition against Napoleon III's imperialistic policies. He protested the declaration of war, negotiated the armistice and peace with Germany, and as the new chief of state suppressed the Commune. Leon Gambetta (1838–82), French lawyer and statesman of Jewish origin, a popular leader of the Opposition. He escaped from Paris during the German siege and organized two armies to continue the war, a measure which was rendered futile because of the treasonable surrender by the commander of the fortress of Metz, who feared the socialists more than the Germans.

291   19   "Prior" and "monks", fanciful characterizations of Adams and his friends. "Secular," in the sense of continuing through ages.

20   Charles William Eliot (1834–1926), became president of Harvard University in 1869, Henry Adams's father having declined the honor a short time before. His introduction of the "elective system" was part of the reforms which he initiated.

292   21   Senator Howe's statement read: "The author is proclaimed to . . . belong to a family in which statesmanship is preserved by propagation—something as color in the leaf of the Begonia, perpetuating

resemblance through perpetual change" (*Wisconsin State Journal,* October 7, 1870).

293 22 Ephraim Whitney Gurney (1829–86). It was at Professor Gurney's home that Henry Adams met his future wife, Marian Hooper (Sept. 13, 1843–Dec. 6, 1885), the sister of Gurney's wife, Ellen. Gurney was then tutoring Marian in Greek. Adams and Marian became engaged on February 27, 1872, and were married on June 27 of that year.

23 The allusion recalls his father's disappointing talk with President Lincoln in 1861 after Lincoln had appointed him minister to Great Britain. Lincoln had casually assumed that Adams's father needed no guidance and switched the conversation from international diplomacy to his own success in filling the Chicago postmastership.

294 24 An echo of the remark attributed to the French author Benjamin Constant: "I am not the rose, but I have lived with her."

25 Abram Steven Hewitt (1822–1903), a philanthropic steelmaker and a noted statesman in support of political reform.

295 26 John Sherman (1823–1900), United States senator and author of the famous Sherman Antitrust Act of 1890.

27 George Hunt Pendleton (1825–89), U.S. senator, 1879–85, secured passage of his pioneer civil service reform bill in 1883 providing for federal civil service examinations; Chester Alan Arthur (1830–86), succeeded to the Presidency of the U.S. after the assassination of Adams's friend President James Garfield; Frederick Theodore Freylinghuysen (1817–85), secretary of state, 1881–85. Freylinghuysen became a good friend of Adams and, apparently unaware of the inadequateness of the post, offered to appoint Adams to the diplomatic mission to Central America at Guatemala City; Mrs. Adams gently dissuaded the secretary of state from making the offer official. Thomas Francis Bayard (1828–98), Democratic senator from Delaware, secretary of state, 1885–98, with whom Adams was also on friendly terms.

297 28 His salary was figured at $2,000 per annum, of which three or four hundred dollars were deducted for rent of his rooms.

CHAPTER XX *Failure* (*1871*)

299 1 Cambridgeport, one of the villages subsequently incorporated into the town of Cambridge.

2 John Richard Dennett (1838–74), also a critic and editorial writer for the *Nation*.

3   Chauncey Wright (1830–75), brilliant scientist-philosopher, evolutionary naturalist, lecturer on psychology, forerunner of William James; Francis Wharton (1820–89), educator and writer of legal treatises (*Treatise on the Conflict of Laws,* 1872), at this period professor of canon law at a theological seminary in Cambridge; John Fiske (1842–1901), American historian, lecturer on philosophy at Harvard, 1869–71, exponent of Darwinian evolution and scientific positivism.

300   4   Henry Warren Torrey (1814–93), taught at Harvard, 1844–86.

301   5   *Anglo-Saxon Chronicle,* a historical compilation by various monks, carried down to the middle of the 12th century, written in Old English; Venerable Bede (673–735), noted scholar and ecclesiastical historian of medieval England who wrote chiefly in Latin.

6   Jean Baptiste Pierre Antoine de Monet de Lamarck (1744–1829), French naturalist whose theory of biological evolution prepared the way for Darwin's definitive theory; Carolus Linnaeus (1707–78), Swiss naturalist who devised the famous Linnaean system of botanical classification of genera and species.

7   Sir Henry Maine (1822–88), English jurist and legal writer, author of *Ancient Law* (1861), *Village Communities* (1871), etc., works used by Adams in his courses at Harvard; John Ferguson McLennan (1827–81), Scottish sociologist noted for his studies of the historical evolution of marriage; Edward Burnett Tylor (1832–1917), English anthropologist, author of *Primitive Culture* (1871) and other important studies of early societies.

8   Adams taught at Harvard 1870–72, 1873–77. He was on leave for the academic year 1872–73 travelling in Europe with his wife on their wedding journey. He taught courses in the history of Europe from A.D. 987, medieval history and medieval institutions, English constitutional and legal history, American colonial and early national history, and graduate seminars, including one in Anglo-Saxon law.

304   9   William I (1797–1888), king of Prussia 1861, proclaimed emperor of Germany January 18, 1871; Pepin (d. 768), king of the Salian Franks; Merwig [Merovaeus, Merovech], supposed founder of the first Merovingian dynasty of the Franks; Othos, medieval German emperor of the Holy Roman Empire; (Frederick) Barbarossa [Red Beard], one of the most famous of the medieval emperors. All reflect the sense of historical grandeur and continuity attached to the coronation of William I.

307   10   Francis James Child (1825–96), professor of English literature and editor of the monumental collection *English and Scottish Ballads* (1857–59); William James (1842–1910), leading American psycholo-

gist and philosopher, author of *Principles of Psychology* (1890), *Varieties of Religious Experience* (1902), *Pragmatism* (1907); brother of the novelist Henry James, who was also a long-time friend of Adams.

11 Adams contributed 22 reviews and review articles to the *North American Review.*

12 Edward the Confessor (1004–66), king of England; Boniface VIII (1228–1303), a famous pope who proclaimed the temporal as well as the spiritual sovereignty of the papacy.

13 A reference to the series of influential exposés of corrupt railroad practices which led to Charles's being appointed a Massachusetts railroad commissioner.

309 14 Samuel Franklin Emmons (1841–1911), worked under the direction of Clarence King.

15 Josiah Dwight Whitney (1819–96), professor of geology at Harvard, author of important reports of various geological and mineralogical surveys.

16 The Union Pacific Railroad was completed May 10, 1869.

310 17 Uintahs, mountain range in northeast Utah; Laramie, at that period a military post newly reached by the Union Pacific Railroad.

18 wapiti, an American elk.

19 Estes Park, one of several great plateaus, called "parks," bordered by high mountains; now part of Rocky Mountain National Park.

311 20 Clarence King (1842–1901) was a graduate of the Sheffield Scientific School at Yale. He became a geologist and mining engineer. In 1867 at the age of 25 he successfully lobbied for a bill authorizing a geological survey of a hundred-mile-wide belt along the new railroad. He published his epochal report, *Systematic Geology,* in 1878, and in the following year was made director of the new bureau of the United States Geological Survey. His descriptive volume, *Mountaineering in the Sierra Nevada* (1872), is rated a minor literary classic. Gay and unpredictable, he led a strange double life; his common-law marriage to a Negro woman of New York was one of the best kept secrets of his intimate friends. See Thurman Wilkins, *Clarence King* (New York, 1958).

21 Alcibiades (450–404 B.C.), a famous general and politician of Athens, renowned for his talents and his personal beauty and notorious for his amours and his love of luxury. Even in camp Clarence King affected elegant dress for dinner. Alexander the Great (356–323 B.C.),

famous king of Macedon, a pupil of the Athenian philosopher Aristotle and one of the greatest conquerors of antiquity. He was idolized as a hero and his practice of being clean-shaven set the fashion for the Graeco-Roman world for 500 years.

CHAPTER XXI   *Twenty Years After* (1892)

314   1   For a full account of the "twenty years" of literary and social success of Adams and his wife in Boston and especially in Washington, of their two important European journeys, of his wife's tragic suicide in December 1885, and of his subsequent travels in Japan and to the South Seas, see Samuels, *Henry Adams: The Middle Years.* Besides the reviews and a few articles which Adams published during his editorship of the *North American Review,* he produced the following works during this long interval: *The Life of Albert Gallatin* (1879); *Democracy, An American Novel* (1880); *John Randolph* (a biography) (1882); *Esther, A Novel* (1884); *History of the United States during the Administrations of Jefferson and Madison,* 9 vols. (1889–1891).

315   2   William Morris Hunt (1824–79), noted American painter of portraits and landscapes, introduced the paintings of Millet and the Barbizon school to Boston, but although a welcome figure in Boston society, he never felt at home in the conservative atmosphere. His death at 55 appears to have been a suicide. His younger brother Richard Morris Hunt (1828–95) became one of the most sought-after architects of his time, especially by the new multimillionaires who could afford great mansion houses whose elegance imitated the chateaux of the Loire. He was a scholarly and dedicated artist whose scrupulous work was hardly understood by his extravagant clients.

3   H. H. Richardson, Adams's college mate, was already a famous architect when he designed and built the houses for Adams and John Hay in Lafayette Square in Washington (1884–85), now replaced by the Hay-Adams Hotel.

4   Charles McKim (1847–1909), American architect, his masterpiece being the Boston Public Library, also designed important buildings for the Chicago World's Fair of 1893; Stanford White (1853–1906), architect, associated with McKim in a wide variety of projects, noted for his brilliant adaptations of Renaissance styles; designed the architectural setting for St. Gaudens' statue, the Adams Memorial, in Rock Creek cemetery in Washington. White's career ended in a tragic scandal when he was shot to death in New York City in 1906 by Harry K. Thaw, jealous over alleged attentions to his wife.

316 5   The mental illness and suicide of his wife which, as he said later, broke his life in "halves" and led him to talk of his "posthumous" existence for years thereafter.

6   For the removal of a wen on his shoulder "which I feared might make me look like a camel if I left it alone" (Adams papers, Henry Adams to Eliz. Cameron, Dec. 6, 1891). The gloom was deepened by his realization of the hopelessness of his attachment for Elizabeth Cameron, the wife of his friend, Senator James Donald Cameron. Their affectionate intimacy continued to the end of Adams's life. On the nature of their intimacy see Samuels, "Henry Adams and the Gossip Mills," *Essays in American and English Literature* (Athens, Ohio, 1967).

7   He left New York August 16, 1890; arrived in Samoa October 7; reached Tahiti February 4, 1891; Fiji Islands, June 15; Australia, July 31; Ceylon, September 5; landed in France October 9, 1891. One of the fruits of his stay in Tahiti was a privately printed history of the people of the island based on the oral traditions which he collected as a guest of the Salmon family, leaders of the Teva clan—*Memoirs of Marau Taaroa Last Queen of Tahiti* (1893, revised, 1901). Adams's letters from the South Seas (in Ford, I) are among the most brilliant and spirited that he ever wrote. La Farge's *Reminiscences of the South Seas* (Garden City, N.Y., 1901) gives a charming picture of their travels and their life among the natives.

317 8   George Bancroft (1800–91), noted American historian and statesman, author of a multi-volume *History of the United States* (1834–1876), resigned as minister to Germany in 1874, resided thereafter in Washington as "dean" of American historians and as an elder statesman. Bancroft, a relative of Mrs. Adams, took a close interest in Adams's historical work as a friend and adviser.

318 9   *Abraham Lincoln: A History,* 10 vols. (New York, 1890), written in collaboration with John G. Nicolay.

10   Searching official archives for additional historical materials on the early relations of the U.S. and France.

319 11   Vailima, the four hundred acre plantation on a mountain shelf near Apia in Samoa, where Adams visited Stevenson and his wife in their "shanty" in a jungle clearing shortly before the building of the manor house.

12   Adams had similarly enjoyed his association with the British governor of the Fiji Islands at Suva and here suggests that the Fijians shared his admiration and sense of inferiority to the British type.

320   13   Calvin Brice (1845–98), rich railroad magnate and able senator from Ohio 1890–97.

14   Grover Cleveland (1837–1908), President of the U.S. 1885–89, 1893–97. The picturesque characterization of the presidential effect upon friends alludes in the case of Cleveland to the fact that he alienated the leaders of his party, which had been out of power for 24 years, by pressing for wider adoption of the merit system in the civil service and by his slowness in meeting their expectations of the spoils of office as they had counted on wholesale dismissals of Republican officeholders to make room for loyal Democrats. Harrison, a Republican, was also committed to support of the Civil Service Act of 1883 and his resistance to congressional pressure for patronage appointments angered many Republican politicians.

321   15   Benjamin Harrison (1833–1901), President of the U.S., 1889–93.

16   "Hosea Biglow's Cornwallis." Hosea Biglow is the homespun hero of James Russell Lowell's *The Biglow Papers,* First Series, 1847. "Cornwallis," annual muster of the militia in Massachusetts during which was reenacted in suitable costumes the surrender of Lord Cornwallis at Yorktown, supposed to have had its origin soon after the Revolution. (*Biglow Papers,* I, 17.)

17   In one of Aesop's "Fables" Zeus answered the plea of the frogs for a king by sending down a worthless and inanimate log. When they protested that the new king did nothing, Zeus sent as a replacement a stork who ate up the frogs.

18   A somewhat idealized view of the role of the Republican party in putting an end to Negro slavery in the U.S. Adams is also alluding to the fact that their friend Secretary of the Interior Carl Schurz, a Republican, had put an end to the disgraceful corruption in the Indian Bureau.

19   Hay had served under President Lincoln, a Republican, as assistant private secretary, and his political associations continued with Republicans like Evarts. His business interests as an associate of his father-in-law, Amasa Stone, the Cleveland railroad magnate, tied him to the Ohio Republicans, especially after the suicide of Stone in 1883 made Hay and his wife millionaires.

322   20   Carl Schurz (1829–1906), German born political reformer, a brigadier general in the Civil War, senator from Missouri, 1869–75; secretary of the interior under President Hayes, 1877–81.

21   John G. Nicolay (1832–1901), an Illinois journalist who became

Lincoln's private secretary. He also wrote *The Outbreak of the Rebellion* (1881) and helped Hay edit Lincoln's writings.

22 *"A la disposicion de Usted!"*, "At your disposition!"

324   23 Rutherford Birchard Hayes (1822–93), 19th President of the U.S., 1877–81, beneficiary of the "stolen" election of 1876 in which Adams had supported Samuel J. Tilden. Adams regarded him as "a third-rate nonentity" (Ford, I, 288). For a more sober evaluation of Hayes's abilities and inclinations at this period see Tyler Dennett, *John Hay: From Poetry to Politics* (1933).

325   24 The collapse of the great London banking house of Baring Brothers in 1891 as a result of the involvement of the firm in a risky Argentine loan touched off a financial recession throughout the world and led to the great depression of 1893. Adams's conservative investments were not greatly affected by the gyrations of the stock market.

327   25 Francis Parkman (1823–93), noted American historian, author of *The Conspiracy of Pontiac* (1851), *The California and Oregon Trail* (1849) and a notable series of books on the French presence in America. He and Adams were on very friendly terms.

26 A characteristic piece of self-depreciation. His publisher, Charles Scribner, felt that the nine volumes met with "exceptional success" in the U.S. Roughly 2,000 sets of the nine volumes were originally published and sold. This, however, fell far below Adams's expectation when he compared the reception of his work with that given to English historians like Macaulay and Gibbon before him. Adams neglects to mention two other "serious readers" of the draft volumes of the *History*, the historian George Bancroft and Charles Francis Adams, Jr., Adams's older brother who made a large number of editorial suggestions. There were also many reviews of the pairs of volumes as they came out, the praise often qualified by important reservations; however, no extended critical essay on the monumental work was published in any of the contemporary literary or historical journals. For a bibliography of the reception of the *History* see W. H. Jordy, *op. cit.*, pp. 298–300. Isaac Wayne MacVeagh (1833–1917), minister to Turkey, 1870–71, was attorney general in President Garfield's Cabinet and active in the civil service reform group with which Adams was associated.

328   27 A humorous reference to King's activities as a mining engineer and prospector.

28 Refers to the flight of the Jews from Egypt under Moses and the forty years' wandering in the Sinai desert as told in Exodus. When fiery serpents plagued the sinful Israelites, Moses made a serpent of

brass which when merely looked at cured snakebite. In the absence of Moses on the Mount, where he was receiving the Ten Commandments, the people under Aaron fashioned an image of a calf out of gold and worshipped it as a god, an act for which they were duly punished with a plague.

29 Last seen by Adams in 1890 on his way to the South Seas.

30 Although mining in the new "western" lands, in Missouri and Wisconsin, had already begun before 1840, the spectacular development of mines in the Michigan peninsula began in the 1840's, followed by the "Gold Rush" of 1849 in California. The great expansion of the railroad system to the West began in the 1840's and its financing required the largest accumulation of capital ever attempted. The capital also "disappeared" into new industries and the rapid expansion of old ones and the development of Western agriculture and stock raising. In this period the buildings were chiefly of wood and their architecture immediately utilitarian. The period was also marked by recurring waves of get-rich-quick speculation in land and transportation and recurring financial panics as of 1837, 1857, 1873, and 1893.

329 31 The musing seated figure, shrouded in a cowled robe, was erected as a memorial to Adams's wife, Marian, who committed suicide during a period of extreme mental depression on December 6, 1885. In tourist books it is sometimes called "Grief"; Adams once wrote that his "own name for it is 'the Peace of God.'" At the cemetery the nameless grave site is referred to as the Adams Memorial. Adams had hoped for some sort of Buddha figure expressive of the idea of Nirvana—oblivion to suffering and the visible world—as at the time he was much interested in the Orient, which he had visited with La Farge in 1886.

32 Kamakura Daibuts, the great bronze image of Buddha called the Dai Butsu at Kamakuru in Japan; Prometheus, in Greek mythology the god who stole fire from heaven to make a gift of it to man and who was punished by Zeus by being chained to a rock in the Caucasus mountains; Michelangelo (1475–1564), greatest of Italian Renaissance sculptors. His sculptures "The Slaves" and the figures on the Medici tombs had greatly impressed Adams by their symbolism. Percy Bysshe Shelley (1792–1822), English Romantic poet whose *Prometheus Unbound* (1820) was a great symbolic poem of the eventual liberation of the human spirit. The array of allusions would suggest that it was man's immemorial fate to achieve the "peace of God" only through suffering. The monument cost in the neighborhood of $25,000, an expenditure that scandalized many persons besides old Civil War vet-

erans on small pensions who stopped to rest on the curved stone bench in front of the statue.

330   33   With his late wife's five young nieces, at a lodge at Aboyne, Scotland. A few years earlier, during an illness, their mother, Ellen Hooper Gurney, wife of Professor Ephraim Gurney and sister of Marian Adams, also had taken her life.

34   An allusion to his somber pose that he had died with his wife.

CHAPTER XXII   *Chicago* (*1893*)

331   1   *fin-de-siècle,* end of the century, i.e. of the 19th century, an intellectual and emotional climate characterized by world weariness, fashionable despair, and emphasis on sophistication, unconventionality, escapism, and revolt against received opinions, especially middle-class opinions of propriety and decorum; in politics an interest in anarchism and nihilism; in art the exaltation of art for art's sake; in literature a preoccupation with symbolism. The phenomenon was limited to a portion of the intellectual and upper classes in Europe and America.

2   Thomas Brackett Reed (1839–1902), speaker of the House of Representatives and the most powerful political figure in Washington, called "Tsar" Reed by those who opposed his autocratic domination of the House through the parliamentary rules which he devised; William Bourke Cockran (1854–1923), Tammany Hall (New York) politician of Irish origin, member of Congress, noted for his fiery oratory on the silver coinage issue; Edward Oliver Wolcott (1848–1905), U.S. senator from Colorado, influential advocate of the free coinage of silver, opponent of the single gold standard.

3   Thomas Francis Bayard (1828–98), secretary of state under President Cleveland, ambassador to Great Britain, 1893–97, a leading opponent of the free coinage of silver. For Adams's interest in the "Silver Question" see *Education,* p. 334 f.

332   4   Senator James Donald Cameron (1833–1918), Pennsylvania-born capitalist and astute politician; president of Northern Central Railroad, 1863–74; secretary of war under President Grant, 1876; Republican senator from Pennsylvania, 1877–97.

5   The marriage took place in 1878, not 1880 (T. T. Sherman, *Sherman Genealogy* [New York, 1920]).

6   Elizabeth (Sherman) Cameron (1857–1944), second wife of Senator Cameron. He was five years older than Henry Adams. Re-

puted the most beautiful young woman in Washington, she was then 21. She became Adams's most intimate friend after his wife's death and a frequent social companion in Paris until World War I ended his annual stay abroad. He idealized her and her daughter Martha as the Madonna and Child of his world. Anna Cabot Mills (Davis) Lodge (1850–1915), Massachusetts-born socialite wife of Senator Henry Cabot Lodge.

7   Theodore Roosevelt (1858–1919), U.S. civil service commissioner, 1889–95, President of the United States, 1901–08, aggressive reform statesman. Adams disapproved of his youthful impulsiveness and egotism but managed to remain on good terms with the President by preserving a diplomatic silence.

8   Sir Cecil Arthur Spring Rice (1859–1918), popular British diplomat, served in British legations abroad and in Washington, became acquainted with Adams in 1887 and carried on an extensive political correspondence with him, appointed ambassador to the U.S. in 1913, recalled in 1918.

9   With Clarence King with whom he became involved as an active Washington supporter of the Cuban revolutionary movement of which King was a prominent partisan.

333   10   See especially his *History of the United States*, I, 29, 114, 115; II, 194 *et seq.;* Index to Vol. IX.

11   Albert Gallatin (1761–1849), Pennsylvania statesman, secretary of the treasury under President Thomas Jefferson, 1801–09, and under President James Madison, 1809–13, and greatly admired by Adams as a model statesman. Adams's biography of him was published in 1879, accompanied by a 2-volume compilation of his papers.

12   "dago," derogatory name applied to persons of Spanish descent, afterwards extended to Italians.

334   13   The hotly debated question of the period whether international trade should be carried on with settlements of balances only in gold or alternatively in gold and silver, at a fixed ratio of silver to gold. The great financial depression of 1893 made the question acute because the enforcement of the single gold standard led to a shortage of gold coin and currency redeemable in gold and a rise in the value of gold with a resulting extreme financial stringency. It should be noted that domestic contracts (bonds, etc.,) usually called for payment in gold coin or gold treasury certificates. For an introduction to the complicated and controversial questions of the Gold Standard and bimetallism see the following articles in the *Encyclopedia Britannica:*

"Gold Standard," "Bimetallism," "Currency," and "Money." Adams makes clear that he had ambivalent feelings towards the issues, feelings that ultimately led to an impasse in his thinking. Thus though he despised the crass materialism of the so-called "gold bugs" (the banking fraternity that supported the single gold standard and monopolistic finance capitalists), he also detested the radical threats to society posed by the growing socialist movement. He abandoned the money question shortly afterwards as largely irrelevant to the great underlying problems of the Western world in favor of the study of the control of Force which he confronts in the chapters "A Dynamic Theory of History" and "A Law of Acceleration." For a discussion of the efforts of Henry Adams and his brother Brooks to resolve the contradictions of capitalist society, see Ch. IV, "Brothers in Prophecy" in Samuels, *Henry Adams: The Major Phase.* For them, as for others, "Capitalism" had a variety of symbolic connotations.

14 Samuel Dana Horton (1844–95), American economist, an early advocate of bimetallism, a system of international settlements based on the maintenance of a fixed ratio between gold and silver and making both available for payments required to be made in specie.

336 15 In the election of 1896 William McKinley, advocate of the single gold standard, defeated for the Presidency William Jennings Bryan, advocate of the free coinage of silver at the ratio of 16 to 1, i.e., 16 ozs. of silver to be regarded as equal in value to 1 oz. of gold.

16 The allusion is to a famous anecdote about Dr. Johnson who when challenged to refute the theory of Bishop George Berkeley that particular objects exist only in the perceiving mind kicked a stone in the road to "prove" that it was real.

337 17 A reference to the disastrous Panic of 1893. As it turned out, their investments were not dangerously impaired.

338 18 Brooks Adams was then working on the manuscript of his *Law of Civilization and Decay,* published in 1895, in which he attacked the finance capitalist as a usurer and attempted to construct a history of the moral decay of society as a result of the rise of a usurious commercial type.

340 19 Academie des Beaux Arts, the chief art school of Paris in which most of the celebrated artists and architects of the period were trained.

20 The two great French houses of fashion. Adams himself had made purchases at Worth's.

21 The dome of the imposing administration building designed by Hunt.

341   22   Daniel Hudson Burnham (1846–1912), prominent Chicago architect whose firm designed the first skyscraper. He was the directing architect of the 1893 Chicago World's Fair and the author of the Burnham Plan for the city of Chicago.

23   Paestum, an ancient Greek city in southern Italy whose ruins are among the most imposing in the Hellenic world; Girgenti (now Agrigento), an ancient Greek city near the south coast of Sicily regarded as one of the most beautiful of the ancient world, of which extremely impressive ruins still remain.

24   Carthage, one of the most famous capitals of the ancient world, situated on the northern coast of Africa, ultimately destroyed by its great rival, Rome.

25   An accurately measured base line for projecting angular measurements in a trigonometrical survey of the earth's surface.

342   26   watt, standard unit of electrical energy; ampere, a standard unit of electrical current; erg, a standard unit of work done in a mechanical system.

343   27   John Percival Jones (1829–1912), English-born mine owner, elected U.S. senator from Nevada, a champion of bimetallism and a supporter of William Jennings Bryan, the eloquent leader of the "Silverites"; Moreton Frewen (1853–1924), an English friend of Adams, a well-known advocate for bimetallism in England and America. The vote for repeal took place on October 30, 1893. It provided the chief issue for the 1896 presidential campaign.

28   Adams took more than a bystander's role in the silver fight, as there is good evidence that he helped write one of Senator Cameron's speeches against repeal of the Sherman Silver Purchase Act.

344   29   These were the elections respectively of Thomas Jefferson and Andrew Jackson, the two great spokesmen for a broadly based democracy of independent farmers and city folk.

CHAPTER XXIII   *Silence (1894–1898)*

346   1   Clarence King's involvement in highly speculative mining ventures made him peculiarly vulnerable to the stock market collapse, particularly because his accounting methods and those of his associates were very sketchy. The crash of 1893 drove him temporarily insane and he was confined for a few months in an asylum. His "want of money" arose in part from his extravagance and in part from his naive trust in his mining associates. Alexander Agassiz had made a fortune out of his connection with the Calumet and Hecla mines in

the Michigan peninsula, a highly prosperous investment which he shared with Boston friends, including Henry Adams, who were let in on the ground floor, so to speak.

2 Adams's investments compared with those of the great capitalists like Rockefeller, Vanderbilt, Carnegie, etc., were trifling, but they did provide him with a very comfortable annual income of from $25,000 to $50,000 in a period of negligible taxes. It should be borne in mind that the *Education* was originally addressed to a small elite group of readers, many of whom were considerably wealthier than Adams.

347 3 As a very prominent financier and politician, Whitney was high in the councils of President Cleveland, and his Washington home and his Fifth Avenue mansion were centers of international high society. One of his sons married the daughter of Adams's closest friend, John Hay.

349 4 Adams's home in Lafayette Square became one of the meeting places of the Washington representatives of the Cuban revolutionists. Adams wrote the historical report in support of the recognition of the Cuban republic for Senator Cameron. It was submitted to the Senate by the committee, December 21, 1896, but no action was taken on it.

5 Probably a reference to Rameses II, one of the most famous of the ancient Egyptian kings, a great builder and conqueror of the Hittites. For his visits to Egypt Adams carefully studied Egyptian archaeology.

350 6 William Hallett Phillips (1853–97), a prominent Washington lawyer who collaborated with Adams in the Cuban revolutionary intrigue.

7 Joseph Paxon Iddings (1857–1920), petrographic expert, associate of Clarence King in the U.S. Geological Survey, associated in the geological survey of Yellowstone Park, 1883–93, became professor of petrology at the University of Chicago in 1895.

351 8 Worthington Chauncey Ford (1858–1941), a longtime friend and economic consultant of Henry Adams, director of the Bureau of Statistics in the State Department; after 1893 he moved to the Treasury as chief statistician; in 1897 he became chief of the manuscript division of the Boston Public Library; in 1902–09 he was chief of the manuscript division of the Library of Congress; in 1909–29 he was editor of the Massachusetts Historical Society. He helped prepare the *Education* for publication in 1918 and edited the letters of Henry Adams in 2 volumes, 1930, 1938.

9 Jean Jacques Elisée Reclus (1830–1905), leading French geographer, author of a monumental universal geography in 19 volumes, par-

tisan of the 1871 Commune, a leader with Prince Kropotkin in the anarchist movement; prosecuted for his anarchistic writings, he took refuge in Switzerland.

352   10   The massacres of Christian Armenians by the Turkish soldiery and populace followed the unsuccessful effort to establish an independent Armenia. The massacres began in 1894 and in spite of the protests of the great powers were not suppressed. In a single massacre in 1896, an estimated 6,000 to 7,000 Georgian Armenians were slaughtered by the Moslem rabble. Estimates of the total number of victims ranged from 20,000 to 50,000; the massacres were accompanied by enormous destruction of property.

11   The Boer War in which the Transvaal Republic and the Orange Free State sought to throw off British rule began in October, 1899. The struggle over "spheres of influence" in China by the Western Powers was becoming acute, having been complicated by the victory of Japan in the Chino-Japanese War of 1894. The Chinese Boxer Rebellion against foreign intervention came in 1900; its failure allowed Russia to establish a virtual protectorate over Manchuria, a protectorate which Russia was forced to divide with Japan after her defeat in the Russo-Japanese War of 1904. The Cuban war with Spain was resumed in 1895. American military intervention came in 1898, ending Spanish rule and establishing the virtual independence of Cuba.

12   The "social gospel" movement among Protestant denominations had already won many thousands of adherents in the large cities; their practical morality aimed at relieving the poverty and the exploitation of the working classes, an activity which gave impetus to the formation a few years later of the Progressive Party and led to many social reforms. See Richard Hofstadter, *Social Darwinism in America,* (Philadelphia, 1944), pp. 105 f.

353   13   Marie de Rabutin-Chantal, Marquise de Sévigné (1626–96), a notable intellectual of the French court, famous for her brilliant letters to her daughter. Her book was another of Adams's favorites.

14   Abigail Adams (1744–1818), wife of President John Adams, pioneer women's rights advocate, noted for her lively and richly observant letters on politics, diplomacy, and social life of the period. Editions of her letters were edited by her grandson, Charles Francis Adams, Henry's father, and by Stewart Mitchell.

354   15   Caen, a city in northwestern France, noted for its two great Romanesque churches, l'Abbaye aux Hommes and l'Abbaye aux Dames, and the beautiful Gothic church of St. Pierre; Coutances, a

town near the English Channel, some 50 miles west of Caen, site of one of the most graceful Gothic cathedrals of Normandy; Mont-Saint-Michel, the remarkable array of fortified abbey buildings surmounted by a Romanesque-Gothic church on a rocky islet of western France, connected by a causeway to the mainland. The party went on to visit the cathedral at Le Mans and the most famous Gothic cathedral of them all, the church of Notre Dame at Chartres, where as Adams wrote at the time, "after thirty-five years of postponed intentions I worshipped at last before the splendor of the great glass God [the famous stained glass windows of Chartres]" (Ford, II, 78). On the same tour he studied the architecture of the cathedrals at Amiens and Bayeux, as well as the noted tapestry at Bayeux depicting the Norman conquest of England in 1066.

355   16   *pulque,* an alcoholic liquor fermented from a Mexican plant.

17   Churriguerresque, in the style of the Spanish architect José Churriguera (1650–1723), whose baroque-like manner was long popular in Spain.

18   Ravenna, on the Adriatic, one of the great art cities of Italy, famous for the Byzantine mosaics of St. Vitale and other churches and chapels.

19   The victory over William Jennings Bryan by McKinley in 1896 marked the ascendancy of Big Business in U.S. politics, the establishment of the gold standard as advocated by the banking community, and the imposition of high tariffs to benefit domestic manufacturers. After the great Panic of 1893 the country was thus launched upon an era of business prosperity and expansion at home and, through so-called "dollar diplomacy," abroad. Adams's intimate friend, John Hay, a liberal contributor to the Republican party, had been actively involved in the campaign. He was rewarded with appointment as ambassador to Great Britain.

356   20   William Woodville Rockhill (1854–1914), diplomat and amateur geologist, author of *Diary of a Journey through Mongolia and Tibet in 1891 and 1892* (1894), assistant secretary of state, 1894–97, and a member of Adams's circle. He was appointed minister to Greece, Rumania, and Serbia in 1897, with headquarters in Athens.

21   The reference is to the repressive measures of the Spanish government which were being resisted by the Cuban guerrillas, to the military coup d'état in Hawaii which forced the dissolute and autocratic king to accept a democratic constitution, and to the attempt to overthrow the dictator-president of Nicaragua in 1896, an attempt that was crushed after several months of heavy fighting.

22   The controversies between the U.S. and the European powers at this period involved the following areas, among others: Samoa, the Sandwich (Hawaiian) Islands, the Bering Sea, the Isthmus of Panama, Venezuela, and Cuba.

23   Marcus Alonzo Hanna (1837–1904), Ohio industrialist, leader of the Ohio Republican hierarchy and political boss of national influence, rescued his friend McKinley from bankruptcy and successfully maneuvered his nomination for the Presidency. He was appointed U.S. senator by the governor of Ohio in 1897 to replace John Sherman.

357   24   Because of his long-standing interest in foreign affairs, Adams was particularly concerned to strengthen the office of the secretary of state and was thus shocked at its being used as a mere instrument of political patronage. Enfeebled in office, Sherman resigned as secretary of state in 1898. He was succeeded briefly by William R. Day who, in the same year, was replaced by John Hay.

25   *embêtement,* stupid annoyance.

26   Noah's dove, Genesis VIII, sent out of the ark when the Biblical flood began to recede.

358   27   King Solomon, in Proverbs XVII, 28.

28   Note Proverbs of Solomon I, especially, "I have stretched out my hand, and no man attended, / But ye have set at naught all my counsel, / And would none of my reproof."

29   "Sophocles" in the 1907 edition was replaced by "Socrates" in the 1918 edition. As Adams did not mark it for correction it has been restored. In the margin opposite "Sophocles" in his corrected copy (1907, Thayer) Adams wrote "Antigone 336–375," a fact which would indicate that the choice of "Sophocles" had been quite deliberate and that he had the plays of Sophocles in mind. The play which would be precisely relevant on the virtues as well as the risks of silence would be *Oedipus Rex.* Note especially the remark of Tiresias, "A fearful thing is knowledge, when to know/ Helpeth no end (trans. Gilbert Murray, *Ten Greek Plays,* 1929, p. 12)." The reference to the great chorus of *Antigone* "Many are the wonders of the world,/ And none so wonderful as Man." would seem to reflect Adams's sense of irony. The substitution of "Socrates" may have been a printer's error or the editors' effort to correct what seemed an irrelevant allusion.

30   In various writings, e.g., "Silence is the eternal duty of man," *Inaugural Address at Edinburgh;* "Silence is the element in which great things fashion themselves together," *Sartor Resartus,* iii, 3; "Silence is more eloquent than words," *Heroes and Hero Worship,*

Lect. ii; "Speech is of time, Silence is of Eternity," *Sartor Resartus* (1836), iii, 3.

31 The clearest expression occurs in Matthew Arnold's poem "The Last Word": "Let the long contention cease!/ . . . Thou art tired; best be still."

32 In the "Chorus" from his *Atalanta in Calydon* (1865): "Silence after grievous things is good . . ./ But silence is most noble to the end."

33 Alfred de Vigny, "La mort du loup" (1843) from *Les Destinées,* somewhat freely translated; more literally, "When one sees what one does on earth and what one leaves/ Only silence is great; all the rest is weakness."

359 34 Byron, *Prophecy of Dante* (1819), Canto III, lines 186–187, 190.

35 From Matthew Arnold's poem "Stanzas from the Grande Chartreuse."

36 Carlton House Terrace, a short street in the heart of historic London near Marlborough House and St. James's Palace.

37 In Homer's *Odyssey:* Odysseus visits the nether world to consult the soothsayer Tiresias and to talk to the heroic dead. Elsewhere Adams uses his Latin name, Ulysses.

360 38 Tannhäuser, the legendary hero knight of Wagner's opera *Tannhäuser* who, having sinned in the cave of Venus, wanders as a pilgrim to Rome to seek absolution. It is denied him, and his years' long painful wanderings take him at last back to the castle of the Landgrave of Thuringia, the Wartburg, in Germany, where the contests of the minstrels are held. In despairing rapture he sings the praise of Venus, who is about to carry him away. The saintly Elizabeth, who loves him, makes her dying prayer for him, and his pilgrim's staff miraculously bursts into bloom to show that he is saved.

39 Saint Germain-en-Laye, on a plateau thirteen miles west of Paris, noted for its Renaissance chateau and the great terrace which provides a spectacular view across the Seine valley. Adams frequently visited the famous museum of prehistoric antiquities located there and subsidized some of its work being carried on by his friend Henri Hubert (1872–1927). The edifice commonly called the Pavillon Henri IV, at one end of the long terrace, is evidently the one intended. The association with the Duke of Angoulême probably arose from the fact that Henry IV had for a time been the protector of the duke and the lover of the duke's sister. Marly-le-Roi, a village not far from Versailles, celebrated as the site of the remains of a sumptuous

chateau of Louis XIV, containing some of the pleasantest promenades in the vicinity of Paris.

40 An echo of the popular saying: "Good Americans, when they die, go to Paris," attributed to a Bostonian, Thomas G. Appleton, and made current by Oliver Wendell Holmes, *The Autocrat of the Breakfast Table* (1858), Ch. 6.

41 Spencer Eddy (1874–1939), private secretary to Ambassador Hay, 1897–98, subsequently clerk in the State Department and diplomat.

42 February 15, 1898, with a loss of 260 men.

43 Karnak, the north half of the vast ruins of Thebes on the Nile in upper Egypt, adjacent to the ruins known as Luxor. The immense temple of Ammon at Karnak is considered the greatest of them all. Adams had previously visited these sites on his wedding journey in 1872.

44 Sphinx, a statue with a lion's body and usually a human head, commonly set up in pairs to guard the approach to a temple. The temple avenues at Thebes were lined with sphinxes.

45 Ephesus, one of the twelve Ionian cities of antiquity in Asia Minor, celebrated for its great temple of Artemis and as a leading commercial center of the ancient world. Its extensive ruins have great archaeological significance.

361 46 Tiryns, a small city of Peloponnesian Greece dating from prehistoric times, mentioned in Homer's *Iliad*. The great palace was excavated by Schliemann and Dörpfeld in 1884–85.

47 Constantine I (surnamed "the Great") (272–337), Roman emperor who made Christianity the state religion and in 330 established Constantinople (formerly Byzantium) as the capital of the Roman empire; Justinian I (surnamed "the Great") (483–565), most famous of all the Byzantine emperors of the Eastern Roman Empire, chiefly remembered for the epochal consolidation of the Roman laws under his direction. The most famous of the many structures built during his reign was the multiple-domed Church of St. Sophia (now a mosque), one of the architectural marvels of the world.

CHAPTER XXIV *Indian Summer* (1898–1899)

362 1 Spanish-American War, April 20, 1898—October 1, 1898, in which Spain suffered disastrous defeats, particularly in the complete destruction of the Spanish fleets at Santiago, Cuba, and Manila Bay in the Philippines. As a result of the war the United States acquired an overseas empire from Spain.

2   A recurring thought in Adams's review of the aims and achievements of his forebears. They had helped found the nation and their statecraft had been directed toward its greatness as an equal power in the world. Grandfather John Quincy Adams had been the author of the foreign policy known as the Monroe Doctrine which he had prepared as secretary of state in President Monroe's Cabinet. Adams's father, in his son's eyes, had done much to force England to respect America during the Civil War and in the Alabama claims negotiation. Finally, the War of 1898 clearly marked the emergence of the United States as a great world power able to hold her own in global competition with the European powers.

3   The Stamp Act of 1765, the British tax on newspapers and documents in the American colonies which became a major grievance leading to the American Revolution.

4   1750, a convenient round number. In actuality his great-grandfather, John Adams, did not become active in the patriot cause until 1765 with his protests against "taxation without consent."

5   A characteristic overstatement of the family policy which had more modestly aimed at freeing the United States from dependence upon England either politically or economically. The idea of a joint Anglo-Saxon mission to advance liberty and progress in the world was expressed by Ambassador John Hay in his 1897 address in London, "A Partnership in Beneficence." Of course the hope for a complete reconciliation of the two English-speaking peoples always existed and social and cultural ties were in fact greatly strengthened during Adams's lifetime.

363   6   Refers to the outburst of anti-British feeling in Germany with the onset of the Boer War in South Africa, German sympathies being strongly on the side of the Boers (Dutch settlers). At the same time Germany adopted a naval program in 1897 aimed at making her a great naval power and thus a threat to British naval supremacy.

7   Anti-imperialists opposed the annexation of the Philippines (Henry's brother Charles was one of the leaders in the movement); but the islands did not become independent until 1945.

364   8   With respect particularly to the establishment by the great powers, including Japan, of spheres of influence in the decrepit Chinese empire through various treaties granting concessions and extraterritorial rights in treaty ports. England, France, Germany, and Russia were the principal beneficiaries, although American trading rights were tacitly conceded.

9   In 1066, marking the Norman conquest of England.

365   10   That is, his appointment as ambassador.

11   Thomas Wolsey (1475–1530), the leading privy councillor of Henry VIII and as archbishop the princely autocrat of the church. Although he had been instrumental in enlarging the power of the king as against the nobility and Parliament, his desire to play an important role in European politics led to his downfall when the French whom he had supported were defeated by the emperor Charles V. He also alienated the secular party in England by his asking the Pope to grant Henry VIII a divorce from Catherine of Aragon. As the Pope had to submit to the dictation of Charles V, the divorce fell through; whereupon Henry VIII took matters into his own hand and brought about the separation from Rome. Wolsey's repentance for his blunders and for his extravagant private life did not avail to save him from the charge of treason, but he died before his trial.

12   Hay's last years were clouded by chronic and debilitating prostate disease, an illness to which he finally succumbed in 1905.

366   13   As assistant private secretary of President Lincoln.

14   An unduly modest statement, as the two friends constantly discussed foreign policy, in which field Hay regarded Adams as an authority. (See Samuels, III, 409.)

367   15   In one of the episodes of Homer's *Odyssey*, Ulysses [Odysseus] makes his escape from the one-eyed giant Polyphemus, son of Poseidon, god of the sea, by getting him drunk and putting out his eye with a great pointed stake. Adams here attaches the story to an ancient Sicilian legend about Polyphemus.

16   Syracuse, the most important Greek city of ancient Sicily. Its long history is a complex record of wars, offensive and defensive, of colonizing and being colonized, of wars with Athens and Carthage and finally of subjugation by Rome. Its greatest splendor was attained as the western center of Greek culture.

17   That is, ancient Rome; Delphi, a mountain town in Greece near the Corinthian gulf, situated on the lower slopes of Mt. Parnassus, containing the impressive ruins of the temple of the world-famous oracle of the Pythian Apollo; Mycenae, an ancient city of Argolis in Greece, whose great temples and palaces were originally excavated by Schliemann in 1876–77, inaugurating a widespread interest in archaeology in which subject Adams became an enthusiastic amateur.

18   Marcus Junius Brutus (85–42 B.C.), Roman leader who joined the conspiracy to assassinate Julius Caesar (100–44 B.C., Roman general and statesman) and who afterwards committed suicide when de-

feated by Octavius the nephew of Caesar at Philippi. The republic
came to an end with the accession of Octavius as the Emperor
Augustus.

19 Cato (95–46 B.C.), a Stoic philosopher and patriot of the republic opposed to Julius Caesar. On learning of Caesar's victory at
Thapsus he committed suicide.

20 Cicero (106–43 B.C.), philosopher, statesman, and most famous
orator of ancient Rome. His orations and other writings were used as
Latin texts when Adams was a student at Harvard.

21 Nero (A.D. 37–68), Roman emperor who became notorious for
his tyranny and ruthless barbarity toward his family and advisers. Accused of having set the fire that destroyed a large part of Rome, he
promptly put the blame on the new sect of Christians and ordered
their persecution. The political assassinations refer particularly to that
of Lincoln and of Adams's friend, President Garfield.

22 Sulla (138–78 B.C.), Roman general and dictator, appointed consul in 80 B.C. He reorganized the government, established colonies, and
was the first to publish a proscription, a list of his enemies who were
declared outlaws to be killed by anyone without fear of punishment.

23 Francis (1182–1226) of Assisi (a hill town in central Italy), a
noted Italian monk, an ascetic and a mystic who founded the order
of Franciscans, dedicated to humility and poverty. Adams was greatly
attracted to St. Francis's intuitionalism and love of nature, i.e. his
mystical pantheism, as may be seen in Adams's *Mont-Saint-Michel
and Chartres,* Ch. XV, "The Mystics," pp. 330–341, which reflects
Adams's ironical skepticism toward pure rationality and even toward
rational skepticism itself as exhibited in the historian Gibbon.

368 24 Church fathers whom Adams studied in the 90's as preparation
for his *Chartres.* St. Ambrose (340–397), bishop of Milan and one of
the great learned Latin "doctors" of the church whose sermons and
theological writings greatly influenced the conversion of St. Augustine
from paganism. He strongly opposed the Arian heresy which asserted
that Jesus was not of the same nature as God and which therefore
tended to deny the divinity of Jesus. St. Jerome (340–420), a learned
and disputatious scholar whose Latin translation of the Bible, called
the Vulgate, was adopted by the Catholic church as the authorized
version. He is also noted as a pioneer in Biblical archaeology.

25 Here lies/ The Lilliputian writer/ The barbarian scholar/ Henry
Adams/ Son of Adam and Eve/ Who first explained/ [the law of]
Soc. Sac and Soc, certain rights of legal jurisdiction belonging to the

lord of the manor in feudal England. The doctoral essays of three of Adams's graduate students and Adams's own essay, "Anglo-Saxon Courts of Law," were published by Adams in *Essays in Anglo-Saxon Law* in 1876.

26   Rudolph Sohn (1841–1917), German legal scholar whose treatise *Procédure de la Lex Salica* was very favorably reviewed by Adams in the *North American Review*, April, 1874. Adams exhaustively annotated his copy of the book.

369   27   A large collection of photographs of churches and details of church architecture which he assembled.

28   La Farge was appointed tutor at Harvard in 1871. He did not do his important murals and stained glass for Trinity Church in Boston until 1876. See Adams's novel *Esther* for an idealized portrait of La Farge in the character of Wharton.

370   29   *cha-no-yu*, hot tea water.

30   Anaradjpura, the great ruined holy city of Buddhism in Ceylon.

31   Okakura [Kakuzo] (1862–1913), a young Japanese scholar whom Adams and La Farge met in Japan in 1886. He was subsequently connected with the Boston Museum of Fine Arts and dedicated his *Book of Tea* (1906) to La Farge. He also published *The Awakening of Japan* (1904).

32   John Humphreys-Johnston(e) (1857–1941). He studied art with John La Farge, became noted for his symbolic paintings and his valuable art collection in his home in Venice.

33   The Boer War, begun October, 1899 (peace was signed May 31, 1902) by the Transvaal Republic and the Orange Free State of South Africa against England. The Boers were the descendants of the Dutch settlers in South Africa. At the conclusion of the war the two defeated republics were annexed to the Cape Colony as part of the British empire; in 1961 the entire Union of South Africa left the British Commonwealth and was proclaimed the Republic of South Africa, dedicated to racial apartheid.

371   34   As a nominal Catholic of French descent.

35   Bourges, a town in central France; its cathedral is one of the most magnificent in the country and its stained glass windows rank with those of Chartres and the Sainte Chapelle in Paris.

372   36   George III (1738–1820), king of England whose arbitrary policies toward the American colonies brought on the American Revolution.

647

37 That is, the right of revolution against arbitrary and oppressive government.

38 Joseph Chamberlain (1836–1914), colonial secretary of England, noted for his advocacy of imperial consolidation. Adams had earlier admired Chamberlain as a progressive politician and was on friendly terms with him as was also John Hay.

373 39 See n. 14 above.

40 Adams's friend Abram Hewitt had been elected Democratic mayor of New York in spite of his reputation as a reformer but when he broke with the Democratic Tammany Hall organization he was defeated for re-election in 1888. The Democratic President Cleveland did not employ his services. Although Hay was a substantial contributor to the Republican party and active in the campaigns, Republican President Harrison did not reward him with an appointment.

374 41 Sir Julian Pauncefote (1828–1902), British ambassador to the United States, 1893–1902; he did much to promote Anglo-American friendship as an able negotiator in the Bering Sea seal-fishing dispute and the Venezuela crisis. He successfully worked out with Hay the Hay-Pauncefote Treaty (1901) providing for equal passage of all nations through the proposed Panama Canal. It conceded the vital right of the U.S. to fortify it. This was the second version of the treaty, the first having been so amended by the Senate that England had rejected it. There was even an earlier draft which Hay had worked on. The tortuous course of the complicated negotiations to revise or replace the 1850 Clayton-Bulwer Treaty with England (providing for joint guarantee of any isthmian canal) is impossible to summarize. At one point Hay was so disgusted with the maneuvering in the Senate in which Henry Cabot Lodge as chairman of the Senate Foreign Relations Committee played a leading role that he tendered his resignation to President McKinley but was persuaded to withdraw it. Cf. the disparaging letter of Henry Cabot Lodge to William Roscoe Thayer (October 17, 1919), ". . . the treaty [the second Hay-Pauncefote treaty] really was made by Mr. Choate [Joseph H. Choate, 1832–1917, ambassador to Great Britain, 1899–1905] and Lord Lansdowne [Henry William Edmund, 1872–1936, sixth marquess], although it bore the signatures of Mr. Hay and Lord Pauncefote." Cf. J. A. Garraty, *Henry Cabot Lodge* (New York, 1953), p. 218. For the details of the whole protracted episode see Tyler Dennett, *John Hay: From Poetry to Politics* (New York, 1933).

375 42 Excerpt from letter of John Hay to Henry Adams, August 5, 1899, printed in *Letters of John Hay and Extracts from Diary*, 3 vols.,

ed. Clara Hay [compiled by Henry Adams] (Washington, 1908), pp. 156–157. In the original transcript in Adams's hand the word "disastrous" appears instead of "monstrous" in the sentence beginning, in the printed excerpt, "To such monstrous shape." The treaty of peace with Spain was ratified by the Senate February 6, 1898, with a *two*-vote majority, according to historian Ray Billington. The sentence, "Is it worthwhile for me . . ." was edited out of the printed edition of the letters as were many other passages which Adams wished to include. To Adams's dismay Mrs. Hay also reduced all names to initials. See Samuels, III, 396–409.

43 In the 9-volume *History* and the biographies of *Gallatin* and *John Randolph.*

44 Clan-na-Gael, a revolutionary organization of American Irish which worked for the overthrow of British rule in Ireland.

45 The other naval powers of Europe were also keenly interested in opposing any arrangement which might increase England's naval supremacy. Count Arthur Paulovich Cassini (1835– ?), Russian ambassador at Washington, 1897–1904, had previously been stationed at Peking, and after leaving Washington was sent to Madrid. In 1913 the *New York Times* reported that he was living in Paris where his brother Count Michael had just died. Presumably both were self-exiled, a fact which may account for his name being omitted from the Soviet *Encyclopedia.* As no further mention of him occurs he evidently died in Paris in obscurity at an advanced age. See also n. 6, Ch. XXXII.

46 Albert Ludwig Karl Von Holleben (1835–1906), German ambassador at Washington.

47 Only a well entrenched bureau chief would have approved of the clumsy system. It exasperated Hay as his many letters to Adams indicate.

48 A gravitational formula of falling bodies, *s* being the distance travelled by a falling object, *g* the acceleration of gravity at the surface of the earth (32 feet a second), *t* the elapsed time of the fall in seconds.

49 Sir Isaac Newton (1642–1727), the most famous of all mathematicians, discoverer of the universal law of gravitation. For Adams he symbolized the intellectual potential of mankind and hence Adams's recurring declaration that the problems of the world required the appearance of a new Newton. Johann Kepler (1571–1630), famous German astronomer who discovered the so-called laws of planetary motion which provided the basis for Newton's discoveries.

377 50 Simon Newcomb (1835–1909), American astronomer, professor of mathematics and astronomy at Johns Hopkins University.

51 Josiah Willard Gibbs (1839–1903), professor of mathematical physics at Yale University, pioneer theoretician of physical chemistry, especially noted for his epochal work *On the Equilibrium of Heterogeneous Substances* (1876–78) in which he set forth the "Rule of Phase" which Adams subsequently (1909) tried to apply analogically to history.

52 Samuel Pierpont Langley (1834–1906), American astronomer and inventor of the first airplane, i.e. heavier-than-air flying machine, the first successful flight being made in 1896; all were unmanned flights. He also invented the bolometer to measure the distribution of heat in the spectrum of the sun.

53 John Bernhard Stallo (1823–1900), emigrated from Germany in 1839, studied chemistry and physics and became a professor at St. John's College, then studied law, appointed a judge in Cincinnati, 1853–55; was a leader of the German community in the Civil War; appointed U.S. minister to Italy, 1885. Published *The Concepts and Theories of Modern Physics* (1882), which was in the main an essay in epistemology, i.e. on the nature and limits of human knowing.

378 54 Rasselas, the disenchanted hero of the philosophical romance *Rasselas* by Samuel Johnson, published in 1759.

55 Palais du Trocadero, an immense building across the Seine River in Paris not far from the Eiffel Tower, constructed for the exhibition of 1878. The area was a fashionable residential district.

CHAPTER XXV   *The Dynamo and the Virgin* (1900)

379 1 Exposition of 1900, opened in Paris April 15 and ran for seven months. It was the largest so far held in Europe.

2 Francis Bacon (1561–1626), Lord Chancellor of England, essayist and philosopher; author of *The Advancement of Learning,* (1605), the great preliminary survey of knowledge and scientific method, subsequently expanded in the *De Augmentis,* a portion of his ambitious effort to create a new natural philosophy to replace Aristotle.

3 "Comedy of Errors," one of Shakespeare's earliest comedies (1594), at one time popular with college audiences for its farcical complications involving two sets of identical twins.

4 King James I, king of England, 1603–25.

5 Based on the theory of "dialectical materialism," i.e. that the mode of production in material life determines the general character of the social, political and spiritual processes of life and that this development moves through predictable phases.

380 6 Gottlieb Daimler (1834–1900), German engineer, invented one of the first small high speed internal combustion engines, patented 1887; pioneer developer of the automobile.

7 A rough approximation. The first practical steam railroad was inaugurated by Stephenson in England in 1825, thirteen years before Adams's birth; the first high speed line was opened in 1830. The Baltimore and Ohio Railroad was begun in 1828 and reached the Ohio River in 1833.

8 His interest in the dynamo had been first aroused at the Chicago Exposition of 1893. Earlier models had already been used for limited lighting and power since the middle of the century. The new high-frequency dynamos greatly increased capacities.

381 9 With the aid of the bolometer which he had invented Langley was able to measure the intensities of the invisible heat-rays in the infrared spectrum.

10 Radium, first isolated by the Curies in 1898, exhibited a phenomenon new to science of an element that spontaneously underwent transformation through radioactive emission, upsetting the conventional distinctions between matter and energy.

11 William Thomson, Baron Kelvin (1824–1907), British mathematician and physicist, noted for discoveries in the realm of thermodynamics and electrodynamics. ". . . as futile as . . .," another example of extreme ironic understatement, a kind of serious facetiousness to emphasize the extreme complexities of these matters.

12 Guglielmo Marconi (1874–1937), inventor of wireless telegraphy (radio telegraphy) about 1895, made first transatlantic communication, 1901.

13 Edouard Branly (1846–1940), French physicist, inventor in 1890 of the Branly "coherer" for detecting radio waves.

14 X-rays, also called Roentgen rays after their discovery in 1895 by Wilhelm Roentgen (1845–1923), the rays being produced by a high voltage discharge in a vacuum tube.

383 15 Copernicus (1473–1543), Polish astronomer, founded modern astronomy by proving the daily rotation of the earth and its rotation around the sun; Galileo (1564–1642), Italian astronomer and physi-

cist, discoverer of the principle of falling bodies, developed the refracting telescope, espoused the Copernican heliocentric theory for which he was condemned by the Inquisition for heresy.

16 Constantine the Great (280?–337), Roman emperor, was persuaded to adopt Christianity, 313; convoked the Council of Nicea, 325, which issued the Nicean Creed.

17 "chemist," druggist; "by way of scandal," an indirect allusion to "venereal" (as in venereal disease) which is derived from Venus, the goddess of love. The cult of the Virgin Mary was generally rejected in the largely Protestant New England of Adams's boyhood.

18 An allusion to the task performed by the legendary hero of Chrétien de Troyes' *Lancelot* (12th cent.), the crossing of a sword bridge to enter a castle and rescue Guinivere. Adams discusses this and other romances of "Christian of Troyes" in his *Mont-Saint-Michel and Chartres.*

19 Lourdes, a famous shrine in Southwest France dedicated to the Virgin Mary, said to be the site of a miraculous visitation of the Virgin to a peasant girl in 1858; much frequented by pilgrims seeking miraculous cures.

384 20 The virgin goddess mother, related closely to the primitive Asiatic goddess of nature and fertility, worshipped in antiquity at her stupendous shrine at Ephesus on the west coast of Asia Minor under the Greek name of Artemis.

21 Lucretius (ca. 99–55 B.C.), from *On the Nature of Things*, I, 21: "And since 'tis thou [Venus] alone/ Guidest the Cosmos," trans. William Ellery Leonard. Cf. *Education*, p. 459 and note.

22 "Lady [Virgin Mary], thou art so great and hast such worth, that if there be who would have grace yet betaketh not himself to thee, his longing seeketh to fly without wings," Dante, *Paradiso*, XXXIII, trans. Carlyle-Wicksteed. "Virgin of the Schools," i.e. of the medieval scholastic philosophers.

23 See n. 13 above.

24 An allusion to the notable paintings of the Virgin at the Louvre in Paris (Leonardo's "Virgin of the Rocks," Raphael's "La Belle Jardinière," etc.) and to the marvelous array of stained glass windows and sculptures honoring the Virgin at the Cathedral of Our Lady at Chartres. Cf. Chs. V–X in Adams's *Mont-Saint-Michel and Chartres.*

385 25 Herbert Spencer (1820–93), British philosopher, famous for his application of evolutionary principles to sociology, author of the monumental *System of Synthetic Philosophy* (1862–93).

26 Walt Whitman (1819–92), whose frank sexual imagery in *Leaves of Grass* (1855) added a new dimension to poetic language. His bold lead was not followed until recent times.

27 Bret Harte (1836–1902), American writer whose story "The Outcasts of Poker Flat" (1869), for example, portrayed sympathetically the gamblers and prostitutes of the California "Gold Rush" days.

28 Probably an allusion to William Morris Hunt (1824–79) and his celebrated "Bathers."

29 Herodias (14?B.C.–A.D.40?), the notorious wife of King Herod of Judea who with the assistance of her daughter Salome tricked the king into ordering the beheading of John the Baptist.

30 Among the inflections lost to English and American speech were most distinctions of masculine and feminine gender. American education had become largely co-educational by 1905, the same education being offered, for the most part, to both boys and girls.

31 Afterwards removed to its permanent site in Central Park, New York City, in 1903; a companion statue of Sherman by St. Gaudens was unveiled in the same year in Washington, D.C.

386 32 *folle,* excessive.

33 Mont Parnasse, a district on the Paris Left Bank whose cafés had long been favorite haunts of artists and writers; Bois de Boulogne, a large wooded park on the fashionable outskirts of Paris.

34 This appears to be Adams's adaptation of a passage in Gibbon's French Journal (Paris, February 21, 1763) quoted in Lord Sheffield's edition of Gibbon's Memoirs (*Miscellaneous Works: With Memoirs* [London, 1796]) as colored by Adams's reading of a passage from the Memoirs itself. a) The Journal: "Nous jettâmes ensuite un coup d'oeil sur l'église de St. Sulpice, dont la façade (le prétexte et le fruit de tant de lottéries) n'est point encore achevée. . . ." [We then cast a glance at the church of St. Sulpice, of which the façade (the excuse for and the fruit of so many lotteries) is not yet finished. . . .]. b) The *Autobiography* (*Memoirs of My Life,* ed. George Bonnard [London, 1966], p. 125): ". . . but the *Catholic superstition* which is always the enemy of reason is often the parent of taste . . . and the parish church of St. Sulpice one of the noblest structures in Paris was built and adorned by the private industry of a late curate. In this outset and still more in the sequel of my tour, *my eye was amused* . . ." [italics added]. For artistic effect Adams imagines Gibbon standing before the masterpiece of Gothic architecture, Amiens cathedral, often called the Parthenon of France.

387   Isis, the most famous of the Egyptian goddesses who absorbed the attributes of all of the ancient female deities as earth- and mother-goddess, commonly represented with cow's horns; Edfu, some fifty miles south of Luxor, and site of the best preserved temple in Egypt, first visited by Adams in 1872–73 and again in 1898.

36   Louis XI (1423–83), an extremely pious and Machiavellian king of France who often dressed like a pilgrim and wore an old felt hat decorated with the leaden figure of a saint.

37   Benevenuto Cellini (1500–71), Italian sculptor and goldsmith; brilliant and turbulent, he worked under Michelangelo and was a protégé of the Medicis. His fascinating autobiography, one of the most vivid ever written, reveals him as a mixture of the consummate artist and the bravo.

388   38   Peter Paul Rubens (1577–1640), one of the greatest and most prolific of Flemish painters. As a young man of 20 Adams first encountered his paintings on a visit to Antwerp cathedral which contained three of Rubens's greatest paintings: "Elevation of the Cross," "Descent from the Cross," and "Assumption of the Virgin Mary."

39   Cnidos (also Cnidus), ancient city in Asia Minor, site of the most famous statue of Aphrodite of the elder Praxiteles; though the original was lost in antiquity, copies exist, the best being in the Vatican.

40   Arnold's "Stanzas from the Grande Chartreuse," recalls Arnold's visit to the imposing mother house of the severely ascetic Carthusian monks in France high in the mountains near Grenoble. Significant portions of their prayers invoke the Virgin Mary. In the pensive lines the poet mourns his loss of the faith which still inspires the monks. The allusion is one of a number which Adams makes to this favorite poem of his.

389   41   Probably an allusion to Zeno of Citium (ca. 366 B.C–ca. 264 B.C.), Greek philosopher, founder of the Stoic school. Two other important ancient Greek philosophers, one an Eleatic the other an Epicurean philosopher, were also named Zeno.

42   Thomas Aquinas (1225?–1274), Italian scholastic philosopher and most important Catholic theologian of the Middle Ages, author of the *Summa Theologiae* and founder of Thomism. Subject of the last chapter of Adams's *Mont-Saint-Michel and Chartres.*

43   Michel Eyquem de Montaigne (1533–92), French essayist and skeptical philosopher; Blaise Pascal (1623–62), French mathematical scientist and philosopher, whose *Pensées* explored the differences

between reason and religion. Sympathetically treated in Adams's *Chartres*.

390 44 A piece of rhetorical emphasis. His chief calculations related to foreign trade, international balance of payments, and the international production of coal and iron from tables of statistics supplied by his friend Worthington Chauncey Ford of the United States Bureau of Statistics.

CHAPTER XXVI *Twilight (1901)*

391 1 An allusion to the mood of the fashionable Anglo-American society in Paris at the turn of the century which devoted its wealth and leisure to the avid pursuit of elegant pleasures, a society in which Adams's intimate friend, the beautiful Mrs. James Donald Cameron, was a prominent figure.

2 The current fashion of pessimism in prominent intellectual circles in France preached that art was decadent and futile. St. Gaudens exhibited his equestrian statue of General Sherman (placed in New York) and his Shaw Memorial (placed in Boston), and a few other notable works. Auguste Rodin (1840–1917) was a celebrated French sculptor whose studio Adams visited a number of times with a view to buying sculptures for friends. Many of his works were then regarded as daringly suggestive in their nudity. His extensive exhibit which included the famous "Thinker" and "The Kiss" at the Pavillon Rodin near the Exposition was immensely popular. Paul Albert Besnard (1849–1934), French impressionist painter, was then noted for the daring unconventionality of his technique.

3 Marquise de Pompadour (1721–64), the brilliant and witty chief mistress of Louis XV of France, the queen of beauty and fashion at his court and a political and financial power in the realm; Comtesse du Barry (1746–93), a remarkably beautiful French adventuress who became mistress of Louis XV in 1769 and achieved complete influence over him. She was guillotined during the French Revolution.

4 Mementos of Napoleon Bonaparte (1769–1821), emperor of France, 1804–14; of his son Napoleon II (1811–32); of his nephew Napoleon III (1808–73), emperor of the French, 1852–70; or of Frederick the Great of Prussia (1712–86) or of Maria Theresa (1717–80), archduchess of Austria and queen of Hungary and Bohemia. Frequenting the auctions at art dealers was a favorite activity of high society.

5 Jean Antoine Watteau (1684–1721), French genre painter of pas-

toral scenes with idealized shepherds and shepherdesses; William Hogarth (1697–1764), English painter and engraver noted for his satirical and realistic sketches of London high and low life; Sir Joshua Reynolds (1723–92), a leading painter of his time and an intimate of the Samuel Johnson literary circle. Jean Marc Nattier (1685–1766), French painter of the court of Louis XV who depicted the female figures in mythological guises.

6 An allusion to the international crisis which developed during the so-called "Boxer Rebellion"—a movement aimed at expelling the European powers from China—when the Europeans were besieged in the Peking legations. After considerable loss of life and vast damage to property, the legations were relieved by an international force of 18,000 men, including 2500 Americans, who suppressed the rebellion by the end of the summer of 1900.

7 Ming vase, greatly prized porcelain vases of the time of the Ming dynasty, which ruled China from the 14th to the 17th centuries. Adams was himself much interested in collecting Chinese ceramics at this time and characteristically generalizes from his own preoccupation.

392 8 Historians have much qualified the importance of Hay's role in the tortuous power politics of the time. His famed "Open Door" policy designed to prevent the dismemberment of China was in fact originated by the British and taken up by Hay when, although paying lip service to the principle, they were quietly abandoning it in favor of spheres of influence and extraterritorial concessions in treaty ports. Hay's highminded statement of American policy toward China did much, however, to allay public anxieties, and the impression was widely held that he had successfully checked European imperialism in China. In his private correspondence Adams expressed serious reservations concerning the actual effectiveness of Hay's diplomacy. The complicated negotiations are fully reviewed in Tyler Dennett's *John Hay: From Poetry to Politics* (New York, 1933). For a searching critique of Hay's diplomacy, see George F. Kennan, *American Diplomacy* (New York, 1951). Hay did play an important indirect role in the rescue of the legations by managing through an agent to get out word from the beleaguered British legation that the Europeans had not been massacred as reported in the press. Hay's resourceful feat won wide acclaim.

393 9 His aggressively nationalist policy provoked the hostility of pro-British factions and of interventionists, especially in 1823 when President Monroe was ready to protest the French invasion of Spain and to recognize the independence of Greece. After much strenuous argu-

ment Secretary of State Adams convinced the Cabinet not to meddle in European affairs and at the same time succeeded in persuading Monroe to enunciate in the Monroe Doctrine the substance of Adams's recommendations concerning the American continents.

10 Count Cassini, the Russian minister to Washington; Von Holleben, the German minister to Washington. Both of these envoys opposed any treaty arrangements between the United States and England which might cause the two countries to act in concert against other European powers. The proposed Isthmian Canal treaty made the two nations arbiters of access to the future canal. The Irish nationalists in the United States were also opposed to any arrangement which might benefit England, and their voting strength was impressive. See also n. 41, Ch. XXIV. Count Cassini's obligation as his country's envoy was of course to oppose through judicious lobbying Hay's efforts to restrict Russian extension of influence in China. Von Holleben had a similar responsibility to his country whose demands for reparations from China as a result of the Boxer Rebellion were the most exorbitant of all.

11 Count Cassini was a member of that faction which favored economic penetration of China by peaceful means, a faction led by Count Serge Yulievich Witte who became minister of finance in 1892 and did much to industrialize Russia. He was therefore opposed to the palace clique which favored strategic railroads and military solutions and which soon brought on the Russo-Japanese War by their activities in Manchuria. Cassini's support, however, of the right of access of the United States to China commerce apparently was mere pretense, as it afterward appeared that he had been acting under orders. The policy of his foreign office was much more cautious and restrictive and its methods have been described as devious and Byzantine. For a more comprehensive and documented account see Edward H. Zabriskie, *American-Russian Rivalry in the Far East 1895–1914*, (1946). Cf. also n. 38, Ch. XXVII; n. 7, Ch. XXX.

394 12 Elihu Root (1845–1937), American lawyer and statesman, secretary of war in the cabinets of Presidents McKinley and Theodore Roosevelt. He reorganized the army and created the general staff. In 1905 he re-entered Roosevelt's Cabinet as secretary of state.

13 *culbute*, literally, a somersault; downfall, catastrophe.

14 Aaron Burr (1756–1836), American politician, Vice President under Thomas Jefferson, killed Alexander Hamilton in a duel, was involved in a mysterious conspiracy to seize control of the Spanish southwest for which he was tried for treason and acquitted, an epi-

sode dramatically recounted in Adams's *History of the United States;*
William B. Giles (1762–1830), U.S. senator, 1804–15, governor of
Virginia, 1827–30, a political enemy of John Quincy Adams; "Sir
Forcible Feebles," in Shakespeare's *Henry IV,* Part II, III. ii. 179,
Falstaff characterizes one of the woebegone recruits as "most forcible
feeble."

15 Marcus Junius Brutus (85–42 B.C.), Roman politician, joined in
the plot against Julius Caesar, a tragic conspiracy dramatized by
Shakespeare; Henry Bolingbroke, Duke of Hereford, leader of the
rebels who overthrew Richard II and who became King Henry IV, a
leading figure in Shakespeare's *Richard II;* Jack Cade, Irish leader
of "Cade's Rebellion" in Kent, England, in 1450. After brief successes which carried them into London the rebels were annihilated.
Shakespeare introduced Cade as a wild rebel in *Henry VI.* Malvolio,
the self-important and conceited steward of Olivia in Shakespeare's
Twelfth Night.

396 16 The exclamation of Arria, the wife of Caecina Paetus, who had
been condemned to die by the emperor Claudius. She set the example
for her husband by stabbing herself and then handing him the
dagger with the words:: "Paete, it does not hurt!" (Pliny the Younger,
Letters, III, 16.)

397 17 Michael Faraday (1791–1867), English physicist and chemist,
discovered electromagnetic induction in 1831 and proved the polarity
of an electrical charge, discoveries which led to the invention of the
dynamo.
  Adams's extensive study of science, referred to in his statement that
"he read all the books he could find," is reflected in his annotations in
the 1907 printing. See Appendix B, Table 6.

18 Marie Curie (1867–1934), Polish-born French physicist and
chemist, discovered radium in 1898 in collaboration with her husband
Pierre (1859–1906).

399 19 *Comus, a Masque,* presented at Ludlow Castle, 1634, by John
Milton (1608–74), a pastoral play of nymphs and shepherds, with
music by Henry Lawes. In Adams's youth *Comus* was a favorite college production. The succeeding line reads: "Not harsh and crabbed,
as dull fools suppose" (*Comus,* line 476). Comus, an imaginary pagan
god, plies travelers with a magic drink which transforms their faces
into those of wild beasts.

20 Charles Doolittle Walcott (1850–1927), geologist and paleontologist, director of the United States Geological Survey, one of Adams's
friends in the Survey, author of a number of important monographs

on North American paleontology published in the *Proceedings* of the U.S. National Museum, 1897–1905. Note that at this point Adams develops further the doubts he entertained in *Education,* Chapter XV, "Darwinism," concerning the theory of evolution and Lyell's uniformitarianism. See the notes to that chapter for his ambivalent early attitude toward the theories of Darwin and Lyell. His sharp contrast between early confidence and subsequent skepticism must be taken as a rhetorical flourish.

400   21   James Croll (1821–90), Scottish geologist and climatologist. Lyell had rejected Louis Agassiz's catastrophe theory of glaciation, suggesting the oscillation of land masses about the poles to explain the changes in climate and supplementing his hypothesis with Croll's theory of glaciation caused by the eccentricity of the earth's orbit and the precession of the equinoxes. Adams had shrewdly attacked both theories in 1867.

22   James Geikie (1839–1915), Scottish geologist, author of *The Great Ice Age* (1874); his *Prehistoric Europe* (1881) argued for five interglacial periods in Great Britain.

23   Eduard Suess (1831–1914), geologist and paleontologist, author of *Antlitz der Erde* (*The Face of the Earth*) (3 vols., 1885–1901).

401   24   Cossacks, a privileged landowning people of Czarist Russia with a central administration at the Ministry of War, noted for their harsh and overbearing rule. Lord Kelvin's early paper in the middle of the century on the age of the earth had denied the claim of Lyell and the Uniformitarians that the earth was several thousand million years old. He won the long controversy in geological circles, but the current researches in the radioactivity of rocks is now disproving Kelvin's hypothesis.

25   See for example Darwin's classic statement of the difficulty in Chapter X, "On the Imperfections of the Geological Record," *The Origin of Species* (1859).

26   *ignoramus,* we do not know; *ignorabimus,* we shall never know; from the famous lecture of Emil Du Bois-Reymond (1818–96), influential German physiologist of French descent. The lecture given in Berlin in 1884 was titled "Uber die grenzen des naturerkennens" ("Concerning the limits of natural science"). It concluded that in the past the natural scientist had confronted the riddles of the physical world and with manly renunciation had said *ignoramus* but had nevertheless felt that in the light of the great achievements of science solutions were always possible. However, in the face of the riddle of what matter and energy are he must once and for all confess the

truth: *ignorabimus.* In his copy of Henry Maudsley, *Body and Will* (1884) Adams underscored this sentence: "The grand conception of the unity of all science may be just as much subjective creation . . . as ever were demons and deities of ancient times." For the background of this skepticism see Samuels, II, 227 f.

27 In the philosophy of Hegel (1770–1831) the dialectical process of thought is described as moving successively through three phases: thesis, antithesis (the contradictory or opposed phase), and synthesis (unification which resolves the contradiction). The process is the product of the compelling necessity of reason and exists in the realm of logic, nature and spirit. The triadic movement builds up through successive syntheses to a more highly organized unity or "larger synthesis." See reference to Hegel's "larger synthesis," *Education,* p. 451.

402 28 *Limulus,* horseshoe or king crab of the American coast, regarded by some biologists of the period as the living survivor, relatively unchanged, of a genus found in one of the oldest geological strata. *Lepidosteus,* a large pike-like genus surviving from Eocene and Miocene geological periods. See *Education,* p. 230.

CHAPTER XXVII *Teufelsdröckh (1901)*

403 1 German, devil's dung; Diogones Teufelsdröckh, central character in Thomas Carlyle's *Sartor Resartus,* the much-troubled German philosopher who passed from the skepticism of "The Everlasting Nay" through "The Centre of Indifference" to "The Everlasting Yea." Cf. n. 19 of "Preliminaries."

2 Joseph Trumbull Stickney (1874–1904), New England poet ("Prometheus Pyrophorous"), successful candidate for doctorate in Paris, 1895–1903, one of the "Harvard exiles," Paris companion of George "Bay" Cabot Lodge (1873–1909), another of the Harvard poets ("Song of the Wave," "Cain," "Herakles"), son of Henry Cabot Lodge. Adams wrote a biography of "Bay" Lodge at the solicitation of the family (1911).

3 "Louise," a new opera (1900) in a naturalistic vein by Gustave Charpentier (1860–1956).

4 The Seine, the river which divides Paris into the Left Bank (containing the university and the Bohemian world of the Latin Quarter) and the Right Bank (the great art galleries, the theatres, and the world of international society and finance).

5 As an intimate of Secretary of State John Hay, Adams had an inside view of the struggle then going on for control of China, the implications of which seemed remote to the Paris of artists and intellectuals who had made the city the intellectual and artistic capital of the world.

404 6 Latin Quarter, on the South or Left Bank, near the university (the Sorbonne) and the neighborhood of the ancient church of St. Germain de Pré, frequented by students since the Middle Ages; Montparnasse, a district near the Latin Quarter, noted for its cafés frequented by artists and writers; Montmartre, the hill district north of the center of Paris and the highest point in the city, crowned by the basilica of Sacré Coeur, a favorite resort of artists; Jean Mounet Sully (1841–1916), a popular French actor.

7 Baireuth or Bayreuth, a town in Bavaria, Germany, home of Richard Wagner (1813–83), famed composer of music dramas about legendary German heroes. His patron, King Ludwig of Bavaria, built a theatre in Bayreuth in 1876 specially designed for the production of Wagner's works. Siegfried, tragic hero of Wagner's tetralogy, *The Ring of the Nibelung;* Brünhilde, the warrior queen and a Valkyrie in the tetralogy and the beloved of Siegfried; *Parsifal.* Wagner's solemn music drama of the quest of the Holy Grail; "Walhalla" (Valhalla), in Nordic mythology the home of the warrior dead, the setting for the final scene in Wagner's *Götterdämmerung* (*The Twilight of the Gods*), fourth part of *The Ring of the Nibelung.* Of *Parsifal,* Wagner's last opera, Adams wrote to Elizabeth Cameron that it was "a mass of flabby German sentimentality which passes patience" (Ford, II, 335).

405 8 An allusion in part to the disastrous floods of the Seine which Adams had witnessed; Etoile, famous star-shaped plaza intersection of several of the great fashionable boulevards of Paris, site of the Arc de Triomphe; Montmartre, see n. 6 above. Probably also an allusion to the occasional revolutionary risings of the city on the Seine which interrupted the amusements of the world of fashion and art.

9 Milka Ternina (1864–1941), celebrated singer of Wagnerian opera, much admired by Adams and his friends for the passionate abandon of her performance.

10 *fluch-motif,* motif of the curse from Wagner's *The Ring of the Nibelung.*

11 Pantheon, the grandiose edifice near the Latin Quarter, superbly decorated and containing the tombs of Rousseau, Voltaire, Victor Hugo, and many other famous Frenchmen.

12 "Grane, Mein Ross," "Grane, my horse," on which Brünhilde rides into Siegfried's funeral pyre. She uses this address in Wagner's *Götterdämmerung*, Act III, sc. 2. This fourth and concluding opera of the tetralogy *The Ring of the Nibelung* had its first performance at Bayreuth in 1876.

406 13 After the death of the German composer Richard Wagner (1813–83) his widow Frau Cosima Wagner and her son Siegfried directed the annual music festival of Wagner's music dramas with authoritarian zeal, rigidly adhering to the elaborate stagecraft established by the master. The "Heiliger Geist," the "Holy Spirit," the third person of the Christian Trinity which figures in Wagner's last opera, *Parsifal*, an opera based on the story of the legendary quest for the Holy Grail. The theatrical religious symbolism struck some critics as a parody of the Eucharist, a matter hinted at by Adams's irony.

14 Georg Wilhelm Friedrich Hegel (1770–1831); Arthur Schopenhauer (1788–1860). Hegel declared that it is the task of the philosopher to find the contradictions latent in incomplete and abstract views and resolve them by dialectical analysis. See n. 27, Ch. XXVI. Schopenhauer, the German philosopher of pessimism, saw man as controlled by the Will, a non-rational and instinctual force which made for never-ending conflict and tension in human affairs.

15 The Hegelian analysis of historical development as consisting of *thesis,* countered by *antithesis,* leading to *synthesis* which in turn serves as thesis for the next opposition in the dialectic process.

16 The Brownian movements of the molecules, first observed by Robert Brown in 1827.

407 17 Prince Peter Kropotkin (1842–1921), Russian geographer and explorer, but most famous as a revolutionary anarchist, author of *Modern Science and Anarchism* (1903).

18 *ouvrier,* workman.

408 19 The uncut ritual beards and earlocks and somber medieval costumes of many of the pious Jews from the ghettoes of Russian Poland were repulsive to his aesthetic sensibilities.

409 20 Khirgis (Kirghiz), a nomadic Mongolian-Tatar people inhabiting southeastern Russia, western Siberia, and Russian central Asia.

21 Kremlin, the walled citadel and administrative center of the Russian government in Moscow.

22 Sir Donald Mackenzie Wallace (1841–1919), British journalist, author of *Russia* (2 vols., 1877); Count Leo Tolstoy (1828–1910), Russian novelist (*War and Peace,* 1865–72, *Anna Karenina,* 1875–6);

Ivan Turgenev (1818–83), Russian novelist (*Fathers and Sons*, 1862; *Smoke*, 1867; Feodor Dostoevski (1821–81), Russian novelist (*Crime and Punishment*, 1866; *The Brothers Karamazov*, 1880); Maxim Gorki (1868–1936), pseudonym of Aleksi Peshkov, Russian writer, author of realistic stories of working-class life; his drama *The Lower Depths* (1903) depicted the outcasts of society.

23   Count Sergei Yulievich Witte (1849–1915), Russian minister of finance, 1892–1903, progressive statesman, promoted industrialization, reformed the currency to attract foreign capital, favored political liberty; Prince Mikhail Khilkov (d. 1909), Russian engineer, worked in the United States and Venezuela; as minister of ways and communications he supervised the development of the Trans-Siberian railroad.

411   24   Jean de La Fontaine (1621–95).

25   From "La Besace" ("The Wallet"), Book I, Fable VII: Jupiter summons his subjects to hear their complaints and redress his mistakes. He invited the monkey to speak first:

> I? why not?
> Have I not four feet as well as the others?
> My face so far has not offended me;
> But as for my brother the bear, he's only a rough draft;
> Nothing, take my word for it, that anyone would paint.

The moral of the fable: men are complacent about their own short-comings and hide their own faults in the back of their wallets while scorning those of others. In the following paragraph Adams plays on the term "bear" as the popular symbol of Russia and figures the monkey and the motor as symbols of the West.

26   See n. 6, Ch. XXV.

412   27   An omnibus reference to Adams's "Anglo-Saxon Courts of Law" in *Essays in Anglo-Saxon Law* (1876) and to his Lowell Institute lecture "The Primitive Rights of Women" (1876). For convenient emphasis he here applies the term "Norse" to his theories of Teutonic and Icelandic origins of social and political institutions. For a critique of those theories see Samuels, I, 247–266.

28   Edward Augustus Freeman (1823–92), English historian, especially noted for his monumental *History of the Norman Conquest* (1867–79), which Adams had reviewed somewhat unfavorably though praising its substantial merits. See the *North American Review*, January, 1872, unsigned.

413   29   Carlyle's *Sartor Resartus* was first published in *Fraser's Magazine*, 1833–34; in book form in Boston, 1836; in England, 1838, the

year of Adams's birth. The hero-philosopher of Carlyle's book had also stood at the North Cape in the course of his wanderings and had encountered a Russian smuggler, a "Hyperborean Bear." (*Sartor Resartus*, Book II, Ch. VIII, "The Centre of Indifference.")

30 Carlyle was a Scottish writer. Important sections of *Sartor Resartus* reflect a great spiritual crisis in the life of Carlyle.

31 On September 6, 1901, five months after his inauguration for a second term, McKinley was shot by an anarchist. The President died September 14. The Vice President, Theodore Roosevelt (1858–1919), a friend of Adams, thereupon became President at the youthful age of 43. Adams, twenty years his senior, did not approve of his exuberant self-assurance in office.

32 Newspapers were published only in morning or afternoon editions according to local time, whereas the Atlantic cables brought news instantaneously without regard to the time of day or the difference in time zones.

414 33 *ne plus ultra,* no more beyond, go no further.

34 Several times restored, the final restoration and repair of the structure had been completed with great ceremony in 1880.

415 35 The year of Adams's first visit to Germany.

36 Picardy, a district of northern France just south of Belgium.

37 Coal was at this period the chief source of fuel for heating, industry and steam navigation the world over and hence the chief source for power; the world rivalry for coal resources resembled that for petroleum of a later day. Coke made from coal was also indispensable for iron and steel making. In addition coal was used to manufacture gas for illumination and cooking.

38 Vyacheslav Plehve (1846–1904), director of the Russian state police, later a member of the council of empire, became minister of the interior in 1902. Witte favored gradual economic penetration of China, as in the joint development of the Trans-Siberian railroad across Manchuria, and he opposed Plehve's appointment to the interior ministry. Plehve advocated military occupation and expansion into Korea, a policy which led to the disastrous war with Japan in 1904. Plehve became infamous especially for his brutal policy of Russification of the alien provinces of Armenia, Poland, Lithuania, and Finland and his encouragement of the pogroms against the Jews of Kishinev. His harsh policies toward the peasants and the working class led to his assassination in 1904. Cf. also nn. 8, 10, 11, Ch. XXVI.

CHAPTER XXVIII *The Height of Knowledge* (1902)

416 1 President Abraham Lincoln, 1865; President James Abram Garfield, 1881; President William McKinley, 1901.
2 Eumenides, also known as the Furies, the avengers of crime in Greek mythology, usually represented as winged women with snakes about them. Figure prominently in the story of Orestes used by Aeschylus (525–456 B.C.) in his trilogy drama *Oresteia*.
3 Adelbert Stone Hay (1877–1901), fell to his death from a college window during a class reunion.
4 All the quotations in the paragraph are from letters of John Hay to Henry Adams, *Letters of John Hay and Extracts from Diary*, 3 vols., ed. Clara Hay [compiled by Henry Adams] (Washington, 1908). The letter referring to King is also printed in Tyler Dennett, *John Hay: From Poetry to Politics* (New York, 1933), p. 161. *"Ça vous amuse, la vie?"*, "So you find life amusing?" an ironic cliché.

417 5 In Adams's eyes the "revolution" was the sudden change in the administration caused by the assassination of McKinley. The accession of Theodore Roosevelt to the Presidency alarmed him as he had a poor opinion of Roosevelt's qualifications for the office. For the ambiguities of Adams's friendship with Roosevelt, see Samuels, III, 244 ff., esp. 251 ff.
6 This idea is explored with great subtlety by Adams in his *Mont-Saint-Michel and Chartres*.
7 Roosevelt continued Hay in his cabinet as secretary of state.
8 Lucius Seneca (4 B.C.?–A.D. 65), famous Roman philosopher and writer, a trusted councilor of the Emperor Nero at the beginning of his reign; subsequently being accused of treason he was commanded by Nero to take his own life.
9 Nero Claudius (A.D. 37–68), Roman emperor, notorious for his profligate and cruel reign.

418 10 Adams avoided visiting the White House, which lies just south of the Square.
11 An echo of Lord Acton's famous phrase: "Power tends to corrupt; absolute power corrupts absolutely," in a letter to Bishop Mandell Creighton, 1887. The idea has inspired numerous maxims since antiquity, but none as succinct as Adams's.
12 Adams's friend Henry Cabot Lodge was now the influential chairman of the Senate Foreign Relations Committee.

420 13 In the figurative sense of propriety or decorum.

421   14   Jane Austen (1775–1817), English novelist (*Pride and Prejudice,* 1813; *Emma,* 1815; etc.)

423   15   Allusion to the Clayton-Bulwer Treaty of 1850 which was superseded in 1901 by the Hay-Pauncefote Treaty giving the United States exclusive control of the proposed canal, a concession which opened the way for the construction of the Panama Canal and its fortification by the United States.

16   Concerning the dispute over the Alaska-Canada boundary.

17   The next step to the "Atlantic System" which Adams advocated to his friend Hay was made possible when the traditional rivalry between France and England was quieted by the Anglo-French Convention of 1904.

18   Jean Léon Jaurès (1859–1914), French socialist politician and editor, killed by an assassin; August Bebel (1840–1913), German Social Democratic statesman and writer on socialism.

424   19   Kaiser William II [Friedrich Wilhelm] (1859–1941), emperor of Germany and king of Prussia, aggressive advocate of Germany as a leading world power. The armaments race among the European powers was now well under way and the new German naval building program challenged English sea power.

425   20   Czar Nicholas II (1868–1918), succeeded to the Russian throne in 1894, made peace proposals in 1898 which led to establishment of the Hague Tribunal; "Mikado" Mutsuhito (reign name, Meiji) (1852–1912), emperor of Japan, 1867–1912.

CHAPTER XXIX   *The Abyss of Ignorance* (1902)

426   1   A magnificent and picturesque ruined castle near Fort William, a borough of Inverness in the Lochaber district of the western highlands of Scotland and a center of the Cameron clan. Mr. and Mrs. J. Donald Cameron had evidently rented the modern castle of Inverlochy owned by Lord Abinger, one and one-half miles northeast of the ruined stronghold. Before going to the Continent, Adams revisited the Gaskells in Shropshire.

2   Other highland clans.

3   An apparent allusion to Aesop's fable of the ungrateful cuckoo in "The Cuckoo, the Hedge-Sparrow, and the Owl." The cuckoo having lost its nest-building instinct lays its eggs in the nests of "host species."

4   Reynolds Hitt (1876–1938), third secretary of the legation, Paris 1901–02; second secretary of the legation, Berlin 1902. At this period

Adams was just finishing his *Mont-Saint-Michel and Chartres* and immersing himself in books on science.

427 5 *vis a tergo,* force from behind; *ennui,* boredom.

6 From section XXVI, "Misère de l'homme," of *Pensées* of Blaise Pascal, 1670 ed. (The translation appears to be that of Adams.)

7 From "The Pulley" by George Herbert (1593–1632), English poet.

428 8 Bernard of Clairvaux (1091–1153), founder of the Cistercian monastery of Clairvaux, France, noted theologian and as a mystic an opponent of rationalistic philosophy, initiator of the Second Crusade.

9 The opposition between St. Bernard and St. Thomas Aquinas recapitulates in very highly condensed form the central issues of Ch. XV, "The Mystics" and Ch. XVI, "Saint Thomas Aquinas," of Adams's *Mont-Saint-Michel and Chartres.* The theological and philosophical problems of the concluding chapters of that book preoccupied Adams during this period. The parallels between the dilemmas of medieval Christian philosophy and modern scientific theory of the turn of the century are developed with impressive erudition in the last three chapters of the *Mont-Saint-Michel and Chartres.* For a criticism of Adams's theology see Robert Mane, *Henry Adams on the Road to Chartres* (Cambridge, Mass., 1971).

429 10 *Energetik,* a term adopted by a school of German natural scientists including Ostwald, Helm and others which conceives the fundamental essence of things to be energy, a conception which appears to be generally held in modern science.

11 Ernst Heinrich Haeckel (1834–1919), a German biologist and monistic philosopher. Adams had studied with particular attention Haeckel's *Welträtsel* (1899) in the French version, *Les Enigmes de l'Univers* (1902). Ernst Mach (1838–1916), Austrian physicist and philosopher of science whose theories rested on a universal physical phenomenalism derived from sensory experience. He stressed the transitional nature of scientific knowledge but was confident of the slow approach to the ideal of a *monistic* view of the world.

12 Probably an allusion to the well-known fairy tale of "Goldilocks and the Three Bears" in the unexpurgated versions in which the bear devours the children. See Mary H. Eastman, *Index to Fairy Tales, Myths, and Legends* (Boston, 1915).

13. Cf. Socrates in the *Phaedrus* of Plato, sec. 235: "As for me all I know is that I know nothing."

430 14 A reference to the perennial problem areas of metaphysics: the nature of being (ontology) and the nature of knowing (epistemology).

The very earliest Greek philosophers sought for the unity which they assumed to exist behind the multiplicity of phenomena or of appearances, a quest which led to endless inquiry into the prerequisite step of knowing how we know. In the *Chartres* in the last three chapters Adams examined how the three schools of philosophy in the Middle Ages—realism, conceptualism, and nominalism—confronted these problems.

15 In philosophy a belief that there is no objective basis of truth, extreme skepticism of all rational inquiry.

16 The great religious controversies inspired by the rise of humanism during the Renaissance and out of which came the Protestant Reformation led Pope Eugenius IV to call a general council in 1450 which reaffirmed the dogmas of the Roman Church and for a time reunited the eastern and western branches of the Church. Adams is here also referring to the rapid rise of scientific study despite the widely recognized conflict between science and conventional religious beliefs. Both the Protestant and Catholic churches were obliged to adopt various compromises with evolutionary and geological theories of cosmic and human origins which conflicted with the literal language of their creeds.

431 17 See also n. 20, Ch. 30 for a brief statement of the kinetic theory of gases.

432 18 David Hume (1711–76), Scottish philosopher and historian who limited human knowledge to experience of ideas and sense impressions and denied the possibility of final verification of their truth (*An Inquiry Concerning Human Understanding*, 1748); George Berkeley (1685–1753), Irish philosopher of subjective idealism most noted for *A Treatise Concerning the Principles of Human Knowledge* (1710) in which he stated that what appeared to be material things existed only in being perceived.

19 Eduard von Hartmann (1842–1906), German philosopher, author of *The Philosophy of the Unconscious* (1869) which asserted the primacy of the Will and carried on the current of pessimism initiated by Schopenhauer.

20 In Goethe's *Faust*, Part I, "A Dreary Day." Faust with the connivance of Mephistopheles has seduced Margaret and she has been imprisoned for her sin. Faust, full of remorse, has just reproached Mephistopheles. Mephistopheles cynically replies that she was not the first girl to be seduced.

21 In the last years of the 19th century a flood of books appeared on the subject of psychology and the science of mind. One of the

most notable works and one which Adams studied carefully was his friend William James's monumental *Principles of Psychology,* published in 1890. Concomitantly there was great interest in abnormal psychology and the medical science of psychiatry. Terms like neurosis and neurotic were already familiar to Adams through the mental illness and nervous breakdowns of friends and relatives in his circle.

433   22   Greek for *psyche.*

23   Melted cheese mixed with beer or ale on toast.

24   Double stars which revolve about one another. Astronomy was one of Adams's hobbies. He was familiar with a number of star atlases. Cf. n. 40, Ch. XXXII.

434   25   In this allusion Adams gives a very free rendering of the basic nature of the generalizations employed by these writers. Buckle's statistical study of social behavior and Comte's attempts to deduce the laws of social dynamics would seem to be somewhat relevant to Adams's thesis. However, Gibbon's procedure was more remote, although it might be said that his controlling thesis was that Christianity and Barbarism destroyed the Roman empire and that these were preponderant "forces."

435   26   Adams's voluminous correspondence reveals that the writing of the second work grew out of the first and that they were not planned simultaneously.

CHAPTER XXX   *Vis Inertiae* (1903)

436   1   Latin term in physics meaning the force of inertia, a property of matter which is its resistance to change of motion, now commonly referred to simply as "inertia." Cf. *Education,* p. 441.

2   Thomas Jefferson (1743–1826), third President of the U.S., 1801–1809; James Madison (1751–1836), fourth President of the U.S., 1809–17. Adams recorded the history of their terms in his *History of the United States during the Administrations of Jefferson and Madison,* a nine-volume work, the research for which was begun in the late seventies. It was published in 1889–91. Adams published the writings of Albert Gallatin (secretary of the treasury under Jefferson) and a biography of him in 1879–80.

3   Sir Michael Henry Herbert (1857–1903), served as British ambassador to the U.S. until his death in September, 1903.

437   4   Baron Hermann Speck von Sternberg (1852–1908), German ambassador to the United States, 1903–08.

669

5 The disclaimer is somewhat disingenuous in the light of his intimate correspondence with Hay on diplomatic matters and Hay's respect for Adams's often superior knowledge of international affairs. See Samuels, III, 176 and 409 f.

438 6 For a more detailed and objective analysis of Hay's role in the geopolitical maneuvering of that period, see Tyler Dennett's *John Hay: From Poetry to Politics* (New York, 1933) and George F. Kennan's *American Diplomacy* (New York, 1951).

7 Count Vladimir Lamsdorf (1845–1907), Russian statesman, minister of foreign affairs, who tried in vain to promote peaceful negotiations with Japan over Manchuria and Korea. Both he and the moderate de Witte were opposed by the minister of the interior de Plehve.

8 President Madison had sent J. Q. Adams to St. Petersburg as the American minister in 1809 at the moment when the Czar had decided to break with Napoleon. The Czar approved the development of American commerce and at the outbreak of the War of 1812 indicated his willingness to act as mediator, an offer that was not acted upon by the belligerents. J. Q. Adams had broken with his own party, the Federalists, in order to support Jefferson's policies, a course of action which cost him re-election to the U.S. Senate in 1808. The success of his mission to Russia led to his appointment as one of the negotiators of the Treaty of Ghent in 1814, then to appointment as minister to England. In 1817 he became secretary of state under Monroe and in 1825 he became President of the U.S.

439 9 When he was private secretary in London to his father who was then minister to England. Russia's hostility to England and France at this period following the Crimean War led her to be strongly sympathetic toward the Northern states, and in 1863 when war threatened over Poland, Russia sent fleets off New York and San Francisco to be ready to attack British commerce, a move that was interpreted as aid to the North.

10 Apparently a reference to the movement toward German unification initiated by Frederick William IV, who succeeded to the throne of Prussia in 1840, a prócess that was not completed until 1870. The unification of the Italian kingdoms took place in 1861. As for Austria-Hungary, the dual state was agreed upon in 1867 and the Austro-Hungarian Empire established.

11 The Anglo-Japanese treaty of 1902 to preserve the territorial integrity of China alarmed the Russian ambassador and he called secretly on Hay for reassurances of the American attitude toward

Russian interests. He also sought to counter the German ambassador's influence. As intimate friend and next-door neighbor of Hay, Adams was privy to the backstairs diplomatic gossip.

440   12   With scare headlines.

13   *vis nova,* new force.

441   14   As warrant for the assumption of equivalence of inertias, Adams relies on H. Poincaré. Cf. *Education,* pp. 456.11, 454. See Appendix B, Table 6, line 441.3.

443   15   Mary Adams (1846–1928), widow of Henry Parker Quincy.

16   Matilda Elizabeth (Davis) Lodge, wife of George Cabot "Bay" Lodge. They were married August 8, 1900. As a result of his marriage George Cabot Lodge left Paris for Boston much to Adams's regret.

17   Edith Kermit (Carow) Roosevelt (1861–1948).

18   Lelia Herbert. Cf. n. 3 above.

444   19   "the serpent," in the Garden of Eden.

20   James Clerk Maxwell (1831–79), British physicist, one of whose most important researches related to the "Kinetic Theory of Gases." At a given temperature the product of the pressure and the volume should be constant in a perfect gas.

21   One of the main squares on the Right Bank in Paris.

22   Thomas Cook & Son was the chief British travel agency, famous for its organized tours.

445   23   Colonial Dames and Daughters of the American Revolution, women's patriotic societies.

24   The *ephemera* or May-fly undergoes extreme transformations in its very short life span which in some species is less than a day. The female is immensely fertile.

446   25   Eocene, the first geological period in which mammals appeared.

26   The epoch of the Homeric poems, the *Iliad* and the *Odyssey,* conjectured to be the early part of the twelfth century B.C. in the closing phase of the Mycenaean age.

447   27   So named in Gounod's opera *Faust.* More usually referred to as "Margaret" in Goethe's *Faust* or "Gretchen." Cf. *Education,* p. 200.

CHAPTER XXXI   *The Grammar of Science* (1903)

449   1   Dante Alighieri (1265–1321), chief Italian poet. In his masterpiece, the *Divine Comedy,* he epitomizes the Christian criticism of his time in his journey through the Inferno, Purgatory, and Paradise.

2 (Oliver) Wolcott Gibbs (1822–1908), the distinguished chemist who was a colleague of Adams at Harvard in the 70's, author of many articles on analytic and inorganic chemistry.

3 Karl Pearson (1857–1936), important English scientist and mathematician. *The Grammar of Science,* a classic in the philosophy of science, was published in 1899. He is regarded as the founder of the science of statistics as applied to biological and social science. In 1902 he established *Biometrika,* a leading journal of statistical theory. The many contentious markings in Adams's copy of Pearson's book (2nd edition, 1900, inscribed by Henry Adams, 1903) show how feelingly Adams responded to Pearson's challenging ideas. He was especially critical of Pearson's refusal to explore philosophical and metaphysical ultimates. For discussions of Adams's quarrel with naturalistic science and scientific materialism, see Jordy *op. cit.,* pp. 228 ff. and Samuels, III, 385, 387.

4 See n. 51, Ch. XXIV. The phrase "the more so . . . his rival Willard Gibbs" was inserted as a correction in the Thayer copy but not adopted by the editors of the 1918 edition. For the problems raised by Adams's error, see Appendix B, Table 2.

450 5 In which he declared we are standing on the brink of an unseen world. See *Smithsonian Institution Reports* for year ending June 30, 1899. He argued for the physicality of so-called telepathic communication.

6 From Preface of first edition, 1899, p. xii. The remaining quotations from Pearson are, in order, Ch. III, Sec. 14 (p. 108), Sec. 12 (p. 137), Sec. 14 (p. 108).

451 7 Pythagoras, 6th century B.C., Greek philosopher and mathematician who sharply distinguished between soul and body and believed in metempsychosis, the passage of a soul from one body to another. Though Herbert Spencer's entire philosophy rested on a materialist basis, he nevertheless felt obliged to postulate "an Unknowable."

8 See reference to "larger synthesis" of Hegel, *Education,* p. 401 and n. 27, Ch. XXVI.

452 9 All of these appeared to have been Christians who in one way or another reconciled their scientific findings with a belief in God, or, as in Darwin's case, in a "Creator."

10 Last lines of the Epilogue of Tennyson's *In Memoriam* (1850). By the time Tennyson wrote "Locksley Hall, Sixty Years After" (1886) he too was filled with doubt, writing: "Chaos, Cosmos! Cosmos, Chaos! Who can tell how all will end?"

11   Adams here incorrectly dated the discovery of Roentgen rays as 1893. The discovery took place in 1895. The date should also be corrected on page 457 of the *Education*.

12   Although recognized as an element, radium differed dramatically from the other elements in that it underwent spontaneous atomic degeneration into other elements. Her discovery was related to the earlier discovery in 1895 of X-rays by Wilhelm Roentgen (1845–1923), which he had produced by passing a powerful electrical current through a vacuum tube.

13   A reference to the epochal discoveries of Johann Kepler (1571–1630) and Galileo Galilei (1564–1642), the latter of whom confirmed the theory of Copernicus that the earth revolved about the sun.

14   *Civitas Dei,* City of God; *Civitas Romae,* the Roman State. See n. 24, Ch. VI. Adams explains the relations of these terms in *Education,* Ch. XXXIII.

453   15   "voyager in strange seas of thoughts alone," a slightly altered line from Wordsworth's tribute to Newton in *The Prelude,* Book III.

16   Wilhelm Ostwald (1853–1932), German physical chemist and inventor. Adams read his *Vorlesungen uber Naturphilosophie* (1902). He also owned a copy of Ernst Haeckel, *Les Enigmes de l'Univers* (trans. from German) (1902). Among other books on science which he studied and usually annotated in the margins were the following: Lucien Poincaré, *La Physique Moderne* (1905); Henry Poincaré, *La Science et l'Hypothèse* (1902); J. B. Stallo, *La Matière et la Physique Moderne* (trans. from English) (1899); Balfour Stewart, *La Conservation de l'Energie* (trans. from English) (1899); Alfred Wallace, *Man's Place in the Universe* (1903); Despaux, *Cause des Energie Attractives* (1902); Heinrich Hertz, *Electric Waves* (trans. from German) (1893); Oliver Lodge, *Electrons* (1906) and *Modern Views of Electricity* (1899). For an analysis of this reading, see Samuels, III, 384 f. See also Appendix B, Table 6.

454   17   Francois Rabelais (1494–1553), noted French satirist, best known for *Gargantua and Pantagruel* (1552–64) in which through the absurd and often bawdy adventures of a fabulous family of giants he ridicules the errors and follies of mankind.

18   Jules Henri Poincaré (1854–1912).

19   From *La Science et l'Hypothèse* (1902), Ch. VIII. The translations are Adams's.

20   *Ibid.,* Ch. X.

455   21   *Ibid.,* Ch. IX.

22   *Ibid.*, Ch. II.

23   *Ibid.*, Ch. III.

456   24   In the theology of Aquinas the universe is in effect an emanation from God. (See the last chapter of *Mont-Saint-Michel and Chartres*.) Spinoza denied the possibility of a plurality of substances, regarding "Substance" as the absolute and ultimate reality. With respect to Kant, Adams apparently alludes to Kant's famous principle of ethics: "Act only on that maxim whereby thou canst at the same time will that it should become a universal law." Although Adams had on the preceding page quoted Poincaré on science as a system of convenient symbols, his reference to Pearson's "medium of exchange" is considerably more elliptical. Since Pearson insisted on the provisional nature of scientific knowledge, Adams concludes that its values have the arbitrary character of a monetary system and are equally subject to revaluation.

457   25   Zeno (490–430 B.C.), Greek philosopher who argued in one of his mystifying paradoxes that since an arrow is at rest at every instant of its flight it is therefore at rest in the whole of its flight.

26   Evidently a round number for the year A.D. 312, the date of the battle of the Milvian Bridge at Rome which signalized the defeat of the Pagan system and the victory of the Christian order. See *Education*, p. 479.

27   This appears to be a very loose approximation of the time at which the compass and gunpowder were introduced into Europe. (Cf. *Education*, p. 482.) The use of gunpowder is recorded in a Florentine document of 1326. The compass in primitive form seems to have come into use as early as the 13th century. Adams is probably referring to the great age of exploration and discovery of the 15th and 16th centuries made possible through the improvement of various aids to navigation.

28   Galileo, by the improvement of the telescope, by discovery of the law of falling bodies, and by other scientific contributions; Bacon, by the immense stimulus his writing gave to use of the scientific method and scientific experimentation.

29   Arthur Balfour (1848–1930), English philosopher and statesman with whom Adams was personally acquainted. The reference is to "On the Future of Science," Balfour's Presidential Address before the British Association, August 17, 1904. It developed further the skepticism of his book *A Defense of Philosophic Doubt* (1879).

458   30   The epigram appears to be Adams's own formulation, epitomizing his research among the physicists.

31   *nacre,* mother-of-pearl.

459 32 From the long poem *De Rerum Natura* (*Of the Nature of Things*) by Lucretius (96?–55 B.C.), Roman philosophical poet of the Epicurean school, a philosophy of enlightened pleasure-seeking based on the conception of the universe as the result of the fortuitous concourse of atoms. The lines quoted are selected from the opening of Book I, i.e. from lines 2, 3, and the beginning of line 4, and lines 21, 22, 23, and the beginning of line 24. The omitted line 1 reads "Aeneadum genetrix, hominum divumque voluptas,"; lines 4 and 5, "concelebras, per te quoniam genus omne animantum/concipitur visitque exortum lumina solis:"; lines 24 and 25, "Te sociam studeo scribendis versibus esse/quos ego de rerum natura pangere conor." Lines 5 through 20 elaborate the praise of Venus. The translation of lines 1 through 5 and 21 through 25 follows with brackets indicating the portions omitted by Adams: "[Mother of Aeneas's sons, delight of men and gods], life-giving Venus who beneath the gliding stars of heaven fills with your presence the sea that bears our ships and the land that bears our crops, [through you every kind of living thing is conceived and comes forth to look upon the light of the sun:] . . . Since you alone control the nature of things and nothing comes forth into the shores of light nor is glad or lovely without you, I crave your help [in writing these verses which I am trying to fashion on the nature of things]." See *Education,* p. 384 where Adams emphasizes *sola,* alone.

460 33 Herman Helmholz (1821–94), German scientist who did important work in physiological optics but is here being mentioned particularly for his contributions toward the theories of electro-magnetic induction and the distribution of energy in mechanical systems.

CHAPTER XXXII *Vis Nova* (*1903–1904*)

462 1 *Vis nova,* the new force or energy.

2 Literally, the Elysian Fields, the magnificent boulevard in Paris which runs from the center of the city at the Place de la Concorde to the Arch of Triumph.

3 General Mikhail Alexeyev (1857–1918), Russian general; the Czar's viceroy in the Far East.

4 In the Place Vendôme in Paris; it was then the fashionable gathering place for Anglo-American and Continental society.

5 The imperial palace of Czar Nicholas II (1868–1918) in St. Petersburg (now Leningrad).

463 6 *blague,* humbug, nonsense. Adams was on friendly terms with Count Cassini but his sympathies lay with the Japanese. During this

period he was on a confidential footing with the Japanese emissary Baron Kentaro Kaneko who greatly appreciated Adams's friendship and advice. See Samuels, III, 630, n. 16. Adams subsequently felt that "Cassini was deliberately sacrificed by his Manchurian gang [i.e., the war party]." (Ford, II, 474.)

464   7 Brooks Adams was now a prominent writer on public affairs, an admirer of Roosevelt as a "strong man," and a close unofficial adviser to the President.

8 Mary Endicott Chamberlain, daughter of Joseph Chamberlain and a favorite among Adams's "honorary" nieces.

9 Joseph Chamberlain (1836–1914), a leading British Liberal statesman, recently resigned from the British cabinet over a colonial tariff issue. Adams had been acquainted with him and his wife for many years.

10 *quos ego*, Latin, literally "whom I." The name of a rhetorical device by which a speaker conveys a threat or menace by starting to speak and then, as emotion seemingly overmasters him, leaving his sentence unfinished as if on the point of turning to violent action. From Neptune's outburst against the disobedient winds in Virgil's *Aeneid*, Book I, line 135.

11 The Anglo-Boer War in South Africa, which had been attended by much suffering among the civilian population, had ended with the defeat of the Boers (Dutch settlers) in 1902. Their struggle to maintain their independence had aroused widespread sympathy in the United States. Chamberlain as colonial secretary had tried in 1897 to conciliate the differences between the Dutch majority and the English minority who as "aliens" were discriminated against by the Boer government. President Kruger of the Transvaal Republic refused to negotiate the grievances. In October 1899 the war began. Initially, Roosevelt, unlike Hay who was strongly pro-British, expressed admiration for the Boers but eventually his sense of American national interests as being linked with those of England led him to support England by a policy of strict neutrality.

465   12 Hay's policy to preserve the territorial integrity of China and to keep China open to trade with all nations on equal terms was threatened by Russian expansion in Manchuria, an expansion which Hay recognized as a threat to U.S. interests. The Anglo-Japanese alliance of 1902 enabled Japan to challenge the Russians. In the ensuing war—1904–05—the Russians were badly defeated.

13 John Singer Sargent (1856–1925), noted American portrait painter and muralist.

466   14   Shawnee, an American Indian tribe in Oklahoma.

15   John Hay, born in Salem, Indiana, spent his boyhood in Warsaw, Illinois, on the banks of the Mississippi. As a law student in Springfield, Illinois, he met Lincoln and accompanied him to Washington to serve as his assistant private secretary in 1861.

16   The judgment is highly relative, if not superficial, certainly with respect to education, as St. Louis did in fact have two thriving universities at this period, Washington University, founded in 1857, and St. Louis University, founded in 1818 as a Latin academy. The public school system was regarded as one of the best in the country. The exaggerated depreciation of the city does, however, add rhetorical force to the praise of the Exposition. The world's fair was held in 1904 to celebrate the centennial of the purchase of the Louisiana Territory from France. The Exposition cost $42,500,000 not including the cost of individual exhibitions.

467   17   Apparently an allusion to the "Visions of Mirza," an allegory of human life by Joseph Addison in his *Spectator* essays, No. 159. (The essay does not, however, use the honorific title "Emir" [an Arabian prince]. "Mirza" is also a title of honor in Persia.) Addison pretends that he had read the visions in an oriental manuscript in Cairo. Mirza recorded that on one of the high hills of Bagdad a shepherd had shown him two visions, one of great misery and one of great beauty.

18   "City of Brass" appears to be Adams's own metaphor for the industrial civilization reflected in the Exposition, inviting a contrast with the "City of God" of St. Augustine which had so greatly influenced the medieval church.

19   The implication is obscure or else mistaken as the fair itself closed with a favorable balance of $1,000,000, an unusual achievement in world fairs.

20   The *New York Times* (July 22, 1904) blamed the press for the generally small attendance. Although Roosevelt opened the fair, he did not return, being much preoccupied with his campaign and with the political convention of that year.

468   21   For Adams's description of the unusual beauty of the Cathedral of Notre Dame (Our Lady) at Coutances, see his *Mont-Saint-Michel and Chartres*, pp. 46–52.

22   Fête Dieu, Corpus Christi day, in the Roman Catholic church the important festival honoring the Eucharist (the sacrament of bread and wine commemorating the death of Christ), held on the first Thursday following Trinity Sunday, the eighth Sunday after Easter. The

festival witnessed by Adams may have been a continuation of the Thursday rites or he may simply have made an error in the day.

23   The Senate bill providing for the celebration of the one hundredth anniversary of the Louisiana Purchase was passed and approved March 3, 1901. It contained the following provision: "The Exposition will be closed on Sundays." In the following year officials of the corporation balked at the provision fearing financial loss, but after a vigorous campaign by the Christian International Reform Bureau the officials contracted to obey the Act in return for the resumption of the Federal subsidy.

469   24   "bag-man," British, a traveling salesman or peddler.

25   See n. 48, Ch. XXIV.

26   From "Stanzas from the Grande Chartreuse" of Matthew Arnold.

470   27   *vitesse,* speed or rate of speed.

28   "Light dissolved in star-showers[,] thrown," quoted from "Stanzas. Written in dejection near Naples" (1818), by Percy Bysshe Shelley (1792–1822).

29   Adams habitually carried binoculars in his quest for stained glass. Touraine, an old province along the Loire near Tours; Champagne, an ancient province north of Paris.

30   *leibwache,* German, bodyguard.

31   Jean Fouquet (ca. 1416–80), court painter of Louis XI, master illuminator of religious books; his precisely executed altarpieces and portraits made a great sensation when first brought together for exhibition in Paris in 1904, an exhibition which Adams had evidently just viewed. Bernardino di Betti, known as Pinturicchio (1454–1513), famous Italian painter of religious frescoes and altarpieces, noted for the minuteness of finish of the heads.

471   32   From the Latin "mea culpa," "I am guilty."

33   That is, more than the traditional Trinity—the Father, the Son, and the Holy Ghost.

34   Particularly as developed by Adams's friend John La Farge.

35   Francis I (1494–1547), king of France, notable chiefly for his wars against Emperor Charles V, who was his successful rival for the imperial dignity; Henry II (1519–59), son of Francis I and king of France, a religious bigot who persecuted Protestants and whose despotic reign was marked by unusual severity in collecting forced loans; Kings of Israel: for the excesses of many of them, see Kings I and II

of the Old Testament; "Tree of Jesse," a favorite ecclesiastical design representing the descent of Jesus Christ from the royal line of King David in the form of a genealogical tree springing from the reclining form of Jesse, father of King David, and culminating in the figure of Jesus or of the Virgin and Child.

36 Thibaut IV, Count of Champagne and King of Navarre (1201–53), most famous of early French lyrical poets, the writers of "courteous" poetry of the Courts of Love, participated in Louis IX's crusade against the Albigensians; Sieur de Joinville, Jean de Joinville (ca 1224–1317), famous for his intimate chronicle history of the reign of King Louis IX [Saint Louis]. He was a native of the province of Champagne of which Troyes was the capital. He followed King Louis in the Seventh Crusade with a retinue of 700 men.

37 The notorious Russian minister of the interior was killed by a bomb thrown by a revolutionary terrorist, July 28, 1904.

38 Hippodrome. An allusion to the wanton destruction and sacking of Constantinople in the Fourth Crusade (1202–04), a crusade in the planning of which Thibaut (d. 1201) of Champagne (Theobald III), father of Thibaut IV (see n. 36 above), played a principal role. In imagination Adams was evidently recalling not only the actors in Jean de Joinville's chronicle history but also those from Troyes who figured in Geoffroy de Villehardouin's *Conquest of Constantinople* (1198–1207), an eyewitness account by one of the leaders of the crusade. Villehardouin was also a native of Champagne. The French crusaders and their mercenary allies, the Venetians, who provided the fleet for the expedition, abandoned their religious objective in order to destroy their commercial rivals whose splendid city was the capital of the Eastern Christian empire. The great city was finally stormed, looted, and burned in large part, the chief beneficiaries of the conquest being the Venetians. Among the priceless trophies carted off from the monumental Hippodrome were the four bronze horses which adorn St. Mark's Square. The city of Troyes is particularly rich in Renaissance churches, the church of St. Pantaleon being especially noted for its sixteenth century stained glass and its multitude of sixteenth century statues.

472 39 A reference to the famous geometrical theorem named after the ancient Greek mathematician Pythagoras (sixth century B.C.) that the square of the hypotenuse of a right-angle triangle is equal to the sum of the squares of the other two sides.

40 Stephen Groombridge (1755–1832). His *A Catalogue of Circumpolar Stars* which was published posthumously in 1838, the year

of Henry Adams's birth, recorded his discovery of star No. 1830, the swiftest moving of all observed stars. The catalogue has been called "one of the most valuable contributions to practical astronomy made during the 19th century."

CHAPTER XXXIII *A Dynamic Theory of History* (*1904*)

476 1 Arthur Balfour (1848–1930), the British philosopher and statesman, in his 1904 lecture on "The Future of Science" had asserted that the 19th century assumptions of science were open to serious question.

2 Archimedes (287–212 B.C.), Greek mathematician and inventor, discoverer of the principle of the lever ("Give me a place to stand and I will move the world."); Aristarchus (flourished ca. 280–264 B.C.), Greek astronomer, calculated the magnitude and distance of the sun and the moon; Ptolemy (ca. first half of the 2nd century A.D.), Alexandrian astronomer, devised a mathematical system of astronomy and geography, placing the earth at the center of the universe, a system that was universally accepted until refuted by Copernicus in the 16th century; Euclid (ca. 300 B.C.), the famous Greek geometer in Alexandria whose *Elements of Geometry* in countless editions has been a standard text for more than two thousand years.

477 3 Adams continued the fine collection of ancient coins begun by his father. It was left to the Massachusetts Historical Society.

4 Diocletian (245–313), Roman emperor who ordered a general persecution of Christians in 303 in an effort to strengthen the old pagan state religion.

5 Pax Romana, the Roman peace, was enforced throughout the Empire by the disciplined legions along the European network of great Roman roads; the Civil Law, codified under Justinian, provided a uniform system of jurisprudence for Europe; Free Trade resulted from the unified economic system of the empire.

478 6 The reference is here to the ancestral tribes, races, and complex racial amalgams out of which these modern nations were formed. The development occurred through the widespread acceptance of Roman civilization and technology.

7 One of the charges made by Edward Gibbon in his celebrated *Decline and Fall of the Roman Empire* (1776–1788). Here put in a much oversimplified form. Cf. Gibbon, Chs. XV, XVI, XXVII, LXXI.

479 8 "With this sign you shall conquer."

9 Theodosius the Great (346–395), famous Roman general and em-

peror of the East, accepted the ecclesiastical authority of Ambrose, the bishop of Milan; in 394 defeated the puppet emperor Eugenius who had been set up by the Frankish general Arbogast.

10   Hercules, the son of Jupiter, the god of physical strength and courage, worshipped by the ancient Greeks and Romans.

11   Robert Jacques Turgot (1727–81), French statesman and economist, presented his idea of social development in his famous discourse of 1750, *The Successive Advances of the Human Mind,* in which he stated: "All epochs are fastened together by a sequence of causes and effects, linking the condition of the world to all the conditions that have gone before it." Auguste Comte in his *Positive Philosophy* (1830–42) postulated that each branch of human knowledge passes through three phases—*Theological* (Fetishism to Polytheism to Monotheism); *Metaphysical,* in which the mind supposes the causes of all phenomena to reside not in supernatural beings but in abstract forces or entities; *Positive,* which rejects the vain search for absolute notions and employs scientific method based on reason and observation.

480   12   Alaric (376?–410), famous king of the West Goths who had served under Theodosius in command of the Goth auxiliaries; he subsequently turned against Rome and sacked the city in 410 A.D.

13   Bishop Augustine of Hippo (St. Augustine) (354–430), most famous of the Church fathers, author of the *Civitas Dei* [*Civitate Dei*], "The City of God." He was also the author of the *Confessions of St. Augustine,* the work cited by Adams in his "Editor's Preface." Augustine was killed in the Vandal invasion of Hippo. By *Civitas Romae* is meant the city of Rome in its imperial extent and dominion. See n. 24, Ch. VI on the Forum vs. the Vatican and n. 20 below.

481   14   Cities in Italy, Sicily, Spain, and France, famous for their masterpieces of medieval Christian church architecture, sculpture, mosaics, and stained glass. The churches of Ravenna and the Cathedral of St. Mark in Venice in Italy, the churches in Palermo, Sicily, especially the cathedral of Monreale, and the cathedral at Cordova, Spain, are most famed for their extraordinary mosaics.

15   Sancta Sofia, the greatest masterpiece of Byzantine church architecture, built by the emperor Justinian, converted into a Moslem mosque in 1453 after the fall of Constantinople which marked the end of the Eastern Roman Empire.

482   16   Justinian (483–565), Byzantine emperor, the most famous of all the emperors of the Eastern Roman Empire, best remembered for the reform and codification of the Roman law, the Justinian Code, made

at his direction. He was active in the great theological disputes of the era. His reign was marked by three great foreign wars. Charlemagne or Charles the Great (742?–814), king of the Franks and emperor of the Holy Roman Empire. His military victories, which greatly extended the empire, reflected great administrative and organizing ability; his interest in ecclesiastical policy gave him the reputation of a great defender of Christianity and as a result he became the subject of many pious legends and epic poems.

17 Nicephoras Phocas (912–969), emperor of the Eastern Roman Empire, 963–969, distinguished as a military leader in the wars with the Saracens.

18 See n. 27, Ch. XXXI.

19 The symbol of Mohammedanism or Islam.

20 The "precise moment" of "the complete triumph of the *Civitas Dei* [the city of God]" of Christianity would seem to be the period when the medieval synthesis of Christianity found expression in the extraordinary multiplication of great churches throughout Western Europe during the twelfth to the fourteenth centuries. The triumph of the city of God of Mohammedanism (the Crescent) seems here identified with the conquest of Constantinople by the Turks in 1453. However, the Turkish or Ottoman Empire did not reach its zenith in Europe until a century later, after more incessant wars, when it extended from near the German frontier to the Persian frontiers. In any case the struggle between the Cross and the Crescent was largely ideological and in both cases led to parallel territorial conquests and political consolidation during the course of a number of centuries.

21 Third century religious movement founded by Mani in Babylonia or Persia as an offshoot of Christianity. He taught that the world was the scene of a perpetual contest between light (the good) and darkness (evil). The object of the religion is to make light prevail. The Manichean doctrine was denounced as heretical in the fifth century and its adherents persecuted. It lingered on in a modified form until the 13th century.

483 22 Johann Gutenberg (1400–ca. 1468), German printer, believed to be the inventor of movable type; Johann Fust (died ca. 1466), German printer, partner of Gutenberg.

23 Martin Luther (1483–1546), German religious reformer and translator of the Bible, a founder of Protestantism; Jean Calvin (1509–64), French Protestant reformer and theologian, whose rigorous theology strongly influenced the first New England settlers.

24 State Street in Boston became in the 19th century the center of banking and finance, though soon outranked as a "bankers' paradise" by Wall Street in New York. It was another irony of history that a "Bible Commonwealth" of religious zealots should in the course of a couple of centuries have been replaced by a secular and worldly culture.

25 John Bunyan (1628–88), English religious writer, famous for his *Pilgrim's Progress, from this World to that to come,* published in 1678.

26 St. Jerome (ca. 340–420), important Church father who made the Latin (Vulgate) translation of the Bible. The parallel with Bunyan is a highly fanciful one, perhaps intending to suggest that St. Jerome's dissatisfaction with the current version of the Bible and his renunciation of pagan literature, a spiritual change resulting from a dream, resembled the later spiritual quest of Bunyan's hero who sought the "Celestial City" of true Christianity. St. Jerome's scholarly effort to establish correct readings obliged him to travel widely through the near East to consult Biblical scholars.

484 27 Giordano Bruno (1548–1600), an Italian philosopher who questioned certain dogmas of the church (transubstantiation and the immaculate conception), for which he was condemned to be burned at the stake by the Inquisition as a heretic.

28 Gottfried Leibnitz (1646–1716), famous German philosopher and mathematician who conceived the ultimate elements of the universe to be centers of force or monads, God being the purely active monad. His ideas concerning the preconceived harmony of the universe and the existence of "sufficient Cause" to explain why this was "the best of all possible worlds" provoked the satire of Voltaire in *Candide* (1758). Ironic echoes of Voltaire's satire of Leibnitz's optimistic phrase recur frequently in the *Education.*

29 Lord Bacon, Francis Bacon. Since the title is rarely used in referring to Francis Bacon in his role as a philosopher, Adams's repeated use of it appears to be faintly ironic to suggest his excessive authority in science.

30 "Nature . . . obeyed," Aphorism III concerning "The Interpretation of Nature" in Francis Bacon, *Magna Instauratio* (1620); "The imagination . . . but weights," misquotes the following sentence from Aphorism CIV, *op. cit.:* "The understanding must not therefore be supplied with wings, but rather hung with weights to keep it from leaping and flying."

485   31 "larger synthesis," the phrase of Hegel as quoted before. See *Education,* pp. 401, 451.

32 Voltaire, the pen name of Francois Marie Arouet (1694–1778), celebrated French writer, religious skeptic and advocate of freedom of thought, especially noted as the greatest satirist of his age. See n. 28 above.

33 Aphorism II, Bacon, *op. cit.*

486   34 "Not by supposition or mere thought but by inquiry learn what nature does and makes." The Latin quotation was added by Adams for the 1918 edition. It is drawn from Bacon's *De Dignitate et Augmentis Scientiarum* (1623), the much enlarged Latin version of his *Advancement of Learning* (1603).

35 The well-known anecdote of Newton and the falling apple was first told by Voltaire, who got it at third hand from Newton's favorite niece who married one of Newton's intimate friends. It was supposed to have happened in 1666 when he was 24. It was never vouched for by Newton himself. Benjamin Franklin proved the electrical nature of lightning by his kite-flying experiment in 1752. James Watt (1736–1819), Scottish engineer, after much experimenting and research invented the condensing steam engine in 1765 which transformed Newcomen's pioneer "steam pump" into a practical engine. His published letters show that his discoveries came through very methodical laboratory experiments as he was a highly trained laboratory technician. The legend of the tea kettle was invented after his death.

36 Joseph Priestley (1733–1804), English clergyman and scientist, discoverer of oxygen. He was sympathetic to the American revolution and the French revolution and spent the last ten years of his life in the United States. His unorthodox opinions as a materialist philosopher caused him to be denied a post as "astronomer" with Captain Cook's expedition to the South Seas. Edward Jenner (1749–1823), discoverer of vaccination against smallpox, first tried out in 1796. There was much factional opposition to vaccination as dangerous or sacrilegious, opposition which still lingers on in a few sects. Robert Fulton (1765–1815), American engineer and designer of the first practical steamboat, the *Clermont,* 1807. In his *History of the United States* Adams had quoted Fulton's account of how his steamboat had been widely ridiculed and dubbed "Fulton's Folly."

487   37 Isis, in Egyptian mythology, the principal female deity, identified with the Nature—and mother—goddesses of the ancient world, was adopted into the Roman religion and became immensely popular.

CHAPTER XXXIV   *A Law of Acceleration* (1904)

489   1   Leonids, a meteor shower in the constellation Leo, occurring annually about November 14; Perseids, a meteoric shower in the constellation Perseus, occurring annually about August 12.

2   The Great Comet of 1843, one of the most spectacular on record, had a tail estimated to be 200,000,000 miles long.

490   3   This figure was more appropriate for 1893 when the Cunard *Lucania* (30,000 H.P.) entered service. When the *Lusitania* was launched in 1907, the year of the private edition of the *Education,* it developed 68,000 H.P.

491   4   At 100° Centigrade the pressure is 14.7 pounds to the square inch; at 200° Centigrade it is 226 pounds to the square inch.

5   Pierre Laplace (1749–1827), famous French astronomer and mathematician. His discovery of the cause of the great inequality in the orbits of Saturn and Jupiter was regarded as the most brilliant advance in physical astronomy since Newton.

6   Thomas Newcomen (1663–1729), with two co-workers invented the atmospheric steam engine, patented in 1705, a relatively crude and inefficient engine which was used to pump water in mines.

7   Alessandro Volta (1745–1827), Italian physicist renowned for his researches and inventions in electricity, invented the voltaic cell, generating electricity through chemical action, the origin of the electric storage battery. The electric "volt" as a unit of measure is named after him.

8   John Dalton (1766–1844), English chemist, perfected the atomic theory of matter about 1804, published in 1810 his *A New System of Chemical Philosophy.*

9   Hermann Boerhaave (1668–1738), a famous Dutch physician and scientist, published pioneer studies of new botanical species, introduced the modern system of clinical instruction in medicine. He made the University of Leyden the world center of medicine.

10   Louis XIV (1638–1715), king of France, 1643–1715, sometimes called the "Sun King" for the splendor of his reign; his court was the most brilliant in Europe and noted for its encouragement of art and literature. His over-ambitious military ventures and vast expenditures nearly bankrupted the nation.

11   Christian Huygens (1629–95), Dutch physicist and astronomer, discovered the rings of Saturn and developed the wave-theory of light.

12   William Harvey (1578–1657), English physician and physiologist, discoverer of the nature of the circulation of the blood, *Essay on the Motions of the Heart and the Blood* (1628).

492   13   Tycho Brahe (1546–1601), Danish astronomer, discovered the variations in the motions of the moon and made other astronomical discoveries which earned him the reputation of being one of the greatest practical astronomers.

14   Leonardo da Vinci (1452–1519), the universal Italian genius, painter ("Mona Lisa," "The Last Supper"), sculptor, architect, scientist, engineer, and musician. His mechanical designs anticipated many modern inventions.

15   Albrecht Dürer (1471–1528), noted German painter and engraver.

493   16   Newton used the Great Comet of 1680 to demonstrate the accuracy of his orbital theories.

494   17   The feasibility of transatlantic steamship crossings was first demonstrated in 1838, the year of Adams's birth, by three rival steamship companies. The first Cunard ship to make the run to Boston was the *Britannia* in 1840. Railroads had begun to radiate out from the eastern cities around 1840; by 1842 New York and Albany were connected by eight independently operated segments, which required a succession of transshipments. Samuel F. B. Morse sent the first electric telegraph message in 1844, from Baltimore to Washington. Daguerreotype, the first successful photographic process, was invented by Louis Daguerre, a French painter and inventor, in 1839.

495   18   The Black Sea. From Shakespeare's *Othello* III. iii. 451–453. "Like to the Pontic sea/ Whose icy current and compulsive course/ Ne'er feels retiring ebb. . . ."

498   19   These occur in the *Critique of Pure Reason* (1781) by Immanuel Kant (1724–1804), the most influential of all German philosophers. An antinomy consists of two contradictory philosophical statements, a thesis and an antithesis, each of which is provable by logical demonstration: 1. The world is finite in time and space; the world is infinite in time and space. 2. Every composite substance consists of simple parts; nothing simple exists anywhere. 3. Causality does not explain all phenomena; all phenomena occur entirely according to the laws of nature. 4. As part of the world or as its cause there is an absolutely necessary being; there is no absolutely necessary being.

CHAPTER XXXV   *Nunc Age* (1905)

499   1   *Nunc Age,* Latin, "Now Go."

500   2   The battle was not for abolition of the great industrial monopolies but for regulation of their power to do harm. In 1904 Roosevelt's attorney general successfully prosecuted the Northern Securities Company, a railroad holding company, as a combination in restraint of trade. Armed with the Supreme Court ruling which reversed an earlier decision, Roosevelt obtained some twenty-five additional indictments.

502   3   Robert Falcon Scott (1868–1912), British explorer whose expedition in the *Discovery* surveyed large areas of the Antarctic and discovered King Edward VII Land. He later reached the South Pole in January, 1912, but died with his four companions during the terrible hardships of the return journey. The quotation is from Scott's *The Voyage of the 'Discovery,'* II (New York, 1905), 176.

4   Purun Dass, character in Rudyard Kipling's story "The Miracle of Purun Bhagat," the prime minister voluntarily turned sunnyasi [sannyasi], a homeless religious mendicant. (Kipling, *Second Jungle Book,* 1895.)

503   5   The Russian Baltic fleet had already reached Madagascar in the Indian Ocean when the news was received of the Japanese victory at Port Arthur. However, when a reinforcement fleet arrived from the Baltic, the commander of the armada decided to proceed. Battle was joined off Tsushima on May 27, 1905, and by the following day practically the entire Russian armada was sunk or captured.

6   Hay had been suffering from prostate disease for some time, increasingly complicated by angina pectoris. He finally succumbed on July 1, 1905, at his summer residence in New Hampshire. Czar Nicholas accepted President Roosevelt's offer of mediation early in June; peace negotiations opened at Portsmouth, New Hampshire, on August 9, and the treaty was signed on August 23rd, replacing Russian influence in Manchuria and Korea with Japanese control.

7   An adaptation of the following passage from Wordsworth's "Ode. Intimations of Immortality":

> The clouds that gather round the setting sun
> Do take a sober coloring from any eye
> That hath kept watch o'er man's mortality.

8   The various arbitration and tariff reciprocity treaties negotiated by Hay were so altered in committee that Roosevelt was obliged to withdraw them.

9 Adams's high praise has been seriously challenged by later writers. See, for example, Tyler Dennett, *John Hay: From Poetry to Politics* (New York, 1933) and George F. Kennan, *American Diplomacy* (New York, 1951).

10 *pax*, Latin, "peace".

504 11 Nervi, a winter resort near Genoa.

12 Nauheim, a famous health resort and spa near Frankfort, Germany.

13 Shakespeare, *Hamlet* V. ii. 368.

14 Pavillon d'Armenonville, a famous and fashionable restaurant on the allée de Longchamp in the Bois de Boulogne, Paris.

Index*

Acceleration, law, 489.

Adams, Abigail, 17, 353; on Catherine Johnson, 17.

Adams, Abigail Brown (Brooks), 23; on English influence, 211.

Adams, Brooks, 360, 464; at Harvard College, 299; on exchanges, 338.

Adams, Charles Francis, 48, 149; taken to Russia, 18; in Boston, 19; marriage, and children, 23; and State Street, 24; nominated Vice-President, 25; slave power, 26; opinion of sons, 26; isolation, 27; political party, 29; reading, 35; family, 36; senatorship agreement, 49; on Europe, 70; in Congress, 88, 99, 101; compared with Seward, 104; minister to England, 110; equipment, 112; impassiveness, 115; social position, 16, 132, 194, 212; Trent affair, 119; trusts Russell, 136, 149; clash with Palmerston, 136; rebel cruisers, 150, 167; interview with Russell, 158; rebel rams, 168; strength of, 208; proposed return to America, 209; collects coins, 213; liking for Washington, 269.

Adams, Charles Francis (1835–1915), 23, 41, 89, 120; at Fort Independence, 112; remonstrates, 129; after the war, 210, 241; railroad studies, 240, 307; gold conspiracy, 270; favors professorship, 293.

Adams, Evelyn (Davis), 442.

Adams, Henry [Brooks], birth, 3, 23; early experiences, 5; encounter with J. Q. Adams, 12; early education, 26; political associations, 29; reading, 36; family atmosphere, 36; dislike of school, 37; visits Washington, 43; impressions, 44; election of Sumner to Senate, 50; student at Harvard College, 55; goes to Germany, 62, 70; college writings, 66; class orator, 66; German gymnasium, 77; musical awakening, 80; at Dresden, 82, 87; in Italy, 85, 88, 208, 235; letters from Italy, 89; at Rome, 90; meets Garibaldi, 94; at Paris, 96; at Washington, 1860, 99, 243; Sumner's break, 108; accompanies father to England, 110; position, 112, 116; newspaper work, 120; proposes to enter army, 129; at Cambridge House, 134; at Fryston, 138; Seward's offer, 145; on Russell, 163, 174; Palmerston, 164; Gladstone, 164; Seward, 174; London society, 195; choice of career, 210; writer, 211, 222, 234; art, 213; buys a Rafael, 216; Darwinism, 224; reviews Lyell, 226; on currency, 233; returns to America, 237;

* Adapted from 1918 Index which was adapted from 1907 Index.

legal tender cases, 250, 277; Sumner's relations, 251; *Edinburgh Review,* 258; gold conspiracy, 270; in London, 284, 316; Harvard professorship, 291, 299; editor *North American Review,* 293, 296, 307; first visit to Harvard College, 299; without office, 322; "History," 325, 327; Paris, 360; "Mont-Saint-Michel and Chartres," 435.

Adams, John, 9, 47, 99, 112, 372; "Works," 31.

Adams, John Quincy, 10, 32, 46, 103, 112; overcomes H. Adams, 12; hobbies, 14; at church, 15; marriage, 17; diplomatic positions, 17; death, 20; restlessness, 28; Russell's resemblance, 167; Secretary of State, 393; in Russia, 438.

Adams, John Quincy (1833–1894), 23; popularity, 35, 241.

Adams, Louisa Catherine, 23; brightness of, 35. *See* Louisa C. A. Kuhn.

Adams, Louisa Catherine (Johnson), 10; described, 16; marriage, 17; wanderings, 17; stricken, 43.

Adams, Samuel, 21.

Adams Building, Washington, 44.

Agassiz, Alexander, 55, 235, 307, 308, 346.

Agassiz, Louis, 60, 227, 307.

"Alabama," the, 150, 152, 153, 167; claims, 285.

Alaric, sacks Rome, 480.

Albert Francis Charles Augustus Emmanuel, Prince consort, death of, 119.

Alexander I, czar, 112, 438.

Alexander II, czar, 439.

Alexeieff, Viceroy, 462.

Alley, John B., politics in 1850, 49, 50.

America, character of man, 297; money in, 328.

Amiens cathedral, 386, 435.

Anarchism, Brooks Adams on, 339; conservative Christian, 405.

Anderson, Nicholas Longworth, 57.

Antietam, battle of, 154.

Antwerp, 74.

Apponyi, Rodolph, Comte d', Austrian ambassador, 135.

Apthorp, Robert East, 76, 80.

Aquinas, Thomas, 389, 428, 435, 456.

Ara Coeli, 91, 209, 235, 340, 470, 477, 497.

Archimedes, 476, 480.

Argyll, Duke of. *See* Campbell.

Aristarchus, 476.

Aristocracy, English, 72.

Arnold, Jane Martha, 125.

Arnold, Matthew, 61, 108, 192, 201, 238, 388, 469; ridicule, 182; on silence, 358.

Arnold, Thomas, 125.

Ashley, Evelyn, 144.

Atkinson, Edward, 242.

Augustin of Hippo [St. Augustine], vii, xxvii, 15, 480.

Aurelian [Lucius Domitius], 91.

Austen, Jane, 228, 421.

Austria, war with France, 83, 84.

Azeglio, Emmanuel Vittorio Tapparelli d', Italian minister, 135.

Bacon, Francis, 379, 451, 457, 484, 485, 491.

Badeau, Adam, character of, 263, 264.

Baireuth, visited, 404.

Balfour, Arthur James, 457, 460, 476.
Balzac, Honoré de, 61.
Bancroft, George, 317, 320.
Bancroft, John Chandler, 82.
Banks in crisis of 1893, 337.
Baring, Thomas, 122.
Barlow, Francis Channing, 210, 248.
Baron Osy, 73.
Barry, Marie Jeanne Gomard de Vaubernier, Comtesse du, 391.
Bartlett, William Francis, 210, 248.
Bates, Joshua, 121.
Baxter, Sarah, Ethel Newcome, 131.
Bayard, Thomas Francis, 331.
Beaumont, Lady Margaret, on foreigners, 196.
Bebel, Ferdinand August, 423.
Beesly, Edward Spencer, 189.
Beethoven, Ludwig van, 80, 81, 82, 85.
Begonia, nature of, 292.
Bennett, James Gordon, 244.
Benton, Thomas Hart, 102.
Berlin, in 1858, 74, 77; university of, 75; gymnasium, 77.
Besnard, Paul Albert, 391.
Bethell, Richard, Lord Westbury, 148, 149; rebel cruisers, 151; foreign enlistment act, 176.
Bille, Torben van, Danish minister, 135.
Birmingham, England, 72.
Bismarck, Otto Eduard Leopold von, 78, 289.
Blackstone, 98.
Blaine, James Gillespie, 261, 280, 281, 321, 331, 394.
Bluebeard, 232.
Boer War, 370, 464.
Boerhaave, Hermann, 491.
Borthwick, Sir Algernon, 135.
Boston, Mass., social tone, 19; want

of healthy resources, 38; women, 40; blackguard, 41; Latin School, 41; mobs, 42; on English eccentricity, 181; simplicity, 241, 269; attitudes, 420.
Boston Courier, Adams writes for, 89, 94.
Boston Whig, 32.
Boutwell, George Sewall, 281, 298; governor, 49; secretary of the treasury, 263, 267; gold conspiracy, 271; voluntary isolation, 273; Hay on, 326.
Bowen, Francis, 72.
Bowles, Samuel, 255.
Brahe, Tycho, 492.
Branly, Edouard, 381.
Bravay, et Cie, rebel rams, 178.
Brice, Calvin Stewart, 320, 331, 343.
Bright, John, 125, 133, 183; attacks Roebuck, 187; power of attack, 188; courage and poise, 190; on criminal sentences, 191; in cabinet, 284.
Brooke, Stopford Augustus, 215, 220.
Brook Farm, 27.
Brooks, Abigail Brown, 23.
Brooks, Ann, 23.
Brooks, Chardon, 23.
Brooks, Charlotte, 23.
Brooks, Edward, 23.
Brooks, Gorham, 23.
Brooks, Peter Chardon, 10; death, 23.
Brooks, Peter Chardon, Jr., 23.
Brooks, Phillips, 55, 235, 315.
Brooks, Preston Smith, assault on Sumner, 76.
Brooks, Sydney, 23, 94.
Brougham, Henry, Lord, 124, 193, 197; audacity, 184.
Browning, Robert, 201; and the guillotine, 92.

Brunnow, Baron, Russian ambassador, 135; on Palmerston, 133.

Bruno, Giordano, 484.

Bryant, William Cullen, 244.

Bryce, James, Viscount, 304.

Buckle, Henry Thomas, 221, 301, 434.

Bull Run, battle of, 118, 129, 152.

Bulwer-Lytton, 39, 201.

Bunyan, John, 483.

Burlingame, Anson, 49, 101.

Burnham, Daniel Hudson, 341.

Burr, Aaron, 394.

Butler, Benjamin Franklin, New Orleans order, 136.

Buxton, Fowell, 184.

Byron, George Gordon, Lord, 358.

Cacciatori, Garibaldi's, 86.

Cain, 12.

Calhoun, John Caldwell, 45, 394.

Calvin, John, 483.

Cambridge, Mass., social, 307.

Cambridge House (Palmerston's), importance of, 134.

Camden & Amboy R.R., 43.

Cameron, James Donald, 332, 343, 385, 426; type, 333; retires, 356; at Surrenden Dering, 364.

Cameron, Elizabeth (Sherman), 332.

Campbell, Lady Elizabeth Leveson-Gower, Duchess of Argyll, 126.

Campbell, George Douglas, Duke of Argyll, 141; friendly to America, 126; faith in Russell, 151, 153.

Campbell, John, Lord, 197.

Canada, troops in, 153; Sumner and cession, 275.

Canning, George, 174, 206.

Caracciolo, Prince, 94.

Carlisle, G. W. F. Howard, 7th earl, 184.

Carlyle, Thomas, 39, 61, 83, 192, 193, 201, 221; Boston and, 33; jibes of, 131; on clothes, 276; on silence, 358.

Cassini, Comte, Russian policy, 375, 393, 437, 439, 463, 465.

Castiglione, Mme. de, 198.

Cavendish, Lord Frederick, 127.

Cavour, Camillo Benso, 92, 95.

Cecil, Robert Arthur Talbot Gascoyne, Marquis of Salisbury, 148, 235, 258.

Cellini, Benvenuto, 387.

Chamberlain, Joseph, 372, 464.

Chamberlain, Miss, 464.

Chandler, Joseph Ripley, 94.

Channing, William Ellery, 27.

Chaos, 406; law of nature, 451.

Charles I, 72.

Charlemagne, 482.

Chartres, 371, 388, 427.

Chase, Salmon Portland, 282; legal tender cases, 250, 278; and Hoar, 277.

Chaucer, 207.

Chester, England, 72, 236.

Chicago exposition, 1893, 339.

Child, Francis James, 307.

China, struggle for control, 391, 436.

Civilization, failure of, 477.

Clay, Cassius Marcellus, minister to Russia, 113.

Clay, Henry, 5, 45, 102.

Clemens, Samuel, 266.

Cleveland, Grover, 324, 331, 373; Brice on, 320; Cuba, 349.

Clinton, Henry Pelham Fiennes Pelham, Duke of Newcastle, on recognizing confederacy, 154, 160; rebel rams, 178.

Cobden, Richard, 125, 133, 183, 191.
Cockran, William Bourke, 331.
Coffin's Point, S.C., 332.
Collier, Robert Porrett, Lord Monkswell, on foreign enlistment act, 150, 167.
Columbus, Christopher, 355, 383, 483, 492.
Compass, the, 482.
Comte, Auguste, 60, 225, 301, 434, 479, 493.
Concord, Mass., philosophy, 27; and the Adamses, 62.
Congressmen, character of, 261.
Conkling, Roscoe, 46, 102, 252, 261, 279, 281, 394.
Conservative Christian anarchist, 405, 406.
Constantine, the Great, 484; sets up the cross, 383, 478.
Cooper, Antony Ashley, Earl of Shaftesbury, 184.
Copernicus, Nicolaus, 383, 492.
Copley, John Singleton, Lord Lyndhurst, 197.
Cotman, John S., 220.
Country and town, New England, 7.
Coutances, fête dieu in, 468.
Coutts, Miss Burdett, 118, 197.
Cox, Jacob Dolson, 271, 277, 282; secretary of the interior, 263, 267.
Cox, Samuel Sullivan, 282.
Crisis of 1893, 337.
Croll, James, 400.
Crookes, Sir William, 450, 452.
Cross, influence of, 383, 478; defence of, 480.
Crowninshield, Benjamin William, 82.
Cruisers, rebel, 150.
Cuba, visited, 349.
Cunliffe, Sir Robert, 190.

Curie, Madame de, 397, 450, 452.
Curtis, Benjamin Robbins, 249.
Cushing, Caleb, on Sumner, 50.

Daguerreotype, 494.
Dalton, John, 491.
Dana, Charles Anderson, 244.
Dana, Richard Henry, 35; character, 29.
Daniels, Conky, 42.
Dante, 449.
Darwin, Charles, 201, 284, 340, 400, 452; effect of, 224.
Davis, Henry Winter, 101.
Davis, Jefferson, to make a nation, 114; Gladstone's recognition, 156, 163, 165; diplomatic agents, 184.
Davis, John Chandler Bancroft, 275.
Degrand, Peter Paul Francis, 20.
Delane, John Thaddeus, 121, 125, 135; at Milnes's, 170.
Dennett, John Richard, 299.
Descartes, René, 389, 484, 491, 495.
Dewey, George, 257.
Dickens, Charles, 35, 39, 61, 201, 421; England of, 72; exaggeration, 181; satires, 182.
Diocletian, Emperor, 477, 498.
Diplomats, complaints of young, 256.
Disraeli, Benjamin, Earl of Beaconsfield, 148, 163, 164, 192, 194, 235, 284.
Dixwell, Epes Sargent, school, 54.
Dohna, Samuel, 255, 263.
Dostoevski, 409.
Doyle, Sir Francis Hastings Charles, 190, 206.
Dresden, 82, 87.
Dudley, Thomas Haines, consul, rebel cruisers, 129.
Dumas, Alexandre, 94, 301, 392.

Dupont, Samuel Francis, 112.
Dürer, Albert, 492.
Dynamic theory of history, 474.
Dynamo, the, 342, 380.

Eaton Hall, 72, 236.
Eccentricity, British, 181.
Eddy, Spencer (Fayette), 360.
Edinburgh Review, 192, 258, 282, 286.
Education, state, 78.
Egypt, visited, 360.
Eliot, Charles William, 300, 304; offer of assistant professorship, 291, 293; commends, 305.
Emerson, Ralph Waldo, 27, 61, 63, 141; protest, 35.
Emir Mirza, 467.
Emmons, Samuel Franklin, 309.
Engrand le Prince, 471.
Ennui, 427.
Erie railroad, 270, 282, 286.
Estes Park, 310.
Euclid, 476.
Eugene [Eugenius], 479.
Europe, influence on youth, 70.
Evarts, William Maxwell, 29, 149, 271, 373; on success, 29; in London, 148, 197; at Cambridge, 204; in Washington, 244, 253; legal tender cases, 249.
Everett, Charlotte (Brooks), 23, 299.
Everett, Edward, 21, 27, 29, 204, 299, 317; eulogy on J. Q. Adams, 21; career, 23; succeeds Webster, 32.
Everett, William, at Cambridge, 204.
Evolution, 91.
Exposition, Chicago, 1893, 339; Paris, 1900, 379.

Falstaff, 229.
Faraday, Michael, 397, 426.
Faust, 432, 447.
Felton, Cornelius Conway, 64.
Fish, Hamilton, 271, 282, 294; secretary of state, 263; kindness of, 266; Sumner and, 274.
Fisk, James, 270, 286, 297.
Fiske, John, 299, 307; on H. Adams, 305.
Forain, Jean Louis, 193.
Forces, development and economy, 379; lines of, 396, 426.
Ford, Worthington Chauncey, 351.
Forster, Jane Martha (Arnold), 125.
Forster, William Edward, 119, 123, 183, 284; described, 125; faith in Russell, 153; education bill, 285.
Fouquet, 470.
France, position in 1858, 83; war with Germany, 286, 290; churches of, 369; science in, 454.
Franklin, Benjamin, xxix, 47, 146, 333, 485, 486, 491.
Free Soil Party, 29, 30, 49.
Freeman, E. A., 412.
Frewen, Moreton, 343.
Friar Bacon, 110.
Friedrich Wilhelm IV, of Prussia, 78.
Frothingham, Ann (Brooks), 23.
Frothingham, Nathaniel Langdon, 23, 27; position, 24.
Frothingham, Octavius Brooks, scepticism of, 35.
Froude, James Anthony, 201, 221.
Fryston, Yorkshire, C. F. Adams at, 119; H. Adams, 138.
Fugitive Slave law, 42.
Fulton, Robert, 486.
Fust, Johann, 483.

Galileo Galilei, 383, 457, 484, 491, 495.

Gallatín, Albert, 333.

Gambetta, 290.

Ganoid, fish. *See* Pteraspis.

Garfield, James Abram, 261, 280, 281, 324.

Garibaldi, Giuseppe, 86, 91, 92, 367; Adams and, 93; at Palermo, 94; in London, 198; Grant and, 265.

Garrison, William Lloyd, 29, 42, 51.

Gaskell, Charles Milnes, 235; meeting with, 204.

Gaskell, James Milnes, 204, 284, 291, 318; described, 206; Mrs., 206, 284.

Geikie, Archibald, 400.

George III, 372.

Germany, education in, 61, 75; in 1858, 82; war with France, 285, 290; imposed on students, 304; a terror to Great Britain, 363; position of, 424, 437; science, 453.

Gettysburg, battle of, 169.

Gibbon, Edward, 301, 367, 434; "Decline and Fall," 91; on cathedrals, 386.

Gibbs, Josiah Willard, 377, 449.

Gibbs, Wolcott, 449.

Giles, William Branch, 394.

Girtin, Thomas, 220.

Gladstone, William Ewart, 149, 182, 192, 202, 206, 262, 284, 289; on confederacy, 115; honesty of, 153; recognizing confederacy, 154, 174; Newcastle speech, 155, 176; rejoinder to Lewis, 161; confession of blunder, 165; Oxford training, 167; on politicians, 179; laughs at Dundreary, 181; uncertainty, 183.

Glass, in churches of France, 470.

Godkin, Edwin Lawrence, 102, 244, 276, 280, 336.

Goethe, Johann Wolfgang von, 62, 81, 82, 432.

Gold conspiracy of 1869, 269, 282, 286, 292.

Gorham, Nathaniel, 46.

Gorki, Maxim, 409.

Gould, Jay, 238, 281, 286, 297; gold conspiracy, 269.

Gracchus, Tiberius, 91.

Grant, Ulysses Simpson, 255, 280, 297, 298, 356, 385; president, 260, 265; cabinet, 262; gold conspiracy, 271; foreign policy, 275; a quarrel with, 276; dislike of Motley, 276; failure of administration, 281, 294.

Granville. *See* Leveson-Gower.

Gray, Horace, 109.

Gray, Thomas, 36.

Great Britain, recognizes belligerency of confederacy, 114; prejudice, 122; intervention, 151; eccentricity, 180; royalty in, 199; manners, 201; English mind, 212; art, 213, 220; historians, 221; treaty relations, 423.

Greek fire, 483.

Greeley, Horace, 244.

Green, John Richard, on Palgrave, 215.

Grey, Sir George, 184; opposes recognition of confederacy, 160.

Groombridge, Stephen, 472.

Grosvenor, 72.

Grote, George, 201.

Grote, Harriet (Lewin), 192.

Guérin, Maurice de, 282.

Guizot, François Pierre Guillaume, 33.

Gunpowder, 483.

Gurney, Ephraim Whitman, 293, 300, 307.
Gutenberg, Johann, 483, 492.

Haeckel, Ernst Heinrich, 429, 453.
Hague, Arnold, 310.
Hallam, Arthur, 206.
Halstead, Murat, 255.
Hamilton, Alexander, 260.
Hamilton, Duke of, 209.
Hampton, Frank, 131.
Hampton, Sarah (Baxter), 131.
Hanna, Marcus Alonzo, 235; senator, 356.
Harrison, Benjamin, 320, 324, 331, 332, 373.
Harte, Francis Bret, 259, 313, 315, 385.
Hartford Convention, 21.
Hartmann, Karl von, 432.
Harvard College, education at, 54; class of '58, 56; class day, 68; influence, 296; history at, 300; value of degree, 305.
Harvey, Peter, 32, 49.
Harvey, William, 491.
Hay, Adelbert Stone, death of, 416.
Hay, Clara (Stone), 360, 366.
Hay, John, 64, 161, 235, 261, 315, 320, 327, 332, 347, 355, 373, 421; Adams meets, 106; in diplomatic service, 210; assistant secretary of state, 317; republican, 321; Life of Lincoln, 322, 325; position with party, 323; memory for faces, 325; Ambassador, 356, 359; success, 362; Secretary of State, 364, 422; troubles, 372; policy, 374; China, 392, 436; Japan-Russia war, 465; at St. Louis, 465; illness, 502; death, 504.

Hayes, Rutherford Birchard, 324, 464.
Hayward, Abraham, 125, 135, 201.
Hegel, Georg Wilhelm Friedrich, 81, 406, 449; "larger synthesis," 451.
Heine, Heinrich, 76, 79.
Helmholz, Hermann Ludwig Ferdinand von, 460.
Henri IV, 42.
Henry VIII, 290.
Herald, New York, 244.
Herbert, Michael, 436, 443.
Hewitt, Abram Stevens, 322, 327, 373; value of, 294.
Higginson, Henry Lee, 41, 210, 235.
Higginson, James Jackson, 82.
Hildreth, Richard, 104.
History, teaching of, 301; methods, 382, 395; dynamic theory of, 474.
Hitt, Reynolds, 426.
Hoar, Ebenezer Rockwood, 257, 271, 282; attorney general, 263, 267; difference with Chase, 277; driven from office, 279.
Hoar, Samuel, 257, 268.
Hofer, Billy, 350.
Hogarth, William, 391.
Holland, Sir Henry, 131; breakfast, 204.
Holleben, Herr von, German policy, 375, 393; recalled, 437.
Holloway, ——, art dealer, 217.
Holmes, Oliver Wendell, 27, 55, 141.
Hooper, Samuel, 253.
Horner, Mary, 127.
Horton, S. Dana, 334.
Houghton, Lord. *See* Milnes.
Howe, Timothy Otis, 292.
Howells, William Dean, 235.
Hughes, Thomas, 127.

Hugo, Victor Marie, anecdote, 143.
Hume, David, 36.
Humphreys-Johnstone, John, 370.
Hunt, Richard Morris, 315, 340, 341, 343, 386.
Hunt, William Holman, 214, 386.
Hunt, William Morris, 213, 315.
Huxley, Thomas Henry, 225, 229.
Huygens, Christian, 491.

Iddings, Joseph Paxson, 350.
Inertia, force of, 440; sex, 441.
"Initials," the, by Baroness von Tautphœus, 87.
Intervention, British, in American Civil War, 151.
Introspection, 432.
Iroquois, 94.
Irish, self obstruction, 393.
Isis, 487.
Italy, 84, 367; an emotion, 89.

Jackson, Andrew, 24, 28, 252.
James, George Payne Rainsford, 71.
James, Henry, 235, 315, 319; novels, 163.
James, William, 307.
Japan, Russia and, 462.
Jaurès Jean Léon, 423.
Jefferson, Thomas, 260, 436.
Jenner, Edward, 486.
Jesse, tree of, 471.
Jews, 3, 79, 195, 238, 285. 272, 408
Jocelyn, Lady Frances Elizabeth, 135.
Johnson, Andrew, president, 209, 261, 374; meeting with, 245.
Johnson, Catherine (Nuth), 16.
Johnson, Joshua, 16.
Johnson, Louisa Catherine, 16.
Johnson, Samuel, 36, 73, 336.
Johnson, Thomas, 16.

Johnston, Humphreys, 370.
Joinville, Sieur de, 471, 483.
Jones, John Percival, 343.
Jowett, Benjamin, 201.
Judkins, ——, 71.
Justinian, 482.

Kant, Immanuel, 62, 81, 449, 456; antinomies, 498.
Kelvin, Lord. *See* William Thomson.
Kepler, Johann, 376, 484, 491.
Khilkoff, Prince, 439, 444.
Kinetic theory of gases, 224, 451.
King, Clarence, 64, 87, 315; on nature's errors, 269; meeting with, 311; on man-atoms, 319; republican, 321; head of Survey Bureau, 322; near success, 328; in 1893, 346, 348, 349; goes to Arizona, 395; death, 416.
King, Preston, 101.
Kinglake, Alexander William, 221.
Kipling, Rudyard, 259; "Mandalay," 316; on steamship, 319; "Purun Dass," 502.
Kropotkin, Prince Peter Alexeievitch, 407.
Kuhn, Charles, 85.
Kuhn, Louisa Catherine (Adams), 86, 88; Italian fervor, 85; death, 287.

La Farge, John, 64, 235, 315, 317, 341, 386; in South Seas, 316; expression, 370; glass of, 371, 470.
La Fontaine, Jean de, on the wolf, 229, 230, 411.
Laird, William, and Son, rebel rams, 168; connection with confederate agents, 186.
Lamar, Lucius Quintus Cincinnatus, 279; confederate agent to Russia,

185; on English allies, 186; Bright
and Roebuck, 187; on slavery,
246; on office, 322.
Lamsdorf, Count Vladimir, 438, 463.
Landor, Walter Savage, 142.
Langley, Samuel Pierpont, 385, 450;
scientist, 377; Paris exposition,
379.
Laplace, Pierre Simon, 491.
Launcelot, Sir, 383.
Lee, Robert Edward, 57, 108, 266;
invasion of Maryland, 152; re-
treat, 154.
Lee, William Henry Fitzhugh
("Roony"), at Harvard College,
57, 58.
Legal tender cases, 249, 277.
Legitimacy and order, 113.
Leibnitz, Gottfried Wilhelm, 484,
491, 495.
Leonardo da Vinci, 492.
Letter to American Teachers, A,
xxviii.
Leveson-Gower, George Granville
William Sutherland, Duke of
Sutherland, 118.
Leveson-Gower, Granville George,
Earl of Granville, 149, 184, 202,
323; on recognizing the confeder-
acy, 154, 160.
Leveson-Gower, Harriet Elizabeth
Georgiana, Duchess of Suther-
land, 118.
Lewis, Sir George Cornewall, 184;
replies to Gladstone, 157, 159; re-
joinder, 161.
Libri, Guglielmo, 218.
Lies of diplomacy, 133.
Limulus, or horseshoe, 230.
Lincoln, Abraham, 98, 103, 121,
297; inauguration message, 106;
described, 107; English prejudice,

122, 136; a nightmare, 130; emancipation proclamation, 155; reëlec-
tion, 208; assassination, 209.
Lindsay, William Schaw, connection
with confederate agents, 186.
Lodge, Anna Cabot Mills (Davis),
332, 353, 404, 442.
Lodge, Elizabeth (Davis), 403, 443.
Lodge, George Cabot (Bay), 403,
405, 443.
Lodge, Henry Cabot, 332, 343, 356,
421; relations with, 353; goes to
Russia, 406.
Lodge, John Ellerton, 31.
London, tone, 33; in 1858, 73; Amer-
ican legation, 171; society, 194;
in 1870, 284.
Longfellow, Henry Wadsworth, 27,
31, 35, 141.
Louis XIV, 491.
Louis Philippe, taste, 40, 195.
Lovejoy, Owen, 101.
Lowe, Robert, 202.
Lowell, James Russell, 65, 83, 141,
259, 307, 308; "Biglow Papers,"
35; influence, 61; meets Bright,
190; on right and wrong, 259.
Lucretius, 384, 459.
Lunt, George, 20.
Luther, Martin, 483.
Lyell, Sir Charles, 127, 309, 398,
400; champions Darwin, 224ff.
Lyell, Mary (Horner), 127.
Lyndhurst. *See* Copley.
Lyons, Richard Bickerton Pemell,
Earl Lyons (1817–87), Minister
to the U.S., 158.
Lytton, Edward George Earle Lyt-
ton Bulwer, 201.

Macaulay, Thomas Babington, 33,
39; method, 221.

McClellan, George Brinton, 129, 137.

McCulloch, Hugh, 263; character, 247.

Mach, Ernst, 429, 453, 460.

Machiavelli, Niccolo, 85.

McKim, Charles Follen, 315.

McKinley, William, 235, 261, 355, 392; policy, 373.

McKinleyism, 423.

McLennan, John Ferguson, 301.

McVeagh, Wayne, 327.

Madison, James, 47.

Maine, Sir Henry, 301, 368.

Maine, sinking of the, 360.

Mals, 87.

Manchuria, Russian designs on, 438, 462.

Mann, Horace, 35.

Manning, Henry Edward, cardinal-priest, 206.

Mansfield Street, Portland Place, 119.

Marconi, Guglielmo, 381.

Markoe, Francis, 101.

Marseillaise, singing by order, 290.

Marshall, John, 47.

Marvin, ——, 41.

Marx, Karl, 33, 60, 72, 225, 351, 379.

Maryland, in 1850, 44.

Mason, James Murray, 204, 394; seizure on Trent, 119; agent of Confederacy, 184.

Massachusetts, senatorship in 1850, 49.

Maupassant, Guy de, 259.

Maurigy's Hotel, London, 116.

Maxwell, James Clerk, 444, 452.

Mexico, visited, 350, 355.

Meyerbeer, 290.

Michael Angelo, 92, 93, 388, 492.

Milan, 85.

Miles, Nelson Appleton, 210.

Mill, John Stuart, 33, 72, 494; a talk with, 126; timidity of, 192.

Mills, Clark, 252.

Milman, Henry Hart, 201.

Milnes, Richard Monckton, Lord Houghton, 119, 123, 185, 195, 201, 206, 285; described, 124; as host, 138; on Hugo, 143; joy over Gettysburg, 169; on Gladstone, 183; not an eccentric, 184.

Mind, American and British, 180; English, 193.

Mommsen, Theodor, 93.

Monroe, James, 269.

Montaigne, Michel de, 389, 454, 485, 492.

Mont-Saint-Michel, 354.

"Mont-Saint-Michel and Chartres," xxviii.

Moran, Benjamin, assistant secretary of legation, 111; secretary, 130, 145.

Morgan, Junius, 121.

Morgan, John Pierpont, 235, 347.

Morley, John, Viscount, on Russell, 160.

Motley, John Lothrop, 27, 274; social taste, 200; returns to America, 237; Grant's dislike of, 276; minister, 284.

Mount Felix, 121.

Mount Vernon, Va., 47.

Mullett, Albert B., 253.

Multiplicity, 12, 449, 455. *See also* Unity.

Murchison, Sir Roderick, 229, 230.

Musset, Louis Charles Alfred de, 142.

Musurus, ——, Turkish ambassador, 118, 135.

Napoleon Bonaparte, 28, 84, 112, 491.

Napoleon III, 96, 138, 208, 285, 289; declares war on Austria, 83, 92; and Gladstone, 156; on intervention, 161; Mexican venture, 162.

Nation, The, 243, 244, 250.

Nattier, Jean Marc, 391.

Nero, 417.

Newcastle, Duke of. *See* Clinton.

Newcomb, Simon, 377.

Newcome, Ethel, Sally Baxter, 131.

Newcomen, Thomas, 491.

New England, contrasts, 7; professions, 32; education of boys, 54; at Washington, 101.

Newman, John Henry, cardinal, 192.

Newport, R.I., social, 241.

Newton, Sir Isaac, 226, 377, 451, 484, 486, 491, 495; on gravitation, 376, 469; comet of, 496.

New York City, in 1905, 499.

Niagara, 112.

Nicolay, John George, 322.

Nietzsche, Friedrich Wilhelm, 485.

Nordhoff, Charles, 255, 264.

North, Frederick, Lord, 174.

North American Review, 281, 286, 353; articles in, 222, 233, 250, 258, 277, 280, 292; position of, 234, 244; Adams as editor, 293, 296, 307.

North-Enders, Boston, 41.

Norton, Charles Eliot, editor *N. A. Review*, 222.

Nuth, Catherine, 16.

Office, poison of, 365.

Okakura, 370.

Oliphant, Laurence, at Fryston, 139.

Olney, Richard, 331.

Ortler Spitze, 86.

Ostwald, Wilhelm, 453.

Owl, The, 139.

Oxenstiern, Axel Gustafsson, 100.

Paley, William, 230.

Palfrey, John Gorham, 27, 35; character, 29; history of, 221.

Palgrave, Cecil (d. of J. Milnes Gaskell), 214.

Palgrave, Sir Francis [Cohen], 214.

Palgrave, Francis Turner, 192, 308; critic, 214, 220; war between Germany and France, 285.

Palgrave, Reginald F. D., 214.

Palgrave, Robert Henry Inglis, 214.

Palgrave, William Gifford, 214.

Palmer, James Shedden, 94.

Palmer, Roundell, Earl of Selborne, 149.

Palmerston. *See* Henry John Temple.

Paris, 96; tone, 33; exposition, 1900, 379; education in, 403.

Parker, Theodore, 27, 29, 42; deism, 35.

Parkes, Joseph, 184; busy-body, 120.

Parkman, Francis, sale of works, 327.

Parkman, George, 20.

Pascal, Blaise, 389, 427, 485.

Patti, Adelina, 200.

Pauncefote, Sir Julian, 374, 393, 436.

Peabody, George, 121.

Pearl, Cora [Emma Elizabeth Crouch], 209.

Pearson, Karl, "Grammar of Science," 449, 453, 456, 495.

Peel, Sir Robert, 33.

Pendennis, Arthur, 286.

Pendleton, George Hunt, 295.

Pennsylvanian, type of, 333.

Perfection, social, 33.

Persia, 71.

Philippe, Louis, 33, 40.

Philippines, the, 363.

Phillips, Wendell, 29, 42.

Phillips, William Hallett, 350.

Phocas, Nicephoras, 482.

Pinturicchio, 470.

Plato, 62.

Plehve, Viatscheslaf Konstantinovich, assassinated, 471.

Poincaré, Jules Henri, 454, 455, 456, 460.

Polk, James Knox, 5, 13.

Pompadour, Jeanne Antoinette Poisson, Marquise de, 391.

Pope, Alexander, 36.

Post, New York *Evening,* 244, 336.

Power, 418, 503.

Prescott, William Hickling, 27.

Press, the, as a career, 211; religious, 352.

Presidents, respect for, 47.

Priestley, Joseph, 486.

Privilege, Bright on, 189.

Pteraspis, ganoid fish, 228, 229, 265, 291, 302, 352, 355, 398, 399.

Ptolemy, 476.

Pumpelly, Raphael, 87, 449.

Punch, on Russell, 164.

Purun, Dass, 502.

Puritans, 483; moral standards, 26; Palfrey on, 222.

Pythagoras, 451.

Quarterly, refuses article, 287.

Quincy, Edmund, 29.

Quincy, Josiah, 15.

Quincy, Mass., 9; want of style, 10.

Rabelais, François, 454; Gargantua, 4.

Radium, 381, 397.

Rafael, Adams buys a, 216, 217.

Railroads, study of American, 240; situation of, 330.

Rams, the Confederate, 167.

Rasselas, 378.

Rawlins, John Aaron, and Grant, 264, 265.

Raymond, Henry Jarvis, 101, 120, 244.

Rebellion, English leaning to, 183.

Reclus, Elisée, 351, 407.

Reed, Thomas Brackett, 331.

Reed, George W., curator of drawings, British Museum, on Rafael drawing, 217.

Reeve, Henry, 125, 258, 282; described, 192; refuses article, 286.

Reichenbach, Hofräthin von, 87.

Reid, Whitelaw, 210, 235, 244, 347.

Religion, in Boston, 34.

Rembrandt, 216.

Renan, Ernest, 61, 201.

Retz, Cardinal de, 276.

Reynolds, Sir Joshua, 391.

Rice. *See* Spring Rice.

Rich, the very, 347.

Richardson, Henry Hobson, 55, 64, 235, 315, 318, 341, 386; in Paris, 213.

Rienzi, Cola di, 91.

Roads, Virginia, 47.

Rock Creek, 268; St. Gaudens' figure, 329.

Rockefellers, the, 235.

Rockhill, William Woodville, 356, 361.

Rodin, Auguste, 391.

Roebuck, John Arthur, connection with confederate agents, 186; encounter with Bright, 187.

Roentgen, Willhelm Konrad, 450.

Rome, in 1870, 89.

Roosevelt, Theodore, 332, 356, 421, 436, 447; outspeaking, 464; \nd the trusts, 500.

Roosevelt, Mrs. Theodore, 443.

Root, Elihu, 394, 464.

Rossini, Giochino Antonio, 94.

Rousseau, xxix.

Rubens, Peter Paul, 74, 388.

Ruskin, John, 192, 387.

Russell, John, Earl, 116, 126, 148, 177, 192, 208, 284; receives rebel emissaries, 115; attitude towards C. F. Adams, 123; insolent replies, 128; as host, 132; foreign secretary, 135; Palmerston's *bêtise*, 137; wish to recognize Confederacy, 149, 152; rebel cruisers, 150; on intervention, 152, 154, 172, 174; Gladstone's speech, 158; gives way, 161; dishonesty, 163; resemblance to J. Q. Adams, 167; rebel rams, 167; weakness, 182; retirement, 212.

Russia, visited, 406; character of, 408; position, 423, 437; rolling of, 439, 448; in Manchuria, 462, 502.

Sac and soc, 368.

St. Francis d'Assisi, 93, 367.

St. Gaudens, Augustus, 64, 315, 341, 391; compensation, 326; figure at Rock Creek, 329; inarticulate, 385; models Hay's head, 465.

St. James's Club, conversation of, 117.

St. Jerome, 483.

St. Louis [Louis IX], 483.

St. Louis, exposition, 1904, 465.

Salem, 244.

Salisbury, Marquis of. *See* Cecil.

Sargent, John Singer, 465.

Savage, James, 41.

Schiller, Johann Christoph Friedrich von, 81.

Schopenhauer, Arthur, 406, 485.

Schurz, Carl, 322.

Scott, Robert Falcon, on seals, 502.

Scott, Sir Walter, 39, 286, 301.

Scott, Winfield, 59; in 1860, 106.

Secessionists, Southern, ignorance of, 100.

Secretaries of legation, in London, 117.

Secretary of State, duties, 375.

Selborne. *See* Palmer.

Sellers, Colonel Mulberry, 279.

Senate, United States, in 1850, 45; treaty delays, 374, 394; obstruction, 393; Secretary of State and, 422.

Senators, United States, 272; in 1850, 45; quality of, 102, 261, 354.

Seneca, 417.

Session, the, 258, 280, 292.

Sévigné, Madame de, 353.

Seward, William Henry, 25, 29, 49, 110, 113, 116, 121, 129, 149; aspirant to Presidency, 89; in 1860, 102; Secretary of State, 103; described, 104; English prejudice, 122; a demon, 130; offer of appointment, 145; propaganda, 146; support by, 171; strength, 174; in 1868, 246.

Sex in art, 385; inertia of, 441, 442, 447.

Seymour, Margaret, Duchess of Somerset, 118.

Shakespeare, William, 62, 229, 232, 379, 394, 492, 504, 505.

Shelley, 470.

Sherman, John, 295, 332; Secretary of State, 356.
Sherman, William Tecumseh, 245.
Shropshire, beauty of, 228.
Silence, praise of, 358.
Silver, question of, 334; repeal of act, 343.
Slave power, influence, 25, 48; fugitive, law, 42; states, 43, 44.
Slidell, John, 184; seizure on Trent, 119.
Smalley, George Washburn, 198, 210.
Smith, Adam, 351.
Smith, Captain John, essay on, 222.
Smith, Sydney, 201.
Socrates, 429.
Sohm, Rudoph, 368.
Somerset, Duchess of. *See* Seymour.
Sophocles, 358.
Sotheby's, London, 213.
South-Enders, Boston, 41.
Sothern, Edward Askew, as Dundreary, 181.
Spaulding, Elbridge Gerry, 277.
Specie payments, 233.
Speck von Sternberg, Baron, 437.
Spencer, Herbert, 385, 451.
Spinoza, Baruch de, 226, 456, 484.
Springfield Republican, 278.
Spring Rice, Cecil Arthur, 332, 356.
Stallo, John Bernhard, 452; "Concepts of Science," 377, 449.
Stanley, Edward George Geoffrey Smith, Earl of Derby, 184, 194, 235.
Stanley, Edward John, 154.
Stanley, Edward Lyulph, 127.
Stanton, Edwin McMasters, 171.
State Street, influence, 21.
Statistics, uncertainty of, 351.
Stelvio Pass, 86.

Sternberg, Speck von, 437.
Stevenson, Robert Louis, 139, 259, 319.
Stickney, Joseph Trumbull, 403, 405.
Stirling-Maxwell, Sir William, at Fryston, 139.
Stoeck[e]l, Baron Edward de, 255.
Storey, Moorfield, 256.
Story, William Wetmore, 93.
Struve, Madame de, 256.
Stubbs, William, 141.
Sturgis, Mr. and Mrs. Russell, 121.
Suess, Eduard, 400.
Sully, Mounet, 404.
Sumner, Charles, 29, 35, 111, 116, 261, 263, 271, 281, 282, 298, 394; ambition and position, 30; senator, 49; in Berlin, 76; quotes Oxenstiern, 99; in 1860, 102; breaks with C. F. Adams, 107; opposes him as minister, 110, 115; English liking for, 122; resumes relations with Adams, 251; quarrel with Fish, 274; Alabama claims, 275.
Sun, New York, 244.
Surrenden Dering, Kent, 364.
Survey of the 40th parallel, 309.
Sutherland, Duke of. *See* Leveson-Gower.
Swinburne, Algernon, 201, 319; at Fryston, 139–144; on silence, 358.

Tacitus, 92.
"Tannhäuser," 360.
Tautphœus, Jemima (Montgomery), baroness von, "The Initials," 87.
Taylor, Richard, 198.
Taylor, Zachary, meeting with, 46.
Temple, Amelia (Lamb Cowper), Lady Palmerston, 137; popularity, 133.

Temple, Henry John, Viscount Palmerston, 92, 125, 148, 149, 151, 284; as Tiberius, 114; dangerous quality, 132; on Butler's order, 136; on recognizing confederacy, 152, 154, 159, 161, 174; simplicity, 164; senility, 168; rebel rams, 177; death, 212.

Tennyson, Alfred, Lord, 35, 39, 92, 201, 206, 224.

Terebratula, uniformity, 228, 266, 291.

Ternina, 405.

Teutonic, the, 318.

Thackeray, William Makepeace, 35, 61, 201; on Lincoln's brutality, 131; satirist, 181.

Theodosius, 479.

Thibaut of Champagne, 471.

Thiers, 290.

Thomson, Sir William Lord Kelvin, 381, 401, 450.

Thüringen, tramp in, 81, 82.

Ticknor, George, 27.

Tilden, Samuel Jones, 373.

Times, London, on Adams's article, 120; slowness of, 170.

Tocqueville, Alexis Henri Charles Maurice Clérel, Comte de, 33, 192.

Tolstoi, 409.

Torrey, Henry Warren, 300.

Town and country, New England, 8.

Treaties, in Senate, 374, 394.

Trent, affair of the, 119, 128.

Trevelyan, Sir Charles Edward, 127.

Tribune, New York, 244, 278.

Tricoupi, S., 135.

Trusts, batle of, 500.

Turenne, 42.

Turgenev, 409.

Turgot, Anne Robert Jacques, 479, 493.

Turner, Joseph Mallord William, 213.

Twain, Mark. *See* Clemens.

Tylor, Edward Burnett, 301.

Tyndall, John, 225.

Unitarianism, Boston, 34.

United States, society in, 237.

Unity, 12, 226, 397, 398, 406, 429, 431, 435, 450, 451, 471, 484.

Valtellina, 86.

Van Buren, Martin, 25, 46.

Vanderbilt, Cornelius, 238.

Van de Weyer, Silvain, Belgian minister, 135.

Venables, George Stovin, 125, 201.

Veronese, Paolo, 198.

Vertebrate, first, 228.

Vicksburg, fall of, 169, 174.

Victoria, Queen, 40, 359; taste, 195.

Vigny, Alfred de, 358.

Virgin, force of the, 383, 468.

Virginia, roads, 47; youth, 57; in 1860, 105.

Volta, Alessandro, 491.

Voltaire, François Marie Arouet de, 140, 391, 485.

Wagner, Richard, 81, 404, 405.

Walcott, Charles Doolittle, 399.

Walker, Francis Amasa, 248; legal tender cases, 277.

Walker, James, 27, 64, 65.

Wallace, Alfred, 409.

Walpole, Sir Spencer, 152.

Walton-on-Thames, 121.

Ward, Samuel, 253, 264, 282.

Washburn, Israel, 101.

Washington, George, 47, 260, 372; slavery and, 47, 50.
Washington, Martha (Dandridge Custis), 48.
Washington monument, Washington, 44, 47.
Washington, D.C., Boston to, 43; in 1850, 44; in 1860, 99; in 1868, 243, 252; society, 256, 296; in 1892, 320.
Watt, James, 486, 491.
Watteau, Antoine, 391.
Watterson, Henry, 255.
Webster, Daniel, 24, 25, 29, 30, 45, 49, 102, 148, 394; representative of Boston, 32.
Weed, Thurlow, 49, 103, 149, 150; in England, 146.
Wells, David Ames, 281.
Wenlock Abbey, Shropshire, 207, 228, 290, 355.
West, the, in 1871, 309; in 1904, 465.
Westcombe, Sir Anthony, 216.
West Indies, Grant's policy, 275.
Westminister Review, 284, 292.
Wharton, Francis, 299.
Whistler, James Abbott McNeill, 220, 370, 371, 386.
White, Stanford, 315, 341, 386.
White House, Washington, visit to, 46.
Whitman, Walt, 385.
Whitney, Josiah Dwight, 309.
Whitney, William Collins, 235, 295, 321, 331, 373; measure of success, 347.

Wide-Awakes, 99.
Wilberforce, Samuel, 201.
Wilde, Hamilton, 92.
Wilhelm I, of Prussia, 78.
Wilhelm II, of Germany, 437, 464.
Wilkes, Charles, 121.
Wilson, Charles L., secretary of legation, 111, 130.
Wilson, Henry, 49.
Winthrop, Robert Charles, 29; succeeds Everett, 32.
Witte, Serge Julievich, Count, 438, 439, 444, 462.
Wolcott, Edward Oliver, 331.
Wolsey, Cardinal, 365.
Woman, American ideas of, 384.
Women, Boston, 40; American, 353, 442, 447.
Woolner, Thomas, 220; sculptor, 215; opinion on Reed, 219.
Wordsworth, William, 36; quoted, 503.
Wren, Sir Christopher, 213.
Wright, Chauncey, 299.
Wynn, Charlotte, 207, 284.
Wynns of Wynstay, 206.

X-rays, 381, 397.

Yellowstone Park, 350.
Yorkshire, England, characteristics, 205.

Zeno, 389.